Black Adult
Development
and Aging

Black Adult Development and Aging

Edited by
Reginald L. Jones
University of California at Berkeley

Cobb & Henry • Publishers
Berkeley, California

Black Adult Development and Aging

Cobb & Henry • Publishers
P.O. Box 4900
Berkeley, California 94704-4900

Book design and typesetting by Cragmont Publications, Oakland, California

Cover design by Mark van Bronkhorst

Manufactured in the United States of America

Library of Congress Cataloging-in-Publication Data

Black adult development and aging.

    Bibliography: p.
    Includes index.
    1. Afro-Americans—Psychology. 2. Aging—United
States. 3. Afro-Americans—Social conditions—
1975- . 4. Afro-American aged. 5. Adulthood—
United States. I. Jones, Reginald Lanier, 1931-   .
E185.625.B54   1989   305.8'96073   89-873
ISBN 0-943539-03-X
ISBN 0-943539-04-8 (pbk.)

Contributors

Norman B. Anderson

Phillip J. Bowman

Benjamin P. Bowser

Linda M. Chatters

Ruppert A. Downing

Rose C. Gibson

Winston E. Gooden

Algea O. Harrison

James S. Jackson

Maurice Jackson

Arthur C. Jones

Syed Khatib

Carolyn B. Murray

Hector Myers

Thomas A. Parham

Howard P. Ramseur

Marva Lloyd Redd

Janice E. Ruffin

Robert Joseph Taylor

Tony R. Strickland

CONTENTS

Preface xi

I. Perspectives

Generational Effects

Generational Effects: The Impact of Culture, Economy and
Community Across the Generations
Benjamin P. Bowser 3

Stages of Development

Stages of Adult Development in Black, Professional Women
Janice E. Ruffin 31

Development of Black Men in Early Adulthood
Winston E. Gooden 63

Black Working Women: Introduction to
A Life Span Perspective
Algea O. Harrison 91

Research Perspectives on Black Men: Role Strain and
Adaptation Across the Black Adult Male Life Cycle
Phillip J. Bowman 117

Identity Development and Tranformation

Nigrescence: The Transformation of Black Consciousness
Across the Life Cycle
Thomas A. Parham 151

Development in Old Age

Social Indices and the Black Elderly: A Comparative Life
Cycle Approach to the Study of Double Jeopardy
Carolyn B. Murray, Syed Khatib and Maurice Jackson . . 167

II. Mental Health

Quality of Life and Subjective Well-being Among
Black Adults
Linda M. Chatters and James S. Jackson 191

Psychologically Healthy Black Adults: A Review
of Theory and Research
Howard P. Ramseur 215

III. Support Systems

Family, Friend, and Church Support Networks of
Black Americans
Robert Joseph Taylor and Linda M. Chatters 245

Human Services and the Black Adult Life Cycle
Ruppert A. Downing 273

Psychological Functioning in African-American Adults:
Some Elaborations on a Model, With Clinical Applications
Arthur C. Jones 297

IV. Special Topics

A Biobehavioral Perspective on Stress and Hypertension
in Black Adults
Hector Myers, Norman B. Anderson
and Tony L. Strickland .311

Alcoholism and Drug Addiction Among Black Adults
Marva Lloyd Redd 351

Life Control Theory: A Perspective on Black Attitudes
Toward Death and Dying
Maurice Jackson 375

V. The Future

Black Adults in An Aging Society
Rose C. Gibson 389

Biographical Sketches 409

Author Index 417

Subject Index 424

Preface

This is a book about the development and aging of Black American adults. The focus is upon the entire adult life span—from early adulthood to old age. However, on occasion pre-adult periods are discussed in order to show continuity between earlier and later stages of development.

The perspective is multidisciplinary, since it is clear that any reasonably comprehensive portrait of human development must draw upon work in a number of fields of study. Therefore, in presenting a portrait of Black adults in the present volume, research and writing have been drawn from several disciplines, including psychology, sociology, economics, social work, and the biological sciences.

Lifespan development in general, and studies of adult development in particular, are relatively new fields of study. While there has been an exponential increase in writings in this area over the past two decades, there has been little attention to Black adults as subjects of investigation, the one exception being the Black elderly in which there is a significant and increasing body of literature. Research and studies on Black early and middle adulthood, however, are rare.

Content analysis of a dozen recent volumes devoted to human development or to adult development revealed they gave little attention to Black populations—a few sentences on occasion, a paragraph, or at most, a chapter on "minority groups." Topics such as the impact of race, of culture, of racism; cohort differences related to race; racial identity development—all areas critical to an understanding of Black adult development—received virtually no attention in these books. In light of the above voids, a volume devoted to Black adult development and aging is timely and needed.

There are no obvious reasons for the absence of studies of Blacks in the adult lifespan literature. Occasionally, a writer will suggest that systematic attention needs to be given to the development of special populations, such as Blacks, women or other groups but, for the most part, these groups are invisible. Such absence may be the result of a belief that findings developed on White middle class males hold for other groups as well. As the present volume unfolds, we will see that such a view is unfounded. There clearly are areas of the Black experience that are unique to Black Americans alone and therefore must be dealt with if a reasonably accurate picture of Black adult development is to be drawn. In particular, history and the impact of racism are two variables that must be accounted for in our theories and explanations. How racism impacts on health and medical care, employment opportunities, career development, and identity development, to name a few areas, must be incorporated into extant theories and models of Black adult development. The integration of literature on these matters, and others, will form an important part of the present volume.

The book consists of sixteen chapters in five parts: Part I, Perspectives; Part II, Mental Health; Part III, Support Systems; Part IV, Special Topics; and Part V, The Future.

Part I presents papers on intergenerational differences among Black adults, stages of development of working and professional men and women at midlife, identity development and transformation, and the Black elderly.

In the first paper in Part I, Bowser discusses the idea of social generation (cohort) as a concept that may help us understand the life experiences of Black adults of various ages. The basic idea is that generations within any group do not experience events and history in the same way. Thus Blacks in their seventies (seniors in 1988) were adults in the 1930's. They were generally poor, and reared in rigidly segregated communities in the North and South. Moreover, they were socialized to expect inferior status and to understand that violations of racial etiquette would be harshly punished. Their parents were strict, authoritarian, quick to punish, and hierarchical. Most were reared in two-parent households and participated in extended social networks. They were clearly reared by Afro-American adults and not by electronic media or peers. They knew about race conflict.

There are important contrasts between seniors and adults who were in their fifties and sixties in 1988. For example, while this latter group also lived in segregated communities and worked mainly in low status jobs, they were decidedly more urban and upwardly mobile than the seniors. Bowser similarly draws economic and social portraits of individuals in their forties, and those in their thirties (baby boomers) as they are seen in a 1988 "snapshot." A description of "baby boomers" is illustrative. Bowser writes that a majority of this group began work after 1970, amidst a series of economic recessions. Memories of Jim Crow and of Civil Rights activism came through their parents and the media. Like their parents of the previous generation, they hold high expectations for continued economic and race progress.

The portraits Bowser draws inform the rest of the book. It is clear that we are not addressing Black adults as a homogeneous group. Rather, we are looking at a group of individuals of varied ages and life experiences who must be viewed in light of the time period of their formative years and of their unique social, economic, environmental and cultural history.

The remaining chapters in Part I, Perspectives, address various stages of adult development, mainly midlife development and development in old age, although there is some attention to issues in the development of young adults, especially around the area of employment.

First, Ruffin looks at stages in the development of Black professional women, using Levinson's life structure paradigm as a framework for her study. Levinson's theory was developed on White middle class men, so Ruffin addresses the relevance of his formulations to the concerns of Black professional women. She found the theory to be useful in some respects and deficient in others. For example, it was necessary to consider how racial identity influenced Levinson's developmental stages, a factor that was not a part of his model.

In the next chapter, Gooden uses Levinson's model as a framework for looking at the development of Black males in early adulthood. Unlike Ruffin's subjects, who consisted of professional women, Gooden's sample includes professional as well as working class subjects. The diverse background of his subjects bring into contrast how Levinson's theory has differential relevance not only as a function of race but of socioeconomic status as well. For example, Gooden found the theory fit the school teachers in his sample better than it did the "street men." And as did Ruffin who studied women, Gooden notes that victimization because of race and class is a part of the story of Black men's early adult development that is not taken into consideration in Levinson's model.

Other perspectives on development in mostly early and middle adulthood are presented in chapters by Harrison, Bowman and Parham, while Murray, Khatib and Jackson address issues related to the Black elderly. Harrison uses historical, economic, social, and psychological data and perspectives to look at Black women in the labor force. Exploitation, lower occupational attainment, and lack of economic parity are among factors that describe Black women's participation in the labor market. Yet, in spite of obstacles, there is evidence of resilience in Black women, across the life cycle. Bowman formulated a role strain-adaptation paradigm that he uses to discuss major problems of Black males at discrete points in the adult life cycle, i.e., pre-adult years, early adulthood, middle adulthood and old age. He notes that successful movement through the life cycle requires the resolution of conflicts and the mastery of tasks related to role strains at the preceeding period. For example, during preadulthood, performance in the student role is critical and early educational preparation is seen as the cornerstone of subsequent adult role accomplishments. In early adulthood, preparation for the world of work is important, and during middle adulthood the provider role is salient. Success in all previous stages influences the degree of role strain in old age. Bowman's paradigm is useful not only in identifying major areas of strain at each life stage, but in looking at maladaptive responses associated with the strains, and in suggesting strategies and resources for ameliorating the problems identified. The model is also useful in highlighting areas needing research.

While writings on mainstream populations give attention to identity as part of the psychology of development, identity development has special meaning for Black populations. In the next chapter, Parham uses a model developed by Cross to speculate about how Blacks deal with racial identity at various points in the adult life cycle. He provides strong support for the thesis that racial identity attitudes are subject to continuous change throughout the adult life cycle. His provocative ideas are pregnant with implications for further research and study.

In the final chapter in Part I, Murray, Khatib and Jackson look at the Black elderly. The authors adopt a life course perspective and the results of two national surveys of the elderly to investigate various social indices of aging. They draw upon available data to look at intraindividual differences within the elderly population in such areas as housing, living arrangements, marital status, income, labor force participation, and physical and mental health. Differences in age subgroupings of the Black elderly are highlighted in the chapter.

Part II concerns mental health. The two papers in this section deal with studies of quality of life and subjective well-being (Chatters and Jackson), and psychologically healthy adults (Ramseur).

In the first paper in Part II, Chatters and Jackson use a lifespan orientation to examine research on quality of life and subjective well-being for Black Americans. The authors explore the background and the meaning of these terms, review pertinent research literature, and look at theoretical models and their relevance to the experiences of Black Americans. Trends in subjective well-being and quality of life for Blacks and Whites, as well as racial differences on those constructs are explored. Needs in theory development and research also are identified.

While there is a sizeable literature on Black psychopathology, relatively little has been written about Black strength, resilience, and adjustment. Because of its emphasis upon theory and research on psychologically healthy Black adults, the chapter by Ramseur is an exception to studies and theories that focus upon Black pathology. In developing his ideas, Ramseur discusses the social/cultural situation of Black Americans, essential elements of an ideal model of adult psychological health, "universal" models of psychological health, and theories of Black personality and identity that have psychological health implications (including studies of self-esteem, racial identity, the "competent" personality, and Black coping resources and styles), and components of a model of healthy Black adults.

The volume includes a number of chapters that provide information of use to service providers. The chapters on support systems (Part III) are most directly relevant. Taylor and Chatters, for example, critically evaluate literature on how family, friends, and church support the development of Black adults. Their adaptation of the support convoy model is a useful vehicle for integrating a widely scattered literature. And as is true in a number of the chapters, the authors look at racial differences between Blacks and Whites as well as subgroup differences among Blacks.

At another level, Downing reports on institutionalized sources of support across the adult life cycle. These include agencies and social services needed to deal with problems unique to each stage of adult development. Thus, Downing describes various family life education services for young adults (e.g., genetic counseling, family planning, adoption), services appropriate in middle adulthood (e.g., Health Services, Preretirement Planning), and services appropriate for later adulthood (e.g., Social Security). An important section discusses elements that enhance the utilization of programs and services among Black adult populations.

Not all problems Blacks face during adulthood can be solved by informal support networks or by social and governmental programs. There are occasions when intervention using individual psychotherapy is appropriate. In a final chapter in the section, Arthur Jones develops a conceptual model useful in framing issues facing Black adults at various stages in the lifespan. He then outlines salient issues within the framework, and presents case studies of commonly encountered clinical assessment and psychotherapy problems the model describes. Included are discussion and cases in the areas of coping with racial oppression, maintaining desired influences with the majority culture, establishing roots within traditional African-American culture, and the influence of personal experiences and endowments.

Part IV introduces three special topics, two of which are related to health—(1) stress and hypertension and (2) substance abuse; and (3) Black attitudes toward death and dying. Health-related problems are of major significance for Black adults and are especially deserving of attention in a book devoted to Black adult development.

In the first paper, Myers, Anderson and Strickland review and discuss the empirical evidence for biological and psychosocial differences in the possible causes, life course, and outcomes of essential hypertension in Blacks and Whites. They also present components of a multi-domain model for research on essential hypertension in Blacks. Their review of literature is of significant value because of its breadth—they critique basic, clinical pharmacologic, epidemiological and clinical studies. Also helpful is a glossary of terms for those of us who are unfamiliar with the many technical terms in the essential hypertension literature.

Next, Redd writes about alcoholism and drug addiction among Black adults. Her primary focus is upon the prevalence of alcoholism and other drug addictions among Blacks, as well as age-related factors in patterns of drug use. In addition to reviewing literature on etiological factors in alcoholism, Redd evaluates the literature on patterns of alcohol consumption, the onset and consequences of problematic drinking and the utilization of alcoholism treatment networks. A similar set of topics is covered with respect to drug addiction.

In a chapter with a quite different focus, Maurice Jackson reviews the literature on attitudes toward death and dying, and introduces his own theory, Life Control Theory, to explain Black death attitudes. Through an informative and wide ranging review that draws upon spirituals, poetry and Black literature, as well as social science studies and research, Jackson disabuses us of erroneous assumptions about Black attitudes toward death seen in popular writings.

In a final chapter (Part V) "Blacks in an Aging Society," Gibson looks to the future. She raises questions about the future of Blacks, at various points on the age continuum, as a result of current demographic trends—an increasing proportion of Black youth in the population, proportionately fewer middle aged Blacks compared to the young and old, and an increasing population of the Black elderly. Implications of these changes in such areas as the health and welfare of Blacks, and other groups, at all points of the age continuum, are poignantly drawn.

The range of methodologies used to support generalizations in individual chapters reflects the current status of research and theorizing about Black adult development and aging. There are many one-shot empirical and racial comparative studies, a few cross-sectional investigations and case studies, but no longitudinal investigations. Each method, of course, has advantages as well as disadvantages. For example, case studies have high internal validity (reasonable hypotheses can be developed about cause and effect relationships) but poor external validity (i.e. generalizability) because of the uniqueness of individual cases. Despite possible shortcomings, I believe we need more, not fewer, case studies; these can be an important vehicle for informing theory development and validation.

Longitudinal studies, because they permit a single individual or group of individuals to be followed over time, thus enabling investigators to assess environmental context and historical periods as variables affecting continuity and change in behavior, have obvious advantages in lifespan developmental studies. Yet, we have virtually no longitudinal studies of Black adults. Some of the authors of individual chapters in the present volume have pointed to areas where longitudinal studies would be of value in advancing our knowledge of Black adult behavior.

Many of the empirical studies summarized in the present volume are the result of comparative studies of Blacks and Whites. The reader is reminded that such studies can only provide information about how Blacks are the same or different from Whites on the variables being investigated; the studies cannot, in themselves, tell us about the behavior of Blacks. If we are to understand the behavior of Black adults, Black adults must be studied. Comparative studies, then, must be viewed as limited in their usefulness in helping us understand the development of Black adults.

Insofar as I know, the present volume represents the first systematic attempt to view Black adult development across the life cycle. The work of authors of chapters in the present volume has not been easy because existing theory and research have been developed from mainstream perspectives. Largely because of the insensitivity of mainstream theory and research to race and culture as variables influencing development, much previous work appears inadequate for explaining important facets of Black adult development and aging. Thus authors have had to sift, evaluate, and synthesize a wide body of literature and, where appropriate, modify existing theories or develop new ones. I believe they have been successful in this endeavor. Authors have suggested modification of extant theories, developed new ones, put forward provocative hypotheses, and provided penetrating critiques and needed syntheses of the existing literature on Black adult development and aging. And, finally, they have suggested many directions for future theorizing and research.

I am grateful to many individuals for assistance in the development of this volume. First, I extend my sincere thanks to the authors of individual chapters. It is they who provide the substance of the book. They have reported on their own work and drawn upon and synthesized a diverse literature to engagingly present penetrating portraits of many facets of Black adult development and aging.

Walter Allen, Gwendolyn Foster, A. J. Franklin, Nancy Boyd-Franklin and John McAdoo provided very helpful reviews of manuscripts. This clearly is a far better book than it would have been without their evaluations and insights. The authors and I are grateful to them for their assistance.

Marlene Kleinman, Sharon Cessar, and Pamela Stafford brought their impressive talents to bear on preparation of the manuscript. I sincerely thank them for their excellent work. I also enjoyed the able assistance of Michele Madlock, Elmire Robinson, Mark Williams, my daughter Julie (an aspiring doctoral student in developmental psychology), as well as Fred and Pauline Felder of Cragmont Publications, and Mark van Bronkhorst, graphic artist.

Finally, my wife Michele provided the kind of nurturance and support of which only she is capable. She has sustained me through the long final days of manuscript preparation and encouraged me to work when I preferred to dawdle and play. Thank you Michele.

Reginald L. Jones
Berkeley, California

Part I
Perspectives

GENERATIONAL EFFECTS: THE IMPACT OF CULTURE, ECONOMY AND COMMUNITY ACROSS THE GENERATIONS

Benjamin P. Bowser

Introduction

Intergenerational differences are important sociological factors that have been underestimated in the modern study of group life (Esler, 1982). What has been generally regarded as age differences throughout the centuries take on an added dimension during times of rapid social change. In this century it is possible for two age groups to live simultaneously with one another and be culturally and historically distinct and literally be puzzled by one another. The specific issue addressed here is to what extent do intergenerational differences effect group organization and cohesiveness. A primary assumption is that these differences are themselves the result of changes in culture, economy and urban social organization. The purpose of this article is to discuss the idea of "social generations" as an issue which may heavily impact Afro-American group life.

The study of intergenerational differences is not new. The idea of a "social generation," described by Karl Mannheim (1928), has simply not been applied in a comprehensive fashion to Black Americans (Allen and Patterson, 1974; Bengtson & Laufer, 1974). Generations within any group do not experience events and history in the same way. Prior experiences, persons with whom perceptions and attitudes are shared, and one's place in society also shape how life experiences are interpreted and how "common points of view" develop (Elder, 1974). In a pluralistic society, transformations in social structure not only impact relations between groups, but they impact relations within each group as well. Mannheim was also interested in the extent to which individuals conformed to the specific generational values, beliefs and norms within their group. This process goes on for all social classes across each generation's life course.

The study of generational differences also represents another view of social class, ethnicity and racial differences in socialization and adult development. Work that highlights life course differences across generations points out that social class and racial differences in aging and adult development do exist (Elder, 1974; 1975). This is in sharp contrast to biophysical and psychological research where race, social class and

3

generational differences are much less visible (Ragan, 1977). It is possible that generational differences among Afro-Americans are just as important a determinant of group status as is racial discrimination. "Social Generations" might further divide social and economic classes in effecting how Afro-Americans as a group are organized and respond to the challenges before them across the decades. The following discussion is an attempt to outline the possible impacts of generational changes on Afro-Americans. The focus is on three key factors—culture, the economy, and urban organization. The background section will be followed by a review of social generational differences for specific cohorts of Afro-Americans.

Effects of Cultural Change Across the Generations

The turmoil of the sixties has been variously attributed to the overwhelming rapidity of change, the collapse of the family, the decay of capitalism, the triumph of a soulless technology and in wholesale repudiation, to the final breakdown of the establishment. Behind these attributions there is a more basic conflict between those for whom the present represents no more than an intensification of our existing cofigurative culture, in which peers are more than ever replacing parents as the significant models of behavior, and (there are) those who contend that we are in fact entering a totally new phase of cultural evolution (Mead 1978, p. 65).

However one explains the challenges of the sixties, rapid social change was certainly one cause. Margaret Mead has a three phase description of cultural change since 1900—prefigurative, postfigurative, and cofigurative, which is very useful in outlining Afro-American generational effects. The significance of these phases is that each describes a different cultural place in which a current generation has had its primary experience. In past history, one cultural phase would last for generations. In this century, cultural transitions are happening in less than a generation, and in doing so are producing unique circumstances.

The Prefigurative

Prior to World War II, elders served as primary socializing agents and reference groups. Correct and appropriate behaviors were embodied in traditions. Owning land was of primary importance as was church membership and participation in family life. In the same way, most southern Whites assumed they were and would always be superior to Afro-Americans. Many Afro-Americans accepted their inferiority. Different racial statuses were reinforced by segregation and an elaborate code

4

for boundaries and behaviors (Dollard, 1937). Furthermore, in the prefigurative mind, the past was expected to continue unchanged into the future.

The Post-figurative

Urbanization of America's population along with the radio, and then television eroded the prefigurative world. Migrants had to learn "city ways" from one another, not traditional elders. Many traditional ways clashed with one another in a world of multiple races and ethnic groups. There was no longer a single correct or appropriate way to do anything. The primacy of land was replaced by the primacy of wage labor. Involvement in church, family and community became optional. Racial discrimination was no longer viewed by Afro-Americans as "God-given" nor was submission to White supremacy accepted as "one's earthly burden" (Rose, 1948). Whites were not superior after all. While urban Whites wanted to maintain racial stratification, they had great difficulty in enforcing traditional forms of segregation in industrial cities. New ways of control had to be devised based on urban rather than rural southern realities.

The Cofigurative

The children of the post-figurative and migrant generation are experiencing yet another cultural transformation. Now adults (elders) share socialization of younger group members with the electronic media. Fictional human and electronic personalities also influence how reality is defined and then responded to. While Afro-American and White youth have many differences, they are the first generation completely reared by a common electronic media. Their sense of self, relations with others and expectations are heavily influenced by media images. With media images blurring direct experience and parental efforts to socialize, there is little to learn from the past and the present is too familiar, boring and is itself optional; one can choose the extent to which one will experience the present or not.

For many young people, electronic media are preferred to direct experience. By selecting a media image you can "be" whatever you want to be without actually having to become it—through dress, behavior and association. For example, in the new music (rock, heavy metal and R & B) what is increasingly important is imagery, not the music. The "boom box" is important not for the music it plays, but rather because its loudness drowns out what is real, present, immediate and alien. Rapping is more imagery and story-telling than music. Primacy is shifting yet again from wage labor to lifestyle—self-concept maintenance. Access to vital

5

information and networks is quickly becoming the new basis for financial and professional salvation. Multiple divorces and remarriages—serial marriage—are likely to become closer to the norm rather than the exception. And in the cofigurative world, racial and class barriers can be maintained or minimized by determining who has access to the various media and specialized communications networks.

Effects of Economic Change Across the Generations

There are good reasons for focusing on economic change. First, an important ongoing cause of race and class inequality is economic gain (Becker, 1957; Thurow, 1969; Bonacich, 1976; Reich, 1982). Economic organization is fundamental to not only how profits and wealth are generated, but also to how race and class inequalities are maintained. It is no coincidence that the three cultures described by Mead are paralleled by three economic transitions in this century. Our first economy was rural, labor intensive and agricultural—prefigurative (Wright, 1978; Price, 1983). As the century progressed, agriculture was mechanized, ceased to be labor intensive and the overall economy shifted its emphasis to centralized and urban based manufacturing—the second economy (Kumar, 1978). We are now entering what some call the "post-industrial" era, where information and knowledge management are the central activities (Bell, 1973; Touraine, 1971)—the third economy within this century. Others call this third economy, advanced capitalism or a further intensification of monopoly and automation (Kumar, 1978).

Post-industrialists claim that new "hi-tech" and service industries will eventually generate enough new jobs to employ a displaced labor force and lead to a new era of economic prosperity (Bell, 1973). This might be very true for the upper middle class. "Hi-tech" and professional services are indeed the brave new world. But there is little evidence that the post-industrial world and the U.S. will generate enough jobs to employ an entire generation of Americans (New York Times, 1985; Luther, 1980). And Afro-Americans will certainly not be first in line for whatever jobs are developed given continuing race and class stratification.

In fact, current management trends are toward automating work and making fewer and fewer employees more and more productive (Chorafas, 1982). Automation of factories has eliminated hundreds of thousands of jobs (Bluestone and Harrison, 1982) and automation of office work is next. It is anticipated that computerization will eliminate thousands of office jobs in the coming decade (Shaiken, 1985; New York Times, 1985). Jobs in manufacturing processes that cannot be automated or robotized are being moved overseas to save labor costs. Finally, it is unlikely that the so-called service industries in the secondary economy will grow large enough to employ an increasingly displaced work-force. It appears that the post-industrialist claim of many new jobs is the equivalent of MacDonald's hamburgers replacing General Motors in the economy. Americans will not continue living in the economic fast lane by selling each other hamburgers, computers and insurance.

Effect of Community Change Across the Generations

American cities came into being and exist to serve industry and trade (Glaab & Brown, 1976). People who live in these cities fulfill roles within the nation's urban economy. As industry, services and trade grew, the city grew. What is less apparent is that urban growth during this century occurred around a succession of newer and more profitable industries. People working in these newer industries were as a rule higher paid, of higher racial and labor status, and were the first to move into newer and better housing (Banfield 1973). Older housing and jobs were in turn passed down to the next status group (Harrison, 1974; Kain, 1968).

Those at the bottom of the urban economy (in the secondary economy) do not realize the full extent to which their opportunities are queued, group specific, structured and unequal. If there is no growth at the top, the opportunity "escalator" does not move. People stay in their current jobs and housing. If there is economic decline, the escalator reverses. Groups at the bottom are the first to be put out of the economy—they lose the jobs and housing they have. But an irony of urban America is that housing at the bottom of the market or end of the queue does not last forever. Low-income housing, like any other housing, must be periodically renovated. But to do so substantially reduces its profitability. Buildings begin to fall apart and not simply from use and abuse. Age takes its toll and has no regard for whether or not alternative housing is available.

A major point (to be elaborated in the next section) is that changes in culture, economy and community are not experienced in the same way by each age group. The primary experiences and current circumstances of each cohort of Afro-Americans will be described in terms of the human and material resources each generation contributes to overall group status. The division of each "generation" by census age groups is arbitrary and is intended to show change over time. Two assumptions have been made for each cohort. First, the primary years of socialization are the teen years and early twenties—adult socialization is established, cultural skills are acquired and work careers are begun. Finally, the primary work years as well as the years of attainment and generational contribution are between 27 and 57 years of age. If we accept these key assumptions, then Afro-American generational effects can be demonstrated.

Generational Differences Across the Decades

The Seventy-two and Older Age Cohort in 1988

It is not an insignificant point that Afro-American elders in 1987 who were adults prior to 1937, have literally witnessed all three transformations of the economy and culture. The younger members of this group were the young people observed by Allison Davis (1941), Charles Johnson (1941), E. Franklin Frazier (1967) and Robert Sutherland (1942) in the 1930s. Their generation were also the subjects in Richard Wright's novels. From the studies of "Negro" youth socialization in the South during the depression we know something about our "seniors'" early experiences. They were poor and were reared in rigidly segregated communities in the North and South. They were socialized to expect inferior status relative to Whites and that violations of racial etiquette would be harshly punished. Their parents were literally the "old school"—strict, authoritarian, quick to punish and hierarchical. Ironically, more recent and detailed studies of Black family life prior to World War II suggested that the vast majority in this age group had both parents present in their households (Gutman, 1976). And the community as well as the family were important extended social networks.

The cultural center for this senior age cohort was their rearing within prefigurative households—traditional, church and elder centered (Mead, 1978). From our current vantage point, this was a generation which was clearly reared by Afro-American adults, not by an electronic media nor by peers. In addition, all of the socializing agents were Afro-Americans—teachers, newspapers, neighbors, ministers and other community professionals. This was also a verbal world. Young people learned from listening to elders' conversations and stories. While a premium was placed on stability, continuity, accommodation to racial etiquette (inferiority) and proper behavior, there was clearly another side to seniors early experiences. They also know and heard about race conflict. Their extended families and communities had members who were Garveyites, victims of and participants in race riots, populists and early union members. There were also those who had fought the night-riders, were lynched, and fought in World War I.

The prefigurative world did not preclude race consciousness. But here, there was a dilemma. During our current seniors formative years, students of Afro-American self-concept reported a pervasive Black self-hatred that centered on color consciousness. This alleged Afro-American self-hatred was common among both the Afro-American masses as well as the small middle class. But at the same time, others pointed to race pride and consciousness. If these observations were accurate, there were probably some who had race pride without self-hatred, others had self-hatred without race pride and still others had both. But the personal histories of seniors in John Gwaltney's *Drylongso* (1980) suggest that this distribution of race pride and self-hatred was not so neatly divided. The dimensions of race consciousness and race hatred varied and were conditioned by the extent to which Afro-Americans were able to resist and subvert Jim Crow in the South (Johnson, 1941) and discrimination in the North.

Finally, World War II brought a major change in the pervasiveness of racial oppression for this generation. The prefigurative world view made the lives that Richard Wright portrayed all the more desperate. The very best Black men could hope for was to be lost in a crowded city—to be Ralph Ellison's "Invisible Man"; White omnipotence just might be forever. But it was during the war years that the masses within the senior generation learned a lot about the "other" colored worlds. They also saw through war that Whites were not omnipotent, after all, and were not destined to remain superior. The prefigurative world view had been broken.

Senior's world of work. By 1940 our current seniors were fully in the labor force as adults (20+ years old). Despite being the last to benefit from the Depression relief efforts and the last to be employed in W.W. II war industries, seniors gained valuable craft skills and work experience. If they had not been displaced by Whites (not all of whom were veterans) after the war, it is possible that racial inequality in the 1950s and 1960s would have been much less. Afro-Americans would have been in skilled jobs and had higher incomes at the beginning of a long period of economic growth. Also most industries had unskilled entry jobs from which one could be trained for more skilled roles. This was an important attribute in both agricultural and manufacturing work that would soon change. With the exception of the latter war years, racial discrimination segregated current seniors throughout their most productive years into low paying, low prestige and less skilled jobs in the nation's older industries. Black senior's labor force marginality continued to increase after the War relative to their White age peers.

Table 1 shows that by 1969 our current seniors relative participation in the labor force had steadily declined for four decades. Conservatives claim that the overall declining labor force participation among Afro-Americans was due to the Great Society welfare programs (Murray 1986). Welfare damaged both the work ethic among Blacks and provided an alternative to gainful employment. But the work experience of the senior generation does not support this claim. Declining Afro-American participation was in place for twenty years before 1960 and the Great Society welfare programs.

There are two alternative and more persuasive arguments than the conservative explanation. In the first, E. Franklin Frazier (1939) pointed out that in the 1930s Afro-Americans were paying a heavy price for

Table 1
The Labor Force Participation Rates of Black and White Males
Who Were 65+ Years Old in 1979

Year	Black Part.	White Part.	% Difference
1939	92.4	95.4	3.0
1949	90.6	95.0	4.4
1959	87.6	94.0	6.4
1969	72.4	81.4	8.9

From U.S. Bureau of the Census, Census of Population, 1980. General Social and Economic Characteristics, Table 87, "Labor Force by Age, Race and Sex: 1940 to 1980." pp. 3132.

migration. The brunt of the Black migrations from the South was experienced by the senior age group. They were the ones who picked up their Southern folk roots and attempted to replant them in the industrial cities of the North and Mid-West. Those who could not adapt and who had misfortunes were legion. Afro-American urban folklore as well as the accounts of scholars and social workers provided direct witness to the personal and economic difficulties of Black migrants in the big cities. Racial discrimination and Frazier's immigrant thesis were the major explanations for Afro-American inequality and maladjustment until these migrations from the South effectively ended in the 1960s.

More recent evidence of Afro-American urban life suggests that the migrant thesis was overdone. Studies of Black community and family life at the turn of the century show two remarkable trends. There were poverty and related problems as described by W.E.B. DuBois in *The Philadelphia Negro*. But then, amidst that poverty, the vast majority of urban Blacks at the turn of the century lived in stable communities and had two adult households (Gutman, 1976; Thernstrom, 1973). From these factors an important question arises. If urbanization has been so destructive of Afro-American life, how could Black people have relatively stable families and communities in large cities such as Boston, New York and Buffalo in 1900, but not in 1935 or 1965? These early city residents were migrants from the South like those who followed them. If city life and organization were in themselves destructive of Afro-American folk culture, then disorganization within Black community life in 1900 should have been far more desperate.

The second explanation for the long-term decline in the senior generation's labor force participation is the following: Afro-Americans have been restricted to work in urban based industries that have matured, been partly abandoned by Whites and are in decline. Each generation's position within the urban economy directly impacts on the stability and quality of community and family life. The present destruction that conservatives blame on modern welfare is primarily due to mounting Afro-American economic marginality. Industry's need for labor matured in the 1950s and has been in decline ever since (Harrison & Bluestone, 1982). And Blacks have had a special place in this evolution of the workforce, at the end of the line. The "last hired and the first fired" is more than a personal testimony; it is the Afro-American's "place" in the industrial economy. Being cut off into permanent low paying and peripheral work is not new for Blacks. The notion of a dual economy is only a more recent phase in Black economic marginality that is now beginning to effect Whites as well.

Housing equity. One role of elders is to provide human support and financial capital to assist younger members. Equity from business, savings, stocks, bonds, property and inheritance are vital to the positioning of younger group members within the economy. Control of wealth is vital. Having no wealth is to be at a distinct disadvantage across the generations. While past comparisons of Black-White economic differences have focused appropriately on income, income is only one component of wealth. Salary income does not fully reflect all resources available to a group. Investments make it possible to assist a sibling through professional school, make a down payment on a "starter" home, provide initial capital to begin a business, pay a grandchild's tuition or support an extensive job search. Even if Black and White people had the same incomes, whoever has invested wealth would have an advantage that could be passed on.

Between 1960 and 1980 the income gap between Whites and Blacks declined. This narrowing gap was used as evidence of progress toward racial equity. But comparisons since 1980 show that the gap is increasing again (see Table 4). What is even more striking are recent comparisons of White and Black financial equity (U.S. Dept. of Commerce, 1986). The median White household had equity worth $39,135 in comparison to $3,397 for Afro-Americans. This is a 12:1 ratio. In addition, the equity held by White households was spread across a variety of sources, while equity held by Blacks was virtually all in family housing. It is not a coincidence that Black equity is held primarily by the seniorage cohort and required a lifetime to accumulate.

This incredible White/Black equity difference reflects a substantial hidden advantage for Whites and disadvantage for Blacks. The 12:1 equity ratio would be lower if Afro-American seniors had not been shut out of work in the primary economy prior to 1960 by racial discrimination. They would have earned more and had more to invest. Then housing segrega-

11

tion has depressed the value of Black held property, leaving community economic decline to devastate whatever Black equity was left. Being long-term property owners and having paid off mortgages has turned out to be a hollow reward due to Afro-American community economic decline. Many attractive Afro-American middle and Working-class communities in the 1940s are now economically depressed enclaves. Longtime residents are trapped in housing that other Blacks could not afford to buy and, for those who could, there was no apparent future equity. The loss of housing equity also means that Afro-American seniors will live out their retirements much poorer than their White peers. It also means that there will be very little equity to pass on to the next generation.

The Fifty-two to Seventy-one Age Cohort in 1988

This second cohort of Afro-Americans entered the work force and began setting up households from 1940 through the 1950s. They were well established by 1960. The older members of this generation can be characterized as seniors. But as one moves down through the years, a very different group comes into view. The younger members were too young to be part of the Negro youth studies of the Depression, so we have no clear picture of them in the social science literature or in novels. After World War II social scientists began moving away from field studies and began to rely more on surveys. Also postwar conservatism and the new "scientific" emphasis ended the pre-War interest in training Black social scientists. As a result, a new age group emerged in the 1950s and Afro-American urban communities continued to transform and very little attention was given to either.

What we do know is that this new Black age group consisted of both migrants from the South and first generation urbanites. They too lived in segregated communities and could only work in low status jobs. Most were reared in prefigurative households and communities, but this is where similarities to seniors end. This second age group was decisively more urban and upwardly mobile than those before them. Frazier pointed out that 25% of urban Afro-Americans in 1950 were "middle-class" in comparison to only 16% in the South (1957). There were more opportunities in the North and Mid-West, while Jim Crow arbitrarily repressed opportunities in the South. This regional difference more heavily impacted those who entered the work force during and right after the War. These differences in circumstance for this second age cohort had cultural effects as well.

Blacks who were 45 to 64 years old in 1980 were the first generation of Afro-Americans who were urban not only in where they lived and worked, but, more importantly, in mind and expectations. In this sense, they were a transitional group between Afro-American seniors and those who were to follow in the 1960s. Frazier observed that the cultural implications of upward mobility and urbanization in the 1950s was that "Negro folk traditions" were compromised and rejected by many. Certainly there were Afro-Americans prior to 1950 who compromised their Southern folkways, but they were not in sufficient numbers or stature to permanently impact the culture. The 1950s was a turning point and the social generation which then entered their prime became a "transitional" age cohort. Higher expectations were no longer held by a few dreamers. The group now had high expectations and newly found housing and post-war government, industrial and manufacturing jobs reinforced expectations.

In addition, the national economy in the 1950s was still centralizing due to technical innovations and the rise of corporations. Distinct cultural regions were being drawn together by interstate highways reducing small town isolation. And what the new highways did not change, television did. Shopping districts of every little town and village became part of the national economy and standardized consumption. Studies of community life in the 1950s recorded the social impacts of this nationalization of regional cultures and economies (Stein, 1960). The maintenance of Mead's prefigurative world required isolation, control, predictability and stability. These new developments seriously undercut prefigurative conditions and propelled the Transitional generation into a new direction. Elders and the "old school" began to carry less and less authority as new ways became acceptable because they were modern and convenient—rearing children, being entertained (movies and T.V.), preserving food (freezing), traveling (auto), etc.

The world of work. One would expect Transitionalists to have higher labor force participation rates than seniors, given the new generation's greater opportunities, optimism and expectations. It turned out that the transitional group had lower labor force participation rates than seniors.

In Table 2 differences in racial labor force participation rates for the transitional age group are compared and there are several surprises. For example, there are progressively lower initial participation rates from the older to younger members of this cohort. There is also a second trend showing progressively lower career-end rates; declining Black participation appears to accelerate after 1960 for both age groups within this social generation. Once again these trends were in place well before the Great Society welfare programs as was the case for Afro-American seniors. Therefore, welfarism cannot be the primary explanation for racial inequality in yet another age cohort.

Long-term decline in Afro-American labor force participation rates relative to Whites might have been due to Blacks working in dirtier, more dangerous and physically demanding jobs than Whites. But if this were the case, how could younger, better educated Blacks who attained newer

Table 2
The Labor Force Participation Rates of Black and White Males Who
Were 45-54 and 55-64 Years Old in 1979

Year	55-64 Cohort		45-54 Cohort		Difference	
Cohort	Blk.	White	Blk.	White	55-64	45-54
1949	86.2	92.8	—	—	6.6	—
1959	89.8	96.3	88.5	95.7	6.5	7.2
1969	85.1	93.3	88.1	96.5	8.2	8.4
1979	62.3	72.2	81.0	91.3	9.9	10.3

From U.S. Bureau of the Census, Census of Population, 1980. General Social and Economic Characteristics, Table 87, "Labor Force by Age, Race and Sex:1940 to 1980". pp. 31-32.

jobs and housing have lower participation rates than older seniors? Could they have had dirtier and more dangerous jobs than seniors? The only reasonable explanation for declining labor force participation rates which fits both the senior and transitional age cohorts is the following: economic growth during the 1940s and 1950s made it possible for jobs and housing to filter down to Blacks who were held in lower status jobs and housing by racial segregation. Meanwhile, the very structure of the economy was in transition. It was dividing into two sectors, primary and secondary, and slowly reducing its need for labor amidst economic growth (Bonacich, 1976). The irony is that, while the economy was rapidly growing in the 1960s, labor force participation rates of those in the most mature and oldest industries were in decline (Bluestone & Harrison, 1982).

The Forty-two to Fifty-one Age Cohort in 1987

By 1960 the post-war personal optimism and desire to modernize was virtually institutionalized. The nation had moved into a new economy and culture. Middle-class aspirations had close to twenty years of development. But underlying Afro-American participation in urban society and post-war optimism was a mounting tension, especially among transitionalists. This tension had nothing to do with adjusting to urban life. Black willingness to continue accommodating racial segregation and discrimination was rapidly eroding. This impatience was the backbone for the civil rights movement. The 1960s ushered in the post-figurative age and promised to provide unprecedented opportunities for a new generation of Afro-Americans. Those who became adults and entered the work force in the 1960s walked into a world totally different than that which either seniors or older transitionists faced. Besides rapid economic growth, "de jure" segregation was outlawed. All of the prefigurative racial codes and etiquette, that had so narrowly confined past generations of Afro-Americans, were under attack and were being dismantled in the South.

This period introduced yet a third generation. The "opportunity" age group was even more urban and post-figurative than the prior group. Their expectations like those of their parents were heavily conditioned by the presumption of continued economic growth and generational mobility. Even those reared in rural areas were heavily influenced by urban culture through television, advertisement and national franchises—from fast food to clothes to movies. Older portrayals of subservient and troubled Negro youth in the 1930s and 40s gave way to television images of young adults able to steadfastly face White mobs, sit-in at "White only" lunch counters and demand employment where their parents were denied. These were unprecedented times and there was little within prefigurative culture to prepare anyone for a world that appeared willing to finally grant Blacks civil rights as Gunnar Myrdal (1944) had predicted. No prior generation had such experiences in their primary years. So the opportunity generation was on its own; they had no authoritarian elders who could lead them through this new world. The new generation placed a premium on change, new beginnings and challenge.

The opportunity generation's world of work. Unprecedented change in prefigurative Southern racial practices and desegregation deflected attention from longterm transitions in the economy. Working class jobs held by the transitional generation during the 1940s and 1950s had been passed down late in each industry's life cycle. Transitionalists were in the labor force of industries that were already mature. Labor intensive activities were becoming obsolete and giving way to automation. The optimism and great expectations of the 1960s was not matched with new working class jobs accessible to Blacks in central cities. The working core of the opportunity generation inherited high expectation but a declining labor market. Cities that had provided previous generations of Afro-Americans with personal freedoms and work unheard of in the South were rapidly becoming economic traps—ghettoes cut off from economic growth. Labor force participation rates for this third social generation show the continued trend of disengaging Afro-Americans from the economy.

By 1970 the Opportunity generation had a lower participation rate in the work force than any prior generation of Afro-Americans at the same time points in their work careers. They had lower participation despite more education, higher expectations, being more urban and entering the

Table 3
The Labor Force Participation Rates of Black and White Males
Who were 35 to 44 Years Old in 1980 (42–51 in 1987)

Year	Black Participation	White Participation	% Difference
1959	82.0	86.8	4.8
1969	87.6	94.7	7.1
1979	86.3	95.2	8.9

From U.S. Bureau of the Census, Census of Population, 1980. General Social and Economic Characteristics, Table 87, "Labor Force by Age, Race and Sex: 1940 to 1980". pp. 31-32.

work force during one of the most dynamic economic periods in this century. The urban riots in the 1960s were partial testimony to the accelerated discarding of Blacks from the work force. Economic disengagement from the primary economy continued unchanged through the 1970s. As a result, the opportunity generation can now vote and eat at a lunch counter in the South, but increasing numbers cannot get adequate employment.

The reality of massive economic disenfranchisement of Afro-Americans in the opportunity generation was initially obscured. More attention was given to those who did manage to get some education and to be the first to integrate middle management, to integrate the faculty and to integrate previously all White neighborhoods. Civil rights activists during the 1960s were drawn heavily from this age group, as well as those who took advantage of new opportunities and were soon to be part of the middle class. Prior to the 1960s and desegregation, the Afro-American middle class was based on providing services to other Blacks. They were physicians, attorneys, teachers, postal workers, small shop keepers, social workers, preachers and entertainers. The size of the middle-class was dependent on the size and prosperity of the community. Housing segregation meant that the Afro-American middle class lived in the community and dominated its leadership. Desegregation changed all of this along with the rapid economic decline of the Black labor force.

Community change. The urban racial enclaves, illustrated by W.E.B. Du Bois in the 1890s (1899), have become over the century sprawling Dark Ghettoes (Clark, 1965). Over half a century, the core of the Afro-American community had transformed from the residencies of those who provided personal services, and did day work, to large cities within cities. The alarm of the early urban ecologists about the size and scale of Chicago's ghetto in the 1920s would turn to shock in the face of southside Chicago or Harlem in the 1960s. But the presence and size of Black urban America in 1960 was no coincidence. The ghettoes of industrial America were large labor reserves for manufacturing and retail industries. But by 1970 the same economic basis that had called Black working class communities into existence in the first place were now forcing their decline.

By 1960 the Afro-American middle class no longer lived "in the community" as they did in small southern towns. The urban Black middle class was in fact segregated within or on the fringes of these huge enclaves. They were twice segregated—away from White and among Blacks. For example, there was Sugar Hill and Strivers Row in Harlem, and then "Pill Hill" on the fringe of Chicago's Southside. The simultaneous economic decline of the community and the expansion of the middle class after 1960 produced the following common experience across the country. The senior and transitional members of the middle class were well established with housing in secure zones and provided services to their Black age peers. The younger opportunity cohort within the middle-class was largely a first generation, upwardly mobile from the working class. They had few financial resources to establish themselves. Nor did they have the organization or will to displace other long term community residents to expand middle income housing for themselves. They more often still held contempt for the very middle class they were now a part of. As a consequence, the opportunity middle class had to find housing where they could and that was outside the community.

Members of the opportunity middle class who provided services to the community found themselves living either in new middle-income high rises near the community—a phase in 1960s urban renewal—or commuting. Others, who took advantage of the new career opportunities in business, education and government, found themselves stretched all over the country and often integrating some distant suburb. The contemporary notion that the new middle class "abandoned" the community is simply inaccurate (Lemann 1986). Certainly there were Afro-Americans who intentionally chose to live and work away from Black people. But their abandonment should not continue to overshadow the fact that the community was in decline and that decline was due to forces older and far more definitive than whether the new middle class lived in or outside of the community. Second, it should be remembered that central cities have generally lacked affordable middle-income housing. And finally, the Afro-American middle class who lived and worked in the community could not have personal contact or serve as role models for the thousands of Blacks who live in the vast ghettoes of "post-industrial" America. Chicago of 1965 or 1987 is not the Chicago described by Drake and Cayton in the late 1930s (1944).

The experience of the opportunity generation since 1960 presents yet another dilemma. How can relative labor force participation rates decline across the generations, while the differences in Black-White family income have decreased over the same period? The latter has been used as an important measure of racial progress since 1960.

Table 4
Afro-American and White Incomes, Medians and Afro-American Incomes as a Percent of Whites

White	1950	1960	1970	1980	1984
Males	2,573	4,319	6,772	13,390	—
Female Heads	—	—	5,620	11,774	—
Male + Female	2,053	3,024	—	—	—
Family	—	5,663	9,958	21,817	27,690
Afro-Americans					
Males	1,361	2,273	4,067	8,296	—
Female Heads	—	—	3,398	7,312	—
Male + Female	973	1,502	—	—	—
Family	—	3,169	6,063	12,598	15,430
A-A / White %					
Males	52%	52%	60%	62%	—
Female Heads	—	—	60%	63%	—
Male + Female	47%	49%	—	—	—
Family	—	56%	61%	58%	56%

From U.S. Bureau of the Census, Census of Population: 1960 U.S. Summary, Table 97; 1970 U.S. Summary, Detailed Characteristics, Tables 245 and 250; 1980 U.S. Summary, Detailed Characteristics, Table 334; Current Population Report, Money Income of Households, Families, and Persons in the U.S.: 1984 (1986).

By looking at the percent that Afro-American income is of Whites income, Table 4 shows progress in reducing income inequity between Blacks and Whites after 1960—the higher the percent, the lower the inequity. Since 1970 that progress has slowed and then reversed itself for family incomes. Certainly a vigorous economy and reform in racial practices were partly responsible. But there is another factor. Women in Afro-American families have historically had a higher labor force participation rate than White married women. In 1970, Afro-American family income reflected a higher proportion of two income households than did White family income. But with increasing numbers of married White women entering the labor force by 1980, the family income gap between the races increased again. A decline in the standard of living and rising prices have forced Whites to do what Afro-Americans had had to do all along—go to work. Also, when median incomes are disaggregated by age and sex, the financial impact of different generational experiences in the labor force becomes apparent.

Table 5
Median Incomes of Males in Constant 1983 Dollars,
Black as a Percentage of Whites by Age, 1949-1983

Age	1949	1959	1969	1979	1983
15-24	66%	71%	91%	75%	61%
25-34	57	58	68	69	65
35-44	53	57	62	65	66
45-54	51	53	59	59	62
55-64	47	49	53	54	52
65+	49	53	57	56	57

From Walter Allen and R. Farley, "The Shifting Social and Economic Tides of Black America, 1950-1980," *Annual Review of Sociology*, Vol. 12, 1986, Table 4, pp. 293-294.

Table 5 shows that the younger are Black male workers, the less the initial gap between White and Black incomes. But Table 5 also shows that Black male incomes decline over the years relative to their White peers—paralleling their declining labor force participation. The decline in income with age is consistent across the decades since 1949. The income difference between Black and White age peers began low at the entry level (15-24 yrs.) between 1949 and 1969, but then began to increase again. Over these three decades income gains in the early years were progressively eroded as each age cohort gained seniority in the labor force. These patterns point to a very different trend than that suggested by William Wilson (1978). The initial decline in income inequality between Black and White families from 1960 to 1970 suggests that younger cohorts of Blacks were progressively better off. What was assumed is that this progressive improvement in incomes would be maintained for each new cohort across the years. If so, we would see a decline in racially specific income over time. What Table 5 shows is that differences between Black and White starting incomes between 1949 and 1969 declined, but whatever gains each cohort made have been progressively eroded over the life of their employment participation.

The Thirty-two to Forty-one Age Cohort in 1987

This last cohort consists of older "baby boomers". It is a relatively large cohort and over the coming decades will have a disproportionate impact on all societal trends. They are also the children of the transitionalists and began entering the labor force in the late 1960s. The majority began work after 1970, amidst a series of economic recessions. Only the older members of this age group had any experience with the prefigurative world as children. Memories of Jim Crow and of Civil Rights activism came through their parents and by watching television while in elementary and junior high school. Like their parents they have very high expectations of continued economic and race progress. Many younger members of this group were recruited into the nation's colleges and universities through affirmative action. But unlike their parents, they have entered an economy that can no longer support continued generational upward mobility.

The older baby boomers are themselves a transitional group. The great expectations of the brief post-figurative days are fading away as the nation's culture now moves rapidly toward a co-figurative world. The senior generation had elders and traditions to rely upon for their socialization and as adult reference groups. After the transitionists, members of the opportunity cohort had each other—peers. For baby boomers, peer reference and socialization are in transition. Electronic media provide increasingly important sources of identity and points of reference. This is the first generation to grow up watching television and to have its own youth oriented music—"Rock 'n Roll". Television has played a critical socializing role through all phases of their development and will continue to do so. For younger and lower class members of this group, they have probably spent as much time watching television as interacting with elders, parents and even peers.

The parents of Afro-American baby boomers had no cultural map into a world of economic growth, urban freedoms and desegregation. Likewise, baby boomers have no cultural map through economic decline and a dual economy. This age group is also the first to be beyond the cultural issues of migrant adjustment to large cities and the effects of losing folk culture. Black baby boomers are by far the most acculturated and assimilated of Afro-American generations. But here lies the problem. E. Franklin Frazier attributed the disorganization of Afro-American community life in the 1930s to the problems of immigrants adjusting to urban life. The cultural skills that Afro-Americans had crafted in the South and that contributed to their survival were suddenly hindrances in big cities.

While Frazier's observation was overdone and later distorted by Daniel P. Moynihan (1986), his point is still important when looking at Afro-American baby boomers.

Baby Boomers do not bring to increasing economic marginality the same cultural skills prior generations of Afro-Americans possessed. Baby boomers have more schooling than any prior generation of Blacks and have even higher expectations for social and economic mobility than their parents. But what they were unprepared for is the actuality of having fewer opportunities than their parents. They will be more marginal to the economy than either their grandparents or parents, despite being better prepared. But there is more here than disappointment. If Frazier's immigrant adjustment thesis was correct, Black baby boomers should be the best adjusted and the most skilled generation of Black urbanites yet. These skills might have been very beneficial if baby boomers had entered a growth economy and the postfigurative culture that they were reared in. But the accelerated break down of baby boomer nuclear families and communities after 1960 suggest that just the opposite is the case. They do not have the same skills in coping with economic marginality as did their parents or Black seniors.

Baby boomers have less of the "folk culture" Frazier observed and was concerned with. But more recent students of Black culture hold that it was this "folk culture" that made Black survival possible in Frazier's "Cities of Destruction" (Jones 1963; Stack 1974). If this counter observation is correct, then there is here both an irony and a dilemma. The irony is that in being prepared to take advantage of new opportunities, coping skills have been lost—the frame of mind necessary to accommodate subordination and economic insecurity. The dilemma is that, even if all of the former generations coping skills were intact, the circumstances baby boomers and future generations face are very different from those that prior generations dealt with. Afro-American baby boomers began their adult community and work careers in the face of unprecedented and massive drug trafficking. They were the primary age group called upon to fight the War in Vietnam. In addition, working class Black baby boomers have had to seek housing outside of the community and for the same reasons that the opportunity middle class did in the 1960s. The deterioration of housing and the community social fabric during the 1970s has made core Black communities increasingly unlivable for those with options.

Afro-American baby boomers are also the first generation for which there is no escape to the South or North. Members of prior generations of Blacks could always return, temporarily and permanently, to the South. When a sibling was sent "down South" it meant more than being sent to another location. It meant being returned to prefigurative roots—to be sent home for care and proper rearing. Southern and prefigurative communities were resources and a base of support for family members struggling in cities. In the same way, southern Blacks could escape to the city and could find better paying jobs and opportunity even within a segregated work force. But today, regardless of whether being in the South, North, city or country, one is part of the same national culture and economy. There is also no escape from drug trafficking, community deterioration and the need to work in what was once called "city work"—factories, offices and services industries. The days when a Southern aunt, cousin, parent or grandparents could add another member to their household are rapidly coming to an end. Finally, war, drugs, economic marginality, deterioration of the core community, electronic socialization and minimal "folk culture" all incline this social generation to greater suspicion, and alienation from institutions. Older baby boomers are a prelude to the next generation where identity and culture will be even more heavily conditioned by electronic images and the media.

The world of work and community. Afro-American labor in the baby boomer cohort is moving from the fringes of a disappearing manufacturing economy into a new secondary and service economy. This new sector is poorly organized, low paying, and a dead-end. One cannot advance through seniority or training out of this sector and into higher paying jobs. This work is very similar to the day-jobs done by Blacks at the turn of the century. The effect of deindustrialization on the Black labor force is reflected again in baby boomers labor force participation rates.

Table 6
The Labor Force Participation Rates of Black and
White Males Who Were 35-44 Years Old in 1979

Year	Black Participation	White Participation	% Difference
1969	35.8	48.9	13.1
1979	83.5	94.3	10.8

From Walter Allen and R. Farley, "The Shifting Social and Economic Tides of Black America, 1950-1980," *Annual Review of Sociology*, Vol. 12, 1986, Table 4, pp. 293-294.

The earlier trend of declining Afro-American male participation in the labor force continues with baby boomers. They have yet lower rates of participation at the same age and point in their labor careers as prior generations of Blacks. What the census unemployment rates do not show are those who are no longer in the labor force. The unemployment rates would be considerably higher if we could account for those who are no longer looking for work in the legal cash economy. A journey through any large urban Black community quickly leads the observer to realize that there is an alternate street economy consisting of unreported cash for services, stolen goods and illegal activities. What was in the 1960s a Black teenage unemployment problem is now a Black adult unemployment problem. The Black teen unemployed in one decade becomes the adult underemployed in the next (Glasgow 1980; Spaights and Dixon 1986).

Comparisons and Conclusions

Group Cohesiveness

Differences in social generations among Afro-Americans provide another dimension to issues regarding Black unity. The idea of Blacks being a united or cohesive group has been assumed by many and is a dream for others. But in reality Black unity is highly conditional. In the prefigurative South, racial discrimination and segregation were an underlying incentive for racial unity. Anyone of African descent, regardless of who they were or what they accomplished, was assigned the same inferior status and out of necessity had to rely on one another for survival. Having to live together also bridged the many differences within the group and reinforced traditions and customs—things in common. But rapid social change during this century has transformed prefigurative ways of maintaining racial subordination and, in doing so, has also transformed the conditions under which Black unity occurs.

In the current postfigurative culture, we recognize that the electric refrigerator modernized the ice-box and air travel has virtually replaced railroads. But we do not fully appreciate that racial domination has also been modernized. Economic racism is displacing biological racism. The prefigurative belief that racial superiority and inferiority was based on innate biological differences justified racial discrimination and called for physical separation—segregation—in order to maintain European racial purity and vigor. Such a basis can no longer be justified, but more importantly, postfigurative Blacks as well as many Whites are less tolerant of it. Instead racial statuses (superior and inferior) can now be justified by alleged differences in work ethics, motivation, competitive and cognitive abilities, management skills and entrepreneurial spirit. These claims are conditional and cultural traits that Whites just happen to have in greater abundance. In addition, racial statuses can be maintained by splitting the economy into primary and secondary sectors. As long as large numbers of Afro-Americans do not gain entry through education into the primary economy, continuing racial inequity is assured with this modern system of dominance; it is no longer necessary to directly segregate or discriminate based on race.

Postfigurative Social Control

In the postfigurative culture, economic racism places Afro-Americans under the same economic controls as poor Whites. One difference is that Black participation in the underclass is on a nearly permanent basis. The few Afro-Americans who do gain entry to the primary economy will not be in sufficient numbers or in enough key roles to threaten those in control of corporate behavior. Nor will they be able to alter the course of business toward greater social accountability. Furthermore, there will be token Afro-American participation in the upper levels of management so that overt racial discrimination is not evident. Even marriage between Black men and White women will be tolerated as long as the women are lower class, the least desired and that the couple not inherit White family wealth. It is also necessary to advocate that anything done for Blacks will also have to be done for poor Whites, women, other minority groups and anyone else. This new requirement makes collective action infinitely more difficult and also makes any government action ineffective.

Desegregation, overt tolerance and the masking of racial discrimination within a new economic organization makes prefigurative Afro-American race unity and race consciousness virtually impossible. Certainly the experiences that were recognized as collectively "Black" prior to desegregation are now becoming less visible and distinct. Alternative bases for a continuing Afro-American cohesiveness will have to be found within a culture and economy in rapid change—from postfigurative to cofigurative. Each of these new cultural phases provide more options and incentives for fragmenting racial identity and collective behavior. In the past there has been a uniform Black racial identity divided by economic class and social values that grew out of a common history and segregation (Drake & Cayton, 1944). In the evolving cofigurative world, collective identities will be heavily influenced, if not defined, by social class related access to powerful and comprehensive medias. Free T.V. will be poor people's access to information, while more technically sophisticated pay networks will be available to those who can afford the fees. In addition, personal experiences will be more directly conditioned by the imagery and content of this media. Present differences in lifestyle, entertainment preference and values can be exaggerated and find social reinforcement in the evolving cofigurative culture.

Social Generation

In one sense, elements of this cofigurative world already exist. Economic marginality has been consistent and a mounting problem for Afro-Americans across the decades. Yet there has been enough cultural change to literally give each age cohort what appeared to be unique generational experiences. Common history, subordination and economic marginality across the generations have been offset by rapid changes in the organization of the economy and national culture. In fact, for well over two decades, 1950 to 1970, three cohorts of Afro-Americans were optimistic and held high expectations of improved economic mobility. In the meantime, they were each losing progressively more jobs and their communities were deteriorating. Afro-Americans are indeed divided by social generations as well as the continuing important differences of economic and social class. But what might be even more problematic is that the social distance across the generations may be as large as the distance between races and economic classes. Afro-American elders carry with them what is left of "Negro folk" culture and as one passes down through the generations that culture becomes less prominent. Elders are simply no longer authorities or primary socializing agents for cofigurative youth. Whatever strengths or weaknesses prefigurative Afro-American life and culture have is being diminished across the generations. But the key question here is what is folk culture being replaced by?

Younger cohorts of Afro-Americans are more culturally assimilated at an earlier age into the public mainstream than were older Blacks. But Afro-American folk culture is not simply disappearing. Rather, it is being replaced by an urban variant of southern Afro-American and rural folkways. As underclass and marginally employed Black youth become increasingly the core population within the Black community, we can expect to see their variation of cofiguration come into being. We can also anticipate that expectations of material progress will continue contrary to actuality. Being urban and tied into mass electronic media means that all social classes will continue to have middle class expectations regardless of their access to real resources.

The Middle Class

The Afro-American middle class is also going through a transition. Opportunity and baby boomer members of the middle class have very different circumstances and generational challenges than older, community based members. It was necessary for the older middle class to be involved in the community—this is where they lived and made their income. For younger class members, who do not live or work in the community, association and involvement in the community as both a psychological and cultural place are optional. Some have more in common with their White class and age peers. Others have learned the value of appropriate and proper behavior among White peers and colleagues. Still others have another and Black cultural world off the job that is closer to

who they are (Staples 1976; Chapter 5). As a consequence, it is very difficult to determine the extent to which the present Afro-American middle
class has assimilated due to the conditional nature of their class behavior.
Finally, it should be remembered that Frazier pointed out that the older
middle class was really not middle class in the classical sense. Being Black
and middle class had more to do with respectability and outward behavior than with real values and class responsibility (Frazier, 1957). New
members of the Black middle class may be just as marginal.

Participation in the Economy

When labor force participation rates are divided by age groups, each
younger cohort shows a declining participation rate. Also the longer any
age group of Afro-Americans is in the labor force the further their participation rate falls behind their White age peers. Conservatives claim that
welfare programs are responsible for declining Black labor force participation. This explanation does not account for the declining participation
of two cohorts of older Afro-Americans who were in the labor force prior
to modern welfare. Nor does it account for the progressive decline in
labor participation as Black age groups get younger, more urban and better educated. The Post-industrialist claim is also questionable. There is no
indication that "hi-tech" industries will employ those displaced by deindustrialization nor will sufficient alternative jobs be created in the U.S. In
this case, deindustrialization has not only affected older Afro-Americans,
it has in fact had a greater negative impact on younger, less established
Black workers. The Split Labor market explanation for declining Afro-
American participation is more appropriate (Kaufman, 1986).
Afro-Americans have been allowed to work consistently on the margins
of the economy and in industries that were near the end of their life cycle.
Growth in jobs and equity are occurring in specialized industries which
constitute a primary or central economy, that Blacks do not have access to.
Whatever is the effect of welfare programs, the long term trend of
declining Afro-American labor force participation is embedded in the
economy and is not a temporary downturn due to recession or slow
economic growth. Not all Blacks are faced with economic doom, but
enough are affected to impact community life as never before. The trend
of declining Afro-American labor force participation raises an important
question. If future profitability means continued automation and employing fewer and fewer, how are the people who are being pushed out of the
economy to support themselves? This is an immediate question for
Blacks, but it is one which will have to be answered in the future for
Whites as well (Hill, 1986).

Impact of Declining Labor Force Participation

Those on the edge of the economy cannot wait until the nation faces up to the consequences of split labor markets and employment downsizing. Urban "peasants" in 1988 do not have rural land and work to return to in the South. They have no alternative but to make it in the money economy with or without salaries. Dividing Afro-Americans into age cohorts provides a circumstance to study the impact of deindustrialization on Blacks. The "so-called" urban crisis of Black family destabilization and community decline is no coincidence. The increasing rate of destruction after 1965 are due to underlying changes as a basis for continuing racial oppression. The withdrawal of government from social support, slow economic growth and deindustrialization combine to accelerate community and family decline. Afro-Americans and labor in general are positioned so that they cannot benefit from the fabulously profitable primary economy.

It is the declining need for labor which makes continued Black community life tenuous and family formation a luxury. Men and women who in past times would be employed are forced to support themselves by hustling, vending, selling drugs and each other and doing whatever they can. It does not take many people in this circumstance to undermine the overall sense of morale, trust and pride within a community. The decline of the U.S. as the major industrial and economic power in the West means that marginal and low status populations are being jettisoned from the economy first. It is possible that the U.S. may end up with shattered "native" economies like third world countries. Recent trends in U.S. Afro-American family formation (Glick, 1982) are approximating family patterns made possible in the "native" economies of the Caribbean—later marriage, child birth independent of marriage and serial relations.

For Future Conflict

The stage is being set for massive unrest. While the primary economy celebrates its vigor and prosperity, the secondary economy is locked into a depression with no end in sight. The numbers of Whites and Afro-Americans who are unemployed and underemployed is growing and they have no place to go—no future. Present conservatives do not understand the need for a liberal social agenda. The New Deal and Great Society programs were never intended to end poverty or discrimination. their function was to reduce alienation, provide hope and buy time. They were magnificent successes. On the other hand, conservatives' control of the economy and national agenda are in the open for all to see without the welfare state to support a large underclass and to confuse who is in control and who benefits. All that is now needed is for the poor and

27

oppressed to find each other—to realize that their problems are not individual.

It is much easier to count those who are successful and there is good reason to celebrate their success (Freeman, 1977). But the so-called underclass is larger than we realize and is not the product of unwillingness to work and unrealistic expectations. It should be remembered that the Afro-American underclass is not new (Drake & Cayton, 1944). What is new is its size and hopelessness. There are no prospects for sufficient new working class jobs on the horizon. The waste of human talent and potential due to under and unemployment in the secondary economy should be added to the list of major issues to be addressed in Afro-American adult development.

References

Allen, D., & Patterson, Z. (1974). The multigenerational family history: A case study of a Black family, *Free Inquiry, 2*, 39-47.

Banfield, E. (1973). *The unheavenly city revisited*. Boston: Little, Brown and Company.

Becker, G. (1957). The economics of discrimination. Chicago: University of Chicago Press.

Bell, D. (1973). *The coming of post-industrial society*. New York: Basic Books.

Bengtson, V., et al. (1974). Time, aging and the continuity of social structure: Themes and issues in generational analysis, Journal of Social Issues, 30, 2, 1-30.

Bluestone, B., & Harrison, B. (1982). *The deindustrialization of America*. New York: Basic Books.

Bonacich, E. (1976). Advanced capitalism and Black-White relations in the U.S.: A split labor market interpretation, *American Sociological Review, 41*, 34-51.

Chorafas, D. (1982). *Office automation: The productivity challenge*. Englewood Cliffs: Prentice-Hall

Clark, K. (1965). *Dark ghetto*. New York: Harper and Row.

Davis, A., et al. (1941). *Deep south*. Chicago: University of Chicago Press.

Dollard, J. (1937). *Caste and class in a southern town*. New Haven: Yale University Press.

Drake, S. C., & Cayton, H. (1944) *Black metropolis*. New York: Harper and Row.

Du Bois, W. E. B. (1899). *The Philadelphia Negro*. New York: Schocken (reprint 1967).

Elder, G. (1974). *Children of the depression*. Chicago: University of Chicago Press.

Elder, G. (1975). Age differentiation and life course, *Annual Review of Sociology, 1*, 165-190.

Esler, A. (1982). *The generation gap in society and history*. Monticello, Ill.: Vance Bibliographies.

Frazier, E. F. (1957). Black bourgoisie. New York: *The Free Press*.

Frazier, E. F.(1939). *The Negro family in the U.S.*. Chicago: The University of Chicago Press.

Frazier, E. F. (1967). *Negro youth at the crossways*. New York: Schocken.

Freeman, R. (1977). *Black elite: The new market for highly qualified Black Americans.* New York: McGraw-Hill.

Glaab, C., & Brown, T. (1976). *A history of urban America.* New York: MacMillan.

Glasgow, D. (1980). *The Black underclass: Poverty, unemployment and entrapment of ghetto youth.* San Francisco: Jossey-Bass.

Glick, P. (1982). A demographic picture of Black families in H. McAdoo (Ed). *The Black family.* Beverly Hills: Sage.

Gutman, H. (1976). *The Black family in slavery and freedom.* New York: Pantheon Books.

Gwaltney, J. (1980). *Drylongso.* New York: Vintage Books.

Harrison, B. (1974). *Urban economic development: Suburbanization, minority opportunity and the condition of the central city.* Washington, D.C.: The Urban Institute.

Hill, E. (1986). Structural unemployment and its social consequences: A sociologist's view, *The Journal of Interdisciplinary Economics, 1,* 101-106.

Johnson, C. (1941). *Growing up in the Black belt.* Washington: American Council on Education.

Jones, L. (1963). *Blues people.* New York: William Morrow.

Kain, J. (1968). Housing desegregation: Negro employment and metropolitan decentralization. *Quarterly Journal of Economics, 82,* 175-193.

Kaufman, R. (1986). The impact of industrial and occupational structure on Black-White employment allocation, *American Sociological Review, 51,* 310-323.

Kumar, K. (1978). *Prophecy and progress: The sociology of industrial and post-industrial society.* New York: Penguin Books.

Lemann, N. (1986). The origins of the underclass. *The Atlantic Monthly,* June, 31-55.

Luther, A. (1980). The dual economy: Internal migration, urban unemployment and differential wages. Stanford University, (PhD) thesis.

Mannheim, K. (1928). The problem of generations, K. Mannheim (Ed.), *Essays in the sociology of knowledge.* London: Routledge (1975).

Mead, M. (1978). *Culture and commitment.* New York: Columbia University Press.

Moynihan, D. (1986). *Family and nation.* San Diego: Harcourt Brace and Jovanovich.

Murray, C. (1986). *Losing ground: American social policy, 1950-1980.* New York: Basic Books.

Myrdal, G. (1944). *An American dilemma.* New York: Harper and Row.

Times, N.Y. (1985, October 7). New studies show growth rate for clerical jobs is starting to slowdown, *New York Times, 9.*

Price, B. (1983). *The political economy of mechanization in U.S. agriculture.* Boulder: Westview Press.

Ragan, P. (1977). (Ed.). *Black and Mexican American aging: A selected bibliography.* Los Angeles: Ethel Percy Andrus Gerontology Center, University of Southern California.

Reich, M. (1982). *Racial inequality.* Princeton: Princeton University Press.

Rose, A. (1948). *The Negro's morale: Group identification and protest.* Minneapolis: University of Minnesota Press.

Shaiken, H. (1985). *Work transformed: Automation and labor in the computer age.* New York: Holt, Rinehard & Winston.

Spaights, E., & Dixon, H. (1986). Black youth unemployment: Issues and problems, *Journal of Black Studies, 16(4),* 385-396.

Staples, R. (1976). *Introduction to Black sociology.* New York: McGraw-Hill.

Stack, C. (1974). *All of our kin: Strategies for survival in a Black community.* New York: Harper and Row.

Stein, M. (1960). *The eclipse of community: An interpretation of American studies.* New York: Harper and Row.

Sutherland, R. (1942). *Color, class and personality.* Washington: American Council on Education.

Thernstrom, S. (1973). *The other Bostonian: Power and progress in the American metropolis: 1880-1970.* Cambridge: Harvard University Press.

Thurow, L. (1969). *Poverty and discrimination.* Washington, D.C.: Brookings Institute.

Touraine, A. (1971). *The post-industrial society.* New York: Random House.

U.S. Department of Commerce, Bureau of the Census (1986). *Money, income of households, families and persons in the U.S.: 1984,* Washington, D.C.: U.S. Government Printing Office.

U. S. Department of Commerce, Bureau of the Census (1983). *Census of population,* 1980, U.S. Summary, Detailed Characteristics, Tables 87, 334. Washington, D.C.: U.S. Government Printing Office.

U. S. Department of Commerce, Bureau of the Census (1971). *Census of population,* 1970. U.S. Summary, Detailed Characteristics, Tables 199, 250. Washington: U.S. Government Printing Office.

U. S. Department of Commerce, Bureau of the Census (1961). *Census of population.* 1960. U.S. Summary, Table 97. Washington, D.C.: U.S. Government Printing Office.

Wilson, W. J. (1978). *The declining significance of race.* Chicago: University of Chicago Press.

Wright, G. (1978). *The political economy of the south.* New York: Norton Publishers.

STAGES OF ADULT DEVELOPMENT IN BLACK, PROFESSIONAL WOMEN

Janice E. Ruffin

Historically, psychologists have devoted greater attention to the study of infancy, childhood, and adolescence than to the adult years. The relatively recent focus on adulthood represents the emergence of a new field: life span developmental psychology. The life span perspective recognizes that development does not stop with adolescence; rather, human development is viewed as a lifelong process. Life span psychologists seek to understand the critical developmental issues for any given period of life and offer explanations for the varying patterns of change which individuals undergo throughout their life courses.

There is general agreement that life span developmental psychology is in its earliest stages of growth. Currently, the field shows the signs of groping, inchoation, and experimentation that characterizes a new field of inquiry (Smelser and Erikson, 1980). Perhaps the most central problem affecting this new field is the absence of a unified, comprehensive theory of adulthood. Such a theory would be based in an integration of biological, psychological, and sociological perspectives. Moreover, such a theory would be grounded in empirical research conducted on diverse populations.

The major impetus for the research reported herein on Black women was that the subgroup is underrepresented in available studies on adult development. To date, such studies have devoted greater attention to males than to females, and to Whites than to Blacks. Given the limited samples upon which conclusions about adult development are based, research on Black women is essential. This chapter proceeds with a brief review of research on adult development, followed by an outline of the issues considered most relevant to Black women.

Research Approaches to the Study of Adult Development

Rossi (1980) has observed that there has been a distinct difference in the approaches of scientists investigating the "life course" versus those of others focusing on the "life span". Life course researchers have as a major focus the search for social patterns in the timing, duration, spacing, and order of life events. Such work done by sociologists, historical demographers, and historians relies on a definition of the life course as "the pathways through the age-differentiated structure in the major role domains of life" (Rossi, 1980, p. 7). By contrast, life span psychologists are more specifically concerned with individual psychological development.

As Rossi (1980) has further clarified, at this point in history, there appears to be two major types of theory within the life-span perspective: "stage theories" and "timing of events" models. In the latter model there is skepticism that any clear and orderly patterns of adulthood exist. Instead of sharply defined stages of development, some argue that change occurs on one or several dimensions of the life course, triggered by specific personal or environmental events. Timing-of-events theorists deemphasize the influence of chronological age in adult development. The assumption is that the phasing and the shifts in self-definition are structured by age norms rooted in culture and society.

Perun and Bilby (1980) have provided a conceptual model of value for visualizing development in terms of a timing-of-events model. They picture changes throughout the life course as analogous to the operation of a disk pack in a computer. Adult development is conceptualized in terms of many dimensions, each internally regulated by a multiplicity of timetables. Each of the constituent dimensions is in simultaneous operation and moves in time at a rate specific to itself. Further, each of the dimensions has its own developmental progression with its own antecedents, transitions, and sequelae (Giele, 1982, p. 7).

The second type of perspective in work on adult development has been labeled the "normative crisis" model or stage theory (Rossi, 1980). These theories tend to follow in the tradition of Erikson's (1950) epigenetic model in which the individual's personality gradually unfolds, from the psychologically undifferentiated infant, to progressively higher and more complex levels of development. Erikson's model is premised on the notion of a patterned sequence of stages; each stage has particular tasks to be accomplished in the physical, emotional, and cognitive spheres.

Stage theories portray adults as continuously tending toward a more individuated and complex self. The assumption is that when the specific tasks of a given stage are unresolved, development in all subsequent stages is impaired. Further, the idea of crisis as a normal part of adult development is incorporated in these stage theories. Crises provide the opportunity for intense self reevaluation, with resultant changes in the self.

Yet, there are often major differences among stage theorists in interpretations of how and why individuals change throughout their adult lives. Erikson's (1959, 1963) conception of the life cycle delineates eight stages which represent a crisis for the developing ego. Other psychoanalysts focus on particular psychosexual events as precipitants of personality change in adulthood (Bibring, 1959; Benedek, 1970). More recently, Gould (1978) has discussed stages in terms of transformation from childhood consciousness to more reality based adult consciousness. Vaillant's (1977) longitudinal study of Harvard undergraduates represented an inquiry into aspects of personality and adaptation. A hierarchy of "ego mechanisms" or defenses was found to be predictive of growth throughout the adult years.

Currently, it appears that there is no paradigm for dealing with changes over the life span that commands consensus. In this author's view, while there are many divergent intellectual traditions within the field, few studies except Levinson's (1978) have moved significantly beyond Erikson's (1963) conception of the life cycle. While Erikson proposed only three stages for the entirety of adult life, Levinson's work provides a more elaborated view of developmental periods in adulthood. Further, Levinson's concept of the life structure avoids a too narrow focus on personality alone, and locates the individual within an external world which also requires examination. Since Levinson's model served as the central framework for the research reported herein on Black women, a brief summary is provided of this model.

Levinson's Life Structure Paradigm

Levinson's theory of adult development is based on his research with a sample of forty men, distributed in age from 35-45 years. Levinson's theory is, fundamentally, a conception of *how* individuals change during the adult years. A pivotal concept within the theory is that of life structure, i.e., the basic pattern or design of a person's life at a given time. Levinson notes: "The concept of life structure...gives us a way of looking at the engagement of the individual in society. It requires us to consider both self and world, and the relationships between them... When I speak of adult development, I mean the evolution of the life structure during the adult years" (pp 41-42).

Levinson's model for development is based in several basic premises. These are: 1) Developmental change is expressed through changes in the life structure; 2) The life structure evolves through a relatively orderly sequence of developmental periods: "It consists of a series of alternating stable (structure-building) periods and transitional (structure-changing) periods" (p. 49); 3). Each developmental period is linked to specific chronological ages; 4) Each developmental period has specific developmental tasks; and, 5) The developmental periods are characteristic of the species and, therefore, are universally observable.

According to Levinson, analysis of the life structure begins with a consideration of its primary components—the choices made by a person. The men in Levinson's sample were found to have two or three central components in their life structures. These central components were: occupation, marriage-family, friendships, peer relationships, ethnicity, religion, and leisure.

One of the most controversial propositions of Levinson's work is that the developmental periods begin at specific chronological ages. That is, the assumption is that there is an average, or most frequent, age for the onset and completion of every era. This is an aspect of the theory which is questioned given the varied and changing meanings of age in our current society.

The sequence of periods in adult development, as proposed by Levinson and his coworkers, is pictured in Figure 1. The sequence begins

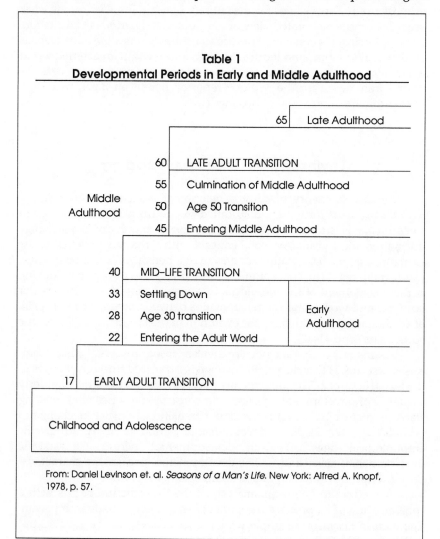

Table 1

Developmental Periods in Early and Middle Adulthood

	65	Late Adulthood
	60	LATE ADULT TRANSITION
	55	Culmination of Middle Adulthood
Middle Adulthood	50	Age 50 Transition
	45	Entering Middle Adulthood
	40	MID–LIFE TRANSITION
	33	Settling Down
	28	Age 30 transition
	22	Entering the Adult World
		Early Adulthood
	17	EARLY ADULT TRANSITION
		Childhood and Adolescence

From: Daniel Levinson et. al. *Seasons of a Man's Life.* New York: Alfred A. Knopf, 1978, p. 57.

with the *Early Adult Transition* (E.A.T.) and is followed by a structure-building period, *Entering the Adult World* (E.A.W.). This structure is modified in the *Age Thirty Transition* (A.T.T.). In the *Settling Down* (S.D.) period, a second adult life structure is built; it is followed by a *Mid-Life Transition* (M.L.T.) which links early and middle adulthood.

Levinson proposed specific tasks for each of the developmental periods, as well as several general tasks for transitional and stable periods. The tasks relate to the evolving life structure, rather than to a developing personality or ego. These developmental tasks were seen to be essential for the evolution of a "satisfactory" life structure. The tasks for each period reflect both the characteristic concerns of a given age group and the demands of the social order. Thus, men were seen to evolve life structures reflecting individual motives as well as societal expectations.

As of this writing, three studies on women have been completed using Levinson's theory (Stewart, 1976; Taylor, 1981; and, Ruffin, 1985). Stewart and Taylor investigated the lives of White women, focusing on the formation of their early adult life structures. Both of these investigators found that Levinson's *descriptions* of the first four devlopmental periods (E.A.T., E.A.W., A.T.T., and S.D.) had applicability to their subjects' lives. However, the fundamental premise that adult lives evolve through a series of alternating stable and transitional periods was not fully supported by Stewart's or Taylor's research.

Further, both of these studies underscored the fact that women's lives evidence variability in the "seasons" in which developmental tasks are accomplished. Women's difficulties in integrating family life with career investment exerted a dominant influence on their life courses. Levinson's theory is challenged, primarily, in terms of its limited explanatory power for women whose lives varied from the almost exclusive career orientation evidenced by Levinson's male subjects.

Gooden's (1980) study of adult development in fifteen Black men also utilized Levinson's theory. Gooden's findings were supportive of Levinson's descriptions of the developmental periods, but his study illuminated the influences of race, social class, and culture on the evolution of these men's life structures. The theory was seen to have limited applicability to men who were unable to achieve economically viable life structures.

The Sociocultural Context of Black Women's Adult Development

The present study on Black women was initiated with a goal of developing hypotheses regarding the interactive effects of age, gender, social class, culture, and race/ethnicity on adult development. Particular attention was given to conceptualizing the cultural milieu within which development occurs.

Three broad issues are addressed in relation to the sociocultural context of Black women's development. These are: 1) Male-female relations within the Black subsociety; 1) Occupational patterns among Black women; and, 3) Socio-historical perspectives.

Male-Female Relations

Jackson (1971) has summarized data relevant to the problem of a low sex-ratio, i.e. the number of males per every one hundred females, within the Black population. Using data derived from census reports, Jackson has concluded that, since 1850, Black men have been becoming more and more scarce in the Black population.

Though there is uncertainty surrounding the accuracy of census data, there is an apparent shortage of Black males in the population (Rodgers-Rose, 1980; Siegel, 1973). In view of this shortage, Jackson (1971) has suggested that Blacks have had a headstart on Whites in developing alternative familial patterns. Three trends have been most notable. First, the number of husband-wife Black families has decreased steadily (from approximately 78 percent in 1950, to a low of 61 percent in 1975) (Rodgers-Rose, 1980, p. 37). Second, the number of Black women heading households doubled between 1950 and 1975 (Rodgers-Rose, 1980, p. 37). Third, both categories of unpaired women (single, never-married and divorced/separated) have shown dramatic increases, although the greatest change has occurred in the number of singles (Rodgers-Rose, p. 37).

Staples (1973) has addressed the fact that the Black divorce rate is, approximately, double that of the White rate (p. 116). He summarizes this situation as one of the interactive effects of economics and racial oppression: "The dissatisfaction of Black women, across class lines, with their marriages reflects the unique situation they face in American society. Their racial oppression leads to economic deprivation, and the two elements interact to make marriage an untenable institution for them" (p. 111). (See also chapter by Tucker and Mitchell-Kernan, this volume).

Occupational Patterns

Black women have also been found to effect unique patterns of relating to the world of work. Epstein's (1973) study of Black, professional women found that they were highly motivated to seek and be successful in a professional career. Epstein's sample of lawyers, dentists, physicians, journalists and business women generally married late, or not at all (over

30 percent). Epstein summarizes the interrelationships between their professional status and their marriage options:

> As this society is presently constituted, it is a serious matter when a young woman cannot depend on marriage as her "primary profession". Yet this is the situation facing the educated Black woman. Lacking the usual guarantee that Prince Charming...will arrive at all, the educated Black girl prepared herself both subtly and directly to adapt if the American dream should fail (p.78).

Black women have always participated in the labor force in higher percentages than White women (Frieze, et al., 1979, p. 151). Their participation has been determined by economic necessity, as well as by their own aspirations and expectations. Economic and social forces may be reflected in Black families' socialization of Black women toward a strong achievement and work orientation (Hill, 1971; Turner, 1972; Epstein, 1973). The concept of sex-role socialization, that has been used to explain the absence of achievement motives among White women, helps to explain the high career aspirations held by Black women.

Socio-historical Perspectives

Black women in the middle years represent an age cohort which has witnessed and experienced a dramatic, profound socio-historical change. This cohort of women has evidenced marked deviation from the "traditional" woman's life pattern. Commenting on the relationship between these social changes and women's life courses, Giele (1982) has noted that, despite feminism and related changes, each age cohort of women since 1900 has at first modeled its life in terms of the traditional ideal. This ideal has, heretofore, consisted of a brief period of work outside of the home, then marriage and settling down.

In many respects, the cohort of Black women studied constituted a transitional group. Born between 1934 and 1941, they grew up with the traditional ideals of their mothers' generation, and yet, they lived a different reality. Their adult lives took place in a social context of changing values in which women want both career success and family life. As such, their lives evidence the need for a new model of women's life courses. As Giele (1982) has noted, such a model is emerging which, rather than holding out a single, optimum sequence of life events, is characterized by several possible options. The new model of women's life courses "recognizes a number of individual variations. It accounts for flexibility, redirection, and multiple possible combinations of timing and sequence. It implies that versatility and freedom of choice are to be valued (p. 122).

This new model acknowledges that social and economic factors have exerted a dominant influence on *all* women's life choices. Rossi

(1980) has observed that the present cohort of middle-aged adults has been subject to a good deal of economic and social stress from large families, overextended budgets, and the need to depart from expected lifestyles as women joined the labor force. Black families have been severely impacted by these economic forces. Recent reports indicate that Blacks continue to receive a disproportionately low share of the total income in the United States; and, though Blacks have had modest economic gains, these have been greater for women than men (Current Population Reports, series P-23, No. 80, pp. 26-28).

Currently, there are several profiles of Black womens' economic status. While a very large subgroup of these women exist at a poverty level, there is a small, but growing number of Black professional women of middle and upper-class status whose incomes are substantial. It is this latter group of Black, professional women who were the subject of this exploratory research. It was assumed that women who were relatively free of economic survival concerns would be the most appropriate population for testing the limits of Levinson's theory.

Further, the social and psychic "revolution" of the 1960s warrants attention in considering Black women's adult development. Pugh (1972) defined the revolution as the "assertedly momentous change in American Black people's assertion of themselves as persons and as a people" (p. 345). Black people of all ages were deeply affected during the 1960s. Vast segments of the community sought to rid themselves of feelings of self-devaluation and inferiority and, instead, acquired a more integrated, positive self and group concept (Pugh, 1972, p. 345).

This study of adult development in Black women investigated the life courses of a specific population of women who entered young adulthood at the time of a historical moment for Blacks. It was assumed that, at least for some young women during this period, the Black revolution had a palpable influence on emerging, still developing identities.

The Study

This exploratory study had as its major objective the *description* of developmental change. The analysis was at two levels: changes within an individual over time (intraindividual change), and differences among subjects in how they changed (interindividual differences). The sample studied and the methods used are briefly described.

The Sample

The sample was comprised of eight women. Practically, since each subject required many hours of the investigator's time, this small sample permitted a more thorough review of each subject's life. Although the sample was too small to permit statistical analysis and interpretations regarding any population, it was sufficiently large to allow for interindividual comparisons.

Five major criteria were used to select research subjects: Age, Race, Professional status, Marital status, and Childrearing experience. Subjects were between 40 and 50 years of age. An effort was made to select women whose ages varied across this range.

Subjects were assumed to have completed four periods of adult life that corresponded to Levinson's model i.e., The Early Adult Transition, Entering the Adult World, The Age Thirty Transition, and Settling Down. Most were in the Mid-Life Transition, while others were in the Entering Middle Adulthood period.

Racially, the sample was restricted to women who were born in the United States. The intent was to include only Black women whose entire life course took place in the United States. The sample was also selected to represent both female and male-dominated professions. Four subjects were from the teaching or nursing professions as these professions have, historically, been female-dominated. The remaining four subjects represented professions that have traditionally included low percentages of women i.e., business and law.

Table 1 summarizes the sample studied. A majority of the subjects had raised children, while one-half of the sample was married. Of the unmarried subjects, two were Single, Never-Married, and two were Divorced. The sample was almost evenly distributed along the 40 to 50 year age range.

Method

Volunteer subjects were recruited through the professional and personal contacts of the investigator, herself a Black woman. It was explained that the research had been designed to explore the adult lives of Black women from the teenage years through the middle years. Subjects were requested to provide 8 to 10 hours of their time for the study.

The central research tool used was retrospective life-history interviewing. In addition, the Thematic Apperception Test (T.A.T.) was administered. In the retrospective method, subjects were asked to recall and reconstruct their life histories, with an emphasis on the span from the late teens to the present.

Table 1
Sample Characteristics*

Subject	Year of Birth	Age When Interviewed	Profession	Marital Status	No. of Children
Annie	1941	41	Nursing	Divorced	1
Eva	1940	42	Education	Never Married	1
Grace	1939	43	Law	Married	2
Helen	1938	44	Law	Married	3
Dora	1938	44	Education	Married	1
Barbara	1936	46	Nursing	Divorced	None
Carol	1935	47	Business	Never Married	None
Fran	1934	49	Business	Married	None

*All names given are pseudonyms.

The Research Questions

Transcriptions of interviews were used to construct biographical accounts of each subject's life. Interpretations were made as to whether lives
gave evidence of an alternation between stable and transitional periods;
an evolution through six developmental periods; the same age ranges for
the periods as outlined by Levinson; and, work on those developmental
tasks proposed by Levinson.

In considering the influences of racial identity on adult development, three specific areas were analyzed. First, we were concerned with
the Dream as a sensitive indicator of Black women's experience of their
possibilities for a successful, satisfying life.

Second, it was anticipated that Black women's development would
reflect varying "coping styles" with respect to racial identity. Such styles
might express differences in perceptions of racial oppression, socio-political stances, and in patterns of interaction with Whites and Blacks. We
were interested in how these various coping styles interfaced with
developmental issues, and for a given individual, influenced work on
developmental tasks.

Finally, we anticipated that racial identity would have a dominant
influence on the life course of a quality exceeding that of any other life
structure component. It was recognized that research on adult development would be much aided by theory on the development of racial

identity throughout the life cycle. However, at this time, there is no single model which can be used to describe such changes. Although several models (Cross, 1978; Harrell, 1979) have been proposed to clarify the patterns used by Blacks in adapting to the racial situation, none discussed adaptive patterns vis-a-vis adult development.

It was determined that changes in racial self-esteem would be an important area to investigate in life-history research. Jenkins' (1982) approach to *The Psychology of the Afro-American* provided a valuable framework for considering racial self-esteem. Jenkins notes that, when we look at the history of Blacks, "we find that they have responded to the situations they confronted with underlying premises of self-worth and competence even though external circumstances did not seem to warrant positive self-appraisals" (p. 19).

Jenkins further clarifies that, at any point in time, personal self-esteem might vary from racial self-evaluation. Studies of self-esteem tend to indicate that when Blacks have low self-esteem about race, they do not necessarily have a correspondingly poor concept about other aspects of themselves (p. 30).

Our examination of the adult life histories of the Black women studied was guided by a newly formulated developmental task. The term "developmental task" was chosen to underscore the universality of this work for all Black people. The newly formulated task was to develop a relationship to race which facilitates a recognition of racism as a social fact; and to develop positive racial self-esteem.

Summary of Findings

This summary discusses the study's findings in several areas: the central components of life structures; the evolution of life structures from the Early Adult Transition through the Mid-Life Transition; and, relationships between racial identity and life structure changes. In order to devote greater attention to the most salient findings, a discussion of the Entering Middle Adulthood period is omitted.

As was noted earlier, the findings provide a descriptive account of life structure evolution. This descriptive approach was judged to be particularly compatible with Levinson's theory. These descriptions permit a glimpse of *how* developmental change is reflected in life structures and, ultimately, allow a focus on the developmental themes germane to the Black women studied.

41

The Central Components

Since the components in each life structure changed across periods, we were interested in what patterns would emerge for the sample as a whole. "Marriage-family" was subdivided into three separate components to accommodate the life patterns of our subjects. The components addressed were love relationships, marriage, and childrearing. Given these subdivisions, each subject's life evidenced the centrality of two or three components. The categorization of subjects as *Integrators, Age 30 Mothers, and Careerists* followed from a consideration of when, or if, childrearing was integrated with other components.

The *Integrators* married between Ages 22 and 26 and began raising children soon thereafter. These three women's life structure components from Entering the Adult World throughout adulthood were childrearing, marriage, and occupation. The *Age 30 Mothers* either married late in E.A.W., and later divorced, or remained unmarried. However, between Age 30 and 32, these two women chose to become mothers. Their life structure components throughout most of early adulthood were childrearing, love relationships, and occupation. The *Careerists* were most divergent from the sequence implicit in Levinson's theory. These three women either remained unmarried throughout early adulthood, effected transitory marital relationships, or married in their late thirties. Their life structure components in early adulthood were love relationships and occupation.

This categorization of the women studied illustrated that developmental stages were produced by experiences related to childbirth, as well as those related to the establishment of separation and autonomy. The *Integrators*, the *Age 30 Mothers*, and the *Careerists* represent distinct patterns of integrating work and family and, consequently, variability in the "seasons" in which certain developmental tasks were pursued.

Also, in contrast with Levinson's male subjects for whom friendships were a peripheral or absent component, we found that friendships were a vital component for all of our subjects. These women's lives showed that their embeddedness in social interactions and personal relationships was a dominant theme throughout early adulthood.

Regarding the other components, except for one subject, religion was a peripheral, or absent component in every subject's life. Finally, we took issue with Levinson's conceptualization of ethnicity as a component of the life structure. Instead, we considered ethnicity to be a feature of the self and, thus, an enduring aspect of adult lives. Issues regarding ethnicity will be discussed at a later point in this summary.

The Evolution of Life Structures

Each life history was examined on the basis of criteria established for the onset and completion of each developmental period. Table 2 outlines the criteria utilized in evaluating when a developmental period began and ended. Table 3 provides an illustration of one subject's life structure evolution from the Early Adult Transition through the Mid-Life Transition.

Our findings regarding the evolution of life structures are discussed in terms of the developmental tasks for the Novice phase, followed by a consideration of tasks for each of the remaining developmental periods.

Table 2
Criteria for the Onset and Termination of Developmental Periods

Developmental Period	Onset of Period	Termination of Period
Early Adult Transition	A) The assumption of "adult" responsibilities. B) Modification or termination of existing relationships with persons and institutions	A) Preliminary life choices made.
Entering the Adult World	A) Preliminary life choices	A) Transitional features manifested.
Age Thirty Transition	A) Transitional features: –Reappraisal of life structure; –Exploration of possibilities for life structure change; and/or –Modification or termination of life structure components.	A) An event symbolizing the end of reappraisal. and/or B) Emergence of Settling Down features.
Settling Down	A) The end of reappraisal. B) Settling Down features: –Attempts toward advancement: –Deepening roots, and anchoring lives more firmly.	A) Culminating events, i.e. events marking the outcome of efforts in this period.
Mid-Life Transition	A) Culminating events	A) The end of reappraisal; and/or B) Enacting life choices made during transition.

Table 3
Developmental Periods in Grace's Adult Life

Developmental Periods	Onset of Period	Key Events	End of Period
Early Adult Transition	H.S. Graduation	Lived with Parents B.S. Degree	First Professional Job
Entering the Adult World	First Professional Job	M.Ed. Degree Guidance Counselor Marriage Childrearing Maternity Leave	Ended Maternity Leave
Age Thirty Transition	Ended Maternity Leave	Educational Conslutant Stable Marriage and Family Dissatisfaction with Teaching Left Teaching	Began Law School
Settling Down	Began Law School	Integrating Roles as Student, Wife, and Mother Financial Problems	Passed Bar Exam; First Job as Lawyer
Mid–Life Transition	First Job as Lawyer	Restabilized Finances Marital Problems Father's Death Development as New Lawyer	Unknown

The Novice Phase

In Levinson's model, the periods beginning with the Early Adult Transition and ending with the Age Thirty Transition constitute a period labeled the *Novice* phase. Tasks common to each period of this phase were: 1) Forming a Dream and giving it a place in the life structure; 2) Forming an occupation; 3) Forming mentor relationships; and, 4) Forming love relationships, marriage and family.

Forming a dream. The concept of the Dream proved to be quite valuable in interpreting the nature of developmental work for our subjects. Generally, both the content of Dreams and their degree of articulation provided indications of subjects' developmental progress.

44

Three varieties of Dreams were expressed in the sample studied. One variation was that of a vague, poorly articulated Dream which subjects gave little definition to, and which exerted minimal influence on life structures. These subjects evidenced substantial difficulty, throughout early adulthood, in achieving emotional independence from their families. A second variation was that of a rather clearly articulated Dream which included occupational and family goals. These Dreams were sometimes revised during the A.T.T. Thirdly, another subgroup evidenced gradual, steady articulation of Dreams relative to occupation, with comparatively slower formation of Dreams relative to marriage-family. This latter subgroups' Dream formation reflected their intrapersonal and interpersonal conflicts in developing intimate relationships.

Forming an occupation. An examination of patterns of relating to occupations revealed three subgroups. One subgroup made early, rather intense career commitments which were not changed, if at all, until the end of the A.T.T. Another subgroup made early choices of occupation about which they remained ambivalent. The remaining subgroup made several shifts during their twenties, but made a firm choice by the end of this phase.

These subgroups paralleled those found by Levinson (1978) in his study of men. Generally, they reflect issues of ambivalence toward occupation, and the problems of achieving clarity about one's personal identity, which have been well documented in the literature. The most salient findings regarding these women's relationship to occupation concern their use of mentors.

Forming mentor relationships. We anticipated that women who had made an occupational commitment would, very likely, have mentoring experiences. However, using Levinson's definitions of mentoring, we found that a majority of our sample did *not* have mentors. Only three women described relationships which could easily be translated into Levinson's terms.

Significantly, all of the mentoring experiences in the present study occurred toward the end of the Novice phase, or after the phase had ended. There is the suggestion that subjects were either too ambivalent about their careers, or were too little invested in them, to seek or be receptive to mentoring before this time in their lives. It is also significant that the only mentoring experiences were with other Black people; two of whom were other women. This suggests that Whites were unavailable to these Black women for mentoring, and/or that the subjects themselves were more receptive to Blacks as mentors.

Forming a marriage and family. The categorization of subjects as *Integrators*, *Age 30 Mothers*, and *Careerists* facilitated analysis of their developmental work in forming a marriage/family. Levinson (1978) defines a central developmental task for the first adult life structure as "exploration" of life choices. An examination of womens' lives relative to this task proved to be illuminating.

Generally, the Integrators married during the E.A.W. following a limited period of exploring relationships with men. For these subjects, as well as the others, the developmental task of forming adult relationships with men was fraught with anxiety about sexual expression and possible pregnancy. Indeed, one subject was married earlier than she preferred because of an unplanned pregnancy. We suggest that the most significant difference between the subgroups is their use of exploration during the Novice phase. The *Integrators* elected to have relatively short periods of exploring relationships with men. They made early long-term commitments to one man and to raising a family.

By contrast, the *Age 30 Mothers* had a relatively longer period of exploring relationships with men. Plans for marriage did not emerge until late in E.A.W. Each woman engaged in relationships with men that reflected their personalities and their attitudes about sexual expression.

The *Careerists* evidenced even further divergence from the traditional sequence of love relationships, followed by marriage and childrearing. Although two subjects were married by Age 25, they were all unmarried by the end of the Novice phase. With considerable variation among the subjects, the bulk of the Novice phase was devoted to career building, with limited or absent desires for family life. Each subject's Novice phase can be characterized as an extended period of exploring love relationships, including sexual expression.

Decisions about contraception were a key element for the *Age Thirty Mothers* and the *Careerists* during the Novice phase. Most of these women made such decisions during the E.A.W., but one woman did not begin to use contraception routinely until the end of her A.T.T., reflecting her ambivalence about sexual expression and, probably, about pregnancy.

Relative to the developmental task of forming a marriage and family, only the *Integrators* evidenced work in both spheres during the Novice phase. The remaining five subjects developed life structures in which either marriage or childrearing, or *neither* sphere was pursued. For reasons owing to their own personalities, and their actual experiences with men, a majority of this sample pursued lifestyles which emphasized autonomous, individualistic interests.

Concerning the additional developmental tasks proposed for the Novice phase, our analysis of subjects' lives provided support for Levinson's conception of tasks for the Early Adult Transition and Entering the Adult World. Given space limitations, they will not be elaborated upon here.

Our findings also paralleled Levinson's in terms of the degrees and forms of change for the Age Thirty Transition. Only three subjects had relatively smooth, nondisruptive transitions. Two further subjects made substantive or dramatic changes in life structures such that there was much discontinuity between life at the beginning of the A.T.T. and at its end. Though there were elements of crisis, these two subjects had a subjective sense of coping effectively. The remaining three subjects had very stressful A.T.T's whose overall character was that of a crisis. Major disruptions occurred and great difficulty was experienced in re-stabilizing lives.

The Settling Down Period

In Levinson's scheme the Settling Down period ordinarily began at Age 32 or 33 and usually ended at 40 or 41. Two major tasks were found to be applicable to the men in Levinson's sample. These were to establish one's niche in society, and to work at advancement. Advancement refers to a broad range of behaviors: building a better life, improving and using one's skills, or becoming more creative, contributing to society and being affirmed by it.

Levinson distinguished five patterns which men evidenced in establishing the second adult life structure. These were: A) Advancement within a stable life structure; B) Serious failure or decline within a stable life structure; C) Breaking Out: trying for a new life structure; D) Advancement which itself produces a change in life structure; and E) Unstable life structure.

For purposes of data analysis, we established the end of the S.D. period according to a specific "culminating event". Levinson defines the culminating event as a marker for the start of the mid-life transition.

Our findings provided some support for Levinson's conception of this developmental period, but also revealed the limited applicability of S.D. conceptions for women's lives. Only half of our small sample was judged to have Sequence A/Advancement outcomes. Their lives were most easily interpreted within Levinson's theory. The next subgroup was characterized as Sequence C/Breaking Out outcomes. These three subjects had S.D. periods which contained elements of stability and transition. Only one of our subjects evidenced an unstable life structure during S.D.

Regardless of the type of outcome for this period, it appeared that *all* subjects were engaged in restructuring their lives. Comingled with subjects' efforts at advancement were prominent transitional elements. We proposed that a more accurate characterization of development during S.D. was a peaking of desires for an *integration* of independence and interdependence strivings.

The one subject with an unstable outcome at the end of S.D. was so evaluated, in part, because of her lack of occupational stability during this period. She avoided economic independence by becoming economically dependent on her lover. Her life illustrated the possibility of maladaptive solutions to the difficult task of integrating independence strivings, particularly through occupational achievement, with parallel needs for interdependence.

The Mid-Life Transition

In Levinson's theory the late thirties mark the culmination of early adulthood. The three major tasks proposed for this period are 1) Reappraising the past, 2) Modifying the life structure, and 3) Mid-life individuation through resolution of the four polarities, i.e. opposing tendencies or conditions within the self. The polarities were young versus old; destruction versus creation; masculine versus feminine; and, attachment versus separateness.

Only three subjects in our sample were judged to have ended the M.L.T. The majority were judged to be in the midst of this transitional period. Our findings with respect to the M.L.T. vary considerably among subjects. Most of these women did *not* evidence work on all the tasks defined by Levinson for this period.

Only two subjects had M.L.T.'s which included intense reappraisal, life structure modifications, and work on all the polarities. This subgroup was labeled *Full Transitions*. Two further subjects were involved in active reappraisal and work on the polarities, but they did not effect major changes in their life structures. This subgroup was labeled *Modified Transitions*. The remaining subjects made modest or major changes in life structures, with limited reappraisal of lives, and with minimal work on the polarities. This subgroup was labeled *Limited Transitions*.

Racial Identity

In Levinson's theory ethnicity is conceived of as a component, whose place in the life structure is individually determined. Levinson's guiding assumption was that, through the life course, components may shift from center to periphery, or vice-versa; formerly important components may be eliminated altogether (p. 44). Clearly, such changes would be possible only if racial identity is not a feature of the self.

When racial identity is conceived of as a feature of the self, its role in life structure evolution is broadened beyond that of a "choice" in adult living. Individuals may be seen to have a wide range of choice in establishing relationships to their racial identities, but life structures would *always* be influenced by race. Based on this revised conception of race, the primary question for this research on Black women was, "How is the overall character of life structure evolution influenced by racial identity?"

As was true for our consideration of life structure evolution, our approach to the analysis of racial identity makes no attempt to systematically review a childhood past. Rather, a descriptive account of each subject's relationship to race during adulthood is provided.

The dream. Our analysis of subjects' Dreams revealed several significant differences in terms of the influence of racial identity. The most obvious differences were determined by the subject's chronological age and the presence or absence of racial segregation at the time Dreams were being formed. All of our subjects were born during a historical era in which racial segregation was an unavoidable fact of life. Born between 1934 and 1941, *every* subject had childhood experiences with segregation and discrimination against Black people. We can only speculate about how each subject's adult Dream was shaped by these early experiences with racism.

However, beginning with the Early Adult Transition, we discerned several specific influences on the Dream. Some subjects' first adult life choices were dramatically restricted by racial segregation. Women who completed high school between 1948 and 1953 were most overtly affected i.e. Barbara, Carol, and Fran. These women were prohibited from freely choosing educational institutions. Their decision-making began with a consideration of whether to attend a predominantly Black, or a racially integrated school.

These three women dreamed of a successful life despite their encounters with a segregated society. Having grown up in a Southern state, they were aware that their life choices would continue to be restricted if they remained in the South. By the end of the E.A.T., all three had relocated to a Northern state to improve their opportunities for a successful life. In effect, they opted to seek a society where Dreams could be more easily pursued, absent the flagrant racism they'd experienced in the South.

The remaining subjects began their adult lives in a Northern state. Their decisions regarding college were made between 1955 and 1959. This period predated civil rights legislation, affirmative action, and other forms of social change which made segregation illegal. These younger subjects did not encounter the flagrant racism experienced by the older subjects during the E.A.T., but each was aware of how few Blacks had achieved in previous generations. Each subject recognized that racism was a social pathology to be contended with in shaping their adult lives. They formed Dreams of occupational achievement despite the odds against their success. In many instances, their Dreams embodied their parent's hope for the next generation.

Dreams were also examined in terms of their explicit attention to racial issues. Half of the sample formed Dreams in which racial issues were so addressed. For example, Annie's Dream of becoming a ballet dancer was revised during the E.A.T. precisely because she despaired of her chances for success as a Black person. She began her adult life on a theme of restricting her choices, avoiding paths which had been infrequently chosen by other Blacks.

Significantly, every one of these subjects chose an initial occupational identity as a teacher, nurse, or social worker. They chose professions which were most economically feasible, and they selected female-dominated professions which emphasize service to others. These particular professions are most frequently chosen by Black women. Thus, their Dream formation was influenced less by individual factors, than by economics and racial/cultural factors.

Coping styles. Every subject's adult life contained indicators of their "coping styles" in addressing racial concerns. By coping styles, we refer to a broad range of behaviors which, taken together, culminate in a pattern of coping with life in a racist society.

The first coping style is represented by Annie only. Her adult life evidences the use of *racial identity as a central organizing theme* for life choices. Beginning in the E.A.W., Annie attempted to use Black cultural nationalism as a rationale for a majority of her life choices. Throughout early adulthood, she conceived of herself as an activist and revolutionary in providing leadership for Blacks. It was not until her mid-life transition that this identity as a cultural nationalist was reappraised and revised.

The second coping style was represented by three subjects. Their adult lives evidence the use of *racial identity as an organizing theme for professional work*. Each woman felt a special responsibility to improve the welfare of Blacks through professional leadership. None had had a particularly elaborate socio-political value system on which to base their work, but all were strongly motivated to use their professional skills to develop programs for Blacks. For example, Barbara spent the bulk of her early adult years in predominantly Black institutions. During her M.L.T. she confronted the advantages and disadvantages of being so affiliated. Her decision to seek a major leadership role in a White institution represented a willingness to adapt to the unique demands of Black leadership in a White institution.

The third coping style evidences the use of *racial identity as a background theme* for various life choices. The remaining subjects can be so described. None of these subjects devoted lives to the welfare of Blacks as a people, but all remained conscious of the racial climate relative to Blacks. Most relied on Black people for a social circle, and had limited social contact with Whites. None developed under a particular socio-political value system, except perhaps that of a belief in self-determination for Blacks.

The background theme for these subjects was quite individually determined. For example, Carol contributed considerable time and energy enabling her nieces and nephews to gain a vocational or college education. She evidenced a strong sense of family loyalty, as well as the conviction that Black families should help the next generation to succeed. And, Grace remained consistently focused on Blacks' need for "self-reliance" in the face of Whites' racist, nonsupportive roles. By the M.L.T. she had become even more strongly convinced of the necessity for self-reliance. Her experiences with racism had reinforced this view on numerous occasions.

Apparently, the mid-life transition represented a critical decision-making period for most subjects. Developmentally, the task of reappraising lives contained crucial questions regarding an optimal fit between "self" and institutional life. Some subjects opted to continue their affiliations with White institutions; but, several chose to continue affiliations with Black institutions only, or opted for limited affiliations with White institutions.

A new developmental task. Our newly formulated task guided the further examination of subjects' lives. The task underscored the importance of recognizing racism as a social fact, and the development of positive racial self-esteem. Further, it was defined to direct our attention to the adaptive mechanism which may be used to cope with racism.

Although each of our subject's lives evidenced the development of positive racial self-esteem, there were significant differences in the means by which this was achieved. Some subjects conducted their lives with ongoing, relatively constant attention to their development as a Black person. These subjects reported important changes in their self-concepts over the adult years. These changes included a transcending of racial perspectives to a more humanistic perspective; a receptivity to assuming leadership in a White institution; a continuing refinement and articulation of theoretical views about interracial dynamics; and, a growing self-affirmation, as opposed to needs for affirmation by Whites. Further, it appeared that the mid-life period represented a crucial period for these subjects' developmental work on racial identity. Other subjects evidenced minimal or absent developmental change in terms of racial identity.

Discussion of Findings

The preceding discussions of subjects' lives in each developmental period has illumminated aspects of Levinson's theory which received support, as well as those which were unsupported by the data. Our findings paralleled Levinson's regarding the centrality of two or three components in a life structure. Generally, these women's developmental work for the Novice phase was comparable to that of Levinson's male sample, with some notable exceptions. The developmental tasks of forming mentor relationships, and of forming a marriage and family, were not applicable to every subject's life. Also, not surprisingly, we found that these women's choices relative to managing sexuality and the potential for pregnancy were pivotal to developmental work during the Novice phase.

Our findings regarding the S.D. and the M.L.T. periods provided only minimal support for Levinson's conception of these periods.

Several areas are discussed in this section; these are 1) the key propositions of Levinson's theory regarding age-linked eras and stable versus transitional periods; 2) developmental patterns; and, 3) racial identity and stages of adult development.

The Key Propositions

Based on his research, Levinson concluded that: "There is a single, most frequent age at which each period begins. There is a range of variation, usually about two years above and below the average" (p. 53). Our findings provided some support for this proposition, but raised questions regarding its limitations. We found that the subjects' age ranges for the first two developmental periods corresponded to those predicted by the theory. However, beginning with the A.T.T., there were several instances in which our assigned age ranges differed from those predicted by the theory.

Apparently, our subjects differed from Levinson's male sample in having shorter Age Thirty Transitions and/or Settling Down periods. These problems in assigning ages to developmental periods have already been discussed by Vaillant and Milofsky (1980). These researchers reviewed Erikson's model of the life cycle in a study with a large sample of men. They reported that "...we found no fixed chronological age at which interpersonl or occupational competence was established" (p. 1358). Vaillant and Milofsky's research, as well as the present study, support the view of adult maturation as an open-ended process. Both men and women are likely to evidence variability in the ages at which developmental tasks are accomplished.

Perhaps the most pivotal proposition in Levinson's theory is that the life structure evolves through a relatively orderly sequence in which stable periods alternate with transitional periods. Our primary finding was as follows: *All subjects evidenced an early adult transition which was followed by a stable, first adult life structure. Thereafter, the sample was evenly divided into subgroups of those whose lives evidenced a continuing alternation between transitional and stable periods, and those whose lives did not.* The first subgroup provides confirmation for Levinson's theory. The second subgroup challenges the theory from several perspectives.

Developmental Patterns

The limits of Levinson's theory for the women studied can be visualized in the grid outlined in Table 4. This graphic illustration illuminates the four life patterns which emerged in the study.

Table 4
Developmental Patterns and Motivational Stances

Developmental Periods	Motivational Stances	
	Self-Discovery	Self-Protection
Alternating Stable and Transitional Periods	(I) Annie Barbara	(II) Carol Dora
Non-Stable Settling Down Period (Breaking Out and Unstable Outcomes)	(III) Grace Helen	(IV) Eva Fran

Subjects who had self-discovery motivational stances, *and* whose life courses evidenced an alternation between stable and transitional periods (Annie and Barbara), corresponded most closely to Levinson's descriptions of development. Changes occurring during their transitional periods reflected exploration of their internal worlds, and an intense reappraisal of existing life structures. The other two subjects (Carol and Dora) who also evidenced alternating stable and transitional periods were characterized as having self-protective stances. Their transitional periods reflected the limited use of reappraisal of life structures. Changes during their transitional periods were stimulated by external, environmental influences, rather than by exploration of their internal worlds.

Significantly, all four of the subjects in this first subgroup sustained a stable career commitment throughout their lives. We speculate that these career commitments provided an anchoring and a continuity which influenced the overall character of lives.

Subjects who did *not* evidence an alternation between stable and transitional periods were so evaluated on the basis of findings regarding the Settling Down period. Within this subgroup, two subjects each were characterized as having self-discovery or self-protection stances.

Three of these subjects used the S.D. period to restructure their lives and to accommodate new professional identities i.e. Fran, Grace, and Helen. Their S.D. periods were not stable in the sense described in Levinson's theory. And, their mid-life transitions reflected continuing efforts to achieve stability. The fourth member of this subgroup, Eva, evidenced continuing problems with stabilizing her life during S.D.

This second subgroup can also be subdivided into patterns of life structure change. Grace and Helen made changes following periods of active reappraisal of their lives. Their pursuit of new occupational identities was aimed at achieving a better fit between "self" and "world". By contrast, Eva and Fran's changes were not a consequence of such reappraisal. Eva left teaching without a clear (internal) picture of her dissatisfactions with the profession. Fran's career change was also made in the absence of a picture of the self to be revised. Neither Eva nor Fran joined issues of career change with those of desired changes in the self.

Importantly, our findings regarding motivational stances do "not" contradict Levinson's conception of developmental periods as such. Theoretically, Levinson maintains that, though everyone lives through the same developmental periods, "...people go through them in radically different ways" (p. 41). However, our findings do raise questions as to whether women's developmental periods are linked to specific chronological ages. Most probably, development proceeds along the staircase pattern which Levinson describes when lives are firmly anchored in a stable occupational identity. When individuals initiate major revisions in occupational identities and, perhaps, other identities, development is unlikely to proceed along the lines of age-linked periods.

Given that women's lives reflect variability in the timing and sequencing of work and family commitments, it was expected that their lives would evidence variability in the "seasons" in which certain developmental tasks were pursued. Our findings provided additional data on this variability in women's lives.

Further, the notion of specific developmental tasks for each developmental period proved to be more applicable for the Novice phase, than for the years from the mid-thirties on. The problem seems to reflect Levinson's conception of the S.D. period as a "culminating life structure". The individual is viewed as advancing toward a level of achievement heretofore unknown; reaching the summit of his/her desires. Such a conception provides insufficient room for individuals, particularly women, who have changed courses in midstream e.g. who have elected to pursue alternate careers. For such individuals, development is less accurately characterized as a culmination, than as a correction and/or revision of early adult life planning.

Finally, with regard to developmental patterns, our data suggest that there are, at least, two alternative conceptions of the changes occurring in these women's lives. Selected aspects of their adult change can be explained within a "timing-of-events" and/or an adult socialization model.

The timing-of-events model suggests that each of the many dimensions of human development has its own developmental progression, with its own antecedents, transitions, and sequelae. This model encourages us to trace an individual's growth and change in specific spheres of adult life. The adult socialization model focuses upon "the sequence of social roles enacted over the adult life course and the ways in which individuals obtain these roles and are prepared to enact them" (George, 1982, p. 29). From this perspective, we are concerned with, primarily, role changes and career changes during the life course.

An examination of adult changes for the women studied reveals that, for some individuals, changes occurred within only one or a few spheres, rather than in the overall character of adult lives. In such instances, transitional periods reflected the influence of specific life events on the life course. For example, Dora's mid-life transition represented changes occurring when her husband suffered a heart attack. Subsequently, she revised her pattern of avoiding first-line administrative positions. Previously, she had been content with "second in command" administrator roles. However, the threat of her husband's death served to encourage her assumption of a "chief" administrative role.

Similarly, role changes and career changes in other subjects' lives served as an organizer of transitional periods. For example, Carol's mid-life transition entailed a relinquishing of responsibilities as a surrogate mother for her brother's children. This key event led to a restructuring of her life in a more autonomous fashion, but the transition was not used for a more extensive reappraisal.

Our data raises the question of whether there are varieties of adult development which help to explain differences in "how" people change. Levinson's theory of the life structure was most applicable to a subgroup for whom self-discovery and self-learning were consistent goals; who used transitional periods for active reappraisal of lives, and whose lives demonstrate a stable relationship to occupation through the adult years.

Yet another variety of adult development would appear to be those individuals who are relatively more responsive to external events as an impetus for change. Such individuals may be unable to use knowledge about the "self" as an organizing framework for life changes; may not use transitions for reappraisal; and, may have transitional periods which reflect the organizing influences of change within one circumscribed sphere upon the overall character of lives. Still other varieties may be seen to combine these different approaches to change, or to vary their approaches across the life course.

Racial Identity and Stages

Several broad issues are germane to a consideration of how racial identity influenced developmental stages in the sample studied. These are 1) issues which these Black women encountered in integrating occupation with marriage and family life; 2) the role of mentoring; 3) ethnicity as a component of life structures; and, 4) developmental themes relevant for stages of adult life.

Unquestionably, the lives of the women studied were strongly influenced by cultural forces affecting marital and family patterns. By the end of the Novice phase, a majority of the sample was pursuing lives in which autonomy and independence were emphasized. Marriages were viewed as either unattainable, undesirable, or impossible to sustain. We suggest that the most primary developmental task of significance to these women's lives was forming the capability of adult peer relations with men, and increasing the capacity for heterosexual intimacy. Our review of their lives was enhanced by tracing their development within love relationships, whether or not these were embedded in a marital relationship. Importantly, our revised developmental task focuses on maturation of the individual's capacity for intimate relationships, not on the adoption of specific roles.

Further, regarding the adaptive patterns of these Black women, note should be taken of their limited use of mentoring as a form of personal and career support. Most women utilized other forms of support to achieve career goals, particularly from their families, or others in the Black subsociety. We suspect that, if mentoring had been defined more broadly to include these alternate means of support, it would better clarify their unique developmental issues. In a recent study on the role of mentoring for Black female administrators, Malone (1981) found that the concept of mentoring was best understood when examined along with other forms of support i.e. from families, the Black community, and other types of professional support (p. 104).

Regarding the role of ethnicity as a component of the life structure, our findings lead us to appreciate the complexities inherent in development along two parallel lines. We propose that continued research on the adult development of Blacks would be aided by the concept of "the Black-White polarity." This conception follows Levinson's notion of the polarity as opposing tendencies or states which are usually experienced as polar opposites.

Throughout history Blackness and Whiteness have represented symbols of culture which contain unconscious fantasies about race. As Kovel (1970) has described, not only has racism been an integral part of American life since slavery, but fantasies about race have energized human culture since the beginning of Western civilization.

Developmentally, work on the Black-White polarity can be viewed as a process of reconciling the coexistence of opposing, contradictory trends within the self. To a large extent, this developmental work entails sustaining positive racial self-esteem in a social context which is based in such primitive symbols. The task of arriving at an integrated view of the "Blackness" and "Whiteness" in oneself and others requires Blacks to resist the assaults on racial self-esteem that are integral to life in a racist society.

Finally, with regard to racial identity, we offer a hypothesis in terms of developmental stages. A description of the cohort itself, and this group's behavior from the early adult years, illuminates several developmental themes.

Without exception, these women began their lives as children of poor, working-class parents. Upon beginning their early adult years, each had been impressed with the importance of education as a means to achieve a successful life. Moreover, every woman began her adult life with the expectation that she would secure an occupational identity and, thus, would become capable of economic self-support.

By their early or mid-thirties, each of these women had achieved some degree of occupational success. Indeed, one of the more interesting aspects of the sample is that, despite their success, most were discontent with their achievements. By the end of their thirties, or in their early forties, a majority of the sample had escalated their efforts at advancement. Within this subgroup, one subject became a doctoral candidate; another earned a doctoral degree; another made a career change to the more lucrative field of organizational consultation; and, two opted to seek careers in the prestigious field of law. Unquestionably, the sample studied was a high achievement-oriented group of women whose educational and occupational accomplishments exceeded that of a majority of women, both Black and White.

Our review of these Black women's lives illuminated the interactive effects of sex-role socialization, work on the Black-White polarity, and developmental imperatives. We suggest that these Black women were socialized to perceive themselves as androgynous i.e. as capable of combining masculine and feminine traits in a positive way. Perceiving themselves in androgynous terms, they had little difficulty integrating an occupational identity into self-concepts. The concept of androgyny has been used in numerous studies on women's socialization. In one study, Galvin (1981) found that Black women were more androgynous than White women.

Further, we suggest that these Black women's achievement aspirations were an integral aspect of work on the Black-White polarity. That is, we assert that the ability to achieve in a racist society requires a transcending of racial stereotypes, and an internalization of healthy racial images. In this regard, we noted that two subjects avoided competition with Whites for the degrees, positions, and other such symbols of success in this society. We suspect that these subjects were (unconsciously) avoiding competition and, perhaps, were protecting themselves from the anxieties of cross-racial contact.

These observations on sex-role socialization and work on the Black-White polarity contribute to a particular view of the Settling Down period. We suggest that, for these Black women, the S.D. period represented *a culmination of aspirations for success in a White world*. Levinson's term of "Becoming One's Own Man" as a description of the latter portion of S.D. was, for these Black women, significantly related to becoming free of internal and external prohibitions against their growth as a Black person. From this perspective, it is particularly interesting to note that, in this small sample, we had three subjects with "Breaking Out" outcomes. Their life structures were revised in the direction of careers which brought higher social status and financial reward.

We have already noted that subjects in the present study, like the larger population of Black women, began their adult lives within one of the female-dominated helping professions. Thus, their career changes during S.D. may also be viewed as "breaking away" from stereotyped notions of Black women's roles. In this sense, they were expanding their perception of what roles were appropriate, and attainable, for themselves as Black women.

Conclusions

The present study represents an examination of the uses and limits of Levinson's (1978) theory for a sample of Black, professional women. Our findings provides inconclusive support for two key propositions i.e., that the life course evolves with alternating stable and transitional periods; and, that there is an average, most frequent age for the onset and completion of each developmental period.

The presence or absence of active reappraisal of lives during transitions is viewed as a key factor influencing developmental work. Data from this study suggests that reappraisal is most likely to occur when subjects are motivated toward self-discovery, and is less likely when subjects are motivated toward self-protection.

This study raises the issue of whether there are varieties of adult development which help to explain *how* people change. Apparently, only some individual's development can be viewed as a process in which transitions are used for intense self reevaluation, with resultant progress toward a more individuated and complex self. Other varieties of development may not utilize transitions for self-discovery, may demonstrate the use of transitional periods for role and/or career changes only, and may not reflect a process of increasing individuation.

In effect, this study on changes in life structures through early adulthood directs our attention to the influences of personality on life changes. By personality we refer to individual differences in dispositions, interpersonal relations, and receptivity to experience. The dispositions of "self-discovery" or "self-protection" can readily be translated into the personality trait of "openness to experience". We noted that, in a recent longitudinal study on personality and aging, "openness to experience" was one of only three traits characterized as an enduring disposition through the life course (Costa, McCrae, and Arenberg, 1983, p. 261).

Future research on stages of adult life would likely benefit from approaches which clarify how personality traits influence the nature of transitional periods. This study's findings suggest that varieties of adult developmental stages reflect, in large measure, whether aging is experienced as a process of learning and self-integration. Thus, adaptation to life at all stages is likely to be powerfully influenced by personality.

Further, in considering the influence of racial identity on adult development, we propose that "forming the capacity for heterosexual intimacy" was the most relevant developmental task for these Black women. Apparently, there are forces within the Black subsociety which culminate in women remaining single, becoming single parents, or becoming divorced in larger percentages than is true within the White population. As Colarusso and Nemiroff (1981) have observed, each culture produces adult personalities that are adaptive to that particular society and which ensure the continuity and cohesiveness of the culture (p. 171). These Black women's lives illustrate how the social context may operate to restrict their choices vis-a-vis marriage. Given limited opportunities for marital roles, alternative patterns may be chosen by necessity. For some of these women, their emphasis on autonomous, independent lifestyles represented an adaptive pattern which is well known, historically, within the Black subsociety.

Finally, we propose that developmental work on the Black-White polarity is specifically indicated for Blacks in a racist society. For the Black women studied, it appeared that such developmental work fostered positive racial self-esteem and, thus, facilitated their growth through the life course. The study illuminated the influences of racial identity at three particular stages i.e. the Early Adult Transition, the Settling Down period, and the Mid-Life Transition.

During the Early Adult Transition, some subjects' life choices were restricted; Dreams were formed in this context of restricted choices. The Settling Down period entailed a peaking of these Black women's aspirations for success in a White world. The period represented a critical time for becoming free of internal and external prohibitions against one's growth as a Black person. Also, the Mid-Life Transition was an important decision-making juncture for most subjects. Developmentally, the task of reappraising lives contained questions regarding an optimal fit between "self" and institutional life.

Although several of Levinson's premises are unsupported by the data, the model proved to be extremely valuable for organizing life history material, and for describing developmental change. The concept of life structure is judged to be quite useful for generating detailed descriptions of these Black women's developmental work. Viewing lives in terms of life structures directs our attention to the pivotal role of "choices" made by a person. Unquestionably, adult development proceeds in an optimal manner when social systems operate to offer unrestricted choices to individuals, particularly vis-a-vis marital and occupational roles. To some extent, the lives of the Black women studied demonstrate the various developmental paths which lives may take in this context of restricted choices.

References

Benedek, T. (1959). Parenthood as a developmental phase: A contribution to the libido theory, *Journal of the American Pychoanalytic Association*, No. 3, 389-417.

Bibring, G. L. (1959). Some considerations of the psychological processes in pregnancy, *The Psychoanalytic Study of the Child*, 14, 113-121.

Colarusso, C., & Nemiroff, R. A. (1981). *Adult development*. New York: Plenum.

Costa, Jr., P. T., McCrae, R. R., & Arenberg, D. (1983). Recent longitudinal research on personality and aging. In K. Warner Schaie (Ed.), *Longitudinal studies of adult psychological development*. New York: Guilford Press.

Cross, Jr., W. E. (1978). The Thomas and Cross models of psychological nigrescence: A review. *Journal of Black Psychology*, 5, 13-31.

Epstein, C. F. (1973). Positive effects of the multiple negative: Explaining the success of Black professional women. *American Journal of Sociology*, 78, 912-935.

Erikson, E. H. (1950, 1963). *Childhood and society*. New York: W. W. Norton.

Erikson, E. H. (1959). *Identity and the life cycle*. New York: International Universities Press, Inc.

Frieze, I., Parsons, J. E., Johnson, P. B., Ruble, D. N., & Zellman, G. L. (1978). *Women and sex roles—A social psychological perspective*. New York: W. W. Norton.

Galvin, Y. R. (1981). Sex, ethnic, and sex role differences in the motive to avoid success. Unpublished dissertation. Psychology, Yeshiva University.

George, L. K. (Nov., 1982). Models of transitions in middle and later life, *The Annals of the American Academy of Political and Social Science*, 464, 22-37.

Giele, J. Z. (Ed.) (1982). *Women in the middle years*. New York: Wiley & Sons.

Gooden, W. (1980). *The adult development of Black men*. Unpublished dissertation, Psychology, Yale University.

Gould, R. L. (1978). The phases of adult life: A study in developmental psychology. *American Journal of Psychiatry*, 129(5), 521-531.

Harrell, J. P. (1979). Analyzing Black coping styles: A supplemental diagnostic system, *Journal of Black Psychology, 5*, 79-84.

Hill, R. B. (1971). *The strengths of Black families.* New York: Emerson Hall Publishers.

Jackson, J. (1971). But where are the men? *Black Scholar*, 30-41.

Jenkins, A. (1982). *The psychology of the Afro-American* New York: Pergamon Press.

Kovel, J. (1971). *White racism: A psychohistory.* New York: Pantheon Books.

Levinson, D., Darrow, C. N., Klein, E., Levinson, M. H., & McKee, B. (1978). *The season's of a man's life.* New York: Alfred Knopf.

Malone, B. L. (1981). Relationship of Black female administrators' mentoring experience and career satisfaction. Unpublished dissertion. University of Cincinnati.

Perun, P. J., & Bielby, D. D. V. (1980). Structure and dynamics of the individual life course. In K. W. Back (Ed.), *Life course integrative theories and exemplary populations.* Boulder, Colorado: Westview Press.

Pugh, R. W. (1972). Psychological aspects of the Black revolution. In R. L. Jones (Ed.), *Black psychology.* New York: Harper & Row.

Rodgers-Rose, L. F. (Ed.) (1980). *The Black woman.* Beverly Hills: Sage Publications.

Rossi, A. (1980). Life span theories and women's lives. *Journal of Women in Culture and Society, 6*, No. 1.

Ruffin, J. E. (1985). An exploratory study of adult development in Black, professional women. Unpublished dissertation, Psychology, City University of New York.

Smelser, N. J., & Erikson, E. H. (Eds.), (1980). *Themes of work and love in adulthood.* Cambridge: Harvard University Press.

Staples, R. (1973). *The Black woman in America.* Chicago: Nelson Hall Publishers.

Stewart, W. (1976). The formation of the early adult life structure in women. Unpublished dissertation, Psychology, Teachers College, Columbia University.

Taylor, S. (1981). Seven women: life structure evolution in early adulthood. Unpublished dissertation, Psychology, City University of New York.

Turner, B. B. (1978). Socialization and career orientation among Black and White college women. Presented at American Psychological Association; Honolulu, Hawaii, 1972. Quoted in R. Barnett and G. Baruch, *The competent woman—Perspectives on development.* New York: Irvington Publishers.

Vaillant, G. (1977). *Adaptation to life.* Boston: Little, Brown & Co.

Vaillant, G., & Milofsky, E. (1980). Natural history of male psychological health: IX. Empirical evidence for Erikson's model of the life cycle. *American Journal of Psychiatry, 137(111)*, 1348-1359.

Washington, D.C.: U.S. Bureau of the Census (1980). Current Population Reports, *The social status of the Black population in the U.S.: A historical view, 1790-1978.*

DEVELOPMENT OF BLACK MEN IN EARLY ADULTHOOD

Winston E. Gooden

Introduction

Psychosocial development during the adult years is emerging as a major area of study among social scientists. While there is a growing body of literature in the field, only a small portion concerns itself with development among Blacks. Several computer searches yielded studies on childhood and adolescent development but very few studies on development in adulthood. Work on adult development of Blacks is in its early stages. Clearly there is much to be done.

The developmental perspective that most directly informs this chapter is that of Daniel Levinson (Levinson, D. F., Darrow, C. N., Klien, E. B., Levinson, M. H., & Mc Kee, B., 1978), so a brief review of some of his concepts is helpful here. Levinson proposes a series of age-linked eras and periods over the life course. The eras span approximately twenty years and include pre-adulthood (0-20), early adulthood (20-40), middle adulthood (40-60), late adulthood (60-80), and late-late adulthood (80+). Within and between each era are periods that are differentiated by the tasks to be accomplished in them (see Table 1). One type of period, the transitional period, is a time in life when one is terminating an era, or a previous period. Transitions bridge two eras or two stable periods in the life cycle. Their primary task is to terminate a time of life, to separate from that time and to initiate a new time of life. The other periods, stable as compared to transitional, are times in which life structures are built and/or enhanced.

Another key concept for Levinson is that of life structure. The life structure is the fabric of life, the interconnected components such as marriage, occupation, key friendships, and relation to parents, that bridge the inner self and the social world. It is the life structure which evolves and develops through the eras and periods of the life course. In transitions, life structures are terminated or modified; in stable periods life structures are built and enhanced.

This chapter is based on the author's doctoral dissertation which sought to use aspects of Levinson's theory as conceptual tools to understand and describe the development of a sample of Black men. Fifteen Black men participated in extensive, in-depth, open-ended interviews in

Table 1
Life and Periods in the Adult Life Course

Eras

	Early Adulthood (17-40)	Middle Adulthood (40-60)	Late Adulthood (60-80)	Late Late Adulthood (80+)
NOVICE PHASE	Early Adult Transition (17-22)	Mid Life Transition (40-45)	Late Adult Transition (60-65)	
	Entering the Adult World (22-28	Entering Middle Adulthood (45-50)		
	Age 30 Transition (28-33)	Age 50 Transition (50-55)		
	Settling Down (33-40)	Culminating of Middle Adulthood (55-60)		

which they described key aspects of their lives in pre-adulthood (0-22), and early adulthood (17-45). The interviews were transcribed and brief biographies written from the transcripts. These biographies were then analyzed using Levinson's theory of development.

Because of space limitations, the lives of only ten men are discussed in the present chapter. All resided in a medium sized Northwestern city and five public school teachers, four of whom were in administrative positions within the school system; and five "street men." This last group has proved difficult to label. They were not chosen based on occupation but rather on their membership in the street corner society that Liebow (1967) describes. The label "street men" is also problematic because street people in the Eighties refer to those who are homeless, adrift, and live on sidewalks and in parks, etc. This was not the situation with the men in the study, all of whom had a home and some form of income. In the 1960's and 1970's "street men" referred to a culture, values and lifestyles as well as a socioeconomic status and not essentially to homelessness.

The focus of this chapter is on development in early adulthood. This era in Levinson's theory includes the following periods: The Early Adult Transition age (17-22) Entering the Adult World (ages 22-28) Thirty Transition Settling Down (ages 33-40), and the Mid-life Transition (ages 40-45). The first three periods form the Novice Phase of early adulthood. This label indicates the sense that the young adult is in an intense time of learning to be an adult in each of the many areas of adult life. One is a novice in occupation, in marriage, in parenting, etc. The developmental tasks to be addressed include formation of a Dream, mentor relationships, occupation and marriage/family.

The Dream is distinct from a daydream; it is the sense of future self which reflects what one wishes to become. While it often includes a particular job and or a family, it transcends those specific achievements to indicate a heroic self-image capable of motivating the young person to the commitment and responsibility that achieving that Dream demands. In its most developed form, the Dream gives shape and substance to the wishes, longing, and fantasies to be a special person in the world of adults. Forming a viable adult life requires, in Levinson's view, the capacity to dream, to form illusions that sustain the striving and effort which brings achievement to fruition.

The mentor relationship is important developmentally because of its connection to the Dream. In Levinson's formulation the ideal mentor relationship involves a mentor who is about a half generation older than the mentee. The mentor may be a sponsor, guide, teacher, advisor, or confidant. Indeed, he or she may play some or all of these roles occasionally but the developmental power of the relationship is based on the mentor's belief in the mentee's Dream. By believing in the mentee's Dream the mentor helps the mentee to believe that the Dream can be accomplished. The mentor is a transitional figure who helps the mentee create a space in which to try out in the imagination and in reality a future self to be realized.

The Novice Phase

Formation of Dream and Mentor Relations Among the Street Men

Dreams. All five street men formed Dreams during the novice phase. Two patterns of Dream formation emerged for the group. The three men who went to high school formed Dreams during these years. These dreams were based on some early sense of preference and proclivity, and were supported by important family members or high school teachers.

One example of this pattern is Lloyd, whose Dream was to become a chef. He had a job as a dishwasher at a major university. While on the job, he met and admired the chief chef who was Black and well known in the community. The chef advised and encouraged him to go to cooking school. Lloyd also attributed the Dream of becoming a chef to the fact that he enjoyed helping his mother in the kitchen during childhood and his teens. The chef and mother were persons with whom he identified, and who he aspired to emulate. Their support was essential in his completing cooking school.

The other pattern of Dream formation involved two men who formed Dreams in their twenties. Neither man attended high school, and they were on their own during most of adolescence. They entered the novice phase without a sense of purpose for their lives. Both worked odd jobs to earn money but had no inner sense of what they wanted to become as adults. The Dream was formed for both of them out of contact with older men whom they came to admire and with whom they identified. Herbert exemplified this pattern. Herbert moved to the Northeast to work in a railroad tie factory. When his job ended he was befriended by an older man who worked as a laborer assisting brick masons. This man helped Herbert get hired, taught him the "ins and outs" of the job and rented him a room. Through this relationship Herbert developed a Dream of being a skilled laborer with steady employment.

The content of these Dreams was primarily nonprofessional; the majority of the Dreams—professional football player, chef, skilled laborer and trucker—were based on physical skills. The one exception, a man who wanted to be a chemist, gave up this dream in his early twenties after flunking out of a local community college. In his mid-twenties he bought into the Black Nationalist Garveyite Dream of returning to Africa.

Let us examine briefly the development of the Dream among the street men. Development involves further clarification and articulation of aspects of the self lived out in the dream, clearer definition of the social roles connected to the dream and pursuit of the occupational goals (for occupationally centered dreams) that will lead to a fulfillment of the dream. Only one of the Dreams formed at the beginning of the novice phase survived to the end of the period. This Dream was articulated through training and eventually found expression in an occupation. The other two dreams were given up early. Two of the later Dreams, formed in the mid twenties, also received support and development. One eventuated into an occupation. The five men in this group reported six Dreams (one man gave up an early Dream and formed a new one in his mid twenties). Three of these Dreams evolved during the novice phase and two were centered on occupations. The third Dream was political in orientation and linked to a strong Black identity. How can we understand the demise of the Dreams that failed? Perhaps there are several reasons for the failure including lack of personal and institutional support, lack of adequate mentoring, and personal deficiencies on the part of the men. Let's look briefly at a Dream that succeeded and one that failed to further clarify these outcomes.

Dean was an outstanding football player who starred on his high school team. In his junior year he decided that he would become a professional ball player. His coach encouraged this aspiration, and Dean reported talking with the head coach of a prestigious state university about a football scholarship. At the end of his junior year, however, Dean had very serious conflicts with his foster mother who demanded that he work and give her his earnings. He escaped to the Army hoping to get away from the conflictual home situation. He planned to turn pro after completing his tour of duty. His military career was marked by conflict, injury and a dishonorable discharge. A leg injury, sustained in the Army, effectively put an end to any hope of playing professional football.

In contrast to Dean, Lloyd pursued his dream of becoming a chef by entering cooking school after graduating from high school. He enjoyed the support of his parents and the chef in the kitchen where he washed dishes. He successfully completed his course and obtained his first job as a short order cook in his early twenties. He aspired to become the head chef in a large restaurant and later to own his own restaurant.

Mentors. The mentoring relationship provides the mentee with a person that believes in him and his ability to achieve the Dream. It often provides external support in the form of guidance, and counsel, but its most crucial aspect is that it provides a figure with whom the mentee can identify and whose confidence the mentee can internalize. If we use the strict definition of a mentor-mentee relationship as defined by Levinson i.e., an intense relationship, lasting from two to eight years ending in a modest friendship or acrimonious break, then only one street man had a mentoring relationship of that length and intensity. With a less strict definition that takes into account relationships that helped the men believe in, clarify or form a Dream, a total of three men had some degree of mentoring during the novice phase. An example of this type of relationship is instructive. Roland became interested in trucking after a few cross-country trips assisting moving van operators. On one trip to Chicago he met Fritz, nicknamed "Flat Head", who owned and operated several trucks. They quickly established a friendship. As incredible as it appears, Roland reported winning a truck gambling with Flat Head and others. The truck was old but operative and Flat Head helped Roland get a contract to haul chickens. Flat Head helped Roland learn the "ropes" of the business. The mentoring relationship, in addition to the positive effects of helping Roland initiate his Dream, had negative aspects as well. Flat Head was a gambler and fighter who lived dangerously. Roland got very involved in this lifestyle and one evening got into a gambling related fight in which he seriously injured his opponent. He fled the area but was soon arrested and sentenced to two years in prison. That effectively ended the Dream of a career as a truck operator/owner.

In all these mentoring relationships we find older Black men taking an interest in, and helping, younger Black men. It is difficult to determine the age differences between mentors and mentees but my general impression is that in two of the three cases the mentor was in a different generation than the mentee. In the two relationships where mentor and mentee were closer in age, friendship was an important aspect of the relationship. Only one of the relationships lasted for several years. This one lasted long enough so the mentee felt he had outgrown the need for advice from the mentor on job related issues. In fact, the relationship evolved into one of peer friendship.

The absence of positive relations to fathers and the high degree of difficulty with male authority figures in their teens reported by these men suggest that mentoring relationships would be very useful not only in helping them form Dreams, but also in helping them develop positive Black male identities and positive images of authority figures. One man who had no mentor, and could recall few if any positive relationships with older males, lamented this gap in his life. At age forty he felt things might have turned out better for him had he had a father figure or older person in his life. Another, recalling his drifting and dissatisfied searching, wondered whether all this time he had been searching for a father. The potential and need for a mentoring relationship clearly exists among this group of men.

Formation of Dreams and Mentors Among the School Teachers

Dreams. Although all five of these men eventually became school teachers, none of them reported an early Dream of becoming a teacher. The decision to teach in four of the five cases was made after the early Dream was relinquished. The four men who formed Dreams in the novice phase saw themselves as future medical doctors or scientists. These dreams were formed during high school and were supported by special teachers and family members. Each of the four dreamed of a future in which intellect would be put to work in a prestigious profession that assisted people. All four men reported doing very well in high school science courses and having special relationships to teachers and principals. The one man in this group who reported no Dream was a marginal student academically, but, a very good basketball player. It was his skill at basketball that formed the nucleus of a positive self image, yet he never formed a Dream of becoming a professional athlete. He went on to college after high school because his high school coach told him a college degree was necessary if he wanted a decent job.

All four Dreams were either drastically modified or given up by the end of the novice phase. The reasons for giving up the dream varied. Two men reported that financial difficulties were the main reason. Absence of funds to complete college forced one man to drop out, work for a while, then transfer to a state school. This was a severe blow to this man's sense of self and future plans. As he recalled these difficult times, he was deeply sad, and moved to tears as he remembered the loss of his youthful Dream. For another the absence of funds for medical school and the pressure to marry his college sweetheart led him to give up the Dream of becoming a doctor. A third man's Dream of becoming a scientist was damaged when he flunked out of college. He returned home and attended a local teachers college, all the while maintaining the belief that he would become a famous scientist. While teaching, he attended night school and worked for several summers at auto plants thus keeping the Dream alive. He finally gave it up in his forties. The fourth man also dreamed of becoming a doctor. This Dream was sustained by excellent work in high school and college. Upon graduation from college he decided to work in a biology lab as a technician and postpone graduate school until he had enough funds. As he worked in the lab and observed doctors in the hospital he decided that he would enjoy being a biologist more than being a doctor. He decided, however, to go to work as a biology teacher and forgo graduate school in biology after his father became seriously ill. He saw himself as the one family member able to help the family emotionally and financially during this time of crisis.

For two of these men leaving the early dream was a deep and very hurtful experience. In both cases they did not voluntarily change or give up the Dream. The men who voluntarily gave up or modified the Dream did not report feelings of loss. These men's experiences are congruent with other research findings. It has been found that those persons who feel forced to change or give up their Dreams are significantly more depressed than those who have no Dreams or modify them voluntarily (Gooden, W.E., & Taye, R., 1984).

The shift to teaching was not made with great enthusiasm or with a clear sense of long-term implications and objectives. Most of these men turned to teaching because it was available and a reasonable compromise with their former Dreams. Those who aspired to be scientists taught subjects in the areas of their original Dream. This provided continuing involvement with subjects that excited them since high school.

Mentors. Only one of these five men reported a strong mentor-mentee relationship during the novice phase. The mentor was a principal at the high school where the mentee taught and a member of the mentee's fraternity. This man felt sustained and supported by the mentor. The other men reported no relationships that could be classified as a mentor-mentee relationship during the novice phase. The group as a whole had many supportive persons who were interested in each man's success. These supportive persons were primarily female family members and high school coaches and teachers. The absence of strong mentoring relationships among this group of men is surprising since given their middle-class southern background, one might have expected Black, professionals to be available to them as mentors. As it turns out, the models who were most available were teachers, and perhaps this is one reason why, after they relinquished their original Dreams, they found teaching an attractive alternative.

Formation of Occupation Among Street Men

Forming an occupation is a major developmental task in the novice phase. This is the time when society expects the person to assume a work role, get trained in the role and begin adequate performance. It also is the time when the person struggles to match valuable aspects of self with occupation and attempts to make work a vehicle for pursuing lifelong goals.

The work life of the street men in the early part of the novice phase was characterized by frequent job changes and work at odd jobs. Their occupational life became more stable in the mid-twenties when most of them were in a job they kept for the remainder of their twenties. To what extent can we say that these jobs were leading toward stable occupational careers? A cursory glance at the major job each man held during the novice phase—janitor, truck driver, construction worker, radio technician, and cook all had possibilities of developing into stable long-term pursuits. In three cases the jobs were connected to a Dream, and as such could have been the vehicle for living out valuable aspects of the self. Each job, except perhaps that of janitor, also had the possibility of enhancing self-esteem through mastery of requisite skills and acquisition of money. What was not often evident, however, was the possibility for advancement to higher positions with better pay. For the most part these were dead-end jobs with very little potential for moving up.

As we examine the work lives of these men in the novice phase we are struck by what can only be described as rapid decline for four of them toward the end of their twenties. All four quit their jobs or were fired and three spent time in jail. Dean provides an example of this pattern of decline. He worked as a janitor at the local high school and, for a few years, performed well. Yet as time went on he became less comfortable with the job and his life. At work his White colleagues displayed racist attitudes. Additionally, his pay was inadequate to meet family needs, so he worked a second job which left him increasingly tired. He remained frustrated because even with the second job his bills continued to mount. He drank as the pressure mounted and this led to tension at home. Eventually he quit both jobs and his drinking got out of control.

Dean's pattern illustrates some of the difficulties these men experience in attempting to form an occupation and integrate it with the rest of their lives. Low pay erodes a sense of being the husband, father, breadwinner; poor relationships with bosses and co-workers deplete rather than enrich work relationships, and the boredom involved in the work itself is often countered by attempts to find excitement that can be costly to family and self. If current work performance is a tangible reminder, in the novice phase, of one's self worth and the possibility that one's Dream will be fully realized, then by the end of the novice phase these men could not have felt as though they had spent a productive novitiate learning how to live as men in the larger world. The message was more likely to be one of current and possible future failure; several were demoralized by this message.

Formation of Occupation Among the School Teachers

All the school teachers worked at odd jobs before and during college but serious participation in occupations began after graduation. Forming of occupation was smoother for the school teachers than for the street men but the process was still difficult. Two patterns of occupational development emerged. One pattern had three men who decided to teach immediately after graduation. These early starters obtained jobs in the education system, two as regular classroom teachers and one as a substitute. Within this pattern of the early starters only one person taught without interruption throughout the novice phase. Teaching was interrupted in one case by the draft and another because of a better paying job in the Army.

The other pattern of occupational development was one in which two men started teaching a few years after college. One of these two worked in a biology lab, until his mid-twenties then, after turning down a request to continue his lab work in another city, began his career as a high school teacher of biology. The second man in this pattern didn't begin teaching until his early thirties. After college he worked as a store clerk, spent two years in the military, worked in a factory and eventually secured employment as a high school teacher.

Four of the five men worked at jobs other than teaching for a year or more during the novice phase. The work outside of teaching indicates several problems these men had starting their professional careers. First, teaching paid very little, and four of them were married in their early twenties. They worked at other jobs in the evenings, and summers, to earn enough money to support the family. In addition to the financial reason, two men were unable to get full-time teaching jobs after college and so were forced to work elsewhere or to substitute teach. The interruption by military service was yet another reason to begin teaching.

Career advancement in the novice phase then consisted primarily of getting started in the occupation. As the novice phase came to an end two men received promotions; both were made chair of their departments. These promotions indicated that they had gotten beyond the entry stage of occupational life.

An important event in the lives of these men is that four of the five began their occupation in regions of the country different from where they lived at the time of the interview. Three worked in the South during the novice phase, one in the Midwest, and one in the Northeast. Four moved to the Northeast in search of better work opportunities and better pay. Three tried jobs outside of teaching. All four who moved felt underpaid and stifled in their previous jobs.

We find that the school teachers became more stable and established in their occupations in the second half of the novice phase. They entered the novice phase with Dreams of becoming scientists and doctors but gave up those Dreams for more practical occupational pursuits as they left college. Despite the college degree, these men did not easily enter the teaching profession. After some pain and difficulty, however, they entered the profession by the end of the novice phase.

How descriptive is the term novice phase of these men's experiences during their twenties? Their life stories, at least in the area of work, indicate that they were novices. They began at entry level positions. As they became proficient in their jobs, deepened their interests, and impressed their superiors, they were gradually given permanent and higher positions. An important developmental task for these men was to form new Dreams to replace the ones relinquished earlier. It was not easy for them to make a central commitment to teaching and to have that occupation become the vehicle for a heroic self-image. Each chose teaching because it was available, yet several sought to teach subjects in the area of the original Dream. Gradually they learned to love teaching and to form a commitment to their students. Still in the novice phase there did not emerge a sense of self as teacher or administrator in the future. While each man was motivated to do well and several pursued graduate education, the sense of self tied to teaching was much more modest than that projected in the early Dreams.

Taken together the street men and the school teachers support the idea that the decade of the twenties is a formative period for occupation. All these men were novices occupationally. Both groups changed jobs frequently and were particularly apt to move from job to job during their early to mid-twenties and to be more stable in the later part of their twenties.

The school teachers were established in occupations by their late-twenties. By then they had more clearly defined interests that were pursued both through work and school. They experienced advancement on the job and had more satisfaction in their jobs than did the street men.

Formation of Marriage/Family Among the Street Men

The development of the capacity to have mature adult relationships that lead to lasting commitments is, for Levinson, a major task in the novice phase of early adulthood. Erikson (1950) points out that the key time for the resolution of the intimacy/isolation crisis is young adulthood. Further psychosocial development for him rests on the resolution of this key crisis. If the formation of the Dream and occupation is tied to developing an identity, i.e., answering the question "Who am I?", the formation of special relations leading to marriage is tied to the question "Who will I love" and "With whom will I share my life?" The stories of the men in this study indicate that they were deeply involved with this task during the novice phase.

All the street men established serious close relationships with women early in the novice phase. Two were married at nineteen and two were married in their early twenties. The fourth man, while not married, began a serious relationship in his early twenties. He lived with a young woman, in his words, "like man and wife." Reasons for getting involved and/or married varied. Three married because their future spouses were pregnant and the men felt, along with the young women and their parents, that marriage was the best thing to do. None of the three felt ready to marry and two said they definitely were not in love with their future spouses. All felt guilt; they married, in part, to assuage the guilt. The other two relationships were based on very strong mutual attraction and caring.

The group as a whole started families early in the novice phase; by the end of the period there were 12 children among them.

All five men reported many relationships before and during marriage. These relationships were characterized as fun and were consciously valued because of the partying, socializing and sex they involved. While it is evident that these relationships gave the men opportunities to learn about women, and explore the possibilities of relating to them, the men did not reflect on relationships in such terms.

Two patterns are striking among these marriages in the novice phase. A pattern of continuous conflict was the case for three marriages. From the outset, these marriages were strained by conflicts about other women, money, and decision-making. In this pattern there is no report of progress in making a relationship work, in forming mutual goals, or in finding ways to decrease conflict and increase harmony. The second pattern, stability, then conflict, was evident in two relationships. In these cases the relationships were basically harmonious; the men had few sustained extramarital affairs, and both spouses maintained stable marriage and family lives until their late twenties. The conflicts that ensued involved, as with the other men, extramarital affairs and financial strain.

By the end of the novice phase all the relationships were at an end. In each situation the wife left or asked the man to leave. The wives seemed to have reached the place where they could no longer tolerate certain behaviors on the part of these men.

What are the sources of difficulty that create such failure in these attempts at developing intimacy and forming stable and long-lasting relationships? Several factors are apparent. In relating to women these men struggled with two competing sets of values. They all wanted long-term stable marriages. They seemed to value this ideal yet they also wanted relationships with women outside of the marriage. The image of self in the first type of relationship is that of a good husband and father who worked hard, earned a decent living and provided for his wife and children. The image of self in the second type of relationship is that of a single young man who is free to do what he pleases with whom he pleases. He is attractive to many women and is perceived by them as a swinger and a good lover. These men grew up in communities where both ideals were present but where, on the streets at least, the second image of self was seen as more heroic. In the lives of these men, there was constant tension between these two images. They went back and forth between them, never fully living in one realm or the other. When there were problems with work such that they felt incapable of maintaining the good provider role, and when there were conflicts in the marriage, they sought compensation in the image of the swinger and lover.

Roland is an example of this pattern. He married his high school sweetheart at nineteen and, to find work, moved to Philadelphia from the South. He was attracted to the fast life of the pool halls, bars etc. and often spent much of his pay on these activities before going home on Friday. This caused severe strain in the marriage. Eventually he took his in-laws advice and moved to Connecticut, where he found a factory job. Things went well for a few months, but again he began to gamble, drink and allow women to take his money. This caused further conflicts with his wife and her family. Roland and his wife were living with his in-laws at the time, and his mother-in-law eventually asked Roland to leave.

After being evicted, Roland worked for awhile then, after a quarrel with his wife, quit the job to "spite her." He took all the money he had, bought new clothes, got a "process hair-do" and, in his words, "hit the road". He drifted from town to town, worked where he could and hustled when he had to. Whenever he made a significant sum of money he returned to his wife and children, gave her the money and stayed a short while before leaving again. He continued this pattern for about three years when, on one of his trips home, he discovered his wife had a relation with another man. He tried to win his wife back but she resisted his efforts. In despair he decided to kill his wife and her lover. He stole a friend's gun but could never bring himself to shoot them. He was so broke and hungry that he eventually sold the gun to buy food. Roland confessed that he felt "torn to pieces" by the ending of his marriage. He was depressed and destitute. He gradually overcame the despair with the help of another woman whom he eventually married.

Another factor that interfered with the development of intimacy among these men was fear of intimacy: the sense that if one fell too deeply in love or let a woman get too close, one would lose all control. Associated with this fear is anger toward women. The physical and emotional abuse these men perpetrated on their wives clearly points to deep seated anger and bitterness that was worked out on those they both hated and cared for. One man confessed during the interview that he never felt able to love a woman. He wondered whether that was due in part to the fact that his mother gave him up for adoption and his foster mother was punitive and controlling.

The inability to handle conflicts successfully also impaired the development of intimacy and the establishment of stable marriages. Conflicts were numerous, often involving money and the wife's or husband's spending. Involved here is also the insidious effect of low wages and unemployment on the self image of these men. Financial conflicts often reminded them of their inability to live up to the model of husband/provider often held by their spouses. Conflicts were often settled, or at least dealt with, through physical fights! In many cases the wife called the police who gave the man the choice of leaving or being arrested. This scenario fueled the men's anger, resentment and feelings of importance. Everyone of these five men had police visits because of a domestic dispute.

Four of the five men did not recall harmonious relations between their mother and father. In all but one case, the father was often not at home. One man recalled that each time he got in trouble as a boy his mother and female relatives would say "you are just like your father." This man became identified by others as developing the same deviant patterns as his dad; it appears this was a self-fulfilling prophecy. Most of these men, therefore, did not grow up with effective examples of positive interpersonal relationships. They did not see the effective resolution of conflict between their mothers and fathers and often they were expected to perpetuate the behavior patterns their fathers exemplified.

For the group as a whole, the role of father did not go much beyond the biological one. Because of frequent separations, these men report very little contact or warm caring relations with their children; and as a result, these men did not seem to receive the affection and attention of their children. One man described this alienation from his children and the fathering role graphically. He said, "They only care about their mother, they don't give a s ____ about me." There is one unusual and noteworthy exception to this pattern. One man, bolstered by a grassroots nationalist organization and ideology, believed in the authority of father. He worked at caring for his children and quit his day job to care for them when his wife left. Unfortunately when she had him jailed, after a fight, he gave up and didn't do much in the way of fathering after that.

During the novice phase all these men attempted to establish stable marital and family relations. They valued, to some degree, the traditional image of responsible father/husband. For a variety of personal and societal reasons they were unable to develop a deep sense of intimacy and to strengthen the marriage they started. At the end of the novice phase they were alienated from their wives and children, and were not far along in their capacity to form and sustain stable lasting relationships.

Development of Marriage/Family Among School Teachers

The exploration of relations with women, which the men described as "fun-oriented," blossomed in college. There was little sense of long term commitment but an intense enjoyment of the attention and company of women. Membership in a fraternity was very important in their process of exploring relations with women as well as bonding with male peers. Several men said they were quite shy as adolescents, but as they entered the fraternity they saw models of more outgoing behaviors. They were rewarded with popularity for dancing and their charm with women. The shyness gradually gave way to more open and outgoing social attitudes. Four of the five men who joined fraternities reported that their social lives revolved around them. They dated women from sororities traditionally linked to their fraternities. They also benefited from the big brother system of the fraternity; these big brothers were models of socializing and often provided help in other areas as well.

The teachers began to settle into more serious relations with women in their early twenties. All were married between the ages of twenty-two and twenty-seven. One pattern in the formation of the marriage is exhibited by three men who reported not being quite ready to marry, but decided to do so in response to external pressure. In one instance, pregnancy was the circumstance; in another, being drafted into the military, and in the third case the wish of the young woman for firmer commitment was given as the reason for early marriage. These three marriages experienced the severest conflicts and came closest to ending in divorce during their twenties. In fact, the only divorce in this group occurred in one of these three marriages. Despite their unreadiness to marry, the three men reported deep attachment to and caring for the women they married.

The contrasting pattern to the pressured marriages was one in which the men felt ready to get married and did so without any obvious external pressure. The reasons given were that they were in love, and felt ready to make a commitment to one woman. The quality of relationships in this pattern was reportedly much more idyllic than the previous pattern. The group had a total of eleven children by the end of the novice phase. Only one man was childless. This man was deeply disappointed when he discovered that he would have no children. He thought about adoption but his wife rejected the idea.

Fathering had several meanings for these men. It meant a greater sense of responsibility. They more acutely felt the need to maintain stable jobs to take care of the financial needs of the family. They were proud of becoming fathers and all felt very attached to their children. Only one man reported being deeply involved in taking care of the children on a day to day basis. For the most part these men worked and left the child-care functions to their wives.

All wives worked: four as school teachers and one as an administrative assistant. The wives were typically on maternity leave during the later stages of pregnancy and the first year after the child was born. The birth of children then, meant a reduction in family income. This increased pressure on the men to find second jobs to supplement their incomes. Four of the men in this group reported working on second jobs throughout their twenties.

There were conflicts in all the marriages. The intensity varied but four men reported severe conflict. All reported money as a source of conflict; there was never enough money to pay the bills. The men typically felt burdened by this and expected their wives to spend less. Several accused their wives of excessive spending. Other reasons given for conflict were extramarital affairs by the husbands, and differences in preference for social activities. For these and other reasons, three marriages came to the breaking point at the end of the twenties, yet only one ended in divorce. The others worked through their conflicts and managed to reaffirm their commitment to their wives and children. Conflicts reduced as they learned to manage money better, resolve differences more effectively and as their earnings increased.

It is clear from these stories that learning to live in a marriage was not always an easy task. These men enjoyed companionship and the attention they received, yet success in the marriage required learning to share decision-making, to value the opinion of another, to share ones feelings, and to learn to be sensitive to the spouse's feelings. Of particular importance was learning to resolve conflicts in a constructive way. The men reported disagreements that often led to hurtful arguments and even acting-out through extramarital affairs, but each gradually learned to use more constructive approaches to the resolution of conflicts.

Levinson suggests that a man often seeks a "special woman" in his twenties who will share his Dream and support him in its pursuit. Like the mentor, the special woman believes in the man and in his capacity to achieve his Dream. While several wives shared the teaching profession none of these relations was described in terms of the woman's connection to the man's Dream. Perhaps it is because most of these men gave up their early Dreams and settled for teaching as a good compromise.

In comparing the school teachers with the street men, several important differences and similarities are evident. Like the street men, the school teachers reported two sets of values regarding male-female relationships. They valued both the image of the responsible husband and father, as well as that of the swinger playboy type. In college, the school teachers reported actively living out the image of the swinger. Several reported having two sets of girlfriends, those on campus that one would consider marrying and those in the community that one related to just for fun. The school teachers were much less likely to live out the image of the swinger after they were married than were the street men. Unlike the street men, most of the school teachers remembered a model of relationship between mother and father that was respectful and committed. No school teacher was typed as being like his "irresponsible father". When conflicts arose between the men and their wives the school teachers were helped by their mothers to think situations through and then to try to resolve them. The street men reported no such resource. The most frequent mediator for them was the police.

Both groups reported that financial problems were core issues around which conflicts developed. The street men, with less stable employment and lower pay, were harder hit in this area. When conflicts around money arose, they were more likely to feel their manhood threatened and to compensate by acting out the swinger image and by giving up the responsible father role.

The street men's relations were much more troubled than those of the school teachers. They were much less able to trust women and seemed to feel that closeness and intimacy could lead to absorption or domination. The school teachers seemed to be able to enter into close relations with women more freely and seemed less afraid of being absorbed, dominated, abandoned, or injured by the women they related to. Hence they were more able, with support and advice from relatives and friends, to work through their difficulties and to sustain their marriages during the novice phase.

Settling Down

The period from age 33 to age 40, called "settling down" by Levinson, is the culminating period of early adulthood, a time when persons dig in and try to bring to fruition the Dreams and projects of early adulthood.

Descriptions of men during this time of life suggest singleminded preoccupation with career advancement, power and success-seeking (Valliant 1977). Climbing the ladder of career success seems an image for the strivings of this time of life.

In this period the Dream of the twenties is concretized into an "enterprise," usually but not always occupationally based. The enterprise or life project is not simply the pursuit of success and advancement, though these are essential ingredients. Its essential hope is the achievement of an inner sense of being "one's own man." The process of becoming one's own man involves efforts at overcoming boyish attitudes and feelings, gaining authority and "speaking with one's own voice." This inner process goes on within the context of work toward success and advancement. Levinson labels the latter portion of settling down as a period of "Becoming One's own Man."

Occupation and Marriage/Family Among the Street Men

The occupational life of the street men shows a mixture of being settled and chaotic attempts to get settled and pursue some meaningful enterprise. Two men seemed to fit a pattern of being settled. Both had stable jobs in their early thirties and worked hard at them. Neither man felt that a career ladder was attached to the job. Their "enterprise" did not consist of pursuing career advancement within the context of work, though work was satisfying. An example of this pattern is Herbert, a skilled laborer. He continued to work steadily in construction during his thirties and enjoyed teaching young workers the "tricks of the trade." Work provided income and was an anchor for his self-esteem. He did not, however, experience any great personal or economic advancement. He did not find in work an arena in which he could learn to exercise authority or advance in status based on his skills; he remained a laborer.

A pattern of periodic work between periods of unemployment was the case for two men. These men had hoped to "make it big" by earning money and becoming successful in some way. The sporadic work they did could not sustain these aspirations and was at best only tenuously connected to heroic images of self. The jobs these men held had little if any prospect of advancement. The men had little authority and few markers to indicate movement to more senior positions. Times of unemployment were frequent. These men were fired from jobs for insubordination, absenteeism, or were laid-off. The interruption of work reduced their income and disrupted a sense of stability.

One man in this group did not work at all during the period of settling down. After separating from his wife and family in his early thirties he entered a V.A. hospital for treatment of alcoholism and an injured arm. His real enterprise was to persuade his wife and children that he was changing in order that they would take him back. Again and again he returned to his family and pleaded his case. Each time he failed to persuade them he returned to drinking. He lived off welfare and disability. At the time of the interview he had given up any hope of reconciliation, and was desperately attempting to end the career of patient that he so skillfully managed during his thirties.

The street men's lives, then, displayed no dramatic success in establishing an enterprise and advancing to its fulfillment. There was little satisfaction in the area of work. The period of settling down resembled the Novice phase for these men in terms of the instability of work and the number of changes. Though these men were more experienced they were unable to build on that experience for further advancement.

When we look at the marriage and family relationships that the street men report, we do not find much advancement beyond the novice phase. By the end of their twenties all five men had ended the primary relationships of their twenties and were out of regular parenting contact with their children. Two men started new relationships that evidenced commitment and a growing level of intimacy. One of the two remarried and credited his new wife with teaching him to love himself, and others. Yet he confessed that he "put her through the mill too." The second of these two men felt committed to the woman he lived with but as with his previous relationship, he refused to marry. His reluctance to marry showed his inability to make a binding and permanent commitment. He was deeply hurt when his girlfriend aborted a pregnancy because he refused to marry her. He wanted the child but could not bring himself to get married. The relationship ended in his late thirties when he withdrew from her after he suffered a stroke. This withdrawal indicated a victory of isolation over intimacy in his life.

The other three men had fleeting relationships, some purely sexual, others with some emotional ties, but of no lasting commitment. Such relationships could have been the basis of efforts to achieve and deepen intimacy and the capacity to care. They might also have provided incentive and support for occupational growth.

The culmination of early adult development is represented by the sense of being "one's own man". To what degree can we say that these five men developed an inner sense of independence, authority, and a capacity to be their own men? As we have seen, they did not rise to positions of authority in any work organization, they were not traditional heads of large families and were not in positions of leadership in local community organizations. Without these obvious external connections can we detect any inner sense of authority and responsibility? Let's examine briefly some of the areas in which these men tried to establish an inner sense of authority.

An example is Roland, who, after a truck accident had to stop driving because of poor vision. He decided to open a very small grocery store.

For several months the business went well. Then Roland was arrested and accused of possessing gambling equipment. He claimed innocence. As he explained, the column in the basement of the store with codes for the "numbers" belonged to the previous store owner. Roland was convicted and spent a year in jail. When he was released, at around age forty, the store was gone. Owning a store was for Roland a way of becoming his own boss, yet even this attempt failed. Roland, a proud man, deeply resented having to collect welfare and disability. The experience of losing the store broke his spirit; he was bitter, and depressed. Like Roland, other street men felt crushed by external factors and inner difficulties. One man got involved in a lodge and sought to hold office. The lodge was split into factions and this street man and a few others tried to start their own group with very little success.

These men were marginal in a double sense. They were outside of the structures of the larger White society and often felt victimized by its rules. They were also outside of the middle-class Black community and thus were unable to enjoy the benefits of belonging to the organizations and systems essential to the community's life. They were not members of churches, parent-teacher groups, tenants groups, or civil rights organizations, etc. They lacked basic ties to the younger generation and to their own generation. Very few useful viable roles were available to them. Their efforts then to become their own men occurred in social and institutional vacuums. Their efforts were likely to be on the margins of legality and this meant the constant threat of punishment by the wider society.

By their early forties three of these men were unemployed and had some type of physical handicap. One had a stroke, another was near blind, and a third had a serious arm injury. Four of the five men were also very heavy drinkers.

This group depended on physical strength to work and had a body based heroic self-image. They valued the strength and good looks of their youth. The demise of their physical abilities was a great blow for these men who had fewer skills and resources on which to build in middle-adulthood. An important challenge for them in middle adulthood will be to find bases for self value other than that of physical prowess. The unemployment and disability made these men dependent on wives, girlfriends, and state government for survival and support. This dependency was very painful for them to accept.

Occupation and Marriage/Family Among School Teachers

A majority of the school teachers had given up their early Dream in their twenties and entered occupations marginally related to the area of

81

their Dreams. Only one man held on to the early Dream and even here his occupation was not a vehicle for the fulfillment of his Dream. His case is worth describing briefly. The Dream was to be a scientist-inventor who became very wealthy as a result of his inventions. This Dream was kept alive by summer school classes toward a masters degree in physics, intense participation in high school science fairs and summer work at General Motors plants. This man gave up his dream in his late forties after his daughter confronted him with the fact that he would not get hired in the automobile industry.

By their thirties, then, the school teachers' primary occupational pursuits were not centered on the achievement of earlier Dreams. Three men were on the second rung of their occupational ladders as department chairs. The others were regular classroom teachers. All had created a place for themselves in public school systems and seemed poised for advancement. Advancement in the school system required ongoing education for certification. Three pursued these courses beyond the school system's requirements. While all of them desired promotions and wanted to advance occupationally, the three who pursued masters degree seemed more willing to sacrifice for advancement. Despite their wishes and efforts however, not all of them advanced occupationally. By the end of their thirties only two teachers received significant promotions.

One man was very angry about the lack of promotion. He had worked hard and felt he was overlooked several times because of favoritism. He considered leaving his school district on two occasions when the opportunity for advancement came in another school district. He did not take these opportunities, however, because his wife and children did not want to relocate.

The central component of these men's lives in their thirties was work. They felt they had become more competent and effective on the job. They enjoyed the contact with students and the challenge of educating the younger generation. One tension they shared was that advancement in the educational system often meant leaving the classroom to become an administrator. The teacher who was promoted to house master, for instance, had to deal with parents and disruptive students quite frequently. Yet, his first love was teaching, and in his earlier years he taught biology to his school's brightest students. Advancement for these teachers then often meant learning to become an effective administrator, yet all enjoyed teaching more than they enjoyed administration. Perhaps this is part of the reason why four of the five teachers considered leaving the field at the end of their thirties.

Let us look at the marriage and family relations of these men in their thirties. At the beginning of their thirties four men were in relatively stable marriages. Two worked on difficulties and disagreements in the late twenties and early thirties and so by the mid-thirties reported stable relationships. Two others reported no significant conflicts. These marriages were stable at the beginning of the thirties and remained that way throughout.

The only divorcee in the group at the beginning of his thirties, attempted but failed at reconciliation with his ex-wife. His two children lived with his parents and this enabled him to have very close contact with them. He started other relationships but was unable to bring his family back together.

Marital and family relations provide a crucial context for development of increased capacity for intimacy and the capacity for caring for the younger generation. When we examine the relations of the school teachers with these developmental potentials in mind we find very prominent individual differences yet a few patterns stand out. For the four married men, family formed a supportive backdrop to their pursuit of occupational goals. The degree and development of intimacy varied, with two men reporting satisfactory relationships, better communication and a stronger sense of closeness in their late thirties than in their late twenties. The decline of a sense of intimacy in the two other relationships is typified by a response by one man to a question concerning how much he and his wife talked. He had reported that when they were young they took long walks in the park and talked a lot. Now he said he knows what his wife thinks and so he doesn't need to talk with her as much.

Unlike the street men, the school teachers were involved in the life of the wider Black community. They were involved in churches, local civil rights organizations, teachers associations, fraternities and local community organizations. These involvements broadened the sense of identity. The developmental implications of these involvements can be best understood by comparing the street men and the school teachers. The street men by and large, did not belong to community organizations in their thirties. Unlike the teachers, they were not able to gain the affirmation of identity through participation in organizations. The middle-adult generation has been described as the dominant generations of any era. Persons in positions of power and authority are more likely to be in the group between forty and sixty than in any other age group. The school teachers participation in organizations allowed them to join their generation. They exercised leadership and responsibility for their community. Street men on the other hand had few ways of joining their generation. They were not in positions of authority in relation to peers or to the younger generation. A part of the despair evident in the lives of the street men comes from a sense of not belonging to their generation in any meaningful way.

Examination of their lives indicates that school teachers, for the most part, strived for advancement occupationally. Several received the affirmation of their value and status from promotion and pay raises, and from their participation in organizations and groups. However, I did not find many "culminating events" that transmitted to these men a sense that they had successfully completed their enterprises. Events that come closest to being culminating, in the sense of bringing to a close early adulthood and carrying a message about the fate of the enterprise, vary for each man. Two men were promoted to higher positions with significant increases in responsibility and authority. These two men fit the pattern of success in which a positive event helps to consolidate a sense of advancement and achievement. One man, angered by the lack of promotion, moved to another school district where he got an administrative position comparable to his previous one but with better pay and promises of early promotion. The event for this man was a mixture of relief and anguish. He subsequently was promoted and eventually became a high school principal. One man struggled with the issue of authority and independence in the context of his marriage. He resigned himself to his position on the job but felt increasingly alienated and oppressed in his marriage. He resolved it by staying in the marriage but gaining greater freedom to build relations outside of it. The fifth man had worked steadily to improve his teaching skills. He was not promoted to administrative positions but felt affirmed as a teacher. At the end of his thirties he became coach of the women's basketball team. This job not only increased his salary but enabled him to coach a sport he loved, and was good at. At forty this man finally was able to become a member of a fraternity he longed to join since college but could not because of financial reasons. Joining the fraternity was a major event; it signaled acceptance by successful middle-class Black men.

As a group the school teachers seemed to have achieved a sense of authority and independence that resonates with "being one's own man".

Conclusions

What conclusions can we draw about the development of Black men as we bring this chapter to a close? One firm conclusion is that development in adulthood is not simply the story of what goes on within a person but is a process that takes place within the context of significant engagements with the world of work, family and community. The inner sense of independence and authority that is the fruit of early adulthood emerges out of the inner struggle of those aspects of self that represent boyhood, smallness, powerlessness, etc., and aspects of the self that represent competence, strength, maturity, and authority. It requires as well the meaningful engagement in work roles, family life or community organizations, if it is not to be purely fantasy. The absence of the external network of institutions that provide roles for each person's engagement is clearly detrimental to development. The street men displayed this most clearly. The four who lived in the public housing project were unemployed at the time of the study. Each man struggled to hold on to a semblance of identity built up in the past. One man still lived off his early dream of becoming a pro football player. Another dressed up each day and sat on a chair in front of his house doing nothing but chatting to others who passed by. His identity, based on being a "sharp dude," is kept going by this ritual of dress, display and joke-telling. Without the engagement in roles that are valued by the community and in relationships of personal significance, development is stunted and life's meaning is held together by fantasy. As Levinson suggests, advancement in the early adulthood requires the establishment of a niche, a psychosocial space made up of vital relations to family, work, community and self, in which one can pursue the fulfillment of the goals of early adulthood. The street men's lives displayed an impoverishment of such psychosocial connections. Mentoring is an example.

When we investigate the availability of mentors in the entire period of early adulthood among the men looked at in this chapter, we find that only four of the ten men had significant mentoring relationships, and only one of these four had a mentor during the period of settling down. Ironically three street men reported having mentoring relationships while only one teacher reported having a mentor. This relationship then, which as Levinson suggests, is a critical aspect of the network of support for development in early adulthood, was not available for most of the Black men studied.

A second broad conclusion had to do with the development of intimacy in committed relationships. George Valliant (1977) suggests that the development of a capacity for intimacy in early adulthood is one of the best predictors of mature ego development and occupational success in middle adulthood. I am struck by the fact that this area is one filled with great difficulty for the men we studied. Nine of the ten men got married in their twenties, and five of these nine divorced before age thirty. Two divorcees remarried so that by age forty, six of the ten men were in marriages. When we look at the quality of intimacy reported by these men we find that of the six who were in marriages at the time of study, two were at the brink of divorce (with very little meaningful contact between the spouses), another was stable but with a very low level of intimacy, and three had a good level of intimacy. Overall then we conclude that these men evidenced relatively little development in the capacity to be intimate and to sustain committed long-term relationships. The issue of developing intimacy in committed relationships is one that is critical not just to Black male development but to the development of the Black family and community.

Both the school teachers and the street men valued marriage as evidenced by the fact that nine of the ten men were married in their twenties. In addition to the view that manhood in some way required the commitment of marriage there was also the competing view that being a *lady's man* was important to a sense of manhood. While school teachers and street men held this view, the street men, it seemed, acted it out in ways that were most destructive. In all five cases there were situations in which marriages or very important relationships were broken because of "affairs". Where affairs existed among school teachers there was secrecy and discretion. For the street men, however, these affairs were often very public. One can argue that affairs were more essential to the self esteem of the street men since for them being out of work often meant being unable to "bring home the bacon" and so be the "man" at home. The inability to provide for their families in a consistent and adequate way was constantly a source of lowered self-esteem. Two strategies used to lessen the pain of feeling like a failure are lowered commitment to wife and family and increased extra-marital affairs with public display of the affairs as testimony to one's manhood.

A third conclusion regards the Dream in the development among Black men. When we examine the Dreams that the men reported we find that eight men said they had Dreams in their Twenties. What are the implications for development of not being able to form or sustain a Dream in early adulthood. Two implications seem important. Men's Dreams seem primarily centered in occupation. One may expect that the Dream provides the motivation to undertake the work of entering and building an occupation in the first half of early adulthood and forms the heart of the struggle for advancement and achievement in the second half of early adulthood. Without this inner drive to be someone special in the world, one settles for more general motivations, e.g., the need to make money, to take care of one's family, or to do something of value. One would predict that for these Black men whose Dreams died young, forming occupations that were connected to something vital and special about self would be very difficult. This was true of the street men. While all of them worked from time to time none of them was able to link specific skills with a work role and Dream to form a deeply satisfying enterprise in early adulthood.

The school teachers also had trouble making their early Dreams the center of occupation. Four of the five had given up their Dreams by the late twenties and all were pursuing the more modest occupation of public school teacher. How can we understand the fate of these Dreams. The school teachers attributed the giving up of their Dream to pursue graduate education to extrinsic circumstances such as lack of money, illness and death of a father. The street men had no single extrinsic circumstance, but certainly they were aware of barriers and the absence of opportunity. In their late teens and early twenties they were on their own and responsible for their own physical well being. For both groups a critical issue was the absence of supportive mentoring figures who could provide models of what they could become and support their effort at fulfilling their Dreams.

Aside from or perhaps through its link to occupational development, the Dream expresses the heroic self. Through pursuing the Dream the young man is able to work on the aspects of himself that are felt to be inferior, weak, and unacceptable. The heroic self-image projected in the Dream provides a protective illusion that facilitates the struggle to become "one's own man". The absence of Dreams and the inability to sustain Dreams deprive Black men of that boundary space between reality and pure fantasy in which to play with images of the adult self and play at becoming more grownup and more whole.

Society has had great difficulty with the Black man as hero. The typical heroic images portrayed for Black men include the athlete, the civil rights leader and the minister. When the men of this study were growing up there was an even greater impoverishment of heroic images for Black men in the wider society. Fortunately for the school teachers and for others of the Black middle class, there have been Black heroes in the roles of teachers, doctors, funeral directors etc. The men on the street corner often had heroes who were ladies' men, dope dealers, and "mean dudes." Unfortunately these heroic roles are rarely sustainable past age 30. Some of the street men were heroes in this countercultural sense; their sense of achievement rested on how "bad" they were.

Summary

This chapter is part of a larger study; space limitation permitted only a partial presentation of our findings here. The study was one of the first attempts to use Levinson's theory with a sample of Black men. Our small sample size requires caution in any attempt to generalize to the entire population of Black men; the in-depth interview used in this study provides rich subjective data but limits the size of the sample that can be used in a given study.

Levinson's theory was very useful in understanding the lives of Black men. Black men's lives seemed to follow the major periods and eras and the men grappled with the major tasks of these periods as Levinson's theory suggests. The developmental perspective was particularly useful in understanding difficulties these men had, and the potential impact of these difficulties on later development.

One danger inherent in using a theory constructed from a study of predominantly White middle-class men is that if the theory primarily reflects White middle-class reality, then the theory may distort the experience of Blacks. Where there is significant divergence between Black and White experience, Black experience may be interpreted as maladjustment. This danger was greatest when looking at the lives of street men. The schoolteachers fit Levinson's model fairly closely in terms of successful outcomes, but the street men seemed less successful when viewed from the perspective of the model. For instance, in structure building periods when the theory expects mens' lives to exhibit a sense of order and cohesion, the street men seemed chaotic and unstructured. There were relatively few times of stability and order during their early adult years. One reason for this is that the theory indicates that marriage/family and occupation are usually the central components of the life structure. In these areas the street men experienced great difficulty. The development of stable life structures was at best very difficult for these street men.

While the theory allows us to describe and discuss what seems to be a central difficulty for this subgroup of men, we must ask whether the theory leads to an unfair stigmatization of this subgroup because it does not live up to White middle-class expectations. Levinson's theory may be vulnerable to this charge because the life structure concept reflects an attempt to bridge internal personality factors and external social factors. To this extent the life structure is always partly determined by the opportunities, limitations and expectations that the society makes available to individual persons. The theory then inherently views development of life structure as co-determined by personal choices, and social imitations and opportunities. *The story of Black adult development is not and cannot be simply an account of personal failure or success but it is inherently the story of how individuals encounter and respond to social opportunities and restrictions in their efforts at forming a viable life.* When we examine the lives of Black men we see that victimization because of race and class are inherently part of their stories. Yet it is never the whole story. To explain these lives as the result of victimization on the one hand or of personal failure on the other, is inadequate. If there is a limitation of the theory for studying Blacks it may be in its lack of explicit alternatives to family and occupation as central components of a life structure. It may be that persons who find these areas unviable because of marginality or low socioeconomic status invest themselves in other types of relationships that give coherence to life and allows for personal development. If this were so we'd expect to learn about those alternatives in the type of in-depth interviews done in this study, but we did not find such alternatives.

Future directions for research on adult development among Blacks are numerous. For instance, we need to study Black women's development throughout the life cycle (see Ruffin Chapter, this volume). We also need to look at childhood antecedents of adult development. One of the shortcomings of the present study was its inability to identify personality factors that could account for the relative success or failure at the developmental tasks of adulthood. This is an important research problem since results in this area would help to decide on specific ways of enhancing development. For instance, the study indicated a low level of mentoring relationships in the sample. The absence of these relationships may be due to the unavailability of potential mentors or to the inability of the men in the study to enter and sustain such relationships, or both.

Studies that examine the personality factors relevant to entering and sustaining mentor relationships would provide very valuable information for establishing mentor relations between younger and older Blacks.

Overall, the area of adult development among Blacks is ready for extensive research. The fruit of such research could be the strengthening of our community through fostering development throughout the life cycle.

References

Erikson, E. H. (1950). *Child and Society*. New York: W. W. Norton & Co.

Gooden, W. E., & Taye, R. (1984). Occupational dream, relation to parents and depression in the early adult transition. *Journal of Clinical Psychology, 40(4)*, 945-954.

Levinson, D. F., Darrow, C. N., Klien, E. B., Levinson, M. H., & McKee, B. (1978). *The seasons of a man's life*. New York: Ballantine Books.

Liebow, E. (1967). *Tally's corner*. Boston: Little Brown & Co.

Valliant, G. (1977). *Adaptation to life*. Boston: Little Brown & Co.

BLACK WORKING WOMEN: INTRODUCTION TO A LIFE SPAN PERSPECTIVE

Algea O. Harrison

Introduction

One of the images of Black women is that of strong resourceful persons who have managed continuously to survive unusual hardships and define their own femininity (Harrison, 1977). This image has been projected in popular and professional writings as a result of individual and group perceptions and assumptions rather than extensive empirical investigations by social scientists. There are critics of this image, however, because of its dehumanizing implications of ignoring human frailties and complexities (Walker, 1983). Yet, it has prevailed in scientific literature, historical materials, and artistic endeavors. One of the contributing factors to this image has been Black women's participation in the labor market over the life span.

Black women's participation in the labor market was an issue in two major social forces for change in recent decades: the civil rights movement, and the women's movement. The social, emotional, and economic implications of labor market participation for Black women were interpreted however, in its relevance to Black men in the civil rights movement and to White women in the women's movement rather than enlightening information regarding Black women independent of the comparison groups.

Both sets of implications had perplexing overtones. Generally, Black females employment was viewed as threatening to the traditional social role of Black men. Some leaders of the civil rights movement proclaimed that among other actions, Black women should leave the marketplace because they were occupying jobs that could be held by men and their actions would reduce the joblessness among Black men (Harrison, 1974). In addition, the push for affirmative action programs was being thwarted by the presence of Black women in the labor market since an employer could hire or promote a Black female and get two minorities for the price of one. According to this perspective, Black working women were destabilizing families and undercutting the progress of the civil rights movement by their presence in the labor market.

The view of Black women in relation to White women was also perplexing. In the early 1950s and 1960s when the current women's movement was gaining interest among women, Black women did not gravitate towards the movement. Generally the reason cited by Black women was that they worked, therefore they did not need to be liberated. In other words, liberation was viewed in a limited manner as relating mainly to woman's right to work. Also, the issues of concern in the women's movement did not impress large numbers of Black women as relevant to their lives. Indeed, the relationship between Black women and White women in social movements has been rocky (See Giddings, 1984 for a more detailed historical discussion). For the majority of Black women the major obstacle in their lives was racism not sexism. Thus, in popular writings, the employment of Black women has been viewed primarily for its relevance to others rather than insightful information regarding Black women. The efforts and works of professionals were not that different. As a result, there is very little empirical research on the psychological impact of employment on Black women. Nevertheless, an examination of issues accompanying the participation of Black women in the labor market across the life span is appropriate and timely. The issues examined in this chapter are as follows: (1) Life span issues, (2) a brief historical review, (3) demographic trends, and (4) employment and family life.

Life Span Issues

What do I want to be when I grow up? This is a question males and females grapple with from early childhood through adolescence and young adulthood and sometimes into middle adulthood. Occupational choices are very seldom made in a short time span. Rather, they are deliberated over an extended period of time. Black girls, like other girls, ponder this question and try out different occupations in play and fantasy. Further, work is important for the individual across the life span and especially for Black females because of their historical participation in the labor market (see discussion below). Work is viewed as the single most dominant influence in the life of an adult, but this is probably more characteristic of males than females (Garfinkel, 1982). Therefore, there are relevant psychological life-span issues for Black working women.

A major issue for young Black females is the availability of role models of Black women in a variety of occupational positions. Young children's occupational aspirations are influenced by the demographic characteristics of persons in the occupations (Obeton, 1984). Generally, Black women have been confined to the jobs that are traditional for women and Blacks (Simms & Malveaux, 1986). Therefore, young Black girls have limited role models of persons like themselves in occupations that are nontraditional (Burlew, 1982). Further, Black girls are influenced by the models of women they see combining wife, worker, and mother roles. The "Superwoman" ideal is *constantly* referred to as a positive model in the Black community (Harrison & Minor, 1978; Hood, 1983). This model imposes constraints in two ways: (1) It is a very hard life style requiring a tremendous energy and ability that some individuals do not possess and thus are made to feel inadequate if they are unsuccessful in their multiple roles and responsibilities; and (2) it is difficult to combine those social roles and become upwardly mobile in professional positions. Generally, Black women hold traditional views regarding the role of women (Gump, 1975) and although Black households are equalitarian (Beckett & Smith, 1981), women are primarily responsible for the household and child rearing tasks. Black women are performing two full-time jobs. And even with assistance from significant others, their daily life is consumed with household and working tasks from sunrise to sunset.

In order to pursue nontraditional high paying occupational careers, Black women have to overcome racism and sexism. This requires tremendous personal sacrifice and attitudinal characteristics that have not been clearly defined empirically. Some women have been successful in combining roles while also occupying high-paying nontraditional jobs. Clearly, research is needed to identify the personal and experiential characteristics of successful Black women. Such information will assist parents and professionals in motivating and aspiring young Black women to actualize their potential whenever the barriers of racism and sexism can be overcome. The research of Barnett and Baruch, (1978) who identified characteristics associated with successful White career-oriented women is suggestive. These researchers found that the parents of these career oriented women provided encouragement, avoided modeling sex role stereotypes, and set high standards for achievement.

The attitudes, abilities, and dispositions begun in childhood impact on efforts to obtain satisfaction as a worker. These attitudes are modified throughout the lifespan, but the family of origin has tremendous influence on the developing person's work attitude (see discussion below of effect of family on work). Family background is a useful predictor of vocational development since it is assumed that socialization affects one's educational and career aspirations. Rutledge (1981) investigated the childhood socialization and present aspirations of a randomly selected sample of Black college females attending a midwestern regional university. She found that the women who had higher educational aspirations had been more positively influenced by significant others, as children had closer relationships with their mother, and spent more time with their fathers. In contrast, the greater the teaching of differences in expectations for males and females, the lower were educational aspirations. This finding is similar to Barnett and Baruch's (1978) results for White career-oriented women who avoid modeling sex role stereotypes.

Rutledge (1981) also found that socioeconomic variables and students' grade point averages had little impact on education and career aspirations in this sample. Clearly, more research is needed on the relationship between socialization in sex role ideology and education and career aspirations among Black women.

Malson's (1981) research is indicative of needed investigations of life-span issues. Using a sample of urban, eastern Black women, she explored three factors contributing to the integrated sex role ideology and behavior of Black women: labor force participation and patterns, early sex role attitudes and role models, and strategies for coordinating family work and paid work. In her report on the research in progress, she found that the sex role ideology for Black women was an integration of non-traditional (employment) as well as traditional (homemaking and child rearing) components. Most respondents said that as children they expected to be employed mothers. Seeing the possibility of combining the wife, mother and worker roles when they were young was provided by the role models of their mother and other Black women who combined those roles. Although some of the subjects' husbands earned enough money to support the household, these women preferred work because they perceived working to be a part of their role as wives and mothers.

In short, occupational choices and decisions slowly evolve over the life span. The availability of role models, the relationship between early socialization and education and career aspirations are some of the life span issues that have been investigated empirically. What is needed is a conceptual framework for generating empirical questions on the issue of the psychological impact of labor market participation on Black women across the life span. Although Black women have an extensive work history, very little is known about the psychological and sociological impact of this history.

Brief Historical Review

In the eighteenth century African women participated in diverse occupations in the labor market. In those regions characterized by female farming traditions they were traders who sold as well as bought (Boserup, 1970). Yet African women came to the shores of America in chains as slaves, except for a few indentured servants, where their efforts in the labor market were not under their control. Within the slave community Black women performed the labors of field workers, house servants, or other jobs ordered by the slave master; they also worked in the master's house (Davis, 1983). In contemporary scientific terminology, slave women were full-time workers with only a fraction of their life devoted to other social roles, e.g., wife, mother, homemaker, etc. From middle childhood to old age the majority of the female slaves performed hard labor in the fields from sunrise to sunset all of their lives. Women from Africa were accustomed to agricultural labor on their continent (Blassingame, 1972), yet slave women not only worked in the fields on plantations, but also labored in foundries, saltworks, mines, laid track for railroads, and were lumberjacks and ditchdiggers (Wertheimer, 1977). When the international slave trade was abolished, southern planters increased their efforts to make breeders out of some of the slave women to assure an adequate supply of slaves. This did not, however, exclude these women from work assignments. The Black women who were free citizens in the North sometimes worked outside the home as housekeepers, laundresses, spinners, weavers, or in other skilled trades. Those who were married to farmers worked beside their husbands maintaining the family land (Wertheimer, 1977).

During reconstruction, Black women continued to be full-time workers and homemakers. Almost 40 percent of all Black women recorded in the 1890 census were employed (Beckett, 1982). For the most part, they continued the work schedule they had during slavery-domestic and field work outside the home combined with wife and mother roles. The legendary Black washerwoman and domestic worker were the chief occupations that supported numerous Black families during this period. Indeed, in 1866 when Black washerwomen in Jackson, Mississippi announced they were charging a standard rate for their services, it was the first instance of collective action on the part of Black working women (Giddings, 1984). Nevertheless, in the regions of the north and south, recent immigrants from Europe and low-skilled native White workers organized formally and informally to keep Black males and females out of the labor market, even for the most menial jobs. In the late nineteenth and early twentieth century, Blacks began to migrate from rural to urban areas in the South to urban areas in the North which slightly increased the labor force participation of Black women. Some Black women were in the professional occupations of nursing and teaching and in 1864 the first Black woman doctor graduated from medical school (Wertheimer, 1977). A few Black women had their own businesses, e.g., selling flowers, cleaning hats, hairdressing, etc. (Harley, 1978). The overwhelming majority (85 percent) of Black working women were employed however as farm laborers and domestic servants in 1910 (Beckett, 1982). Racism and sexism prevented Black women from being employed in the jobs created in America's rapidly expanding manufacturing industries. Yet economic necessity dictated that most Black women work.

During reconstruction, whether or not to support the women's suffrage movement was a controversial issue. Nevertheless, some Black leaders began to stress economic security for Black men and women (Terborg-Penn, 1978) as a means of uplifting the race and eliminating poverty. Indeed, Delang, co-editor with Frederick Douglas of the influential Black newspaper, The North Star, exclaimed before the surge of the women's rights movement that Blacks must not have a traditional attitude toward the role of women. Black women were important to the upward mobility of the race through their roles as socializing agents and economic providers, and therefore should be encouraged to seek high levels of education and careers (Terborg-Penn, 1978). Nevertheless, most Blacks continued to perceive the struggle against racism as the most prevalent social issue, although they supported women suffrage and female participation in the political arena. The view of Dubois reflected an important opinion for that era, votes for women meant votes for Black women (Giddings, 1984). Indeed, Dubois in his speeches and writings welcomed women into leadership roles (Davis, 1983).

During the decade of World War I, Blacks continued their migration to urban centers where they encountered few employment options other than low wages and unskilled positions for males as well as females. When the supply of White male workers was decreasing because of the war, a few Black men and women were employed in the factories in northern urban areas (Harley, 1978). Black women industrial workers, however, were employed in the most menial, dangerous, and undesirable jobs, e.g., sweepers, cleaners, ragpickers, pressers, etc. (Scott, 1980).

Consequently, a majority of the unskilled Black women had to continue to work as domestic servants, a work arena that was totally ignored by the emerging labor movement. As workers in jobs that were exhausting, exploitative, and demanding beyond human expectations (e.g., textile workers) were being organized by the labor movement for better working conditions, the occupations dominated by Black women and equally as exploitative were not considered. Indeed, for all their clamor of being treated unfairly by the system, the workers in the early labor movement did not want Black men, much less women, in the manufacturing and industrial jobs (Wertheimer, 1977). Meanwhile, Black colleges began to graduate Black women in increasing numbers in the professional positions of school teacher, nurse, and social worker (Scott, 1980).

Between World War I and World War II, Black women made very few occupational gains, although the country was making technological progress that created skilled jobs and increased white-collar positions that were occupied by White women. In 1910, a majority of Black working women were in agriculture. However, in 1940 the majority were in domestic service positions, a category that had increased by over 50 percent (Beckett, 1982). When the United States entered World War II, the labor market participation of Black women changed very little. During the decade of World War II, the labor force participation rate of Black women over the age of 14 was 37.3 in 1940 and 37.1 in 1950 (Bancroft, 1958). With Black and White males entering the armed services, there was a tremendous need for workers in the defense industries. White women were used to fill the void. Blacks were leaving the rural areas, north and south, and moving to the large urban areas in search of opportunities to improve their lives. Black women could not enter, in any large numbers, the defense industries as workers because of racial discrimination. White women especially did not want Black women to compete for the better paying defense jobs. The exclusion of Black women from those jobs assured White women a source of cheap labor for the domestic servants they needed so they could enter the labor market.

During the decades of the sixties and seventies the employment of Black women in traditional female professions, federal civil service positions, white-collar positions, and semi-skilled jobs increased. By the eighties more Black women were in the labor market than ever before. However, they continued to suffer the double discrimination of racism and sexism although two major social forces for change had emerged during the decades between the end of World War II and the eighties. The activities, goals, and policies of the civil rights movement were directed mainly at the concerns of Black men; the women's movement was focused on the aspirations of White women, and issues of concern to Black women were not the focal point of either social movement (Simms & Malveaux, 1986). Black women have continued to make progress in the labor market, yet they remain the most vulnerable group of workers. Unemployment is a constant threat since they are the most marginal group in the labor force with the fewest resources to fall back on (Giddings, 1984).

One of the trends of the past decade has been the feminization of poverty. Currently, female head of households are increasingly becoming impoverished, regardless of their labor force participation (Pearce & McAdoo, 1981). Nevertheless, during this period the number of Black women in public sector employment and the traditional female professions has increased. It was easier for Black females to enter the traditional female professions than for Black males to enter the traditional male professions. Yet, Black women continued to suffer the double discrimination of race and sex which has fostered occupational segregation and wage discrimination (Scott, 1980). In comparison to men of both races, and White women, Black women are at the bottom in income distribution (see discussion below). In the future, as occupations become more sex and race integrated, Black women probably will be the first group to suffer unemployment as a result of a shrinking economy (Giddings, 1984). Manufacturing jobs are disappearing from the U.S. labor market. These jobs have traditionally served as an economic basis for mobility in the working class, and have been a leading source of income to improve the quality of life. As a result of the changing U.S. economy during the last decade, the class structure is becoming increasingly polarized and the middle class is disappearing (Jaffee, 1986). There is a decline in high wage industrial manufacturing jobs (where there is a high concentration of Black workers) along with an expansion in high technology and information service jobs (where Blacks are not concentrated in substantial numbers).

According to Jaffee (1986), "It is in the interest of manufacturing firms to employ variable capital (labor) versus constant capital (machine equipment). When demand then declines, it is labor that bears the cost of the economic downturn through layoffs, rather than business through equipment (p. 313)." The decline in manufacturing jobs will negatively impact Black women in two ways: (1) they will probably be pushed out of a shrinking economy as competition for jobs increases from other workers—Black men, White men, and White women—downward slide in the labor market; and (2) the subsequent decline in employment and decrease in wage standards among Black men will force more Black women into the labor market for family-related economic reasons.

In summary, Black women have been in the labor market, involuntarily and voluntarily, throughout their life span and since their arrival on this continent (as slaves). Historically, their labor has been exploited by the political and economic systems in spite of major social and for humanitarian efforts—the labor, civil rights, and womens' movements. In the past decades, Black women have made employment gains in traditionally female professional positions and low level white-collar positions in mainly public sector agencies. Nevertheless, the largest percentage labor as domestic servants and unskilled employees. The general lack of diverse employment opportunities for Black working women in an expansive, sophisticated economy reflects the effects of double discrimination—racism and sexism—that have plagued this group historically. Currently, there is a growing dichotomy within this group. Along with the feminization of poverty, there is, in contrast, upward mobility among selected professional Black women.

Demographic Trends

Employment Rates

Currently Black females are participating in the labor market at the highest rates since the U.S. Bureau of Labor Statistics started recording their presence. In 1984 the participation rate was 55.2 percent as compared to 49.5 percent in 1970, 48.9 percent in 1975, 53.2 percent in 1980, and 54.2 percent in 1983. The participation rate figures are for persons 16 years and older. Except for the slight decline (-.6) between 1970 and 1975, the participation rates have continued their historical climb. The labor market rate for Black female participation is projected to continue to increase with expected rates of 59.0 percent for 1990 and 61.2 percent for 1995 (Statistical Abstract of the United States 1986). This steady increase in labor market participation for Black females is in contrast to the decline in labor market participation by Black males. For Black males there has been a decline in the past decade from 76.5 percent civilian labor force participation in 1970 to 70.8 in 1984. Moreover, it is projected that the rates for Black male participation will change very little in the next decade; the projected rates are 70.4 for 1990 and 70.5 for 1995. The greatest difference in rates for Black males occurred between 1970 (76.6 percent) and 1975 when the rates dropped to 71.0 and continued at that approximate level with rates of 70.6 in 1980 and 1983. Importantly, the labor force participation rates for Black males and females are converging. The difference score between rate of labor force participation for Black males and females is declining: the difference between the two groups was 27.0 in 1970 and 17.4 in 1980, and it is projected that this trend will continue to decline with a difference score of 11.4 in 1990 and 9.3 in 1995 between the projected rates of labor force participation of Black males and females.

As the Black male labor force participation rates decline so that it converges with Black females, the labor force participation rates of White females is converging on Black females by their increase in labor force participation. The labor force participation rate of White females was 42.6 in 1970 with an increase to 53.3 in 1984. Their participation rates parallel Black females in that there has been a steady increase in the past decade with a projected continued increase. The participation rates were 45.9 percent in 1975, 51.2 in 1980, and 52.7 in 1983. The projected rates are 58.1 in 1990 and 60.0 in 1995. Interestingly, the labor force participation rates of White males is *similar* to Black males in that there has been a steady decline since 1970. The drop between 1970 and 1975 was not as dramatic as Black males—80.0 to 78.7; however, the level is similar in that there has been very little change over the decade and the projected rate is at approximately the same level. The actual figures are 78.2 percent in 1980, 77.1 percent in 1983, and 77.1 percent in 1984. The projected figures are 77.4 percent for 1990, and 77.0 percent for 1995 (Statistical Abstract of the United States 1986). Thus for Blacks and Whites, the labor force participation rates for females is increasing and the trend is expected to continue in contrast to the decline and then leveling off participation rates for males.

When age of Black females participating in the labor force is considered, the percent of employed workers increases steadily with age and is relatively high throughout the life span. The percent of Black females employed for the 16-19 age category is 57.4 and this increases to 95.3 for 65 years and older. A large percentage of Black females are employed during the prime childbearing years, with 74.4 percent for the 20-24 age category and 84.6 percent for the 25-34 age category. The rate increases for the remaining age categories: 90.6 for ages 35-44, 91.5 for ages 45-54, and 94.2 for ages 55-64. Indeed, the percent of labor force employed figures for Black females and males are very similar with females having a higher percent in the older age categories. The rates for Black males are 57.3 for ages 16-19, 73.4 for ages 20-24, 85.0 for ages 25-34, 89.6 for ages 45-54, 92.1

for ages 55-64, and 92.3 for 65 years and older. The above data are for persons seeking work because they are able to participate in the labor market and were 16 years old and over in 1984 (Statistical Abstract of the United States 1986).

Occupational and Educational Attainment

As in past decades, the majority of Black women workers are concentrated in the service occupations. When the data are examined for occupational group and educational attainment however, higher educational attainment is beginning to advance Black females in the labor market although not as much as it does for White males and females. When the percentage rates are examined by occupational category for Black females (Statistical Abstract of the United States 1986) with less than four years of high school, over half are employed in service occupations (62.3 percent). The remaining third are somewhat evenly divided between low-level white-collar positions: technical/sales/administrative (16.1 percent) and operators/fabricators (17.1 percent). The distribution of workers in categories changes when data are considered for those with four years of high school: the largest percentage of workers then move to the technical/sales/administrative category (43.6 percent) with only 28.8 percent in the service category; little change in the operators category (17.7 percent); and 6.5 in the managerial/professional category. When Black women workers have completed one year of college or more, the distributions again change with the greatest change in the managerial/professional, from 6.5 to 37.9. The percentage of workers in the service industry drops to 9.7 percent and 3.9 percent for operators, with very little change in technical category (47.3). Clearly, staying in school and also acquiring advanced education have marketplace rewards for Black women. Nevertheless, the advances have to be compared to what happens to White males, an appropriate comparison group when the relationship between educational attainment and occupational categories are examined. Research studies of the value Black women place on work, their acceptance of the work ethic, and their ambition have found that they are similar to White men; however, their expectation of success in the marketplace and sense of control over their work life are lower than any other demographic group (Scott, 1980).

White males with four years of high school or less are concentrated in occupations that are heavily organized by labor which gives some degree of job security and protection against exploitation. Staying in school and completing high school does not change the percentage distribution that much; White males are concentrated in high paying semi-skilled and skilled jobs. When they complete one year of college or more however, 47.5 are in managerial/professional positions. The labor market rewards for completing one year of college or more are even more dramatic for White females. When White women workers complete one year or more of college, just about all of the women in this category in the labor force become concentrated in two occupational categories: managerial/professional (45.8 percent) and technical (42.8). The payoff at this level of educational attainment for Black males is less clear. Black males with high school diplomas are distributed across the occupations as follows: 5.2 managerial, 14.0 technical, 22.6 service, 17.4 precision production, 38.0 operators, and 2.8 farming; when one year or more of college are completed, the percentages change to 32.1, 24.8, 17.3, 10.1, 14.8, and 1.0 respectively. Notably, the attainment of a managerial/professional position in the labor market is strongly influenced by the educational achievement, gender, and ethnicity of the person.

The number of Black females enrolling in college has increased steadily over the past two decades with the highest number, 961,000, in 1981. The data are for Black and other races. In 1984 there were 906,000 Black and other race females enrolled in college as compared to 450,000 in 1972. The general trend of an increase in college enrollment between 1972 and 1984 for Black females is the same for other salient groups, Black males, White females, and White males. The percentage of Black females completing college has also increased over the past two decades (Statistical Abstract of the United States 1986, data for Black females only). In 1960 the percent of the Black female population completing four years or more of college was 3.3 with a steady increase in 1970 (4.6), in 1980 (8.3), and in 1984 (10.4). Thus in the past 14 years the number of Black females completing four years or more has tripled and parallels the change in occupational attainment. The increase in level of educational accomplishments was similar for Black males. In 1960 the percent of the Black male population completing four years or more of college was 2.8 with an increase to 4.2 in 1970, 8.4 in 1980, and 10.5 in 1984. Generally the data for White males and females follow the same trend.

Income Distribution

Although there have been gains in occupational and educational attainments for Black women, they still remain at the bottom of the income distribution by when compared to other salient groups. In 1983, the median income for Black females was $5,543 as compared to 6,421 for White females, 8,967 for Black males, and 15,401 for White males. When the mean figures are used there is no change in the ranking—White males are at the top (18,823), followed by Black males (11,501), White females (8,885), and Black females (7,872). The income of Black women is crucial when it is considered that a large percentage of Black children depend solely upon the resources of their mother for the quality of their lives.

Families headed by Black women are the most poverty-stricken families. Over one-half of Black families headed by women are in poverty. Although families headed by Black men are often in poverty, female-headed families constitute two-thirds of all Black families in poverty (Simms, 1986). In 1983, the median income for Black female headed families was 7,999 compared to 15,552 for male headed families (U.S. Department of Commerce, 1984). The Black family with the highest income was a married couple with two-earners, 26,389. Married couples with one earner ranked under the male headed families with 13,821, but ahead of female-headed families. When the household head was employed full-time however, the income distribution was in the same rank order, yet the quality of life improved somewhat. The income distributions are married couple two earners (31,363), male head (23,946), married couple one earner (21,765), and female head (16,055). Of all family types, Black female-headed families continue to have the lowest income.

Often Black women have been restricted to low-paying jobs with limited advancement potential because of racism and sexism (Simms & Malveaux, 1986) despite the popularized myth of a double advantage (Epstein, 1973). The families maintained by these women with limited income are the most economically disadvantaged (Simms, 1986; Pearce & McAdoo, 1981), and are a source of concern for the Black community and public agencies concerned with human services. In the past decade, the Black community and other community organizations have mobilized their resources and mounted a campaign to provide support for the existing families and attempted to affect private attitudes and public policies that facilitate the growth of this family grouping.

In summary, Black working women have a continuous history of labor market participation and the participation rates are projected to increase over the next decade. Indeed for Blacks and Whites the labor force participation rates for females are expected to continue to increase contrary to the decrease and leveling off for males. Importantly, education has marketplace value for Black working women, although not as much as it does for White working males and females. It is not surprising therefore that the number of Black females enrolled in college has increased steadily over the decades. Nevertheless, the position of Black women at the bottom in terms of income distribution—in comparison to Black men, White men, and White women—has not changed. Families headed by Black women are the most poverty stricken families. Concerned persons and agencies have initiated efforts to affect attitudinal and public policy changes that deal with the growth of this type of family grouping. The impact of these efforts has been a decline in the growth rate of households headed by Black women.

Employment and Family Life

There has been increased participation of American women in the paid labor force since the 1960s. Popular wisdom and social scientists suggest that these trends are a reflection of the feminist movement, economic pressures on families, and social forces from changing life styles. As a result of women in the work place and other social forces, the stresses, adjustments, and coping strategies for women are changing. Women have had to grapple with managing the demands of the work-place and family simultaneously. Seemingly, the pressures and stress would be more manageable if they are part of one's expectations of life roles. Black women plan to work throughout their adult years and do not view employment as incompatible with family life (Burlew, 1982). Indeed, Black females generally enter the labor market with marginal jobs while teenagers and stay in the labor market until retirement in their sixties (see discussion above).

During their working years, Black women seldom voluntarily leave the work force. The majority of this group of workers are clustered in low-paying and unskilled jobs without the protection of organized labor and modern fringe benefits. Consequently, their employment histories have been interrupted with lay-offs, loss of jobs, transfers, etc. During their fertility years, Black women do not stay out of the labor market for long periods of time because of childbearing. The general trend is to take off work for a short period of time and return to the work place.

Black women have incorporated employment into their life styles although they have been exposed to the traditional female model of full-time homemaker. There are numerous factors influencing the incorporation of employment into their family life-style e.g., socialization of sex roles, modeling, economic factors, community consensual defini-tion of femininity, etc. According to Giddings (1984), "Historically, necessity has made Black women redefine the notion of womanhood to integrate the concepts of work, achievement, and independence into their role as women (p. 356)." Thus in the lives of Black women, the employ-ment system and the family system converge and influence one another.

How the interaction between employment and family systems effect and shape one another has been the subject of discussion by social scien-tists. Mortiner and London (1984) noted that work affects family life by providing social status and economic resources, setting external con-straints on family organizations and activities, and affecting the attitudes, values, and personalities of the members. On the other hand, family life effects work in a number of ways. The family socializes each new genera-tion of workers, instilling basic attitudes and values toward work. The employment of mothers also implicitly transmits messages regarding the legitimacy of employment for women. Also, family economic needs pro-vide a major motivation to seek employment and to be successful in the occupational career. The employment of Black women has effected their family life in the areas described by Mortiner and London in a manner unique to their cultural history and political-social-economic systems interacting with the Black community.

Effect of Work on Family

The work status of the wage earner sets external constraints on family organizations and activities, provides the economic resources and social status for the family, and affects the attitudes, values, and personalities of family members.

Lamphere (1986) in her examination of the lives of immigrant women, specifically Italian, Colombian, and Portuguese, as workers and family members between 1915 and 1977, asserts that work/production enters the home and family life in subtle and overt ways. The families' daily schedule (e.g., eating, sleeping, leisure time, etc.) was determined largely by the organization of work patterns of the working members of the family. Further, the wages paid to male workers determined whether other family members would have to work outside the home for wages to maintain the household.

Within the 62 year time period studied by Lamphere (1986) the increased participation of women in the paid labor force changed the family status of the women who worked. At the turn of the century mothers worked at home supporting the labor of their working daughters as well as the men in the family. In the 20th century there was a "transition from an era of 'working daughters' to one of 'working mothers' (Lamphere, 1986, p. 118)."

Currently the most rapid increase in labor force participation in the last two decades has been among "working mothers"—single and married women with children (Beckett & Smith, 1981). It is predicted that approximately seventy percent of the children in America will have two working parents by 1990 (Brazelton, 1986). No longer is it culturally unacceptable for mothers to be in the work force. As more mothers enter the labor market it can be speculated that participation in the work force will effect fertility rates. Labor force participation has a negative relationship with fertility rates. Working women tend to have fewer children spaced closer together in age than women who are full-time homemakers. The group of American women who have the highest labor force participation rate and lowest fertility rate of any demographic group of women is college trained Black females (Scott, 1980).

In addition to the relationships between labor force participation and fertility rates, work also has an effect on families by setting the family's social status and economic resources. The income from the employment of wives has supplemented the income of the wage earner husband in the Black community since emancipation. In the mid-1970s among two-parent Black middle-class families, 62 percent of all wives worked full- time as compared to 24 percent of similar White families. If wives were not working in the average upper middle-class Black family, the family would be short $9,000.00 in reaching the category of upper-class; in comparison, upper middle-class White families would have been short only $4,000.00 (Landry, 1987). According to Landry (1987) not only in the 1970s and 1980s but historically, once within the middle class, "Black families have depended far more upon the economic contribution of wives to approach or maintain the living standard associated with that class (p. 7)." This additional income has raised the standard of living for numerous Black families and increased their economic resources. Nevertheless, the family work pattern that characterizes most Black families is dual wage-earners, the group that has been examined the least for the impact of work on family life. The family work pattern that has been researched most by social scientists is dual career families.

Rapoport and Rapoport (1969) coined the phrase dual career family to describe the family pattern that was emerging from White women reaching higher levels of education and occupational attainment which had been accelerated by the womens' movement and affirmative action programs. Subsequently, social scientists initiated studies of this group, the subjects were working wives who were doctors, lawyers, or college professors. Studies examining the life-style of these couples for the impact of work on family life were important since this group's behavior was projected as the "norm" for all working couples. It was assumed that their experiences would serve as models for all working couples since it was grounded in gender equality, women working for personal instead of economic reasons, and their numbers would increase given that women were entering the labor market in record numbers (Benenson, 1984). Generally, the findings suggested that these White middle and upper class families exhibited a neo-traditional pattern, husband dominant wage earner with economic assistance from wife; and wife responsible for household/child rearing tasks with some assistance from husband. They also reflected the substantial differential between male and female earnings at the top managerial and professional levels.

Studies of dual career Black families, on the other hand, have professional women that are teachers, nurses, social workers, and low-level white-collar positions. These families are often the "pillars" of the community and are more equalitarian in their outlook. The husband and wife salaries are more likely to be in the same range. The wife, therefore, is more likely to be an equal economic partner rather than an assistant. Historically, the economic relationship of Black working husband and wives has been characterized by more equalitarian roles and economic parity (Staples, 1981). There is a sharing of household/child rearing tasks, although the woman is mainly responsible for these activities. Regardless of socioeconomic level, Black husbands have an equalitarian perspective and positive attitude towards their wives working (Beckett, 1976; Beckett and Smith, 1981). However what must be kept in mind in evaluating these findings is that the demands of the professional positions of these wives do not arouse strong conflicts between work and home in terms of overtime hours, travel, etc.

Some social scientists have criticized this approach of studying dual career families for insights into the impact of work on family life. One of the leading critics, Benenson (1984) noted that this research trend operated out of false assumptions and importantly the incidence figures of these couples are so small they cannot be considered representative. Married women in the seven high level professions frequently used in these studies accounted for only 1.13 percent of all wives in the labor force in 1982. Notably, it cannot be assumed that their numbers will increase significantly, given persistent gender discrimination, occupation and wage segregation, and the limited number of positions available in these careers. The family work patterns that will yield the most information regarding the impact of work on family life is dual wage earner families.

The greatest occupational gains for women have been in clerical, service, and low level white-collar wage earning positions. Among Black families there emerged a working class dual earner pattern in which husbands held semi-skilled blue-collar jobs and wives held clerical or traditional female professional positions. Professional Black women tend not to exclude men with less social status and education from the pool of eligible men to marry (Burlew, 1982). The evidence suggested that these families were organized along the traditional sex role patterns in division of labor with women assuming the full-time social roles of wife, mother, and worker. Social support systems and improved housecleaning technology have lightened the harshness of their burden somewhat. Nevertheless, the lot of most Black working women in terms of demands on their time and energy has changed very little over the years since emancipation.

In trying to juggle the demands of several social roles, the occupational status of most working Black women has been a factor. Work is the only source of income for the dual wage earner family so the family members are driven to meet the demands of employment even at the expense of family relationships. Black working women, however, have a tendency to prioritize the family demands over employer demands (Harrison & Minor, 1978). Blue-collar male and female jobs are characterized by inflexible work schedules that allow little time off for personal business and often impose forced overtime or rotating shifts on workers. A common crisis in families with two employed adults and single working parent is the problem of a sick child. Northcolt (1983), in a Canadian survey of the area of Edmonton, found that it is the female parent who is more likely to stay home whether she works full-time or part-time. In this study with a quality of life theme, the subjects showed ideological support for an equalitarian sexual division of household tasks and child care; the behavioral realities, however, reflected a traditional division of labor. The wives of most wage earners tend to be employed in jobs that have low wages, little or no fringe benefits, poor working conditions, and little or no opportunity for advancement (Mortiner & London, 1984). For employed female-heads of household, the working conditions of their job impedes their efforts to spend "quality" time with their children. These women rely on social support systems to relieve the stress in their lives from combining all of the social roles (McAdoo, 1986). Indeed, no significant differences exists between single and married mothers in the extent to which they are involved in a kinship network nor in the type of help that they give or receive (McAdoo, 1980).

In short, the efforts of Black women to meet the demands of employment as well as family roles have become a part of their self image. This is reasonable given that a large percentage of Black women contribute economically to the maintenance of self over the life span. Indeed, labor force participation by Black women is unaffected generally by social class, marital status, the presence or absence of children, or spouse's negative attitude toward womens' employment (Scott, 1980). Black women are more likely to work throughout the life span and husbands are more likely to accept this (Beckett, 1982), although they have lower status jobs for less pay and work longer years than other major demographic groups in society. Moreover, in Burlew's (1982) sample of college women in a mid-western university who elected to pursue nontraditional careers, their early work experience gave them the self-confidence to pursue nontraditional female educational programs. Interestingly, in Murray and Mednick's (1977) review of literature for insights into Black women's achievement orientation, the motivation for entering nontraditional fields by Black women was not oriented from ego needs, these authors concluded. Rather the "encouragement to enter nontraditional areas such as law and politics is couched in other directed (serve the needs of Black people) rather than competitive and self-directed terms (Murray & Mednick, 1977, p. 251)." It is reasonable to speculate that the satisfaction from being working members of society, contributing to the general welfare of the community, and financially supporting and psychologically nurturing the family are the reasons Black women have been able to maintain a healthy self-esteem in spite of the negative messages from the cultural milieu concerning their group (Harrison, 1987). The media and society promote the White standard of beauty which is the antithesis of Black beauty (Harrison, 1974); promotes the idea that Black women enjoy a double advantage (Epstein, 1973), which is in stark contrast to their reality (Fulbright, 1986); and pressures them to be submissive to Black men as a means of refuting the myth of the Black matriarchy (Copeland, 1977; Harrison, 1979; Hood, 1983). Yet, Black women feel good about themselves and have high respect for the competence of other Black working women (Epstein, 1973). Although it is not clear how functioning in a negative and hostile environment can shape positive personality traits among Black women, Fleming (1983) has illuminated the issue in her study of Black women in Black and White college environments. The findings indicated that the adverse conditions of predominantly White colleges were more likely to encourage self-reliance, assertiveness and self-confidence among Black women. Clearly more research is needed in this area.

Generally, work has affected the large number of Black females in the labor market and specifically their definition of femininity and the daily living patterns of families. On the other hand, the family social system has also affected the labor market.

Effect of Family on Work

One of the most noticeable effects of family on work is in the socialization process. Black working women have influenced the ideology and accomplishments of their children. The family is the earliest socializing agent of future workers and the primary source of basic attitudes and values concerning the meaning of work. Also from the perspective of life span issues, the family has a powerful impact on the vocational preference and eventual occupational destinations of its younger members (Mortiner & London, 1984). Employed mothers implicitly transmit messages regarding the legitimacy of employment for women, and family economic needs provide a major motive to seek employment and to be successful in an occupational career.

Mullins and Sites (1984) have empirically examined the impact of the educational and occupational accomplishments of Black mothers on their children. In their study of eminent Black Americans and their historic origins, the social scientists randomly selected a sample of persons from the list published in 1978 of Who's Who Among Black Americans. They traced the ancestry of their sample from the antebellum period to the present. Because of the continuing presence of racism in America, Blacks could not accumulate great capital wealth to pass on to their children, so high societal position had to be achieved in each generation rather than passed on through ascription. Mullins and Sites (1984) found that the social stratification patterns through generations could be accounted for by antebellum freedom, lighter skin color, urban residence, and importantly the higher education and occupational attainment of the mother. In the absence of large wealth and the presence of discrimination, the mother's social origin and achievement were important factors in providing the social resources that facilitated the individual's achieving eminence. Black women have participated in the labor market since emancipation, yet the rate of employment (66.9 percent) among mothers of eminent Blacks was atypical of women in the Black population (38 percent) in 1940. Similar findings of the importance of mother's educational and occupational attainment on the upward mobility of families was found by McAdoo (1981). McAdoo investigated factors among Black families associated with mobility in four generations living in a middle atlantic city. She found that the mobility of the families would not have been possible without the dual income and could not be maintained without the continued employment of both parents. Families where there was upward mobility in each generation had mothers that were better educated than other family patterns. Brookins (1985), using a sample of 36 Black families in a northeast metropolitan area with a mother, father, and one child 6 to 8 years old, found a positive relationship between maternal employment and children's egalitarian sex role ideologies and occupational choice. As maternal employment increased so did children's range of occupational choices and belief in men and women equally performing household tasks and activities.

The findings of Brookins (1985), McAdoo (1981), and Mullins and Sites (1984) are consistent with other studies regarding the effect of maternal employment among Black women on their children. Furthermore, examination of data from several studies suggested that the feminine behavior model presented by Black mothers shaped the sex-role perceptions of Black children towards a more androgynous attitude and less stereotypic view of sex roles (Harrison, 1981). Burlew's (1982) investigation of differences in the backgrounds, attitudes, and career related expectations of Black college females pursuing traditional (e.g., teaching, social work, and nursing) and nontraditional (e.g., sciences, engineering, pre-law, and business) careers for women supported this position. The results indicated that although 90 percent of all subjects' mothers worked at some time either full-time or part-time, mothers of nontraditional subjects were likely to be better educated and more likely to have worked in nontraditional fields than mothers of traditional subjects. These findings are consistent with other studies which indicated that Black females tended to be influenced in their career preference by the same sex parent and same sex model (Obleton, 1984).

Although there are large numbers of their members in the labor force, Black women tend to hold traditional views of the feminine role (Gump, 1975) and these sex role concerns have a mediational effect upon achievement orientation (Murray & Mednick, 1977). Murray and Mednick (1977) surmised that the motivating factor for Black women in their effort to achieve is family concerns rather than self-actualizing reasons. Their conclusions were based on the findings of several studies indicating that Black women generally aspire to traditional careers that offer economic security rather than risk-taking careers that are potentially self-fulfilling. Thus, family considerations impact on the work patterns and aspirations of Black women. Their career aspirations and achievements reflect the internalization of traditional roles, yet they tend to see working, rearing children and fulfilling a wifely role as a valued lifestyle.

Interestingly, there is a relationship between a strong commitment to work and health problems. Howenstein and his colleagues (Howenstein, Koal, & Harburg, 1977) in their investigation of the relationship between work status, work satisfaction, and blood pressure levels among married Black and White women found significant effects. Women who were more committed to the work role (worked by choice, rated various job activities or opportunities as personally more important) had higher blood pressure levels, as did those women who were relatively low on indicators of job achievement. Indeed, women in two-job families experienced significantly more work-family role strain than men as suggested from the findings by Keith and Schafer (1980).

Keith and Schafer (1980) interviewed 135 two-job White families in a study designed to investigate the relation between stress and time spent at work by both spouses. Working wives in two-job families experienced significantly more work-family role strain than their husbands. Hours per week spent at work was the most important variable in explaining work-family strain; as their spouses spent more time at work, the level of strain expressed by women increased. Negative perception of their financial situation relative to others and devaluing of husband's performance as a provider also influenced the level of depression among working wives. Harrison and Minor (1978) investigated a similar issue in their study of interrole conflict between wife, worker, and mother roles among Black working wives. One hundred and four women completed a questionnaire on how satisfied they were with their role performance and the type of coping strategy used to handle interrole conflicts. The social status of the role sender differentiated the response of the women whenever there was conflict between family and work. If the conflict was between the husband's demands and the demands of work, the women generally negotiated with the husband to alter his demands and come to agreement on a new set of expectations. If the role sender was a child, however, the women chose a different type of coping strategy to handle work-family conflicts. Generally the women coped with mother and worker conflicts by establishing priorities, partitioning, and separating roles, changing attitudes toward roles, and the expectations and perceptions of the role sender may remain unchanged. In other words, the women attempted to make internal changes in attitude and perceptions to reduce role conflicts between family and work. Usually the demands of the mother role was prioritized over the worker role. Interestingly, husband's approval of wife working did not influence the women's satisfaction with their worker role, the greatest influence on career satisfaction was whether or not the subject was a professional worker as compared to a nonprofessional. Similarly, Landry and Gendreh (1978) found in their study of employed Black and White working and middle-class wives that husband's attitude may deter White middle-class wives from working, but has little negative impact on Black wives. They also found Black middle-class wives are more likely to work because of economic reasons than White middle-class wives. In contrast, Black working class families also have an economic need, yet strong opposition from their husbands deterred them from working. In Harrision's and Minor's working class sample of working wives, husband's approval did not influence their satisfaction with the workers role. Thus, once wives decided themselves to work, the attitude of their husbands did not relate to their role satisfaction.

In summary, historically Black women have had to combine work and family-life and they have internalized employment into their self-image. Black women's views of the role of women have been shaped over the life-span. The empirical findings discussed suggest the need for a conceptual framework that will generate empirical investigations of life-span issues among this population of women. These findings are just the beginning of an examination of the interrelatedness of work, self, and gender identity among Black women. Contributing to the economic well-being of the family is as important to the Black woman as the more traditional female attitudes and behaviors (e.g., nurturing, supportive, and caring adult). Black women's employment has impacted on the family resulting in a more equalitarian perspective and positive attitude towards wives' employment among Black husbands, a tendency toward egalitarian division of household/child rearing tasks in Black families, a stabilizing factor in family life styles, and a positive view towards self and other Black women. The family life patterns of employed Black women have impacted on work through the socialization process. Children of working mothers have been shaped by their educational and occupational attainments in their choice of educational programs, career goals, occupational attainment, attitude toward sex roles, and upward mobility between generations.

Summary and Conclusions

Historically Black women have had high, stable levels of labor force participation over the course of the life cycle. Since their arrival on this continent as slaves, Black women have performed manual jobs most persons envision as only for males (e.g., lumberjacks, field hands, etc.), and as only for females (e.g., laundress, washerwoman, cook, etc.); and professional jobs some envision as only for males (e.g., doctors, bankers, engineers, etc.) and as only for females (e.g., nurses, teachers, social workers, etc.). Nevertheless, their work history can be summarized as being exploited by the political and economic systems because they have had little option as to whether to enter the labor market, or occupational choices, once involved. Further they have had very little return in terms of occupational attainment and income distribution for the positive attitude, energy, effort, and persistence they have devoted to the labor market. The activities of three humanitarian forces—civil, womens', and labor movements—have not created economic parity for Black women with other demographic groups (White males, White females, and Black males). Yet, Black women continue to enter the labor market in record numbers and are projected to be the demographic group of women with the largest percentage of workers in the labor force in 1995. Currently, there is a growing economic division among Black working women, with a small percentage advancing professionally, the vast majority laboring at low status and low paying jobs, and a considerable portion in between as clerks and low level white-collar workers. Notably, Black womens' participation in the labor market has generally been unaffected by the expected factors (e.g., husbands' attitudes, social class, poor working conditions, etc.).

Given the history and extent of Black womens' participation in the labor market, they have had to combine employment and family life out of necessity. Their employment has placed constraints on and impacted their family life. Indeed Black college trained women have the highest and most stable labor force participation rate and lowest fertility level of any group of women. The employment record of women has shaped the Black family into generally an equalitarian entity with sharing of economic, household tasks, and child rearing activities among adults. This dual wage earner family pattern is the norm among Black families.

Black women have and continue to participate in the labor market with the least return for their attitude and behavior of any demographic group and yet they have maintained a positive self-image of themselves and other working Black women. Black women have had to work for economic reasons and their working has legitimized employment of women in the Black community. Their employment has impacted their children and influenced their sex role ideologies, career goals, and occupational attainments; and the upward mobility of Black families. Employment continues to be an important aspect of Black womens' lifestyle.

Although Black women have participated extensively in the labor market over the life span, very few empirical investigators have investigated the psychological impact of these events. Life span issues investigated empirically were the relationship between early socialization, education, and career aspirations; and the impact of role models on developing personality of Black females. More conceptual discussion and empirical investigations of employment on Black women is needed. We need to know what are the dominant psychological mechanisms (e.g., modeling, learning from reinforcement, etc.) and external conditions (e.g., female-heads of household, low salaries for Black males, etc.) that impact on their developing sex role ideology. What factors maintain the ideology and what factors will more likely provoke change. In the decade of the 60s and 70s, studies indicated that Black women generally held traditional views regarding the role of women and were comfortable with the contradictory view of working women. Future investigations are needed to see if this view is still prevalent and if changed what factors contributed to the change. Our knowledge of Black women is very limited although the study of women has emerged in recent years as a viable area of academic research. The focus in this area has been mainly on White women. Clearly more research is needed on Black women generally, and specifically how they incorporate (internally and externally) employment into their self-concept and life plans.

References

Bancroft, G. (1958). *The American labor force: Its growth and hanging composition.* New York: John Wiley and Sons.

Barnett, R. C., & Baruch, G. K. (1978). Women in the middle years: A critique of research and theory. *Psychology of Women Quarterly, 3,* 187-197.

Beckett, J. O. (1982). Working women: A historical review of racial differences. *The Black Sociologist, 9,* 4-26.

Beckett, J. O. (1976). Working wives: A racial comparison. *Social Work,* 463-471.

Beckett, J. O. & Smith, A. D. (1981). Work and family roles: Egalitarian marriage in Black and White families. *Social Service Review,* 314-326.

Benenson, H. (1984). Women's occupational and family achievement in the U.S. class system. *The British Journal of Sociology, 21,* 19-41.

Blassingame, J. (1972). *Slave Community.* New York: Oxford.

Boserup, E. (1970). *Woman's Role in Economic Development.*

Brazelton, T. B. (1986). Issues for working parents. *American Journal of Orthopsychiatry, 56,* 14-25.

Brookins, G. K. (1985). Black children sex-role ideologies and occupational choices in families of employed mothers. In M. B. Spencer, G. K. Brookins & W. R. Allen (Eds.), *Beginnings: The social and affective development of Black children,* 257-271. Hillsdale, N. J.: Lawrence Erlbaum.

Burlew, A. K. (1982). The experiences of Black females in traditional and nontraditional professions. *Psychology of Women Quarterly, 6,* 312-326.

Copeland, E. T. (1977). Counseling Black women with negative self-concepts. *Personnel and Guidance Journal, 55,* 397-400.

Davis, A. (1983). *Women, Race and Class.* New York: Vintage Books.

Epstein, C. (1973). Positive effects of the multiple negative: Explaining the success of Black professional women. *American Journal of Sociology, 78,* 912-935.

Fleming, J. (1983). Black women in Black and White college environments: The making of a matriarch. *Journal of Social Issues, 39,* 41-54.

Fulbright, K. (1986). The myth of the double-advantage: Black female managers. In M. C. Simms & J. M. Malveaux (Eds.), *Slipping through the cracks: The status of Black women,* 33-45. New Brunswick, N. J.: Transaction Books.

Garfinkel, R. (1982). By the sweat of your brow. In T. M. Field, A. Huston, H. C. Quay, L. Troll, & G. E. Finley (Eds.), *Review of Human Development*. New York: Wiley.

Giddings, P. (1984). *When and Where I Enter*. New York: Morrow.

Gump, J. (1975). A comparative analysis of Black and White women's sex-role attitudes. *Journal of Consulting and Clinical Psychology, 43*, 858-863.

Harley, S. (1978). Northern Black female workers: Jacksonian Era. In S. Harley & R. Terborg-Penn (Eds.), *The Afro American woman: Struggles and images*. Port Washington, N. Y.: Kennikat Press.

Harrison, A. O. (1987). Images of Black women. In S. Dix (Ed.), *The American women 1987-88: Women and research*, 257-261. New York: W. W. Norton.

Harrison, A. O. (1974). The dilemma of growing up Black and female. *Journal of Social and Behavioral Science, 20(2)*, 28-40.

Harrison, A. O. (1981). Attitudes toward procreation among Black adults. In H. P. McAdoo (Ed.), *Black Families*, 199-208. Beverly Hills: Sage.

Harrison, A. O. (1977). Black women. In V. O'Leary (Ed.), *Toward Understanding Women*, 131-146. Monterey: Brooks/Cole.

Harrison, A. O., & Minor, J. H. (1978). Interrole conflict, coping strategies, and satisfaction among Black working wives. *Journal of Marriage and Family, 40*, 799-806.

Harrison, A., Serafica, F. & McAdoo, H. (1984). Ethnic families of color. In R. D. Parke (Ed.), *The Family Review of Child Development Research*, 329-371. Chicago: The University of Chicago Press.

Hood, E. (1983). Black women, White women: Separate paths to liberation. *The Black Scholar, 11(7)*, 26-37.

Household and Family Characteristics: (1985). U.S. Bureau of the Census, Washington, D.C.

Howenstein, L. S., Koal, V. S. & Harburg, E. (1977). Work satisfaction and blood pressure among married Black and White women. *Psychology of Women Quarterly, 1*, 334-349.

Jaffee, D. (1986). The political economy of job loss in the United States, 1970-1980. *Social Problems, 33(4)*.

Keith, P. M. & Schafer, R. B. (1980). Role strain and depression in two-job families. *Family Relations, 29*, 483-488.

Lamphere, L. (1986). From working daughters to working mothers: Production and reproduction in an industrial community. *American Ethnologist, 13*, 118-130.

Landry, B. (1987). The new Black middle-class (Part II). *Focus, 15*, 6-7.

Landry, B. & Jendrek, M. P. (1978). The employment of wives in middle-class Black families. *Journal of Marriage and the Family, 40*, 787-798.

Malson, M. R. (1981). Black women's sex role integration and behavior: Report on research in progress. In A. O. Harrison (Ed.), *Conference on Empirical Research in Black Psychology*, 42-49. Rochester, M. I.: Oakland University Press.

McAdoo, H. P. (1986). Strategies used by Black single mothers against stress. In M. C. Simms & J. M. Matveaux (Eds.), *Slipping Through the Cracks*, 153-166. New Brunswick, N. J.: Transaction Books.

McAdoo, H. P. (1981). Patterns of upward mobility in Black adults. In H. P. McAdoo (Ed.), *Black Families*, 155-169. Beverly Hills: Sage.

McAdoo, H. P. (1980). Black mothers and the extended family support network. In L. F. Rodgers-Rose (Ed.), *The Black Woman*, 125-144. Beverly Hills: Sage.

Mortiner, J. T. & London, J. (1984). The varying linkage of work and family. In P. Voydanoff (Ed.), *Work and Family*, 20-35. Palo Alto: Mayfield.

Mullins, E. T. & Sites, P. (1984). The origins of contemporary eminent Black Americans. *American Sociological Review, 49*, 672-685.

Murray, S. R. & Mednick, M. T. (1977). Black women's achievement orientation: Motivational and cognitive factors. *Psychology of Women Quarterly, 1*, 247-259.

Northcott, H. C. (1983). Who stays home? Working parents and sick children. *International Journal of Women's Studies, 6(5)*, 387-394.

Obleton, N. B. (1984). Career counseling Black women in a predominantly White coeducational university. *Personnel and Guidance Journal*, 365-368.

Pearce, D. & McAdoo, H. (1981). *Women and children alone and in poverty*. National Advisory Council on Economic Opportunity. Washington, D.C.

Rapoport, R. N. & Rapoport, D. (1969). The dual career family. *Human Relations, 22*, 3-30.

Rutledge, E. O. (1981). Socialization and aspirations of Black college females. In A. O. Harrison (Ed.), *Conference on Empirical Research in Black Psychology*, 59-71. Rochester, M.I.: Oakland University Press.

Scott, P. B. (1980). Black women and the work experience. In D. G. McGuigan (Ed.), *Women's lives: New theory, research and policy*. Ann Arbor: University of Michigan.

Simms, M. C. (1986). Black women who head families: An economic struggle. In M. C. Simms & J. M. Malveaux (Eds.), *Slipping Through the Cracks*, 141-151. New Brunswick: Transaction Books.

Simms, M. C. & Malveaux, J. M. (1986). *Slipping Through the Cracks*. New Brunswick: Transaction Books.

Staples, R. (1981). Race and marital status: An overview. In H. P. McAdoo (Ed.), *Black Families*, 173-175. Beverly Hills: Sage.

Statistical Abstract of the United States 1986. Bureau of the Census (Washington, D.C.: GPO, 1986).

Terborg-Penn, R. (1978). Black male perspective on the nineteenth-century woman. In S. Harley and R. Terborg-Penn (Eds.), *The Afro-American Woman: Struggles and Images*. Port Washington, N.Y.: Kennikat Press.

U.S. Department of Commerce, Bureau of the Census, *Detailed population characteristics, United States Summary, 1980 Census of the Population*. (Washington, D.C.: GPO, 1984).

Walker, A. (1983). *In Search of Our Mothers' Gardens*. New York: Harcourt Brace Jovanovich.

Wertheimer, B. M., (1977). *We were There: The Story of Working Women in America*. New York: Pantheon.

RESEARCH PERSPECTIVES ON BLACK MEN: ROLE STRAIN AND ADAPTATION ACROSS THE ADULT LIFE CYCLE

Phillip J. Bowman

Introduction

Over the past two decades, the modern women's movement and related changes in gender roles have spurred a significant increase in literature on the role of men in American society (Farrell, 1974; Fasteau, 1975; Goldberg, 1977; Hapgood, 1979; Harrison, 1978; Hoffman, 1980; Krigel, 1979; Nichols, 1975; Pleck, 1976; Pleck & Pleck, 1980; Pleck & Sawyer, 1984). Studies highlight the privileged access to power, wealth and respect among males in America. However, ongoing social and economic changes have resulted in a number of gender role complexities. To be sure, White males still represent a distinctly powerful group which continues to experience disproportionate success in all sectors of society. However, although Black males appear to share similar values for achievement, they remain at far greater risks for persistent failure in educational and other major life roles (Allen & Farley, 1985).

The past decade has witnessed a growing interest in the special economic, social and psychological circumstances of Black males (Evans & Whitehead, 1988; Gary, 1981; Staples, 1982; Wilkinson & Taylor, 1977). Nevertheless, the unique problems faced by Black males in America remain both controversial and ill understood. Race, gender and class appear to interact in complex ways to place Black males at disturbing risks for persistent school failure, familial estrangement, homicidal violence, stress-related illness and a range of other psychosocial problems (Bowman, 1980; Heckler, 1985; Gary & Leashore, 1982; McAdoo, 1984). Despite such risks, studies also indicate that many Black men continue to defy the odds by excelling in student work, family, community and national leadership roles (Allen, 1981; Bowman, 1985; Cazenave, 1981; Franklin & Meier, 1982; Gary, 1981; McAdoo, 1981; Walton, 1985).

This chapter critically evaluates major research perspectives in the literature on Black men as a basis for formulating a more integrative adult development approach. An exhaustive review of existing literature will not be attempted. Rather, the focus is on the classification, analysis and synthesis of research perspectives which characterize our current knowledge on Black men in America.

An adult development approach to role strain and adaptation has two main features germane to the improvement of research on Black men. First, a role strain and adaptation model provides a coherent theoretical framework for integrating disparate empirical findings from past studies. This integrative model considers the influence of both external and internal factors in explaining both maladaptive and adaptive behavior patterns. Moreover, a focus on adult development provides a basis for better understanding distinct role strain and adaptation issues at different stages of adulthood. Emphasis is placed on the importance of successful adaptation to salient role strains at early stages of adulthood for effective navigation of role barriers during later stages.

Existing Research Perspectives

Recent reviews of literature on Black men in the United States clearly document the particular difficulty that Black males face in all sectors of American society (Cazenave, 1981; Gary, 1981; Staples, 1982). These reviews also levy strong criticism against traditional research which tend to narrowly focus on Black males as deviant or pathological. Despite critics, victim blaming studies that concentrate on deficits within Black males themselves still predominate in the psychological and social science literature (Evans & Whitehead, 1988). However, social scientists have begun to formulate alternative research paradigms which provide the basis for a more balanced, accurate and meaningful understanding of Black males. Divergent approaches that focus on concepts such as institutional racism, adaptive behaviors and cultural strengths have been offered to help redress limitations of pathology studies (Ashante, 1981; Gary, 1981; Taylor, 1981).

As illustrated in Table 1, existing studies on Black males tend to reflect four competing themes—*pathology, oppression, coping* and *ethnicity*. These four distinct research perspectives differ in two major ways: (1) the degree of emphasis on maladaptive or adaptive behavioral patterns, and (2) the degree of emphasis on internal or external causal factors in analysis of these behavior patterns.

Although some studies incorporate more than one theme, the tendency is to emphasize one theme at the expense of the others. Distinctions between these four research orientations have important practical as well as theoretical implications. The focus on positive aspects of the Black male experience in coping and ethnicity studies favor non-intervention policies. However, pathology research calls for therapeutic changes in Black men, while oppression studies support policy initiatives directed at

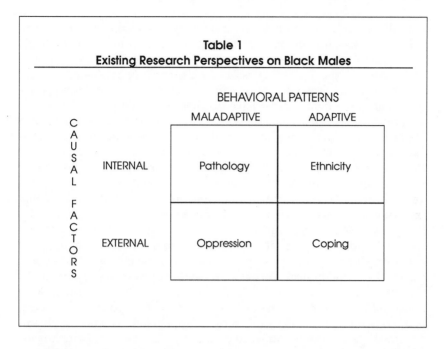

Table 1
Existing Research Perspectives on Black Males

BEHAVIORAL PATTERNS

		MALADAPTIVE	ADAPTIVE
CAUSAL	INTERNAL	Pathology	Ethnicity
FACTORS	EXTERNAL	Oppression	Coping

broader social changes. Each perspective is briefly highlighted below along with related theoretical and empirical literature.

Pathology Perspective

Pathology researchers have chosen to focus on maladaptive behaviors, and seek to support the hypothesis that cultural or psychological deficits are primary causal factors. This perspective dominated early research on Black males and continues to be well represented in more recent literature (Evans & Whitefield, 1988; Gary, 1981). Studies guided by the pathology perspective have often been restricted by serious conceptual and methodological problems (Abrahams, 1970; Auletta, 1982; Hetherington, 1966; Miller, 1958; Rubin, 1974; Shinn, 1978). Critical questions should be raised about research that not only focus narrowly on deviant life styles, but also overgeneralize from small samples of low income Black males with rather extreme psychosocial problems. In an insightful review, Gary (1981) noted that these studies have resulted in a distorted social science literature that largely depicts...

> ..."Black males as 'street corner men,' pimps, deserters, criminals, hustlers, or ineffective family heads. Moreover, the Black male has been projected as psychologically impotent and castrated, dependent, incredulous, nebulous, irresponsible and suspicious (p. 11)."

119

In addition to studies on small biased samples, pathology researchers have also employed archival and epidemiological methods which involve statistical analysis of larger datasets (Cannon & Locke, 1977; Gary & Leashore, 1982; Kessler & Neighbors, 1985; Miller & Dreger, 1973). Archival studies based on the decennial census, institutional records and other data sources have documented widespread patterns of social pathology among Black males. Epidemiological studies have also found a greater incidence and prevalence of some patterns of psychopathology among Black males. These pathology-oriented statistical studies have helped frame the bleak but popular portrait of Black males as essentially deviant and pathological.

The major benefits from archival and epidemiological work are that they provide the best available estimates of psychosocial risks faced by Black males. Moreover, detailed risk analysis among can monitor changes in social and psychological distress over time, identify subgroups at greatest risk for various problems, isolate possible etiologic factors and guide the development of early prevention measures (Gary, 1978; Georges-Abeyie, 1984; Heckler, 1985; Neighbors, Jackson, Gurin & Bowman, 1983). Despite larger samples and some potential benefits, pathology-oriented statistics on Black males, remain extremely problematic; they are too often framed in denigrative White-Black comparisons which are used to advanced victim blaming ideologies with questionable scientific or practical value (Miller & Dreger, 1973; Neighbors, 1985; Ryan, 1971).

Oppression Perspective

Similar to pathology research, oppression studies focus on maladaptive rather than adaptive aspects of the Black male experience. However, rather than blame internal psychological or cultural deficits, external societal barriers are emphasized as the root causes of widespread maladaptive behaviors (Clark, 1965; Glasgow, 1980; Kunjufu,1982; Liebow, 1967; Staples, 1982; Stewart & Scott, 1978; Valentine, 1978; Wilkinson & Taylor, 1977). Oppression researchers reject the pejorative tone of pathology studies and emphasize the victimization of Black males by race and class barriers. These researchers employ a variety of concepts such as institutional racism, internal colonialism, underclass entrapment and urban poverty to help explain the external sources of prevalent psychosocial problems among Black males. For example, Gary (1981) formulated an oppression model which focused on institutional racism; he showed how discriminatory organizational practices, especially in economics and education, impose devastating pressures and frustrations on Black males. Similar to other oppression researchers, Gary emphasized the manner in which institutional barriers restrict employment options of Black males and place severe pressure on their family relations. He concluded that Black males too often employ a variety of self-destructive "psychological and social coping mechanisms, including suicide, homicide, crime and vice, drugs, and alcohol, for dealing with the racial oppression of these institutions (p. 14)." The emphasis may differ, but a focus on destructive effects of external barriers on maladaptive behavior summarizes the central theme in oppression studies on Black males.

Coping Perspective

Problem-oriented research, whether emphasis is on pathology or oppression themes, tends to divert attention away from Black males who manage effective responses to stressful obstacles. Coping researchers, while they often acknowledge oppressive barriers, look beyond maladaptive to more adaptive response patterns (Bowman, 1985; Cazenave, 1981; McAdoo, 1981; Neighbors et al., 1983). Coping researchers emphasize the importance of understanding processes that enable many high risk Black males to avoid devastation, to struggle against adversity and to even excel despite discouraging odds. A coping perspective may well focus on critical aspects of the Black male experience, but we still lack a coherent theoretical model or a substantial evidentiary base (Bowman, 1985; Taylor, 1981).

Taylor (1981) reviews the stress-coping paradigm and its implications for guiding future inquiry on Black males; he concludes that...

...."the challenge of future research is to delineate the process through which Black males achieve and maintain mental health in spite of conditions inimical to its development. What is required is a theoretical framework that takes account of the multiple possibilities for individual adaptation within the parameters imposed by the conditions of social life (p. 142)."

To develop a viable coping model, carefully designed studies should systematically examine factors that foster adaptive functioning of Black males in naturally occurring student, work and family roles (Allen, 1981; Bowman, 1985; Cazenave, 1981; McAdoo, 1981; Kunjufu, 1986). Coping studies may also help explain collective efforts among Black men who actively participate in organizations which work to reduce race and class barriers (Gary, 1981; Morris, 1984; Walton, 1985; Yearwood, 1980).

Ethnicity Perspective

Ethnicity studies on African-Americans have focused on adaptive modes of cultural expression rather than maladaptive "reactions" to op-

121

pression. Emphasis has been placed on the cultural foundation of authentic and "proactive" responses to institutionalized barriers. Indigenous ethnic or cultural adaptations among Black males have been examined in music, language, literature, religion, family and other areas of social life (Baratz, 1973; Drake & Cayton, 1945; Hannerz, 1969; Hill, 1971; Keil, 1966; Layng, 1978; Tinney, 1981). Rather than material culture, traditional emphasis has been placed on retention of core psychological aspects—attitudinal and expressive behavioral patterns (DuBois, 1903; Herskovits, 1935; 1955). As with any ethnic group, these subjective aspects of African-American culture are transmitted across generations and are often adapted in response to changing social or ecological imperatives (Triandis, 1972; Triandis, Lambert, Berry, Lonner, Hernon, Brislin & Draguns, 1980-1981).

Ethnicity researchers disagree with the tradition of scholarship which concludes that the most conspicuous thing about Black Americans is their lack of indigenous ethnic culture (Frazier, 1939; Glazier & Moynihan, 1963; Miller, 1958; Myrdal, 1964). As Hannerz (1969:195) notes:

> "To them, Black people are only Americans, without values and culture of their own to guard and protect, and without an opportunity to view themselves as other ethnic groups do. Thus they would be less likely to organize themselves to take care of their own social problems." In opposition to this view, ethnicity researchers focus on adaptive cultural patterns among African-Americans that differ in style and/or substance from European-American, middle class cultural forms.

Among ethnicity researchers, a sharp divergence exist regarding the origins of distinct cultural patterns among Blacks in America. One view is that Black American ethnic patterns are basically reactions to American racial oppression which are devoid of African origins (Hannerz, 1969; Keil, 1966). In contrast, others view these patterns as distinctly African adaptations rather than mere cultural residues of oppression (e.g., Herskovits, 1935; 1941; Sudarkasa, 1980; 1981). In this latter tradition, Afri-centricity has emerged as an increasingly popular conceptual framework to guide ethnic studies on Black males in America (Akbar, 1979; Ashante, 1981; Baldwin, 1981; Myers, 1985). The Afri-centrist focuses on the unique African heritage as the prime source of adaptive African-American cultural patterns. Afri-centric research on Black males may help identify indigenous ethnic resources that facilitate adaptive over pathological response to oppressive role barriers. Ethnic organizations, extended kinship bonds, flexible family roles, group consciousness and religion may all be sources of empowerment for Black males as they struggle with discouraging barriers in cherished social roles (Berry & Blassingame, 1985; Hill, 1971; Levine, 1977; Morris, 1984; Nobles, 1974a; b; Sudarkasa, 1981; Yearwood, 1980).

Toward An Integrative Life Span Approach

A focus on pathology, oppression, coping and ethnicity illuminates disparate aspects of the Black male experience in America. Pathology research has reinforced a pejorative victim blaming ideology, but also provides a systematic basis to monitor the incidence and prevalence of maladaptive behaviors among high risk Black males. Oppression studies, which emphasize the destructive effects of race and class barriers, often depict Black males as helpless victims. Coping studies, with their emphasis on adaptive responses to societal barriers, may undermine the devastating effects of growing underclass entrapment among Black males in urban America. Finally, while ethnicity studies may help identify indigenous cultural resources among Black males, the origins and adaptive psychosocial functions of these resources remains controversial.

Despite insights provided by the four research orientations, each has limitations and neither alone can adequately explain the Black male experience in America. Research findings generated by each of the four perspectives should be considered as only one aspect of the complex "social reality" of Black males. Moreover, each of these critical aspects of the Black male experience can be better understood if integrated into a more inclusive theoretical model. Hence, a research approach is needed that incorporates unique features of each perspective into a more comprehensive, balanced and culturally-sensitive social psychological paradigm. As suggested earlier, in order to be viable, such an integrative research paradigm should have at least two basic features. First, it must be built on a coherent *theoretical base* that clarifies interrelationships between phenomena emphasized in the four existing perspectives. Secondly, it must provide a *life cycle framework* to study how these interrelated phenomena operate as Black men move through various stages of adulthood.

Role Strain and Adaptation: A Theoretical Model

A growing literature on role strain processes provides a coherent basis to conceptualize the relationship between oppression, pathology, coping and ethnicity variables in future research on Black males (Allen & Vande Vliert, 1981; Barnett & Baruch, 1985; Baruch & Barnett, 1986; Bowman, in press; Eron & Peterson, 1982; Kessler, Price & Wortman, 1985). Based on a national study of Black husband-fathers, Bowman (1985) offered a role strain-adaptation approach which raises the following questions: (1) Are harmful psychological effects of oppressive race and class barriers mediated by difficulties in major life roles? (2) What social psychological mechanisms increase vulnerability for pathological responses? (3) Can these mechanisms be reversed to facilitate adaptive coping

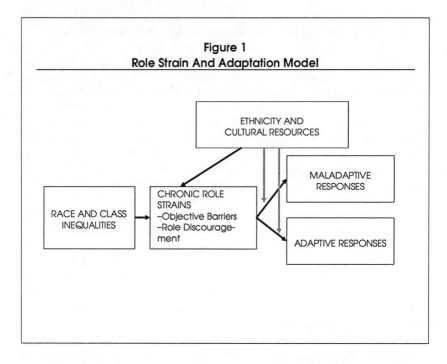

Figure 1
Role Strain And Adaptation Model

responses? (4) How might ethnic resources reduce vulnerability and promote adaptive coping with oppressive role barriers? Role strain and
adaptation studies on Black males should build on existing theoretical
literature to systematically investigate these crucial issues.

To guide future inquiry, a role strain-adaptation model is presented
in Figure 1 which specifies interrelationships between the four classes of
variables emphasized in existing literature. This model focuses on the
nature, antecedents and consequences of chronic strains in major life roles
that threaten the quality of life among Black American males. Role strain
may be defined as objective difficulties, or subjective reactions to such
difficulties, faced by people as they engage in valued social roles (Good,
1960). Role strain can be produced either by barriers in the social environment, by personal limitations, or by conflicts at the environment-person
interface (Kahn, Wolfe, Quinn, Snoek & Rosenthal, 1964). When obstacles
frustrate the achievement of goals in valued life roles, role difficulties may
be perceived as either personally uncontrollable or more manageable. The
manner in which role difficulties are perceived, interpreted and evaluated
may largely distinguish maladaptive from adaptive behavioral responses
(Bowman, 1985; Pearlin, 1983; Sarbin & Allen, 1968).

As with others in society, Black males are socialized to highly value
success in major life roles as students, workers and family members (e.g.,
Cazenave, 1981; Merton, 1968; Pearlin, 1983). In a social psychological
sense, we come to think of ourselves largely in the terms of these central

societal roles we play in life. Equally important, our self-evaluations may depend heavily on success or failure in playing specific roles we learn to cherish during various adult stages. Despite the high stakes Black males place in major life roles, they must more often cope with discouraging role barriers, repeated failure, and frustration (Allen & Farley, 1986; Bowman, in press; Green, 1982). In a review of literature on Black males, Cazenave (1981) raised a critical question for future inquiry: "What happens to Black men who accept society's notion of what it takes to be a man but are denied the resources to 'earn' their masculinity through traditional channels?" To address this issue, the model highlighted in Figure 1 emphasizes the importance of understanding both maladaptive and adaptive responses to chronic role strains. The role strain-adaptation model does not ignore the high risks for maladaptive behavioral patterns among Black males.

However, unlike pathology research, the structural antecedents and sociocultural ecology of maladaptive patterns are emphasized. Sociological research has demonstrated how oppressive race and class systematically impede the performance of Black and other minorities in major life roles (Merton, 1968; Staples, 1982). Moreover, ethnic studies have identified indigenous cultural resources which may mitigate destructive effects of such role strains and promote adaptive coping (Gary, 1981; Hill, 1971). Social psychological studies can further clarify specific cognitive mechanisms that differentiate maladaptive (arrow 1) from adaptive (arrow 2) emotional and behavioral responses. Subjective reactions such as role discouragement and self-blame may be very distressful. However, culture-based empowerment processes may reaffirm a sense of personal efficacy and motivate adaptive coping strategies (Bowman, 1984; 1985; in press). Cultural resources may function in three main ways to reduce hopelessness and facilitate adaptive coping. First, ethnic resources may better enable Black males to avoid or navigate around objective barriers that impede successful role performance (arrow 3). Secondly, cultural resources may directly reduce maladaptive responses and promote adaptive coping behavior (arrows 4 and 5). Finally, as moderating mechanisms, ethnic resources may "buffer" deleterious effects of role barriers and "accentuate" positive effects (broken arrows 6 and 7).

In summary, two central assumptions guide this integrative role strain-adaptation perspective. First, in addition to objective barriers, the manner in which Black males respond to such barriers is a crucial determinant of their longterm role outcomes. Secondly, ethnicity enables some Black males to cope with oppressive role obstacles in adaptive ways rather than become dispirited, bedeviled or devastated victims. In the next two sections, an adult life cycle approach to role strain and adaptation is formulated to further clarify processes depicted in Figure 1. This model identifies distinct role strain and adaptation issues which confront

Black males at each stage of adulthood. The analysis of *role strain processes* highlights successive shifts in salient goals, oppressive role barriers and critical coping tasks across the adult years. This is followed by an analysis of two distinct *role adaptation processes*, where a discussion of pathology and ethnicity issues help clarify differential modes of coping across the adult life cycle.

Role Strain Processes Across The Life Cycle

Role strain processes among Black men and other at risk groups can be better understood in light of the proliferating literature on adult development (Batles & Brim, 1980; George, 1980; Hughes & Noppe, 1985; Huych & Hoyer, 1982; Kimmel, 1980; Newman & Newman, 1983; Powell, 1983; Stevenson-Long, 1979; Troll, 1982; Van House & Worth, 1982). Despite a growing number of studies, the work of Erick Erickson on the adult life cycle has clearly been the most influential in the last half of the 20th century (1966; 1968; 1980). Erickson, as well as other life span researchers, suggests that males of all races move through four sequential stages during the adult life cycle: preadult years, early adulthood, middle adulthood and old age. In line with Erickson's psychosocial model, healthy development requires one to settle pivotal conflicts and master related growth tasks at each stage. Therefore, during each adult period, mental health among Black men may largely depend on successful resolution of conflicts and mastery of tasks related to salient role strains.

Developmental Issues

While Erickson's analytical system provides a rich point of departure, a viable life span approach to psychosocial development among Black men must have several unique features. Going beyond existing life span paradigms, Table 2 highlights three role strain concepts which can help explain effects of specific psychosocial risk factors faced by Black men in America. The focus on *salient role performance goals*, *pressing role barriers* and *critical role conflicts* at each stage of adulthood provides a conceptual framework for a unique life span approach. A perceived "gap" between salient goals and pressing barriers in a major life role may produce a critical intra-role conflict during each adult stage. Moreover, student, work, family and elderly role conflicts have special developmental effects during the pre, early, middle and older adult years respectively. Hence, intra-role conflicts in each of these four major life roles have especially critical psychosocial consequences during its corresponding adult

Table 2
Critical Role Strain Processes Across the Adult Life Cycle

	SALIENT GOALS	PRESSING BARRIERS	CRITICAL CONFLICTS
PRE ADULT YEARS: Student Role Strain	Educational Preparation	Ineffective Public School	Student Role Discouragement vs. Educational Achievement
EARLY ADULTHOOD: Work Role Strain	Career Consolidation	Post-industrial Displacement	Job Search Discouragement vs. Occupational Attainment
MIDDLE ADULTHOOD: Provider Role Strain	Familial Fulfillment	Chronic Employment Problems	Provider Role Discouragement vs. Husband/ Father Success
OLD AGE: Elderly Role Strain	Dignified Aging	Inadequate Retirement Provisions	Elderly Role Discouragement vs. Functional Health

stage (i.e. student-preadulthood, work-early adulthood). However, conflicts within a given role may occur during more than one adult period.

At each stage of adulthood, a critical developmental task for many Black men is to overcome discouraging barriers to achievement in a salient life role. Salient role performance goals shift systematically as people move from one stage of adulthood to the next. From late adolescence to old age, salient goals typically shift from educational preparation, to career consolidation, to familial/social fulfillment and finally to dignified aging. Among Black men, failure in earlier student roles too often combine with additional role barriers in subsequent adult stages to increase their psychosocial risks. A succession of adult role barriers may threaten cherished values by frustrating role efforts and eliciting discouragement or even hopelessness. During each period, extreme role discouragement may produce a perplexing approach-avoidance conflict. A strong approach tendency to seek salient goals in a valued life role is often repelled by an opposing tendency to avoid the stress of repeated failure. Hence, such intra-role conflict may severely test the strength of motivation and value commitment in major adult roles.

At each adult stage, if discouragement in the salient life role reaches the level of hopelessness, the risks for pathological responses to role barriers may significantly increase. Such extreme discouragement in student, work, family and elderly roles respectively may increase risk for identity confusion, isolation, stagnation and despair as Black men proceed from adolescence to old age. The more extreme the level of role discouragement or hopelessness, the more likely the corresponding pattern of psychosocial distress will be expressed in severe symptoms. For example, extreme student role discouragement may seriously erode a positive sense of identity and produce severe role confusion during adolescence. A sense of hopelessness in the student role may also have far reaching developmental consequences by placing individuals at much greater risks for chronic work, family and elderly role strains in later adult life. As Black men proceed through adulthood, most manage to avoid being devastated by ineffective schools, labor market displacement, chronic joblessness and poverty. In psychosocial development terms, they somehow overcome a succession of role barriers to develops a sense of identity, intimacy, generativity and integrity in their journey from adolescence to old age (Erickson, 1963). In all cultures, indigenous ethnic resources are transmitted across generations to facilitate coping with normative role strains as individuals progress through adult life stages (Herskovits, 1955). Moreover, it also follows from culturally guided social learning studies that success in a major life role at one adult stage increases a sense of personal empowerment and the likelihood of role successes in subsequent stages (Gibson, 1986). Therefore, personal empowerment which is rooted in culture and prior role success appears crucial for successful adaptation to subsequent adult role strains. Indeed, cultural groups in all multi-ethnic societies face the challenge of preparing their members to overcome normative obstacles that impede performance in competitive adult roles (Goode, 1960; Pearlin, 1983). However, African-Americans face the additional challenge of devising cultural strategies to overcome race and class barriers which dramatically reduce the odds of excelling as students, workers, and family providers (Bowman, 1985; 1988; in press; Merton, 1968).

Preadulthood: Student Role Strain

Of all the important roles played by Black males during the preadult years, none has more crucial psychosocial implications than the student role. To be sure, early educational preparation is the cornerstone for career consolidation and subsequent adult role accomplishments. Therefore, student role success is not only a pivotal resource for healthy identity development during adolescence, but also for navigating the difficult transition to gainful employment in adulthood. Among adolescents, student role achievements increase a sense of competence, purpose and commitment which enable individuals to energetically pursue future career and family. While academic difficulty is a central concern for many youth, Black males face especially discouraging odds in the student role. For example, the Black male dropout rate in urban public schools is catastropic reaching 72 percent in New York High Schools (Riley, 1986). Although less dramatic nationally, Black male academic performance in high school lags far behind White males, White females and Black females. Even when Black males do graduate from high school, they are more likely than Black females to be functionally illiterate and less likely to enter college; and the few who do enter college are less likely to graduate (Hatchett, 1986).

For many Black males, the central role conflict during the preadult years involves student role discouragement versus school achievement. Organizational practices in ineffective public schools too often frustrate efforts of Black male students to prepare educationally for a successful transition to adulthood (Edmonds, 1979; Hatchett, 1986). Systemic barriers facing Black males in public schools result in repeated academic failure, widespread role discouragement and identity confusion (Bowman, in press; Green, 1982). During adolescence, intense student role conflicts can seriously thwart a sense of personal competence, generate aimlessness, and erode social commitments. Therefore, adaptive coping with student role discouragement in favor of school achievement becomes a critical task. In the face of discouraging odds, effective student role adaptation can enable high-risk Black males to proceed into early adulthood with much better prospects for employment and related life goals.

Early Adulthood: Work Role Strain

In many adult development models, young adulthood is signaled by the end of educational preparation for the world of work. In any society which requires a skilled labor force, school achievement during the preadult years is the major prerequisite for a successful transition to early adulthood. Strong academic preparation provides a few Black American males with a solid foundation to navigate obstacles in their pathway to career consolidation (Bowman & Howard, 1985; Bowman, Gurin & Howard, 1984; Wilson, 1978). In the transition from adolescence to adulthood, the predominant role expectations shift from "doing well in school" to "getting a job". This salient role shift is not only imposed by society, community, and family but is also personally reinforced as these social expectations are internalized into one's own value system. Hence, the work role becomes the major life arena for role strain processes during early adulthood. However, the transition from school to work among many problem-plagued Black males is restricted by both unsolved student role conflicts and pressing labor market barriers.

Because of post-industrial labor market shifts, the historical problem of menial jobs among Black men is increasingly compounded by chronic joblessness. Rapid displacement of unskilled jobs by automation has combined with ineffective public schools to increase the economic obsolescence of Black men in the American labor market. A growing gap between labor market demands and public school preparation promises to further escalate chronic joblessness among Black males well into the 21st century (Bowman, 1987). Nationally, Black youth unemployment is consistently higher than for any other group and exceeds 50 percent in some areas. Black males who never find a regular job must seek alternative means to survive, some as members of a growing urban underclass (Glasgow, 1980; Green, 1982; Wilson, 1978; 1987). Given early adult role pressures to get a job, postindustrial displacement, chronic unemployment, and discouragement in job search become major psychosocial risk factors for young Black men (Mangum & Seninger, 1978; Wool, 1978).

Job search discouragement versus occupational attainment represents a critical work role conflict as young Black men attempt to overcome educational and labor market barriers to a decent career. Discouragement in job search can be especially stressful for young Black men who leave public schools ill prepared for a post-industrial labor market. In a nationwide study of joblessness, young Black adults looked more actively for employment than older Blacks (Bowman, 1984; Bowman, Gurin, & Howard, 1984). However, the majority of the young jobless had become discouraged and many had already given up hope of finding a decent job. For young Black men, this sense of hopelessness in job search represents a serious threat to any goals of forming a personal occupational identity or settling down as a responsible family provider. Hence, job search discouragement may not only frustrate efforts to build and maintain a stable economic base for oneself, but also impede the establishment and maintenance of loving family relationships. Psychosocial studies suggest that basic human needs for intimacy may be seriously threatened by isolation among jobless young males because work and love become more intertwined in early adulthood (Erickson, 1980; Powell, 1983; Smelser & Erickson, 1980) than in other periods. As fathers and husbands, young Black males may become increasingly bewildered and distressed by job search discouragement in a post-industrial economy with decreasing need for unskilled labor. In the struggle to adapt to growing economic displacement, they must respond to a set of pressing questions: Should I continue to look for a decent job? How will I support myself without marketable skills? Will I ever be able to get married or assume responsibility for my children? What realistic options do I have for using my natural talents to achieve personal life goals? Maladaptive or adaptive responses to these questions have immediate psychosocial consequences during young adulthood and also carry over into middle adulthood.

Middle Adulthood: Provider Role Strain. As Black males move into middle adulthood, conventional gender and family roles make their performance as fathers and/or husbands especially critical issues (Erickson, 1980; Erickson & Erickson, 1981). Traditionally, family expectations for husband/fathers have emphasized the breadwinner role, while wife/mothers have been viewed primarily as tenders of hearth and children. Indeed, women increasingly share mutual expectations as responsive sex partners, companions, confidants, decision makers and accountants. However, despite increasing flexibility in gender roles, the "provider" and "caretaker" roles still appear to carry differential weights in the personal identities of men and women (Duvall, 1977; Troll, 1982). Among contemporary middle aged men, Black and White, the provider role remains at the core of their masculine identity. However, because marginal employment among Black men, their family's economic stability has long depended on working Black women (McAdoo, 1981). However, the provider role continues to be a salient aspect of the masculine identity among both middle and low income Black males (Cazenave, 1981; Liebow, 1967; Marsiglio, 1987). Chronic role strains faced by young Black males as students and workers carry-over into serious provider role problems when they reach middle adulthood. Studies on Black males reveal that success as a breadwinner becomes a major source of personal pride, but provider role failure and hopelessness can be psychologically devastating (Cazenave, 1981; Liebow, 1967). While provider role failure may be bothersome to younger men, such role strain may become an especially sensitive issue for the middle aged. In personal attempts to delay provider role commitments, younger adults may be more able than the middle aged to remain hopeful in the face of persistent employment problems. During middle age, chronically jobless Black men may be at special risk for a sense of hopelessness regarding long held goals in the family provider role. Economically marginal Black husband/fathers must face the stark reality that if they have been unable to adequately provide for their children by middle age—they probably never will. This realization may instigate a "mid-life crisis" as men come to terms with the prospect that their persistent provider role problems may be irreversible. As many Black men move through middle age, their increasingly desperate provider role efforts are often frustrated by chronic employment problems rooted in inadequate schooling and post-industrial labor market barriers. Hence, the critical role conflict for these middle aged Black men involves provider role discouragement versus husband/father contribution. In explaining his concept of generativity, Erickson (1980) observes that the major task of middle adulthood is to fulfill valued familial and social goals. According to his psychosocial theory, success in the care and guidance of the next generation is a major determinant of psychological well-being during middle age. Therefore, by middle age, men who have repeatedly failed to meet familial responsibilities may be left with a more extreme sense of discouragement, hopelessness and stagnation. When middle aged men negotiate chronic provider role failures with adult children, feelings of stagnation can be aggravated by father-child encounters. Such long-term provider role problems make the link between work and love especially problematic in father-child relationships. The guilt and distress associated with provider role failure may be intensified by encounters with "maturing" children, who become stressful reminders that past hopes of meeting the needs of their young children are now foregone conclusions. Extreme discouragement as fathers and/or husbands may increase vulnerability to feelings of impoverishment, defensive self-indulgence and other expressions of psychosocial stagnation. A central challenge among middle aged Black men who face provider role discouragement is to mobilize available resources in the interest of adaptive rather than maladaptive coping.

Old Age: Elderly Role Strain. Older Black men who have overcome discouraging barriers in past student, work and family provider roles may experience fewer mental and physical health problems; they can readily view their past lives as meaningful and continue productive activities. Adequate retirement provisions, new hobbies and contentment with a less mobile life style become benchmarks of successful aging. Unfortunately, a succession of past failures in major life roles often culminate in serious difficulties among the Black elderly (Hamilton, 1975; Jackson, 1971; Taylor & Taylor, 1982. Reflection on these successive role strains during old age may result in a tendency to regard oneself and one's life as failures. In addition to past role barriers, inadequate retirement provisions may also become a major psychosocial risk factor among Black men in the elderly role. Pressing economic hardships may severely discourage older Black men in their efforts to cope with emerging feelings of despair and growing physical decline. Hence, elderly role discouragement versus functional health emerges as a critical role conflict for large numbers of aged Black men. Among the Black elderly, economic status is strongly associated with their higher risks for mental and physical health problems (Chatters, 1983; Jackson, 1971; Jackson, Chatters, & Neighbors, 1982). Economic difficulty erodes the life quality of many elderly Americans, but abject poverty represents an even more serious threat to older Blacks. Chronic poverty among the Black elderly is rooted in an "unstable" employment history and gives way to serious psychological distress and health care problems (Hamilton, 1975; Jackson & Gibson, 1985). Estrangement from familial support systems may further exacerbate the harmful effects of a menial money supply on functional health problems of older Black men (Taylor, 1983).

During old age, positive mental health among Black men requires them to maintain a level of integrity or to effectively cope with despair. Despite the importance of present economic well-being, integrity in the elderly role may depend even more on past role successes that promote identity, intimacy and generativity (Erickson, 1980; Erickson & Erickson, 1981). However, elderly Black men must too often seek integrity in spite of a lifetime of role failures as students, workers and family providers. Earlier experiences of identity confusion, isolation and stagnation may erode their sense of integrity and generate despair. In the face of successive role strains, despairing Black men must somehow cope with feelings of regret as they look back over their lives during their waning years. According to Erickson (1963), this "despair expresses the feeling that the time is now short, too short for the attempt to start another life and to try out alternate roads to integrity (p. 269)." Therefore, a major psychosocial challenge for many older Black men is to cope with such feelings of despair in adaptive rather than maladaptive ways.

Adaptation Across The Life Cycle

The foregoing analysis incorporates both oppression and coping themes into an integrative life span approach to role strain among Black men. During each stage of adulthood, I have suggested that (1) *oppressive* barriers in a major life role threaten cherished goals and (2) that adaptive *coping* with role discouragement emerges as a critical developmental task. More meaningful role strain-adaptation research on Black males must extend this focus on oppression and coping to also incorporate phenomena emphasized in pathology and ethnicity models. With a focus on differential adaptation to chronic role strains, pathology and ethnicity respectively can be conceptualized as maladaptive and adaptive coping patterns. In the next section, pathology findings on Black men are placed in this perspective by examining modal shifts in maladaptive responses to critical role conflicts during each adult stage. To place ethnicity research in perspective, various cultural patterns are then identified as resources which promote more adaptive coping with such critical role conflicts.

Maladaptive Response Patterns: Pathology In Perspective

To guide future inquiry, Table 3 highlights a range of psychosocial problems often associated with Black males. As responses to chronic role strains, these maladaptive patterns may vary systematically across the

Table 3
Maladaptive Psychosocial Response Patterns
Across the Adult Life Cycle

	STRUCTURAL RESPONSES	SELF-PROTECTIVE MECHANISMS	CLINICAL CATEGORIES
PREADULT YEARS: Identity/Role Confusion	Rebellion	Fantasy/ Identification	Conduct Disorders/ Delinquency
EARLY ADULTHOOD: Isolation/ Estrangement	Innovation	Displacement/ Compensation	Antisocial Disorders/ Crime
MIDDLE ADULTHOOD: Stagnation/ Self- indulgence	Retreatism	Denial/ Emotional Insulation	Substance Use Disorders/ Alcoholism
OLD AGE: Despair/ Disgust	Helplessness	Repression/ Suppression	Psychosomatic Illness/ Disability

adult life cycle. In the preceding sections, I noted that Black males who fail to cope effectively with critical role conflicts during early adult stages may well be at elevated risk for psychosocial problems during subsequent stages. Psychosocial problems prevalent among Black males at different stages of adulthood can be better understood as maladaptive responses to stage-specific role strains. Extreme student, work, family and elderly role discouragement may result in a variety of psychosocial problems because of shifting role conflicts and related life cycle changes.

As Black men proceed from adolescence to old age, a succession of unresolved conflicts in major life roles may produce a corresponding series of psychosocial development problems—role/identity confusion, isolation/estrangement, stagnation/self-indulgence and despair/disgust (Erickson, 1963; 1980). As outlined in Table 3, each of these stage-specific psychosocial problems may be expressed in three modal response patterns—structural strategies, self-protective mechanisms and clinical symptomatology. Black males may be prone toward particular modes of coping with structural role barriers during different adult periods (Merton, 1968; Kaplan, 1980). Rebellion, innovation and retreatism appear to predominate during the pre, early and middle adult years respectively. At each adult stage, structural role barriers may frustrate adaptive coping efforts and seriously threaten self-esteem (Pearlin, 1983). Self-protective mechanisms, may also help Black males better manage stress during each stage (Powell, 1983). However, if intense role conflicts produce unmanageable distress, maladaptive response patterns may include more severe symptomatology. As suggested in Table 3, such clinical patterns may also shift systematically as Black males move from one stage of the adult life cycle to the next (Eron & Peterson, 1982; Gallatin, 1982).

Preadult years. During the preadult years, chronic student role discouragement may precipitate several maladaptive response patterns. As shown in Table 3, existing research suggests that adolescent Black males are at very high risk for identity confusion, rebellion, fantasy and overidentification with delinquent peers (Clark, 1965; Hatchett, 1986; Miller, 1958). Their identity or role confusion may be expressed in various patterns of rebellion against authority. Black male students can become especially hostile when repeated academic failure produces a sense of rejection or makes cherished life goals seem impossible to attain. Acting out fantasies and gang delinquency may become alternative means for young Black males to re-affirm their sense of self worth outside student roles. Within inner cities, legitimate attempts to establish a sense of manhood are to often frustrated in an economically depressed, restrictive and even life-threatening environment. Perhaps the most disturbing expression of identity confusion among adolescent Black males is the high incidence of assaultive behavior and homicidal violence (Georges-Abeyie, 1984; Wolfgang & Cohen, 1970). Black males under 18 years of age have the highest arrest rates for forcible rape and robbery of all age/race/gender groupings. Indeed, these preadults account for a large portion of the violence that occurs in urban communities. They are not only the prime perpetrators, but also the most frequent victims of homicidal violence during the transition from adolescence to adulthood, a pattern which persists well into middle age.

Early adulthood. In early adulthood, research suggests that many Black youth become hopeless in job search, which increases psychological distress—global life dissatisfaction, a sense of powerlessness and low self esteem (Bowman, 1984; Bowman, Jackson, Hatchett & Gurin, 1982). However, more empirical research is needed to clarify the link between job search discouragement and other prevalent psychosocial problems among young Black men. For example, work role discouragement during early adulthood may exacerbate a tendency for adolescent role confusions to carry-over into a sense of isolation and estrangement. If Black men completely give up hope of finding a decent job, their feelings of estrangement may be expressed in more severe terms. Adolescent patterns of rebellion, fantasy and delinquency may give way to more innovative strategies, compensatory mechanisms and adult crime as illustrated in Table 3. Hustling, street life and other accessible means to maintain an economic livelihood may be adopted by Black males if they perceive that barriers to a legitimate career are insurmountable (Kaplan, 1980; Valentine, 1978). Moreover, structural entrapment among a growing urban underclass may foster a variety of compensatory activities to reduce feelings of inadequacy and enhance self-esteem. Literature on violent crime and antisocial disorders also reveal that young Black men too often displace hostility from work-related frustration on those closest to them—family members, acquaintances and other vulnerable segments of the Black community (Bowman, 1980; Gary & Brown, 1975; Georges-Abeyie, 1984).

Middle adulthood. In the middle adult years, extreme provider role discouragement among Black fathers and husbands may precipitate severe feelings of stagnation. Long-term underemployment or joblessness among middle aged Black men may make cherished goals in the family provider role appear hopeless. A national study of Black husband-fathers cited earlier found that those who experienced provider role discouragement were clearly at greater psychological risk (Bowman, 1985). This study examined multivariate effects of three indicators of provider role discouragement—primary provider role expectancy, husband role expectancy and father role expectancy—on a measure of global life happiness. Findings revealed that husband's expectancy of failure in efforts to provide for wives was particularly distressful, accounting for even more variance in global unhappiness than actual unemployment. Provider role discouragement among husbands and/or fathers may not only erode perceived life quality but also produce other maladaptive response patterns. Future inquiry should seek to unravel a broader range of psychosocial risks associated with family provider role conflicts among middle aged Black men.

As suggested in Table 3, intense family provider role conflicts during middle age may threaten the achievement of generativity, increase feelings of stagnation and elevate risks for severe psychosocial problems (Erickson, 1980; Erickson & Erickson, 1981). Among middle aged Black men, extreme feelings of stagnation may be expressed in retreatism, denial, emotional insulation and substance abuse. If chronic joblessness among Black men continues into middle age, a growing sense of hopelessness may lead many to retreat altogether from long held provider role goals. To reduce impending guilt, self-protective mechanisms may include tendencies to undermine provider role problems, to describe them in least threatening terms, or to even deny that children exist. Patterns of retreatism and denial may be especially prevalent among Black men who struggle with provider role distress in the nation's prisons, or otherwise socially isolated from their children and families (Gary, 1981; Georges-Abeyie, 1984; Wilkinson & Taylor, 1978). Chronic provider role strain together with such social isolation may increase tendencies toward emotional insulation as a self-protective mechanism. Moreover, a tendency for younger Blacks to cope with problems through polydrug experimentation may give way to a greater dependency on alcohol or other substances as they grow older (Gary, 1981; Harper, 1976).

Old age. For those Black men who reach old age, earlier failures as students, workers and family providers may culminate in serious elderly role conflicts, disgust and despair. As suggested earlier, their sense of despair may grow directly out of past experiences of stagnation, estrangement and identity confusion (Erickson, 1980). Extreme levels of despair among older Black men may result in repression, feelings of helplessness, or psychosomatic illness (See Table 3). In this final stage of life, those with a succession of past failures in adult roles may be more likely to view themselves and their lives with disgust. As self-protection, role failure experiences which are most threatening to self-esteem may be unconsciously or consciously barred from one's memory. However, intra-punitive beliefs that past role failures were primarily one's own fault may severely erode self-esteem and precipitate a sense of helplessness (Miller & Norman, 1979).

Role strain-related learned helplessness may stifle motivation, cause depression and help explain the severe health problems of elderly Black men (Seligman, 1975; Gallatin, 1982). A Black male born in 1982 has a life expectancy of only 64.9 years, compared to 73.5 years for Black females, 71.5 years for White males and 78.8 years for White females. Moreover, morbidity data reveal that older Black men are at highest risks for a wide range of health problems and more often report physical disability (Gary, 1981; Heckler, 1985; Howard-Caldwell, 1986). Higher risk for physical illness among older Black men has been most clearly linked to diet as well as psychosocial factors such as poverty, social isolation and stressful events (e.g., Heckler, 1985). However, chronic strains in major life roles may also be prominent in the motivational, emotional and physical health problems of elderly Black men.

Adaptive Cultural Resources: Ethnicity In Perspective

While some Black males are devastated by successive role strains, the majority manage more adaptive modes of coping as they move from one adult stage to the next. As they progress from adolescence to old age, most achieve a measure of positive identity, intimacy, generativity and integrity. Some even overcome discouraging obstacles to excel against great odds in student, work, family and elderly roles. The factors that enable some Black men to cope and even excel despite discouraging race and class barriers that devastate others remain a mystery. Unfortunately, scientific studies have yet to unravel social psychological factors that enable many Black men to avoid devastation, struggle effectively against discouragement and overcome pressing role barriers. Guided by an Afri-centric perspective, role strain and adaptation research on Black men can break new ground by identifying ethnic resources and related mechanisms that facilitate adaptive coping.

Table 4
Adaptive Ethnic Resources Across the Adult Life Cycle

	COMMUNITY NETWORKS	FAMILIAL RELATIONSHIPS	PERSONAL BELIEF SYSTEMS
PREADULT YEARS	Rite of Passage Rituals	Race-related Socialization	Ethnic Achievement Orientations
EARLY ADULTHOOD	Self-help Support Groups	Flexible Family Roles	Racial Consciousness & System Blame
MIDDLE ADULTHOOD	Para-kin Relationships	Cohesive Family Bonds	Religion
OLD AGE	Indigenous Institutions	Consanguineous Relationships	Spirituality

Table 4 specifies a set of African-American cultural resources that may facilitate instrumental coping with role strains at each stage of adulthood (Hill, 1971; Jones & Matthews, 1977; Nobles, 1973; 1974a; b; Sudarkasa, 1975). We need to better understand how ethnic patterns at the community, familial and personal levels facilitate adaptation to specific role strains at each stage of adult life. A growing literature suggests that authentic African-American resources, which have been transmitted across generations, are periodically modified to foster adaptation to changing life circumstances (Berry & Blassingame, 1982; Harding, 1981; Herskovits, 1935; 1955; 1941; Levine, 1977). Rather than monolithic "Africanisms", studies need to clarify evolving African-American cultural patterns which promote effective coping with shifting race and class barriers. During each generation, effective African-American "adaptations" require both (1) the preservation of traditional core patterns, and (2) the incorporation of old core patterns into new strategies to meet pressing imperatives.

Guided by a Euro-centric bias, "culture of poverty" and related theories have assumed that no adaptive African-American culture exist (e.g., Auletta, 1982; Miller, 1958). According to this conventional view, the prevalent problems facing Black males are rooted in the lack of European-American middle class values (Hannerz, 1969). In contrast, Afri-centric scholars focus on indigenous resources within Black community life as the major source of individual and collective efforts to cope with chronic role adversity. Hence, ethnic strengths may not only reduce individual vulnerability, but also serve as prime sources of collective efforts to overcome discouraging racial barriers (Akbar, 1981; Bowman, 1985; Hill, 1971; Jones, 1980; Morris, 1984). Future studies on Black men should seek to clarify how specific ethnic resources enable many to defy the odds at each stage of adult life.

Preadult years. During the preadult years, parents are primary sources of empowerment for those who must struggle against discouraging barriers in the student role. Black parents may mobilize a variety of ethnic resources to help their children effectively cope with academic discouragement, resolve identity confusion and overcome pressing barriers (Bowman, 1977; Bowman & Howard, 1985; Hare, 1985; West, 1987). As outlined in Table 4, Black parents may find "rites of passage" rituals, race-related socialization and ethnic achievement orientations important cultural resources. Black adolescent boys may experience more academic success and less identity confusion if formal passage rituals were common in Black communities (Hare, 1985). As with the Jewish bar mitzvah, such transition rituals convey core ethnic realities as well as the privileges and responsibilities of manhood. Formal rites of passage ceremonies are rarely practiced in Black American communities today, but they were imperative in traditional African societies (Kenyatta, 1938).

Despite the infrequency of formal passage rituals, 64% of the young Black males in a recent nationwide study revealed that their parents informally transmitted proactive messages to them about their ethnic status (Bowman & Howard, 1985). These Black parents transmitted specific messages to their sons regarding the virtues of ethnic pride, adaptive responses to racism, racial equality and interracial coexistence as well as individual character development. The 36% of the young Black males who could not recall such parental messages expressed a sense of powerlessness in the face of life's barriers. In contrast, those whose parents emphasized adaptive responses to racism were the most successful students, while clear character building messages were linked to strong sense of personal empowerment. Moreover, commitments to ethnic achievement goals for community development, advancement and survival also tend to increase student motivation and success (Bowman, 1977).

Early adulthood. Research on Black men in the early adult years need to identify specific community support networks, family arrangements and belief systems that enable some to overcome discouraging work role barriers. Indigenous Black community organizations (i.e. Urban League, faternal associations) have long coordinated self-help groups to foster adaptive responses to shifting sources of work-related discouragement. Recently, emphasis has been on difficult employment transitions into a competitive post-industrial labor market. However, some Black male support groups have also focused on provider role responsibilities, drugs and related psychosocial problem solving. Flexible family roles, which involve multiple earners and shared household duties, may reduce familial disruption associated with pervasive job search discouragement among young Black fathers and husbands (Bowman, in press; Hill, 1971; Nobles, 1974). Studies also suggest that system-blame which strategically focuses on labor market barriers may reduce intrapunitive self-blame and motivate more adaptive individual coping (Bowman, 1984; Bowman, et al., 1982). Moreover, system-blame ideology may combine with other dimensions of ethnic consciousness to increase readiness for collective strategies (Baldwin, Duncan & Bell, 1987; Bowman, 1977; Gurin & Epps, 1974; Jackson, McCullough & Gurin, 1981).

Middle adulthood. Within Black communities, para-kin support networks among men may foster social bonding which reduces distress associated with family provider role discouragement during middle age (Gary, 1981; Liebow, 1967).

However, findings from a study cited earlier suggest that cohesive family bonds and strong religious commitments may be even more powerful resources for coping with provider role difficulties (Bowman, 1985). This national study of Black husband-fathers found that those two cultural resources accounted for more variance in a measure of life happiness than supportive friendships, multiple family earners, or system blame ideology. Future inquiry should further unravel the adaptive effects of extended families and religious beliefs among middle aged Black men. For example, these indigenous ethnic resources may: (1) directly reduce the level of provider role discouragement, (2) directly reduce maladaptive coping (or increase adaptive coping responses), and (3) buffer the discouragement—coping relationship (Kessler et al., 1985).

Old age. As indicated in Table 4, an additional set of ethnic resources may combine with those already mentioned to help Black men replace despair with a sense of integrity during old age. The Black church, consanguineous "blood ties", and spirituality may become especially crucial to dignified aging among Black men in the elderly role. During this final chapter of life, the Black church has been a very dependable ethnic institution which provides a wide range of material, informational and emotional support (Chatters, 1983; Taylor, 1983). Ethnic patterns in consanguineous kinship ties with children may also become a relatively reliable source of support for elderly Black men and women (Sudarkasa, 1980; 1981). In traditional Black families, adult children often become a primary source of economic and social support for aged parents (Chatters, 1983; Taylor, 1983). In emotional terms, the child-grandparent relationship may foster a special sense of integrity as the past and future come together in the present. Mead (1972) suggests that grandparents offer children a link to the past, and children give grandparents a feeling for the future of humanity—as both learn from one another about the discontinuities and continuities of life. Intrinsic religious beliefs, characterized by strong spiritual motivation, may also help elderly Black men transcend feelings of despair or disgust; such spirituality may enable many to achieve a sense of integrity regardless to past shortcomings (Jennings, 1983; Mbiti, 1970; Oliver, 1975).

Summary and Conclusions

In stark contrast to growing literature on the role of White men, existing studies on Black men emphasize either pathology, oppression, coping or ethnicity themes. A classification matrix with four cells provides a basis for better understand and critically evaluating these competing research perspectives. Systematically, each of these four approaches differs in emphasis on maladaptive-adaptive and internal-external dimensions of the Black male experience. Pathology research, such as culture of poverty studies, has painted a denigrative portrait by blaming Black males themselves as the major cause of their own problems. Rather than blame the victim, oppression studies have emphasized external causes such as institutional racism to explain the widespread maladaptive behavior among Black males. Coping and ethnicity studies have focused on adaptive rather than maladaptive aspects of the Black male experience. Coping studies emphasize adaptive responses to stressful life conditions, while ethnicity research examines indigenous cultural patterns which foster adaptive modes of coping.

The role strain-adaptation paradigm provides an integrative framework for more meaningful research on Black men across the adult life cycle. Oppression, pathology, coping and ethnicity studies present different but not incompatible views on the experience of Black males. A focus on both role strain and adaptation processes has special appeal because it provides a theory-driven conceptual framework to systematically link essential elements from each perspective. Two basic notions in this integrative theoretical approach are (1) that oppressive role barriers can result in either pathological or adaptive coping, and (2) that ethnicity can facilitate adaptive response patterns. This role strain-adaptation model not only offers a reasonably parsimonious framework, but also builds on a diverse theoretical and empirical literature (Barnett & Baruch, 1985; Bowman, 1985; Goode, 1960; Kahn et al., 1964; Merton, 1968; Pearlin, 1983; Sarbin & Allen, 1969). Therefore, studies guided by this integrative model can go beyond past research on Black males which has primarily been descriptive, rather than theoretical and predictive.

Perhaps the major virtue of the role strain-adaptation paradigm formulated in this paper is its explanatory power across the adult life cycle. A life cycle perspective avoids misconceptions that occur if we only focus on role strain at a particular life stage and fail to notice the continuity in role strain and adaptation processes across the life course. In a life span framework, the interrelated concepts of development and adaptation have unique explanatory power (e.g., Allen & Vliert, 1981; Gibson, 1983; Neugarten, 1970; Newman & Newman, 1983). To develop means to grow out of, to evolve from—where experiences at one life stage not only follows but emerge directly from preceding life experiences. The related concept of adaptation involves a continuing process of incorporating past experiences into new patterns to strategically meet the challenge of changing life demands without undue compromise. In adult development, adaptation involves preserving old patterns while also transforming them into new forms to cope with additional demands as one moves from one stage of adulthood to the next.

Among high risk Black men, chronic role strains and related psychosocial problems do not just occur at a point in time. Rather, they evolve out of interactions between past role experiences, immediate role barriers and adaptive efforts. Early adulthood evolves from childhood and builds directly upon the adolescent experience, while at the same time forming the basis for experiences of middle adulthood, old age and life's final transition. However, development at each stage not only emerges from previous role experiences, but also depends on adaptation to new role barriers and conflicts. At each critical period of adulthood, Black males must build on previous role experiences in efforts to adapt to pressing role barriers which threaten cherished goals. For example, maladaptive coping with student role barriers increase risk of chronic strains in major life roles throughout adulthood. However, successful student role adaptation becomes a cornerstone for adaptive coping with subsequent work, family and elderly role barriers.

As suggested by Allen (1978), the scientific value of a life cycle approach depends on its ability to stimulate research. Systematic empirical research is crucial to both theory building and practical intervention. To help build a viable life cycle theory of role strain and adaptation, empirical studies on Black males should investigate several questions: *As Black males traverse the adult life cycle, what is the nature of salient role strains at each stage? How are such strains interrelated from one stage to the next?* Cross-sectional studies can help describe objective and subjective dimensions of naturally occurring role strains, but longitudinal data are necessary to chart precise linkages between successive student, work, family and elderly role strains. *During each critical adult period, how do salient role strains increase risks for specific maladaptive response patterns?* Studies must be designed to carefully unravel harmful effects of objective role barriers, discouragement and other subjective aspects of chronic role strain. *How do various ethnic resources operate to facilitate adaptive coping with critical role strains during each adult stage?* Afri-centric research may help clarify cultural resources which enable some Black males to maintain a sense of hope, vitality, persistence and to excel against discouraging odds. At each stage of adulthood, ethnic resources may not only reduce feelings of being overwhelmed, "put off" or dispirited, but also motivate both individual and collective coping strategies.

Unfortunately, traditional boundaries between basic and applied research have resulted in serious discontinuities between theory and practice. However, Durbin (1983) and others suggest that the utility of any theoretical model must ultimately be tested through its application by the practitioner. Research based on a life span approach to role strain and adaptation may help inform a wide range of practitioners concerned with problems of high-risk Black males. Policy-makers, community leaders and professionals can design interventions to eradicate pressing role barriers, mobilize adaptive ethnic resources, and promote individual coping at each stage of adulthood. Within local communities, intervention that mobilizes ethnic resources to promote personal empowerment may be especially timely. Reaffirmation of culture-based community, familial and personal resources may empower a larger number of Black males to resolve critical role conflicts on the side of successful adult development. A basic assumption is that Black men are at greater risks for maladaptive responses to chronic role strains when they are alienated from indigenous cultural resources—community support systems, cohesive extended families, ethnic commitments and strong religious beliefs.

Indeed, reaffirmation of African-American cultural strengths may foster personal empowerment by (1) mitigating the potentially devastating psychological effects of successive role strains and (2) motivating adaptive strategies to better navigate role barriers. However, policy-makers become extremely critical in primary prevention to reduce the high exposure of Black males to a succession of adult role barriers. Responsive educational, employment, family and geriatric policies can significantly reduce objective barriers that place Black males at higher risks for successive strains in major adult roles. Educational policy may well be the most important of all the primary prevention activities we may undertake. Responsive policies are needed in urban public schools as well as in higher, adult and continuing education. For example, "effective school" policies cannot only prevent pervasive academic failure during the pre-adult years, but also reduce risks for chronic work, family, and elderly role strains at later stages of adulthood.

In conclusion, culture-based empowerment and responsive policy initiatives may both be necessary to prevent the destructive effects that discouraging role barriers appear to be having on Black American men of all ages. Without such initiatives, the current incidence and prevalence of maladaptive response patterns may have far reaching familial, community and societal impact as we move into the 21st century.

References

Abrahams, R. (1970). *Deep in the jungle.* Chicago: Aldine.

Akbar, N. (1979). African roots of Black personality. In W. D. Smith et al. (Eds.), *Reflections on Black psychology.* Washington, D. C.: University Press of America.

Akbar, N. (1981). Mental disorder among African-Americans. *Black Books Bulletin., 7,* 2.

Allen, V., & Vande Vliert, E., (Eds.) (1981). *Role transitions.* New York: Plenum.

Allen, W. R. (1978). The search for applicable theories of Black family life. *Journal of Marriage and the Family,* 117-129.

Allen, W. R. (1981). Moms, dads, and boys: Race and sex differences in the socialization of male children. In L. E. Gary (Ed.), *Black men,* 115-130. Beverly Hills, CA: Sage.

Allen, W. R., & Farley, R. (1985). The shifting social and economic tides of Black America, 1950-1980. In R. H. Turner, & J. F. Short (Eds.), *Annual Review of Sociology.* Palo Alto, CA: Annual Reviews Inc.

Antonucci, T. C., & Jackson, J. S. (1984). Physical health and self esteem. *Family and Community Health, 8,* 1-9.

Ashante, M. K. (1981). Black male and female relationships: An Afrocentric context. In L. E. Gary (Ed.), *Black Men,* 75-83. Beverly Hills, CA: Sage.

Auletta, K. (1982). *The Underclass.* New York:Random House.

Baldwin, J. (1981). Notes on an Afrocentric theory of Black personality. *The Western Journal of Black Studies, 5,* 172-179.

Baldwin, J. A., Duncan, J. A., & Bell, Y. R. (1987). Assessment of African self-consciousness among Black Americans from two college environments. *Journal of Black Psychology, 13,* 27-41.

Baratz, J. C. (1973). Language abilities of Black Americans. In K. S. Miller, & R. M. Dreger (Eds.), *Comparative studies of Blacks and Whites in the United States,* 127-184. New York: Seminar Press.

Barnett, R., & Baruch, G. K. (1985). Women's involvement in multiple roles, role strain and psychological distress. *Journal of Personality and Social Psychology*, *51*, 578-585.

Baruch, G. K., & Barrett, R. (1986). Role quality, multiple role involvement and psychological well-being among midlife women. *Journal of Personality and Social Psychology*, *51*, 578-585.

Battles, P. B., & Brim, O. G. (Eds.) (1980). *Life span development and behavior*. New York: Academic Press.

Berry, M. F., & Blassingame, J. W. (1982). *Long memory: The Black experience in America*. New York: Academic Press.

Bowman, P. J. (1977). *Motivational dynamics and achievement among urban Black students: A situationally relevant-path goal expectancy approach*. Unpublished dissertation, University of Michigan.

Bowman, P. J. (1980). Toward a dual labor market approach to Black-on-Black homicide. *Public Health Reports*, *95*, 555-556.

Bowman, P. J. (1984). A discouragement-centered approach to studying unemployment among Black youth: Hopelessness, attributions and psychological distress. *International Journal of Mental Health*, *13*, 68-91.

Bowman, P. J. (1985). Black fathers and the provider role: Role strain, informal coping resources and life happiness. In A. W. Boykin (Ed.), *Empirical Research in Black Psychology*, 9-19. Washington D. C.: National Institute for Mental Health.

Bowman, P. J. (1988). Post-industrial displacement and family role strains. Challenges to the Black Family. In P. Voydanof, & L. C. Majka (Eds.), *Families and Economic Distress*. Beverly Hills, CA: Sage.

Bowman, P. J. (in press). Psychological expectancy: Theory and measurement in Black populations. In R. L. Jones (Ed.), *Handbook of tests and measurements for Black populations*.

Bowman, P. J., Gurin, G., & Howard, C. S. (1985). *A longitudinal study of Black youth: Issues, scope and findings*. Ann Arbor, MI:Survey Research Center.

Bowman, P. J., & Howard, C. S. (1985). Race-related socialization, motivation and academic achievement: A study of Black youth in three-generation families. *Journal of the Academy of Child Psychiatry*, *24*, 134-141.

Bowman, P. J., Jackson, J. S., Hatchett, S. J., & Gurin, G. (1982). Joblessness and discouragement among Black Americans. *Economic Outlook U.S.A.*, 85-88.

Cannon, M., & Locke, B. (1977). Being Black may be detrimental to one's health: Myth or reality? *Phylon*, *33*, 408-428.

Cazenave, N. A. (1981). Black men in America: The quest for "manhood". In H. P. McAdoo (Ed.), *Black families*, 176-186. Beverly Hills, CA: Sage.

Chatters, L. M. (1983). *A causal analysis of subjective well-being among elderly Blacks*. Unpublished dissertation, University of Michigan.

Clark, K. B. (1965). *Dark ghetto*. New York: Harper & Row.

Drake, S., & Cayton, H. (1945). *Black metropolis*. New York: Harcourt/Brace (republished 1964 by Harper Torchbooks).

DuBois, W. E. B. (1903). *The souls of Black folk*. Greenwich, CT: Fawcett (republished 1961).

Durbin, R. (1983). Theory building in applied areas. In M. D. Dunnette (Ed.), *Handbook of industrial and organizational psychology*, 17-40. New York: John Wiley.

Duvall, E. (1977). *Marriage and family development* (5th Ed.). New York: Lippincott.

Earl, L., & Lohmann, M. (1978). Absent fathers and Black male children. *Social Work, 33,* 413-415.

Edmonds, R. (1979). Effective schools for the urban poor. *Educational Leadership.*

Erickson, E. H. (1963). *Childhood and society.* New York: Norton.

Erickson, E. H. (1966). The concept of identity in race relations. In T. Parsons & K. B. Clark (Eds.), *The Negro American.* Boston: Beacon Press.

Erickson, E. H. (1968). *Identity, youth and crisis.* New York: Norton.

Erickson, E. H. (1980). *Identity and the life cycle.* New York: Norton.

Erickson, E., & Erickson, J. (1981). On generativity and identity. *Harvard Educational Review, 51,* 249-269.

Eron, L. D., & Peterson, R A. (1982). Abnormal behavior: Social approaches. *Annual Review of Psychology, 33,* 231-264.

Farrell, W. (1974). *The liberated man.* New York: Bantam Books.

Fasteau, M. (1975). *The male machine.* New York: McGraw-Hill.

Franklin, J. H., & Meier, A. (1982). *Black leaders of the 20th century.* Urbana: University of Illinois Press.

Frazier, E. F. (1939). *The Negro family in the United States.* Chicago: University of Chicago Press.

Gallatin, J. (1982). *Abnormal psychology: Concepts, issues and trends.* New York: MacMillan.

Gary, L. E. (Ed.) (1981). *Black Men.* Beverly Hills, CA: Sage.

Gary, L. E. (Ed.) (1978). *Mental health: A challenge to the Black community.* Philadelphia: Dorrance.

Gary, L. E., & Brown, L. P. (Eds.) (1975). *Crime and its impact on the Black community.* Washington D. C.: Institute for Urban Affairs and Research, Howard University.

Gary, L. E., & Leashore, B. R. (1982). High-risk status of Black men. *Social Work,* 45-54.

George, L. K. (1980). *Role transitions in later life.* Monterey, CA: Brooks/Cole.

Georges-Abeyie, D. (1984). *The criminal justice system and Blacks.* New York: Clark Roardman Co.

Gibson, J. T. (1983). *Living: Human development through the life span.* Reading, MA: Addison-Wesley.

Glasgow, D. G. (1980). *The Black underclass.* San Francisco, CA: Jossey-Bass.

Glazer, N., & Moynihan, D. P. (1963). *Beyond the melting pot.* Cambridge, MA: MIT Press.

Goldberg, H. (1977). *The hazards of being male: Surviving the myths of masculine privilege.* New York: Signet.

Goode, W. J. (1960). A theory of role strain. *American Sociological Review, 11,* 483-496.

Green, L. (1982). A learned helplessness analysis of problems confronting the Black community. In S. Turner, & R. Jones (Eds.), *Behavioral modification in Black populations: Psychosocial issues and empirical findings,* 73-93). New York: Plenum.

Green, W. J. (1980). Generations without work. *RF Illustrated: The Rockefeller Foundation, 4,* 14-15.

Gurin, P., & Epps, E. (1974). *Black consciousness, identity and achievement.* New York: John Wiley & Sons.

Hamilton, R. N. (1975). *Employment needs and programs for older workers—especially Blacks.* Washington, D. C.: National Center on Black Aged.

Hannerz, U. (1969). *Soulside: Inquires into ghetto culture and community*. New York: Columbia University Press.

Hapgood, F. (1979). *Why males exist*. New York: William Morrow.

Harding, V. (1981). *There is a river: The struggle for freedom in America*. New York: Harcourt Brace Jovanovich.

Hare, N. (1985). *Bringing the Black boy into manhood: The passage*. San Francisco, CA: Black Think Tank.

Harper, F. D. (1976). *Alcohol use and Black America*. Alexandria, VA: Douglas.

Harper, F. D. (1981). Alcohol use and abuse. In L. E. Gary (Ed.), *Black men*, 169-179. Beverly Hills, CA: Sage.

Harrison, J. (1978). Warning: The male sex role may be dangerous to your health. *Journal of Social Issues, 34*, 65-86.

Hatchett, D. (1986). A conflict of reasons and remedies. *The Crisis, 93*, 36-46.

Heckler, M. H. et al. (1985). *Report of the Secretary's task force on Black and minority health*. Washington, D. C.: U. S. Department of Health and Human Services (Also see related subcommittee reports and commissioned papers).

Hendricks, L., Ceasar, S., & Gary, L. (Eds.) (in press). *Issues in racial and comparative research*. Washington, D. C.: Howard University Institute for Urban Affairs and Research.

Herskovits, M. J. (1935). Social history of the Negro. In C. Murchinson (Ed.), *A Handbook of Social Psychology*, 207-267. Worchester, MA: Clark University Press.

Herskovits, M. J. (1941). *The myth of the Negro past*. New York: Harper & Brothers.

Herskovits, M. J. (1955). *Cultural anthropology*. New York: Knopf.

Hetherington, E. (1966). Effects of parental absence on sex-typed behavior in Negro and White males. *Journal of Personality and Social Psychology, 4*, 87-91.

Hill, R. (1971). *The strengths of Black families*. New York: Emerson Hall.

Hoffman, S. (1980). *The classified man: Twenty-two types of men*. New York: Conward, McCann, & Geoghegan.

Howard-Caldwell, C. S. (1986). *Motivation and patterns of medical services utilization among Black male veterans and non-veterans*. Unpublished dissertation, University of Michigan.

Hughes, F. P., & Noppe, L. D (1985). *Human development across the life span*. New York: West.

Huych, M. H., & Hoyer, W. J. (1982). *Adult development and aging*. Belmont, CA: Wadsworth.

Jackson, J. J. (1971). Aged Blacks: A potpourri towards the reduction of social inequities. *Phylon, 32*, 260-280.

Jackson, J. S., Chatters, L., & Neighbors, H. (1982). The mental health status of older Black Americans. *Black Scholar, 13*, 21-35.

Jackson, J. S., & Gibson, R. (1985). Work and retirement among Black elderly. In Blau (Ed.), *Work, leisure, and retirement among Black elderly*. JAI Press.

Jackson, J. S., McCullough, W., & Gurin, G. (1981). Group identity development within Black families. In H. P. McAdoo (Ed.), *Black Families*, 252-264. Beverly Hills, CA: Sage.

Jennings, R. M. (1983). *Intrinsic religious motivation and psychological adjustment among Black Americans*. Unpublished doctoral dissertation, University of Michigan.

Jones, D., & Matthews (Eds.) (1977). *The Black church: A community resource*. Washington, D. C.: Howard University Institute for Urban Affairs and Research.

Jones, R. (1980). *Black psychology.* New York: Harper & Row.

Kahn, R. L., Wolfe, D. M., Quinn, R. P., Snoek, J. D., & Rosenthal, R. A. (1964). *Organizational stress: studies in interrole conflict and ambiguity.* New York: Wiley.

Kaplan, H. B. (1980). *Deviant behavior in defense of self.* New York: Academic Press.

Keil, C. (1966). *Urban blues.* Chicago: University of Chicago Press.

Kenyatta, J. (1938). *Facing Mt. Kenya: The tribal life of the Gikuyu.* New York: Vintage Edition (1965).

Kessler, R. C., & Neighbors, H. W. (1986). A new perspective on the relationships among race, social class and psychological distress. *Journal of Health and Social Behavior, 27,* 107-115.

Kessler, R. C., Price, R. H., & Wortman, C. B. (1985). Social factors in psychopatholoy: Stress, social support and coping processes. *Annual Review of Psychology, 31,* 531-572.

Kimmel, D. (1980). *Adulthood and aging.* New York: Wiley.

Krigel, L. (1979). *On men and manhood.* New York: Hawthorn.

Kunjufu, J. (1982). *The conspiracy to destroy Black boys.* Chicago: African-American Images.

Kunjufu, J. (1984). *Developing positive self-images and discipline in Black children.* Chicago: African-American Images.

Layng, A. (1978). Voluntary associations and Black ethnic identity. *Phylon, 39,* 171-179.

Levine, L. W. (1977). *Black culture and Black consciousness.* New York: Oxford University Press.

Liebow, E. (1967). *Tally's corner: A study of street corner men.* Boston, MA: Little, Brown.

Mangum, G. L., & Seninger, S. F. (1978). *Coming of age in the Ghetto: A dilemma of youth unemployment.* Baltimore: John Hopkins University Press.

Marsiglio, W. (1987). Commitment to social fatherhood: Predicting adolescent males intentions to live with their child and partner. *Journal of Marriage and the Family,* 82-91.

Mbiti, J. (1970). *African religions and philosophy.* New York: Doubleday.

McAdoo, H. P. (1984). Poverty equals women and their children. *Point of View,* 8-9.

McAdoo, J. L. (1981). Involvement of fathers in the socialization of Black children. In H. P. McAdoo (Ed.), *Black families,* 225-238. Beverly Hills, CA: Sage.

Mead, M. (1972). *Blackberry winter.* New York: Morrow.

Merton, R. K. (1968). *Social Theory and Social Structure.* New York: Free Press.

Miller, I. W., & Norman, W. T. (1979). Learned helplessness in humans: A review and attribution-theory model. *Psychological Bulletin, 86,* 93-119.

Miller, K. S., & Dreger, R. M. (1973). *Comparative studies of Blacks and Whites in the United States.* New York: Seminar Press.

Miller, W. (1958). Lower-class culture as a generating milieu of gang delinquency. *Journal of Social Issues, 14,* 5-19.

Morris, A. (1984). *Origins of the civil rights movement: Black communities organizing for change.* New York: Free Press.

Myers, L. J. (1985). Transpersonal psychology: The role of the Afrocentric paradigm. *The Journal of Black Psychology, 12,* 31-42.

Myrdal, G. (1964). *The American dilemma.* New York: McGraw-Hill (First edition 1944, Harper & Row).

Neighbors, H. W., Jackson, J. S., Bowman, P. J., & Gurin, G. (1983). Stress, coping and Black mental health. *Journal of Prevention in Human Service, 2*, 5-29.

Neugarten, B. L. (1970). Adaptation and the life cycle. *Journal of Geriatric Psychiatry, 4*, 71-87.

Newman, B. M., & Newman, P. R. (1983). *Understanding adulthood*. New York: Holt, Rinehart, & Winston.

Nichols, L. (1975). *Men's liberation: A new definition of masculinity*. New York: Penguin.

Nobles, W. (1973). Psychological research and the Black self-concept: A critical review. *Journal of Social Issues, 29*, 11-31.

Nobles, W. (1974a). Africanity: Its role in Black families. *Black Scholar, 5*, 10-17.

Nobles, W. (1974b). African root and American fruit: The Black family. *Journal of Social and Behavioral Sciences, 20*.

Oliver, M. O. (1975). Elderly Blacks and the economy: Variables of survival-personal integration, style, pride and positive spirit. *Journal of Afro-American Issues, 3-4*, 324-336.

Pearlin, L. I. (1983). Role strains and personal stress. In H. B. Kaplin (Ed.), *Psychosocial stress: Trends in theory and research*, 3-32. New York: Academic Press.

Pleck, J. (1976). The male sex role: Definitions, problems and sources of change. *Journal of Social Issues, 32*, 155-163.

Pleck, E., & Pleck, J. (1980). *The American man*. Englewood Cliffs, N. J.: Prentice Hall.

Pleck, J., & Sawyer, J. (Eds.) (1984). *Men and masculinity*. Englewood Cliffs, N. J.: Prentice Hall.

Powell, D. H. (1983). *Understanding human adjustment: Normal adaptation through the life cycle*. Boston: Little, & Brown.

Riley, N. (1986). Footnotes of a culture at risk. *The Crisis, 93*, 23-45.

Rubin, R. (1974). Adult male and the self attitudes of Black children. *Child Study Journal, 4*, 33-44.

Ryan, W. (1971). *Blaming the victim*. New York: Pantheon.

Sarbin, T. R., & Allen, V. L. (1969). Role theory. In G. Lindzey, & E. Aronson (Eds.), *Handbook of Social Psychology*, 488-568. Reading, MA: Addison-Wesley.

Seligman, M. E. P. (1975). *Helplessness: On depression, development and death*. San Francisco, CA: Freman.

Sheehy, G. (1976). *Passages: Predictable crises of adult life*. New York: Dutton.

Shinn, M. (1978). Father absence and children's cognitive development. *Psychological Bulletin, 85*, 295-324.

Smelser, N., & Erickson, E. (Eds.) (1980). *Themes of work and love in adulthood*. Cambridge, MA: Harvard University Press.

Staples, R. (1982). *Black masculinity: The Black man's role in American society*. San Francisco, CA: Black Scholar Press.

Stevenson-Long, J. (1979). *Adult life: Developmental processes*. Palo Alto, CA: Mayfield.

Stewart, J., & Scott, J. (1978). The institutional decimation of Black American male. *Western Journal of Black Studies, 2*, 82-93.

Sudarkasa, N. (1980). African and Afro-American Family Structure: A comparison. *The Black Scholar*, 37-60.

Sudarkasa, N. (1981). Interpreting the African heritage in Afro-American family organization. In H. P. McAdoo (Ed.), *Black Families*, 37-53. Beverly Hills, CA: Sage.

Sudarkasa, N. (1975). An exposition on the value premises underlying Black family studies. *Journal of the National Medical Association, 67*, 235-239.

Taylor, R. J. (1983). *The informal support networks of the Black elderly: The impact of family, church members and best friends*. Unpublished dissertation, University of Michigan.

Taylor, R. J., & Taylor, W. H. (1982). The social and economic status of the Black elderly, *Phylon, 43*, 295-306.

Taylor, R. L. (1981). Psychological modes of adaptation. In L. E. Gary (Ed.), *Black men*. Beverly Hills, CA: Sage.

Tinney, J. S. (1981). The religious experience of Black men. In L. E. Gary (Ed.), *Black men*, 269-276. Beverly Hills, CA: Sage.

Triandis, H. C. (1972). *The analysis of subjective culture*. New York: Wiley-Interscience.

Triandis, H. C., Lambert, W., Berry, J., Lonner, W., Hernon, A., Brislin, R., & Draguns, J. (Eds.) (1980-1981). *Handbook of cross-cultural psychology, 1-6*. Boston: Allyn & Bacon.

Troll, L. E. (1982). *Continuations: Adult development and aging*. Monterey, CA: Brooks/Cole.

Valentine, B. (1978). *Hustling and other hard work*. New York: Free Press.

Van Hoose, W. H., & Worth, M. R. (1982). *Adulthood in the life cycle*. Dubuque, IA: Brown.

Walton, H. W. (1985). *Invisible politics: Black political behavior*. Albany: State University of New York Press.

West, J. M. (1987). Clarifying the parental role in helping Black youth make a successful transition from adolescence to adulthood. Dissertation, The University of Michigan.

Wilkinson, D., & Taylor, R. (1977). *The Black male in America*. Chicago, IL: Nelson-Hill.

Wilson, W. J. (1978). *The declining significance of race: Blacks and changing American Institutions*. Chicago, IL: University of Chicago Press.

Wolfgang, M. E., & Cohen, B. (1970). *Crime and race*. New York: Institute of Human Relations.

Wool, H. (1978). *Discouraged workers, potential workers, and national employment policy*. Washington, D. C.: National Commission on Employment Policy (Report No. 24).

Yearwood, L. (Ed.) (1980). *Black organizations: Issues and survival techniques*. Lanham, MD: University Press of America.

NIGRESCENCE:
THE TRANSFORMATION OF BLACK
CONSCIOUSNESS ACROSS THE LIFE CYCLE

Thomas A. Parham

Introduction

In recent years, several models describing changes in Black people's racial identity have been proposed as a means of conceptualizing the "Negro to Black" conversion experience (Cross, 1970, 1978; Thomas, 1971; Jackson, 1976; Williams, 1975). These models, while appearing to be somewhat distinctive, seem to delineate several common assumptions. First is the notion that all Black people are not alike and one way of exploring this within group variability is by examining their racial identity attitudes. Second is the assertion that the development of a Black person's racial identity and/or the progression through the various stages of racial awareness are often fueled by racist and oppressive conditions created by White society.

Through these models, Black scholars have sought to articulate the transformations of Black people's racial identities from negative to positive self-perceptions. Thomas (1971) for example, detailed a five-step process which he proposed as necessary conditions for Black people to eradicate "Negromachy" (a confusion of self-worth and dependence on White society for self-definition). Jackson (1976) presented a Black Identity Development Theory (BID) which describes the process by which a Black person develops a positive racial identity. Likewise, Williams (1975) has proposed nine major "response sets" and eleven subsets in suggesting that there exists in each Black person a response specificity or tendency which directs his or her behavior with regard to racial issues.

Perhaps the most well publicized model of psychological nigrescence (nigrescence is defined as the process of becoming Black) was developed by Cross (1971, 1978) who contended that the development of a Black person's racial identity is characterized by movement through four distinct psychological stages. The stages, ranging from least to most self secure are as follows: Pre-encounter, Encounter, Immersion, and Internalization. While some researchers have attempted to expand the descriptive aspects of the Cross model (Milliones, 1973; Davidson, 1974; Williams, 1975), other scholars have sought to extend its application by exploring the relationship of racial identity to counselor preference (Parham and Helms, 1981; Porche and Banikiotes, 1982) and other psychological constructs such as self-esteem and self-actualization (Parham and Helms, 1985a, 1985b).

Despite the recent attention in the psychological literature, a limitation of the Cross (1971) model and the research emanating from it (Parham & Helms, 1981, 1985a), is the lack of a developmental perspective in identity formation, and reliance for the most part on college student populations as subject samples. Such narrowly focused research has helped to implicitly perpetuate the notions that: a) the development of Black people's racial identity is confined to an individual's college years (usually late adolescence/early adulthood); and b) an individual's racial identity development is resolved once a person has completed a singular cycle through the stages.

There exists however, other literature which suggests that identity formation continues throughout an individual's entire life span (Erikson, 1963, Levinson, 1978). Can it also be said that the formation of a person's racial identity continues throughout life as well? In support of an affirmative answer to this question, some scholars suggest that Black people may in fact struggle with their racial identities through many stages of the life cycle particularly since they are confronted on a daily basis with racist and oppressive conditions (Wilkins, 1982; Malcolm X, 1965; Jenkins, 1982). Jenkins (1982) for example, who addresses the process of nigrescence in his analysis of the life of Malcolm X, describes the similarities between the stages of racial identity and several phases of Malcolm's life (p. 132). In "A Man's Life—An Autobiography", Wilkins (1982) reflects on different phases of his life during which he manifests varying degrees of Blackness. Even Malcolm X (1965) himself details how his life was characterized by a movement through a series of stages in which his identity was transformed from anti-Black to pro-Black. But perhaps Baldwin (1963) said it best when he wrote..."to be (Black) in this country and to be relatively conscious is to be in a constant state of rage almost all of the time." Baldwin seems to imply that the constant exposure to racist and oppressive conditions creates a never-ending encounter experience for most Black people.

The following N of one case study is presented as an example of the lifetime of struggle which is implicated in the writings cited above. Data were obtained via a questionnaire which the respondent completed as part of a pilot study.

> Mary is a fifty year old, Black female, residing in a large metropolitan city of the Western United States. She grew up in a predominantly Black community in a large midwestern city, and remembers receiving lots of positive comments and support from her parents, school teachers, and other community residents. For Mary, growing up Black was seldom an issue since the entire community was Black. Her iden-

tity was almost characterized by a sense of ambivalence. She reports that her racial identity attitudes have changed over the course of her lifetime as a result of both positive and negative experiences with Blacks and Whites.

At age 17, Mary intended to enroll in an all-Black teachers college, but because of the desegregation order (Brown vs Board of Education, 1954) the college integrated. She recalls feeling somewhat angry and frustrated at the efforts to integrate Black and White college campuses and students. To many, integration seemed to resemble assimilation of the Black into the White, especially since "most of the concessions (closing buildings and demotions of school personnel) were made by the predominantly Black colleges". Despite these attitudes, Mary did enroll, and in time, resolved her negative feelings and began to recognize the need to view Whites as individuals: some were racist, and some were not.

After marrying, Mary and her family relocated to another midwestern city. At age 28, she found herself confronted with more encounters of a racist and discriminatory nature, and subsequently filed a fair housing suit against that city and state. The seven year experience of having to seek justice through litigation again left Mary with feelings of intense anger and hostility towards White people. She also reports that this negative experience was coupled with her absorption of large amounts of Black power oriented literature written by authors such as Stokley Carmichael, H. Rapp Brown, and Malcolm X.

Mary is now a professional in a supervisory capacity with a large public school system. Despite her success and position on the job, she reports feeling slightly paranoid and suspicious of individual Whites, and thus, restricts her contacts with Whites whenever possible. She also perceives that her vocal pro-Black attitudes are treated with apprehension by many of her White colleagues. While some of her Black colleagues are supportive of her racial identity attitudes and opinions, others feel that she is oversensitive, and encourage her to "maintain the status quo" rather than "rock the boat". She seemed to imply that many of her Black colleagues fear that one outspoken Black person may damage relations between Whites and other Blacks, or jeopardize potential opportunities for them on the job. With the exception of one White friend, her personal life is characterized by an all-Black peer group and affiliations with predominantly Black social clubs.

The case study presented above provides a framework for examining changes in identity states which occur at different points in an individual's life. If the above example is the least bit indicative of a larger sample of Blacks, then what is needed in the literature is a model which explicitly describes the relationship between stages of racial identity and stages of the life cycle. Such information would contribute substantially to our knowledge of Black personality development. Despite the need for a more comprehensive view of the nigrescence process, existing models have failed to address this relationship. Readers should be reminded, however, that many of the nigrescence models, including the one proposed by Cross (1971), originally were meant to address "the phenomenon of identity metamorphosis within the context of a social movement and not the evolution of identity from childhood through adult life (Cross, 1978).

The purpose of this chapter then is to attempt to expand the descriptive characteristics of the Cross model by presenting a model of psychological nigrescence which hypothesizes the changes in racial identity that a Black person can experience at various points in the life cycle process.

Racial Identity Attitudes

Cross (1971) introduced a description of the "Negro-to-Black" conversion experience by suggesting that the development of a Black person's racial identity is often characterized by his or her movement through four distinct psychological stages: Pre-encounter, Encounter, Immersion-Emersion, and Internalization.

Pre-encounter

In this stage, the individual is prone to view the world from a White frame of reference. He or she thinks, acts, and behaves in ways which devalue and/or deny his or her Blackness. The person has accepted a deracinated frame of reference, and because their reference point is usually a White normative standard, he or she develops attitudes which are very pro-White and anti-Black.

Encounter

This stage is characterized by an individual experiencing one or many significant (shocking) personal or social events which are inconsistent with his or her frame of reference. For example, a Black person who views his/her race as not important and wishes to be viewed and accepted simply as a "human being" is denied access to living in an exclusive neighborhood because of skin color. These encounters successfully shake a person's self-image of non-Black or "be like White" and make them vulnerable to a new interpretation of self in relation to the world. The encounter stage appears to involve two phases. The first is the realization phase where an individual recognizes that their old frame of reference or view of the world is inappropriate, and he/she begins to explore aspects of a new identity. The second phase (decision) occurs when the person, first cautiously, then definitely, decides to develop a Black identity.

Immersion-Emersion

This stage represents a turning point in the conversion from the old to a new frame of reference. The period of transition is characterized by a struggle to repress or destroy all vestiges of the Pre-encounter orientation while simultaneously becoming intensely concerned with personal implications of the new found Black identity (Cross, 1978). The person begins to immerse him or herself into total Blackness, clinging to various elements of Black culture while simultaneously withdrawing from interactions with other ethnic groups. While the degree of overt manifestations of Blackness is high (i.e. Black clothes and hairstyles, attendance at all Black functions, linguistic style, etc.), the degree of internalized security about one's blackness is minimal. At this stage, everything of value in life must be Black or relevant to Blackness. This stage is also characterized by a tendency to denigrate White people while simultaneously glorifying Black people (Pro-Black/Anti-White attitudes).

Internalization

This stage is characterized by the individual achieving a sense of inner security and self confidence with his or her Blackness. The resolution of conflicts between the old and new worldview become evident as tension, emotionality, and defensiveness are replaced by a calm secure demeanor (Cross, 1978). This stage is also characterized by psychological openness, ideological flexibility and a general decline in strong anti-White feelings. While still using Black as a primary reference group, this person moves towards a more pluralistic, non-racist perspective (Cross 1978). "As internalization and incorporation increases, attitudes toward White people become less hostile, or at least realistically contained, and pro-Black attitudes become more expansive, open, and less defensive" (Cross, 1971, p. 24). The withdrawal from contact with other ethnic groups which characterized the Immersion-Emersion stage is gradually replaced by a willingness to renegotiate relationships with people from other ethnic groups.

Levels of Racial Identity

The present model proposes that within the context of normal development, racial identity is a phenomenon which is subject to continuous change during the life cycle. While the psychological nigrescence research certainly documents how a person's racial identity can change from one stage to another (i.e. Pre-encounter to Encounter to Immersion-Emersion to Internalization) during the late adolescence/early adulthood period, previous research has failed to detail how the various stages of racial identity will be accentuated at later stages of life. This manuscript seeks to describe how the stages of racial identity are manifested at two additional phases of life, middle-adulthood and late adulthood and how each phase of life is characterized by a central underlying theme.

Middle-Adulthood

Middle-adulthood is a period in which individuals attempt to confront and successfully integrate developmental tasks which are physical, psychological, and social in nature. Physically, bodies begin to change and energy levels begin to moderate; psychologically, adults attempt to mentally adjust to changes taking place around them; socially, adults continue to evolve a standard of living consistent with their work status, and begin to relate more to various social institutions for their sake, as well as for the sake of growing children and aging parents (Bloom, 1980).

Generally, the issues addressed by each middle-adulthood person appear to be both intrapsychic as well as psychosocial. Gould (1978) discusses how adult consciousness progresses as an individual masters fears and false assumptions left over from childhood consciousness. Neugarten (1975) defines salient issues in adulthood which characterized the middle-adult person. These include:

a) achieving a sense of self-utilization;

b) increased awareness of physical vulnerability;

c) modified time perspective;

d) planning for further accomplishments in life, and...

e) taking stock, structuring, and restructuring life experiences.

Similarly, Levinson (1978) suggests that middle-adulthood is a time of life when individuals are more or less living out their commitments to various life structures (an underlying design of a person's life at a given time). Levinson further suggests that those middle-adulthood years are characterized by alternating periods of stability and transition of the life cycle, during which men (and by implication women) question previous life decisions, and slightly modify or completely change initial life structures.

Issues faced by individuals engaged in working through these middle-adulthood transitions are often phenomenological. It is entirely likely then that the phenomenology of an issue can be peculiar to both an individual or a group of individuals. This suggests that Black people (generally) may experience a different (from Whites) interpretation of reality based upon their collective life experience, and consequently may face an additional issue to confront in their passage through middle adulthood. An example of this phenomenon is provided by Turner and Darity (1973) who found that fears of genocide (acts committed with intent to destroy, in whole or part, a national, ethnic, racial, or religious group) are very prevalent in Black communities across America. Interestingly, Turner and Darity found that 62.6% of their sample agreed with the statement "As Blacks become more militant (pro-Black), there will be an attempt to reduce the Black population". In light of their findings one might speculate that the middle-adulthood period of life may be the most difficult time to struggle with racial identity because of one's increased responsibilities and increased potential for opportunities. As such, Black people can never lose sight of the fact that their ability to "make it", or to excel in mainstream America depends greatly on their ability to assimilate their values, behaviors, and lifestyles into what the White culture indicates is legitimate.

Middle adulthood then, appears to be a time when many Black people (like their White counterparts) become entrenched in many of society's institutions (i.e. family, work, church, civic organizations). As such their level of racial identity (degree of Blackness) and corresponding attitudes and behaviors are likely to be manifest within the various institutions of which each person is a part. It seems logical then that this middle adulthood period is characterized by a theme of institutionalization.

Pre-encounter. The middle-adulthood Black person with pre-encounter attitudes is very likely to be an individualistic achiever, preferring to adopt the Eurocentric standard of rugged individualism and materialism. This person is likely to have an internally focused locus of control and may deny the extent to which his or her race is an inhibiting factor in their life (Gurin & Epps, 1975). Generally speaking, he or she may believe that successes and/or setbacks are influenced by talent and effort alone. Their lifestyles are analogous to Ellison's (1952) "Invisible Man" which symbolizes the invisibleness of Blackness that must be displayed in order to make it in mainstream America and have access to the resources and opportunities of the dominant culture. As such, while there may be strong verbal attempts to deny the degree to which race may be important, there is an intuitive recognition that the ability to successfully negotiate one's way through life may be contingent upon how well he or she conforms to a White normative standard of values, behaviors, attitudes, and lifestyles. As such, the lack of awareness which characterizes early life pre-encounter attitudes and behaviors is less likely in a midlife person; conscious choices are often made where identity is concerned.

In attempting to gain the approval of White friends and colleagues, these individuals may disassociate themselves from other Black friends and co-workers, preferring instead to restrict their social and professional interactions to White-oriented activities (Davis & Watson, 1982). In part, such behavior helps to maintain an investment in a "non-Black" self-image.

At home, individuals with pre-encounter attitudes are likely to encourage their children to de-emphasize their Blackness in favor of adopting values and behaviors which are more consistent with and less threatening to their White counterparts. Children may be asked/required to dress, groom, and behave in ways which parents believe will make them more acceptable to Whites, and draw less attention to their Blackness.

It is also important to note that some Black parents, especially mothers, who in de-emphasizing Blackness to their children, may be trying to shield and protect them from a harsh reality of what it means to be Black in America that they as parents have experienced first hand. Thus, the de-emphasis on Blackness may be motivated by a maternal (parental) need to protect rather than a personal need to denigrate Blackness.

Encounter. Because of increased responsibilities (children, family), and investments in acquired material positions (income, housing, jobs), individuals who experience encounters in middle-adulthood are likely to experience them with a greater emotional intensity.

Consistent with the previous life stage, the individual will somehow be reminded that the only person forgetting he or she is Black is him or herself. The encounter can be initiated by Whites (i.e. no promotion on job, not receiving rewards promised, racially degrading experience), or by Blacks (i.e. friends who confront you about your lifestyle and behavior, and ethnic loyalties).

The experience is analogous to Davis and Watson's (1982) characterization of Black corporate manager's style of "Wading":

> ...Waders are new entrants (either recent college graduates or persons who moved into positions after years with a company) to the mainstream of corporate life. ...For Blacks, the prestige and even the titles have tremendous psychological importance... Most waders expect, after a while, to shove off and swim toward the midstream, and then start swimming upstream. In the beginning, most do not know that the stream is so full of turbulent currents and stagnant pools, so full of well-tailored flotsam and jetsam, so perilous with undertows

and eddies, so crowded with false promises and poor drainage that it is much more difficult to swim than the wader first imagines (p. 152).

In some cases, it is even possible that the encounter might be self-initiated in the sense that it emerges from a personal perception. For example, parents may begin to interpret the consequences of their lifestyle choices (i.e. sending their children to predominantly White schools, living in predominantly White neighborhoods) through their children's attitudes and behaviors, and become distressed at what they see and hear from their children.

Recent issues of *Ebony* (Gaines-Carter, 1985) and *Newsweek* (Williams et al, 1985) magazines highlighted this phenomenon in articles which talked about the sense of frustration felt by upwardly mobile, middle-class Black parents whose children have grown up with no sense of a Black identity.

Once the person becomes disillusioned with the treatment he/she receives or the behaviors and attitudes he or she displays, they again become vulnerable to a new interpretation of the world.

Immersion-emersion. The middle-adulthood Black person with immersion-emersion attitudes is likely to feel the same sense of anger, hostility, guilt, and frustration as his or her early adulthood counterpart. Likewise, the decision to develop and display a strong sense of Blackness is just as real. Unlike persons in the previous life stage however, their feelings and behaviors are likely to manifest themselves in more institutionalized ways.

Individuals at this stage, if employed, are likely to work toward goals which help to promote or maintain a sense of Black presence. For example, they may work to improve the affirmative action policies on the job in hopes of creating more opportunities for Blacks. If they are associated with an educational institution, they may stress the importance of teaching Black oriented courses. In some respects, these persons are similar to what Davis and Watson (1982) call "splashers", in that they are likely to make waves on the job or stir up commotion with regard to racial injustice. ...Other Blacks in the job setting may consider splashers crazy, until they are needed to protest a personal racial injustice (p. 160).

These individuals will likely avoid White parties and social affairs unless there are significant numbers of Blacks present. Typically though, their relationships with friends and associates will be restricted to other Blacks. Persons with Immersion-Emersion attitudes are likely to join or maintain memberships in all Black organizations. They are also likely to be very concerned about the type of education their children receive, and may institute efforts to supplement traditional schooling with more culturally relevant educational and social experiences. Because of the recognition that one must still survive in a White dominated environment, the anger and hostility which characterized the Immersion-Emersion stage is likely to be expressed in more passive-aggressive ways by middle-adulthood Blacks. For some however, maintaining a sense of biculturalness is very difficult because acting in a "socially appropriate" manner (acting White) represents a conflict with recently modified self-definitions of Blackness.

Internalization. The internalized middle-aged adult has resolved his or her feelings of guilt and anger and now feels comfortable with self. This inner security with Blackness is evident in renegotiated relationships with members of other ethnic groups. In these situations, the internalized Black ethnic groups will often *insist* on being acknowledged for being Black while recognizing and appreciating other ethnic heritages.

The internalized individual will likely channel some of his/her working energies into areas which lend themself to a more universal ethnic perspective. For example, there may be an identification with work colleagues who also are recognized for being an oppressed group. The internalized individual is also likely to be more accepted by White colleagues at work, especially when compared to his/her Immersion-Emersion counterpart, because Whites are less likely to feel threatened. Also, the sense of anger and hostility which characterizes the Immersion stage, and helps to maintain social distance, has usually dissipated enough to make approaching an internalized Black person more comfortable for whites, or other colleagues of different ethnicities.

The theme of universal connectedness is also likely to be seen as parents interact with children. Parental assistance in the form of advice giving may encourage youngsters to be proud of their ethnic heritage, while simultaneously learning to respect differences in other people. Parents are likely to incorporate some vestiges of Black life and culture into their lifestyles, and will try to expose their children to as much cultural information as possible.

Late Adulthood

Late adulthood is a period when Black individuals begin to gain an appreciation for the fullness of life, and must adjust to many inevitable changes. Late adulthood is characterized by many unique developmental tasks which include integrating and appreciating one's life experiences (Erickson, 1963). The challenge presented to many late adulthood persons is to find use for what knowledge and skill he or she has already obtained in a lifetime of learning and adapting (Butler, 1980). In making life adjustments, late adulthood persons must teach themselves to conserve their strength and resources where this is necessary, and to adjust to those changes and loses (physical, economic, social) that occur as a part of the aging experience (Butler, 1980).

While much of the psychological literature comments on the changes in social circumstances and physical well being of the older members of our society, there also seems to be general agreement that major developmental tasks of this era include a period of self-assessment and reflection on past activities and accomplishments in life (Erikson, 1963; Butler, 1980; Havighurst, 1956; Levinson, 1975). Erickson (1963) talks about the need to combine, integrate, and appreciate one's life experiences and come to terms with the finality of life. Butler (1980) talks about the need to review past activities with a reorientation towards the future. In a similar manner, Levinson (1978) talks about the need to arrive at some appraisal of one's life. As such, this period of life seems to be characterized by a theme of reflectiveness.

Due to the inner-connectedness and extended nature of many Black families, late adulthood persons are likely to have extensive contact with relatives and friends from younger generations. Because many of these persons retain vigorous bodies and sound minds, efforts to sustain some sense of youthfulness are directed at increased participation in social activities, as well as various forms of vicarious living through the younger generations.

Pre-encounter. As the late-adulthood, pre-encounter individual reflects back on his or her life, he or she is likely to contrast their sense of accomplishment in comparison to the accomplishments of their White peers. Their Eurocentric value structure may compel them to measure personal worth and satisfaction in terms of the amount of individual productivity achieved and personal power (control) that has been obtained. He or she is likely to feel a sense of satisfaction (integrity) if the amount of productivity and power achieved is consistent with expectations from life structures in early and middle-adulthood. They are likely to see accomplishments in life as personal achievements which other Blacks could have attained if they had only tried harder to assimilate. If for some reason the individual is dissatisfied with his or her assessment, then some measure of disappointment and despair are likely to be felt. As such, he or she may develop the notion of disappointment, "if only I had been more mainstream, or external disappointment, "if other Blacks had worked harder, I'd have been better off". Regardless of whether the Pre-encounter person achieves a sense of integrity or disappointment, he or she is likely to attribute success or failure to individual talent and effort, or intra-talent and effort. Pre-encounter persons may even feel some disdain and disgust at Black people) for having been "too Black".

Because many late-adulthood persons are often interested in imparting information on younger generations, messages on race related issues given by Pre-encounter individuals are likely to provide encouragement to assimilate. Such encouragements are likely to be given in conjunction with the relating of a personal or group life experience which reinforces the need for a deracinated frame of reference.

It is also likely that social interactions outside of the family may be confined to predominantly White groups, even if the individual has an option of selecting a more culture specific network.

Encounter. The encounters experienced by late adulthood persons are likely to represent intense emotional experiences. The meaning of frustration, discrimination, and degradation may even be exacerbated because of the frailties and vulnerabilities of old age (Butler, 1980).

The type of encounter experiences may also depend on the stage of late-adulthood in which it occurs. For example, if he or she is at pre-retirement age, then encounters are likely to be actual experiences which parallel those discussed in earlier sections of this paper. On the other hand, the act of reflecting on one's life experience may signal an encounter for a post-retirement person. While taking stock on one's life, negative reflections may lead him or her to question previous lifestyle priorities and assumptions. It is important to remember that "personal reflections" may focus on the specific life experiences of the individual, or the general experiences of Blacks as a people. These negative reflections may lead him or her to the realization that denial of one's "Blackness" was tantamount to a life without real integrity. As such, the individual may feel a sense of guilt, anxiety and betrayal, which in turn may compel (motivate) a person to develop a stronger sense of Blackness.

While the focus in the encounter stage has centered on negative experiences and/or perceptions, positive experiences and reflections can also provide the bases for an encounter experience. As such, the importance of positive ethnically oriented experiences should not be discounted.

Immersion-emersion. Late-adulthood persons with immersion-emersion attitudes are likely to experience the full intensity of emotions which usually accompany this stage. These persons are likely to feel a strong sense of anger, frustration, hostility and guilt. In contrast to immersion-emersion persons at earlier stages of life however, the person in late adulthood may be prone to hold feelings inside rather than to display them overtly.

As the person with immersion-emersion attitudes begins to reflect back on life, he or she is likely to base their positive assessments on the degree to which life's experiences have incorporated some measure of "Blackness." Also, an individual with these attitudes is likely to structure the remaining years of his or her life in a way such that being Black is a major focus.

If the individual has achieved any measure of success in life, then he or she is likely to experience feelings of pride and satisfaction. If there is a perception that he or she has been less successful than originally expected, then he or she may experience more negative feelings of frustration, anger, resentment, and even despair. That individual is also likely to attribute the causes for their lack of success to racism and discrimination perpetuated by White society.

It is entirely possible that some people could remain fixated in the immersion-emersion stage throughout their entire life. However, if he or she has experienced a recent encounter or immersion into Blackness experience, they are likely to feel disappointment and disgust with themselves for their previous denial of Blackness, which gained them nothing in life.

As the late adulthood person with Immersion-Emersion attitudes interacts with younger generations, their efforts may be directed at instilling in young people a strong sense of Black pride. Younger persons may also be encouraged to become receptive to experiences and information which heighten their sense of Black awareness.

Social activities for the late adulthood person with Immersion-Emersion attitudes are likely to be consciously restricted to all Black groups. If such groups are not available, then he or she will probably withdraw into social isolation, interacting with Whites on limited occasions, and only on a need-to-do basis.

Internalization. Late-adulthood persons with internalization attitudes are likely to feel the same sense of security with their racial identity as other internalized persons do at earlier stages of life.

If his or her internalized attitudes have been present for many years, a person is likely to reflect back on life in a positive manner because of the internalized security with one's identity resolution.

The sense of satisfaction may also be due to the fact that the internalized person will have little if any unfinished business with respect to identity development. As such, reflections on life may be characterized by a lack of anxiety.

Pre-retirement persons with internalization attitudes are likely to have fairly good relationships with other work colleagues from different ethnic backgrounds. He or she will feel pride in his/her level of racial consciousness but may not feel the need to manifest that racial pride in overt ways. Since his or her remaining years in the work force are limited, work activities for the internalized person may involve making a last-ditch effort to impact their jobs with contributions which contribute to the betterment of all oppressed persons.

Post-retirement persons with internalization attitudes have already begun the disengagement (framework) process. As such, the racial identity attitudes are likely to be more reflective in nature, at least where their former career or job is concerned. He or she is also likely to try to rearrange his/her priorities in life to accommodate more time for leisure activities. Such activities will likely include relating to racially different persons in a receptive way.

Relationships with members of the younger generations may be characterized by a sense of biculturalness. That is, the late-adulthood person will probably attempt to impress upon younger generations the necessity to develop cross-cultural skills as well as an appreciation for other cultures, in addition to one's own.

Analysis of the Case Study

The case study of "Mary" presented earlier helps to facilitate our understanding of how the nigrescence process is manifest at different stages of the life cycle.

Initially, Mary's sense of racial consciousness appears to have been more latent than visible. Growing up in an all Black community made focusing on race a less salient issue since being Black was the norm. As such, her identity may have been characterized by a sense of ambivalence.

In analyzing Mary's life thus far, her changes in racial identity correspond to the changes proposed by Cross (1971, 1978) in his model of psychological nigrescence. Also consistent with the hypothesis generated by Cross is the fact that Mary's movement from stage to stage appears to have been triggered by her perceptions of racist and oppressive conditions created by White society.

As a seventeen-year-old, Mary appears to be confronted with a personal encounter experience where her racial identity attitudes quickly change from ambivalence, to frustration, and then to anger. Pro-Black-anti-White attitudes are also evident.

Over time, however, her negative and angry feelings towards Whites in general diminish, and she develops a more realistic picture of Whites as individuals, while still maintaining pro-Black attitudes.

The transition from late twenties to early thirties signaled a turbulent time for Mary. Again she was confronted with experiences which reinforced her beliefs about White people as racist. The latest encounters not only left Mary angry and bitter, but they also helped to motivate her re-immersion into Blackness, and her obsession with absorbing massive amounts of Black literature written by "militant Blacks".

The duration of her struggle (legal action) and the emotional intensity involved appear to have had a profound effect on Mary. Her current lifestyle is characterized by very strong pro-Black attitudes, suspiciousness of White people, a predominantly Black social and peer group, and feelings of tension from other Black colleagues who feel Mary is "too

Black". Most importantly, Mary reports feeling very comfortable with both her lifestyle and her racial identity attitudes.

Summary

This chapter has attempted to extend the parameters of the Cross model of racial identity development. The model proposes that the development of racial identity attitudes is a phenomenon which continues throughout the life span, and that racial identity attitudes are subject to continuous change over time.

The model also contends that racial identity attitudes will manifest themselves in different ways at various stages of the life cycle process. These differential manifestations are each characterized by an underlying theme which influences an individual's behavior with regard to racial issues.

Scientific inquiry typically proceeds to two levels: discovery and confirmation. This manuscript proposed a framework for understanding racial identity development at different phases of the life cycle. While the concepts are theoretical in nature, they are intended to stimulate further empirical investigation in the nigrescence area. Only time and more research will tell whether the ideas contained within this paper have any merit.

References

Baldwin, J. (1963). *The fire next time*. New York: Dial Press.

Bloom, M. (1980). *Life span development*. New York: MacMillan.

Butler, R. N. (1980). Successful aging. In M. Bloom (Ed.), *Life span development*. New York: MacMillan

Cross, W. E. (1971). The Negro to Black conversion experience: Towards a psychology of Black liberation. *Black World, 20(9)*, 13-27.

Cross, W. E. (1978). The Cross and Thomas models of psychological nigrescence. *Journal of Black Psychology, 5(1)*, 13-19.

Davis, G., & Watson, G. (1982). *Black life in corporate America*. Garden City, NY: Anchor Press.

Ellison, R. (1952). *Invisible man*. New York: Random House.

Erikson, E. (1963)., *Childhood and Society*. (2nd ed.). New York: Norton.

Gaines-Carter, P. (1985). Is My post-integration daughter Black enough? *Ebony*, vol XL, 54-56.

Gould, R. (1978). *Transformations: Growth and change in adult life*. New York: Simon and Schuster.

Gurin, P., & Epps, E. (1975). *Black consciousness: Identity and achievement*. New York: John Wiley.

Havighurst, R. (1956). *Potentialities of women in the middle years*. New York: McKay.

Jackson, B. (1976). Black Identity Development. In L. Golubschick and B. Persky (Eds.), *Urban Social and Educational Issues*, 158-164. Dubuque: Kendall-Hall.

Jenkins, A. (1982). *The psychology of of the Afro-American*. New York: Pergamon Press.

Levinson, D. (1978). *The seasons of a man's life*. New York: Alfred Knopf.

Malcolm X (1965). *Autobiography of Malcolm X*. New York: Grove Press.

Milliones, J. (1973). Construction of the developmental inventory of Black consciousness. (Doctoral Dissertation, University of Pittsburg, 1973). *Dissertation Abstracts International*, August, 1974, 35-02, 1241-A. University Microfilm No. 74-18, 415.

Neugarten, B. L. (1975). Adult personality: Toward a psychology of the life cycle. In W. C. Sye (Ed.), *The human life cycle.*. New York: Jason Aronson.

Parham, T. A., & Helms, J. E. (1981). Influence of a Black students racial identity attitudes on preference for counselor race. *Journal of Counseling Psychology, 18(3)*, 250-256.

Parham, T. A., & Helms, J. E. (1985a). Relation of racial identity attitudes to self-actualization and affective states of Black students. *Journal of Counseling Psychology, 32(3)*, 431-440.

Parham, T. A., & Helms, J. E. (1985b). Attitudes of racial identity and self-esteem of Black students: An exploratory investigation. *Journal of College Student Personnel, 26(2)*, 143-146.

Porché, L. M., & Banikiotes, P. G. (1982). Racial and attitudinal factors affecting the perceptions of counselors by Black adolescents, *Journal of Counseling Psychology, 29*, 169-174.

Thomas, C. (1971). *Boys no more*. Beverly Hills: Glenco Press.

Turner, C., & Darity, W. A. (1973). Fears of genocide among Black Americans as related to age, sex, and region. *American Journal of Public Health, 63(12)*, 1029-1034.

Wilkins, R. (1982). *A man's life: An autobiography*.

Williams, D. A., Jackson, T. A., and Weather, D., Joseph, N., and Anderson, M. (1985). Roots III: Soul on Ice. *Newsweek, 23, 82-84*.

Williams, I. (1975). An investigation into the developmental stages of Black consciousness (Doctoral Dissertation, University of Cincinnati). *Dissertation Abstract International*, November, 1975, 36-05, 2488-B. (University Microfilms No. 75-25, 934).

SOCIAL INDICES AND THE BLACK ELDERLY: A COMPARATIVE LIFE CYCLE APPROACH TO THE STUDY OF DOUBLE JEOPARDY

Carolyn B. Murray, Syed Khatib, and Maurice Jackson

Introduction

The literature on the elderly, particularly the comparative literature on Black and White elderly, is dominated by the theme of "double jeopardy." This concept, first popularized in the 1960's (Tally & Kaplan, 1956; National Urban League, 1964), asserts that the adverse living conditions of Black elderly in America is compounded by the social fact of their overall treatment as minority group members (National Council on Aging, 1971; Jackson & Wood, 1976; Dowd & Bengston, 1978; Jackson, Kolody, & Wood 1982; and National Caucus and Center on Black Aged, 1987).

The present paper contributes to that literature by examining the double jeopardy theme employing a life cycle frame to investigate social indices of aging. We argue here that race and/or ethnicity are the primary ingredients which heavily impact, if not determine, the social well-being of the Black elderly, and that the elderly status of Blacks in America compounds the adversity of their treatment as a racial group. Employing current census data, the directness of the age/race link between the social well-being of the White elderly and that of the Black elderly will be examined over the life cycle.

Life Cycle Approach

The process of aging begins at birth and continues until death (Honzik, 1984). The study of the life cycle is an investigation of the transitions that occur as one becomes elderly. There are no absolutes in transitions; however, these transitions are most often, though not always (e.g., biological changes, life events, role acquisitions, etc.) marked by chronological age—birth, early childhood, adolescence, young adulthood, middle age, old age and death. Aging is important since it, along with race and gender, is often considered to be a biological and organizing constant in society. Everybody (who lives) grows old and thus experiences the various role assignments associated with different points along the age continuum.

Social and biological scientists point out that while studying the aged is of paramount importance, data on old age gain descriptive and explanatory value when interpreted within a frame of information concerning the whole biography. They argue persuasively that observed age differences are not only products of aging per se, but also are due to specific properties of cohorts or specifiable events (see Bowser, chapter 1, this volume). However, in spite of this recognition by social scientists that the aging process is conditioned by broader social and historical contexts, the existing literature on the life cycle experiences of the Black elderly is extremely limited.

In terms of methodology, there are three major types of life cycle research of interest to gerontologists (Munnichs & Olbrich, 1985). The most informative is the longitudinal approach in which the researcher has followed the participants from youth, keeping track of them over their entire adulthood. The advantage of this research is that investigators can make use of the knowledge of the biographies of their aging participants to discover the process by which aging occurs. After conducting an extensive literature review to locate longitudinal research pertinent to the Black elderly, we came to the conclusion that a void exists in the literature utilizing this approach.

A second approach is cross-sectional research which describes and explains development in a relatively late period of life. Here the researcher may identify one group of participants just prior to their entering old age, and another group who has already entered old age. These groups are followed for a relatively short period of time to assess the process of aging from the young-old (55 to 64 years of age) to the middle-old (65 to 74 years of age) or old-old (75+). Slightly more research on the Black elderly exists employing this approach; however, more research is needed and should be carried out given its time and cost-effectiveness advantage over longitudinal research.

The third and final research approach is the comparative. This approach makes intergenerational comparisons between younger and/or middle-aged and/or older individuals, tested at the same points in time and correlated with each other. Interpretations of intergenerational data are limited to direct observational or measured differences, rather than on the process of aging. A considerable body of comparative research which examines issues relevant to the Black elderly is available. Much of this research, however, focuses on racial differences, social class differences, urban/rural differences, and to a lesser extent, comparisons among younger, middle aged and/or elderly adult Blacks; there is a dearth of comparative studies which employ a life cycle frame to investigate social indices of Black aging.

The measurement and analysis of the life cycle is of special interest to gerontological demographers, particularly because of the relation of the process of aging and the life course to characteristics of the older population (Riley, Johnson, & Fonner, 1972; Siegel, 1980). The problem posed for the demographer has been to identify sources of variation in specific demographic aspects of the life course, to try to separate their effects, and to analyze the relative contribution of each factor to the demographic change under study. According to the double jeopardy theme one source of variation contributing to life course differences between the Black and White elderly is their differential treatment throughout the life cycle. The present chapter presents 1980s demographic data on comparative social indices of Blacks and Whites at different adult ages to investigate our double jeopardy hypothesis.

With the current debate concerning the impact of governmental policies on the well-being of the elderly as a backdrop, the time is propitious for critically viewing the social indices of elderly social well-being. Within this paper, the social indices focused on include population characteristics, geographical distribution and mobility, housing, living arrangement, marital status, income status, labor force participation, and physical and mental health.

Two National Surveys

The observations presented above provide a context for interpreting the results of two surveys conducted by Louis Harris Associates for the National Council on Aging in 1974 and 1981. These surveys employed multi-stage random cluster sampling with an over-sampling of those aged 65 and over, and non-Whites (Blacks and Hispanics). This procedure produced a sample of 3,427 in 1974 and 4,254 in 1981 of whom 619 Blacks were interviewed in the first survey and 497 in the second. It should be noted that in these, as in most national surveys, institutionalized people (i.e., those in the military, hospitals, and prisons) were exluded.

The surveys also over-sampled individuals over 64 to provide in-depth information about the elderly in America. This procedure provided an over-sample of 479 Black elderly in 1974 and 274 in 1981. Because the survey was a cluster sample, a disproportionate number of Blacks were, low income, residents of the South, and inhabitants of urban areas.

The two surveys provide a rare opportunity to investigate a trend in societal thinking over a seven-year time span. While the respondents were not the same people in the two surveys, the sampling methodology, utilizing specific weighting procedures, provide a reliable basis of comparison of not only Blacks with Whites, but—more important for present concerns—of the perceptions of Blacks in 1974 with those of Blacks in 1981.

The results of the surveys show that, with respect to most issues, there were few significant differences between the '74 and '81 samples, although there were predictable differences between Blacks and Whites within both samples. These Black-White differences, however, tended to disappear when the income level for both was controlled—a phenomena not uncommon to sociological research in America.

However, with respect to particular issues such as health, there were significant differences, not only between Blacks and Whites for both surveys, but also between Blacks in 1974 and Blacks in 1981. In addition, to data from the surveys, we will employ a life cycle perspective to examine other studies and census data which compare elderly race-sex groups with their younger counterparts.

Population Characteristics

At the beginning of this century, less than 1 in 8 Americans was age 55 and over and 1 in 25 was age 65 and over. By 1984, 1 in 5 Americans was at least 55. America is growing older, with its elderly population increasing far more rapidly than the other population elements (U.S. Senate Special Committee on Aging, 1985/86). In the last two decades alone, the 65-plus population grew by 54 percent while the under 65 population increased by only 24 percent. But the 85+ population is the fastest growing age group in the country. The primary causes for this increase in older Americans are the lower annual rate of births prior to 1920 on one end, and increased longevity due to major achievements in disease prevention and health care on the other (Soldo & Manton, 1986).

The Black population has a smaller proportion of elderly than the White population. Since 1970 the percentage of the Black population recorded at 65 or over has remained at 7 to 8 percent, while Whites 65 or over are at least 13 percent of the overall White American population (Phillips, 1986). This difference is a result of higher fertility and higher mortality below the age of 65 for the Black population. Still, the Black elderly form the fastest growing segment of the Black population. Between 1970 and 1980, the Black elderly population increased 16 percent (Matney & Johnson, 1983). Furthermore, though Whites presently are disproportionately represented in the elderly population, it is projected in the next century that the Black elderly population will grow at a faster rate than the White.

Geographic Distribution and Mobility

Life cycle (aged-related) migration patterns played an important role in the racially selective suburbanization of metropolitan populations that took place in the immediate postwar decades. The 1890 Census, the first for which urban-rural data for Blacks were available, showed most Blacks (80%) resided in rural areas and 9 out of 10 Black Americans lived in the Southern region (U.S. Bureau of the Census, 1980). Urbanization did not become the norm for Blacks until the years after 1940—fed by the large influx of Blacks to northern cities looking for employment. Thus, a disproportionate number of today's Black elderly were most likely a part of that migration, while younger adult Blacks were most likely to be born in an urban environment. During this period, the members of successive upwardly mobile White population cohorts chose suburban destinations. At the same time, Black city residents at all status levels were prevented from moving into suburban locations due to a variety of well-known discriminatory mechanisms (Taeuber, 1975). This concurrent process of White suburbanization and Black centralization led to city populations that are disproportionately comprised of Blacks and low income Whites, and the associated problems of private disinvestment, reduced public services, environmental deterioration and crime (Frey, 1984).

In a recent publication disseminated by the U.S. Bureau of the Census (December, 1983), it was stated that "Blacks are moving to suburbia but not beyond"(p. 10). However, 55 percent of the Nation's Black population in 1982 still remained in central cities, compared to 59 percent in 1970. In contrast, only 23 percent of the White population lived in central cities of metropolitan areas in 1982; 43 percent lived in suburbs, and 34 percent lived in non-metropolitan areas. In 1970, the proportions were 28 percent, 40 percent, and 32 percent, respectively. Put simply, the most recent census indicated that Blacks were significantly more urbanized than Whites, but this trend is beginning to reverse itself with a higher annual rate of growth among Blacks than among Whites in the suburbs (U.S. Bureau of the Census, 1980).

The greater suburban movement of Blacks can be linked to rising Black social status, some elimination of past discriminatory practices and improvements in race relations. This opening of suburban residential opportunities also tends to be most evident for Blacks born since 1945 (Pettigrew, 1980; Frey, 1984). On the average, elderly persons tend to move far less often than younger persons. Approximately one-fifth of Black elderly live in rural areas—a somewhat lower proportion than White elderly (about one-fourth)—and over 59 percent are concentrated in the Southeastern States. Of the remainder, most live either in the North Central or Northeast regions (U.S. Senate Special Committee on Aging, 1985/86). However, whether they live in urban ghettos or rural slums, elderly people are generally left behind in old decaying areas. Housing is the most visible sign of this deprivation.

Housing

Most Americans, especially the elderly (73%), compared to the non-elderly (65%), live in single-family owner occupied homes (Kart, 1981). Furthermore, non-elderly householders were much more likely than elderly householders to have home mortgages (Jackson, 1985).

Housing, while an asset for many elderly people, represents a serious problem for some of them. For elderly homeowners who do not have to budget for mortgage or rental payments, or who can sell their homes at a profit, housing can be an asset. However, for many elderly persons who own older homes, the cost of repair and maintenance can be prohibitive. And, for renters or owners with a mortgage, monthly housing payments can be a substantial burden.

In 1980, 57.7 percent of all Black families headed by elderly persons owned their own homes, and 42.2 percent were renters. This compared to 72.1 percent and 27.9 percent, respectively, for elderly White families (NCCBA, 1987). Among the elderly Black families who lived in rental units, only 6 percent lived in public housing and less than 1 percent lived in subsidized units (Hill, 1978). The majority of homeowners lived in families, while the overwhelming majority of renters lived alone.

Data from the 1981 Louis Harris poll tell a different story. Seventy percent of the Whites versus 44% of the Blacks had paid off their mortgages. However, about one of three elderly Blacks found their houses to be unsuitable. This finding is supported by a recent study of racial differences in well-being among elderly persons utilizing services at nutrition sites in Cleveland, Ohio. It found that the Black elderly, in contrast to their White counterparts, lived in poorer housing, and were less satisfied with their living environment (Comptroller General of the United States, 1977). Thus, in terms of home ownership, though Black elderly (66%) in the 1981 Harris poll generally reflected the 1977 census data (70%) for Blacks, the findings also illuminated the need for a finer distinction of the home ownership category in terms of whether the mortgage was paid off, the conditions of the property, the surrounding community, and other costs (i.e., taxes, insurance, etc.).

Moreover, recent budget cuts have aggravated housing problems for elderly Blacks. Large numbers of elderly Blacks are discovering that their housing situation is practically impossible. Rising property taxes and maintenance costs make it difficult for elderly persons to remain in their homes (NCCBA, 1987). For instance, according to a report issued by the National Caucus and Center on Black Aged (1987), on the average, 30 percent of the elderly Black person's income is paid towards rent and increasing utility bills, and there are many cases where rent and utilities exceed the elderly's monthly income.

This situation is worsened by the fact that many elderly Black persons are forced to live in crime-infested neighborhoods, because they cannot find alternative housing due to limited income; and discrimination in housing. These are especially important distinctions given that Blacks are less prepared for retirement and have considerably less income after retirement than do their White counterparts.

Living Arrangements

One of the major trends characterizing the change in household[1] (see footnotes at the ned of chapter) composition during the 1970's has been a substantial increase in the number of families[2] maintained by women with no husband present. In 1982, the majority of Black families were still maintained by married couples. However, since 1970, the percentage of all Black families maintained by married couples has significantly declined from 68 to 55 percent. Almost 41 percent of 6.4 million Black families were maintained by women. The comparable percentages for Whites during this period increased from only 9 percent to 12 percent (Matney & Johnson, 1983).

During the middle years (ages 35-64) about the same percentage (roughly four-fifths) of Blacks and Whites live in family units (see Table 1). While 94 percent of all elderly live in the community, a slightly higher proportion (96%) of Black elderly do (Phillips, 1986). Over two-thirds (67%) of elderly noninstitutionalized persons lived in a family setting in 1983. However, as shown in Table 1, in 1984 two-fifths of elderly Black women and one-third of elderly Black men did not live in families. This living arrangement was more so for elderly White women (over half) and least for elderly White men (one-fifth). Relatively more elderly Blacks than Whites are widowed, divorced, or separated; thus, a smaller proportion live with their spouses (Harel, 1985). However, sharing a home with a grown child, usually a daughter, is a common arrangement for elderly Blacks. According to Hill (1978), it should be emphasized, however, that because of their desire to be as self-reliant as possible, the Black elderly are much more likely to take others into their households rather than permit themselves to be taken into the households of younger relatives.

The strength of the Black elderly is further exemplified by the fact that Blacks, in contrast to elderly Whites, are more likely to have young children living with them. This is especially true for family units headed by elderly Black women (Hill, 1978). Moreover, as shown in Table 1, within family units elderly Black women (as are Black women in general) are much more likely than elderly White women to be primary householders. Two-fifths of all Black families headed by women 65 and over had children under 18 years old living with them, compared to only one tenth of families headed by elderly White women. Similarly, while only 4 percent of White husband-wife families with heads 65 years and over had dependent children living with them, more than five times as many (22%)

Table 1
Percent Distribution of the Living Arrangements of Aged Blacks and Whites by Sex and Age, United States, 1984

Living Arrangements and Age	Percentage Distribution			
	Black Women	Black Men	White Women	White Men
% in Families				
35—39 years	91.1	77.0	91.5	84.9
40—44 years	88.5	77.0	93.1	87.7
45—54 years	87.1	80.4	90.7	89.1
55—64 years	75.5	75.5	80.4	88.9
65—74 years	61.2	76.8	62.9	86.4
75+ years	55.6	67.9	46.6	77.5
% Householder				
35—39 years	48.0	54.0	15.9	74.8
40—44 years	39.2	60.6	17.3	80.0
45—54 years	36.4	60.9	14.0	82.1
55—64 years	32.0	65.4	10.6	82.9
65—74 years	24.9	63.4	9.3	79.8
75+ years	22.3	55.9	10.1	68.0
% not in Families				
35—39 years	8.6	23.0	8.0	15.0
40—44 years	11.5	23.0	6.5	12.2
45—54 years	12.9	19.6	9.1	10.8
55—64 years	24.3	24.5	19.5	11.0
65—74 years	38.6	22.9	37.0	13.5
75+ years	44.4	32.1	53.3	22.5
% Non Family Householder				
35—39 years	6.6	15.5	6.5	10.8
40-44 years	9.3	19.8	5.1	9.5
45-54 years	12.0	13.5	8.1	8.6
55-64 years	22.6	21.1	18.4	9.6
65—74 years	36.9	20.3	36.1	12.1
75+ years	43.1	28.6	51.6	20.8

Source of raw data: U.S. Bureau of the Census, Current Population Reports, Series P-20, No. 399, *Marital Status and Living Arrangements: March 1984*, U.S. Department of Commerce, Bureau of the Census, July 1985, pp. 23-24.

**Table 2
Percent of Persons Married 15 Years and Over, by Age,
Sex, and Race, United States, March 1984.**

Age	Percent Married					
	Blacks			**Whites**		
	Both	**Males**	**Females**	**Both**	**Males**	**Females**
Total, 15+ years	35.9	39.4	31.9	59.1	61.6	56.9
35—39 years	47.8	53.8	42.9	76.0	76.1	75.9
40—44 years	55.5	64.3	48.4	78.6	80.1	76.6
45—54 years	55.1	62.5	49.3	79.9	82.6	77.2
55—64 years	52.3	65.2	42.7	76.3	84.6	69.0
65—74 years	44.4	62.4	31.4	64.2	81.7	50.6
75+ years	29.7	52.7	16.3	39.9	68.4	23.5

Source of raw data: U.S. Bureau of the Census, Current Population Reports, Series
P-20, *Marital Status and Living Arrangements: March 1984*, U.S. Department of
Commerce, Bureau of the Census, July 1985.

elderly Black two-parent families had dependent children living with
them (U.S. Bureau of Census, 1976). Thus, elderly Blacks, and especially
elderly Black women, play an important role in the Black family.

Marital Status

Across the life span men, regardless of race, were more likely to be
married than their female counterparts. In addition, Blacks were less
likely to be married than Whites, and Black women were the least likely to
be married of the four groups (see Table 2). With regard to the elderly, in
1970, 55 percent of elderly Black men were living with their spouses, compared to 70 percent of elderly White men (Hill, 1978). Recent statistics
compiled and disseminated by the American Association of Retired Persons (Phillips, 1986) show that the proportion of elderly men living with
their spouses has increased among both Blacks (54.9%) and Whites
(74.2%). However, still for both Whites and Blacks age 65 and older, the
majority of men (74.2 and 56.9%, respectively) are married while the majority of women (51.1% and 57.7%, respectively) are widowed.

This picture can be attributed to the fact that elderly women outnumber elderly men three to two, a considerable change from 1960 when
the ratio of elderly females to elderly males was five to four. Among
Blacks age 60-64, there are 80 men for every 100 women, while for Whites
there are 87 men for every 100 women. This situation worsens with age.
By age 75 there are 63 Black men for every 100 Black women, and 61

White men for every 100 White women (Phillips, 1986). These differences are caused by a combined effect of the higher age specific death rates for adult men, the tendency for men to marry younger women, and the tendency for more men than women to remarry after the death of a spouse (Williams, 1980). Thus, on the average, women live longer than men and, therefore, are more likely to end up living alone.

Summary. Currently, the Black elderly are the fastest growing segment of the Black population, and it is projected for the next century that their proportion will grow at an even faster rate than the comparable proportion of White elderly. In terms of residential patterns, Blacks are characterized as urbanized, while Whites in general are more suburban or rural. This demographic pattern was fostered and maintained by barring members of Black population cohorts from selecting suburban destinations at all ages of the life cycle (Frey, 1984). The elderly among them is no exception; however, while this pattern is reversing itself with a higher annual rate of growth among Blacks in general than among Whites moving to the suburbs, the pattern for elderly Blacks is not changing in that direction. Rather, it is holding constant: elderly Blacks have inherited the old and dilapidated housing of the urban ghettos and rural slums.

This situation is further exacerbated by the fact that elderly Blacks of whom many are disproportionately living on extremely inadequate incomes, also are more likely than their White cohorts to head families with persons under 18 years of age living with them, or to live alone. Further exacerbating the living conditions of the Black elderly are federal cutbacks in spending for social programs.

Income Status

Inadequate income and lack of benefits characterize the life experiences of Blacks from youth to old age (Jackson & Gibson, 1985). The median income for Black males and females ($8,989 and $5,542, respectively), continues to lag behind that of their White counterparts ($15,359 and $6,403, respectively) (U.S. Bureau of the Census, 1985). While the income levels for Black married couples was climbing during the decade of the 1970's, this group experienced a decline in the proportion they constituted of all Black families, dropping from 64 percent in 1972 to 55 percent in 1982 (Matney & Johnson, 1983).

In 1970, about 8 million Blacks (34 percent) and 17 million Whites (10 percent) had incomes below the poverty level. By 1981, the number increased to 9 million for Blacks (34 percent) and 22 million for Whites (11 percent) (Matney & Johnson, 1983). Thus, the decline in Black family median income reflects, in part, the increase in the proportion of families maintained by females with no husbands and the lack of income gain for these families.

Elderly Americans as a group have a lower economic status than other adults in our society. This largely results from changes in status often associated with aging: retirement from the work force, the death of a spouse, and/or a decline in health (Harris & Associates, 1981). However, it is also true, as indicated by Jackson and Wood (1976), Manuel (1982), and by recent findings of the U.S. Commission on Civil Rights (1982), that because of socioeconomic and racial discrimination, most elderly Blacks still are highly likely to be "multiply disadvantaged" by age, poverty, and race in contrast to their White counterparts (Watson, 1983). The high rate of inflation experienced over the past two decades further exacerbates this situation.

By any standard, the Black elderly are the most economically disadvantaged of any of the elderly groups (NCCBA, 1987). Overall, 35 percent live below the poverty level, as compared to only 13 percent of the White elderly. For rural Blacks, 1 out of 2 live in poverty, contrasted with about 1 of 4 White rural elderly.

Though the income of elderly Blacks improved during the 1970s, narrowing the income gap with elderly Whites (Hill, 1978), still the Black elderly consistently have had substantially lower money incomes than their White counterparts. By 1985, the median income for elderly Black men was about $4,113, while that for elderly Black women was $2,825, compared to $7,408 for elderly White men, and $3,894 for elderly White women (Phillips, 1986). Furthermore, the Black elderly are more likely to have their sole income from one or two government sources (Social Security and/or Supplemental Security Income) or to have no income. And while Social Security constitutes a greater proportion of the income for Blacks 65 years and older than it does for elderly Whites, the proportion of elderly Blacks receiving Social Security is less than that for elderly Whites. A major source of this difference is that a larger proportion of elderly Blacks—especially the very old—worked in occupations which were not covered by Social Security or were only partially covered during their working years (NCCBA, 1987).

Those worse off are older women, particularly those living in rural areas and the "oldest-old" (85 or older). In 1984, nearly 3 out of 5 (56.6%) elderly Black women living alone had an income below the poverty level. Almost 21% of rural White women live in poverty, but 68% of rural Black women do, making them the most impoverished of any group of elderly (Phillips, 1986).

These statistics are best reinforced by the self-reported perceptions of the elderly participating in the 1974 and 1981 Louis Harris surveys. In general, the attitude of the elderly concerning their own financial well-being changed from the majority (52%) in 1974 *dis*agreeing with the statement that "older people today are worse off financially than older people 10 or 20 years ago," to a majority (54%) in 1981 agreeing with this statement. Black elderly Americans agreed even more strongly (60%) that older persons were worse off financially by 1981 a turnaround from 1974 when only a 44-41% plurality felt they were worse off (Harris & Associates, 1981).

Disturbing racial differences also have been found regarding adequacy of income among the elderly. While a majority of White elders (52%) were consistently getting by with a little extra income or had the capacity to buy pretty much anything they wanted with their 1980-81 incomes, a large majority of Blacks (80%) were regularly just scraping by or were in real financial difficulty. Additionally, while 42 percent of the elderly had been able to save or invest some of their income during 1979-1980, older Blacks (18%) were among the least likely to have saved or invested (Harris & Associates, 1981).

This picture is even bleaker given that 3 in 5 (61%) of the elderly Black participants in the Louis Harris 1981 survey used their savings to pay bills and expenses. One in 3 (38%) elderly Blacks reported having no savings reserve at all, compared to only 1 in 11 (9%) of elderly Whites (Harris & Associates, 1981). Moreover, between 1980 and 1982 the only two Black groups whose median total money income rose were married couples with wives in the paid labor force and unrelated men. By contrast, with the sole exception of aged female householders, White groups were better off in 1982 than in 1980 (Jackson, 1985).

Labor Force Participation

Across the life-cycle Black men and women experience significantly higher unemployment rates and higher underemployment rates than their White counterparts. About 11 million Black persons were in the civilian labor force in 1982, an increase of 2.7 million (31 percent) over 1972.(Matney & Johnson, 1983). According to a special report issued by the U.S. Bureau of the Census (Matney & Johnson, 1983), between 1972 and 1982 the number of employed Black persons grew by 1.4 million (19 percent), whereas the number of unemployed Black persons increased by 1.3 million (140%, from 900,000 in 1972 to 2.1 million in 1982).

Of those employed in 1980, Blacks were overrepresented in certain occupations. For example, although Blacks comprised about 10 percent of the total civilian labor force, they constituted 14 percent of all operators, fabricators, and laborers, and 18 percent of all service workers. In contrast, Blacks were underrepresented in managerial and professional specialty occupations (6%) and technical, sales, and administrative support occupations (8%). This situation was even more evident at the detailed occupational level. For example, Blacks accounted for over one-half (54%) of all the workers who were private household cleaners and servants, and one-fourth of all postal clerks and nursing aides, orderlies, and attendants. Conversely, Blacks were only 3 percent of all physicians, lawyers, and engineers, and 4 percent of managers and administrators (Matney & Johnson, 1983).

While most elderly persons (over 65) are not in the labor force, there are differences in the employment characteristics of elderly Blacks and Whites. About the same percentage (13%) of Blacks and Whites continue to work after age 65. Elderly Blacks, however, are concentrated in lower paying jobs. Furthermore, among men, Blacks have lower levels of life-time labor force participation than Whites. They also are more likely to have experienced long periods of unemployment due to discrimination and other causes. Not only do Black men accumulate less work experience, they also are more likely to leave the work force earlier. Thus, Black men, to a greater extent than their White counterparts, fall into the category of discouraged workers. Discouraged workers are those who are not working and, although they would like a job, are not looking for one because they do not think they can find one. They no longer appear in either unemployment or employment statistics. These disparities in the proportions of Blacks and Whites with jobs, or employment ratios, exists for all age groups, although they are particularly pronounced for young adults (aged 20-24) and elderly adults (aged 55 +).

In general, for elderly persons who need or want to continue to work, unemployment due to age discrimination is a serious problem. Older workers who are unemployed, stay out of work longer than younger workers, suffer a greater earning loss in subsequent jobs than younger workers, and are more likely to become discouraged, giving up the job search altogether. Thus, age further compounds this problem.

Summary. Overall, elderly persons who work full time tend to have incomes similar to younger persons of the same race and sex. Thus, occupational participation figures for elderly Blacks reflect the limited opportunities they have experienced during their younger years. As pointed out by Jackson and Gibson (1985) "Blacks are less well off economically than Whites, their economic deprivation is due, in the main to their disadvantaged labor force position over time" (p. 198). Furthermore, given that younger Blacks are still disproportionately concentrated in the lower paying jobs, and they are twice as likely as their White cohorts to be unemployed, an improvement in this situation does not appear to be in sight. Moreover, given the uncertain future of Social Security, Medicare, and other programs that favor the elderly, this situation may actually worsen.

In short, nearly every aspect of the lives of elderly Blacks is different from the average situation of elderly Whites, partially because, in general, elderly Blacks do not have as much money (NCCBA, 1987). Thus, the data not only supports the thesis that elderly Blacks on the average experience "double jeopardy", but most also experience "triple jeopardy", because they are old, Black and poor (NCCBA, 1987).

Health

It is a truism that health and mobility decline with advancing age, with the majority of elderly persons in their younger retirement years being relatively healthier than those in their older years. By the eighth and ninth decades of life, the chances of being limited in activity and in need of health and social services increase significantly (Nagi, 1976). Currently, almost a third of the nation's personal health care expenditures benefit the elderly. However, the elderly frequently bear a significant financial burden for health care. During the 1980's, the average out-of-pocket cost of health care equaled 15 percent of the elderly's income—the same as before Medicare was enacted (U.S. Senate Special Committee on Aging, 1985/86).

The patterns of illness and disease have changed in the past 80 years. Acute conditions were predominant at the turn of the century, while chronic conditions are now the more prevalent health problem for elderly persons (National Center for Health Statistics, 1981). Three out of four elderly persons die from heart disease, cancer, or stroke. Moreover, the types of conditions experienced by elderly people vary by sex and race. Elderly men are more likely than elderly women to experience acute illnesses that are life threatening, while elderly women are more likely to have chronic illnesses that cause physical limitations. Osteoporosis (a bone disease characterized by reduction in bone density accompanied by brittleness and associated with a loss of calcium from the bones), for example, is much more common among elderly women (in particular elderly White women) than men, while coronary heart disease is much more common among elderly men.

Differences in life expectancy between Blacks and Whites, however, strongly suggest the existence of health problems among certain segments of the population. The disparity between the death rates of Blacks and Whites (excess death) affect certain age/race groups more than others. Compared to Whites, Blacks have twice the rate of infant mortality. The disparity is smaller through age 24, followed by a sharp rise in excess deaths thereafter through age 64. Homicide was the major cause of excess deaths occurring in Blacks, especially Black males, age 25 to 44 years. Excess Black deaths between the ages of 45 to 69 were due mainly to cancer, heart disease, stroke, diabetes, and cirrhosis.

The health situation of elderly Blacks has been generally poorer than that of elderly Whites (Harel, 1985). For example, hypertension has been regularly more prevalent among Blacks 65 to 74 years old (45%) than Whites (33%), according to health data from 1971 to 1975 (U.S. Bureau of the Census, 1976). The Black elderly have also been more likely to be sick and disabled, and to see themselves as being in poor health than the White elderly (Jackson & Harel, 1983; Harel, 1985). Elderly Blacks have higher rates of chronic disease, functional impairment, and indicators of risk, such as high blood pressure. At age 65-75, the mortality of Blacks is higher than that of Whites. However, Blacks of extreme old age (75+) have lower mortality rates. This "survivor effect", or mortality crossover, has been attributed to hardiness among survivors in a population that has a higher early-age death rate. Overall, however, the Black elderly suffer more illnesses and die earlier, compared to Whites.

The bottom line is that economic deprivation has taken its toll throughout the lives of Blacks. It has caused, for example, many Blacks to skimp on their diets. This has produced deteriorating physical conditions and generally poorer health than for aged Whites (NCCBA, 1987).

The findings from both the 1974 and 1981 Harris polls parallel these data, with elderly Blacks reporting poorer health than their White counterparts. It was somewhat surprising, however, to find a drastic change in the perceptions of Blacks regarding the following question: "Older people today are healthier than older people were ten or twenty years ago?"

The combined (all racial groups) sample produced a 69 percent agreement rate to this question in 1974 and a 68 percent agreement figure in the 1981 sample. Agreement rates were shown to be higher for this (health-related) question than for a similar question concerning financial status, but lower than that obtained from a similar question concerning educational status. This pattern of responses held generally constant for both 1974 and 1981, with the possible exception of a more pessimistic view of financial status in the latter survey.

However, when the total sample is analyzed along the racial dimension, significant differences in response to the health question occur not only between Blacks and Whites—which, again, one might expect given the economic disparity between the two groups—but also between the 1974 and 1981 Black samples. The 1974 sample of Blacks revealed a 57 percent agreement rate with respect to the health question, while the 1981 sample showed a 37 percent rate of agreement. This seven-year 20 percent decline in perceptions regarding health is paralleled by a 8 percent decline in perceptions regarding finances, but—given margins of error—the financial decline is perhaps not nearly as significant as that regarding health.

It is perhaps worth noting that this decline has occurred despite advances in American medical care during the same seven-year period. However, as pointed out by the NCCBA report (1987) on the Black elderly, they are victims of the country's two-tier health system, in which the poor receive "welfare medicine", or in other words grossly inadequate health care, while the more affluent or those with adequate health insurance receive quality health care.

Mental Health

Many psychiatric problems are not as frequent for elderly persons as for younger persons, but cognitive impairment is a serious problem. According to recent studies by the National Institute of Mental Health (NIMH), persons 65 years and older were found to have the lowest rates of all age groups for eight mental disorders. However, the NIMH studies found mild cognitive impairment in about 14 percent of elderly males and females, and severe impairment in 5.6 percent of elderly men and 3 percent of elderly women (U.S. Senate Special Committee on Aging, 1985/86). Alzheimer's disease is the leading cause of cognitive impairment in the elderly. Another indicator of mental health problems, suicide rates (although extremely low when compared to other causes of death) are higher for elderly persons than for younger age groups (National Center for Health Statistics, 1981).

Suicide rates among elderly White men have dominated the national trends in suicide because they have generally been much higher than the rates for other race and sex groups. White male rates remain significantly higher than the other three race and sex groups, White men having increased their rate 15.6 percent from 17.80 persons in 100,000 for 1969/71 (3-year averaged rate) to 20.58 persons in 100,000 for 1979/81 (3-year averaged rate). However, an even greater increase of 37.60 percent in the suicide rate has occurred for Black men who, from 1969 to 1971, exhibited a 3-year averaged rate of 7.83 persons per 100,000, in contrast to 10.75 persons per 100,000 average rate for the period between 1979 and 1981. The suicide rate increased steadily with age for White males, with a high at age 85+ of 53.28 persons per 100,000 averaged rate for the 3-year period between 1979 to 1981 (Manton, Blazer, & Woodbury, 1987). Black men, however, showed a peak in their rate of suicide of 23.61 persons per 100,000 between the ages of 25 and 29, then a decline, and a leveling off after ages 45 to 49. The age at which the Black male's rate of suicide peaks corresponds to the age at which he is expected to be making a living, supporting a family, and competing in the market place. However, due to racism and discrimination inherent in the major institutions of the society (i.e., the educational system, labor market, justice system, etc.), many by this time have already become disillusioned, discouraged workers, or institutionalized.

The suicide rate for White females has actually declined from 7.10 persons per 100,000, average rate for the 3-year period between 1969 and 1971, down to 6.44 persons per 100,000 for the 3-year period 1979 to 1981. The rate shows a peak during the menopausal period (i.e., 45 to 55) which also probably coincides with changes in household composition due to adult children leaving home. For Black women, the suicide rate is much lower than for any of the other 3 race and sex groups, with no change in the 3-year average rate of 2.68 persons per 100,000 and 2.48 persons per

100,000, respectively. Furthermore, there is no specific pattern in their rate of suicide (Manton, Blazer, & Woodbury, 1987).

Thus, the data suggest that suicide in late life is not a homogeneous phenomenon, and it is specifically more characteristic of the advantaged group (e.g., Whites, especially males), than it is of the disadvantaged group (e.g., Blacks, and especially Black women, the most disadvantaged group).

Summary. Though elderly Blacks are less likely to commit suicide, which is an indicant of mental health, they are more prone to serious chronic physical illnesses. These findings should come as no surprise when one takes into account that Black people experience discrimination and racism that serves to expose them to the dirtiest, most hazardous, low paying jobs. Coupled with a lifetime of unhealthy living and working conditions, poor health care, and income that does not lend itself to a nutritious diet, it is apparent why a racial gap in health exists between Blacks and Whites.

Conclusions

The over all picture of the elderly as living comfortably is grossly misleading when the Black elderly is considered. A synthesis of the literature and the demographic information reviewed in this chapter—on geographical distribution and mobility, housing, living arrangement, marital status, income status, labor force participation, and health and mental health—strongly suggests that a significant correlation exists between the young adult experiences of Blacks and their experiences in old age; Blacks are discriminated against racially and thus are disadvantaged economically at all points along the life cycle. In fact, the evidence shows that a cumulative process of systemic discrimination from youth through elderhood either initially reduces the life chances of Blacks—particularly Black males—and then systematically stagnates or severely limits options of overcoming that process throughout the life span or it kills—either abruptly, or slowly, by degrees. For Blacks who survive into elderhood, the chances of enjoying a quality well-being are small indeed. Again, this is the consequence of the cumulative effect of the inadequacy and lack of benefits which, in effect, characterize the general life span experiences of Blacks in America, from youth to old age. This adversely affects family stability, living conditions, and health. Thus, it is not surprising that Blacks are more likely to be unmarried, to live in central cities, and to have shorter life spans than their White counterparts, regardless of age.

The preponderance of evidence shows that through 1981 the Black elderly had less chance of a successful social well-being in retirement than did their White counterparts. On measures of population proportion and life expectancy, the Black and White elderly both were experiencing rapid increases, though given the traditionally larger population proportion of White elderly compared to Black elderly and the greater life expectancy for Whites overall than for Blacks, the gaps between the groups largely remained. However, a much more telling and significant set of factors—the economic status of the elderly (income, employment, housing, and health)—demonstrated a very serious difference in the living conditions and access to the well-being of elderly who are Black and elderly who are White. The Black elderly tended to be more poverty-stricken, less rewarded (and more discouraged) in seeking supplemental employment, less able to afford decent housing, and more debilitated in terms of health problems than their White counterparts. These consequences are systematically related much more than they are a result of individual inadequacy and incompetency among the Black aged.

Thus, it can be said that the majority of elderly Blacks now encounter the "double jeopardy" of age and race, and a disproportionate number experience "triple jeopardy" because they are old, Black and poor.

In fact, suicide was the only significant statistic in which the Black elderly did not "lead." Although the data showed an increase among Black males, that percentage increase and the overall rate among Black males was still very small compared to White males. Black females demonstrated no appreciable increase in their already low suicide rates.

Since 1981 the federal administration has had a powerful impact on the level and quality of services available to the elderly. It will be very instructive to do timely research now on the status of the Black elderly, especially looking at whether the Black suicide rate has significantly increased given the government's ability to make an already marginal existence by the Black elderly a truly hopeless situation.

As poignantly stated in a very recent NCCBA report (1987), "a nation as powerful as the United States clearly has the capacity to assure that its senior citizens can live in dignity and self-respect. What is needed is commitment [to all its elderly] and an action plan " (p. 17) to achieve it.

Notes

1 A household consists of all the persons who occupy a housing unit. A house, an apartment or other group of rooms, or single room is regarded as a housing unit when it is occupied or intended for occupancy as separate living quarters; that is, when the occupants do not live and eat with any other persons in the

structure and there is direct access from the outside or through a common hall (U.S. Bureau of the Census, 1985, p. 37).

2 The term "family" refers to a group of two or more persons (one of whom is the householder) related by birth, marriage, or adoption and residing together; all such persons (including related subfamily members) are considered members of the same family. Thus, if the son of the householder and the son's wife are in the household, they are treated as part of the householder's family. However, a lodger and his wife not related to the householder or an unrelated servant and his wife are considered as additional families, not a part of the householder's family. These unrelated subfamilies are not included in the count of total families (U.S. Bureau of the Census, 1985, p. 38).

3 Excess deaths expresses the difference between the number of deaths actually observed in a minority group and the number of deaths that would have occurred in that group if it experienced the same death rates for each age and sex as the White population (National Center for Health Statistics, 1981).

References

Comptroller General of the United States. (1977). The well-being of old people in Cleveland, Ohio. Washington: U.S. General Accounting Office.

Dowd, J. A. & Bengston, V.L. (1978) Aging in minority populations: An examination of the double jeopardy hypothesis. *Journal of Gerontology, 33,* 427-436.

Frey, W. H. (1984). Life course migration of metropolitan Whites and Blacks and the structure of demographic change in large central cities. *American Sociological Review, 49,* 808-827.

Harel, Z. (1985). Nutrition site service users: Does racial background make a difference? *The Gerontologist, 25*(3), 286-291.

Harris, L. & Associates. (1981). *Aging in the eighties: America in transition.* A survey conducted for the National Council on Aging.

Harris, L. & Associates. (1974). *A survey on aging: Experience of older Americans vs. public expectations on old age.* A survey conducted for the National Council on Aging.

Hill, R. (1978). A demographic profile of the Black elderly. *Aging,* Nos. 287-288, U.S. Department of Health, Education, and Welfare, Administration of Aging, 297-303.

Honzik, M. P. (1984). Life-span development. *Annual Review Psychology, 35,* 309-331.

Jackson, J. J. (1985). Aged Black Americans: Double jeopardy re-examined. *Journal of Minority Aging, 10*(1),25-61.

Jackson, J. S., & Gibson, R. C. (1985). Work and retirement among the Black elderly. In Z. S. Blau (Ed.) *Current perspectives on aging and the life cycle, 1,* p. 193-222.

Jackson, M. & Harel, Z. (1983). Ethnic differences in social support networks. *Urban Health, 9*, 35-38.

Jackson, M., Kolody, B. & Wood, J. (1982). To be old and Black: The case for double jeopardy on income and health. In R. C. Manuel (Ed.), *Minority aging*, pp. 77-82, Westport, Connecticut: Greenwood Press.

Jackson, M. & Wood, J. L. (1976). *The Black aged: Aging in America*. (No. 5), Washington D.C.: National Council on Aging.

Kart, C. S. (1981). *The realities of aging: An introduction to Gerontology*. Boston: Allyn and Bacon, Inc.

Manton, K., Blazer, D. & Woodbury, M. (1987). Suicide in middle age and later life: Sex and race specific life table and cohort analyses. *Journal of Gerontology, 42*(2), 219-227.

Manuel, R. C. (1982, March). *A re-examination of the double jeopardy hypothesis*. Paper presented at Norfolk State College.

Matney, W. C. & Johnson, D. L. (1983, July). *America's Black population, 1970 to 1982: A statistical view*. Washington, D.C.: United States Department of Commerce, Bureau of the Census.

Munnicks, M., & Olbrich, C. (1985). *Life-span and change in a gerontological perspective*. Orando: Academic Press.

Nagi, S. (1976). An epidemiology of disability among adults in the United States. *Millbank Memorial Fund Quarterly, 54*, 439-467.

National Caucus and Center on Black Aged, Inc., (NCCBA). (1987, July). *The status of the Black elderly*. A report prepared for the Select Committee on Aging, House of Representatives 100 Congress 1st session. Comm. Pub. No. 100-622. U.S. Government Printing Office, Washington, D.C.

National Center for Health Statistics. (1981). *Monthly Vital Statistics Report.* Provisional Data, *29*, No. 13.

National Council on the Aging. (1971). *Triple jeopardy: Myth or reality.* Washington, D.C.: National Council on the Aging.

National Urban League. (1964). *Double jeopardy: The old Negro in America today*.New York: National Urban League.

Pettigrew, T. F. (1980). Racial change and the intrametropolitan distribution of Black Americans. In P. Solomon (Ed.) *The prospective city*, Cambridge, MA: M.I.T. Press.

Phillips, M. (1986). *A portrait of older minorities*. The American Association of Retired Persons, Minority Affairs Initiative, Pamphlet.

Riley, M. W., Johnson, M. & Fonner, A. (1972). *Aging and society. Vol. 3. A sociology of age stratification*. New York: Russell Sage.

Siegel, S. J. (1980). On the demography of aging. *Demography, 17*(4), 345-364.

Soldo, B. & Manton, K. (1986). The graying of America: Demographic challenges for socioeconomic planning. *The Journal of Socio-Economic Planning Sciences.*

Talley, T. & Kaplan, J. (1956, December). The Negro aged. *Newsletter*, Gerontological Society, p. 6.

Taeuber, K. E. (1975). Racial segregation: The persisting dilemma. *Annals of the American Academy of Political and Social Science, 442*, 87-96.

U.S. Bureau of the Census. (1976). Household and family characteristics. *Current Population Reports*, Series p-20, No. 311.

U.S. Bureau of the Census. (1980). *The social economic status of the Black population in the United States: An historical view, 1790-1978*. U.S. Department of Commerce, Special Studies, Series p-23, No. 80.

U.S. Bureau of the Census. (1983, December). Current Population, Reports, Special Studies. *Population Profile of the United States: 1982.* Series p-23, No. 130.

U.S. Bureau of the Census. (1985, July). Current Population Reports, Series p-20, No. 399. *Marital Status and Living Arrangements: March 1984,* U. S. Department of Commerce, Bureau of the Census.

U.S. Commission on Civil Rights. (1982, June). *Minority elderly services: New programs, old problems, part I.* Washington, D.C.: Government Printing Office.

U.S. Senate Special Committee on Aging. (1985/86). *Aging in America: Trends and projections.* Prepared in conjunction with American Association of Retired Persons, the Federal Council on Aging, and the Administration on Aging.

Watson, W. H. (1983). Selected demographic and social aspects of older Blacks: An analysis with policy implications. In R. L. McNealy & J. L. Colen (Eds.) *Aging in minority groups,* pp. 42-49, California: Sage Publications.

Williams, B. S. (1980). *Characteristics of the Black elderly.* United States Department of Health and Human Services, Office of Human Development Services, Administration on Aging, National Clearinghouse on Aging.

Part II
Mental Health

QUALITY OF LIFE AND SUBJECTIVE WELL-BEING AMONG BLACK AMERICANS

Linda M. Chatters and James S. Jackson

Introduction

Over thirty years of work have been devoted to examining the quality of life (QOL) and subjective well-being (SWB) of the general U.S. population. Quality of life and subjective well-being (a type of social indicator as suggested by Andrews, 1982) research evolved from a shared background (Schuessler & Fisher, 1985) and the distinction between these efforts is largely obscured. Both approaches focus on individual expressions of satisfaction or happiness with one's life (global and domain-specific), examine these reports at the aggregate level (e.g., cities, nations), conduct cross-national and international comparisons, and examine trends in these reports across time. Perhaps the most useful distinction is that QOL research is more directly aimed at policy outcomes and is more readily applicable to rhetorical uses within a political and social policy context (Schuessler & Fisher, 1985). For the purposes of this discussion, QOL and SWB will be used interchangeably.

Despite a long tradition of work, research on adult Blacks has generally failed to provide a coherent and comprehensive picture of QOL/SWB processes for this group (Campbell, Converse & Rodgers, 1976; Jackson, Chatters & Neighbors, 1986). SWB research among Black Americans generally has been fragmented and involved small and unrepresentative samples. Subjective well-being research among older (i.e., 55 years of age and above) Blacks within the gerontology literature has been more numerous, but similarly suffers from the use of restricted samples of respondents. Emergent perspectives and research on the adult Black population, coupled with a current general interest in pursuing integrative approaches to SWB, suggests that a reconsideration of these issues and their significance to Black Americans is both timely and potentially rewarding.

While SWB research has been approached from a number of disciplines (i.e., gerontology, psychology, sociology), age (or stage of life) has proved to be an important demarcation for the efforts of many. The topic is primarily divided into work which is either oriented toward the general adult (i.e., non-gerontological) population or has an exclusviely gerontological focus. Other work examines life-cycle variations in well-being as present during early adulthood and marriage, parenthood and childrearing, post-childhood, and retirement. Further, SWB research has employed both survey research and experimental methods, single-item and multiple-item measures of well-being, a variety of analytic procedures, and substantially divergent samples of respondents. It is only recently that researchers from these disparate traditions have begun to recognize the need for work which provides for collaboration in research ideas, a more explicit understanding of how these disparate efforts relate to one another, and an integrative approach to SWB across the life span (Diener, 1984; Herzog, Rodgers & Woodworth, 1982).

Contemporary assessments of the well-being literature (Diener, 1984; George, 1981) indicate that while there is not a strict consensus of thought, a conventional definition of SWB is emerging. Subjective well-being, as the overarching construct, is commonly characterized by a focus on subjective experience as opposed to objective conditions, the explicit inclusion of positive indices, and the use of an overall evaluation of life (Diener, 1984). Gerontological conceptions of SWB are distinctive in that they frequently incorporate specific references to age or time of life and contain ideological elements (Diener, 1984; George, 1981; Kozma & Stones, 1978). Current definitions underscore the fact that SWB encompasses several associated, but discrete concepts, such as life satisfaction, happiness, morale, and psychiatric symptomatology (George, 1981).

These well-being concepts diverge from one another in several critical ways. Specifically, they differ in whether they involve primarily cognitive vs. affective processes, measure positive vs. negative experiences, involve transitory mood states as opposed to more enduring judgments, and utilize current vs. lifetime experience as their frame of reference (Kozma & Stones, 1978). Extensive reviews of the SWB literature provide a general orientation to this work (Diener, 1984; Diener & Griffin 1984; Adams, 1971; Lohmann, 1977; Schuessler & Fisher, 1985), and discussions of conceptual and methodological considerations, major correlates, and psychometric and structural properties (Larson, 1978; George, 1981; George & Bearon, 1980).

Given that the focus of the present chapter is on SWB theory and research as they pertain specifically to the adult Black population, it is important and appropriate to ask whether or not the concept in its current expression has relevance and significance for minority groups. The historical development of the topic of SWB (particularly the paucity of work addressing status group differences in its meaning), disputes regarding conceptual definitions and connotations, the challenges to measurement, and problems in comparability across investigations, suggest that a considerable amount of work remains to be completed.

The general inquiry into these issues, however, does not presuppose that the investigation of subjective evaluations of life quality within minority populations is without significance. However, it is important to know whether or not SWB exhibits conceptual equivalence across racial groups (and indeed, across other important social status categories such as socioeconomic status and gender), and that we understand what is meant when members of minority groups report on their levels of life quality. The potential policy implications and applications of quality of life indicators argues that we should be thoroughly cognizant of their significance to individuals, their relation to objective life circumstances, and the particular aspects of personal experience that they embody.

Researchers in the area have emphasized the similarities across racial groups in the observed relationships involving SWB evaluations (Andrews & Withey, 1976). Others (Jackson, Herzog & Chatters, 1980; Herzog, Rodgers & Woodworth, 1982; Campbell et al., 1976), however, have observed that the patterns of relationships within Black samples are slightly different than those for the general population. These divergences are potentially indicative of the operation of different mechanisms in the development of SWB across racial groups (Jackson et al., 1980). The generally inferior status position of Blacks in economic, social, and political spheres within American society, suggests that the processes underlying the development of perceptions of well-being might diverge from those in the majority group (Jackson, Chatters & Neighbors, 1986). The nature of these potential differences has not been adequately delineated or explored in past efforts.

The present chapter attempts to address these concerns and questions regarding SWB evaluations among the adult Black population. Specifically, the discussion focuses on the theoretical models which underpin their use and their relevance to the experiences of Black Americans. The chapter itself incorporates a life-span orientation and uses that perspective as its pivotal organizing theme. Consequently, the chapter begins with a discussion of the life-span viewpoint and its general relevance for understanding SWB among Black Americans. A background of SWB research and of the various explanatory models of well-being is then provided. Following that, trends in SWB for Blacks and Whites and overall racial differences in SWB are explored.

Finally, a review of research on the life quality of Black Americans will be presented. The scarcity of previous systematic research among Black Americans suggest the need to explore the influences of sociodemographic factors within a representative sample of this population group. A collection of studies of well-being, which are based on a national sample of the adult Black population (i.e., the National Survey of Black Americans), allow the investigation of the effects of social status factors on reports of life quality. The role of socioeconomic resources (i.e., income and education) in determining well-being evaluations among this group is accorded particular attention for a number of reasons. Specifically, models of SWB which imply that socioeconomic resources are critical determinants of well-being (either directly or through mediating factors) are prominent in the literature. Conflicting evidence regarding their significance for well-being is possibly due to the lack of samples of Black adults in which there exists an adequate and representative range on demographic factors. The availability of a representative national sample of Black adults, permits the investigation of these issues. Age status is also granted special notice due to the observed age differences in these perceptions and the possibility that age and age cohort effects may moderate the relationship between socioeconomic resources and well-being (Campbell et al., 1976; Janson & Mueller, 1983; Herzog et al., 1982; Veroff, Douvan & Kulka, 1981; Jackson, Herzog & Chatters, 1980). The chapter concludes with a discussion of current models of SWB and areas requiring further theoretical work and investigation are discussed.

Life-span Perspectives on Black Development

A central thesis of this chapter is that a life-span perspective on SWB is crucial to understanding the nature of these and other social-psychological processes among Black Americans. A life-span orientation to SWB suggests that personal adjustment in middle and late adulthood is a reflection of developments which occur over the lifetime of the individual. While the idea of lifelong development is hardly a novel one, it is only recently that life-span models of development have received serious and systematic treatment. An example of a life-span approach suggests that the generally lower levels of education (relative to younger persons) present among current cohorts of older individuals, reflects the prevalent societal mores and expectations for educational achievement that were in operation during their formative years. An appreciation of age group (i.e., cohort) differences in average levels of education is important for understanding the differential influence of education as a predictor of other behaviors.

Black-Adult Development and Aging

The utilization of a life-span approach is particularly appealing among Black Americans because it is a succinct means to organize a variety of factors and forces which impinge on the development of Blacks. Specifically, because a life-span perspective suggests that past life circumstances have an impact on present status, age cohort and period (i.e., historical) influences are given prominence. Present cohorts of middle and older age Blacks have lived through a period of substantial change in race relations within American society and in the status position of Blacks as a group. These changes have meant that over several decades, the distribution of economic, educational, occupational, political, and other personal and social resources for Blacks has been radically altered. Accordingly, the structure of societal opportunities and rewards for Blacks as a group has undergone substantial change. These age cohort and/or historical period differences in the social and political environments of successive cohorts of Black Americans means that they are likely to view their position within society (and potentially their satisfaction with that status) in very different ways.

Further, it is often assumed that relationships involving these objective status indicators (e.g., between income level and SWB) are essentially invariant across age groups. However, differences in the conditions of one's earlier life could also relate to differences in the predictive capabilities of objective status measures for SWB evaluations. As a consequence of differences over time in the resources available to Blacks as a group, contemporary cohorts of older Blacks could view objective status indicators as much less important for determining their sense of well-being (Veroff et al., 1981). Consequently, the predictive capabilities of these measures could be diminished among this cohort of Blacks, but heightened among younger groups.

While the discussion has focused on changes in objective status measures and their relationship to SWB, another relatively unexplored area of interest concerns differences in political ideology socialization which are evident among successive cohorts of Black Americans (i.e., the impact of the Civil Rights Movement, the Brown vs. The Board of Education decision, Voter Rights Act), and its potential for affecting the well-being evaluations of Blacks. The widening of social and political opportunities for Black Americans could mean that as a group they would begin to converge with Whites and become more similar in the correlates and structure of well-being. It is also possible that to the extent that these advances are isolated among the middle-classes, a widening cleavage could emerge and more firmly entrench differences between upwardly mobile Blacks and the Black lower and under-classes (Jackson, Chatters & Neighbors, 1986).

Life-span Issues in SWB Models

Life-span issues are evident in several gerontological models of SWB (Herzog et al., 1982). Particular life-span conceptualizations emphasize that the life course constitutes a pattern of social roles and obligations (Rosow, 1985; Hagestad & Neugarten, 1985). The loss of major life roles (e.g. spouse, worker) with advancing age, as well as the lack of roles which are regarded as socially important, result in a dearth of meaningful outlets for older individuals. As a consequence, older persons assume a roleless state with concomitant ambiguity regarding normative behaviors and expectations. Further, there is an inability to draw upon roles and their fulfillment as sources of satisfaction and well-being in old age (Witt, Lowe, Peek & Curry, 1980).

Another life-span approach focuses on both the availability of socioeconomic and personal resources over the life course as well as current levels of resources in understanding adjustment in old age and SWB evaluations. One line of thought suggests that documented declines in personal health status and income with increasing age will potentially influence (i.e., depress) the SWB levels of older persons. Further, the experience of lifelong disadvantage is thought to facilitate adjustment to old age (i.e., reflecting a smaller discrepancy between middle-age and old age levels of these resources), whereas a marked difference between resources prior to and those available in old age (e.g., pre- and post-retirement income) results in poor adjustment (Dowd & Bengtson, 1978; Ortega, et al., 1983). Despite the presence of life-span themes in these models, the exclusive focus on older adults within the gerontological literature has ignored the question of whether the identified processes are applicable to younger groups.

The Background of Subjective Well-Being Research

The issue of SWB has had a long history within the field of adult development and aging. Gerontological treatments of SWB emerged from a tradition of research which had as an early focus the delineation of optimal or successful patterns of aging. Prominent among these efforts were theories and models of aging which were largely prescriptive in nature. The disengagement and activity theories of aging were influential in generating myriad empirical investigations concerning the issue of subjective well-being in aging. However, they were by in large, unsuccessful (as originally formulated) in accurately describing SWB processes and the factors which governed them.

Following this, research focused on the conceptualization and measurement of SWB concepts which were independent of implicit value connotations and assumptions regarding optimal aging. Scales of SWB for use among specifically older populations (Lawton, 1975; Morris & Sherwood, 1975; Neugarten, Havighurst & Tobin, 1961; Wood, Wylie & Sheafor, 1969; Kozma & Stones, 1980), as well as investigations of single-item measures and multi-item scales intended for more general applications were developed. The variety of work on SWB resulted in vast differences in how it was defined and measured, with the attendant difficulties of lack of conceptual and methodological precision (George, 1981). Similarly, divergences in the methods (i.e., samples, age ranges, and analysis procedures) which were exercised across studies impeded comparative work (Jackson, Herzog, & Chatters, 1980).

An interest in subjective well-being which parallels that of social gerontology arose out of a line of investigation which was concerned with population-based reports of life quality. Research on the quality of life (QOL) and social indicators generally refer to broad-based programs of work which are geared toward the development of sets of both objective and subjective indices through which societal change can be objectively measured and monitored (Land, 1975). Focused on various facets of life, this work attempts to assess how individuals perceive and evaluate objective conditions (i.e., subjective indicators), as well as their factual reports regarding those conditions (i.e., objective indicators).

Subjective and objective social indicators are distinct not only in the content they tap, but also in their relationship to one another and other measures. Generally, subjective and objective measures are only weakly correlated. Rather than being isomorphic with one another, subjective and objective indicators are viewed as providing complementary information on life quality (Andrews, 1982; Rossi & Gilmartin, 1980; Campbell, Converse & Rodgers, 1976). In addition to work which investigates global evaluations of life (i.e., general life satisfaction and happiness), other research on life quality assessments examine domains of life concerns (e.g., evaluations of family, work, leisure).

Interpretations of Subjective Well-Being

Progress toward theoretical explanations of SWB evaluations has been limited (Diener, 1984) and research on SWB has been criticized as being fragmented and largely atheoretical (George, 1981; Jackson, Herzog & Chatters, 1980). While various theoretical models of SWB have been advanced, the task of clearly elaborating these approaches (e.g., the development of explicit theoretical propositions, construct definition) and proposing the specific manner in which they are related to one another has yet to be completed (Diener, 1984). Reflecting the fragmented character of SWB research, work which is focused on gerontological samples and research among the general population are relatively isolated from one another. Gerontological approaches to SWB have frequently incorporated specific age referents in item content which limit their usefulness when applied to the general adult population (Diener, 1984). Further, although social gerontological models of SWB commonly embody life-span themes and implications (which would be useful in the development of general theory), they have remained relatively unexplored (Herzog, Rodgers, & Woodworth, 1982). Non-gerontological conceptualizations of SWB, on the other hand, typically ignore the potential influence that age has on these evaluations. Despite this, several theoretical orientations to SWB are articulated in the literature (George, 1981; Herzog, Rodgers, & Woodworth, 1982; Kozma & Stones, 1978) and provide a basis for understanding these phenomena among adult Blacks. The separate presentation of these models of SWB is somewhat misleading, since these interpretations of well-being contain comparable ideas and perspectives (e.g., life-span orientations).

Disengagement and Activity Perspectives on SWB

Within the social gerontology tradition, the debate between disengagement and activity theories of aging underscored two general explanations of SWB (George, 1981). The *disengagement perspective* suggested that with the coming of old age, the relationship between the individual and society underwent a profound alteration. Old age witnessed a mutual withdrawal of individual and society to establish a new equilibrium predicated on relinquishing or disengaging from social roles and obligations. The disengagement argument suggested that older individuals, faced with declining opportunities to obtain satisfaction from social roles, progressively disengaged from them and invested in other goals (i.e., intrapsychic).

In contrast to the disengagement perspective, the *activity theory* of aging suggested that activity (and more specifically social activity and interaction) generated a sense of well-being (Diener, 1984). Subjective well-being was achieved by maintaining levels of activity and involvement which were characteristic of middle-age. Activity itself, is a central concept in several formulations in gerontology such as continuity and role theories (Horan & Belcher, 1982), and social gerontologists defined activity very broadly to include both social behaviors and interaction and solitary activities.

The empirical evidence for these models of aging was not overwhelming, and both theories as originally formulated were regarded as obvious oversimplifications of aging processes (George, 1981; Herzog, Rodgers, & Woodworth, 1982). Similar to research on other groups of older adults, older Blacks failed to exhibit a normative and universal pattern of disengagement from social roles and activities. Rather than one exclusive progression of events (whether of continued activity or disengagement from social roles), diversity in patterns of social aging were observed.

Resource Models of SWB

A concern with objective circumstances and their relationship to subjective evaluations of life quality was reflected in studies of the sociodemographic correlates of SWB (George, 1981). The *resource model* of SWB suggested that the personal and economic resources (e.g., income, health, marital status) that an individual possessed or that are characteristically associated with particular social status positions (i.e., race and gender) were important in maintaining SWB (Herzog, Rodgers, & Woodworth, 1982). The utilization of a resource model to explain SWB evaluations among the Black population predicts that levels of well-being should reflect trends in Black performance in political, economic, and social spheres. Socioeconomic status measures would then function as general monitors of the status of Blacks as a group and bear a positive relationship to overall evaluations of life quality (Jackson, Chatters & Neighbors, 1986). Empirical evidence documenting trends in SWB for Black Americans indicates a substantial disparity between improvements in the objective life conditions and subjective evaluations of life quality (Jackson, Chatters & Neighbors, 1986).

Conceptualizations of the relationship between resources and SWB which proposed a one-to-one correspondence between resources and well-being demonstrated generally weak relationships (Andrews, 1982). Others (Diener, 1984; Andrews, 1982) suggested that subjective judgments of life domains are closer in the causal sequence to overall SWB, and further, domain judgments incorporate a variety of subjective factors which function to mediate the relationship between objective conditions and SWB (Michalos, 1980; Herzog, Rodgers, & Woodworth, 1982). Relationships between domain satisfactions (e.g., satisfaction with income) and overall evaluations of life quality demonstrate generally higher correlations than those involving objective status indicators (e.g., actual reported income) and well-being (Diener, 1984; Campbell, 1981).

Within the field of gerontology a special form of a resource model, the *double jeopardy hypothesis,* was advanced to explain the social status position of elderly groups and their adjustment in aging. Specifically, for older Blacks (and other racial minorities) the problems of old age were accompanied and compounded by a life history of racial discrimination within the wider society. Double and multiple jeopardy hypotheses (National Council on Aging, 1971; Lindsay, 1971) of various forms (i.e., combining the adverse effects of age, race, gender, and poverty) suggested that older people who possessed a devalued position on several of these social status indicators, were in precarious circumstances in terms of social and eocnmic resources. This disadvantaged situation was predicted to be evident in the overall evaluations of life quality of older minority adults as well. In support of a double jeopardy interpretation, real discrepancies in objective status position (favoring White elderly) have been noted for the aged of racial minority and majority groups (Dowd & Bengtson, 1978). It has been less clear, however, whether jeopardy hypotheses are adequate to explain differences in SWB evaluations across racial groups. Several investigators have failed to find significant racial differences in well-being for older adults (Jackson & Walls, 1978; Ward & Kilburn, 1983), while others (Register, 1981; Jackson, Kolody, & Wood, 1982) report lower SWB among older Blacks.

A competing model of the relationship between age and race statuses suggested that advancing age functioned to diminish those racial inequities which existed in earlier periods of the life cycle (Dowd & Bengtson, 1978). In effect, the *age-as-leveler hypothesis* stated that across racial groups, as individuals approached old age they became more alike on status position indicators due to the overriding importance of the influence of age status. A corollary assumption suggested that adjustment to aging was less formidable for minority elderly because the apparent status differentials before and after reaching old age were less acute than that among majority elderly (Ortega, Crutchfield & Rushing, 1983). The age-as-leveler hypothesis has had only limited support. Social status disparities between racial groups in their progression from middle-aged to older age are, in some instances, more pronounced (Dowd & Bengston, 1978). The evidence suggests that membership in a racial minority group apparently has an enduring and lifelong effect on the social status position of current cohorts of elderly (Jackson & Gibson, 1985). A review (J. J. Jackson, 1985) of research on the double jeopardy and age-as-leveler hypotheses suggests several deficiencies including the absence of adequate theoretical development, the lack of clearly defined and testable hypotheses, and the need to employ appropriate methodologies to distinguish between age differences, age changes, and cohort and historical period effects in SWB (Schaie et al., 1982).

Judgment Theories of SWB

As suggested in the previous discussion, the relationship between objective circumstances and overall evaluations of those conditions is not identical. Cognizant of the discrepancies between objective circumstances and subjective evaluations, the general class of *judgment theories* of SWB incorporated a relativistic viewpoint. Judgment theories suggested that a sense of well-being arose from subjective processes involving comparisons of one's own status with important points of reference (Diener, 1984; Michalos, 1980, 1985). The relevant reference points could be other people (i.e., social comparison), aspirations for one's own situation, past life circumstances, or adjustments and adaptations to present events and circumstances. Judgments or comparisons of status position between societal groups and comparisons of one's own status relative to expended effort (e.g., relative deprivation and status inconsistency hypotheses, respectively) have often been utilized to explain reported levels of well-being observed in the Black population. The apparent discrepancy between trends in SWB reports for Blacks over many years and the manifest social, economic, and political improvement of Blacks as a group, suggests that there are substantial divergences between expectations for advancement and actual achieved progress (Jackson, Chatters & Neighbors, 1986).

Other writers (Carp & Carp, 1982) have proposed that perceptions of societal inequities as reflected in differentials in social status position may be more predictive of the SWB of older adults than the discrepancies between individual aspirations and achievements. In relation to the subjective well-being of adult Blacks, similar processes can be posited consisting of comparisons between one's status in relation to same- and different-race peers as well as self-comparisons of one's life at earlier stages in the life cycle (i.e., aspirations versus achievements).

Observed positive relationships between age and SWB evaluations (Clemente & Sauer, 1976; Alston, Lowe & Wrigley, 1974; Czaja, 1975) prompted interpretations which utilized judgment theory reasoning to explain differences in well-being. One model proposed a decline in aspiration level and expectations with increasing age (Campbell, Converse, & Rodgers, 1976). The comparison of one's current situation employing these reduced aspiration and expectation levels produces a diminished discrepancy between relevant reference points and an enhancement of SWB. A related explanation based on adaptation or accommodative processes, suggests that over time exposure to events and conditions tends to produce satisfaction with those circumstances (Diener, 1984; Herzog, Rodgers, & Woodworth, 1982).

The expectation of differences between major age groups or cohorts in the determinants of SWB is based in part on the notion that the choice of relevant reference points for comparisons may be influenced by life history and experiences. Some evidence suggests that sociodemographic factors have a differential influence on the SWB evaluations of Blacks of various age groups (Jackson, Herzog & Chatters, 1980; Jackson, Chatters & Neighbors, 1986). In particular, for older Blacks who have experienced lifelong disadvantage in these areas, income and education (and the implied comparisons along these dimensions) are less central determinants of well-being.

For younger cohorts of Blacks who have witnessed widening opportunities in these areas, the role of income and education may be more important and assume a more central role in predicting well-being (Jackson, Herzog & Chatters, 1980). Glenn (1980) suggests that difficulties in actualizing expected occupational and economic gains is a possible explanation for lowered reports of happiness among younger cohorts of the general population. In a related vein, Veroff et al. (1981) suggest that having achieved a particular level of social or economic status, the impact of income on well-being is diminished among middle-aged persons. Among younger individuals who are yet achieving in these areas, income plays a more central role in well-being evaluations.

Aging, Stress and SWB

In recent years, researchers have begun to examine whether aging itself constitutes a special disadvantage in terms of the levels of stress which are encountered. While models of *aging and stress* are yet evolving, notions of stress are implicit in much of the writing on aging, and indicate that this period of life has unique, identifiable life events or occurrences that convey presumptive stress (e.g., widowhood, retirement, declining health). Others (House & Robbins, 1983) have suggested that the physical changes associated with aging may constitute risk factors for poor health outcomes. Finally, similar to research on the general adult population, there is interest in whether social and psychological factors are important in resisting the effects of stress for older persons as well.

Empirical research on stress and coping among older populations has been slow to develop because of a number of methodological and conceptual limitations (Chiriboga & Cutler, 1980; House & Robbins, 1983; Lazarus & DeLongis, 1983). Specifically, life event and stress methodologies have been criticized for their failure to reflect the events of later life in terms of general representativeness, content validity, and appropriate weighting systems. These scales have received criticism in similar areas in connection with research on racial minority groups.

The literature on stress and adaptation documents several age differences and variations. Older persons have been found to report fewer life events than younger persons and the attendant disruption or stress is less severe (Masuda & Holmes, 1978). However, given the noted criticisms of the life event approach, these findings are regarded as tentative. Other work which examines individual's responses to identical events (i.e., natural disasters) suggests that older victims have less severe reactions and experience lower levels of distress (Bell, 1978; Huerta & Horton, 1978) than younger ones. Emergent work on stress and adaptation focuses on events which are less traumatic in nature than life events. These approaches examine stress and adaptation in relation to role strains, chronic problems, the timing and scheduling of normative life transitions, and daily hassles. Researchers have begun the work of isolating these events and investigating their impact on physical and mental well-being in a systematic manner (House & Robbins, 1983).

Comparative Trends and Racial Differences

Social indicator measures have been used in large national surveys of the American population over a number of years. These efforts, however, have provided relatively little information regarding the life quality of Black Americans (Campbell, 1981). The small numbers of

Blacks who comprise the subsamples of these surveys are of questionable representativeness. As a consequence, generalizations to the larger Black population should be undertaken with caution (Diener, 1984; Jackson, et al., 1980). Taken together, the results of several investigations indicate that over a number of data collections and points of time, Blacks view their lives less positively than do Whites (Andrews & Withey, 1976; Jackson, Herzog & Chatters, 1980).

A recent examination (Jackson Chatters & Neighbors, 1986) of comparative trends in SWB used data from a number of national surveys of the general population, non-national surveys, and two national surveys of the general population. The national data on the Black population were taken from the National Surveys of Black Americans and the National Black Election Study conducted by the Institute for Social Research (The University of Michigan). Distributions for reports of satisfaction with life for the general population and for Black Americans indicates that evaluations for Blacks and Whites were roughly similar in 1965. Subsequent years demonstrate a decline in satisfaction for Blacks, followed by an upturn in reports of satisfaction for 1978. This trend culminates in 1980 with the highest reported levels of both satisfaction and dissatisfaction for the Black population. Jackson et al. (1986) suggest that the trends possibly reflect an increasing polarization in reports of life satisfaction among particular demographic subgroups of the Black population. In contrast, reports of life satisfaction for the general population remained fairly constant during this period. Turning to happiness ratings, lower levels of happiness were found for Blacks in 1957. Both Blacks and Whites demonstrated first a decline in reports of being very happy, followed by an upswing in subsequent years. While reports of unhappiness declined over the years, Black Americans were consistently more negative in their evaluations than were members of the general population.

Studies of SWB among older Black adults have documented racial similarities and differences on a variety of dependent measures (Jackson, 1971a). Black elderly have been found to score both lower (Register, 1981; Alston, Lowe & Wrigley, 1972; Donnenwerth, Guy, & Norvell, 1978; Lipman, 1966; Youman, 1963) and higher (Messer, 1968; Kivett, 1982; Campbell et al., 1976; Bengtson, 1979; Linn, Hunter & Perry, 1979) than White elderly on SWB measures. Other studies (Sauer, 1977; Clemente & Sauer, 1974; National Council on the Aging, 1975; Rubenstein, 1971; Spreitzer & Snyder, 1974; Ortega et al., 1983) report no differences between Black and White elderly when socioeconomic status and other factors are controlled. As a whole, this work is characterized by the use of a variety of methodological and analytic procedures. In particular, the use of bivariate versus multivariate analysis and differences in the set of control variables which are examined in multivariate treatments represent significant sources of variability. As a consequence, it is difficult to say with certainty whether there are consistent race differences in SWB and the exact nature of those effects.

Correlates and Predictors of SWB

A group of studies which examine the correlates and predictors of SWB among older Black adults indicates that health status is a preeminent concern, with better health being consistently and positively related to reports of well-being (Ball, 1983; Himes & Hamlet, 1962; Ehrlich, 1973; Jackson, Bacon, & Peterson, 1977; Sauer, 1977; Chatters, 1977; Jackson, Herzog, & Chatters, 1980; Jackson, Chatters, & Neighbors, 1982; Chatters, 1983). Marital status differences indicate that being married is important for well-being among this group (Ehrlich, 1973; Jackson, Bacon, & Peterson, 1977; Jackson, Herzog, & Chatters, 1980; Chatters, 1983; Jackson, Chatters, & Neighbors, 1982; 1986).

Socioeconomic status measures have been inconsistently related to SWB among older Blacks. Education is a positive predictor of SWB in several studies (Himes & Hamlet, 1962; Jackson, Bacon, & Peterson, 1977; Chatters, 1977), while in others, education bears no independent relation to well-being (Sauer, 1977; Jackson, Herzog & Chatter, 1980; Chatters, 1983; Jackson, Chatters & Neighbors, 1982; 1986). In a study of older Southern Black women (Himes & Hamlet, 1962), home ownership was significantly related to SWB. However, negative findings for income are reported for several investigations (Ehrlich, 1973; Jackson, Bacon, & Peterson, 1977; Sauer, 1977; Chatters, 1977; Jackson, Herzog, & Chatters, 1980; Chatters, 1983; Jackson, Chatters, & Neighbors, 1982; 1986).

There is little support for gender differences in SWB among older Black adults (Sauer, 1977). Jackson et al. (1982) report a significant bivariate finding for gender and life satisfaction, but subsequent multivariate analyses indicate no independent effect for gender (Chatters, 1983). A national study of Black adults (Jackson, Chatters & Neighbors, 1986), found regional differences in reports of SWB which favored Southern older respondents. Several studies report that social interaction factors are related to higher SWB levels among older Black adults (Ortega et al., 1983; Ball, 1983). In contrast, investigations of voluntary association participation and interaction with family and friends indicate no independent effects on morale, while solitary activities were a significant predictor in one report (Sauer, 1977).

Age status is a fairly pervasive and consistent positive predictor of SWB (Campbell, Converse & Rodgers, 1976; Veroff et al., 1981; Campbell, 1981). Witt et al., (1980) observe that, over several years, a trend in the relationshp between age and SWB from negative to weak positive has occurred. They explain this trend by citing the introduction of important control variables in studies of SWB during that time. Negative findings for the relationship between age and SWB among older Blacks have been reported (Sauer, 1977; Vaughan et al., 1984). However, research which controls for relevant sociodemographic factors indicates that age and SWB are positively related (Ball, 1983; Chatters, 1983; Jackson, Chatters & Neighbors, 1982; 1986; Jackson, Herzog & Chatters, 1980; Janson & Mueller, 1983).

Age Cohort and Resource Analyses of SWB

This section of the chapter highlights a series of investigations of race and age interactions for well-being among national samples of the general population, as well as research conducted on a nationally representative sample of the adult Black population (i.e., the National Surveys of Black Americans). These analyses focus specifically on the operation of age cohort differences and socioeconomic resource factors in determining well-being assessments. As a whole, this work suggests that the past life experiences of current cohorts of older Blacks has had an important impact on their present status. These influences are expressed through a number of factors which both directly bear on SWB as well as act to moderate the relationships between SWB and other variables. Relying on cross-sectional data, this work is admittedly limited on its ability to address the several potential influences (i.e., cohort, period, and aging) on SWB evaluations. Nonetheless, they provide the preliminary work on several interesting hypotheses concerning age differences in SWB.

The presence of national data on Black Americans provides several unique advantages over past efforts. First, these data provide adequate numbers of Black respondents for analyses (i.e., multivariate and bivariate). Second, the data are representative of a wider range of variability on demographic factors and thus, allow for subgroup analyses. Third, as a consequence of increased sample representativeness, it is possible to perform more meaningful comparisons between racial groups (i.e., allow the examination of relationships while controlling for effects which are due to race vs. socioeconomic status).

Jackson, Chatters & Neighbors (1982) examined the mental health status of older Black adults (55 years of age and above) using both traditional and social indicators of global well-being. Overall, respondents reported high levels of well-being (i.e., life satisfaction and happiness) and moderate levels of significant personal problems. Age comparisons revealed that the oldest of the sample (75 years and above) were more likely than their younger counterparts to indicate that they did not have a personal problem. One possible explanation for the difference in reports of a personal problem could be that older adults are less burdened with problems arising from familial and employment conflicts or transitions. Alternatively, very old adults may represent a special group with reference to their physiological, psychological, and social functioning.

Demographic variables were significantly related to traditional measures of psychological distress as well as the global well-being items. The findings indicate that age was positively related to general well-being and that the youngest cohort of respondents (55 to 64 years) were most likely to have a personal problem. Other significant findings indicate that men and married persons reported less severe personal problems than their counterparts, and married persons additionally reported higher levels of general well-being. Higher levels of income and education were inversely related to problem seriousness, while education had a curvilinear relationship with overall happiness. This relationship may reflect the fact that persons with moderate levels of education (i.e., high school graduates) have the greatest gap between life aspirations and achievements. Evaluations of health status were positively related to the global well-being measures and negatively related to problem seriousness.

Collectively, the findings indicate that these different aspects of SWB demonstrate a considerable level of congruence. The global SWB measures, in particular, displayed the anticipated relationships to more intensive and direct measures of psychological distress and self-reported symptomatology. Further, although not tested in a causal manner, the pattern of findings suggests that while socioeconomic resources were generally inadequate for directly predicting SWB, they may be important for determining intermediate factors such as discrete psychological events (i.e., distress) which, in turn, affect SWB.

A study of the causal relationships among health concerns, stress, and subjective well-being among a sample of older Blacks (Chatters, 1983), investigated the effectiveness of demographic factors as resources for well-being. The tested model hypothesized that instead of influencing well-being directly, demographic factors represented important resources which affected discrete physical and mental health outcomes. These intermediate factors, in turn, had a direct bearing on well-being. In partial support of the model, SWB evaluations (i.e., happiness and life satisfaction) were relatively independent of demographic factors and largely affected by intermediate health concerns and stress. Further, demographic factors exerted significant influences on intermediate causal elements such as health status and level of stress and they, in turn, directly affected the final outcome measures.

In an attempt to explore the distinctive relationship between age, race, and SWB, investigators have conducted age subgroup analyses across Black and White adults. Campbell et al. (1976) compared young (18 to 34), middle-aged (35 to 54), and older (55 years of age and above) Blacks on reported levels of well-being and found that older Blacks demonstrated higher levels of both happiness and life satisfaction than did younger groups. Although Blacks generally scored lower than Whites on SWB, older Blacks were more positive about their lives than were older Whites. Work by Herzog et al. (1982) confirms that younger Blacks are less happy than other age-race groups, while older Blacks and Whites demonstrate comparable levels of happiness.

A secondary analysis by Jackson et al. (1980) aggregated the Black subsamples of 12 datasets from surveys conducted over a number of years at the Institute for Social Research, the National Opinion Research Center and several U.S. universities (see Jackson et al., 1980 for the specific details regarding aggregation procedures). The total aggregated dataset contained approximately 3,5000 Black respondents, 31% of whom are 55 years of age and above. The analyses focused on the possible differential impact of: 1) background and demographic factors, 2) social activity, and 3) family factors on subjective well-being within three age groups (18-34 years, 35-54 years, and 55 years and above).

Among the oldest group of respondents, being older, married, and in self-reported good health were related to higher levels of happiness. For middle-aged respondents (35-54 years), being married, in good health and male were related to greater happiness, while being married and of relatively higher income were predictive of greater happiness among young (18-34 years) respondents. In terms of life satisfaction ratings, satisfaction with health was the only significant predictor of life satisfaction for the oldest respondents. Among young and middle-aged groups, satisfaction with health retained its significance as a predictor of life satisfaction; for the middle-aged, age and marital status were also significant predictors.

Summarizing the results for older Black adults, a small group of background and demographic factors were predictive of subjective well-being. Self-perceived health, marital status, and age demonstrated the most consistent pattern of relationships.

Comparisons of the regression equations for happiness and life satisfaction reveal that age, marital status, and self-reported health had independent effects on happiness, while for life satisfaction, satisfaction with health was the only significant predictor. Overall, background and demographic factors accounted for very little of the variance in happiness and life satisfaction scores.

Jackson, Chatters and Neighbors (1986) investigated reports of subjective life quality within the entire adult age range of the NSBA sample. The purpose of the analyses was to highlight the important conceptual role of economic well-being in life quality evaluations and to assess the role of age (and age cohorts) for the relationships between sociodemographic factors and well-being. Overall, the findings provided little support for a major role of achieved status variables such as income and education in well-being, and only partial support was found for a moderating effect of age cohort in these relationships. The analyses for separate age cohorts did reveal that education was an important predictor for well-being among the youngest groups of respondents, but was ineffective in explaining well-being among middle-aged and older Black adults. Age, itself, was a significant and positive predictor of well-being only among the oldest group. Other significant relationships included higher well-being among married respondents and Southern residents. The general failure of income and education to significantly impact on well-being, suggests that low achieved status does not directly lead to lowered assessments of life quality. Effects for socioeconomic factors may be transmitted indirectly through other status dimensions (e.g., health and levels of experienced stress) or through perceptions of attainments in relevant life domains.

Conclusions and Directions for Future Research

The expanse of topics and issues that have been examined in relation to SWB, coupled with the paucity of existing data on Black adults, makes the task of providing recommendations for future research difficult. Recent efforts to integrate the variety of research on SWB (Diener, 1984; Schuessler & Fisher, 1985) have been valuable in providing an appreciation of the commonalities and differences in conceptualizations of SWB. Prior to that, literature reviews of SWB were characteristically confined within particular disciplinary traditions. Survey research and experimental methodologies are reviewed and evaluated in this work and suggestions for needed work both within and across substantive research areas are provided.

Two areas of research, the qualitative meaning of SWS evaluations and age differences in SWB structure and components, are in particular need of further work. Research on the qualitative meaning of SWB evaluations should concentrate on the use of single-item measures in survey applications. Methodological studies addressing the meaning of close-ended responses to SWB items will provide valuable information concerning the content validity of these items. The use of structured probes for single-item measures may reveal the nature of judgemental processes and the relevant reference points used in these evaluations. The underlying rationale for responses to these items may vary in predictable ways as a function of membership in social status groups. It is clear that social status position has an important influence on well-being evaluations. What has been less apparent and generally lacking in SWB theory is the rationale behind these differences. In an attempt to ground SWB evaluations in life circumstances, other work should examine the relationship between SWB and reactions to discrete occurrences such as stressful life events, natural disasters, and personal problems.

Age status and cohort differences in SWB and in the processes which underlie these evaluations have been a prominent concern of researchers. The power of discrete historical events and broad socialization influences to shape behaviors and attitudes has been documented. Cohort differences in life experiences and in modifying the role of status factors as determinants of well-being are interesting lines of research. Further work on age differences should explore the existence of possible period and cohort effects in shaping outlook and generalized feelings of well-being.

With regard to theory development, the juxtaposition of varied approaches to SWB invites researchers to actively explore these identified areas of commonality and divergence in their work. In general, a broadening of perspective is warranted in existing theories to include a consideration of the possible mechanisms by which membership in particular social status categories (e.g., age, race, and gender) impacts upon well-being.

Current approaches to SWB which have traditionally incorporated-life-span notions into their theories and models should explicitly examine and develop these life-span implications and extend present investigations to study the patterns of concerns which comprise SWB across the life cycle. Theories of SWB from other disciplines should be sensitive to life-span issues and concerns as well. Researchers should be aware that their methods, in particular scale construction, may incorporate age or other biases (e.g., item content).

Further, these efforts clearly demonstrate the dearth of information on SWB processes among the Black population. An emphasis on simple comparative research has done little to explain the nature of racial differences in SWB. In addition to work examining these processes among exclusively Black samples, comparative research on Blacks and Whites should be conducted in which sufficient sample sizes and variability on background factors within each group allows meaningful comparisons and the ability to separate out the effects of race and socioeconomic status. An integrated approach to research and theory helps to delineate racial and socioeconomic status similarities, potential differences in the processes underlying SWB, and a broader understanding of the nature of subjective well-being.

References

Adams, D. L. (1971). Correlates of satisfaction among the elderly. *The Gerontologist, 11,* 64-68.

Alston, J. P., Lowe, G. D., & Wrigley, A. (1974). Socioeconomic correlates for four dimensions of self-perceived satisfaction. *Human Organization, 33,* 99-102.

Andrews, F. M. (1982). Subjective social indicators, objective social indicators, and social accounting systems. In F. T. Juster & K. C. Land (Eds.), *Social indicators and social accounting systems*. New York: Academic Press.

Andrews, F. M., & Withey, S. B. (1976). *Social indicators of well-being*. New York: Plenum.

Ball, R. E. (1983). Marital status, household structure, and life satisfaction of Black women. *Social Problems, 30*, 400-409.

Bell, B. (1978). Disaster impact and response: Overcoming the thousand natural shocks. *Gerontologist, 18*, 531-540.

Bengtson, V. L. (1979). Ethnicity and aging: Problems and issues in current social science inquiry. In D. E. Gelfand and A. J. Kutzik (Eds.), *Ethnicity and aging: Theory, research, and policy*. New York: Springer Publishing.

Campbell, A. *The sense of well-being in America: Recent patterns and trends*. New York: McGraw-Hill, 1981.

Campbell, A., Converse, P. E., & Rodgers, W. L. (1976). *The quality of life: Perceptions, evaluations, and satisfactions*. New York: Russell Sage Foundation.

Carp, F. M., & Carp, A. (1982). Test of a model of domain satisfactions and well-being: Equity considerations. *Research on Aging, 4*, 503-522.

Chatters, L. M. (1977). The influence of selected attitudinal and personality variables on life satisfaction among urban Black elderly. Unpublished manuscript, The University of Michigan.

Chatters, L. M. (1983). A causal model of subjective well-being among elderly Blacks. Unpublished dissertation thesis. The University of Michigan.

Chiriboga, D. A., & Cutler, L. (1980). Stress and adaptation: Life span perspectives. In L. W. Poon (Ed.), *Aging in the 1980's: Psychological Issues*. Washington, D.C.: American Psychological Association.

Clemente, F., & Sauer, W. J. (1976). Racial differences in life satisfaction. *Journal of Black Studies, 7*, 3-10.

Czaja, S. J. (1975). Age differences in life satisfaction as a function of discrepancy between real and ideal self-concepts. *Experimental Research on Aging, 1*, 81-89.

Diener, E. (1984). Subjective well-being. *Psychological Bulletin, 95*, 542-575.

Diener, E., & Griffin, S. (1984). Happiness and life satisfaction: Bibliography. *Psychological documents*.

Donnenwerth, G. V. Guy, R. F., & Norvell, M. J. (1978). Life satisfaction among older persons: Rural-urban and racial comparisons. *Social Science Quarterly, 59*, 578-583.

Dowd, J. J., & Bengtson, V. L. (1978). Aging in minority populations: An examination of the double jeopardy hypothesis. *Journal of Gerontology, 33*, 427-436.

Ehrlich, I. F. (1973). Toward a social profile of the aged Black population in the U.S.: An exploratory study. *Aging and Human Development, 4*, 271-276.

George, L. K. (1981). Subjective well-being: Conceptual and methodological issues. In C. Eisdorfer (Ed.), *Annual Review of Gerontology and Geriatrics, Vol. 2*. New York: Springer.

George, L. K., & Bearon, L. B. (1980). *Quality of life in older persons: Meaning and measurement*. New York: Human Sciences Press.

Glenn, N. D. (1980). Values, attitudes, and beliefs. In O. G. Brim, Jr. & J. Kagan (Eds.), *Constancy and change in human development*. Cambridge, MA: Harvard University Press.

Hagestad, G., & Neugarten, B. L. (1985). Age and the life course. In R. Binstock & E. Shanas (Eds.), *Handbook of aging and the social sciences*. New York: Van Nostrand Reinhold.

Herzog, A. R., Rodgers, W. L., & Woodworth, J. (1982). *Subjective well-being among different age groups*. Ann Arbor, MI: Institute for Social Research, The University of Michigan.

Himes, J., & Hamlett, M. (1962). The assessment of adjustment of aged Negro women in a southern city. *Phylon, 23*, 139-147.

Horan, P. M., & Belcher, J. C. (1982). Lifestyle and morale in the southern rural aged. *Research on Aging, 4*, 523-549.

House, J., & Robbins, C. (1983). Age, psychosocial stress and health. In B. B. Hess & K. Bond (Eds.), *Aging in society: Selected reviews of recent research*. Hillsdale, NJ: Erlbaum. Huerta, F., & Horton, R. (1978). Coping behavior of elderly flood victims. *Gerontologist, 18*, 541-545.

Jackson, J. J. (1971a). The Blacklands of gerontology. *Aging and Human Development, 2*, 156-167.

Jackson, J. J., & Walls, B. E. (1978). Myths and realities about aged Blacks. In M. R. Brown (Ed.), *Readings in gerontology*, (2nd edition). St. Louis, MO: Springer Publishing.

Jackson, J. J. (1985). Race, national origin, ethnicity, and aging. In R. H. Binstock & E. Shanas (Eds.), *Handbook of aging and the social sciences*, (2nd edition). New York: Van Nostrand.

Jackson, J. S., Bacon, J. D., & Peterson, J. (1977). Life satisfaction among Black urban elderly. *Aging and Human Development, 8*, 169-180.

Jackson, J. S., Chatters, L. M., & Neighbors, H. W. (1982). The mental health status of older Black Americans: A national study. *The Black Scholar, 13*, 21-35.

Jackson, J. S., Chatters, L. M., & Neighbors, H. W. (1986). The subjective life quality of Black Americans. In F. M. Andrews (Ed.), *Research on the Quality of Life*. Ann Arbor, MI: Institute for Social Research, The University of Michigan.

Jackson, J. S., & Gibson, R. C. (1985). Work and retirement among the Black elderly. In Z. Blau (Ed.), *Current perspectives on aging and the life cycle*. Hartford, CT: JAI Press.

Jackson, J. S., Herzog, A. R., & Chatters, L. M. The meaning and correlates of life satisfaction in older (and middle aged) Blacks: A secondary analysis. Final Report AOA Grant No. 90-A-1025. The University of Michigan, Ann Arbor, MI, 1980.

Jackson, M., Kolody, B. & Wood, J. L. (1982). To be old and Black: The case for double jeopardy on income and health. In R. C. Manual (Ed.), *Minority aging: Sociological and social psychological issues*. Westport, CT: Greenwood Press.

Janson, P., & Mueller, K. F. (1983). Age, ethnicity, and well-being. *Research on Aging, 5*, 353-367.

Kivett, V. R. (1982). The importance of race to the life situation of the rural elderly. *The Black Scholar, 13*, 13-20.

Kozma, A., & Stones, M. J. (1978). The measurement of happiness: Development of the Memorial University of Newfoundland Scale of Happiness (MUNSH). *Journal of Gerontology, 35*, 906-912.

Land, K. C. (1975). Social indicator models: An overview. In K. C. Land & S. Spilerman (Eds.), *Social indicator models*. New York: Russell Sage Foundation.

Larson, R. Thirty years of research on the subjective well-being of older Americans. *Journal of Gerontology*, 1978, *33*, 109-125.

Lawton, M. P. (1975). The Philadelphia Geriatric Center Morale Scale: A revision. *Journal of Gerontology*, *30*, 85-89.

Lazarus, R. S., & DeLongis, A. (1983). Psychological stress and coping in aging. *American Psychologist*, *38*, 245-254.

Lindsay, I. (1971). *Multiple hazards of age and race: The situation of aged Blacks in the United States*. Special Committee on Aging, U. S. Senate.

Linn, M. W., Hunter, K. I., & Perry, P. R. (1979). Differences by sex and ethnicity in the psychological adjustment of the elderly. *Journal of Health and Social Behavior*, *20*, 273-281.

Lipman, A. (1966). *Responsibility and morale*. Proceedings of the 7th International Congress of Gerontology. Wien: Wiener Medizinische Akademie.

Lohmann, N. (1977). Correlates of life satisfaction, morale, and adjustment measures. *Journal of Gerontology*, *32*, 73-75.

Masuda, M., & Holmes, T. H. (1978). Life events: Perceptions and frequencies. *Psychosomatic Medicine*, *40*, 236-261.

Messer, M. (1968). Race differences in selected attitudinal dimensions of the elderly. *Gerontologist*, *8*, 245-249.

Michalos, A. C. (1980). Satisfaction and happiness. *Social Indicators Research*, *8*, 385-422.

Michalos, A. C. (1985). Multiple discrepancies theory (MDT). *Social Indicators Research*, *16*, 347-413.

Morris, J. N., & Sherwood, S. (1975). A retesting and modification of the Philadelphia Geriatric Morale Center Scale. *Journal of Gerontology*, *30*, 77-84.

National Council on the Aging, Inc. (1971). *Employment prospects of Blacks, Chicanos, and Indians*. Washington, D.C.: National Council on the Aging.

National Council on the Aging, Inc. (1975). *The myth and reality of aging in America*. Washington, D.C.: The National Council on the Aging, Inc.

Neugarten, B. L., Havighurst, R. J., & Tobin, S. S. (1961). The measurement of life satisfaction. *Journal of Gerontology*, *16*, 134-143.

Ortega, S. T., Crutchfield, R. D., & Rushing, W. A. (1983). Race differences in elderly personal well-being: Friendship, family, and church. *Research on Aging*, *5*, 101-118.

Register, J. C. (1981). Aging and race: A Black-White comparative analysis. *The Gerontologist*, *21*, 438-443.

Rosow, I. (1985). Status and role change through the life cycle. In R. H. Binstock and Shanas, E. (Eds.), *Handbook of aging and the social sciences* (2nd edition). Van Nostrand Reinhold: New York.

Rossi, R. J., & Gilmartin, K. J. (1980). *The handbook of social indicators: Sources, characteristics and analysis*. New York: Garland.

Rubenstein, D. I. (1971). An examination of social participation found aomng a national sample of Black and White elderly. *International Journal of Aging and Human Development*, *1*, 172-188.

Sauer, W. (1977). Morale of the urban aged. A regression analysis by race. *Journal of Gerontology*, *32*, 600-608.

Schaie, K. W., Orchowsky, S., & Parham, I. (1982). Measuring age and sociocultural change: The case of race and life satisfaction. In R. C. Manuel (Ed.), *Minority aging: Sociological and social psychological issues*. Westport, CT: Greenwood Press.

Schuessler, K. F., & Fisher, G. A. (1985). Quality of life research and sociology. *Annual Review of Sociology, 11,* 129-149.

Spreitzer, E., & Snyder, E. E. (1974). Correlates of life satisfaction among the aged. *Journal of Gerontology, 29,* 454-458.

Vaughan, D. A., Kashner, J. B., Stock, W. A., & Richards, M. (1984). A structural model of subjective well-being: A comparison of ethnicity. *Social Indicators Research, 16,* 315-332.

Veroff, J., Douvan, E., & Kulka, R. A. (1981). *The inner American.* New York: Basic Books, Inc.

Ward, R. A., & Kilburn, H. (1983). Community access and satisfaction: Racial differences in later life. *International Journal of Aging and Human Development, 16,* 209-219.

Witt, D. D., Lowe, G. D., Peek, C. W., & Curry, E. W. (1980). The changing association between age and happiness: Emerging trend or methodological artifact? *Social Forces, 58.,* 1302-1307.

Wood, V., Wylie, M. L., & Sheafor, B. (1969). An analysis of a short self-report measure of life satisfaction: Correlation with rater judgments. *Journal of Gerontology, 24,* 465-469.

Youmans, E. G. (1963). Aging patterns in a rural and an urban area of Kentucky. *University of Kentucky Agricultural Experimental Station Bulletin,* 681.

PSYCHOLOGICALLY HEALTHY BLACK ADULTS: A REVIEW OF THEORY AND RESEARCH

Howard P. Ramseur

> ... the Negro has no possible basis for a healthy self-esteem and every incentive for self-hatred. (A. Kardiner and L. Ovesey, *The Mark of Oppression* 1951, p. 297)

> ...the experience of being Black in a society dominated by Whites does *not*, as is sometimes incorrectly assumed, lead to deep and corrosive personal demoralization. Blacks live with greater stress, but they have the personal and social resources to maintain a perspective which keeps the stress external, does not permit it to become internalized or to disrupt personal integration (J. Veroff, E. Douvan, and R. A. Kulka, *The Inner American* 1981, p. 437).

Overview

What are the psychological and social characteristics of psychologically healthy Black American adults? How do these characteristics develop and change over the life cycle? Until now these significant questions have not been comprehensively addressed. They have not been addressed partly because of the lack of consensus and conceptual clarity in the literature about what represents "psychological health" or "healthy development" for adults, Black or White. In addition, the idea that Black American adults could be psychologically healthy, however defined, is one that mainstream social scientists and much of the lay public would find unacceptable. The vast literature on Blacks in psychology, sociology, social work, and psychiatry converges on the assumptions embodied in the quote from Kardiner and Ovesey (1951) above. That is, given the social and cultural conditions under which Black Americans live, psychological health is an impossibility. These assumptions led social scientists to a theoretical and research focus on low self-esteem, self-hatred, and psychopathology among Black American adults.

The 1960s and 1970s saw theoretical and empirical challenges to mainstream social science theories, particularly to their predictions that Black adults were self-hating or had self-esteem lower than White Americans. Recently, some social scientists have moved beyond the main-

215

stream view, or simply challenging it, and have begun to explore sources and mechanisms underlying "positive" Black psychological characteristics. They have focused on specific aspects of psychological functioning or development they have defined as healthy, e.g., high self-esteem, positive racial identity, or adaptive coping styles. While a number of interesting empirical findings have emerged in each area, little general theorizing about Black adult psychological health over the life cycle, or about the implications of these findings for psychological treatment, has occurred.

This chapter will review theory and research on psychological health among Black American adults by discussing the social/cultural situation of Black Americans, the essential elements of an "ideal" model of adult psychological health, "universal" models of psychological health, and theories of Black personality and identity that have psychological health implications. The chapter will then turn to empirical research and associated theorizing in three areas theorists have linked to Black psychological health: self-conception (self-esteem and racial identity), the "competent" personality, and Black coping resources and styles. Finally, the chapter will examine the implications of recent theory and empirical research for creating models of Black adult psychological health and for future research.

Models of Psychological Health

How should "psychological health" be defined? How does it change over the adult life cycle? While the social science literature contains hundreds of differing theoretical definitions and dozens of empirical studies of adult psychological health, no theory or model has achieved a consensus or accumulated a convincing body of empirical evidence to address these questions. In addition, while existing models of psychological health claim to be "universal", that is applicable and explanatory for all persons, in fact, they usually have little or nothing to say about the unique social/cultural circumstances of Black Americans and the impact of such circumstances on Black adult psychological health. Existing theories of Black adult psychological health will be reviewed by focusing on the unique social/cultural situation of Blacks and the issues that it raises, by discussing what an "ideal" model of adult psychological health ought to encompass, and by examining the two existing bodies of theory: "universal" models of psychological health and models of Black personality and identity.

The Social/Cultural Context of Black Americans

Black adults must live and adapt to a unique social and cultural environment as well as history in the United States. That environment and the necessity that they adapt to it has implications for any model that claims to define and understand psychological health for Black American adults. Certain issues seem important in characterizing the aspects of that environment that are relevant to psychological health: White racism, the need to adapt to White institutions and culture, adapting to the Black community—family, institutions, and culture, and coping with poverty and political powerlessness (See Jones, 1972; Pierce, 1974; Barbarin, 1983; Cross, 1984, for extended discussions).

Pierce (1974) argues that the overriding psychiatric (psychological) problem for Blacks is the "withering effect of racism" (p. 512). Jones (1972) and Pierce (1974) have extensive discussions of racism and its impacts on Blacks and the Black community. While Pierce defines White racism as behavior that results from the attitude that White skin (and Whites) are always superior to Black skin (and Blacks), Jones has a more detailed discussion of the different levels of racism: individual, institutional and cultural. For Jones, individual racism refers to individual acts of discrimination or violence and attitudes of prejudice and paternalism that grow out of a belief in the genetic inferiority of Blacks to Whites. Institutional racism refers to institutional patterns—of resource allocation, entry, expectation, or outcome—that consistently led to different and more negative status for Blacks than for Whites. Cultural racism refers to the ideologies and values that undergird the other forms of racism; racist values that are perpetuated by the mass media, schools, and churches. While Jones (1972) and other writers emphasize different themes, three key racist cultural themes emerge from a survey of the literature: 1) Blacks as unattractive and not socially valuable; 2) Blacks as unable to be effective in the world: unable to achieve, to effectively manage people or events, unable to compete with Whites; and 3) what Pettigrew (1964) calls Id-oriented stereotypes—Blacks as sexually and aggressively impulsive and uncontrolled. These, then, may be key cultural themes of racism to which the Black individual (and community) are forced to adapt.

Most Black Americans must adapt to both the Black community and its culture as well as White American culture and institutions. While most Blacks live, have families, social friends and churches within the Black community, they still must adapt to White-run schools, workplaces, military settings and media, an adaptation that often requires them to juggle different values, behavioral styles and aspirations. This situation has led some social scientists to postulate that many Blacks become bicultural; i.e., able to function in both cultures.

There is another aspect of social reality that Blacks must adapt to as well. Cross (1984) exhaustively documents a family poverty rate and an adult unemployment rate for Black Americans that are double those for Whites. He notes the family income and wealth gap and lower access to quality medical and other social services that Blacks suffer from as well. Cross also demonstrates the continuing relative political and economic powerlessness of Blacks and the Black community. He links these social conditions to the historic and current discrimination and institutional racism that he sees as continuing constraints and frustrations for Blacks. Barbarin (1983) points out that these social conditions mean more stressors for Blacks and fewer resources than Whites have to cope with them.

In summary, Black adults must adapt to racism in its different variants, Black and White cultures, poverty, and political powerlessness. They often have the support of Black families and friends, the Black community and its institutions, and Black culture in their attempts to successfully adapt. Which issues and conflicts are the central ones they must adapt to, given the social/cultural context, and which psychosocial characteristics are "adaptive" or "healthy" for Black adults are questions any adequate model of Black adult psychological health must address.

An "Ideal" Model of Adult Psychological Health

What are the elements of an "ideal" model of adult psychological health? Certain essential elements emerge from the comprehensive discussions of psychological health of Jahoda (1958), Smith (1961), Lazarus (1975), and others. An ideal model should explicitly describe and define the essential personal, social, and behavioral characteristics of the psychologically healthy adult over the entire adult life cycle. It should differentiate levels of psychological health for adults in various areas of functioning. An ideal model should also explain gender differences as well as family, social, and cultural factors that are significant. It should be amenable to empirical investigation and have a body of empirical findings supporting it. Clear links to a theory of personality and to a more general psychological theory would be another aspect of an "ideal" model. The underlying value premises of the model and their impact on its structure and empirical predictions would also be explained. An "ideal" model would also define what are healthy or positive psychosocial characteristics for Black Americans, and explain how they develop and are maintained. Given the unique and adverse social situation of Black Americans, understanding the psychological, family, and community resources utilized by Blacks to achieve and maintain psychological health would be of central importance. Defining how healthy psychosocial characteristics of Black adults might differ from those of White American adults would also be a task for an "ideal" model.

"Universal" Models of Psychological Health

What do existing "universal" models of psychological health contribute to an understanding of Black adult psychological health? This
review of existing models will utilize the work of George and Brooker
(1984), who analyzed conceptions of psychological health and came up
with four categories that grouped them. Modifying their format by drawing on the work of Lazarus (1975) yields six categories that will organize a
brief discussion of existing "universal" models of psychological health.
The categories are: 1) freedom from illness; 2) being average; 3) an ideal
personality type; 4) using multiple criteria to determine psychological
health; 5) a developmental/life-span perspective; 6) a stress/adaptation
approach.

Freedom from symptoms or illness is the most medical model of
psychological health. Health is the absence of illness, and implicitly the
ability to function adequately. Psychological health defined as being essentially like the average or "modal" member of society, or the notion of
being "adjusted" to one's social/cultural surroundings were once common models in the literature. However, both concepts are little used now.
"Adjustment" seems to evoke conformity and blandness for many
theorists, and a culture-bound notion that they want to transcend. The
notion of health as the absence of illness has also been criticized by
theorists (see Maslow, 1968) who stress the importance of "positive"
characteristics like creativity, "growth," and self-actualization in psychological functioning.

The "ideal personality" approach has a number of exponents, with
S. Freud and his notion of the "genital character" and A. Maslow's notion
of the "self-actualizer" being the most widely known. Freud actually
wrote little about psychological health. He is reputed to have said that the
healthy person should be able to "love and to work," that is, to make a
balanced commitment to a heterosexual love "object" and productive
work. The abilities to have unconflicted sexual and emotional expression
and to work productively are expressions of the full maturity of the "genital character." The final stage of psycho-sexual development, the genital
stage, is reached by those whose sexual, emotional, and interpersonal
development was not damaged and fixated at an earlier psychosexual
stage. The genital character is an ideal of balanced psychological forces,
functioning, and rationality that is never actually attained by any individual.

A. Maslow (1968), writing from a humanistic perspective, says a
healthy person is a "self-actualizer," someone who is moving towards
fulfilling (or has fulfilled) their unique human potential. We all have an
inherent motivation towards growth or self-actualization, Maslow felt,
that would flower if society allowed more primitive needs to be satisfied
(e.g., hunger, safety). Maslow investigated the personality characteristics

of self-actualizers by reviewing biographies of prominent figures and his friends and drawing up a list of common traits. He arrived at fifteen, ranging from accurate perception of reality, the ability to be intimate with others, and the capacity to have mystical experiences, to creativity. Self-actualizers are rare, and probably should be seen as the Olympic athletes of mental health—if, as many wonder, they exist.

Marie Jahoda's (1958) classic discussion of the six themes of "positive mental health" perhaps best represents the "multiple criteria" approach to psychological health. "Positive mental health" refers to the stance that psychological or mental health is more than the absence of symptoms of mental disorder, it involves the presence of "positive", "healthy" characteristics. Based on the social science literature and discussions with colleagues, she came up with six aspects of the healthy person: 1) positive and realistic attitudes towards the self; 2) growth and self-actualization,; 3) integration or a balance of psychological forces and consequently stress resistance; 4) autonomy; 5) accurate perception of reality; and 6) environmental mastery—the ability to love, work, and play, efficiency in problem solving, etc. Jahoda did not specify how, or if, the six criteria are interrelated.

Erik Erikson's (1968) elaboration and extension of Freud's model is probably the most sophisticated example of the developmental/life-span approach to psychological health. Erikson examines the human life cycle in terms of eight different stages of ego development. Each stage is a crisis or turning point that involves a basic psychological issue that can have a healthy or pathological outcome that has implications for the next stage of life. Erikson emphasizes the role of social and cultural factors on development, as well as sexual and unconscious ones, and analyzes their impact on personality development over the whole life cycle. He postulates that four stages (of eight) are in adulthood: V) Ego identity vs. role confusion—where the healthy outcome is identity and role confusion the pathological outcome; VI) Intimacy vs. Isolation; VII) Generativity vs. Stagnation; and VIII)Ego Integrity vs. Despair. Erikson emphasizes that the outcome of each of these stages is a dynamic balance; with health representing a favorable ratio, not perfection. His work is the basis for much of the recent life-span developmental research focusing on mid-life.

A large literature has developed in recent decades that examines the stress/adaptation model and the links between stress, coping mechanisms, and the level of subjective well-being or distress experienced by an individual or group. The stress/adaptation model incorporates social and situational factors as well as those internal to the individual; it also allows a focus on the process of resolving problems—coping—from an environmental and intra-psychic viewpoint.

Stress has been defined in many ways; but, all definitions involve an environmental demand to which the person must react, one that is perceived of as at least potentially exceeding the person's ability or resources to meet it. Coping refers to efforts to master environmental demands when a previous response is unavailable or ineffective. The stressor and the coping response(s) are linked by the cognitive appraisal of the stressor and the internal/external resources of the individual. Cognitive appraisal refers to the significance and meaning attached to the stressor. Internal resources refer to individual factors; i.e., personality traits, racial identification, social class, and cultural beliefs. External resources refer to family or social ties, work relationships, church affiliation, etc. Outcome refers to either short or long-term psychological distress and symptoms or adaptive behavior and subjective health. The model then is: stressor(s), an appraisal of the stressor(s) and the person's internal/external resources which in turn produces a coping response that leads to an adaptive or distressful outcome. There is also feedback between elements of the model; i.e., the outcome can modify the coping response and/or appraisal of the stressor (see Cervantes and Castro, 1985; and Barbarin, 1983 for extended discussions).

While all existing models of psychological health fail to meet the criteria for an ideal model, each has its areas of strength and weakness. "Freedom from symptoms" and being average" or "adjusted" have the virtues of being straightforward and potentially measurable. However, their atheoretical nature, and for "adjustment," culture-bound stance, limit their usefulness. The "ideal personality" model, especially Freud's "genital character," has the asset of being tied to personality theory and more general psychological theories. It also presents a unified, detailed picture of the psychological healthy adult, and in Freud's case a picture of development and pathology. However, the lack of a social/cultural framework for understanding adult psychological health and the neglect of development(s) during the adult years are real weaknesses. The difficulty in empirically defining and investigating the model as well as the implicit assumption that either no actual adult or very few are psychologically healthy limits the usefulness of this model.

The multiple criteria, developmental, and stress models all seem to meet more criteria of an ideal model, and to be more useful in understanding psychological health among Blacks. The multiple criterion approach specifies that psychological health has a number of definable dimensions that may be related, but may also be independent of one another. Implicit in the approach is the notion that the dimensions are measurable and can be empirically investigated. However, variants of this model are often not tied to theory, don't have a developmental or social/cultural perspective, and haven't considered gender differences. The developmental approach, particularly as exemplified by E. Erikson, meets a number of the demands of an ideal model. Because it discusses the whole life cycle, points to the importance of society and culture, and is clearly linked to theory, Erikson's approach has a number of strengths. Erikson also points out that psychological health is a matter of a "dynamic balance" or a favorable ratio of positive to negative psychological aspects—not perfection—a useful corrective. Unfortunately, while Erikson points to central issues and ego strengths in each stage, he never gives enough definition and detail to facilitate empirical definitions of his concepts. In fact, relatively little empirical investigation of his work has occurred. The stress/adaptation model has a number of strengths too: it inherently takes the social/cultural environment of the person into account, can look at different points in the life cycle, is open to empirical measurement and investigation, and is linked to social/psychological theory. However, work based on this model has generally been focused at the group level of analysis, rather than the individual person. Therefore, applying findings to assess or describe a psychologically healthy individual is often difficult.

R. Lazarus (1975), in a comprehensive review of existing models and research on psychological health, makes two observations that are important for a discussion of "universal" models. First, after surveying the lists of central characteristics of the psychologically healthy adult created by various theorists, Lazarus points out a central issue: the role of values. The question of why "autonomy" is considered an essential characteristic of health and "creativity" is not, confronts the role that the values of the theorist, investigator, or community play in defining psychological health. Lazarus argues that it is impossible to objectively define "optimal," "effective," or "healthy" functioning because at least implicit in the discussion is a conception of what is a good or desirable behavior, emotion, or way of life. Lazarus argues that theorists and investigators need to explicitly face this inevitable aspect of describing or defining psychological health and attempt to empirically investigate the consequences of favoring one value over another (e.g., autonomy over creativity). Implicit in his discussion is the question of whose values, or which community's perspective will determine what are "healthy" or "positive" characteristics or functioning.

Lazarus (1975) also addresses the issue of the central characteristics of the psychologically healthy person. He does so by surveying the major theorists and attempting to identify areas of consensus on central characteristics. He identifies five: 1) Acceptance of self; 2) The ability to be intimate with others; 3) Competence (Freud's work?); 4) Accurate perception of reality; 5) Autonomy and independence (Lazarus, 1975, pp. 16-18).

Relating the social/cultural realities facing the Black individual and the central characteristics of the healthy person listed by Lazarus, it seems clear that the social/cultural context facing the Black individual compromises or renders more difficult attainment of a positive status on Lazarus' characteristics. For example, Lazarus lists acceptance of self and a sense of competence as key aspects of the healthy person; certainly for Blacks, given their unique social/cultural circumstance and its demands, attaining both is a more complex and problematic enterprise than it is for their White American peers. Unfortunately, existing "universal" models of psychological health give little guidance in understanding that complex process.

Traditional Theories of Black Personality and Identity

While little direct theorizing or research on the topic of psychological health among Black adults occurred in mainstream social science literature, a substantial literature on Black personality and identity was produced. Given the prevailing assumptions and findings about Black personality or Black identity, little needed to be said about psychological health; rather, the focus was on emotional disorder and social pathology among Blacks. An examination of the underlying assumptions of mainstream work about Black personality, and those of the "mark of oppression" approach, that has had the greatest impact on mental health researchers, will point out the assumed barriers to Black psychological health more clearly and put recent work in context.

The mainstream view of Black personality and identity has a number of variants; but the basic model is that living in a racist White society, where Blacks are viewed and treated as inferior, and where they are in poverty in a powerless community, leads Blacks early in life to internalize the beliefs and negative feelings about themselves and other Blacks conveyed by the White community. Explanations of exactly how the internalization occurs and its precise impacts vary with the theoretical orientation of the writer (see Kardiner and Ovesey, 1951; Karon, 1958; Pettigrew, 1964; Thomas and Sillen, 1972).

The most influential example of the psychological approach has been Kardiner and Ovesey's *Mark of Oppression* (1951). The study was clearly influential in some of the theorizing in Grier's and Cobbs (1969 discussions of Black psychology and Moore's (1982) discussion of the psychosocial status of Black women.

Kardiner and Ovesey were Freudian psychiatrists who set out to understand the "basic personality" of the American Negro. Adherents of the "culture and personality" school, they used Freudian ego psychology, anthropology, and sociology to link cultural values with personality development. The central idea was that a group of people who live under the same institutional and environmental conditions will have similar mental and emotional processes, or a "basic personality" in common. Since American Blacks live under similar caste and social class barriers they should possess a basic personality that differs from that of American Whites. To understand "Black personality," Kardiner and Ovesey used White Americans as a background control group with which they contrasted the 25 Black New York City residents they studied. Their subjects were psychoanalytically interviewed from 20 to 100 sessions and administered the Rorschach and T.A.T. tests. Male and female as well as lower and middle class Blacks were studied; 12 were patients in psychotherapy, 11 were paid subjects, and two volunteered.

Kardiner and Ovesey concluded that Blacks do have a "basic personality" that is different and more damaged than that of White Americans. Black personality is centrally organized around adapting to social discrimination (racism). Racist behavior by Whites reveals an unpleasant image of the self to the Black individual who internalizes it and feels worthless, unlovable, and unsuccessful. In essence, he or she feels low self-esteem that eventually is elaborated into self-hatred and idealization of Whites. In addition, the frustrations of racist behavior arouse aggression, cannot be expressed because of the caste situation, so it must be controlled and contained. Kardiner and Ovesey argue that this repressed aggression most often leads to low self-esteem, depression and passivity. Since the caste situation and poverty disturb family life, the Black family's socialization practices lead to a restricted emotional range, inability to be emotionally intimate, and poor conscience mechanisms. Kardiner and Ovesey do not point to significant male/female differences in Black basic personality. They do see middle-class Blacks as somewhat better off because of more stable family life than lower class Blacks. These "defects in adaptation" (the "Mark of Oppression") Kardiner and Ovesey concluded, lead to low self-esteem, self-hatred, repressed rage, depression, and in general a "wretched internal life" for all American Blacks (Kardiner and Ovesey, 1951, p. 81).

Grier and Cobbs (1969) use a number of elements of this approach in their discussion of Black psychology in the book *Black Rage*. They seem to differentiate between a male and female basic personality. Black male personality revolves around the control of aggression through repression, passivity or explosion. The family, particularly mothers, socializes males against the direct expression of aggressiveness in childhood and their social roles in adult life reinforce the lesson. Black women have their feminine narcissism (self-love) wounded because they cannot be the White ideal of femininity; their central concern then is seen as maintaining self-esteem. Cobbs and Grier see turning away from heterosexual life towards maternal functions or becoming depressed as typical ways of coping with this dilemma.

While the "Mark of Oppression" model and traditional social science approaches have substantial theoretical and empirical support (see McCarthy and Yancey, 1971; Taylor, 1976 for reviews), challenges to their image of the Black person, their theoretical assumptions about Black reactions to racism, methodology, and their empirical evidence have recently developed. Social scientists have questioned the model's assumptions, pointing out that given the social and cultural diversity of the Black community, postulating one reaction pattern to racism or one set of personality traits seems unreasonable. The notion that Blacks, in the

1980's, are always cognitively or behaviorally passive in the face of racist images or behavior is also seen as untenable. Some observers have also noted that the Black family, institutions, and community can serve as mediators of the negative messages from White society (see Barnes, 1980) and as sources for alternative frames of reference and significant others for Black children and adults (see Taylor, 1976). In addition, Black identity need not be negative or only have an insignificant effect on the psychological functioning or behavior of the Black individual (see Cross, 1980).

The most striking challenge to this tradition has been the undermining of its empirical supports; that is, recent studies with findings that run counter to the predicted personality characteristics of Blacks. In fact, Black children and adults have been shown to have equivalent levels of self-esteem when compared with Whites (see McCarthy and Yancey, 1971; Taylor, 1976 for reviews; Hays and Owens, 1972; Edwards, 1974; Veroff, Douvan, Kulka, 1981; Jensen, White, and Galliher, 1982), and to show no more symptoms, diagnoses of psychopathology, or reported psychological distress than Whites (Yancey, Rigsby, and McCarthy, 1972; Veroff, Douvan, & Kulka, 1981; see Neighbors, 1984 for review). In addition, the prediction of more repressed aggression or more aggression directed against other Blacks rather than Whites receives only mixed support in a brief review of studies by Guterman (1972, 231-233).

One model of Black psychological health that grew out of this tradition is that of the "Black Norm," which was developed by Grier & Cobbs (1969) in their book *Black Rage*. The "Black Norm" is a body of personality traits that all American Blacks share. "It also encompasses adaptive devices developed in response to a peculiar environment", which are seen as "normal devices for making it in America" for Blacks (p. 178). The Black Norm consists of cultural paranoia, cultural depression and masochism, and cultural anti-socialism. While providing little detail for their formulations, Grier and Cobbs seem to say that American Blacks share a mistrust of Whites as individuals, distrust White society's laws, and have each developed a sadness and an "intimacy with misery" in reaction to racism. Grier and Cobbs say little about variation by age, class, gender, or region in these characteristics, nor do they provide any non-clinical empirical evidence for them.

To summarize, how useful are existing theories in explaining and describing Black adult psychological health over the adult life cycle? Clearly, no existing theory meets the criteria for an "ideal" model of adult psychological health outlined earlier. A number of the "universal" theories have positive points and ideas; e.g., Erikson's life-cycle perspective, and his idea that health is a dynamic balance, not perfection. However, all of them leave large areas unexplored, often the social/cultural factors that have an impact on health—a crucial lack for a model of Black American adult psychological health. While theories addressing Black personality and identity do discuss social and cultural factors, their focus on the "inevitable" pathological outcome and impact for the Black adult, and their assumption of little diversity in reactions to social factors and in the Black community limit their explanatory usefulness as well.

While no existing theory will serve as a satisfactory explanatory or descriptive model of Black adult psychological health, it is possible to synthesize aspects of existing theory, the discussion of the social/cultural situation of American Blacks, and Lazarus' "consensus" characteristics to point out central issues an adequate theory would address. Based on the work cited earlier, several psychological issues can be hypothesized as important for the Black individual throughout the adult life cycle: 1) maintaining an overall positive conception of the self; 2) maintaining a positive conception of Blacks as a group and a positive sense of connection and involvement with the Black community and its culture; 3) maintaining an accurate perception of the social environment (including its racism); 4) adapting to both Black and White community/cultures and using effective, non-destructive ways to cope with both; 5) developing and maintaining emotional intimacy with others; 6) maintaining a sense of competence and ability to work productively. How successfully an individual confronts these issues and the balance between successful and dysfunctional adaptation may be the measure of psychological health for a Black adult. Certainly, an adequate theory of Black adult psychological health would have to describe and explain how the Black person developed and maintained a positive status on these issues.

Recent Empirical Research

The findings of recent empirical studies of self-esteem and psychological distress cited above stand in stark contrast to the conclusion that no Black American adults are able to successfully adapt to the key psychological tasks that face them. Investigations of Blacks in several other areas also challenge the mainstream view and address issues central to Black psychological health as well—specifically studies in the areas of racial identity, the competent personality, and coping with stress. Unfortunately, no general model and little theorizing has emerged from this work. In addition, only scattered work has emerged in other areas related to psychological health, like intimacy and interpersonal relations or involvement in group or individual political action to combat racism—an important lack. Existing research will be reviewed in the areas of (positive) self-conception—self-esteem and racial identity, competent personality, and coping with stress in order to assess current findings and draw theoretical implications where appropriate. This review will cite studies that are central to the area discussed or ones that illustrate important trends in the literature. Comments in each area will be based on cited studies as well as a wider reading of the literature.

Self-conception

Self-conception, variously defined and conceptualized, has been at the heart of much of the research and theorizing done about Black Americans. Low self-esteem, self-hatred, and a negative racial identity have been the characteristics traditionally attributed to Black children and adults. Recent research on self-esteem and racial identity challenges these traditional findings and offers new evidence about how some Blacks positively adapt to one of the central psychological tasks facing them: establishing and maintaining a positive sense of self—both individually and as a member of a group.

Self-esteem Self-esteem is usually defined as the evaluative dimension of the self-concept. The person is thought to have global, i.e., overall, self-esteem that can range from very positive to very negative. Global self-esteem is often thought to be the summing up of the person's self-esteem in a number of specific areas, ranging from physical self to academic self. Adult self-esteem is typically measured using paper and pencil personality or self-esteem inventories or projective tests or, more rarely, interviews.

A number of comprehensive reviews and excellent studies of Black self-esteem have been published in the last 15 years. Perhaps the most comprehensive was done by Cross (1985), who reviewed 161 studies of Black self-concept done between 1939 and 1977, studies conducted using child and adult subjects. Some 101 of these studies involved self-esteem; of those, 71% showed Black self-esteem to be equal to or exceed that for White, 16% found Whites with higher levels of self-esteem, and 13% had mixed results. Taylor (1976) in a comprehensive review of theory and studies of child and adult self-esteem, reached similar conclusions. Large sample studies of Black and White adult self-esteem by Yancey, Rigsby, and McCarthy (1972) and by Heiss and Owens (1972) found that the two groups had essentially equal overall self-esteem. Veroff, Douvan, and Kulka (1981), using national survey data, found Blacks and White American adults to have equivalent overall self-esteem and equivalent self-esteem in a number of areas. Unfortunately, little information investigating Black self-esteem at different points in the adult life cycle exists.

What are the sources of positive Black self-esteem? Discussing children and youth, Taylor (1976) and Gibbs (1985) found that the key factor for the level of the Black child's self-esteem is the general attitude of significant others towards the child. Parents, peers, and teachers are significant others for Black children. For the vast majority of Black children, and by extension Black adults, these significant others are Black. Therefore, a Black social context is their primary source of social comparisons and self-evaluation—evaluations that are often positive. Barnes (1980) also argues that, under certain conditions, the Black family and community can act as mediators or filters of negative, racist images and messages for the Black child or youth (and adults). McCarthy and Yancey (1971) argue that Black adults use other Blacks as significant others, that they use criteria of worth relevant to the Black community to evaluate themselves, and that a "system-blame" explanation of failure is available to cushion blows to self-esteem. Heiss and Owens (1972) empirically investigated these ideas with a large-sample study of Black and White adults. They looked at global self-esteem and how these adults evaluated different aspects of the self (e.g., self as parent, intelligent, athlete). While they found rough equality overall between groups, there was variation between each race on different traits (and by the four race-sex groups as well). They argued that their results indicated that variation occurred because of the variations in the type of significant others used by Blacks, likelihood of Blacks using dominant society standards of evaluation (vs. Black community ones), and differences in the availability of a system-blame explanation for each aspect of self-esteem.

In summary, recent research points out that: 1) Blacks and Whites have equivalent global self-esteem; 2) Blacks often use other Blacks, not Whites, as their significant others; 3) other mechanisms may be available to insulate Black self-esteem, e.g., a "system blame" explanation of negative events, or the use of Black cultural (vs. White) standards of evaluation; and 4) Blacks and Whites may not have equivalent evaluations of different aspects of the self.

Racial Identity

Racial identity has been discussed extensively in the social science literature using various terms and measures. Black identity, group identity, group self-concept, "sense of peoplehood", "sense of Blackness" are all terms used and measured by workers in the field. No consensus on concept definition, measurement technique, or links to personality theory has emerged, however. Much of the work in the field seems to assume that Black identity is strongly linked to personal self-esteem, but usually makes that link a theoretical postulate rather than empirically demonstrating it.

Cross (1985), in a comprehensive review of 22 studies of "reference group orientation" (group identity, race awareness) done from 1968 to 1977 found that in 68% (15 studies) Black subjects (children and adults), showed positive Black identities, in 27% (6) negative ones, and in 5% (1) a mixed pattern. Surveying studies back to 1939 and one longitudinal study, he argues that "Black parents present both the Black and White worlds to their children...Black children, and perhaps Black people in general, have a dual [Black and White] reference group orientation" (Cross, 1985, p. 169). Cross sees this dual reference group orientation as adaptive and healthy for Black Americans.

Although few studies have investigated the racial identities of Black adults a number have looked at the racial identities of Black adolescents. Gurin and Epps(1975) investigated Black identity and self-hatred by interviewing 600 southern Black college students in 1965 as part of a larger study. They found what they saw as a typical pattern of Black identity: a predominantly positive Black identity for most Black students and a small subgroup of students who had a predominantly negative identity. Ramseur (1975) looked longitudinally at the racial identities of Black freshmen and cross-sectionally at a sample of Black upperclassmen at Harvard College. He found two independent dimensions: "Salience of racial issues" and "Acceptance of Black ideology". Both dimensions were significantly linked to race-related social/extracurricular activities at college, but not to academic achievement. Gibbs (1974) interviewed 41 Black college student clients at Stanford's Counseling Center and categorized them based on their orientation towards the dominant White culture at the university. Her categories were affirmation, assimilation, separation, and withdrawal. Affirmation was the most adaptive mode, involving "movement with the dominant culture". It was a mode marked by "self-acceptance, positive[Black] identity... high achievement motivation, and autonomous self-actualizing behavior" (Gibbs, 1974, p. 736).

Perhaps the best known and most widely researched model of Black identity and identity development is Cross's (1980) model of the conversion from "Negro" to "Black." He has sometimes referred to his (and Charles Thomas') perspective as that of "psychological Nigrescence," the process of becoming "Black." He describes five stages: 1) Pre-encounter—the person is a "Negro" and accepts a "White" view of self, other Blacks, and the world; 2) Encounter—some shocking personal or social event makes the person receptive to new views of being Black and the world. This encounter precipitates an intense search for Black identity; 3) Immersion—an emotional period ensues where the person glorifies anything Black and attempts to purge him or herself of their former world-view and old behavior, 4) Internalization—the person makes his/her new values their own and Blacks their primary reference groups. This stage and the next, Internalization-Commitment, are characterized by positive self-esteem, ideological flexibility and openness about one's Blackness; 5) In the fifth stage the person finds activities and commitments to express his or her new identity.

Cross clearly sees the person in stage Five-Internalization-Commitment as the "ideal," that is, psychologically healthy Black person. They have made their new pro-Black identity and values their own. They have a "calm, secure demeanor" characterized by "ideological flexibility, psychological openness and self-confidence about one's Blackness" (Cross, 1980, p. 86). Blacks are a primary reference group, but the person has lost his prejudices about race, sex, age and social class. He or she also struggles to translate their values into behavior that will benefit the Black community. Cross seems to see the "Negro to Black" conversion process as an Afro-American model of self-actualization under oppressive social conditions. Blacks in Stage Five would then be Black self-actualizers. Cross has yet to follow up this idea, and says elsewhere that basic personality structure remains the same after the process. It seems that key aspects of racial identity change, however.

Cross (1980) points to a number of studies that seem to validate his stage model and to say that his stages exist independently and occur in the sequence he describes. However, the family and social conditions that lead all Blacks to the "Pre-encounter" stage or that support the Stage 5—Internalization/Commitment phase are unspecified. In addition, class, gender, and regional differences in the prevalence of people at different stages and theorizing about those differences are largely missing from his work as well (For a comprehensive review of research in this area see Cross, Parham, & Helms, in press; for a treatise applying Cross' notions across the adult life cycle, see Parham, this volume).

In summary, 1) many Blacks have a predominantly positive racial identity, with perhaps a minority having a negative identity; 2) Black identity has links to behavior; and 3) Black identity can have links to other attitudes and personality characteristics. However, the issue of whether an individual's type (positive, negative) of Black identity is linked to their level of personal self-esteem seems unresolved. While Cross (1985), Clark (1982), and Houston (1984) find no evidence for such a link, Gibbs (1974), Parham and Helms (1985a, 1985b) and Wright (1985) do find empirical evidence for it.

Competent Personality

M. B. Smith (1968) describes competence as an important aspect of personality functioning. He bases his discussion on the theoretical work of Robert White (1960) and his empirical study of "competent" Peace Corps volunteers. Smith sees the competent person as having views of the self, the world and behaviors that fit together, and are trans-cultural (and trans-racial). The person has positive self-esteem, but more importantly a sense of potency and efficacy in the world—a sense he or she can cause desirable things to happen. The person also has "hope" about the world—an attitude that effort can achieve results in the real world. Smith also describes a behavioral component to competence, since he expects the competent person to set "realistic," moderately challenging goals for himself. Tyler (1978), with a conception of competence similar to Smith's, explored the idea that competence is a configuration of personality traits, attitudes toward the world, and behaviors. Focusing on Rotter's Internal-External control dimension, level of trust (rather than Smith's hope) and an "active coping orientation" that has behavioral attributes like realistic goal setting, he surveyed three samples of college students. He found that the configuration held across the three samples and was independent of social desirability and aptitude.

Unfortunately, studies focusing on "competent" adult Blacks are sparse. Ramseur (1982), in a study of stress and and coping mechanisms among "successful" (competent) Black administrators at White universities, surveyed the literature and interviewed six "successful" male and female Black administrators. The interviewed administrators were found to have high self-esteem and realism about the self and their work environment. They were also planful and had set career strategies for themselves in ways that pointed to a high sense of internal control. These administrators also seemed to positively identify with being Black and took a pragmatic view of race-related issues and problems they confronted.

While the group of studies examining competent Black adults is small, a number of studies have had adolescents as their focus. Looney and Lewis (1983) examined 11 "competent" working-class Black adolescents and 11 upper-middle class White ones. The Black (and White) youngsters were strikingly secure and open, were described as "doers"—active and self-assertive, as generally good students, and as having wide networks of friends. The authors described their "competent" families, all of whom were two-parent ones, as having open communication, openness with affection, a focus on efficiently solving problems, as encouraging the development of autonomy, and as showing high emotional support of members. Lee (1984,1985) studied competent Black adolescents in a rural county in the deep South. In his 1984 study of these academically and socially "successful" students, Lee found them to have "positive, but realistic" views of the self, an internal locus of control, high achievement motivation, and strong social networks outside the family. Students described their families as having a high degree of open communication, and their parents as "strict", or close to it, in terms of rules and discipline. Lee rated most of them as having low to moderate levels of "Black consciousness". Griffin and Korchin (1980) initially interviewed 16 junior college faculty members for their descriptions of the "ideal" competent personality for an adolescent Black male. These faculty members then nominated "competent" Black male students (13) who were studied along with "average" peers (10) who volunteered for the study. Faculty members, both Black and White, saw competent male Black adolescents similarly: as able to adapt to many different settings—academic and social; as goal oriented, with realistic, flexible goals; and as able to be disciplined and self-confident in the face of difficult conditions. Both competent and average students scored as "well-adjusted," on Offer's self-image questionnaire and in general seemed to be functioning effectively. Competent males, however, were more inner-directed, more ambitious, goal-striving more vigorously, and less concerned with their acceptability to others than were their "average" peers.

The ability to draw conclusions from the studies in this area is limited by a number of methodological problems. The differing definitions of "competence" used in the studies, small sample sizes, the usual lack of a control group, the focus on adolescents as subjects (see studies by Edwards, 1976; Griffin & Korchin, 1980; Looney and Lewis, 1983; Lee, 1984, 1985), and the lack of discussion of gender differences combine to limit the force of conclusions that can be drawn. However, trends do emerge: 1) Positive self-esteem, a high sense of efficacy, active coping strategies ("a doer"), being achievement oriented, and having good social relations, are characteristics that seem to regularly occur together; 2) At least a mildly positive identification with Blacks and a pragmatic view of race relations were also regularly present; and 3) Certain family backgrounds seem most common for competent Black individuals: high family stability, both marital and residential, high emotional support generally, and encouragement of academic achievement. Clear rules and regulations at home ("strictness") was another common finding, along with "competents" being first-borns.

Stress/Adaptation

In recent years, the stress/mediation/coping model has inspired a great deal of empirical work involving Black adults.

A number of studies have looked at links between aspects of stress, (appraisal, coping resources, coping styles) and the level of psychological well-being or distress of Black adults. This section will briefly review work on the role of appraisal of stress, external and internal coping resources, and the coping styles of Black adults.

Appraisal. Do Blacks and Whites differ in their appraisal of the severity or meaning of different stressors? Little systematic information exists on these questions, but there are some suggestive studies. Komaroff, Masuda, and Holmes (1968) compared Whites, Blacks, and Mexican-Americans on their assessment of the amount of adaptation required by certain life-change events (e.g., marriage, moving). The three groups of low income subjects rank-ordered the items in similar fashion, with Blacks and Mexican-Americans in closest agreement.

Barbarin (1983) in a review of stress and appraisal among Black families, points to three factors that might be important in Blacks' appraisal of stress: religious orientation, causal attributions of undesirable events to racial discrimination, and "paradoxical" control beliefs. He argues that personal religiosity and involvement in organized religion can enhance coping by providing a basis for optimism and a cognitive framework for understanding stressful episodes. He also found in an empirical study (Barbarin et al., 1981) that Blacks more frequently interpret negative life outcomes in terms of individual and institutional discrimination than do Whites. In addition, based on that 1981 study, he argues that Blacks often have "paradoxical" control attributions. This means they have a sense of personal efficacy but at the same time the sense that Blacks as a group have little control over their destiny. Overall, then, his work suggests that religious orientation, perception of discrimination, and sense of control over stressful events may be significant factors in Blacks' appraisal of stress. His work also suggests a type or style of appraisal that differs from that of White Americans.

External coping resources. A number of researchers have examined the topic of external resources that Blacks use to cope with stress (see also chapter by Taylor and Chatters, this volume). A quote cited by George and McNamara (1984) summarizes many of the findings well:

> We know Black people have a history of being religious and oriented towards their kinship and friendship networks for buffering the stresses of life, but we were surprised by the extent to which the data [from American Blacks] reveal family and church to be essential elements in the lives of our respondents (*ISR Newsletter*, 1983: 7).

Neff (1985), in a brief review, points out that adjusting for age and social class, Blacks show higher levels than Whites for church attendance, interaction with friends, enjoyment of clubs, and help from both friends and relatives. Blacks also more often had a family member nearby, had contact with relatives living close by, and were somewhat more likely than Whites to perceive relatives as available sources of help.

Blacks have also been found to rely more than Whites on informal social networks (family, friends) than formal ones to cope with stress (Gibson, 1982; Barbarin, 1983). Neighbors, Jackson, et al. (1983) found that for *all* socio-demographic groups of Black adults in a national survey sample, informal social networks were used first and more substantially than formal sources of help. Gibson (1982), in a reanalysis of national survey data from 1957 and 1976, looked at middle-aged and elderly Black adults' resources and coping styles. She found that Blacks in middle and late life were more likely to seek help from friends (1957) and from a combination of family members (1976) than were Whites. That is, Whites were more likely to only turn to a spouse or one family member with their worries than were Blacks. This difference held even when all social variables were held constant. Gibson also found that Blacks shifted from talking with friends in middle years to multiple family members in later years.

In addition, other studies point to the importance of supportive social and kin networks. For example, Holahan, et al. (1983) studying working-class Black and White women in Austin, Texas found that although Black women reported more psychological symptoms than White women, the difference was explained by a race and social (network) integration interaction. Black women with high social network scores (friends, neighborhood contacts, job) showed mental health levels similar to White women. Those Black women low in social integration showed mental health scores in the pathological range. All measures of social integration showed a much greater relation to mental health scores for Black women than White. Dressler (1985) studied the ability of the extended Black family to buffer stress in a Black community in a small Alabama town. He linked recent stressful events, chronic stress, kin and non-kin support, and depression for Black subjects. Those Black adults who perceived their kin to be supportive reported fewer symptoms of depression. The number of kin and non-kin support sources were not related to depression. However, there was no buffering effect for chronic stressors, like economic problems. Interesting gender differences arose as well. Extended kin support was far more beneficial for males than females. For females over 34, extended kin support was as powerful in reducing symptoms of depression as economic stressors in creating them. Females 17-34 years old received no benefits in protection from depression through extended kin support. Dresser defined support as money, information, and help with tasks for both sexes.

Internal coping resources. Religion has historically played a powerful role in the life of the Black community and for Black individuals. It apparently continues to do so given recent research findings. George and McNamara (1984) note that studies have found Blacks to be more frequent church attenders than Whites. Their re-analysis of 1972-1982 national survey data which looked at religion, subjective life satisfaction, and health produced several striking findings: 1) For Blacks, far more than for Whites a sense of well-being seems markedly enhanced by religious attendance and by stated strength of religious affiliation, at *all* levels of age, education and income. Black women seem to derive most life satisfaction from church attendance and Black men from stated strength of religious affiliation ("religiosity"). For both sexes, their respective measures of religious involvement are highly predictive of global happiness, subjective health, and satisfaction with family life.

Bowman (1985) used a national survey sample of Black husband/fathers to examine the links between stress (employment difficulties and consequent difficulties fulfilling the provider role in the family), coping resources, and psychological well-being (here, "subjective life happiness"). Bowman examined five coping resources—multiple economic providers, family closeness, non-kin friendship, racial ideology (system-blame), and religious orientation. He found that religious orientation had a much stronger positive effect on the level of life happiness among Black fathers than did family cohesion or any other informal coping resource investigated.

Harrison, Bowman, and Beale (1985) used a national sample of Black working mothers to investigate the links between stress (role strains from being a worker and a mother), coping resources, and psychological well-being. They examined five coping resources—religious orientation, family closeness, best friend, child care availability, and child care advice. They found that religious orientation was the most important coping resource followed by family closeness. They also found that the five coping resources together significantly offset the stress from role strain these Black mothers experienced and therefore positively affected their psychological well-being.

Coping styles. Neighbors, Jackson, et al. (1983), Barbarin (1983), and Gibson (1982) found prayer to be the most common coping response to worries or stressful episodes for Blacks. Moreover, prayer was used substantially more by Black adults at all age ranges than by Whites. Neighbors found that the coping response ranked "most helpful" by Blacks after prayer was an instrumental one: "Facing the problem squarely and doing something about it." Neighbors found that among subjects with economic difficulties lower income people were more likely to use prayer as a coping strategy; and that overall a majority of Blacks using prayer found that it made economic troubles "easier to bear" (Neighbors & Jackson et al., 1983). Perhaps there is a fusion of external resource (church association) with internal resource (religiosity), and coping style (use of prayer) for many Black adults.

Lykes (1983) studied how 52 successful Black women coped with incidents of racial and sexual discrimination over their life histories. The women were 70 or older at the time of the study and Lykes worked from transcripts of their oral histories. She linked situational variables (racial composition of workplace, type of discrimination identified), personal factors (perception of the control of the outcome, source of the problem) and coping (direct, instrumental, and flexibility). The study and findings are complex, but Lykes was able to look at the stress-mediation-coping process for individual "competent" Black women over time, and provide useful insights. In part, she found that these Black women were discriminating and adaptive in their use of coping responses in response to situational demands and constraints. She also found that directness (confrontation vs. indirect) and flexibility (use of several strategies) of coping were independent dimensions of coping style for these women.

Several findings emerge from these studies of stress and coping:

while Black adults may not differ from others in their appraisal of the stressfulness of particular events, they may have a cognitive framework for appraising stress that is significantly different from that of White Americans. In addition, Blacks seem to rely on informal social networks (kin, friends, church) to buffer stress to a significantly greater degree than White adults. Religious involvement—church attendance, "religiosity"— is also an important factor in buffering stress for many Black adults. There are some suggestive findings that point to typical patterns of coping with stress, that is, coping styles, among Black adults that may differ significantly from those of their White peers.

Conclusions

What are the social and psychological characteristics of psychologically healthy Black adults and how do they change over the life cycle? No existing theory or model satisfactorily addresses these questions. While "universal" models of psychological health offer some positive perspectives and ideas, they generally have little to say about the impact of the unique social-cultural context of Black Americans. Other models that focus on Black personality and identity have generally assumed a pathological reaction and a lack of diversity in reactions to the social/cultural context by Blacks. While neither body of theory provides an adequate model, taken together, along with work on the social and cultural situation of American Blacks, they do provide a basis for hypothesizing about the central psychological issues for Black adult psychological health. Those issues are: 1) maintaining an overall positive self-conception; 2) maintaining a positive group (Black)identity and community connection; 3) maintaining an accurate perception of the social environment—including its racism; 4) effectively adapting to the social environment confronting a Black individual—coping with its stressors and adapting to both Black and White cultures; 5) developing and maintaining emotional intimacy with others; 6) maintaining a sense of competence and the ability to work productively.

What are the major findings of recent empirical research in areas that theory indicates are important for Black adult psychological health? In the area of self-conception recent research has pointed out that many Black adults have positive self-esteem, that they use Blacks as significant others, and that they use a Black social context for their social comparisons and self-evaluations. In addition, Black adults may use "system-blame" explanations of failure to protect their self-esteem. Other studies point out that many Blacks have positive or largely positive racial identities and that racial identity has links to behavior and other personality characteristics. Cross (1980) offers a stage theory of Black identity development that has empirical support for some of its propositions and Parham (this volume) has extended these notions across the Black adult life span. Black adults may also have a cognitive framework for appraising stress that is significantly different from their White peers. They also appear to use different internal and external resources to buffer stress: relying on informal social networks and religious involvement to a greater degree than do Whites. These different types of appraisal and resource use may be tied to unique Black coping styles. Other research on competence indicates that positive self-esteem, a sense of personal efficacy, active coping strategies, achievement orientation, good social relations and a positive racial identity may regularly occur together to form what might be called a "Black competent personality". Certain family backgrounds and childrearing practices also seem associated with these characteristics.

What are the implications of these theories and recent research? Several central ones stand out: 1) Some Black American adults possess "positive" or "healthy" psychological characteristics and functioning. Theories or models that postulate universal pathology or pathological outcomes are clearly unhelpful and do not fit current findings; 2) Particularly in the area of self-esteem, some of the sources and mechanisms that maintain these "healthy" characteristics are being identified, theorized about, and empirically investigated; 3) Developing new models and expanding current theory is a vital task at this point, particularly work outside of the area of self-esteem. For example, a rigorous definition of the dimensions of Black identity and its links to other aspects of self-conception, personality, and behavior would be extremely useful. A clear definition and conceptualization of the Black "competent personality" would also be helpful. Examining emotional intimacy and interpersonal relations among Blacks would be a valuable addition. Forging theoretical links with other traditions and newer theories in psychology and sociology are other necessities. Rutter's (1979) discussion of "protective factors" and more recent discussions of the "invulnerability" of some children in the face of stress have obvious relevance; 4) Empirical research using adult subjects, with large samples, sophisticated designs and statistical rigor, is sorely needed. New research needs to be guided by theory and to be sensitive to gender differences and the diversity by class, region and home country within the American Black community. For example, research that investigated the actual degree of association of the characteristics said to comprise the "Black competent personality" and that looked at gender, class, and regional differences would be extremely valuable. 5) Perhaps the model of the "competent personality" has the ability to unite and make sense of recent research findings on self-concept, personality characteristics, and behavioral coping styles. It also offers a link to a theoretical/research tradition in psychology that has been fruitful. Finally, recent theoretical and empirical findings and the increasing research interest in areas this chapter identified as central to understanding Black adult psychological health mark this as an important period for the field.

References

Barbarin, O. (1983). Coping with ecological transitions by Black families: A psychosocial model. *Journal of Community Psychology, 11*, 308-322.
Barbarin, O., Maish, K., & Shorter, S. (1981). Mental health among Blacks. In O. Barbarin, P. Good, O. Pharr, & J. Siskind (Eds.), *Institutional racism and community competence.*
Rockville, MD: U.S. Department of Health and Human Services (DHHS Publication #ADM81-907).
Barnes, E. J. (1980). The Black community as a source of positive self-concept for Black children: A theoretical perspective. In R. Jones (Ed.), *Black Psychology,* 106-138. New York: Harper & Row.
Bowman, P. (1985). Black fathers and the provider role: Role strain, informal coping resource, and life happiness. In W. Boykin (Ed.), *Proceedings.* Seventh Conference on Empirical Research in Black Psychology, 9-21. Rockville, MD: N.I.M.H.
Cervantes, R. C. & Castro, F. G. (1985). Stress, coping, and Mexican American mental health: A systemic review. *Hispanic Journal of Behavioral Sciences, 7(1),* 1-73.
Clark, M. L. (1982). Racial group concept and self-esteem in Black children. *Journal of Black Psychology, 8(2),* 75-89.
Cross, T. (1984). *The Black power imperative: Racial inequality and the politics of non-violence.* New York: Faulkner Books.
Cross, W. E. (1980). Models of psychological nigrescence: A literature review. In R. Jones (Ed.), *Black Psychology.* New York: Harper & Row.
Cross, W. E. (1985). Black identity: Rediscovering the distinction between personal identity and reference group orientation. In M. Spencer, G. Brookings, & W. Allen (Eds.), *Beginnings: The social and affective development of Black children,* 155-173. Hillsdale, NJ: Lawrence Erlbaum Associates.
Cross, W. E., Parham, T. & Helms, J. (In press). Nigresence revisited: Theory and Research. In R. L. Jones (Ed.), *Advances in Black Psychology.*
Dressler, W. W. (1985). Extended family relationships, social support, and mental health in a southern Black community. *Journal of Health and Social Behavior, 26,* 39-48.
Edwards, D. W. (1974). Blacks versus Whites: When is race a relevant variable? *Journal of Personality and Social Psychology, 29(1),* 39-49.
Edwards, O. L. (1976). Components of academic success: A profile of achieving Black adolescents. *Journal of Negro Education, 45,* 408-422.
Erickson, E. (1968). *Identity, youth, and crisis.* New York: Norton.
Gary, L. E. (Ed.) (1978). *Mental health: A challenge to the Black community.* Philadelphia: Dorrance & Co.
George, A., & McNamara, P. (1984). Religion, race and psychological well-being. *Journal for the Scientific Study of Religion, 23(4),* 351-363.

George, J. C., & Brooker, A. E. (1984). Conceptualization of mental health. *Psychological Reports, 55,* 329-330.

Gibbs, J. T. (1985). City girls: Psychosocial adjustment of urban Black adolescent females. *Sage, 2(2),* 28-36.

Gibbs, J. (1974). Patterns of adaptation among Black students at a predominantly White university: Selected case studies. *American Journal of Ortho-Psychiatry, 44,* 728-740.

Gibson, R. (1982). Blacks at middle and late life: Resources and coping. *Annals of the American Academy of Political and Social Science, 464,* 79-90.

Grier, W., & Cobbs, P. (1969). *Black rage.* New York: Basic Books.

Griffin, Q. D., & Korchin, S. J. (1980). Personality competence in Black male adolescents. *Journal of Youth and Adolescence, 9(3),* 211-227.

Gurin, P., & Epps, E. (1975). *Black consciousness, identity, and achievement: A study of students in historically Black colleges.* New York: John Wiley & Sons, Inc.

Guterman, S. (1972). *Black psyche: The modal personality patterns of Black Americans.* Berkeley, CA: Glendessary Press.

Harrison, A. O., Bowman, P., Berale, R. (1985). Role strain, coping resources, and psychological well-being among Black working mothers. In W. Boykin (Ed.), *Proceedings.* Seventh Conference on Empirical Research in Black Psychology, 21-29. Rockville, MD: N.I.M.H.

Heiss, J. & Owens, S. (1972). Self-evaluations of Blacks and Whites. *American Journal of Sociology, 78,* 360-370.

Holahan, C. J., Betak, J. F., Spearly, J. L., Chance, B. J. (1983). Social integration and mental health in a biracial community. *American Journal of Community Psychology, 11(3),* 301-311.

Houston, L. (1984). Black consciousness and self-esteem. *Journal of Black Psychology, 11(1),* 1-7.

Institute for Social Research (1983). Black Americans surveyed. *I.S.R. Newsletter,* 5-6. Ann Arbor: Institute for Social Research.

Jahoda, M. (1958). *Current concepts of positive mental health.* New York: Basic Books.

Jensen, G. F., White, C. S., & Galliher, J. M. (1982). Ethnic status and adolescent self-evaluations: An extension of research on minority self-esteem. *Social Problems, 30(2),* 226-239.

Jones, E. E., & Korchin, S. J. (1982). *Minority mental health.* New York: Praeger.

Jones, J. M. (1972). *Prejudice and racism.* Reading, MA: Addison-Wesley Publishers.

Kardiner, A., & Ovesey, L. (1951). *The Mark of Oppression: Explorations in the personality of the American Negro.* New York: World Books.

Karon, B. P. (1958). *The Negro personality: A rigorous investigation of the effects of culture.* New York: Springer.

Komaroff, A. C., Masuda, M., & Holmes, T. H. (1968). The social readjustment rating scale: A comparative study of Negro, Mexican, and White Americans. *Journal of Psychosomatic Research 12(2),* 121-128.

Lazarus, R. (1975). The healthy personality—A review of conceptualizations and research. In L. Levi (Ed.), *Society, stress and disease* (Vol. 2). *Childhood and adolescence,* 6-35. New York: Oxford U. Press.

Lee, C. C. (1984). An investigation of psychosocial variables related to academic success for rural Black adolescents. *Journal of Negro Education, 53(4),* 424-434.

Lee, C. C. (1985). Successful rural Black adolescents: A psychosocial profile. *Adolescence, 20(77),* 129-142.

Looney, J. G., & Lewis, J. M. (1983). Competent adolescents from different socioeconomic and ethnic contexts. *Adolescent Psychiatry, 2,* 64-74.

Lykes, M. B. (1983). Discrimination and coping in the lives of Black women: Analyses of oral history data. *Journal of Social Issues, 39(3),* 79-100.

Maslow, A. (1968). *Towards a psychology of being.* (2nd ed.) Princeton, NJ: Van Nostrand.

McCarthy, J., & Yancey, W. (1971). Uncle Tom and Mr. Charlie: Metaphysical pathos in the study of racism and personal disorganization. *American Journal of Sociology, 76,* 648-672.

Moore, H. B. (1982). The Black sisterhood: A second look. *Women and Therapy, 1(3),* 39-50.

Neff, J. (1985). Race and vulnerability to stress: An examination of differential vulnerability. *Journal of Personality and Social Psychology, 49(2),* 481-491.

Neighbors, H. W. (1984). The distribution of psychiatric morbidity in Black Americans: A review and suggestions for research. *Community Mental Health Journal, 20(3),* 169-181.

Neighbors, H., Jackson, J., Bowman, P. & Gurin, G. (1983). Stress, coping, and Black mental health: Preliminary findings from a national study. *Prevention in Human Services, 2,* 1-25.

Nobles, W. W. (1976). Extended self: Rethinking the so-called Negro self-concept. *Journal of Black Psychology, 2(2),* 15-25.

Parham, T., & Helms, J. (1985a). Relations of racial identity attitudes to self-actualization and affective states of Black students. *Journal of Counseling Psychology,* Vol. 32 3, 431-440.

Parham, T., & Helms, J. (1985b). Attitudes of racial identity and self-esteem of Black students: An exploratory investigation. *Journal of College Student Personnel,* Vol. 26, 143-147.

Pettigrew, T. W. (1964). *A profile of the Negro American.* Princeton, NJ: VanNostrand.

Pierce, C. (1974). Psychiatric problems of the Black minority. In A. Arieti (Ed.), *American Handbook of Psychiatry,* (2nd ed.), 2, 524-534.

Porter, J. & Washington, R. (1979). Black identity and self-esteem: A review of studies of Black self concept 1968-1978. *Annual Review of Sociology, 5* 53-74.

Ramseur, H. (1975). Continuity and change in Black identity: Black students at an interracial college. Cambridge, Mass: Unpublished Ph.D. dissertation, Harvard University.

Ramseur, H. (1982). Major sources of stress and coping strategies of Black administrators at White universities. *Proceedings.* First National Conference on Black Administrators at White Universities. Cambridge, MA: Massachusetts Institute of Technology Black Administrators Association.

Rutter, M. (1979). Protective factors in children's responses to stress and disadvantage. In M. Kent & J. Rold (Eds.), *Primary Prevention of Psychopathology, 3,* 49-79. Hanover, NH: University Press of New England.

Simmons, R. G. (1978). Blacks and high self esteem: A puzzle. *Social Psychology, 41(1),* 54-57.

Smith, M. B. (1961). "Mental health" reconsidered: A special case of the problem of values in psychology. *American Psychologist, 16,* 299-306.

Smith, M. B. (1968). Competence and socialization. In J. Clausen (Ed.), *Socialization and Society,* 270-320. Boston: Little, Brown and Co.

Smith, W. D., Burlew, A. K., & Mosley, M. H. (1978). *Minority issues in mental health.* Reading, Mass.: Addison-Wesley.

Spurlock, J. (1986). Development of self-conception in Afro-American children. *Hospital and Community Psychiatry, 37(1)* January, 66-70.

Stock, W. A., Okun, M. A., Haring, M. J., Witter, R. A. (1985). Race and subjective well-being in adulthood: A Black-White research synthesis. *Human Development, 28,* 192-197.

Taylor, R. L. (1976). Psychosocial development among Black children and youth: A reexamination. *American Journal of Orthopsychiatry, 46(2),* 4-19.

Thomas, A. & Sillen, S. (1972). *Racism and psychiatry.* Secaucus, N.J.: Citadel Press.

Thomas, C. S. & Comer, J. (1973). Racism and mental health services. In C. Willie, B. Kramer, & B. Brown (Eds.), *Racism and Mental Health.* Pittsburgh: University of Pittsburgh Press.

Tyler, F. (1978). Individual psychosocial competence: A personality configuration. *Educational and Psychological Measurement, 38,* 309-323.

Veroff, J., Douvan, E., & Kulka, R. A. (1981). *The inner American: A self-portrait from 1957 to 1976.* New York: Basic Books.

White, R. (1960). Competence and the psychosexual stages of development. In M. Jones (Ed.), *Nebraska Symposium on Motivation 1960,* 97-141. Lincoln: University of Nebraska Press.

Wilcox, C. (1973). Positive mental health for Blacks. In C. Willie, B. Kramer, & B. Brown (Eds.), *Racism and Mental Health.* Pittsburgh: University of Pittsburgh Press.

Wright, B. (1985). Effects of racial self-esteem on personal self-esteem of Black youth. *International Journal of Intercultural Relations, 9(1),* 19-30.

Yancey, W. L., Rigsby, L., & McCarthy, J. D. (1972). Social position and self-evaluation: The relative importance of race. *American Journal of Sociology, 78,* 338-359.

Part III
Support Systems

FAMILY, FRIEND, AND CHURCH SUPPORT NETWORKS OF BLACK AMERICANS

Robert Joseph Taylor and Linda M. Chatters

Introduction

The concept of informal social support and support networks has been a consistent theme in research and writings on Black Americans. Formal and informal support networks developed in part as the result of a particular set of conditions in American society in which Black Americans were systematically excluded from diverse spheres of activity, in particular economic, political, educational, and civic arenas. Lacking access to social institutions and roles within larger society, Black communities developed parallel institutions and mechanisms to serve their needs. It has been a common practice of theoretical treatments to view Black networks and institutions strictly as compensatory reactions to exclusion from mainstream society. This perspective unfortunately views Black institutions as mere imitations of their counterparts in wider society. As such, Black institutions have been frequently characterized as, at best, poor substitutes or caricatures of White institutions, and at worst, dysfunctional organizations which in effect impede the development of Black communities and individuals. This perspective, whether in its more benign or perjorative form, fails to appreciate the truly innovative and adaptive features of these networks and organizations.

A long tradition of theory and research in the social sciences has documented the critical position and functions of supportive networks in the economic, social, and political development of Blacks. These supportive networks, organized within family, church, and neighborhood settings, exert diverse and far-reaching influences on individuals, families, and communities. The most widely investigated of support networks are those which are organized within the family, although church and neighborhood networks are receiving increasing attention in the literature.

Research and theory acknowledge that individuals in the United States are not isolated from their kinship networks, but are members of modified extended families (Dono et al., 1979). The modified extended family is characterized by frequent interaction, close affective bonds, and the exchange of goods between family members (Bengtson & Cutler, 1976;

Troll et al., 1979). Members of modified extended families typically live within visiting distance, interact by choice, and are connected to one another by means of mutual aid and social activities.

Current definitions of social support emphasize that it is provided in a variety of forms, including the provision of instrumental or material aid (e.g., food, money, transportation, running errands), cognitive aid (e.g., advice, counseling) and emotional assistance (i.e., visiting, companionship) [see Antonucci, (1985) for a discussion of definitions and measurement approaches to social support]. The diversity in types of assistance means that face-to-face interaction and proximity of family members are not strictly prerequisites for receiving support. Despite the significance of informal support for Black individuals and communities, few explicit theoretical models of assistance have been advanced to understand these relationships. What is available in the literature is largely descriptive of support networks and relationships. Work in the area of social support, however, has begun the task of model development.

Overview of Chapter

The present chapter reviews the literature on the support networks of Black Americans with an emphasis on recent research. Both familial and nonfamilial (i.e., friend, neighbor, and church member) support relationships are examined. The chapter begins with a discussion of current life course perspectives on social support processes. Research focusing on two factors which influence the exchange of support (i.e., living arrangements and kinship interaction) is then examined. A review of ethnographic research on familial support is next presented, followed by a review of survey research findings on the family support relationships of Blacks. Next, competing theoretical models of kin and non-kin supportive relationships are disussed, followed by an examination of research on friendship and church support networks. Literature examining both racial differences and subgroup differences among Blacks will be reviewed for each topic presented. Particular emphasis is given research which investigates the support networks of elderly Blacks.

Life Course Perspectives on Social Support

Except for a few models addressing helper choice, research on informal assistance, and particularly support relationships among Black Americans, has been largely descriptive and lacking in theoretical grounding. Even less attention has been devoted to understanding life course variation in the nature of supportive relationships. This section of the chapter will: 1) briefly review research on the nature of age differences in support, 2) present a life course model of social support known as the support convoy, and 3) discuss available research among Black Americans within the context of the convoy model.

Age Differences in Social Support

Empirical research on social support has identified discrete changes in the nature of helping relationships across different age groups. Specifically, age variations in support indicate that older persons are less likely than younger individuals to provide assistance to network members and are less likely to receive assistance from family (Antonucci & Depner, 1981; Lee, 1980). Network size, however, appears to be unaffected by advancing age.

Research among the Black population provides some evidence for age differences in social support relationships as well. Taylor and Chatters (1988) examined the role of church members as providers of assistance to adult Blacks and found that older respondents were less likely than younger persons to receive support. A more focused analysis among older Black adults (Taylor & Chatters, 1986a) found that the relationship between age and support was moderated by other factors. For elderly persons with children, advanced age was associated with increases in the frequency of assistance from church members. Among childless elderly, increases in age were associated with dramatic decreases in the frequency of support. This finding suggests that adult children function as linkages to church support networks for their elderly parents. Similarly, age was differentially related to levels of support dependent upon whether the older person was a church member. Those who were church members received roughly comparable levels of assistance. Nonmembers who were of advanced age received significantly more support than their relatively younger counterparts. Among this group of older persons, age may be a particularly critical factor in the allocation of support resources.

Age differences however, provide only a limited understanding of possible life course changes in social support. First of all, the evidence for age differences in supportive relationships is based on cross-sectional data in which the influences of cohort and period effects are unknown. Age differences in supportive behaviors observed in current cohorts of adults may in fact be reflective of unique socialization experiences and/or exposure to historical events. Longitudinal designs are needed to investigate lifelong patterns of involvement in supportive relationships. These studies will help to determine whether the social isolation found among some elderly and age differences in supportive behaviors are in actuality the result of aging or a continuation of lifelong tendencies which are unique to select cohorts of the adult population.

Second, aging represents only one aspect of the phenomenon of life course progression. The notion of the life course embodies more than chronological aging, and encompasses the nature, pattern, and timing of life roles and events. The life course, as a constellation of life events and roles, is subject to variation as the result of factors such as social status (e.g., race, socioeconomic status) as well as differences due to historical and social change. As such, aging is merely a proxy for these diverse influences and provides a rough indicator of how supportive behaviors may change in relation to the course of one's life.

Convoys of Social Support

One perspective which addresses the nature of support networks across the life course is based on the notion of the support convoy (Antonucci, 1985; Kahn, 1979; Kahn & Antonucci, 1980). Specifically, the support convoy represents in a broad sense the constellation of support providers that an individual has at any one point in their lives. The determinants of the convoy, the manner in which it is organized and functions, and its effects on the focal individual are discrete components of the convoy model. The convoy as a dynamic entity, develops and changes over time and in response to particular life occurrences and major role changes. College education, entry into the work world, changes in career and employment patterns, marriage, the birth and rearing of minor children, launching of adult children, geographic relocations, divorce, retirement, and widowhood are the types of life roles and events which both initiate and modify the nature of an individual's support convoy.

Over the course of life, convoy membership changes as old members are lost and new ones gained, ultimately affecting the structural and dynamic characteristics of the convoy. Structural features of the support convoy include its size, composition or homogeneity (membership similarity), stability (length of membership), connectedness (network members who know each other), symmetry (reciprocity of relationships), and complexity (members who share support functions). The dynamic aspects of the support convoy relate to the fact that the convoy model itself is longitudinal and based on supportive relationships as they endure and change over time (Antonucci, 1985, p. 99). Thus, in addition to increases and decreases in members, the nature of relationships with convoy members who have had a continuing association with the focal individual may be transformed.

The history of the support relationship has an influence on the types of supportive functions which are elicited from convoy members. A shared history of reciprocal assistance predisposes the enlistment of specific convoy members. This past record of aid constitutes a "support reserve" which establishes obligations and normative expectations for assistance. The support convoy model is compatible with other models of support transactions. Specifically, models of assistance to older individuals frequently emphasize the importance of filial obligations and bonds for enlisting support persons and the matching of support tasks (i.e., in terms of difficulty and commitment) to support providers (Cantor, 1979; Shanas, 1979). Inherent in these formulations is the notion that assistance transactions involve a sense of obligation which derives from familial relationships and/or a shared history of reciprocal aid.

Support Convoys and Black Americans

The notion of the support convoy, because it is tied to the concepts of life roles and events, is a particularly adaptable and flexible framework which can be used to understand supportive networks and relationships among subgroups of the population. Different population groups, as defined for example by race, gender, and socioeconomic status, vary in the nature, timing, and sequencing of important life roles and events (Hagestad & Neugarten, 1985). Differences in the timing and sequencing of life events and roles are possible, as well as differences in the types of events themselves. For example, we know that labor market history and experiences will be very different for persons of diverse racial and socioeconomic backgrounds. Low income groups and racial minorities, in contrast to traditional work and employment patterns, may be faced with conditions of chronic unemployment and underemployment. The convoy model accommodates these differences because it incorporates the influences of person (e.g., age, gender, race) and situation (e.g., resources, opportunities) characteristics in the formation and functioning of the convoy. As such, it provides a useful framework for understanding support relationships across diverse groups and may be particularly helpful in exploring the effects of unique cultural and social structure factors.

Ethnographic work on the support networks of Black Americans, although not directly addressing the notion of a support convoy, is suggestive of similar mechanisms. In particular, long-term bonds of association and mutual assistance with both kin and non-kin give rise to a sense of shared obligation among support participants. Living arrangements and kin and non-kin interaction patterns suggest a similarity with the properties of support convoys.

Recent survey research efforts have highlighted the role of family relationships and feelings of family closeness in the selection of helpers to the informal support networks of older Black adults (Chatters et al., 1985, 1986). These studies show that relationships which embody the strongest sense of filial obligation and a history of reciprocal assistance (i.e., spouse and children) are most commonly enlisted first as support providers. In the absence of these preferred providers, other individuals are recruited. Similarly, expressed feelings of affective closeness to family members facilitated the use of family helpers over other categories.

The significance of Black churches as a source of assistance to Black Americans and their similarities with the support convoy model have been demonstrated in recent work (Taylor & Chatters, 1986a; 1986b; 1988). Blacks are often affiliated with a church at an early age and develop long-term associations with them. Churches are integrally involved with a variety of life events and transitions such as marriage, the birth of children, personal illness, and death of significant others. Several studies suggest that church involvement variables (i.e., frequency of attendance, perceived importance of church attendance and religion, church membership) are important as determinants of the receipt of support from church members (Taylor & Chatters, 1986a; 1988). These findings are congruent with research on informal support networks, and suggest that support from church members is a reward for one's past record of participation in church activities.

Analyses focusing on the types of assistance provided by the church and other support groups (i.e., family and friends) have noted that Black churches are preeminent in the provision of emotional and spiritual support, as well as help during illness. In some instances, however, churches provided financial assistance, material goods, and services (Taylor & Chatters, 1986a; 1986b; 1988). These findings suggest that Black churches are an integral component of the support networks of Black Americans. The reciprocal nature and long-term commitments to a church suggest that it is amenable to a support convoy interpretation.

The notion of a support convoy is a potentially worthwhile area for future research on life course changes in the nature and functioning of the support networks of Black Americans. The findings which are to be reviewed in subsequent sections of this chapter were not derived from a support convoy perspective.

However, because different aspects of the convoy model (i.e., its longitudinal focus, structural and dynamic properties, emphasis on a history of past association and reciprocal assistance) are found throughout this work, it may be a useful context in which to view the discussion. The ultimate usefulness of the support convoy perspective for understanding support among Black Americans will be determined empirically. We will return to the convoy model at the end of the chapter in our discussion of future directions for research.

Familial Support Networks

Living Arrangements of Blacks

A considerable amount of research in the family literature has focused on the living arrangements and household structure of Black Americans. One of the most consistent findings has been that Blacks are more likely than Whites to reside in extended households (Allen, 1979; Angel & Tienda, 1982; Gutman, 1976; Hofferth, 1984; Morgan, 1982; Sweet, 1973; Tienda & Angel, 1982; Williams & Stockton, 1973), a racial difference which is maintained even when measures of socioeconomic status are controlled. Billingsley's (1968) seminal work on Black families outlined a typology of extended family structures in which differences in family structure were viewed as responses to economic hardship. Accordingly, it was expected that because extended family structures were an adaptation to scarce economic resources, low income Blacks would be more likely to adopt this pattern than would their higher socioeconomic status counterparts. In support of his argument, Billingsley presented case studies which demonstrated that greater economic stability among middle and upper-income Blacks enabled them to maintain conventional nuclear families. An analysis of Census data (Allen, 1979) found that Blacks were more likely than Whites to reside in extended households. Controls for socioeconomic status diminished, but did not entirely eliminate racial differences in family structure.

Research focusing on the living arrangements of elderly adults also indicated that aged Blacks were more likely to reside in extended households than aged Whites (Mitchell & Register, 1984). Although older Blacks were less likely than older Whites to live with a spouse, they were less likely to live alone and more likely to live with two or more persons (Rubenstein, 1971). Other work suggested that elderly Blacks were more likely than older Whites to reside with children and grandchildren (Shanas, 1979; Mitchell & Register, 1984) and to take children and grandchildren, nieces and nephews into their households (Mitchell & Register, 1984). Among widowed elderly, Blacks had more children living with them than did Whites (Lopata, 1979) and aged Blacks were more likely than older Whites to raise the children of others (Hirsch et al., 1972).

Collectively, this body of work indicates that Blacks of all ages use extended family arrangements to pool limited resources, mitigate economic deprivation and, consequently, create more viable economic units. Unlike earlier efforts (e.g., Frazier, 1939; Moynihan, 1965; Rainwater, 1970), this research views extended family patterns as valid and realistic adaptations to restricted economic opportunities and racial discrimination. The sociological literature on family supports, however, is

251

less concerned with the detailed investigation of how extended family arrangements contribute to the economic well-being of Blacks.

Economic research on intrafamily transfers (Morgan et al., 1962; Moon & Smolensky, 1977) examines the economic benefits which accrue from extended household arrangements. Characteristically, family members in these situations provide economic assistance through a variety of means including direct financial aid, purchases of major gifts (e.g., washer, dryer), and payment for specific services (e.g., educational tuition, nursing home care). Although extended family living arrangements are undertaken for a variety of reasons, economic necessity is clearly one of the most important. Joint residency of two or more nuclear families in an extended family household itself represents a significant form of intrafamily transfer, and among certain groups (e.g., single parents, the young and old, the poor), "doubling up" in extended households has an important bearing on economic welfare. Morgan et al. (1962), investigated the economic benefits of extended households and found that 3 out of 4 nonnuclear adults (i.e., extended kin) improved their economic situation by residing with relatives, while only 5% were adversely affected. Further, residency in extended households is a less expensive method than direct cash transfers of providing for needy relatives.

Recent work by Angel and Tienda (Angel & Tienda, 1982; Tienda & Angel, 1982) on comparative living arrangements documents the greater degree of extendedness among Black families and the mechanisms through which extended families mitigate economic hardship. Tienda and Angel (1982) found that Blacks, in comparison to Whites, were 14% more likely to reside in an extended household and more likely to have a non-nuclear adult residing in the household. Further, these racial differences were maintained when controls for measures of socioeconomic status (i.e., education, employment status, earnings) were utilized. Blacks were not, however, more likely than Whites to have a non-nuclear adult residing in the household who was economically active. Among both Blacks and Hispanics, extended family structures were more prevalent in households which were headed by single parents than in households in which both spouses were present.

Angel and Tienda (1982) found that under conditions of social and economic distress, Black families relied on immediate family and non-nuclear relatives residing within the household for monetary support. The relative contributions of a wife, adult children, and non-nuclear relatives constituted a greater share of the total household income for Blacks than for Whites. Further, adult children and non-nuclear relatives contributed a significant share of the household income in both single and two parent headed families. Apparently, the lower earnings of Black heads of household require that other family members supplement family income to achieve a desired standard of living, or in many cases, simply to meet daily needs. Despite the additional income provided by non-nuclear members, a considerable number of Black households had incomes below the poverty level, suggesting that the economic contributions of non-nuclear members generally failed to offset the labor market disadvantages faced by Blacks.

There are other important economic support benefits which accrue to extended living arrangements. The presence of non-nuclear adults within the household allows for the internal reallocation of market and domestic responsibilities. For example, the presence of another adult in the household on a permanent basis who assists with day care and other household duties, may enable a single parent with a young child to secure employment outside the home (Tienda & Angel, 1982). Similar types of support benefits of extended family households have been documented in research on Black families. Ladner (1971) and Aschenbrenner (1973, 1975) found that many Blacks resided in three-generational households where, among other things, grandparents cared for grandchildren while their own adult children worked. In some instances, Black grandparents informally adopted their grandchildren and cared for them into adulthood (Ladner, 1971). This pattern, in which grandparents functioned as the primary agent of socialization of grandchildren, was found to be more common among Blacks than Whites (Mitchell & Register, 1984).

Despite the significance of this work for understanding extended relationships within households, survey research studies (i.e., Angel & Tienda, 1982; Hofferth, 1984; Morgan, 1982; Tienda & Angel, 1982) likely underestimate the full degree of extended relations within Black families. Ethnographic research demonstrates that, in many instances, several nuclear families reside in separate, but proximal residences (i.e., in the same apartment building or neighborhood) and fully cooperate in the daily tasks of living (e.g., share meals, assist in household tasks) (Aschenbrenner, 1973, 1975). In essence, the functions of extended relations are maintained across physically separated households. Survey research efforts which are based on samples of individual households, generally fail to gather information on extended arrangements which exist across separate households. The survey research findings reviewed here document the prevalence of extended households and their economic benefits, but are less able to examine the nature of extended families which occur across households. This limitation suggests that an approach combining both ethnographic and survey research procedures may provide the most comprehensive picture of extended family patterns.

Kinship Networks of Urban Blacks Families

The detailed investigation of the family and friend interaction patterns of urban Blacks (Blumberg & Bell, 1958; Feagin, 1968; Meadow, 1962; Martineau, 1977), provided important information in rebuttal to the pathology-centered portrayal of Black lifestyles in urban communities (e.g., Moynihan, 1965; Frazier, 1939). The resulting profile of kin interaction demonstrated that the majority of respondents in these studies had frequent contact with their relatives; 65% of the respondents in Meadow's study, 46% of the respondents in Blumberg and Bell's study and 71% of the respondents in Martineau's study reported weekly contact with relatives. This work also demonstrated that urban Blacks lived near their relatives and that residential proximity was positively associated with level of kinship interaction. Feagin's (1968) data on social support exchanges indicated that one out of five respondents reported giving aid to a relative with financial difficulties. Types of informal social support included help in moving from one residence to another, emotional support, and financial advice.

A study of racial differences in kinship relations (Hays & Mindel, 1973) found that Black families interacted with kin on a more frequent basis and perceived them as more significant sources of aid. Black families also had more extended kin residing in the same household than did White families. Furthermore, comparing racial groups on an indicator of social support (i.e., child-rearing assistance), Blacks received help more frequently and received a greater amount of assistance from extended kin than did White families.

Although these findings are important, generalization to the broader Black population on the basis of these small sample area studies is problematic. These investigations were based on nonprobability samples of northern, urban, Blacks. The work of Hays and Mindel (1973) and Martineau (1977) were based on relatively stable sample populations, whereas samples in other studies (i.e., Blumberg & Bell, 1958; Feagin, 1968; Meadows 1962) consisted of recent migrants to these areas. A further limitation of these studies was that demographic (i.e., gender, age, income, education, marital status) and familial differences (e.g., family proximity) were rarely investigated. Overall, this body of research can be characterized as being largely descriptive of the kin and friend interaction patterns of urban Blacks.

Ethnographic Research on Familial Support Among Blacks

Ethnographic studies provide a rich source of information on kinship and support networks among Blacks (Aschenbrenner, 1973, 1975; Kennedy, 1980; Martin & Martin, 1978; Shimkin et al., 1978; Stack, 1972, 1974). A consistent theme in these studies is that informal support networks are an important component of individual and family survival. A major emphasis of this literature is the structural and functional aspects of the informal support networks of family units. In terms of structural features, research has indicated that the primary social unit is the extended or modified-extended family as opposed to the nuclear family. These extended patterns occurred across households so that it was not uncommon for married adult children to reside in the same neighborhood or apartment building as their parents. Although each household operated as separate economic units, extensive cooperation and support was evident across households. Extended family members participated in support networks which were characterized by general responsibility for child care, joint household cooperation in domestic tasks (i.e., meal preparation, grocery shopping), financial assistance, and the provision of care for aging parents and grandparents.

Martin and Martin (1978) used the term mutual aid in their examination and description of the support networks of Black extended families. Both financial (e.g., personal loans, help paying bills, assistance with small purchases) and emotional support (e.g., personal advice and comfort) were important features of the mutual aid system. In some instances, financial support was given on a regular basis to dominant family figures who, in turn, used this money to ensure that the basic needs of all family members were met. Helping dependent family members was socially reinforced and family members received support without being stigmatized. Similarly, Kennedy (1980) emphasized the concept of reciprocity in his analysis of extended family relationships among Blacks. Participation in reciprocal support relationships was one of the most important factors in the maintenance of strong familial bonds. Family members typically knew who needed help as well as the type and amount of assistance required. Family members who failed to provide needed assistance to others were considered negligent in their family obligations.

The functional characteristics of informal support networks (i.e., elastic household boundaries, lifelong bonds to three-generational households, and an elaborate exchange network), are viewed as adaptive responses to socioeconomic conditions of chronic poverty and unemployment (Stack, 1972, 1974). Further, because of adverse economic conditions, extended families are viewed as the most enduring family form among Blacks of lower class status.

Although ethnographic studies provide extensive information on the support networks of Blacks, a major limitation of this work is its lack of generalizability. In particular, these studies tend to focus on low-income, and to a lesser extent, urban Blacks. Absent from these investigations are Blacks who are middle-class, reside in racially heterogeneous neighborhoods, or who are socially isolated from family members.

Racial Differences in Support Exchanges

Using data from the Panel Study of Income Dynamics, Hofferth (1984) examined racial differences in participation in informal support networks among families with minor children. Blacks were more likely than Whites to reside in extended family structures, but were less likely than Whites to receive money from outside relatives. There were, however, no racial differences in the extent to which respondents gave money to other relatives. Subgroup analysis focusing on female-headed families indicated that Blacks were less likely than Whites to receive money from the informal support network.

Morgan's (1982) examination of racial differences in support transfers (using the 1980 Panel Study of Income Dynamics data), instituted a crucial control for income level. Given the relatively low socioeconomic status of Blacks vis-a-vis Whites, and the fact that the measures for money exchanges involved sums of over $500 a year, controls for income were clearly important for understanding the nature of possible race differences. In addition, Morgan's analysis was not limited to an examination of families with children under 18. Blacks were more likely than Whites to indicate they could both give and receive of their time to others for support activities (e.g., services), but were less likely to receive financial assistance. Blacks were also 4.3% more likely to report that emergency help was available from distant relatives or friends. On a regular, non-emergency basis, Blacks were: 1) 3.5% more likely to report giving $500 or more in the last year to relatives who resided outside the household, 2) 5.5% less likely to have received $500 or more from friends and relatives and 3) 10.4% less likely to provide housing for others.

Gaudin & Davis (1985) examined racial differences in the support networks of lower socioeconomic status, rural mothers. Black mothers generally had networks which were smaller and less supportive than did White mothers. Although there were no significant racial differences in the mean number of relatives in the network and the frequency of contact with network members, Whites had more neighbors as members of their networks than did Blacks. Among Black mothers, kin resided in closer proximity and their networks were more geographically stable than those of their White counterparts. However, instrumental and affective help was more readily available from the social networks of White mothers. In summary, rural, low socioeconomic status Black mothers exchanged less support within their networks than did White mothers.

Gibson (1982) examined race, life-stage (i.e., middle- and late-life), and cohort differences (i.e., comparing national data collected in 1957 and 1976) in the use of informal helpers in coping with psychological distress. Her analyses revealed that Blacks utilized a more diverse pool of informal helpers than did Whites. In both middle and late-life, Blacks tended to be more versatile in utilizing both family and friends. In contrast, Whites in middle-life were more likely to limit help seeking to spouses and to replace spouses with a single family member with the onset of old age.

Support Network of Blacks

Investigations of support among all-Black samples have been reported in the literature. McAdoo (1978) found that 66% of her respondents reported receiving substantial amounts of help from family members, while only 10% indicated receiving no assistance at all. The amount of help received was unaffected by socioeconomic status; both affluent and nonaffluent respondents received similar amounts of assistance. The rated importance of the type of help received differed for mothers and fathers; mothers rated child care as most important, while fathers rated financial help as most important.

McAdoo's (1980) examination of the informal support networks of Black mothers indicated that although family and friends were both important elements of support networks, family members were more integral components. Two-thirds of all mothers received a great deal of help from family, while 4 out of 10 reported receiving assistance from friends at levels comparable to that from family. In terms of support reciprocity, respondents reported receiving more assistance from family than they themselves gave, whereas they tended to give more help to friends than they received from friends. Child care, financial, and emotional assistance were the most prevalent types of reciprocal support received from both family and friends. Parental status differences for friendship support networks revealed that single-parent families received greater amounts of help from friends than did two-parent families. Similarly, in terms of reciprocal support, financial assistance was mentioned more frequently by single-parent families, whereas emotional aid was more prevalent among two-parent families. The only observed demographic difference indicated that although both urban and suburban mothers received more help from families than friends, city residents tended to rely on family to a greater extent than persons in the suburbs.

Taylor, Jackson, and Quick (1982) investigated the impact of demographic factors and family variables on the frequency of informal support. Persons with relatively lower incomes and fewer years of education were less likely than their counterparts to receive support from family members on a frequent basis. These results challenge the assumption that "need" is the overriding factor for receiving assistance and that social support has unusual prominence among lower income Black Americans. Socioeconomically advantaged respondents were more likely than disadvantaged persons to receive family support on a frequent basis. The relationships between the family variables and the receipt of support suggested that the quality of kin relations and frequency of interaction were important arbiters of informal support transactions. The existence of demographic differences in the receipt of support indicates that the family support networks of Black Americans are more diverse than previously thought. Further, the receipt of support from family members is related to qualitative and affiliative aspects of kin relations.

Taylor's (1986a) analysis of the absolute probability of receiving support (contrasting those who received help vs. those who didn't) from extended family members found that both family and demographic factors are important predictors of assistance. Logic analysis indicated that income and age were the only demographic variables that were significantly related to the probability of receiving support. Income level was positively related to receiving aid from family. An inverse association between age and support prompted the speculation that other variables might influence this relationship. An interaction term combining age and whether a respondent had a child was created and found to be a significant predictor. Older respondents with children were significantly more likely to receive support than older respondents without children. This finding substantiates the importance of adult children in the informal social support networks of elderly Blacks (Taylor, 1986a).

Among the family variables, having an available pool of relatives, frequent interaction with family members, and close familial relationships were prerequisites for receiving support. Demographic factors, such as gender and marital status, which have been strongly related to receiving support in other work (see Antonucci, 1985; Troll et al., 1979; Bengtson et al., 1976), failed to achieve significance.

Other research utilizing the National Survey of Black Americans data investigated the role of the informal support network in coping with a serious personal problem. Neighbors and Jackson (Neighbors et al. 1983; Neighbors & Jackson, 1984) examined patterns of informal and professional assistance in response to an identified personal problem. The majority of respondents utilized informal help solely (43%), or a combination of both informal and professional help (44%). Four percent of respondents used only professional support, while 8.7% did not receive any outside assistance for their problem. Gender, age, income, and problem type were related to these four patterns of informal and professional help seeking: 1) women were more likely than men to seek both informal and professional help; 2) older respondents were less likely than younger respondents to seek informal help only; 3) persons with physical health problems were more likely than persons with other types of problems to seek both informal and professional assistance; and 4) respondents with emotional problems were least likely to seek help from either source.

Racial Differences in Support Networks of the Elderly

Research examining racial differences in support exchanges among the elderly are mixed. Shanas (1979) found that a higher proportion of White elderly reported that they gave help to their children and grandchildren, whereas elderly Blacks were more likely than Whites to receive help from children. Although Cantor (1979b) failed to find racial differences in the amount of support that elderly received from children, both Black and Hispanic elderly provided greater amounts of help to children than did White elderly. Mindel et al., (1986) found that controlling for income, elderly Blacks received more formal support than elderly Whites, whereas the amount of informal support received was similar.

Utilizing the Myth and Reality of Aging data, Mitchell and Register (1984) found that when controlling for socioeconomic status, aged Blacks received more assistance than aged Whites; no racial differences in giving aid were evident. In addition, an examination of the type of social support exchanged between the elderly and their children and grandchildren (Jackson, 1980) revealed only one racial difference. Among higher income aged, Black elderly were much more likely than White aged to give child-rearing assistance and financial help.

Mutran's (1985) examination of racial differences in intergenerational family support has the advantages of both a multivariate analysis approach and the use of a national sample. Black families were more involved in exchanges of help across generations, and in comparison to aged Whites, elderly Blacks gave more help to children and grandchildren. Elderly Black parents were also more likely to receive help from adult children, but this effect was reduced in the presence of controls for socioeconomic status. The decomposition of race and socioeconomic status effects revealed that elderly Blacks tended to receive more help from their children as a result of generally lower incomes and fewer years of formal education. Mutran (1985) argues that both cultural and socioeconomic status factors are important in understanding racial differences in support transactions.

Support Networks of Aging Blacks

In a cross-cultural study of minority aging, Stanford (1978) found that 7 of 10 elderly Blacks indicated providing help to others. The type of help given by older Blacks was physical help or normal household chores (19.8%), help during an illness (16.8%), financial (12.98%), transportation (10.9%), talking/counseling (4%), and foods/meals (1%).

Using the elderly subsample of the National Survey of Black Americans data, Taylor (1985) examined the correlates of the frequency of support from extended family. The descriptive findings indicated that the family was extensively involved in the informal social support networks of elderly Blacks. Elderly respondents reported significant levels of interaction with family members, residential proximity to immediate family and other relatives, extensive familial affective bonds, and a high level of satisfaction with family life. In addition, over half of the respondents indicated receiving assistance from family members.

Regression analysis indicated that proximity of relatives and family contact were positively associated with the frequency of receiving support. For the demographic factors, women, persons with few years of formal education, and higher income respondents all received support more frequently than their counterparts. In addition, Southerners received support more often than residents of the Northeast region. Further analysis indicated that adult children were a primary source of assistance to elderly Blacks. Among childless elderly, however, having an available pool of relatives was of singular importance.

Two sets of analyses examined the impact of socio-demographic, health, and family factors on the size and composition of the informal helper networks of elderly Blacks (Chatters, Taylor & Jackson, 1985, 1986). Respondents were asked to choose from a list of 12 informal helpers who would help them if they were sick or disabled. The informal helper list consisted of immediate family members (spouse, children, siblings), other relatives (cousins, aunts, uncles), and non-kin (friends, neighbors, coworkers). Thirty-four informal helpers were generated from this initial list and a total of 3 mentions for informal helpers were used.

Taken together, the studies provide valuable information regarding the health support networks of older Blacks. First, it was clear that health factors, per se, had little influence on either size or composition of the helper network. The second general conclusion is that various socio-demographic statuses of the individual were clearly important in determining both the size and composition of the helper network. Marital status was the most important, influencing network size, overall composition, and the selection of specific helpers. Married older Blacks had larger helper networks comprised of immediate family and which exhibited a preference for spouse as helper. The absence of spouse among unmarried elderly, resulted in smaller and more diverse networks. Additionally, there was a tendency for older women to have larger networks than men. The significance of region for the size and composition of the helper network was particularly intriguing and suggested that Southern residents had larger networks which were more likely to include a diverse group of helpers. Finally, these analyses confirmed the influence that close familial relations and confidence in friend vs. relatives as support resources have on network characteristics. Feelings of closeness were positively related to network size and the selection of immediate family members to the network, while a stated preference for friends over relatives was related to choosing a more diverse (i.e., including non-kin)helper network.

Non-kin Sources of Informal Support

Previous research suggests that the social interaction occurring within the context of family and friend relationships is of particular importance to both elderly (Jackson, 1972, 1980) and non-elderly Blacks (McAdoo, 1978). The family, particularly spouse, children, and siblings, is viewed as the most important source of assistance, and is distinguished from other groups by the permanence of relationships and the operation of explicit normative expectations for affection and mutual assistance (Branch & Jette, 1983; Horowitz & Shindelman, 1983). Friendships, unlike kinship ties, are based on individual choice which is reflected in the high degree of participant similarity on factors such as age, gender, and socioeconomic status (Dono et al., 1979). Further, because expectations to assist are less explicit, the motivation to provide support to a friend emerges from a history of reciprocal assistance (Antonucci, 1985). Despite these differences, recent work has begun to document the importance of neighbors (Cantor, 1979a) and church members (Taylor & Chatters, 1986a, 1986b) as sources of support.

Theories of the Role of Kin and Non-kin Sources of Support

Two alternative theories of informal support networks are germane to a discussion of kin vs. non-kin sources of assistance. Although these theories were developed to understand helping relationships as they pertain to the elderly, they are nonetheless useful for examining informal support networks across the life span. The hierarchial-compensatory model as proposed by Cantor (1979a) postulates that elderly adults exercise an ordered preference for the groups which are selected for support needs. In accordance with this model, the elderly prefer assistance from a particular group regardless of the nature of the task. Help from other groups is sought only when the preferred group is unwilling or unable to provide support. Kinship groups are typically viewed as the most appropriate source for support, followed by other groups (i.e., friends, neighbors, church members, and coworkers), and lastly by formal organizations (Cantor, 1979a; Dono et al., 1979).

In contrast, the task-specific model (Dono et al., 1979; Litwak, 1960; Litwak & Szelenyi, 1969) emphasizes both the type of support received and characteristics of the source of support. According to this model, family and relatives are generally viewed as the most appropriate group for providing both extensive long-term help (e.g., home health care) and advice and comfort. However, because modified-extended family patterns are characterized by the geographic dispersion of family members, only those tasks which do not require proximity are seen as appropriate for kin. Neighbors, because of their proximity, are better equipped to deal with time-urgent tasks (e.g., emergencies) and daily social interaction, but do not typically perform tasks which require long-term commitments. Friends provide support which emphasizes peer group concerns and problems, as well as similarity of experience. Unlike neighbors, however, relationships with friends typically involve long-term commitments (Cantor, 1979a; Dono et al., 1979; Litwak, 1960; Litwak & Szelenyi, 1969).

Both hierarchical-compensatory and task-specific models suggest that normative expectations for filial obligation operate in specifying kin as the most appropriate source of aid. The task specific model, however, incorporates a specific consideration for the nature of relationships with particular helper groups.

Ethnographic Research On Non-kin Support Providers

Ethnographic research on Black families emphasizes the integral role of non-kin in informal support networks (Aschenbrenner, 1973, 1975; Kennedy, 1980; Martin & Martin, 1978; Shimkin et al., 1978; Stack, 1972, 1974). Ladner (1971) and Liebow (1967), in fact, argue that for certain subpopulations in Black communities (i.e., Ladner's adolescent girls and Liebow's street corner men), friends tend to be the more dominant and influential members of the support network. Friendships often took the form of kin relationships, so that it was not uncommon for unrelated older individuals to be given the surname of "Aunt" or "Uncle" or to be referred to as a "play mother or father." Friendships that were referred to in kinship terms resulted in an intensification of bonds of mutual obligation in what would normally be a casual relationship (Aschenbrenner, 1973). Generally, pseudo-kin were full participants in the informal support network. As an example, Kennedy (1980) found that regardless of whether family membership was based on blood, marriage, or mutual consent, remaining in the family was based upon the completion of expected duties.

Liebow's (1967) study of the street corner society of a group of poor Black men has contributed to our understanding of the special characteristics of supportive interpersonal relationships among Black Americans. Liebow focused on the informal social support that these men received from close friends. These friendships, which were based upon primary face-to-face relationships, involved relatives, coworkers, and people who lived in the same area and spent much of their time on neighborhood streets. Because much of the informal support which was exchanged centered around the basic prerequisites of daily living, Liebow argued that friends were of special importance to the street corner men's sense of physical and emotional security. The more friends a street corner man had or believed he had and the stronger the friendship bonds, the greater his self-esteem. Kinship ties were frequently manufactured to explain friend relationships. The most common form of the pseudo-kin relationship between two men was known as "going for brothers." When two men "go for brothers", they agreed to present themselves as brother to the outside world and to deal with one another on the same basis. Going for brothers represented a special case of friendship in which the usual obligations, expectations, and loyalties of the friendship relations were publicly declared to be at their maximum (Liebow, 1967).

Most researchers argue that support from both kin and friends is important in maintaining the social support networks of Blacks (Aschenbrenner, 1973, 1975; Ladner, 1971; Liebow, 1967; Stack, 1972, 1974). Researchers differ, however, in the importance attached to friends as members of the support network. Martin and Martin (1978) argued that friends play an extremely limited role in Black extended family networks. They stated that Blacks with scarce resources felt little obligation to friends or anyone else outside the boundaries of the extended family (Martin and Martin, 1978). Stack (1972, 1974) and Aschenbreener (1973, 1975) argued that although friends were important to the support networks of Blacks, the primary and most stable members of the network were relatives. Friends tended to change and move in and out of various social networks, while assuming a stable position in their own kinship network.

While Aschenbrenner (1973, 1975), Stack (1972, 1974) and Martin and Martin (1978) have agreed that friendship and pseudo-kinship relations are not the most enduring form of relationship, Liebow (1967) is the only researcher who has viewed the pseudo-kinship relation as explicitly negative. Liebow argued that by trying to interpret a friendship relation as a kinship relation, the street corner men attempted to lend structural support to a typically fluid and unstable relationship. Liebow's findings and interpretation may be due to the low-income, unemployed status of the street corner men he studied or the "cultural deviant" perspective that he utilized to guide his analysis (Allen, 1979).

Friendship Networks of Blacks

Several researchers have investigated both the kinship interaction pattern and the friendship networks of urban Blacks (Feagin, 1968; Martineau, 1977; Meadow, 1962). Overall, this research documents that urban Blacks have frequent contact with friends. Meadows (1962) reported that 43% of the Blacks in her sample visited friends at least three times a week, while Martineau (1977) found that 40% of the respondents interacted with friends three times a week and 75% interacted with friends at least once a week.

The importance of friends as support providers has also been noted in the research of Gibson (1982) and McAdoo (1978, 1980). Utilizing data from two national probability samples, Gibson (1982) found that friends and neighbors were integral components of the support networks of middle- and late-life Blacks. Data collected in 1957 indicated that Blacks in both middle- and late-life were twice as likely as Whites to utilize friends and neighbors in coping with psychological distress. These differences were not as large in the 1976 data set, although the racial difference in use of friends and neighbors was maintained.

McAdoo's work on the support networks of Blacks in general (1978) and, Black mothers in particular (1980), also documents the importance of the friendship role. Although kin generally had the more dominant role, 1 of 5 Blacks and 1 of 4 Black mothers indicated that friends provided the most support. Analyses of the type of support given and received indicated that respondents were more likely to exchange emotional support with their friends and financial assistance with family.

Chatters et al., (1985, 1986) found that friends and non-kin associates were present in the helping networks of older Black adults. They were particularly prominent in the networks of elderly Blacks who were unmarried, childless, and who characterized family relations as not being affectively close. Similar to the models of kin and non-kin support, these results reinforce the primacy of kin sources of aid as well as the importance of helper availability in selecting individual helpers. Of particular significance for helper selection was the role played by family factors which assess the quality of family relationships.

Churches as a Supportive Network

Both historically and contemporaneously, religion and religious institutions have played a crucial role in the lives of individual Black Americans and the development of Black community life. The primacy of religion and religious institutions to Blacks is evidenced by the social (Taylor & Chatters, 1986a, 1986b), psychological (Gibson, 1982; Neighbors et al., 1983), and political mobilization (Morris, 1981) functions they perform. This is in addition to their role in promoting and enhancing spiritual well-being. A recent analysis indicated that Blacks reported a number of primary ways the church has helped the condition of Blacks (Taylor, Thornton, & Chatters, 1987). Among them were: 1) spiritual assistance, 2) having a sustaining and strengthening influence, 3) giving personal assistance, 4) providing guidelines for moral behavior, 5) acting as a source of unity, 6) serving as a community gathering place, and 7) being active in attaining social progress. The multifaceted roles and functions of churches in Black communities make them second only to the family as an important social institution.

The significance of religion for Black Americans is revealed in data on religious behaviors and attitudes. Racial comparisons of religious participation indicate that Blacks of all ages display higher levels of religious commitment than Whites. Religious commitment has been examined using a variety of indicators such as church attendance, frequency of prayer, subjective importance of religious beliefs, and reports of having had a religious experience. Research has indicated that Blacks were more likely than Whites to: 1) attend religious services on a frequent basis (Nelsen et al., 1971; Sasaki, 1979), 2) engage in daily prayer (Greeley, 1979; Sasaki, 1979), and 3) report that religious beliefs are important (Gallup, 1984; Sasaki, 1979).

Research among elderly adults also indicates that older Blacks are more religious than older Whites. Hirsch et al. (1972) showed that aged Blacks were more likely than aged Whites to pray regularly, listen to religious programs, and read the Bible. Taylor (1986b) also found that elderly Black adults were extensively involved in religious pursuits. One-half reported attending church on at least a weekly basis, 3 out of 4 were official members of a church, and 3 out of 5 characterized themselves as being "very religious". Multivariate analyses indicated that gender, marital status, urbanicity, and age were significantly related to the various measures of religious participation.

Research on the social participation of the elderly provides additional insight into the importance of religion and the church in the lives of elderly Blacks. One of the strongest and most consistent racial differences in the leisure patterns of the aged is that Blacks were more likely than Whites to participate in religious activities (Clemente, Rexroad & Hirsch, 1975; Heyman & Jeffers, 1970). Furthermore, research on exclusively Black samples indicates that church and church-related activities were the most frequently reported types of voluntary association participation (Lambing, 1972).

Historical (Frazier, 1974) and present-day evidence suggests that Black churches are extensively involved in the provision of support to their members. Church members exchange material, emotional, and spiritual assistance with one another, as well as providing information and advice. Other examples of more formal supportive relationships within churches are found in the various organizations designed to assist church members and others in the community (e.g., food and clothing programs, visiting programs to the sick and shut-in). Finally, the church is particularly prominent in the role it plays in the positive appraisal of self (i.e., self-worth and esteem) and the affirmation of shared beliefs and attitudes held by the congregation.

A recent analysis investigated the impact of church members as a source of informal social support to elderly Black adults (Taylor & Chatters, (1986a, 1986b). This analysis indicated that for older Blacks, frequency of church attendance was a critical indicator of both frequency and the amount of assistance received. Findings for the type of support received indicated that church members provided a variety of assistance. Although it is not surprising that a large percentage of respondents indicate that they received help in a spiritual or religious manner (e.g. "We pray together"), it was unexpected that almost one out of five of those who received church support reported receiving either financial assistance, goods and services, or total support. These findings suggest that the church may be a more integral component of the support networks of elderly Blacks than has been previously thought.

Conclusions

A developing body of primarily qualitative studies on the family lives of Blacks has investigated the critical nature of informal social support networks. Although somewhat meager, the quantitative data also indicates that Blacks interact with family and friend networks on a frequent basis and that these networks provide the basis for the exchange of goods and services. Despite these efforts, there remains a paucity of quality research on the support networks of Blacks as compared to the breadth and depth of concerns evident in the literature on Whites. At present, there is little published research on the supportive relationships of subgroups of the Black population such as single mothers, childless elderly, and those who are divorced, widowed, or remarried. Little work exists on such critical indicators of support as family interaction, and affection. In addition, few studies examine intergenerational support exchanges and reciprocal support relationships. While research on the familial networks of Blacks is extremely limited, work on friends, neighbors, and church members as sources of informal support is practically nonexistent.

The body of research on the support networks of Black Americans is representative of a variety of approaches and perspectives. It is clear from a review of this work that the collection of findings have a bearing on many of the concerns and issues evident in emerging life course perspectives on social support, in particular the support convoy notion. Information on living arrangements and household composition of Black Americans suggests that these situational factors may have an influence on the structural and functional features of the convoy. Similarly, differences in memberships and participation in organizations like the church will have an important influence on the nature of the convoy. Expressed attitudes concerning the nature of support relationships involving both kin and non-kin enforce the idea that mutual obligation and past performance in supportive roles are important for understanding present helping behaviors, in much the same manner as a support reserve. The characteristics of extended family relationships which emphasize the importance of long-term association and interaction reinforce the notion of the convoy as a dynamic entity embodying a longitudinal focus. Although these findings are in large measure consistent with the support convoy model, because they were not developed with that perspective in mind they are only suggestive of possible areas of future inquiry.

In addition to work exploring the notion of the support convoy among Black Americans, there are other research areas deserving of attention. The general paucity of research on the social support networks of Black Americans indicates that there are many areas which require a significant amount of work. Many of these issues have been raised in connection with specific research topics (e.g., examinations of the support networks of subgroups of the Black population).

Methodologically, research utilizing diverse samples of the Black population and the employment of multivariate procedures will help to clarify the independent effects of factors on support and illuminate the nature of both subgroup and racial differences in these behaviors. More work needs to be conducted in which ethnographic and survey research approaches are utilized in combination. Both methods are important in comprehending the dynamic and multifaceted aspects of the support process. Finally, longitudinal studies of supportive networks will help to determine what are the eventual outcomes of participation in these groups. This work will be particularly important in establishing the long-term economic benefits of support networks for low income Black Americans (i.e., movement out of poverty status). An increase in the volume of work, coupled with an improvement in the quality of research efforts will enhance our knowledge of the informal social support networks of Black Americans.

References

Allen, W. R. (1979). Class, culture, and family organization: The effects of class and race on family structure in urban America. *Journal of Comparative Family Studies, 10,* 301-313.

Angel, R., & Tienda, M. (1982). Determinants of extended household structure: cultural pattern or economic model? *American Journal of Sociology, 87,* 1360-1383.

Antonucci, T. C. (1985). Personal characteristics, social support behavior. In E. Shanas & R. H. Binstock (Eds.), *Handbook of aging and the social sciences.*

Antonucci, T. C., & Depner, C. E. (1981). Social support and informal helping relationships. In T. A. Willis (Ed.), *Basic Processes in Helping Relationships*. New York: Academic Press.

Aschenbrenner, J. (1973). Extended families among Black Americans. *Journal of Comparative Family Studies, 4,* 257-268.

Aschenbrenner, J. (1975). *Lifelines: Black families in Chicago*. New York: Holt, Rinehart & Winston.

Bengtson, V. L., & Cutler, N. E. (1976). Generations and intergenerational relations: Perspectives on age groups and social change. In R. H. Binstock & E. Shanas (Eds.), *Handbook of aging and the social sciences*. New York: Van Nostrand Reinhold.

Billingsley, A. (1968). *Black families in White America*. Englewood Cliffs, NJ: Prentice Hall.

Blumberg, L., & Bell, R. R (1958). Urban migration and kinship ties. *Social Problems, 6,* 328-333.

Branch, L. G., & Jette, A. M. (1983). *Older's use of informal long term care assistance. The Gerontologist, 23,* 51-56.

Cantor, M. H. (1979b). Neighbors and friends: An overlooked resource in the informal support system. *Research on Aging, 1,* 434-463.

Cantor, M. H. (1979a). The informal support system of New York's inner city elderly: Is ethnicity a factor? In D. E. Gelfand & A. J. Kutzik (Eds.), *Ethnicity and aging: Theory, research and policy*. New York: Springer Publishing Co.

Chatters, L. M., Taylor, R. J., & Jackson, J. S. (1986). Aged Blacks' choices for an informal helper network. *Journal of Gerontology, 41,* 94-100.

Chatters, L. M., Taylor, R. J., & Jackson, J. S. (1985). Size and composition of the informal helper networks of elderly Blacks. *Journal of Gerontology, 40,* 605-614.

Clemente, F., Rexroad, P. A. & Hirsch, C. (1975). The participation of the Black aged in voluntary associations. *Journal of Gerontology, 30,* 469-472.

Dono, J. E., Falke, C. M., Kail, B. L., Litwak, E., Sherman, R. H., & Siegle, D. (1979). Primary groups in old age; Structure and function. *Research on Aging, 1(4),* 403-434.

Feagin, J. (1968). The kinship ties of Negro urbanites. *Social Science Quarterly, 69,* 600-665.

Frazier, E. F. (1974). *The Negro church in America*. New York: Schocken.

Frazier, E. F. (1939). *The Negro family in the United States*. Chicago: University of Chicago Press.

Gallup Report (1984). *Religion in America.*

Gaudin, J. M., & Davis, K. B. (1985). Social networks of Black and White rural families: A research report. *Journal of Marriage and the Family, 47,* 1014-1022.

Gibson, R. C. (1982). Blacks at middle and late life: Resources and coping. *Annals of the American Academy of Political and Social Science, 464,* 79-90.

Greeley, A. M. (1979). Ethnic variations in religious commitment. In Robert Wuthnow (Ed.), *The religious dimension: New Directions in quantitative research*. New York: Academic Press.

Gutman, H. (1976). *The Black family in slavery and freedom: 1750-1925*. New York: Pantheon Books.

Hagestad, G. O., & Neugarten, B. L. (1985). Age and the life course. In R. Binstock and E. Shanas (Eds.), *Handbook of aging and the social sciences* (2nd ed.). New York: Van Nostrand Reinhold.

Hays, W., & Midel, C. (1973). Extended kinship relations in Black and White families. *Journal of Marriage and the Family, 35*, 51-56.

Heyman, D. K., & Jeffers, F. C. (1970). The influence of race and socioeconomic status upon the activities and attitudes of the aged. In E. Palmore (Ed.), *Normal aging: Reports from the Duke longitudinal study, 1955-1969.* Durham, NC: Duke University Press.

Hirsch, C., Kent, D. P., & Silverman, S. L. (1972). Homogeneity and heterogeneity among low-income Negro and White aged. In D. P. Kent. R. Kastenbaum, & S. Sherwood (Eds.), *Research planning and action for the elderly: The power and potential of social science,* 400-500. New York: Behavioral Publications.

Hofferth, S. L. (1984). Kin networks, race, and family structure. *Journal of Marriage and the Family, 46*, 791-806.

Horowitz, A., & Shindelman, L. W. (1983). Reciprocity and affection: Past influences on current caregiving. *Journal of Gerontological Social Work, 5*, 5-21.

Jackson, J. J. (1980). *Minorities and aging.* Belmont, CA: Wadsworth.

Jackson, J. J. (1972). Comparative lifestyles and family and friend relationships among older Black women. *Family Coordinator, 21*, 477-486.

Kahn, R. L. (1979). Aging and social support. In M. W. Riley (Ed.), *Aging from birth to death.* Boulder, CO: Westview Press.

Kahn, R. L., & Antonucci, T. C (1980). Convoys over the life course: Attachment, roles and social support. In P. B. Baltes and O. G. Brim (Eds.), *Life-span perspective for social psychology.* New York: Academic Press.

Kennedy, T. R. (1980). *You gotta deal with it: Black family relations in a southern community.* New York: Oxford University Press.

Ladner, J. (1971). *Tomorrow's tomorrow: The Black woman.* Garden City, NY: Doubleday.

Lambing, M. L. B. (1972). Social class living patterns of retired Negroes. *Gerontologist, 12*, 285-288.

Lee, G. R. (1980). Kinship in the seventies: A decade review of research and theory. *Journal of Marriage and the Family, 42*, 923-934.

Liebow, E. (1967). *Tally's corner: A study of Negro streetcorner men.* Boston: Little Brown & Co.

Litwak, E. (1960). Occupational mobility and extended family. *American Sociological Review, 25*, 9-21.

Litwak, E., & Szelenyi, I. (1969). Primary group structures and their functions: kin, neighbors, and friends. *American Sociological Review, 34(4)*, 465-481.

Lopata, H. Z. (1979). *Women as widows.* New York: Elsevier.

Martin, E., & Martin, J. (1978). *The Black extended family.* Chicago: University of Chicago.

Martineau, W. (1977). Informal social ties among urban Black Americans. *Journal of Black Studies, 8*, 83-104.

McAdoo, H. P. (1980). Black mothers and the extended family support network. In L. Rodgers-Rose (Ed.), *The Black woman.* Beverly Hills, CA: Sage Publications.

McAdoo, H. P. (1978). Factors related to stability in upwardly mobile Black families. *Journal of Marriage and the Family, 40*, 762-778.

Meadow, K. I. (1962). Negro-White differences among newcomers to a transitional urban area. *Journal of Intergroup Relations, 3*, 320-330.

Mindel, C. H., Wright, R., & Starrett, R. A. (1986). Informal and formal health and social support systems of Black and White elderly: A comparative cost approach. *The Gerontologist, 26,* 279-285.

Mitchell, J. S., & Register, J. C. (1984). An exploration of family interaction with the elderly by race, socioeconomic status and residence. *The Gerontologist, 24,* 48-54.

Moon, M., & Smolensky, (1977). Income, economic status and policy toward the aged. In G. S. Tolley & R. V. Burkhauser (Eds.), *Income support policies for the aged.* Cambridge, Massachusetts: Balinger Publishing.

Morgan, J. N. (1982). The redistribution of income by families and institutions and emergency help patterns. In Duncan, G. J. & Morgan, J. N. (Eds.), *Five thousand American families—patterns of economic progress: Volume X, Analyses of the first thirteen years of the panel study of income dynamics.* Ann Arbor, MI: Institute for Social Research.

Morgan, J. N., David, M., Cohen, W., & Brazen, H. (1962). *Income and welfare in the United States.* New York: McGraw-Hill.

Morris, A. (1981). Black southern sit-in movement: An analysis of internal organization. *American Sociological Review, 46,* 741-767.

Moynihan, D. (1965). *The Negro family: The case for national action.* Washington, D.C.: U.S. Government Printing Office.

Mutran, E. (1985). Intergenerational family support among Blacks and Whites: Response to culture or to socioeconomic differences?*Journal of Gerontology, 40,* 382-389.

Neighbors, H., & Jackson, J. (1984). The use of informal and formal help: Four patterns of illness behavior in the Black community. *American Journal of Community Psychology, 12,* 629-644.

Neighbors, H., Jackson, J. S., Bowman, P. J., & Gurin, G. (1983). Stress, coping and Black mental health: Preliminary findings from a national study. *Prevention in Human Services, 2,* 5-29.

Nelsen, H. M., Yokley, R. L., & Nelsen, A. K. (1971). *The Black church in America.* New York: Basic.

Rainwater, L. (1970). *Behind ghetto walls: Black families in a federal slum.* Chicago: Aldine.

Rubenstein, D. I. (1971). An examination of social participation found among a national sample of Black and White elderly. *International Journal of Aging and Human Development, 2,* 172-188.

Sasaki, M. S. (1979). Status inconsistency and religious commitment. In Robert Wuthrow (Ed.), *The religious dimension: New directions in quantitative Research.* New York: Academic Press.

Shanas, E. (1979). *National survey of the aged. Report of Administration on Aging.* Washington, D.C.: Department of Health and Human Serivces.

Shimkin, D., Shimkin, E., & Frate, D. (1978). *The extended family in Black societies.* Chicago: Aldine Publishing Co.

Stack, C. B. (1974). *All our kin.* New York: Harper & Row, Publishers.

Stack, C. B. (1972). Black kindreds: Parenthood and personal kindreds among urban Blacks. *Journal of Comparative Family Studies, 3,* 194-106.

Stanford, E. P. (1978). *The elder Black.* San Diego, CA: Campanile Press.

Sweet, J. A. (1973). *Women in the labor force.* New York: Seminar Press.

Taylor, R. J. (1985). The extended family as a source of support to elderly Blacks. *The Gerontologist, 25,* 488-495.

Taylor, R. J. (1986a). Receipt of support from family among Black Americans: Demographic and familial differences. *Journal of Marriage and the Family, 48,* 67-77.

Taylor, R. J. (1986b). Religious participation among elderly Blacks. *The Gerontologist, 26,* 637-642.

Taylor, R. J., & Chatters, L. M. (1986a). Church-based informal support among elderly Blacks. *The Gerontologist, 26,* 637-642.

Taylor, R. J., & Chatters, L. M. (1986b). Patterns of informal support to elderly Black adults: Family, friends, and church members. *Social Work, 31,* 432-438.

Taylor, R. J., & Chatters, L. M. (1988). Church members as a source of informal social support. *Review of Religious Research, 30.*

Taylor, R. J., Jackson, J. S., & Quick, A. D. (1982). The frequency of social support among Black Americans: Preliminary findings from the National Survey of Black Americans, *Urban Research Review, 89,* 1-4, 10.

Taylor, R. J., Thornton, M. C., & Chatters, L. M. (1987). Black American's perception of the socio-historical role of the church. *Journal of Black Studies, 18,* 123-138.

Tienda, M., & Angel, R. (1982). Headship and household composition among Blacks, Hispanics, and other Whites. *Social Forces, 61,* 508-531.

Troll, L. E., Miller, S. J., & Atchley, R. C. (1979). *Families in later life.* Belmont, CA: Wadsworth.

Williams, J. A., & Stockton, R. (1973). Black family structures and functions: An empirical examination of some suggestions made by Billingsley. *Journal of Marriage and the Family, 35,* 39-49.

HUMAN SERVICES AND THE BLACK ADULT LIFE CYCLE

Ruppert A. Downing

Introduction

Adulthood is a critical period in the human life cycle. Specialists in human development typically identify the span of adulthood in three basic phases: early adulthood, middle adulthood and later adulthood (Kimmel, 1974; Kennedy, 1978; Bloom, 1980). Meyer (1976) describes the life cycle in terms of age specific tasks/needs, expected crises/problems and institutional arrangements for service delivery. Successful movement through the life cycle assumes the availability of organizationally responsive institutions and services, and informal networks to meet needs as they occur. The notion set forth in this chapter is that institutions and services should not replace individual and collective self-help networks but rather should function in a supportive role. Self-help refers to individual and group structures for mutual aid and accomplishment of a special purpose (Encyclopedia of Social Work, 1977). During each of the phases of adult life there are a variety of decision points, situational crises, and developmental tasks which impact upon successful social, physical, and mental maturity. Kimmel (1974) using the construct of a human life line identified the following as some of the decision points and developmental tasks which represent milestones during the adult years:

1) voting
2) beginning an occupation
3) marriage and parenthood
4) death of parents
5) children leaving home
6) grandparenthood
7) retirement
8) death of a spouse
9) great grandparenthood
10) death

The decisions, crises, and developmental tasks faced at various points in the adult life cycle traditionally constitute normal or expected crises. For Blacks and other persons of color, race and visibility profoundly influence adaptational strategies employed to meet the normal decisions/tasks required for appropriate progression through the adult life cycle. They are unlike White Europeans who were more easily assimilated into American society. Racism, a system of logic, thought, speech and action, whether consciously or unconsciously determined whose goal is the maintenance of White supremacy, is a fact of life for Blacks in American society (Welsing, 1974). Embodied in this definition is the element of personal attitudes and beliefs which influence actions and institutionalization of the same. Briefly stated, Blacks progress through the "normal" adult life cycle in a non-receptive and hostile environment, where race has been a significant factor in determination of need, planning, utilization, and delivery of human services. Table 1 outlines some of the developmental tasks/decisions, supports/services needed, barriers encountered, and relevant issues involved. While space does not allow for a discussion of every item shown in the Table, a discussion of selected areas will follow.

Early Adulthood

Young adulthood is the transition period of the adult life cycle when a person takes on the rights and responsibilities of adult life which include the right to vote, to bear arms, to marry, and to procreate. The Black individual enters this transition period with a dual mind set: the need for competence in dealing with reality, and the capacity to transcend reality. Chestang (1980) clearly states the dilemma when he states:

> The Black man is not a marginal man but a bicultural man. He does not live on the fringes of the larger society; he lives in both the larger society and the Black society. The experience of functioning in two cultures results in dual responses. We emphasize dual responses because we are not suggesting duality of personality, but two ways of coping with tasks, expectations, and behaviors required by his condition. They converge in the adequately functioning Black individual as an integrated whole (p. 46).

Early adulthood is also that period of transition from adolescence where self-image is being developed within a family and community to independence and decision-making in a wider social context. Decision-making is directed toward specific goals such as mate selection and marriage, employment or career choices, and participation in the political arena (Devore, Schlesinger, 1981). One option in this decision-making process is singlehood. During early adulthood biological development peaks and signs of the aging process become more visible.

Table 1
Developmental Tasks/Decisions for Black Adults

Point in Life Cycle	Typical Development Tasks/Decisions	Supportive Institutions and Needed Services	Barriers Encountered	Issues Encountered
Early Adult	1. Independence/Self Development 2. Selection of mate (Marriage) 3. Beginning Family (Married or Single) 4. College (Higher Education) 5. Career Choice	1. Family & Friendship Network 2. Family Life Education 3. Family Planning 4. Genetic Counseling 5. Information & Referral Services 6. Educational/Mentor (Teacher/Educator) 7. Ethnic Sensitive Service Provider 8. Church	Color/visibility Hostile Enviornment Lack of Enviornment Institutional Racism Service Providers Lacking Ethnic Sensitive Training	Availability of Black Service Provided Funding for "Ethnic" Genetic Disease Service Programs Undercount in census data and its impact on political representation and allocation of federal dollars
Middle Adulthood	1. Attention to Health and Mental Health 2. Economic Security 3. Retirement Planning 4. Maintenance of Marital & Family Relationships 5. Emancipation of Children	1. Health Care Services 2. Financial Planning 3. Kinship Network 4. Pre-retirement Counseling 5. Affirmative Action Programs 6. Pension Investment 7. Church	Lack of responsible research Politically Conservative Policy (Cuts under Reagan Administration) Assumptions Used to Organize Services	Emergence of Black Human Service Agencies
Later Adulthood (Aging)	1. Physical Care 2. Retirement 3. Bereavement (loss) 4. Death 5. Income Maintenance	1. Home Health Care 2. Nutritional Services 3. Retirement Counseling 4. Legal Services 5. Information 6. Kinship Support Network 7. Church 8. Advocacy Services 9. Daycare Centers	Underutilization of Available Services Lack of Federal, State, Local Financial Support	Minority Specific vs. Minority Blind (Legislation & Policy Decision) Integration of Social Services System Assistance and Family Assistance

Family Life Education Services

One of the major decisions facing the young adult is whether to pursue further education or enter the world of work. Education is a needed service for the Black young adult. In a technological society, strong emphasis needs to be placed upon career counseling and making appropriate decisions. One can choose technical school which will certify acquisition of certain skills and early entrance into the world of work, or career counseling which urges early exposure to the occupational world or college/graduate school. The nature of the job market has shifted toward jobs requiring higher levels of education and educational service must be of high quality. Hare (1988) states that the cornerstone of a healthy adult is the capacity to take care of one's own and one's own self. To accomplish this task educational guidance and preparation for employment must be in place. Even under optimal conditions of preparation, the young adult has to deal with the reality of job discrimination, underemployment and less pay for equal work.

Given the priority of decisions and tasks mentioned above, a vitally important service needed is family life education. Family life education as a service focuses on providing opportunities to explore issues related to individual and family goals. The family life education process includes the imparting of information which serves as a resource and support for making sound decisions and completing developmental tasks successfully. The educational emphasis could include information regarding social and mental health, sexuality, reproduction, contraception, and child growth/development. Somerville (1970) noted that family life educators' ability to function effectively is related to their familiarity with social/economic realities facing Black families, forced adaptations resulting from that reality and a level of self-awareness that allows the family life educator to meet the needs of the population.

Genetic Counseling

Genetic counseling is another preventive service of importance in making decisions about mate selection, marriage, and employment. Persons with genetic disorders need a wide range of professional services to support and clarify decisions which could have generational impact over time. Sickle cell anemia, an incurable hereditary blood disorder, is illustrative of a disorder for which genetic counseling is appropriate. Estimations are that 45,000 to 75,000 Blacks actually have sickle cell anemia and approximately 2,000,000 are carriers of the sickle cell trait (Battle, Barnett, 1985). With the sickle cell disorder, genes for abnormal hemoglobin are passed on from parents to children resulting in a person with sickle cell anemia or a healthy carrier with sickle cell trait (Battle, Barbett, 1985). The issues which arise regarding public awareness, and funding for needed services such as diagnostic work, individual/genetic counseling, and adequate follow-up activities further illustrate the need to improve the delivery of services to Black adults and their families. Weaver (1976) indicates that because of sickle cell's association with the Black community, Blacks have acted to heighten public attention with the goal of securing federal assistance in screening, counseling, education, and research. He further makes the following comments relative to racial implications of heightened public awareness of sickle cell anemia:

> Now that the Anglo community has learned of sickle cell anemia, new forms of anti-Black discrimination have appeared: some employers reportedly reject all trait carriers; the New York State Health commission reports that 13 major life insurance firms charge trait carriers additional premiums; the Air Force has declared trait carriers ineligible for pilot or co-pilot positions; several states have introduced compulsory screening laws. Thus, not only are economic hardships being worked on Blacks, but serious civil liberties issues are raised by the nonvoluntary, racially directed blood testing. Yet there is little or no evidence that being a trait carrier opens one to special risks: Careful, controlled studies of carriers of the trait are few and far between, so the matter is clouded by a slew of impressions and erroneous notions (Weaver, 1976, p. 85).

In terms of federal responsiveness to needed services for sickle cell victims, the Sickle Cell Act of 1972 provided heightened awareness and financial support for state and local programming. With expiration of the Sickle Cell Act and passage of the Genetic Disease Act of 1976, diseases of genetic origin could be funded from a centralized source. This, however, raised an important issue illustrative of analyzing existing human service policies from the perspective of service delivery to Blacks. Battle and Barnett (1985) note the implication of this kind of analysis with the following statement:

> Prior to the Genetics Act, sickle cell anemia programs had some independence and a special area of responsibility. The question now is whether the Genetic program can provide continued comprehensive services that are needed by sickle cell anemia patients in conjunction with the other eight disorders which are better understood by the public, in contrast to sickle cell patients who are mostly Black and whose needs and problems are less understood (p. 213).

Family Planning Services

Early adulthood is also a typical time to begin a family. Some persons at this decision point will choose marriage and natural parenthood, while some will choose singlehood and adoption. Additionally, single natural parenthood is sometimes a decision undertaken and, given available statistical data, typically a problematic choice.

Family planning services, particularly birth control, have been the subject of much controversy. The general problem has centered around the issue of genocide. Genocide is defined as acts committed with intent to destroy, in whole or in part, a racial group (Turner, Darity, 1980). While there are differences in viewpoint about contraceptives between male and female, both voice concerns about the possibility of genocide in America.

Fears are heightened during periods of intense racial tension. Even in 1988, in an atmosphere of political conservatism, racial tension has increased. Although family planning services are not inherently bad, any national population policy should demonstrate that it is concerned about the health and wealth of Black people (Willie, 1971). There is reluctance to accept limitation of family size through family planning services when these services are not offered as part of a comprehensive approach to health care (Gould, 1980). Acceptance of family planning services may be enhanced by recruitment of Black service providers and increased ability of Blacks in communities to influence the manner in which services will be delivered. Family planning is an appropriate service to be available for young adults who are in a period of transition in acquiring the rights and responsibilities of marriage and procreation.

Adoption Services

Adoption services for Blacks have been beset by myths and stereotypes. Historically, traditional child welfare agencies and opponents of Black families have marketed a view presenting Blacks as not having an interest in adoption, Black children being unadoptable, and the inability of Blacks to provide a suitable home atmosphere. Aldridge (1974) cites the problem as agencies' insensitivity to the positive history of Black families and "the designing of policies whereby home ownership, money, prestige, and education have been given far more weight in determining whether a family can adopt as opposed to a family's ability to nourish, love, and rear a child"(p. 409). Such a stance deliberately excludes and alienates Blacks from the traditional agency adoption services system. The ability or willingness to hire and/or train culturally sensitive staff, to extend services beyond the agency walls through aggressive outreach, to have involvement with potential Black adoption resources through informal/formal community networks, and to undertake the task of developing policies and procedures commensurate with the values and lifestyle of the Black target population demonstrates agency commitment. Community education efforts would also enhance the utilization of available adoption services. The emergence of Black welfare agencies such as the Afro-American Family and Community Services in Chicago and programs such as Homes for Black Children in Detroit have demonstrated that adoption services can and will be used by Black couples and single adults (Aldridge, 1974). The unique effort in the State of Illinois, "One Church, One Child" program, is further evidence that aggressive outreach can and will produce positive results. This effort, which was begun in 1980 at Holy Angels Church in Chicago by Father Clements, had 50 participating churches in two years. After its inception, federal support was obtained through a $150,000 grant from the U.S. Department of Health and Human Services (Hotline, 1982).

Middle Adulthood

Theorists such as Daniel Levinson (1977), and Bernice Neugarten (1968) have described the middle adult period of the life span as a time of reappraisal and important decision making.

Zacks (1980) describes this period of the adult life-cycle as a time of inner struggle, psychological turmoil, realizing that some of life's dreams have not come true, and recognizing that time is running out for making long-desired changes in one's life. Zacks (1980) further cites self-actualization as a key element in the successful mastery of developmental tasks. Self-actualization is the striving to realize ones' ideals about excellence and those things which make life meaningful and worthwhile. Middle adulthood is a time in life when significant physiological changes occur such as a gradual decline in physical prowess, change in physical appearance, and changes in the reproductive system. Nichols (1986) notes that in midlife "there is a modest decline in the elemental drives and a gradual diminution of physical powers"(p. 39). Changes however slight, provide clues that one is not the person one used to be at an earlier point in the human life-cycle. Neugarten (1968) presents evidence of differences in perception of middle adulthood among men and women. She cites the fact that women tend to define their age status within the context of the timing of events within the family life cycle such as emancipation of children into the adult world. Men tend to perceive their age status based on factors outside the family context such as career expectations versus career achievements in the work world (Neugarten, 1968).

Health problems such as heart disease, vascular lesions, ulcers, malignant neoplasms, and infection account for a death rate in middle adulthood which exceeds that of the general population (Stevens-Long, 1979). The leading cause of death in middle adulthood is cardiovascular disease and accounts for approximately 40% of the deaths (Stevens-Long, 1979). General life stress, the number and type of life changes a person experiences, is associated with the incidence of heart attacks.

For Blacks in the United States the middle adulthood phase of the

279

adult life cycle, with its demands for self-actualization to accomplish developmental tasks and sound decision-making, is complicated by what DuBois described as the "dilemma of twoness"(Blackwell, 1985, p. 344). This concept is based upon the recognition that Blacks are in America but not of America in the sense that being Black limits privilege in a society viewed, theoretically, as being open to all persons regardless of race/color (Blackwell, 1985). Needed human services during middle adulthood must be considered within the above mentioned context.

Health Services

According to Dr. Herbert Nickens, director of the Office of Minority Health at the Department of Health and Human Services, "Black health status is clearly the worst"in the United States (O'Brien, 1987, p. 1). Diseases such as heart disease, cancer, cirrhosis, are health problems that have hit Blacks harder than Whites (O'Brien, 1987). The delivery of health care services presents one of the most pressing needs for survival and quality of life. Factors which strongly affect health care services delivery and utilization are life-style behavior, lack of information, and Black manpower shortage. More specifically, these factors are significant in making Blacks more susceptible to disease, death and the receipt of an inadequate quality of health care (Brown, 1987). Dr. John O. Brown, then President of the National Medical Association, in a 1986 speech at the Morehouse School of Medicine, Atlanta, Georgia emphasized the following:

> In six key areas (cancer, cardiovascular disease, diabetes, homicide and accidents, chemical dependency and infant morality) the Task Force found that Black Americans are victimized by diseases and die at a higher rate than White Americans. Homicide was cited as the leading cause of death for Black men aged 14 to 44 years. Blacks have the highest overall cancer rates for both incidence and mortality of any population group in the United States. Black men under the age of 45 are 10 times more likely to die from hypertension than White men. Heart disease rates are twice as high in Black women as in White women. The Task Force also reported that Blacks are twice as likely to die from cirrhosis as Whites. And the most distressing, infant mortality and the incidence of low birth weight among Black babies is still more than double that of White babies (Brown, 1987, pp. 260-261).

Life Style Behavior. Key to enhancing the utilization of available health care services is an understanding of the "patterned way of life that has special meaning to the individual and his/her social group" and is transmitted generationally through learning (Bailey, 1987, p. 389). This concept of culture may be defined as a system of shared beliefs, values, customs, behaviors, and artifacts that members of a society use in interpersonal relationships guiding their belief/actions, and coping with familiar and new life situations (Bailey, 1987). The fact is that Blacks, out of necessity, must deal with two distinct "worlds" for survival and the general meeting of needs. Adaptation to these two worlds has resulted in a distinct life-style response to receiving and using human service resources available. Chestang describes the meeting of essential needs and adaptation to a dual existence in the following way:

> Slavery severed the Black's cultural connection with their homeland, and Blacks were forced to adopt the only culture they knew, the American culture. At the same time, their participation in American society was circumscribed and conditional. Blacks identified with a larger American culture, but the opportunity to derive the benefits of that identification was denied them....Because sustenance needs (e.g., employment, economic resources, political power, and so forth) could only be met in the wider society, Blacks had to venture into that world. Their needs for nurturance, however, (e.g., family, friends, supportive institutions, and so on) were in the Black community (Chestang, 1983, p.17).

An illustration of how adaptation to survival in American society over time (and looking to traditional supports and institutions in the Black community to meet basic needs) influences life style behaviors related to acquiring needed services is the following case:

> Miss N., an 84 year old, had worked well past the traditional age 65 retirement. Although she had gained eligibility for benefits under social security during her primary working years, Miss N. refused to apply for benefits. She had continued working, since from her view, she did not want "welfare aid". Her periodic health problems were indicative of the fact that some provision would need to be made for both financial and medical support. Miss N.'s work with the church missionary society and membership in benevolent/secret societies solidified her belief that when the time came she would be able to call upon this resource for both financial and in-kind help. The fact that her sister was receiving social security benefits, and had been for many years, was not persuasive enough. Based on her experiences of going through the application and interview process for public assistance as a young adult and being racially intimidated by the welfare worker, Miss N. had vowed that she would never again bother with "government welfare" (Black Elderly Project, 1975).

Life style behaviors related to health care-seeking behavior were studied by Bailey using a combination of informant oriented and participant observation methods (Bailey, 1987). Data were analyzed from informal interviews, semi-structured interviews, individual life history profiles, and participant observation carried out in hypertension screening clinics in the Detroit Metropolitan area. The following care-seeking behaviors were identified:

281

1) Illness appears (perceived symptoms).
2) Individual waits for a certain period (days or weeks).
3) Allows body to heal itself (prayer or traditional regimens).
4) Evaluates daily activities (reduces work or stress).
5) Seeks advice from a family member or close friend (church leader and/or traditional healer).
6) Attends health clinic or family physician (Bailey, 1987, p. 390).

These patterns of behavior were associated with cultural factors such as maintaining a traditional health regimen, believing in spiritualism, trusting in individual moral strength, and believing in obedience to authority structures (Bailey, 1987).

Disease states such as hypertension may also be linked to life style behavior. Duh and Willingham (1986) hypothesized that salt retention, a key factor in hypertension in Blacks, is culturally based and evolved as an adaptive behavior. This ecological perspective suggests that tropical climates where Blacks originated causes increased salt loss through perspiration and as an adaptation for survival Black kidneys "learned" to retain salt through an evolutionary process (Duh & Willingham, 1986). This evolutionary process required that salt be taken into the body in amounts that allowed the kidneys to retain it and that the tongue adapt to be less sensitive to salt. Given this evolutionary background and being transported to America where less salt is needed for survival, Blacks in the United States may be likely to have excessive salt intake and retention (Duh & Willingham, 1986). An additional factor related to the high incidence of hypertension is the response to stress. A key factor in Blacks' response to stress is the social situation of being Black in a color conscious society that emphasizes competitiveness, individual achievement and equal opportunity. The implication here is that if one works hard one will likely experience success. For Black Americans who struggle with institutionalized racism and extreme pressures of poverty, responses of frustration, anger, and resentment contribute to increased blood pressure. Duh and Willingham (1986) suggest the following to providers of health care services.

> Approaching the hypertensive patient from an ecological view (that is, examining those features of his life style, environment, and ancestral history that may contribute to the disease) and taking time to counsel him may increase not only the patient's understanding of the illness but also enhance his compliance with therapy involving salt restriction. Each of us responds better to individual attention than to impersonal instruction; therefore, a little more time spent for this ecological discussion might save lives (Duh & Willingham, 1986, p. 619).

Life style factors such as smoking, drinking, eating patterns, occupational exposure to carcinogens contribute to the high incidence of cancer in Blacks. The State of Ohio Governor's Task Force on Black and Minority Health indicated that advertising and marketing dollars and energy are used to promote high risk behaviors rather than reduce them in Black and ethnic minority communities. Of particular concern is cigarette and alcohol advertising. The Task Force noted the following:

> Cigarette advertisements are the main revenue source of two national Black publications followed by ads for alcohol, which represented 20 percent of the advertisements in a national Black women's magazine. Promotion activities are shifting to sponsorship of cultural, civic, sports and entertainment events in Black and Hispanic communities (Governor's Task Force State of Ohio, 1987, p. 47).

Bang and associates suggest that the dietary habits of Blacks relative to high consumption levels of fats and low consumption levels of vegetables may result in excess incidence of cancers of the prostate, colon, and esophagus (Bang, Perlin, Sampson, 1987).

It seems clear that an ecological perspective in understanding life style behavior and its relationship to health status assists in assessing both obvious and subtle factors relative to quality of health.

Health education. Health education is very important in health care delivery and utilization of health services. As an intervention, health education focuses on producing desirable changes in health behavior. For this kind of intervention to be successful, cultural, social and racial variables should be an integral part. Health educators need to know what people are thinking, have a broad definition of health, an in-depth understanding of factors impinging upon health, and realization of the effects of racism (Bailey, 1987).

A 1980 study by the American Cancer Society revealed a belief that cancer was the main concern of Whites while hypertension and sickle cell disease are the primary health concerns of Blacks (Bang, Perlin, Sampson, 1987). Such a belief is probably reflective of the fact that health information marketing strategies have targeted Blacks for information on hypertension and sickle cell disease but marginally regarding cancer.

A U.S. Department of Health and Human Services task force on Black and Minority Health indicated that "scientific literature supports an hypothesis that differences in cancer experience between nonminorities and Blacks may be largely attributable to social or environmental factors rather than genetic or biologic differences" (Secretary's Task Force on Black and Minority Health, 1985, p. 94). Other contributing factors include nutritional status/dietary patterns, educational level, awareness of cancer preventive concepts, and an acceptance of cancer as a current and potential threat. Additional findings of the 1980 American Cancer Society study indicated that 69 percent of Blacks think that they are not likely to get cancer and only 25 percent could name five to seven of cancer's warning signals (Bang, Perlin, Sampson, 1987). A Howard University Cancer Center study revealed that nearly seven out of ten Blacks believed that surgery can cause cancer (Bang, Perlin, Sampson, 1987).

The factual information and research studies cited clearly indicate a need for accurate and relevant health information. Such an educational effort should be focused on increased awareness of health problems and their related risk factors. Regardless of the content of the educational effort, incorporation of social, cultural, and racial elements should be present to help assure success.

Manpower in health care. Members of minority groups have been the primary providers of health care delivery and educational systems and this is reflected in the dearth of health care services and practitioners in minority communities. More specifically, the Black manpower shortage is evidenced by the following:

1) Blacks are less than three percent of all physicians in the United States
2) The number of Black Ph.D.s in biological sciences (including MDs and Ph.D.s) is 0.25 percent of thetotal in the United States
3) Six percent of medical students in the United States are Black (Peniston, 1987, p. 144).

Black physicians are two-and-one half times more likely to practice in low income and rural areas than majority doctors and this will increase the discrepancy in health care services to Black people (Evans, 1987).

In addition to physicians, shortages are evident in other health care areas. In 1980, data revealed that only 2.5 percent of all dentists, 3.3 percent of all pharmacists and slightly more than 8 percent of all registered nurses were Black (Nickens, 1987). In contrast, Blacks make up 19 percent of dietitians, more than 40 percent of the midwives, 22 percent of the practical nurses and more than one-fourth of the nurses aides, orderlies and attendants (Nickens, 1987). This underrepresentation in the more prestigeous and higher paying jobs in health has been described as Blacks being relegated to the "cotton fields" of the health care industry (Williams, 1987). Increases in the number of Black health care providers will have a direct bearing on the utilization of health care services, particularly because of greater mutual cultural sensitivity.

The influx of foreign medical graduates to the United States has created an apparent but not real surplus of physicians (Brown, 1987). The 1980 report of the Graduate Medical Education National Advisory Committee (GMENAC) predicted an emerging surplus of physicians (Hanft, 1984). In spite of predicted surpluses in health manpower, both GMENAC and the Southern Regional Education Board have indicated that the "emerging surplus" does not include a surplus of minority health professionals (Iglehart, 1986). Whether or not there will be an increase in

Black health professionals will depend on increases in school enrollment, the matching of admission and graduation figures, improved secondary and higher education opportunities in science, and adequate funding for scholarships.

Planning For Retirement

Retirement is a condition in which a person is forced or allowed to be employed less than full time and income is derived from benefits earned as a job holder (Atchley, 1976). The middle adult phase of the life cycle is a time when active preparation is undertaken for establishing a stable career/employment situation and undertaking pre-retirement planning. Stable career/employment situations suggest taking time to assess one's employment in light of factors such as changing family obligations, changing economic pressures and advisability of making a career change prior to retirement. For Blacks in the work force this kind of reflection about employment may be tempered by limits on mobility due to institutional racism. This may be particularly true among professional athletes who, within an open system, might opt for a position as head coach/manager or other top administrative position for which they are qualified. The obvious absence of Blacks in these positions is evidence of institutionalized limitations. The labor union movement is another example where mobility of Blacks from the rank and file to top leadership positions seems limited as evidenced by their absence. Although being challenged in court, affirmative action programs have given support to opening areas of employment formerly closed to Blacks.

Pre-retirement planning. With the growing need to plan adequately for retirement in the later adult phase of one's life, the number of retirement planning programs have increased. Torres-Gil (1984) in discussing a general profile of most retirement planning/preparation programs noted the following:

> The field of retirement planning and preparation,...has yet to serve a heterogeneous population that differs by sex, language, race, and socioeconomic status. The retirement literature concentrates exclusively on a population that is White, educated, and relatively affluent, implying that techniques and educational models used by retirement-planning specialists for that population can be just as useful for individuals who are of a different race, ethnicity, and/or language (Torres-Gil, 1984, p. 109).

Given the generalized profile of Blacks as being employed in jobs without adequate pension coverage, having health problems which force early retirement, needing to work in old age, having no accumulated pension/vesting rights, and having a perception that retirement is inappropriate for their situation, the content and marketing strategies of pre-retirement programs must change. Blacks who are employed in state or federal civil service programs will likely be vested in pension programs and may be a good group to target for retirement planning programs. Persons who have worked for the postal service, who have made the military a career, are included among this group. Additionally, Blacks who have had employment where strong unions have established generous health and pension benefits are good candidates for retirement planning programming.

The retirement planning process uses two basic approaches: pre-retirement education and pre-retirement counseling. Pre-retirement education is the sharing, individually or in groups, of objective facts that will influence them when they retire (Peterson, 1984). Topics in education can include financial planning, problems in private and public pension plans, medicare/medicaid benefits, volunteer work, alternate employment options and planning for health care. Pre-retirement counseling is a helping process designed to help persons deal with emotional responses toward retirement. Resolving anxieties and feelings about prospects of retiring and the objective facts presented in the educational approach is an important aspect of making an appropriate transition from work status to non-work status in later adulthood. Pre-retirement planning is not just for the affluent Black person but can also be relevant to persons, who for a variety of reasons, have limited resources to invest and save (Torres-Gil, 1984).

In both the education and counseling approaches to pre-retirement planning it is imperative that there is sensitivity to the history, cultural traditions, and current situations of Blacks. Marketing strategies, for example, might include recruitment of Black retirement specialists, community outreach, and use of the oral tradition in communication of information about the need/value of retirement planning. Regardless of occupational level, a positive orientation to retirement is strongly influenced by exposure to formal retirement planning programs, exposure to media presentations, and personal discussions about retirement (Atchley, 1976).

Later Adulthood

Later adulthood marks the period of time in the life cycle when there is a shift from the middle years to old age. Today people are living longer and it is predicted that by the year 2030 the median age in the United States will be about 40 years and there will be approximately 65 million persons over the age of 65 (Joe, 1988). For the elderly, generally, issues of income and health are priority issues. Fisher (1988) describes the traditional fear of old people as the loss of their health and savings without knowing which will run out first.

Black elderly in the United States are, collectively, one of the most disadvantaged groups in society (see chapter by Murray, Khatib and Jackson, this volume). The Census Bureau projection of 3 million Black aged sixty-five and older by the year 2000 would result in a 46 percent increase of older Blacks (Beaver, 1983). Aged Blacks are the poorest of the poor among all the elderly and no other major aged racial or ethnic group including Hispanics, Indians and Asians, has a higher poverty rate (Simmons, 1987). In 1985, 31.5 percent of Black elderly were poor Black elderly women who live alone were the most disadvantaged with a poverty rate of 54.5 percent. Given the above cited statistics, the economic need of the Black elderly is obvious. The condition of poverty is also related to other problems, including poor health, poor housing, living in high crime areas, and lack of adequate supportive services.

Service Delivery: Federal Programs

The federal government has programs designed for the delivery of services to the elderly. Table 2 summarizes programs for older people under the Older Americans Act of 1965 as revised and amended. Elderly Blacks are underrepresented in some programs serving the elderly. This fact has been presented in hearings on problems of the Black elderly and confirmed in reports/studies such as a 1982 Civil Rights Commission Report and studies funded by the Administration on Aging (Simmons, 1987).

The Older Americans Act of 1965 as revised and amended provides for a range of program services for and on behalf of the elderly, including provisions for creation of the Administration on Aging, development of programs to help older persons, development of training, research and demonstration programs, and health education training. Specifically, elderly Blacks' participation in the Older Americans Act supportive and nutrition services programs has declined (Simmons, 1987). For Title II-B supportive services the participation dropped 10.7 percent in 1985 (Simmons, 1987). A lesser pattern of decline in the Title III-C nutrition program has also been noted (Simmons, 1987). Dancy makes the point that even if Black elderly do not share the view that services are charity, contemporary Black elderly, who tend to be a low-income group, may regard services as low quality or not attuned, culturally, to their needs (Dancy, 1977).

Table 2
Programs for Older People Available
Under the Older Americans Act

Program	Program Type	Program Benefit	Program Administration
Title III–A Community Planning and Coordination (1965)	—	Planning Coordinate Technical assistance	Area-wide Agency on Aging (AAA)
Title III–B Social Services (1973) Senior Centers (1978)	Not means-tested Not means-tested	In-kind (depending on each community)	Local agencies Local senior citizens councils
Title IIIC Nutrition Services (1973)	Not means-tested	In-kind	Local project sponsor
Title V Community Service Employment	Meanstested	In-kind	Local project sponsor

Source: Dobestein, Andrew, *Serving Older Adults: Policy, Programs and Professional Activities*; Prentice-Hall, Inc., New Jersey, 1985.

Utilization of Programs and Services: Symbolism and Modeling

Symbolism and modeling are important elements which enhance participation in and utilization of programs and services.

Symbolism. Symbolism is the "perceptions of objects and human interaction in the environment that lead to behavioral responses of cooperation and rejection"(Downing & Copeland, 1980, p. 298).

Modeling. Modeling is "demonstration through presence and behavior, for the purposes of learning and self-enhancement, with the goal of active participation of others in community processes" (Downing & Copeland,

1980, p. 301). To enhance Black elderly participation in and utilization of services it is necessary to be sensitive to racial, cultural, and communication issues. Attitudes and perceptions regarding past experiences often result in low expectations of services. For example, many older Blacks grew up during a time when racism was blatant and openly practical. They were not accepted by the American society or its institutions and the culture they knew in America was hostile. The aged Black focused energy, over time, in developing survival techniques, behaviors and attitudes which have not been relinquished (Johnson, 1978).

Regarding the cultural significance of communication, Johnson has noted:

> Most elderly Blacks experience difficulty in communicating which results from a language barrier which is culturally based. There is still a tendency for many elderly Blacks to speak in the Black vernacular. Often service agency staff complain that they do not understand what the older person is attempting to communicate and his needs are not fulfilled. However, this could be rectified by having available Black professionals to meet the needs of the clients. Associated with the language barrier is reading ability. The education level of most elderly Blacks is low and there are instances in which information is made available but which they cannot decipher (Johnson, 1978, p. 38).

The establishing of community-based agencies and services, hiring of Black staff, appointment of Black board members, and implementation of outreach program services is an integral part of symbolizing and modeling culturally syntonic services for the Black elderly. Holmes and associates found in their research that the strongest predictors of greater utilization of services by minority elderly are staffing patterns, and location of program offices in minority neighborhoods (Holmes and Associates, 1979). This would suggest that greater efforts should be made to hire Black (minority) staff in proportion to their representation in the target population served. Holmes further indicates that agencies which have offices in minority neighborhoods with minority staff are better able to overcome cultural, racial, language, and transportation barriers to the utilization of needed services.

Economic Sufficiency

One of the most pressing problems, given the poverty among the Black elderly, is economic sufficiency or retirement income security. Retirement income security is the ability to financially maintain self and dependents through Social Security, private pension, employment or a combination of such (Thomas, 1987). The employment patterns of elderly Blacks has been such that the retirement years are often entered into without the individual being vested in a pension plan. Vesting refers to the acquisition of full legal benefits made possible by an employer's contribution to a pension plan (Foner, Schwab, 1981). Changes in the pension laws under the Tax Reform Act of 1986 which lower the required period of vesting to five years, should improve the opportunity of Blacks entering retirement with pension benefits.

Table 3
Summary of Social Security Programs

Program	Kind of Program	Type of Benefits	Administrator of Program
Title I Old Age Assistance (1935–1972)	Assistance (Need-tested)	Cash	State Government (now rescinded)
Title II Social Security Retirement (1935)	Insurance (Entitlement)	Cash	Federal Government (Social Security Administration)
Disability (1950)	Insurance (Entitlement)	Cash	Federal Government (Social Security Administration)
Title XVI Supplemental Security Income (Former OAA)	Assistance (Need-tested)	Cash	Federal Government (Social Security Administration)
Title XVIII Medicare (1965)	Insurance (Entitlement)	In-kind	Federal Government (Social Security Administration)
Title XIX Mecaid (1965)	Assistance (Need-tested)	In-kind	State Government
Title XX Social Services (1974)	Assistance (Need-tested)	In-kind	State Government

Source: Dobestein, Andrew, *Serving Older Adults: Policy, Programs and Professional Activities*, Prentice-Hall, Inc., New Jersey, 1985.

Social Security. Social Security legislation initiated in 1935, and since amended, has provided benefits which have become the mainstay of retiree income. Table 3 summarizes programs provided through Social Security. Gayle Thompson in a published study of Social Security benefit trends for Blacks for the period of 1960-73 noted that Blacks were heavily represented among young beneficiaries but underrepresented among aged beneficiaries (Thompson, 1975). The historical context of social and occupational access to opportunities available in society reveals, in part, reasons for the benefit status of Blacks in the Social Security System. The Thompson study gives the following reason:

> A more plausible explanation for the race difference in beneficiary rates among the older population is that elderly Blacks, especially the very aged, are less likely than Whites to have achieved insured status under OASDHI. Although the 1950 and 1954 amendments to the Social Security Act extended coverage to farm laborers and domestic workers—occupations in which there are relatively large numbers of Blacks—some Blacks may have been too old at the time to benefit from the extension of coverage. In addition, early labor-force withdrawal for health reasons, the seasonal or casual nature of the work, and perhaps some underreporting of earnings may have affected the ability of older domestic and migratory workers to acquire the necessary quarters of coverage for insured status (Thompson, 1975, p. 31).

Although the Social Security Act provides for a major source of support for individuals in financial need, the benefits are not intended to be the recipient's sole source of financial support. Rather it is assumed that savings and other supplementary sources of support will be available to the individual. Blacks tend to be among the most disadvantaged retirees and receive less, or average, in Social Security benefits than their White counterparts (Foner & Schwab, 1981).

Advocacy Services

Given the status of the Black aged in terms of delivery of human services, services utilized, and services needed, advocacy services are important. Advocacy suggests being partisan in viewpoint and using available expertise exclusively to serve the interest of those one represents. Included among advocacy services are negotiation initiative, responsible research, and legislative initiative.

Negotiation initiative. Negotiation initiative is a process by which local communities and agencies bring together—through documented evidence—local, state and national definitions of service needs and program implementation in the interest of a specific group—for example, the Black elderly (Downing & Copeland, 1980). Advocacy through negotiation initiative is possible if the target group is thoroughly understood, needs are documented with sound data, and interpretation of the data is accurate and appropriate. The work of groups such as the National Caucus and Center on Black Aged (NCBA), created in 1970 to advocate nationally, is an example of how negotiation initiative has been used. Their work in providing employment, training and housing services for Black elderly needs to be continued and expanded. Additionally NCBA has been involved in working cooperatively with the Congressional Black Caucus (CBC) to heighten awareness regarding the elderly and their condition in the United States.

Responsible research. Responsible research, which goes beyond the concept of manufacturing knowledge through scholarly pursuits, is an advocacy service when findings are brought to the attention of agencies and decision-makers. The work of Black researchers such as Jacquelyne Jackson of Duke University, a founder of the National Caucus on the Black Aged, illustrate advocacy through responsible research. Federal legislation and national, state, and local programs and policies have been influenced by advocacy through responsible research. For example, situations such as underutilization of services, lack of equity in distribution of available resources, and need for more trained Black service providers has been identified and communicated to legislators, agency administrators and educators.

Legislative initiative. Legislative initiative as an advocacy service has often been neglected. Groups such as the Congressional Black Caucus (CBC), National Caucus and Center on Black Aged (NCBA), and the National Association of Black Social Workers (NABSW) have recommended and lobbied for legislation on the behalf of Black elderly. Jackson (1980) has identified a critical issue in the legislative area: is there a need for minority-specific or minority blind legislation? Minority-specific legislation targets provisions for given ethnic groups and eliminates group and or individuals that are unnamed from status as beneficiaries. Minority blind legislation does not target particular groups or individuals as sole legal beneficiaries (Jackson, 1980). Historically, minority-specific legislation has included the Fourteenth Amendment and legislation related to American Indian tribal rights. In the area of aging, Jackson (1980) cites Title VI under the Comprehensive Older Americans Act Amendments of 1978 for providing Indian Tribes and tribal organizations with direct funding.

Given the data available which reflect the quality of life related to factors such as race, health, employment and income, Blacks have historically not received maximum benefit from the provisions of the Social Security Act. For example, life expectancy statistics are indicative of the fact that Blacks, although contributing to the social security system, would not live long enough to collect retirement benefits at age 65 or older (Report No. 92-450, 92nd Congress, 1971). Some professionals have proposed altering the Social Security laws to provide earlier benefit payments to Blacks and other minorities because of health, employment, life expectancy and related racial factors (Report No. 92-450, 92nd Congress, 1971). This kind of legislative proposal would be an advocacy service. Jackson (1980) cites need to raise customary fees charged by minority professionals who charged lower fees in the past because their patients were low income. This would take into account previous patterns of discrimination and could be provided for, now that Medicare/Medicaid payments are available.

Summary

Historically Blacks have struggled to survive in a hostile color conscious society. This chapter has explored the adult life cycle in terms of developmental tasks and decisions as well as human services needed to support this process. While every aspect of human adult development and human service delivery could not be fully explored, a grid was developed to outline the following: 1) stage of development; 2) developmental tasks/decisions/crises; 3) supportive institutions and needed services; 4) barriers encountered; and 5) issues encountered.

Governmental programs are available to support, not supplant, family and individual effort. To truly accomplish this objective the human service delivery system and the family need to move toward full integration to provide for existing needs. In order to enhance the utilization of available services, emphasis must be placed on increasing the numbers and availability of Black service providers. Moreover, decision-making must be based on responsible research, accurate interpretation of data, and outreach activity. Advocacy for human services for Black adults must be continued, coordinated and expanded.

References

Aldridge, D. P. (1974). Problems and approaches to Black adoptions. *The Family Coordinator, 23*, 407-410.
Atchley, R. C. (1976). The sociology of retirement. New York: Wiley.
Bailey, E. J. (1987). Sociocultural factors and health care-seeking behavior among Black Americans. *Journal of National Medical Association, 79*, 389-392.

Bang, K. M., Perlin, E., & Sampson, C. C. (1987). Increased cancer risks in Blacks: A look at the factors. *Journal of National Medical Association, 79*, 383-388.

Battle, S. F. & Barnett, A. P. (1985). Status of the National Genetic Disease Act: Its effect on Black Americans, the delivery of comprehensive services. *The Western Journal of Black Studies, 9*, 209-213.

Beaver, M. L. (1983). *Human service practice with the elderly*. Englewood Cliffs, New Jersey: Prentice-Hall.

Blackwell, J. E. (1985). *The Black community: Diversity and unity*. New York: Harper & Row.

Bloom, M. (1980). *Life span development*. New York: Macmillan.

Brown, J. O. (1987). Crisis in health care for Black Americans. *Journal of National Medical Association, 79*, 260-261.

Chestang, L. W. (1983). The policies and politics of health and human services: A Black perspective. In A. E. Johnson, (Ed.) *The Black Experience: Considerations for health and human services*, (17-25). Davis, Ca: International Dialogue Press.

Chestang, L. W. (1980). Character development in a hostile environment, *Life span development*, (pp. 40-50). Macmillan.

Dancy, J. (1970). *The Black elderly*. Ann Arbor, Michigan: Institute of Gerontology, University of Michigan.

Devore, W. & Schlesinger, E. G. (1981). *Ethnic-sensitive social work practice*. St. Louis, Toronto, London: C. V. Mosby.

Downing, R. A. & Copeland, E. J. (1980). Services for the Black elderly: National or local problems? *Journal of Gerontological Social Work, 2*, 289-303.

Duh, S. V. & Willingham, D. F. (1986). An ecological view of hypertension in Blacks. *Journal of the National Medical Association, 78*, 617-619.

Evans, G. (1987). Black admissions to medical school less likely report says. *Black Issues in Higher Education, 4*, 1.

Fisher, B. M. (1988). Health and money: The enduring dilemmas of aging. *The Purdue Alumnus, 75*, 10-11.

Foner, A. & Schwab, K. (1981). *Aging and Retirement*. Monterey, Ca: Brooks/Cole.

Gould, K. H. (1980). *Contemporary social work: An introduction to social work and social welfare*. New York: McGraw-Hill.

Hanft, R. (1984). Minorities and the health professions in the 1980's. *Health Affairs, 3*, 71-83.

Hare, B. (1988). Black youth at risk. *The State of Black America 1988*, (81-93). New York: National Urban League, Inc.

Holmes, D., Holmes, M., Steinbach, L., Hausner, T. & Rochelean, B. (1979). The use of community-based services in long-term care by older minority persons. *The Gerontologist, 19*, 389-397.

Hotline (1982). Illinois Department of Children and Family Services, *2*, 9-10.

Iglehart, J. K. (1986). Trends in health personnel. *Health Affairs, 3*, 130-131.

Illinois Board of Higher Education (1975). Black Elderly Research Project #74-1775-006, Case Example. Springfield, Illinois: Illinois Board of Higher Education.

Jackson, J. J. (1980). *Minorities and Aging*. Belmont Ca.: Wadsworth.

Joe, B. E. (1988). The aging of America: How shall we provide for a graying society, and what will it mean? *Purdue Alumnus, 75*, 8-9.

Johnson, R. (1978). Barriers to adequate housing for elderly Blacks. *Aging*, 38.

Kennedy, C. E. (1978). *Human development: The adult years and aging*. New York: Macmillan.

Kimmel, D. C. (1974). *Adulthood and aging: An interdisciplinary developmental view.* New York: Wiley & Sons.

Levinson, D. J., (1977). The mid-life transition: A period in adult psychosocial development. *Psychiatry, 40,* 99-112.

Meyer, C. H. (1976). *Social work practice.* New York: The Free Press.

National Association of Social Workers, (1977). *Encyclopedia* of Social Work, Self-help groups, 1254-1260. Washington, D.C.: National Association of Social Workers, Inc.

Neugarten, B. (Ed.) (1968). *Middle-age and aging.* Chicago: University of Chicago Press.

Nicols, M. P. (1986). *Turning forty in the 80's: Personal crisis, time for change.* New York: W. W. Norton.

Nickens, H. (1987). Health care crisis aggravated by shortage of minority providers. *Black Issues in Higher Education, 4,* 4, 8.

O'Brien, E. M. (1987). Minorities, especially Blacks, face health care crisis. *Black Issues in Higher Education, 4,* 1, 15.

Peniston, R. L. (1987). A racial view of medical education. *Journal of the National Medical Association, 79,* 143-145.

Peterson, J. A. (1984). Pre-retirement counseling. In H. Dennis (Ed.), *Retirement preparation: What retirement specialists need to know.* Lexington, Mass: Lexington, Heath.

Simmons, S. J. (1987). The Black elderly: A forgotten statistic. *Point of View,* 11-13.

Somerville, R. M. (1970). Contemporary family materials for education counseling family services. *The Family Coordinator, 19,* 279-280.

Stevens-Long, J. (1979). *Adult life and developmental processes.* Palo Alto, Ca.: Mayfield.

The Governor's Task Force on Black and Minority Health. (1987). *Final Report,* 11-50. Columbus, Ohio: The Governor's Task Force on Black and Minority Health.

Torres-Gil, F. (1984). Retirement issues that affect minorities. In H. Dennis (Ed.), *Retirement preparation: What retirement specialists need to know,* 109-128. Lexington, Mass: Lexington, Heath.

Thomas, R. J. (1987). Retirement security-a priority for Blacks. *Point of View,* 14.

Thompson, G. (1975). Blacks and social security benefits: Trends, 1960-73. *Social Security Bulletin,* 30-40.

Turner, C. & Darity, W. A. (1980). Fears of genocide among Black Americans as related to age, sex, and region. In M. Bloom (Ed.), *Life span development,* 306-307. New York: Macmillan.

Washington D.C. Department of Health (1985). Report of the Secretary's Task Force on Black and Minority Health, (pp. 87-94). Washington: U. S. Department of Health and Human Services.

Weaver, J. L. (1976). *National health policy and the underserved: Ethnic minorities, women, and the elderly.* St. Louis, IL.: Mosby.

Welsing, F. (1974). The Cress theory of color-confrontation. *Black Scholar, 5,* 32-40.

Williams, M. (1987). Health care crisis aggravated by shortage of minority providers. *Black Issues in Higher Education, 4,* 4.

Willie, C. V. (1971). Perspectives from the Black community. *Population Reference Bureau,* Selection No. 37, pp. 1-12. Washington D.C.

Zacks, H. (1980). Self-actualization: A midlife problem. *Social casework: The Journal of Contemporary Social Work,* 223-233.

PSYCHOLOGICAL FUNCTIONING IN AFRICAN-AMERICAN ADULTS: SOME ELABORATIONS ON A MODEL, WITH CLINICAL APPLICATIONS

Arthur C. Jones

In a previous article (Jones, 1985) a model was presented describing the various psychological adaptation tasks African American individuals must face in order to negotiate effective living. Figure 1 summarizes the model. As shown, four major areas, relatively independent as well as interrelated, are seen as important. These include developing a means of coping with racial oppression, maintaining desired influences with respect to the majority culture, establishing roots within traditional African American culture, and the influence of personal experiences and endowments. It was suggested that an understanding of how different individuals approach these four tasks can facilitate a clinician's assessment process and can permit a therapist to view the infinite variety of patterns presenting themselves in different clients.

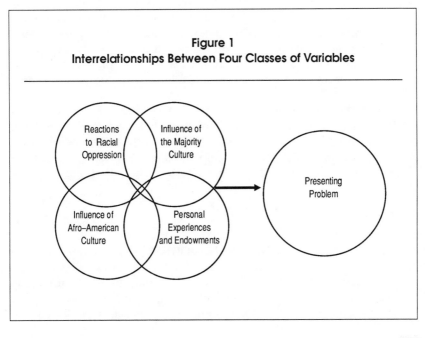

Figure 1
Interrelationships Between Four Classes of Variables

Reactions to Racial Oppression

Influence of the Majority Culture

Influence of Afro–American Culture

Personal Experiences and Endowments

Presenting Problem

This conceptual model is useful in framing the issues facing individuals at various stages in the life span, from infancy to old age. The current article attempts to outline some salient issues within this framework for individuals during adulthood, with a focus on commonly encountered clinical assessment and psychotherapy problems.

Reactions to Racial Oppression

Racial oppression is a fact of life for all African Americans, regardless of social class or geographical location. This is a natural outcrop of the need of the majority Anglo culture to have objects of projection for various undesirable personal characteristics (Kovel, 1971). Certainly, many ethnic and religious groups have been victims of political and social oppression at various times in history. The psychological defense mechanism of projection appears to explain well the dynamics of such oppression. However, the powerful symbolic meanings mediated by color make African peoples particularly vulnerable to such projections. Some colors have nearly universal symbolic meanings (e.g., red as a symbol of passion, fury, anger, etc.). However, when it comes to skin colors, cultures tend to ascribe negative or undesirable characteristics to skin colors different from their own, and these negative attibutions are propelled by powerful emotional forces (Zahan, 1977). In the United States (and in the West generally), the colors Black and brown have been the selected carriers of negative projections (Kovel, 1971). The continued "high visibility" of African people (because of skin color) serves to maintain this convenient use of dark-skinned people as a projective repository of undesirable personal characteristics. Thus, despite "progress" on some fronts, the spectre of White racism is likely to continue to loom indefinitely.

With the onset of adulthood, various tasks present themselves, including the consolidation of gender identity and the establishment of a niche for oneself in society (Erikson, 1980). In early adulthood, this also requires that the individual develop strategies for dealing with experiences of racial oppression. The issues surrounding this task are numerous.

Male Development

For African American males, face-to-face confrontations with racism are particularly intense at the time the young adult is consolidating his masculine identity. His efforts in this area are accomplished in the context of challenges from the majority culture, dominated by White males. Problematically, White males themselves encounter intensely difficult and personally threatening experiences during this phase of development. As Monick (1987) points out, societal domination by White males compensates underlying feelings of insecurity accompanying attempts to develop masculinity and to be freed from the unconscious psychological domination of family roots. In the process, White male's insecurity is expressed in part via the collective projection of threatening personal material onto African American males, who are in turn viewed consciously as threatening (virile, powerful, violent) and therefore requiring some means of depotentiation. Eugene Monick, a White male, seems to understand this process well in his recounting of a personal experience:

> I remember walking into the office of a senior priest in New York... The cardinal rector was seated with a male friend, chatting. As I rounded the corner of his room, he greeted me with a great smile, "How are you, boy?" Had I been willing to risk the money his parish gave my mission I would have replied, "Just fine, mother-fucker." My rage was enormous. I can feel it today, twenty years later. I knew then, with little psychoanalytic knowledge, that he meant to demean, *to imply that I was his "nigger."* (1987, p. 103, italics mine).

Monick's ready use of the "nigger" analogy to describe his personal experience highlights his awareness of the cultural dynamic: disempower the "nigger" before he uses his awesome power and virility to get you! The true test of an adaptive response to this cultural dynamic is whether the young man (or *old* man, for that matter) can develop a sense of himself that is grounded from within, in his own soul, and not simply reactive to White male-initiated racism. Some of the stereotypical roles played out by some African American males (e.g., hypermasculinity, compulsive "womanizing," etc.) reflect failures in adaptation, manifested in attempts at compensation for underlying wounds of insecurity inflicted by the majority culture. On the other hand, true integration of confident masculinity frees one from such pathological patterns.

African American males often have to be creative in their personal, strategic reactions to racism, and there is no one "right" approach (Jones, 1985). The essential ingredient of a successful adaptation strategy is that it include a conscious understanding of the issues involved as well as a conscious, deliberate choice of actions, based on secure self-anchoring. This is in contrast to reactive strategies that mask unconscious self doubts and insecurities.

Case Example

A 29-year-old man suffering from severe anxiety attacks reported the following dream: "I am riding in a fancy red sports car, with a small white leather interior. I am wearing a tailored blue suit, sunglasses, and a red silk tie. I drive through the front gate outside the building where I work. As I drive through the gate the roof of my car falls off. I am shocked by this, but I continue to drive on. Then the side door falls off. I begin to get very nervous, but I continue. Slowly, my car begins to fall apart, bit by bit, until I am sitting in the seat with just the steering wheel and nothing else. Then, as I sit there in a total panic, I notice my clothes beginning to fall off, until I am finally naked. I am terrified!"

This man was at a point in therapy where he was becoming aware of the feelings of vulnerability and transparency accompanying the hyper-masculine posture he had adopted in his attempts to deal with racism, particularly in his work setting. As he struggled with the feeling of panic he had experienced in the dream, associated with being stripped of his outward persona, down to his bare essentials (literally!), he was forced to work on finding a greater degree of genuine, inner strength in his battles with racism. This was difficult and took some time, but he slowly began to experience a more solid self assuredness, accompanied by a marked reduction in his anxiety symptoms. Although he continued to encounter instances of personal and institutional racism, he focused more on the behaviors needed to confront these experiences (e.g., initiation of a law-suit), and no longer had the need for a "macho" image to assert his manhood. Ironically, he reported feeling more strongly masculine than ever before.

Female Development

African American women face tasks similar to their male counter-parts in confronting the myriad effects of racism. There have been some particularly hazardous patterns. Again, cultural projection has under-girded much of the process. Often, Black women have been seen as projective objects of White males' unintegrated sexual passions, yet stripped of the delicate "pedestal" status assigned White females. With many of their Black men internally demasculinized (see above), some African American females have been left having to "do it all" (work, raise children, etc.), with little pay or personal reward. Moreover, the essen-tially White women's liberation movement has offered very little to the African American woman, whose dual struggles with racism and sexism have been far different from the experiences of middle-class White females. In fact, White women have sometimes been viewed as co-equal oppressors, in partnership with White males.

As with men, these struggles for African American women have had multiple consequences. The hazards faced include the risk for developing hardened, defensive stances in which any outward expression of femininity is experienced as threatening. This has left some women cut off from important parts of themselves, feeling the risk is too high to lay bare these vulnerable inner dimensions. From a psychological standpoint, the outcome can sometimes be contained in the trap of a reactive stance against racism without a centered, consciously conceived adaptive strategy.

Case Example

A 35-year-old professional woman sought therapy because she felt depressed and increasingly distant from her husband. She felt a dilemma, because the confidence and assertiveness she had worked hard to develop over the last few years (and which had resulted in a highly successful professional career) seemed to be liabilities at home. She felt angry that her husband seemed to devalue these traits. After some self exploration she discovered that the cold, businesslike persona that she had used successfully in the professional world was also being used indiscriminately at home. She was shocked at becoming aware of how pervasive this had been. She also realized that she had not felt "like a woman" in years. Following a series of conjoint sessions with the husband (who had to confront his own male insecurities), her marital relationship began to improve, including increasing emotional closeness to her husband. To her surprise, her husband began to be more supportive of her career pursuits. She found herself amazed that she had unwillingly allowed her strategy for dealing with racism and sexism on the job to spread to her home life.

The point of this case example, again, is the necessity for conscious awareness in selecting the type and range of reactions to racial oppression, with the very real danger for African American men and women of permitting unconscious issues to reap undesired and sometimes harmful effects. Clearly, these undesired effects can be prevented or reversed with conscious attention and awareness.

Influence of the Majority Culture

African Americans, perhaps more than any other American ethnic minority group, face numerous paradoxes and ironies in their straddling of two cultures, traditional African, and Anglo American. Despite opportunities that may arise for "success" within the majority culture, ultimate exclusion from that culture is continually reinforced because of the perpetual forces of racism, as discussed above. In addition, internalization of majority culture values carries with it the risk of loss of anchoring to oneself and to one's community. At the same time, it is impossible to function within an ethnic minority vacuum, since the influence of the majority culture is present all around us in the print and electronic media, pervasively permeating even the most economically impoverished homes in physically segregated African American communities. Survival and personal growth require some way of selecting those aspects of the larger culture that are compatible with one's values and temperament, avoiding the excesses and aberrations that are frequently reflected in the mental health problems of American society. Unfortunately, for some African Americans internalization of majority culture influences occurs on an unconscious level, with the undesired consequence of self alienation (Luther X, 1974). A part of this pattern at times is the exaggerated mimicry of the worst aspects of Anglo American society, elucidated so clearly by Frazier (1962) over 25 years ago and sadly still present today in some segments of the African American community.

The extent of immersion in the majority culture is wide-ranging, including an infinite variety of attitudes and perspectives. Clinically, it is impossible to define an absolute standard in terms of degree of immersion and its correspondence in optimal mental health functioning (Jones, 1985). However, it is critical that one develop the ability to select consciously one's specific stance and perspective without compromising personal integrity.

Case Example

A couple in their mid thirties requested marital counseling. The wife was concerned that her husband, a young corporate executive, was "spending too much time with White folks," and that his interest in some of the activities of his White colleagues (e.g., golf, jogging, skiing) extended far beyond what she perceived as obligatory professional contact. The wife was herself a professional person who prided herself on her anchoring in the African American Community and her ability to "leave the White folks at work!"

Clinical exploration revealed a number of underlying issues, including problems in trust that had developed in the five-year history of this couple's marriage. However, the racial issues raised by the wife were seen as important, independent of the basic trust problems. This couple had begun their marriage with the commitment of remaining connected to the African American community as they climbed their respective professional success ladders. Yet, as they talked about it, it was clear that material success was also important to them, as well as their ability to engage in competitive individual achievements. The wife had simply become the spokesperson for both of them concerning the anxieties they both felt as they negotiated the balance, as they saw it, between "Blackness and success." They remained committed to their material and professional aspirations, but increased their awareness of the hazards of excess.

For contemporary African Americans, ignorance or attempted avoidance of the pervasive influence of the majority culture is synonymous with massive psychological denial. However, vigilance and awareness can promote balance and sanity in the choice of values and behaviors that match one's sense of self and integrity.

Influence of Traditional African–American Culture

A core aspect of mental health for all human beings is the ability to experience oneself as part of a larger group, with a unique history and set of cultural values and traditions (McGoldrick et al., 1982). African Americans sometimes lose track of this important fact. Nobles (cf. 1980a, 1980b) has helped to elucidate the specifics of African American cultural traditions, including such factors as group orientation ("I am because we are and because we are, therefore I am"), spirituality, and fluid expression of affect. These cultural emphases are present everywhere in African American communities: in church music and services, in professional group gatherings, in barbershop and beauty parlor conversations, in jazz club jam sessions, etc. "Soul" is alive in all of these settings, the unique spirit that is infused into places where consciously self-anchored African Americans gather. As mentioned earlier, the ability to embrace this spirit and, by extension, to embrace oneself (Luther X, 1974) often provides the "glue" that permits healthy emotional functioning during all subphases of adult life. This topic has been discussed extensively in another article (Jones, in press), with illustrations drawn from autobiographical and fictional writings by African American authors. An example worth repeating here is the character of Avey Johnson from Paule Marshall's (1984) novel, *Praisesong for the Widow*. Avey Johnson is a staid, aging widow whose journey on a luxury cruise liner provides the occasion for an introspective review of her life. A dream one night precipitates an emotional crisis. In the dream, Avey encounters her Aunt Cuney, a deceased aunt whom Avey, as a child, had visited during summer excursions to a sea island off the coast of South Carolina. Aunt Cuney had repeatedly taken the young Avey to a spit of land overlooking the ocean and had told the child a story of African Ibo ancestors who had come to the island as slaves. According to the story, the visionary Ibos had turned abruptly away from the island and walked across the water towards Africa. The recollection in the dream of this story provides the symbolic backdrop for an inner transformation in Avey, who through a dramatic series of events restores her connection to herself and her people, a con-

303

nection she had experienced as a child and young adult, but had lost in her (and her deceased husband's) struggle against racism. The author leaves to the reader's imagination how the new self awareness is to be put into practice in Avey's life, but the novel ends in a spirit of renewal and hope.

As in Paule Marshall's allegorical novel, many African American adults, particularly in middle and old age, face real-life crises stimulated by lost connections with themselves via lost cultural rootedness. Sometimes a reanchoring (or in some cases anchoring for the first time) can serve to restore a proper inner balance, permitting a reorienting to outer life.

Case Example

A couple in their late forties sought help for their teenage daughter, who was enrolled in a predominantly White school and had recently begun to associate with "punkers." The parents were panicked and outraged by their daughter's behavior. In fact, they had been worried for some time about their daughter's "White" interests and apparent rejection of "Black" interests (e.g., choice of punk rock over rhythm and blues, disenchantment with the Black church, etc.). After some exploration, the parents were able to see how they themselves had set the stage for their daughter's behavior. They had assumed that their own internalized Black pride would automatically be passed on to their daughter. Inadvertently, in their move to obtain a "better" life for themselves and family, they had cut themselves off from important ties to their community. They had to acknowledge that not only had their daughter been adversely affected, but they themselves had suffered as well. They seemed to have lost the spontaneity and vibrancy they had felt when they were younger, poorer and more closely involved with "the ghetto." While they determined that they did not want to give up their material success, they were committed to finding new ways to reconnect to the waning "soul" in their lives.

Personal Experiences and Endowments

Obviously, life as an African American requires constant attention to issues relevant to race and culture, as has been the focus of the discussion thus far. However, each person has a set of personal experiences and endowments that, relatively independent of race, also affect psychological functioning.

These varied personal factors operate sometimes as strengths and sometimes as limits on functioning. For example, physical handicaps or a personal background of parental abuse are factors that would impede effective functioning in adult life, independent of cultural issues. Conversely, a high level of intelligence and multiple talents would normally enhance functioning. This may seem too obvious to mention. However, Black and non-Black clinicians frequently make the mistake of focusing disproportionately on racial and cultural factors, ignoring other issues that are critical to the assessment of developmental maturity and prognosis in psychotherapy.

Case Example

A man in his late twenties sought therapy because of a deepening depression that had developed over the last six months. The depression had begun following the breakup of a relationship with a woman whom he had dated for four years. He had ended the relationship for reasons that not even he himself understood: vague feelings of discomfort and a desire to "see other people," even though nothing in the relationship was particularly unsatisfactory. His girlfriend had begun to hint at her desire for marriage, and the client was unsure why this made him uncomfortable, since he had felt for some time that he wanted to marry her. Now, to his chagrin, he found himself mistrusting not only his girlfriend, but African American women generally. The therapist, operating from an Afrocentric theoretical perspective, began to focus on the client's self esteem deficits, and particularly problems in his sense of himself as an African American. After several sessions with this focus, the client revealed in an emotional moment that he had been beaten severely by his mother when he was a young child, and that the beatings never seemed to be related to any specific misbehaviors on his part. His mother was later hospitalized for mental illness. He had never told anyone outside the family about this and in fact had tried himself to forget about it. With the emergence of this new material, the therapy shifted in focus to the pervasive effects of these early childhood experiences, particularly with respect to the client's inability to commit to intimate relationships. The client was able to report a history of problems in this area beginning with his first dating experiences as an adolescent. He began seeing his girlfriend again, feeling new hope that things could possibly work out.

In this case, it was the revelation of the childhood abuse that forced the therapist to shift the focus from questions of racial identity to the issue of past abuse and its effect on intimacy. Fortunately the client was able to take an active role in facilitating this shift. If this shift had not occurred, the case could have concluded with a "resistant" client and a premature termination. This underscores the need for clinicians, in their zeal for promoting self-awareness, to avoid the trap of ignoring important points of personal background that are relevant to assessment and therapy.

Overview

It should be clear that the concept of balance is critical to the achievement of adaptive functioning in adulthood as viewed from this model. Dealing with racism is impossible without adequate cultural rootedness, which in turn is impeded without attention to the question of where one stands vis-a-vis the majority culture, etc. All factors overlap and have reciprocal effects on each other, requiring balancing and blending for healthy functioning.

One assumption made here is that a central unconscious balancing factor can assist in this process. This underlying, spiritual guiding factor is present unconsciously in all individuals. When made conscious it has the effect of aiding each person in fulfilling his or her personal "destiny." If one can tap into this inner "guide," growth can proceed naturally. Unfortunately, most of Western psychology is silent on this critical human process. An important exception is the psychology of C. G. Jung (1972), whose concept of the "Self" captures this idea of an underlying spiritual core that helps direct life and restore imbalances. African Americans, rooted in spiritual traditions, appear particularly adept at approaching life from this perspective.

Current trends in African American psychological theory parallel this emphasis on spirituality and "natural" growth, and the potential for African Americans to experience themselves in this way. Akbar (1976, 1977, 1984) has been perhaps the clearest in his elucidation of this orientation.

Recently, an anthropologically-oriented work by a Jungian analyst (Buhrmann, 1987) has in fact corroborated the pervasiveness of this spiritual focus in traditional African "therapy" and healing, and has validated empirically the richness of specific African healing traditions as a source of knowledge about human growth and healing. Buhrmann conducted an extensive study of the sophisticated training procedures required of the *amaggira* (traditional healers) among the Xhosa people of South Africa. The study uncovered interesting parallels to the process of training Jungian analysts in the West, including the requirement for one's own personal introspection, the need for special abilities in dealing with spiritual processes, and certification by mentors that the individual *iggira* (singular of *amaggira*) has experienced some of the difficult, painful growth processes that will be part of the lives of future patients. There is a particularly strong emphasis on paying attention to one's dreams as a source of spiritual wisdom. Buhrmann concludes that Westerners have much to learn from the Xhosa (and other traditional African peoples) with respect to the invocation of natural spiritual growth processes in the treatment of psychological (and physical) ailments. If this is true for White Europeans, it is even more true for African Americans, who have much to gain from immersion in these proven methods from African cultural traditions of making contact with the inner resources that can establish and restore imbalances in living, in line with the ideas that have been sketched in the present article. Using this approach, each individual discovers a unique point of balance for the various spheres of personal experience. One is aptly reminded of what Akbar (Luther X, 1974) asserted nearly 15 years ago: that self knowledge and awareness may in fact be the key to African American (human?) mental health.

References

Akbar, N. (1976). *The community of self.* Chicago: Nation of Islam Office of Human Development.

Akbar, N. (1977). *Natural psychology and human transformation.* Chicago: World Community of Islam in the West.

Akbar, N. (1984). *Chains and images of psychological slavery.* Jersey City, NJ: New Mind Productions.

Buhrmann, M. V. (1987). *Living in two worlds: Communication between a White healer and her Black counterparts.* Wilmette, Illinois: Chiron Publications.

Erikson, E. H. (1980). *Identity and the life cycle.* New York: W. W. Norton.

Frazier, E. F. (1962). *Black bourgeosie.* New York: Collier.

Jones, A. C. (1985). Psychological functioning in Black Americans: A conceptual guide for use in psychotherapy. *Psychotherapy, 22(2s),* 363-369.

Jones, A. C. (In press). Rootedness and the striving African American: Implications for self development and psychotherapy. In R. L. Jones (Ed.), *Advances in Black psychology.* Berkeley, CA: Cobb & Henry.

Jung, C. G. (1972). *Two essays on analytical psychology.* New York: Princeton University Press.

Kovel, J. (1971). *White racism: A psychohistory.* New York: Viking.

Luther X. (Weems). (1974). Awareness: The key to Black mental health. *Journal of Black Psychology, 2(1),* 30-37.

Marshall, P. (1984). *Praisesong for the widow.* New York: E. P. Dutton, Inc.

McGoldrick, M., Pearce, J. K., & Giordano, J. (Eds.). (1982). *Ethnicity and family therapy.* New York: Guilford Press.

Monick, E. (1987). *Phallos: Sacred image of the masculine.* Toronto: Inner City Books.

Nobles, W. W. (1980a). African philosophy: Foundations for Black psychology. In R. L. Jones (Ed.), *Black psychology (Second Edition). New York: Harper & Row.*

Nobles, W. W. (1980b). Extended self: Rethinking the so-called Negro self concept. In R. L. Jones (Ed.). *Black psychology* (Second Edition). New York: Harper & Row.

Zahan, D. (1977). White, red and Black: Colour symbolism in Black Africa. In Spring Publications (Ed.), *Color symbolism.* Dallas: Spring Publications.

Part IV

Special Topics

A BIOBEHAVIORAL PERSPECTIVE ON STRESS AND HYPERTENSION IN BLACK ADULTS

Hector F. Myers, Norman B. Anderson,
and Tony L. Strickland

Introduction

In the past decade we have witnessed a significant increase in basic, clinical, pharmacologic, epidemiologic and behavioral research on essential hypertension in Blacks (See Gibson & Gibbons, 1982, Anderson, In press (a) and the Report from the Task Force on Black & Minority Health, 1980 for comprehensive bibliographies and reviews of the subject). Most of the studies have focused on ascertaining the bases or causes of the observed differences in morbidity (see glossary of terms at end of chapter) and mortality from hypertension between Blacks and Whites. This research has been largely comparative in nature, and has focused primarily on identifying similarities and differences between Blacks and Whites on various factors relevant to this disease. Unfortunately, most of the studies to date have pursued their primary research questions within narrow disciplinary domains and have relied exclusively on the research tools specific to their disciplines. For example, pharmacologic and clinical studies have typically evaluated the impact of specific drugs, biochemical interventions or treatment procedures on specific biological mechanisms known to control blood pressure (Weiner, 1979; Luft, Grim & Weinberger, 1985). On the other hand, epidemiologic and sociopsychological studies typically focus their attention on social status, health habits and psychological factors as potential contributors to differential risk, morbidity and mortality from essential hypertension in Black and White populations (Syme et al., 1974; Harburg et al., 1978; James, 1985). Although these studies are addressing the problem of essential hypertension in Blacks, there is little comparability and overlap in the samples, in the measures taken, in the presumed causal mechanisms studied, or in the level of analysis conducted. Therefore, there is little opportunity for an integrative, synergistic perspective on the problem to emerge. Therefore, a major obstacle faced by current research on essential hypertension is the absence of an

The preparation of this manuscript was supported in part by NHLBI/NIH grant No. RO1-HL31707, to the first author.

integrated, multidisciplinary perspective that considers multiple contributing factors and different levels or domains of analysis within the
same study (e.g. physiological mechanisms, neurohormonal processes,
psychosocial factors and behavioral attributes).

This chapter reviews and discusses the empirical evidence for biological and psychosocial differences in the possible causes, in the life
course, and in the outcome of hypertensive disease in Blacks and Whites.
Second, the basic rationale for an integrative, multi-domain, biobehavioral perspective for research on hypertension will be presented, and
the basic components of such a model outlined. Third, a brief review of
current biobehavioral research addressing the question of Black-White
differences in cardiovascular functioning will be presented. And, finally, a
brief discussion of new research directions, and the implications of their
findings for improving the health status of Black Americans will be
addressed.

Black-White Differences in Essential Hypertension

All of the available medical and epidemiologic evidence over-
whelmingly identifies Black adults as running the greatest risk of
developing essential hypertension, of suffering disproportionately from
the pathological consequences of this disease, and of running the
greatest risk of early mortality from this disease and its sequelae of all
U.S. population groups (Finnerty, 1971; NCHS Report, 1981; Gillum,
1979; Thompson, 1980; Langford, 1981; Prineas & Gillum, 1985). In the
U.S., essential hypertension in some age groups of adults has been reported to be twice as prevalent in Blacks as compared to Whites.
Further, Blacks have higher average resting blood pressures and higher
prevalence of hypertension than Whites at all SES levels, all ages, and in
both gender groups (Syme et al., 1974; Hypertension Detection & Follow-Up Program (HDFP), 1977; Black Health Care Providers Task Force
Report (NBHCPTF), 1980). According to a recent report from the
National Center for Health Statistics (NCHS), Blacks were 1.23 times
more likely to suffer from essential hypertension than Whites across all
age groups. This excess morbidity rate is evident throughout the entire
life span. For example, the Black excess morbidity rate for ages 1-24 was
1.62, for ages 25-44 it was 1.98, for ages 45-64 it was 1.70, for ages 65-69
it was 1.49, and for ages 70 and above it was 1.11. As these data indicate,
the greatest Black-White discrepancy in morbidity occurs among young
and middle-aged adults (i.e. ages 25-44 and 45-64), and the lowest occurs among the aged (i.e. ages 70+). (See Table 1)

Table 1
MORBIDITY RATES BY RACE AND GENDER: U.S., 1979-1981*
(Rates per 100,000 population)

Ages	White Men	Black Men	White Women	Black Women
1-24	799.64	998.68	823.14	1,606.51
25-44	7,860.88	11,163.09	5,743.67	15,184.56
45-64	21,835.73	32,937.57	23,132.68	42,812.12
65-69	30,327.36	43,166.84	38,661.45	58,079.25
70+	29,323.36	35,734.89	44,980.19	48,630.09
All Ages	11,350.93	10,136.40	12,777.34	16,580.31

Relative Risk Based on White Morbidity

Ages	All Blacks	Black Men	Black Women
1-24	1.617	1.249	1.952
25-44	1.977	1.420	2.644
45-64	1.702	1.508	1.851
65-69	1.485	1.423	1.502
70+	1.113	1.219	1.081
All Ages	1.231	1.120	1.298

*Data reported from the National Center for Health Statistics, Morbidity, U.S., HIS, 1979-1981. Selected Chronic Circulatory Diseases Database, 1985.

Evidence also indicates that there is different target end-organ damage associated with more severe hypertension in Blacks and Whites. Hypertensive Blacks often show more cardiographic and radiographic evidence of left ventricular enlargement, yet run a lower risk of coronary heart disease than Whites. On the other hand, Black hypertensives run a greater risk of strokes, end-stage renal disease (i.e. severe kidney dysfunction requiring regular kidney dialysis), and are more likely to suffer from primary aldosteronism, pheochromocytoma, and coarctation of the aorta than their White counterparts (Gillum, 1979; Thompson, 1980; Finnerty, 1971; Curry & Lewis, 1985; Shulman, 1985). In the Gillum (1979) and Anderson (In press, a) reviews, researchers are warned against overinterpreting evidence that suggests that the biological mechanisms governing blood pressure in Blacks and Whites may be fundamentally different. The most reasonable hypothesis of the causes of Black-White differences in blood pressure, given the present state of knowledge, appears to be some combination of differences in renal physiology interacting with environmental factors to impact cardiovascular functioning.

The course of hypertension in Blacks also appears to be different, with typically earlier onset, earlier development of the more pathological and severe forms of the disease, especially in Black men, and earlier mortality (Stamler, 1980; NBHCPTF, 1980; Tyroler et al., 1984; Neaton et al., 1984). Across all age groups, Black men are 2.47 times more likely to die from hypertensive disease than White men (i.e. 27.62 vs. 11.20) and Black women are 2.02 times more likely to die from this disease than White women (i.e. 29.32 vs 14.52). Black women are slightly more likely to die from hypertension than Black men (i.e. 1.05 times), but Black men are likely to die at a younger age. In fact, the mortality rate for hypertension is higher in Black men compared to Black women until age 80 (see Table 2).

TABLE 2
MORALITY RATE BY RACE AND GENDER: U.S., 1979-1981*

Ages	White Men	Black Men	White Women	Black Women
20-24	0.08	0.49	0.05	0.40
25-29	0.27	2.12	0.10	1.62
30-34	0.48	5.63	0.23	3.05
35-39	1.02	11.83	0.45	7.21
40-44	2.52	26.01	1.15	15.63
45-49	4.86	39.85	2.59	28.20
50-54	9.03	62.76	4.47	44.26
55-59	16.05	88.60	8.24	62.54
60-64	24.67	113.32	14.94	88.24
65-69	38.84	146.81	26.28	124.12
70-74	59.20	194.75	47.37	177.47
75-79	95.45	238.73	85.60	244.34
80-84	150.62	323.77	157.47	343.40
85+	278.05	427.95	316.61	467.50
All Ages	11.20	27.62	14.52	29.32

*Data reported from the National Center for Health Statistics, Mortality, U.S., HIS, 1979-1981. Selected Chronic Circulatory Diseases Database, 1985.

Finally, there is clinical evidence suggesting that compared to Whites, Black hypertensives respond differently to anti-hypertensive medications. Blacks often show comparatively greater blood pressure reduction to diuretics and lesser reduction from beta-adrenergic blockers (Langford, 1981; Kilcoyne et al., 1974; Hall, 1985). These differences in treatment response have been attributed to the greater tendency of Black hypertensives to have lower plasma renin levels, especially older Black adults. This is a further indication of differences in kidney function between the two ethnic groups (Chrysant et al., 1979; Langford, 1981; Gillum, 1979; Luft, Grim & Weinberger, 1985).

It is this evidence of racial differences in morbidity and mortality, and related differences in the pattern of physiological functioning, in risk for end-organ damage, and in response to pharmacologic intervention that has stimulated recent interest in the causes of racial differences in hypertension. This research on the causes of racial differences in hypertension can be roughly grouped into four major categories: (a) studies of biological differences, (b) studies of genetic/familial differences, (c) studies of socioeconomic differences, and (d) studies of sociopsychological and behavioral differences.

Biological Differences

In two recent reviews of Black-White differences in hypertension (Gillum, 1979; Anderson, In press, a), the empirical evidence of racial differences in renal physiology, endocrine function, autonomic nervous system function, and cardiac anatomy and function are discussed. The authors note that the most frequently cited explanation for Black-White differences in hypertension is the evidence of Black-White differences in renal physiology. These include the tendency of Black hypertensives to have lower circulating plasma renin levels, lower sodium and potassium excretion rates, and higher plasma volume levels than White hypertensives. The hypothesis has been offered that Blacks may have evolved more efficient mechanisms for sodium conservation (e.g. high sodium reabsorption in the proximal tubules of the kidney), and therefore more Blacks than Whites may be "salt sensitive", and less able to excrete the excess sodium that is common to the modern diet (Luft et al., 1979; 1985). Results from the Evans County, Georgia study (Grim et al., 1980), and from national dietary recall studies (Langford, Watson, Douglass, 1980; Frisancho et al., 1984) also reported that while there are no consistent Black-White differences in sodium intake, Blacks consistently report lower dietary intakes of potassium and calcium. Thus, it is speculated that the greater prevalence of hypertension in Blacks may not only be due to possible differences in sodium handling, but may also be due to a relative deficiency in dietary intake of potassium which also affects renal handling of sodium (Langford, Langford & Tyler, 1985).

The recent work by McCarron and his colleagues on the role of calcium in hypertension suggests that dietary intake of calcium and the mechanisms controlling calcium metabolism should also be included in the sodium-potassium equation (McCarron, Morris & Cole, 1982).

315

Evidence indicates that Blacks have lower dietary intake of calcium, and of vitamins C and A than Whites, and that calcium is an important factor in the metabolism of sodium and potassium (Langford, Langford, & Tyler, 1985).

Additional evidence of biological differences in Blacks and Whites that might be implicated in population differences in disease rates include differences in mineralocorticoid secretions by the adrenal cortex, and greater tendency in younger Blacks to develop hypertension when adrenal cortical abnormalities are present (Russel & Massi, 1973). Evidence has also been provided for possible differences in sympathetic tone as indicated by the higher prevalence of lower plasma renin levels in Blacks, lower heart rates in Black hypertensives, and lower DBH levels (dopamine-beta-hydroxylase) in both Black hypertensives and normotensives than in Whites (Lovenberg et al., 1974).

Finally, Gillum (1979) reported evidence suggestive of greater pulse pressure, more left ventricular hypertrophy, and more cardiac enlargement at each blood pressure level in Blacks than in Whites. The author cautions, however, that much of the evidence of biological differences between Blacks and Whites is still inconclusive, and therefore, conclusions drawn from this evidence would be speculative at best. Nevertheless, the preliminary evidence provides interesting hypotheses about possible biological sources of racial differences in hypertension.

Genetic/Familial Sources of Differences

The preponderance of the scientific evidence to date supports the hypothesis of a strong genetic contribution in hypertension in both Blacks and Whites, and that the disease is probably polygenically determined (Hayes, Tyroler & Cassel, 1971; Grim et al., 1984; Miller & Grim, 1983). Unfortunately, many investigators have taken the previously cited indications of possible biological differences in Blacks and Whites as convincing evidence of a genetic basis for Black-White differences in hypertension rates. Watkins (1984) and Cooper (1984) argue quite eloquently that several factors cast doubt on this proposition. First of all, "Black" is more of a sociopolitical category than a biological one. Ethnic similarity and identity should not be confused with unequivocal evidence of genetic homogeneity (Patterson, 1983). In fact, the peculiar history of Blacks in the U.S. is one of considerable miscegenation, and therefore, the U.S. Black population is genetically quite heterogenous. Second, if the predisposition for higher blood pressure has a genetic basis, then dark-skinned people all over the world should share this common tendency towards elevated blood pressure. The world epidemiologic data on Africa and the Caribbean indicate no such consistent tendencies. In fact, the evidence seems to link high prevalence of hypertension in Blacks in these areas to environmental factors such as urbanization, diet, lifestyle and other by-products of the pressures of acculturation (Watkins, 1984).

Of equal importance in this discussion is the need to evaluate the evidence of genetic factors in hypertensive disease. Except for the compelling work on twins, most of the evidence of a genetic basis for this disease is based on indirect evidence. For example, there is ample evidence that a family history of hypertension is a major risk factor for this disease regardless of race, SES or gender (Epstein, 1984; Watt, 1986). This familial disease link is supported by evidence of moderate blood pressure concordance rates in families (Zinner, Levy & Kass, 1971; Zinner, Rosner & Kass, 1985), and moderate heritability estimates from population based, family aggregation studies of blood pressure (Hayes, Tyroler & Cassel, 1971; Moll et al., 1983). However, increased family concordance in blood pressure and increased risk for hypertension does not prove genetic transmission of the disease.

Somewhat more direct evidence for a genetic basis for Black-White differences in hypertension is provided by studies of the relationship between blood grouping, skin color and blood pressure in the U.S. These studies suggest that darker skin and purer African ancestry are associated with higher resting blood pressures and greater risk for this disease (Boyle, 1970; Keil et al., 1977; 1981; Miller et al., 1979; Harburg et al., 1973; 1978a, b). Black theoreticians have also postulated theories that are somewhat consistent with this genetic model of determination. They argue that melanin, the factor that determines skin color and functions as a neurotransmitter, operates neurochemically to enhance physiological sensitivity and responsivity to environmental stimuli. Therefore, darker skinned Blacks are biologically more responsive to external stimuli, be they positive or negative (McGee, 1976). This theory, although not yet supported by empirical evidence, does recognize the significance of environmental factors even when a genetic predisposition is postulated.

Regardless of which theory is investigated, the conclusions drawn from these data must be treated with considerable caution. Investigators face considerable problems defining and measuring skin color, most fail to separate the biological attributes of race from their psychological and social meaning and from social class, and most studies used small, non-representative Black samples (Tyroler & James, 1978; Cooper, 1984; Patterson, 1983).

In addition, and as noted previously, these investigators ignore the fact that the association between skin color, racial admixture and blood pressure is not consistently evident in Black populations outside of the U.S. (Watkins, 1984).

The strongest and most compelling direct evidence of genetic influence in hypertension is provided by studies of White twins both adopted and reared together. These studies provide evidence of a very strong linear association between blood pressure concordance and genetic similarity (Rose et al., 1979, 1980; Miller & Grim, 1983; Mongeau & Biron, 1981; Annest et al., 1979a, b). Preliminary results from a study of a small sample of Black twins indicated that blood pressure heritability estimates in Black twins are comparable to those reported for White twins (Grim & Cantor, 1986).

In sum, present evidence does support a genetic contribution in blood pressure. However, the available evidence falls short of supporting the hypothesis that there is a genetic basis for Black-White differences in rates of hypertension that are independent of and more important than socio-environmental factors. Future research should continue to pursue hypotheses about biological differences between the two groups, but care must be exercised in the definition of the groups (i.e. who are identified as Black and White), in the size and representativeness of the samples selected, and in the hypothesized relationships tested (i.e. simple direct effects vs interactions).

Socioeconomic Status Differences

Present epidemiologic evidence consistently points to an inverse relationship between socioeconomic status and both level of resting blood pressure and prevalence of essential hypertension (Stamler, 1980; HDFP, 1977; NBHCPTF, 1980; James, 1985). Since Blacks are disproportionately overrepresented in the low SES groups, a significant proportion of the variance in the observed Black-White differences in hypertension risk is undoubtedly attributable to their overall lower educational, income, and occupational status (Syme et al., 1974; Keil et al., 1977; Stamler, 1980; James, 1985).

However, this association between low SES, race and hypertension risk must be carefully evaluated. The tendency to treat socioeconomic status as a simple demographic descriptor on which subjects are classified only helps us to understand which groups are at greatest risk. It does not tell us much about *how* or *why* these characteristics are associated with enhanced risk. In an effort to clarify the latter two questions, several recent papers have suggested that socioeconomic and sociocultural factors that impact health should be subsumed under the generic construct of social status, and that this construct be conceptualized and measured multi-dimensionally. Distinctions between socio-structural factors and related sociopsychological attributes associated with social status are recommended (Myers et al., 1984; Watkins & Eaker, 1986). Socio-structural factors refer to such factors as race, education, occupation, income, marital status, and social mobility, all of which define social status through their social meanings, and through social institutions and practices that control life opportunities and obstacles faced by Blacks. Sociopsychological factors, on the other hand, include the host of in-

dividual differences in experiences, personal attributes, resources and liabilities that contribute to individual vulnerability or resistance in the face
of external social conditions. These include personality characteristics, the
appraisal of life stresses, stress coping styles, the availability and use of
social supports, the management and expression of anger, anxiety and
similarly strong emotions, etc. In assessing the impact of SES on health,
careful attention must be given to distinguishing between objective, con-
crete events and experiences that Blacks face from the subjective
interpretations and meanings conferred on these experiences and events.
Both individual and collective group meanings must be considered
(Myers, 1982; James, 1984; Kasl, 1984). Both the socio-structural and
sociopsychological components of social status are believed to interact
through biobehavioral mechanisms to define health status and illness
risk. However, they also operate through social policy to impact the
availability of health services, the quality of health care provided in the
management of illness, and in the final analysis, they impact mortality
risk (Myers, 1985).

Recent evidence also indicates that race and gender mediate the
meaning and role that SES has on health and well-being (James, Harnett
& Kalsbeek, 1983; James, 1984; Kessler & Neighbors, 1986). In the case of
Blacks, it is difficult to completely separate the contributions of
race/ethnicity from SES as attributable risk factors, especially when we
recognize that institutional racism has insured a nonrandom distribution
of educational and occupational status and income with respect to race
(Hogan & Pazul, 1982; Washington & McCloud, 1982). Also, both race and
SES exert their effects through a host of health beliefs, habits and behaviors that impact most detrimentally on the lowest SES groups, on
darker skin Blacks, and on men (Jackson, 1981). However, Kessler &
Neighbors (1986), argue quite successfully that the relative contributions
of each of these factors on health can be determined if the appropriate
statistical procedures are used. For example, they demonstrated empirically that previous studies indicating that it was SES and not race that was
the primary predictor of psychological distress were incorrect. When a
more appropriate statistical treatment of the data was used, i.e. one that
considered the possibility that race and SES could function interactively,
the evidence indicated that the effect of SES on well-being was mediated
by race such that low SES and Black was associated with greater psychological distress than either race or SES by itself. Taken as a whole, these
data suggest that socioeconomic factors play an important role in the observed Black-White differences in risk and in the prevalence of essential
hypertension. However, there is still additional research needed to disen-
tangle the independent contributions of race, gender and SES on the
etiology, course and outcome of this disease.

Sociocultural and Sociopsychological Differences

One of the major hypothesized sources of racial differences in hypertension has been the sociocultural, with particular attention focused on dietary habits. As noted earlier, primary focus has been on dietary abuses of sodium and unsaturated fats, and the resultant excess body fat and body weight as the major culprits. Research has consistently linked increased risk for essential hypertension to obesity, and this link is particularly evident in the poor and in Black women (Gillum, 1979; Stamler, 1980). Data on the prevalence of obesity in Blacks and Whites, and in males and females between the ages of 20-24 years indicate that the obesity rate for White males and females and for Black males was 15%, while for Black females it was 23%. This pattern of excess weight in Black women continues with age such that by ages 55-64, 50% of all Black women are obese (Bonham & Brock, 1985). Similar rates were observed in a national report by DHEW, 1978), which noted obesity rates among Black women ages 20-44 years of 25%, 45% among those ages 45-64 years, and 30% among those 65 years and older. In comparison, we find rates of 12.8%, 8% and 5.8% among Black men in the respective age cohorts.

This tendency towards obesity among Black women has been attributed to both genetics and to dietary abuses of unsaturated fats and carbohydrates (Stamler, 1980). While some have offered primarily cultural explanations for these dietary differences (e.g. a predilection for soul food), social class and rural-urban residency factors are probably as significant in determining these dietary differences as is culture (i.e. relatively less access to more nutritious but more expensive foods among the poor).

It should be noted that the relationship between obesity and high blood pressure appears to be stronger and more direct in Whites than in Blacks (Boyle et al., 1967; HDFP, 1979). Perhaps for Blacks, and especially for Black women, other biological (i.e. sodium metabolism) and socio-environmental factors (e.g. stress) play a more direct role in the etiology of hypertension, while obesity plays a more indirect, contributory role. In any event, additional research is needed to further specify the contribution obesity makes in this disease relative to other known dietary and non-dietary risk factors in Blacks.

The previously reported evidence of lower sodium excretion rates among Blacks despite no significant differences in sodium intake suggests that dietary sodium may be potentially more pathogenic for Blacks (Grim et al., 1980). Of course, support for this hypothesis does not prove that sodium is a cause of hypertension, but it would help to explain why excess dietary sodium appears to increase overall morbidity risk in "salt sensitive" Blacks and in those who possess other known risk factors. Additional studies are clearly needed to clarify this issue of salt sensitivity as a risk factor, and to consider the possible contributory role that dietary calcium and potassium intake might play in this regard.

Another major area in which considerable research interest has been demonstrated is in the exploration of socio-ecological and psychological differences between Blacks and Whites that might account for greater Black vulnerability to hypertension.

This research emphasizes the role of socio-ecological and psychological stresses attendant to race and social status, to personality characteristics, and to coping styles as the central factors of interest. Sociopsychological studies have failed to demonstrate the existence of a specific "hypertensive personality" both in general and specific to Blacks (Harrell, 1980). However, provocative evidence has been reported in two large epidemiologic studies in Detroit and Charleston, North Carolina that indicate a strong association between elevated blood pressure, prevalence of hypertension and a high level of community disorganization (Nesser, Tyroler & Cassel, 1971), exposure to high socio-ecologic stresses, both alone (James & Kleinbaum, 1976) and in interaction with skin color and reactive anger management (Harburg et al., 1973; Gentry et al., 1982; Diamond, 1982). These data indicate that sociopsychological factors interact to create a pattern of person-environment transactions that are more pathogenic in general, and specifically more pathogenic for hypertension (Lazarus & Launier, 1978; Lazarus, 1978; Myers, 1982).

More recently, James et al. (1983) also suggested that poorly educated Black men who believe that hard work and determination can overcome social obstacles despite their limited resources (i.e. high John Henryism) are at significantly greater risk for hypertension than better educated or less active coping Black men. This "high risk" coping style is conceptually consistent with observations that higher pressor responses occur under conditions of effortful coping with an uncontrollable behavioral stressor (Obrist et al., 1978), and when neither flight nor fight responses are available or appropriate (Ostfeld & Shekelle, 1967). Dohrenwend & Dohrenwend (1970), Syme (1979) and Myers (1982) suggest that this state of effortful coping under conditions of high uncertainty and perceived uncontrollability is the "normal" socio-structurally determined state of existence for a significant percentage of the Black population. This peculiar pattern of person-environment transactions is also likely to play an important role in the disproportionate risk for essential hypertension run by Blacks (James, 1985).

Pitfalls of Racial Differences Research

Great care must be exercised in addressing the causes of Black-White differences. There is legitimacy to the pursuit of this knowledge, especially in light of the existing evidence of racial differences in risk, disease course, and in disease outcome. Unfortunately, however, the history of science is replete with evidence of gross abuses of racial differences research that has been used to justify racist and discriminatory social policies and practices. (See Thomas & Sillen's book *Racism in Psychiatry*, 1972 for a historical review of research on racial differences in psychiatry, and Robert Guthrie's book *Even the Rat Was White*, 1976 for a review of the treatment of race in experimental psychology). In addition, most of the studies of racial differences can be criticized for their small and nonrepresentative samples, their failure to control for social class or other sources of within-group variability, or to give adequate attention to the sociopolitical, economic and psychological dimensions of their variables. Thus, many investigators make faulty causal assumptions about the genetic and biological basis for the racial differences observed, and make unjustified generalizations to the population as a whole. A good example of this problem is the research on skin color and blood pressure. Researchers interested in questions about racial differences must recognize the complexity of the issues addressed, and the political underpinnings and implications of their research. Failure to do so raises serious questions about the scientific integrity and utility of such research.

To add to the complexity of the problem, we must also note that all of the available evidence point to multiple, interacting factors as causally implicated in hypertension (i.e. Page's [1960] mosaic theory of the hypertension), as well as in the observed racial differences in essential hypertension (Anderson et al., In press, a). However, the evidence of racial differences in hypertension falls short of articulating any coherent pattern of relationships or mechanisms through which the hypothesized causes interact to result in different patterns of risk and different types of hypertensive disease in Blacks and Whites. One obvious missing link is the absence of a consistent pattern of racial differences in cardiovascular stress reactivity as measured by physiological, endocrine, behavioral and psychological indexes. Careful consideration of the role that race and social class might play in mediating stress-exposure, stress-reactivity and stress-coping should also be given (Myers, 1982).

The Biobehavioral Perspective on Essential Hypertension

In several seminal papers, the biological, clinical, and behavioral evidence in hypertension is reviewed, and an eloquent argument is made for taking an integrated, multi-disciplinary and multi-domain approach in studying this disease (Schwartz et al., 1979; Lazarus, 1979; Shapiro & Goldstein, 1982; Krantz & Manuck, 1984; Matthews et al., 1986). Such an approach has been labeled "biobehavioral" to reflect the focus on the direct and concurrent effects of biological, psychological and behavioral processes in the pathophysiology of this disease. Essential hypertension is characterized as a disease of disordered homeostasis or disregulation of the biological mechanisms that control blood pressure. This disregulation is believed to result from frequent exposure to stress, and, in turn, frequent acute pressor responses are continuously being elicited over time. This pattern of "hyperreactivity" ultimately results in the resetting of the blood pressure control mechanisms to a higher resting level (i.e. chronically elevated resting blood pressure), which ultimately defines the disease of essential hypertension (Schwartz et al., 1979; Krantz & Manuck, 1984).

In recent years, biobehavioral researchers have focused their attention on the role that these short-term increases in cardiovascular activity during exposure to behavioral or environmental stressors play in the development of essential hypertension (See Krantz & Manuck, 1984, and Matthews et al., 1986 for a comprehensive review of this literature). This "reactivity" may be characterized by any of a number of adjustments occurring in various combinations or patterns. These cardiovascular adjustments, which are mediated by the sympathetic nervous system (SNS), may include increases in systolic and diastolic blood pressure, cardiac output, muscle blood flow, vascular resistance, and hormonal secretions. These adjustments are also directly affected by the emotional state and cognitive processes of the person as they act on, react to, and cope with their daily living environments. Therefore, the broad outlines of a biobehavioral model of essential hypertension can be depicted by linking the two major domains of influences, the biological and the sociopsychological or behavioral. In this model, stress is viewed as the catalyst that activates affective and cognitive processes, on the one hand, and biological (i.e. SNS) processes on the other (Kaplan, 1979).

Consistent with a biobehavioral perspective, it is hypothesized that individuals who exhibit exaggerated reactivity (i.e. those that are "hyperreactive") may be at greatest risk for the development of hypertension (Eliot, Buell and Dembroski, 1982; Folkow, 1982; Obrist, 1981). Although this hypothesis has yet to be confirmed by prospective epidemiologic studies, it is supported by converging evidence from both animal (Schneiderman, 1983) and human experiments (Matthews et al., 1986). Laboratory experiments on humans have found that: (1) White hypertensives tend to exhibit cardiovascular hyperreactivity relative to normotensive subjects in response to laboratory stressors (Frederickson, Dimberg, Frisk-Hamber and Storm, 1982; Hollenberg, Williams & Adams, 1981; Steptoe, Melville & Rose, 1984); (2) Whites with a parental history of hypertension frequently exhibit greater cardiovascular responses to stress than the offspring of normotensives (Ditto, 1986; Falkner, Kushner, Onesti & Angelakos, 1981; Jorgenson & Houston, 1981; Manuck & Proietti, 1982), and (3) White adults display a different pattern of cardiovascular reactivity in different settings and while engaging in different activities (Pickering et al., 1982; Mann, Miller-Craig & Rafferty, 1985). The latter evidence underscores the impact of the environmental setting or context on stress and cardiovascular reactivity.

If we extrapolate from this evidence in Whites to explain Black-White differences in hypertension, we would hypothesize that if cardiovascular hyperreactivity is in fact associated with a heightened susceptibility to hypertension, then Blacks should show a great tendency to respond to stress with exaggerated cardiovascular reactions than Whites.

Biobehavioral Research on Hypertension in Blacks

Cardiovascular Stress Reactivity to Laboratory Stressors

Efforts are currently underway to apply a multidimensional, biobehavioral perspective to the question of what are the biological and psychological bases for the differences in hypertension disease risk between Blacks and Whites. The central focus of these efforts to date is primarily on laboratory stress reactivity measured on physiological, neurohormonal, behavioral and psychological parameters. Specifically, investigators often measure such *physiological* indexes of stress reactivity as changes in systolic and diastolic blood pressure, heart rate, pulse pressure, forearm blood flow, and skin conductance. *Neurohormonal* indexes frequently studied include serum electrolyte concentrations, urine electrolyte excretion rates (i.e. sodium, potassium, calcium, creatinine, etc.), and changes in plasma catecholamines concentrations (i.e. epinephrine, norepinephrine and cortisol).

The *psychological* parameters frequently investigated include anger response style (e.g. suppressed (In) vs expressed (Out) anger; reflexive vs reflective anger), trait anxiety, level of subjective distress, chronic life stresses and coping, life change stresses (life events), level of social supports, depression, Type A behavior pattern, and psychological defensiveness. Finally, the *behavioral* parameters are usually defined in terms of the types of stressor tasks faced, and include such varied stressors as active coping tasks (e.g. mental arithmetic, videogames), interpersonal stresses and conflict (e.g., stressful interviews, role play, anger-arousing conflict interaction tasks), cognitive-perceptual tasks (e.g. the Stroop Color Conflict task, videogames), dietary or chemical stresses (e.g. caffeine, alcohol, tobacco), passive physical stresses (e.g. cold pressor test), active physical exercise stresses (e.g. handgrip strength task, running in place, the step task, bicycle ergometer, treadmill exercise stress), and finally, naturally occurring stresses (job stresses, driving on the freeway, arguing with a family member, etc.). (See Light, 1987 and Schneider-man, Kaufman & Carver, In press, for a review of these approaches).

For purposes of organization and clarity, our review of the available studies of Black-White differences in cardiovascular reactivity will be organized into two major sections, (1) studies investigating differences in reactivity in normotensives adults, and (2) studies of differences in reactivity in hypertensives. In each section, distinctions between reactivity to physical and to psychosocial stresses will be made. Finally, the small body of research on Black-White differences in response to caffeine will also be reviewed.

Studies of Normotensive Adults

Physical stressors. There have been comparatively few studies of ethnic differences in response to physical stressors in normotensive adults. In a study by Anderson, Lane, Muranaka, Williams and Houseworth, (in press) blood pressure, heart rate, forearm blood flow, and forearm vascular resistance were measured during the application of an ice pack to the foreheads of 10 Black and 10 White males (ages 18-22). This procedure has been shown to elicit profound peripheral vasoconstriction (Abboud & Eckstein, 1966). In response to the cold stimulus, Black subjects exhibited significantly greater increases in systolic and diastolic blood pressure and forearm vascular resistance. Since no ethnic differences were observed in heart rate, the hyperreactivity among Blacks was primarily vascular in nature rather than cardiac. In a second study by Venter, Joubert & Strydom (1985) heart rate and blood pressure responses to the head-up tilt were compared in sixteen South African Black and White adults matched on age, sex and body mass. Tilting from supine to 40 degrees, and from 40 degrees to 80 degrees caused significant increases in heart rate and diastolic blood pressure in both groups. White subjects had higher systolic pressures than Blacks when tilted to 80 degrees. No significant heart rate or diastolic differences were observed. The authors hypothesized that ethnic differences in systolic BP response to tilting might be due to quantitative and/or qualitative differences in cardiac beta-1 adrenoreceptors.

Researchers at Indiana University have conducted an elegant series of studies on the effects on sodium loading in Black and White adult subjects (for review see Grim et al., 1984; Luft, Grim and Weinberger, 1985). To investigate the effects of volume expansion and contraction in males (Luft, Grim, Fineberg and Weinberger, 1979; Luft, Grim, Higgins, Weinberger, 1977), subjects were fed a 150-mEq/day sodium diet and given an intravenous infusion of 2 liters of normal saline (volume expansion). Sodium depletion was induced by a diet containing 10 mEq of sodium and three 40-mg doses of furosemide (volume contraction). Following sodium loading (expansion) Blacks excreted significantly less sodium in urine than Whites. In another study, blood pressure responses to six different levels of daily sodium intake (10, 300, 600, 800, 1200, 1500) were examined in Black and White males (Luft et al., 1979). At intakes of 600 mEq/day or greater, Black subjects showed consistently and significantly higher blood pressures than Whites. No significant blood pressure differences were observed at the lower intake levels. Thus, while research has failed to demonstrate racial differences in sodium intake (Grim et al., 1980), this study suggests that Blacks may be more susceptible to the deleterious effects of sodium on blood pressure (i.e. more Blacks may be "salt sensitive" than Whites).

Psychosocial stressors. Few studies have compared the cardiovascular responses of normotensive Blacks and Whites during psychosocial stressors. In one recent study, Morell, Myers, Shapiro, Goldstein & Armstrong (In press) measured heart rate, blood pressure and skin conductance responses to mental arithmetic (i.e. serial addition) in 34 Black and 42 White normotensive males, selected for family history of hypertension. These groups were compared during screening, and at three experimental periods: at baseline or pre-MA period (5 mins.), during the mental arithmetic task (MA period) (5 mins.), and during recovery or the post-MA period (5 mins.). Although there were no differences in screening blood pressures, Blacks exhibited significantly higher diastolic blood pressures, and Whites exhibited higher heart rates and skin conductance levels during the baseline period. Blacks also showed higher diastolic levels during the MA task. However, when the baseline differences were statistically removed, no significant diastolic differences remained, but higher systolic levels in the White subjects were uncovered. There were no significant race and family history interactions.

In an earlier report from that same study, Myers et al. (1985) compared SBP, DBP, and HR reactivity of Black and White normotensive males to a series of psychological stressors (i.e. mental arithmetic, Type A interview, the Stroop color conflict task, and a racial conflict film) and to two physical stressors (i.e. handgrip task and the exercise treadmill test). The preliminary results indicated few overall racial differences in reactivity. However, White males reacted to the acute psychological stressors with higher SBP and HR responses than Blacks, while Blacks evidenced greater SBP and DBP reactivity to the physical stressors than Whites. Contrary to expectations, neither group evidenced marked physiological reactions to the racially loaded conflict film. The latter may have been due to the passive nature of this stressful task which afforded the subjects ample opportunities to screen or to cognitively mediate the full impact of the events depicted in the film.

Caffeine and stress. There has been increasing interest in the hemodynamic effects of caffeine, both alone and in combination with various psychological stressors (Shapiro, Lane & Henry, 1986). This drug, which is found in a wide variety of foods, and rivals nicotine and alcohol as one of the most frequently used psychotropic substances, has a variety of physiological effects on the central nervous system. The most relevant of these effects is small to moderate blood pressure increases in normotensives and mild hypertensives, especially when caffeine is combined with psychological stress (Shapiro, Lane & Henry, 1986; Robertson et al., 1978; Shapiro & Goldstein, In press). The presence of a parental history of hypertension also appears to exacerbate the cardiovascular impact of caffeine and stress, at least in White and Chinese males who regularly consume caffeine (Greenberg & Shapiro, In press; Greenstadt, Yang & Shapiro, In press).

To date, two studies have investigated whether caffeine, both alone and in combination with psychological stress would produce different patterns of blood pressure reactivity in Black and White adults. A study by Myers, Shapiro, McClure & Daims (1986) examined blood pressure reactivity to caffeine (250 mg) and mental arithmetic stress in a sample of 40 healthy, normotensive Black and White male regular caffeine consumers. Comparisons on family history of hypertension were also made. These investigators found dose-related increases in systolic blood pressure (SBP) to 250 mg of caffeine and to the combination of caffeine and stress in both racial groups. However, there were no overall race or family history differences in reactivity observed. A second study by Strickland (1986) tested for race and parental history differences in reactivity to caffeine (250 mg) and mental arithmetic stress in 48 healthy, normotensive Black and White adult women who were not regular caffeine consumers. This investigator also failed to find any significant overall race or parental history differences in reactivity, but unlike in men, caffeine alone had no significant effect on blood pressure or heart rate in these young women. However, Black women with a parental history of hypertension reacted to the stress of the mental arithmetic task with significantly higher diastolic blood pressure (DBP) responses and slower DBP recovery than the other groups.

These results suggest that caffeine has different cardiovascular effects depending on whether it is consumed under stressful or non-stressful conditions; whether the consumer is male or female, or Black or White; whether they have a family history of hypertension, and whether they are regular or infrequent consumers of caffeine. At least among Black adults, the available evidence seems to indicate that Black men appear to be more reactive to caffeine and to stress, while Black women appear to react more to psychological stress than to caffeine. Having a parental history of essential hypertension seems to confer additional risk to Black women, but apparently not to Black men. Additional studies are needed to verify these preliminary results, as well as to investigate the long-term cardiovascular effects of regular caffeine use as a potential enhancer of risk for essential hypertension in Black adults.

Hypertensive Adults

Physical stressors. Two studies compared Black and White hypertensives on cardiovascular reactivity to physical stressors. Rowland et al. (1982) evaluated blood pressure and heart rate reactivity in 16 Black and 16 White adult males and females with mild-to-moderate hypertension. In addition to gender, subjects were matched on age, blood pressure, and socioeconomic status. Tasks consisted of isometric handgrip, upright bicycle exercise, and the cold pressor test. No significant differences in heart rate or blood pressure responses between Black and White hypertensives were obtained on any of the tasks.

Dimsdale, Graham, Ziegler, Zusman and Berry (In press) infused norepinephrine in Black and White normotensives and hypertensives on two extremes of dietary sodium intake: 10 mEq/day and 200 mEq/day. A highly significant dose-response relationship was found for norepinephrine dosage and blood pressure. Among hypertensives on the high salt diet, Black subjects had steeper dose-response slopes than White subjects.

Psychosocial stressors. Several recent studies have also investigated ethnic differences in reactivity to psychosocial stressors among hypertensives or those with casual elevated blood pressure. Frederickson (1986) examined cardiovascular and non-cardiovascular reactivity in three groups of Black and White subjects: established hypertensives, borderline hypertensives, and normotensives. The task consisted of 16-signaled reaction time tasks where a 110 decibel white noise was delivered contingent upon poor performance, while measures of heart rate, blood pressure, respiration, skin conductance, and skin and muscle blood flow were obtained (muscle and skin vascular resistances were later calculated). Although resting cardiovascular activity was similar in Black and White hypertensives and normotensives, heart rate (HR) and systolic pressure (SBP) increased less in Black hypertensives and normotensives than in their White counterparts. Skin conductance changes were also attenuated in the Black subjects. Additionally, muscle and skin vascular resistance increased during the task in Black subjects irrespective of diagnosis, but not in Whites, suggesting enhanced vascular resistance among Blacks.

In another study of Black and White hypertensives, Nash, Jorgensen, Lasser and Hymowitz (1985) examined heart rate and blood pressure responses of 98 Black and White mild hypertensives to the videogame PACMAN and to the Stroop Color Conflict task. The investigators found that while no significant race or gender effects were observed on blood pressure, a significant heart rate effect emerged. Black subjects, regardless of gender, exhibited lower heart rate changes to the tasks. It was noted that the ethnic group differences could have been mediated by affective responding, since White subjects reported more task-related anxiety and frustration than did Blacks.

Schneiderman (1986) measured a variety of cardiovascular and humoral responses in Black and White male and female borderline hypertensives and normotensives to several challenging tasks (i.e. Type A interview, videogame, bicycle ergonometer, cold pressor test). Also, ambulatory monitored blood pressure was assessed at home and at work. Black females and White males exhibited greater epinephrine and heart rate reactivity to the tasks than Black males or White females; this relationship was reversed on plasma renin reactivity. In an analysis of the predictability of home and work blood pressure by the laboratory responses, Schneiderman found that the best predictor of home or work blood pressures for all groups was the laboratory baseline blood pressure; blood pressure during the videogame added significantly to the prediction of work blood pressure. Among Whites, the best predictor of ambulatory systolic blood pressure was the systolic responses during the videogame. In Blacks, on the other hand, diastolic responses to the cold pressor test was the better predictor of ambulatory diastolic pressure.

Falkner, Kushner, Khalsa & Katz (1987) examined the effects of sodium loading on cardiovascular responses to mental arithmetic in three groups of subjects: 45 representative Blacks, who were selected from a larger group of participants in an epidemiologic study; 45 borderline hypertensive Blacks who were also enrolled in the larger study; and 45 age- and gender-matched normotensive Whites. Cardiovascular reactivity to mental arithmetic and tilting was measured before and after sodium loading. Following sodium loading, Blacks showed the greatest increase in resting mean arterial pressure (MAP) indicating greater sodium sensitivity. The Black borderline hypertensives had the highest MAP levels at baseline and during stress, both before and after sodium loading. However, White subjects exhibited greater MAP changes from baseline to stress before and after the sodium intervention.

Light et al. (1986) have conducted perhaps the most comprehensive assessment of Black-White differences in stress reactivity. Cardiovascular and renal responses in Black and White subjects, selected for normal or borderline systolic blood pressure were examined in three studies. In the first study, they compared subjects on four stressors and found that Black borderlines showed greater increases in SBP to all four stressors than their White counterparts. Heart rate (HR) and DBP responses did not differ in the hypertensives, and the highest HR values were observed in the normotensive Blacks.

In a second study of ethnic differences in physiologic responses with and without beta-blockade during a competitive reaction task, Light et al. found increased cardiac output in the hypertensives prior to beta-blockade, but the increases were larger in the White hypertensives than in Black hypertensives. After beta blockade, however, cardiac output fell more noticeably in the Black hypertensives, and remained lower than in White hypertensives during stress. This indicates that there is less of an increase in beta-adrenergic activity in Blacks during stress, but greater beta-adrenergic activity at rest. Also, stress produced greater decrease in total peripheral resistance in Whites than in Blacks prior to beta blockade. However, following beta-blockade, the greatest increase in peripheral resistance was observed in Black borderline hypertensives.

In a final study, Light et al. examined renal and cardiovascular responses in *8* Black and *8* White subjects under four experimental conditions following sodium and water ingestion; pre-task rest, competitive task, post-task rest 1, and post-test rest 2. These procedures were tested with and without beta-blockade. They found that without beta-blockade renal function fell in all groups, but the decrease was more marked in Blacks during post-task rest. Also, both with and without beta-blockade Blacks showed a significantly greater drop in their glomerular filtration rate during post-task rest. Blacks also excreted less fluid and less sodium during post-task rest both with and without beta-blockade. And, finally, while Blacks and Whites showed similar stress-induced SBP and DBP increases, the blood pressures of Blacks remained more elevated than in Whites during the post-task rest periods.

Within-Group Variability in Reactivity Among Blacks

As noted in the findings reported previously, there is considerable heterogeneity among Blacks in resting cardiovascular activity, particularly in blood pressure. For example, blood pressure levels in Blacks vary with SES, age, stress coping style, obesity, and other factors. It is probable then that the magnitude or pattern of cardiovascular responses to laboratory stressors also varies among Blacks. A substantial body of literature exists on White samples pertaining to reactivity differences in persons most at risk for cardiovascular disease compared to those at reduced risk (e.g. Type A vs Type B adults, those with a parental history of hypertension vs those without, etc.). Besides those studies that compared Blacks and Whites that were summarized in the last section, there are a few studies that have addressed individual differences in stress reactivity among Blacks.

At least three studies have investigated reactivity differences in Blacks as a function of Type A behavior. In a study of middle-aged Black women, Anderson et al. (1986) found Type A behavior assessed via structured interview to be significantly associated with SBP and DBP increases during the interview but not during mental arithmetic stress. Family history of hypertension did not predict cardiovascular response to either task, either alone or in combination with Type A. In a similar study with Black college-age women, and including forearm blood flow to BP and HR measures, Anderson et al. (in press, b) found that Type A behavior interacted with parental history of hypertension, such that in Black women with a parental history, Type A was significantly associated with increased SBP responses during the structured interview. Watkins & Eaker (1986) cite a study by Clark & Harrell (1982) which found a significant association between Type A behavior assessed using the Jenkins Activity Survey and diastolic blood pressure reactivity in Blacks.

Finally, Anderson, Williams, Lane, and Houseworth (In press, b) found that among college-aged Black women, those with a family history of hypertension exhibited significantly smaller SBP and FBF responses than their negative family history peers. This pattern of reactivity is somewhat contrary to that reported by Light et al. (1986) and by Strickland (1986), who found greater reactivity associated with a positive parental history of hypertension.

Life-Span Perspective on Biobehavioral Research on Hypertension

While a considerable body of clinical, epidemiological and biomedical research on essential hypertension in Blacks has been accumulated (See Gillum, 1979, Hall, Saunders & Shulman, 1985; Secretary's Task Force Report, 1985 for comprehensive reviews), very little has been done to develop an integrative picture of this disease across the life span. For example, we know that hypertension develops earlier in Blacks than in Whites, and that the greatest racial difference in morbidity for this disease occurs between ages 25-44 (NCHS Report, 1981). However, we know comparatively little about the pattern of early development of this disease in Black vs White children and adolescents. Also, while there is growing provocative evidence of different biological processes and psychosocial factors underlying the development and course of hypertension in Blacks and Whites, there is very little research on how these factors may make different contributions to hypertension morbidity and mortality at different life stages in both groups. Therefore, before we conclude this chapter, we would like to offer a preliminary review and conceptualization of the interplay of biological and psychosocial factors that contribute to essential hypertension in Blacks during childhood and adolescence, in adulthood, and in the aged.

Hypertension Research in Children & Youth

Until recently, there was limited valid information on which to compare blood pressure status in Black and White children and youth. Recent studies on infants and children (ages 0-5 years) by Schachter, Kuller & Perfetti (1984a,b) provide early indications of racial differences in cardiovascular status. Comparing heart rates and blood pressures of 392 healthy, full-term Black and White children at birth and at 2, 6, 15, 24, 36, 48 and 60 months of age, they found no race, gender or SES differences in BP levels. Body size was only modestly correlated with BP, and parent-child blood pressure was only weakly associated. However, Black infants had higher resting heart rates at birth through six months, they showed a more dramatic slowing of heart rate during the first five years than Whites, and offspring of parents with a family history of hypertension had slower heart rates than those without such a parental risk factor. The authors conclude that a slower heart rate during early childhood may be a better index of risk of adult hypertension than elevated blood pressure.

However, both cross-sectional and longitudinal epidemiologic studies of Black and White children in the Minneapolis Childrens' Blood Pressure Study (Prineas et al, 1980), the Philadelphia Blood Pressure Study (Katz et al, 1980), and the Bogalusa Heart Study (Voors et al, 1977, 1976) indicated that in children ages 5-14 body mass (wt/ht3) becomes the best predictor of blood pressure, and that Black children over age 10 evidence higher systolic and diastolic blood pressures than White children.

Black children are also more likely to be represented in the upper 95th percentile of blood pressures. This tendency towards higher blood pressures in Black children has also been associated with lower plasma dopamine B-hydroxylase and renin levels, lower sodium and higher potassium excretion rates (Berenson, Cresanta & Webber, 1984), as well as with larger stress-reactive blood pressures and lower heart rates to exercise and to video-game stresses (Voors, Webber & Berenson, 1980; Murphy et al, 1986). This pattern of enhanced cardiovascular reactivity in Black children was particularly sensitive to the race of the experimenter, such that Black children were more stress-reactive with Black experimenters than with Whites (Murphy et. al., 1986).

Obesity also becomes a major contributor to enhance the risk for high blood pressure in adolescence, especially for Black females. Also, lower socio-economic status and higher socio-ecologic stresses appear to confer additional risks for hypertension, especially for Black teenage males (Kotchen et. al., 1974; Kilcoyne, 1973).

Thus, the evidence seems to indicate that there are some early Black-White differences in blood pressure, body mass, and in electrolyte function which appear to stabilize by late adolescence. Obesity and socio-economic status, both directly and indirectly (e.g. through stress, diet, life style, etc.) appear to enhance pre-existing biological vulnerability to this disease in Black adolescent males and females. More studies focusing on differences among Black children and youth in stimulated vs. unstimulated blood pressure, electrolyte function, renin level, and in neuroen-dochrine function as a function of gender, SES, age, socio-ecologic contexts, activity level, body mass, etc. are clearly needed.

Research on Hypertension in Black Adults

The evidence on the contributors in hypertension and its sequelae in Black adults has been reviewed in detail earlier in this chapter and need not be repeated here. Suffice it to say that much of what we know about the pathogenesis and course of this disease comes from studies on young and middle-aged adult hypertensives. What is missing, however, are more integrative studies of the biological and psychosocial changes that are specifically linked to major adult life stages (e.g. early employment vs. mid-career changes vs. retirement; early marriage vs. first becoming parents vs. raising teenagers; coping with a recent marriage vs. coping with divorce; fulfilling multiple competing social roles over time, etc.). For example, do Blacks who differ in biological risk for hypertension (i.e. positive vs. negative family histories) evidence different psychological, neuroendochrine and hemodynamic response patterns to major life tran-sitions such as career changes, divorce, entering their 40s, retirement, etc.? Are these patterns of influences different for Black men and women? Stu-dies addressing these issues would make a significant contribution to our understanding of how psychosocial processes at different life stages im-pact biobehaviorally on the development and course of hypertension in the Black population.

Research on Hypertension in the Black Aged

Anderson (In press, d) provides a comprehensive review of the ex-tant knowledge of hypertension in the Black aged. He notes the higher morbidity and mortality in older Blacks to hypertension-related vascular diseases (e.g. heart disease, stroke), as well as to renal disease and renal failure as compared to Whites (Shulman, 1985). Anderson notes that there is current evidence of age-related biological differences between older Black and White hypertensives, including lower renin levels, lower sodium excretion rates, lower potassium and calcium intakes, along with greater sodium/potassium ratios, and decreased creatinine clearance. There is also evidence of significantly greater prevalence of obesity, espe-cially in Black women, and in Blacks above the poverty line. It should be noted, however, that while obesity is a strong predictor of high blood pressure in Whites, this association is not as strong in Blacks (Boyle et. al., 1967; Tyroler, Heyden & Hames, 1975). Perhaps the high prevalence of obesity among older Blacks makes it a weaker differentiator of normotensive and hypertensives. In any event, more research is needed to clarify this unexpected finding.

There is comparatively less information on the role and impact of psychosocial factors and behavioral factors on hypertension in older Blacks. For example, there is very little research on stress reactivity in older Blacks. We don't know whether the pattern of neuroendocrine reactivity to stress in younger hypertensives continues to be evident in older hypertensives, or whether gender differences in reactivity are evident at both younger and older ages. Answers to these questions would help to clarify whether laboratory stress-reactivity is a reliable index of hypertension risk in both younger and older Blacks.

There is also some provocative evidence which suggests that older Blacks may be less cardiovascularly vulnerable to socio-ecologic stresses and to lower socio-economic status (Harburg et. al., 1973; 1978a; HDFP, 1977). Syme (1979) suggests that this age-related difference in vulnerability to high stress and low social status may reflect reduced efforts to attain a better quality of life given the odds. In other words, Blacks who survive to old age may have become more philosophical and better able to cope with their social conditions, and are no longer fighting to overcome them. These data suggest that age-related changes in stress appraisal and coping may contribute beneficially to reducing the risk of hypertension and to hypertension related co-morbidity, despite other risk factors such as obesity and problems with electrolyte management. Such changes may also simply reflect the attributes of survivorship for Blacks. In any event, there is considerable need for more research on these factors in older Black adults.

Summary and Future Directions for Research

Essential hypertension is one of the major health problems facing Blacks in the U.S. and in most industrialized societies. It is the leading contributor to the excessive rates of cerebrovascular, renal and cardiac disease morbidity and mortality in Blacks. The causes for the high morbidity rate is at present unclear. However, it is very doubtful that a comprehensive understanding of this problem can be attained by narrow biological explanations, but requires a more comprehensive examination of multiple interacting factors. In this chapter, we have reviewed the available literature on hypertension in Blacks, paying particular attention to the biological, socioeconomic and sociopsychological factors believed to be implicated in the excessive rates of hypertensive disease in Blacks. Current epidemiologic and clinical evidence identify racial differences in such factors relevant to hypertension as differences in renal function and in the metabolism of sodium; differences in dietary intake of potassium and calcium; differences in body mass, especially in Black women; differences in socioeconomic status, in exposure to insidious ecologic stresses, and in sociocultural experiences; and finally, differences in the impact of psychological responses to frustrating social obstacles (e.g. impact of reflexive anger, and an active, effortful coping style). These differences are believed to contribute to the observed racial differential in morbidity and mortality from hypertension.

We propose an integrative, biobehavioral perspective for investigating the problem of enhanced risk for hypertension in Blacks. This model seeks answers to this question in the interplay between factors and processes in the psychosocial, behavioral and biological domains rather than in any of these domains by themselves (i.e. seeking biological explanations to the exclusion of psychosocial contributors). The available evidence of Black-White differences in cardiovascular stress reactivity in laboratory experiments was reviewed as examples of studies investigating whether biobehavioral stress reactivity might be the mechanism underlying the racial differential in high blood pressure. This evidence indicates that although no firm conclusions can be drawn about racial differences in stress reactivity at this time, there are two noteworthy trends that have begun to emerge. The first concerns the possibility that Blacks respond to acute stressors with decreased cardiac reactivity (i.e. reduced heart rate or cardiac output) as compared to Whites (Frederickson, 1986; Light et al., 1986; Anderson et al., In press, a). Although speculative at this time, these findings may indicate that cardiac influences, perhaps beta-adrenergically mediated, may be less significant to the development of hypertension in Blacks than in Whites. Biomedical evidence of lower plasma renin activity (Luft et al., 1985), decreased responsiveness to beta-adrenergic blockade in Black hypertensives (Hall, 1986), and lower resting heart rates in young Black normotensive adults (Persky et al., 1979) provides partial support for this hypothesis.

A second trend suggests that Blacks may show a propensity toward blood pressure reactivity mediated by peripheral vasoconstriction (Frederickson, 1986; Anderson et al., 1986; Strickland, 1986; Light et al., 1986). Thus, alpha-adrenergic hyperreactivity, as indexed by peripheral vasoconstriction, may prove to be an important contributor to high blood pressure in Blacks.

Considerable additional research is needed to further elucidate these trends, including consideration of possible within-group differences due to gender, age, blood pressure group, family history of hypertension, and SES. Future biobehavioral studies must also venture beyond the safe but limiting confines of the experimental laboratory. Results of laboratory studies, although intriguing, suffer from built in constraints on external validity that are inherent in studying reactivity to acute stressors in a few individuals in the contrived settings of research laboratories. Life stresses that are most likely to contribute to the development of diseases such as hypertension are likely to be chronic and long term rather than acute, and they exert their effects during the normal daily lives and in the natural living environments of the individuals at risk (i.e. in Black communities).

Two exciting methodologies offer considerable promise as more naturalistic extensions of the biobehavioral research paradigm. These are the family interaction paradigm and the developments in the technology for ambulatory blood pressure monitoring. In recent years there have been several studies of blood pressure reactivity to interpersonal conflict stress in couples and families (Ewart et al., 1983; Hafner et al., 1983; Baer, 1983). These studies are based on the concept of "family psychosomatics", which recognizes the powerful role that family context plays in shaping health beliefs and behaviors, in enhancing or buffering risk for a variety of psychological and physical illnesses, in shaping stress-coping and adjustment to illness, and in enhancing blood pressure concordance (Grolnick, 1972). This concept was subsequently elaborated by Baer (1983) into an appealing strategy for research on hypertension.

Research by Speers et al. (1986) on married couples reported moderate to high levels of concordance in health behaviors (e.g. eating habits) and in blood pressures. The blood pressure concordance rates in spouses were comparable to those reported for genetically related parent-offspring and sibling pairs. They also noted that BP concordance increased with length of marriage, which supports an environmental contribution in high blood pressure.

In a study of blood pressure reactivity in White couples, Ewart et al. (1983) demonstrated increased blood pressure reactivity in couples discussing a real marital problem. Their blood pressures increased as a function of the degree of marital distress experienced, the level of conflict expressed, and the degree of reliance on conflict avoidant coping strategies (i.e. anger-in). The latter has also been confirmed in studies with White hypertensive couples (Hafner et al., 1983), and in studies of family interactions in both Black and White families with a hypertensive father (Baer et al., 1980; Baer, 1983). These studies indicate that families with a hypertensive father evidenced more reactive blood pressures (i.e. greater pre-post BP changes) and a higher frequency of conflict-avoidant, nonverbal behaviors (i.e. gaze aversion) during a family conflict discussion and role play conflict task than normotensive families. These data suggest that families with a hypertensive father may develop, perhaps through parental modeling, a greater tendency to cope with conflicts by interpersonal distancing and avoidance (i.e. anger-in) see Myers, 1986 for a detailed review of this research.

While this work was largely conducted on White couples and families, the focus on intrafamilial dynamics as a potentially powerful contributor to or protector against the development of hypertension in biologically at risk Blacks should make a significant contribution to the field. Such a study is currently underway testing for differences in blood pressure reactivity and conflict coping styles in Black hypertensive and normotensive mother-daughter dyads during a family conflict discussion by McClure & Myers. The results of this pilot study are expected to provide a direct empirical test of the extent to which family conflict reactivity contributes to enhanced risk for hypertension in Blacks.

The second exciting new development which promises to revolutionize stress reactivity research is the ability to measure blood pressure in the natural environment with ambulatory monitoring devices. Studies using this technology have shown that blood pressure varies greatly during a 24-hour period, with pressures tending to be highest while at work and lowest during sleep (Pickering et al., 1982). Studies by Pickering et al. (1982, 1985) indicate that clinic measures of blood pressure do not reliably reflect pressures at other times and in other settings, and that target organ damage secondary to high blood pressure appears to be more closely associated with 24-hour ambulatory blood pressures than with clinic pressures.

Given all of the evidence that Blacks and Whites differ in socioeconomic status, in exposure to socio-ecologic stresses, and in exposure to stresses associated with racism and discrimination, ambulatory monitoring of blood pressure over time and in the natural course of daily living could provide the necessary data to determine the extent to which these social differences contribute to the observed racial differences in hypertension morbidity and mortality. The one published study to date that compared 24-hour BP patterns in Blacks and Whites found no significant racial differences (Rowlands et al., 1982). However, preliminary results of a recent study with a small sample of Black normotensives, on the other hand, suggested that Blacks may maintain higher resting blood pressures during sleep than those reported for Whites in other studies (Harsfield, personal communication).

Unfortunately, there are many conceptual and methodological problems that remain to be resolved in order to make full use of the ambulatory BP monitoring technology. Among them are the ability to reliably separate valid physiological responses from artifacts (e.g. due to noise, movement, etc.), the need to reliably link physiologic responses to identified stressors in the natural setting (i.e. what was the person reacting to at the time the reading was taken), as well as to link these responses to the psychological state of the respondent (i.e. how did the person feel at the time the reading was taken). Despite these technical complications, this is an exciting new approach to the biobehavioral study of blood pressure and it should be applied to the study of hypertension in Black adults.

In conclusion, biobehavioral studies of Black-White differences in stress-induced cardiovascular reactivity have gained prominence as a useful approach in identifying the bases for the observed racial differences in essential hypertension. Although present findings are inconclusive with respect to the causes of these racial differences, they suggest that perhaps decreased cardiac reactivity and increased peripheral vascular reactivity in Blacks compared to Whites may be part of the puzzle. Future biobehavioral studies on this question would be greatly improved by (1) recognizing the heterogeneity of the Black population and exercising greater care in defining and selecting Black adult samples (e.g. including better gender, age, SES distributions in Black samples); (2) by focusing more on differences among Blacks, such as in life stages, gender and in SES, rather than on differences between Blacks and Whites; (3) by using more interpersonally complex and personally meaningful stress tasks that are likely to produce results that are more generalizable outside of the research laboratory, and (4) by making better use of the available technology for ambulatory blood pressure monitoring to assess stress-reactivity to more chronic stresses and under more naturalistic conditions.

References

Abboud, F. M. & Eckstein, J. W. (1966). Active reflex vasodilation in man. *Federation Proceedings, 25*, 1611-1617.

Anderson, N. B., Williams, R. B., Lane, J. D., Haney, T. S., Simpson, S., & Houseworth, S. J. (1986). Type A behavior, family history of hypertension and cardiovascular responsivity in Black women. *Health Psychology, 5*, 393-406.

Anderson, N. B. (In press, a). Ethnic differences in resting and stress-induced cardiovascular and humoral activity: An overview. In N. Schneiderman, P. Kaufman, & C. Carver (Eds.), *Research in cardiovascular behavioral medicine: A handbook of research methods, measurement and experimental design.* NY: Plenum.

Anderson, N. B., Williams, R. B., Lane, J. D., & Houseworth, S. J. (In press, b). Family history of hypertension and cardiovascular responses in young Black women. *Journal of Psychosomatic Research.*

Anderson, N. B., Lane, J. D., Muranaka, M., Williams, R. B., & Houseworth, S. J. (In press, c). Racial differences in blood pressure and forearm vascular responses to the cold face test. *Psychosomatic Medicine.*

Anderson, N. B. (In press, d). Aging and hypertension among Blacks: A multidimensional perspective. In J. Jackson (Ed.), *The Black American Elderly: Research on Physical & Psychological Health.* N.Y.: Springer Publishing Co.

Annest, J. L., Sing, C. F., Biron, P., & Mongeau, J-G. (1979a). Familial aggregation of blood pressure and weight in adoptive families. I: Comparisons of blood pressure and weight statistics among families with adopted, natural or both natural and adopted children. *American Journal of Epidemiology, 110(4)*, 479-491.

Annest, J. L., Sing, C. F., Biron, P., & Mongeau, J. G. (1979b). Familial aggregation of blood pressure and weight in adoptive families. II: Estimation of the relative contributions of genetic and common environmental factors to blood pressure correlations between family members. *American Journal of Epidemiology, 110(4)*, 492-503.

Baer, P. E. (1983). Conflict management in the family: The impact of paternal hypertension. *Advances in Family Intervention, Assessment and Theory, 3*, 161-184.

Baer, P. E., Vincent, J. Williams, B., Bourianoff, G. G., & Bartlett, P. (1980). Behavioral response to induced conflict in families with a hypertensive father. *Hypertension, 2*, 70-77.

Berenson, G. S., Cresanta, J. L. & Webber, L. S. (1984). High blood pressure in the young. *Annual Review of Medicine, 35*, 535-560.

Bonham, G. S. & Brock, D. W. (1985). The relationship of diabetes with race, sex and obesity. *American Journal of Clinical Nutrition, 41*, 775-783.

Boyle, E. (1970). Biological patterns in hypertension by race, sex, body height and skin color. *JAMA, 213*, 1637-1643.

Boyle, E., Griffey, W., Nichaman, M., & Talbert, C. (1967). An epidemiologic study of hypertension among racial groups of Charleston County, South Carolina: The Charleston Heart Study, Phase II. In J. Stamler, S. Stamler, & T. Pullman (Eds.), *The Epidemiology of hypertension*, 193-203. NY: Grune & Stratton.

Chrysant, S., Danisa, K., Kem, D., Dillard, B., Smith, W., & Frohlich, E. (1979). Racial differences in pressure, volume and renin interrelationships in essential hypertension. *Hypertension, 1*, 136-141.

Clark, V., & Harrell, J. (1982). The relationship among Type A behavior styles used in coping with racism and blood pressure. *Journal of Black Psychology, 8*, 89-99.

Cooper, R. (1984). A note on the biological concept of race and its implications in epidemiological research. *American Heart Journal* (Supplement), *108(part 3, no. 2)*, 715-723.

Curry, C. L., & Lewis, J. F. (1985). Cardiac anatomy and function in hypertensive Blacks. In W. D. Hall, E. Saunders, & N. B. Shulman (Eds.), *Hypertension in Blacks: Epidemiology, pathophysiology and treatment*, 61-70. Chicago: Year Book Medical Publishers.

Diamond, E. L. (1982). The role of anger and hostility in essential hypertension and coronary heart disease. *Psychological Bulletin, 92(2)*, 410-433.

Dimsdale, J. E., Graham, R., Ziegler, M. G., Zusman, R., & Berry, C. C. (In press). Age, race, diagnosis and sodium effects on the pressor response to infused norepinephrine. *Hypertension*.

Ditto, B. (1986). Parental history of essential hypertension, active coping, and cardiovascular reactivity. *Psychophysiology, 23*, 62-70.

Dohrenwend, B. S., & Dohrenwend, B. P. (1970). Class and race as status-related sources of stress. In S. Levine & N. A. Scotch (Eds.), *Social Stress*, 111-140. Chicago, IL: Aldine Publishing Co.

Eliot, R. S., Buell, J. C., & Dembroski, T. M. (1982). Blood pressure, ethnicity, and psychosocial resources. *Psychosomatic Medicine, 48*, 509-519.

Epstein, F. H. (1984). How useful is a family history of hypertension as a predictor of future hypertension? *Annual of Clinical Research, 16* (Supplement), 43, 32-34.

Ewart, C. K., Burnett, K. F., & Taylor, C. B. (1983). Communication behaviors that affect blood pressure: An A-B-A-B analysis of marital interaction. *Behavior Modification, 7(3),* 331-344.

Falkner, B., Kushner, H., Onesti, G., & Angelakos, E. T. (1981). Cardiovascular characteristics in adolescents who develop essential hypertension. *Hypertension, 3,* 521-527.

Falkner, B., Kushner, H., Khalsa, D. K., & Katz, S. (1987). The effect of chronic sodium load in young Blacks and Whites. Paper presented at the Annual Meeting of the Society of Behavioral Medicine, Wash., D.C.

Finnerty, F. A. (1971). Hypertension is different in Blacks, *JAMA, 216,* 1634-1635.

Folkow, B. (1982). Physiological aspects of primary hypertension. *Physiological Reviews, 62,* 347-504.

Frederickson, M. (1986). Racial differences in reactivity to behavioral challenge in essential hypertension. *Journal of Hypertension, 4,* 325-331.

Frederickson, M., Dimberg, U., Frisk-Hambert, M., & Strom, G. (1982). Hemodynamic and electrodermal correlates of psychogenic stimuli in normotensive and hypertensive subjects. *Biological Psychology, 15,* 63-74.

Frisancho, A. R., Leonard, W. R., & Bollettins, L. (1984). Blood pressure in Blacks and Whites and its relationship to dietary sodium and potassium intake. *Journal of Chronic Disease, 37,* 515-519.

Gentry, W. D., Chesney, A. P., Fary, H. E., Hall, R. P., & Harburg, E. (1982). Habitual anger-coping styles: Effect on mean blood pressure and risk for essential hypertension. *Psychosomatic Medicine, 44(2),* 195-202.

Gibson, G. S. & Gibbons, A. (1982). Hypertension among Blacks: An annotated bibliography. *Hypertension, 4(1),* Part II.

Gillum, R. F. (1979). Pathophysiology of hypertension in Blacks and Whites. *Hypertension, 1,* 468-475.

Greenberg, W., & Shapiro, D. (In press). The effects of caffeine and stress on blood pressure in individuals with and without a family history of hypertension. *Psychophysiology.*

Greenstadt, L., Yang, L., & Shapiro, D. (In press). Caffeine, mental stress and risk for hypertension: A cross-cultural replication. *Psychosomatic Medicine.*

Grim, C. E. & Cantor, R. M., (1986). Genetic influences on blood pressure in Blacks: Twin studies. Paper presented at the American Federation of Clinical Research.

Grim, C. E., Luft, F., Miller, J., Meneely, G. Batarbee, H., Hames, C., & Dahl, K. (1980). Racial differences in blood pressure in Evans County Georgia: Relationship to sodium and potassium intake and plasma renin activity. *Journal of Chronic Diseases, 33,* 87-94.

Grim, C. E., Luft, F., Weinberger, M., Miller, J., Rose, R., & Christian, J. (1984). Genetic, familial and racial influences in blood pressure control systems in man. *Australian & New Zealand Journal of Medicine, 14,* 453-457.

Grolnick, L. (1972). A family perspective on psychosomatic factors in illness: A review of the literature. *Family Process, 11,* 457-486.

Hafner, R. J., Chalmers, J. P., Swift, H., Graham, J. R., West, M. J., & Wing, L. M. (1983). Marital interaction and adjustment in patients with essential hypertension. *Clinical & Experimental Hypertension, 5(1),* 119-131.

Hall, W. D., Saunders, E., and Shulman, N. (Eds.) (1985). *Hypertension in Blacks: Epidemiology, pathophysiology and treatment.* Chicago, IL: Year Book Medical Publishers.

Harburg, E., Erfurt, J., Hauenstein, L., Chape, C., Schull, W., & Schork, M. A. (1973). Socioecologic stress, suppressed hostility, skin color and Black-White male blood pressure: Detroit. *Psychosomatic Medicine, 35,* 276-296.

Harburg, E., et al., (1978a). Skin color, ethnicity and blood pressure. I: Detroit Blacks. *American Journal of Public Health, 68(12),* 1177-1183.

Harburg, E. et al., (1978b). Skin color, ethnicity and blood pressure. I: Detroit Whites. *American Journal of Public Health, 68(12),* 1184-1187.

Harrell, J. P. (1980). Psychological factors and hypertension: A status report. *Psychological Bulletin, 87,* 482-501.

Hayes, C. G., Tyroler, H. A., & Cassel, J. C. (1971). Family aggregation of blood pressure in Evans County, Georgia. *Archives of Internal Medicine, 128,* 965-975.

Hollenberg, N. K., Williams, G. H., & Adams, D. F. (1981). Essential hypertension: Abnormal renal vascular and endocrine responses to a mild psychological stimulus. *Hypertension, 3,* 11-17.

Hogan, D. P., & Pazul, M. (1982). The occupational earning returns to education among Black men in the north. *American Journal of Sociology, 87,* 905-920.

Hypertension Detection and Follow-up Program Cooperative Group (1977). Race, education and prevalence of hypertension. *American Journal of Epidemiology, 106,* 351-361.

Hypertension Detection and Follow-Program Cooperative Group (1979). Five-year findings of the hypertension detection and follow-up program: Mortality by race, sex and age. *JAMA, 242,* 2572-2577.

Jackson, J. J. (1981). Urban Black Americans. In A. Harwood (Ed.), *Ethnicity and medical care,* 37. Cambridge, MA: Harvard University Press.

James, S. A. (1984). Socioeconomic influences on coronary heart disease in Black populations. *American Heart Journal, 108(3, Part 2),* 669-672.

James, S. A., (1985). Psychosocial and environmental factors in Black hypertension. In W. Hall, E. Saunders, & N. Shulman (Eds.). *Hypertension in Blacks: Epidemiology, pathophysiology and treatment.* Chicago, IL: Year Book Medical Publishers.

James, S. A., Harnett, S. A., & Kalsbeek, W. (1983). John Henryism and blood pressure differences among Black men, Journal of Behavioral Medicine, 6, 259-278.

James, S. A. & Kleinbaum, D. G. (1976). Socioecologic stress and hypertension-related mortality rates in North Carolina. *American Journal of Public Health, 66,* 354-358.

Jorgenson, R. S., & Houston, B. K. (1981). Family history of hypertension, gender and cardiovascular reactivity and stereotype during stress. *Journal of Behavioral Medicine, 4,* 175-189.

Kaplan, N. M. (1979). Stress, the sympathetic nervous system and hypertension. *Journal of Human Stress, 4(3),* 29-34.

Kasl, S. V. (1984). Social and psychological factors in the etiology of coronary heart disease in Black populations: An exploration of research needs. *American Heart Journal, 108(3, Part 2),* 660-669.

Katz, S. H., Hediger, M. L., Schall, J. I., Bowers, E. J., Barker, W. F., Aurand, S., Eveleth, P. B., Gruskin, A. B., and Parks, J. S. (1980). Blood pressure, growth and maturation from childhood through adolescence: Mixed longitudinal analyses of the Philadelphia Blood Pressure Project. *Hypertension, 2 (Suppl. I),* I-55-69.

Keil, J. E., Sandifer, S. H., Loadholt, C. B., and Boyle, E. Jr. (1981). Skin color and education effects on blood pressure. *American Journal of Public Health, 71,* 532-534.

Keil, J. E., Tyroler, H. A., Sandifer, S. H., & Boyle, E. (1977). Hypertension: Effects of social class and racial admixture: The results of a cohort study in the Black population of Charleston. South Carolina. *American Journal of Public Health, 67(7),* 634-639.

Kessler, R. C., & Neighbors, H. W. (1986). A new perspective on the relationships among race, social class and psychological distress. *Journal of Health & Social Behavior, 27,* 107-115.

Kilcoyne, M. M. (1973). Hypertension and heart disease in the urban community. *Bulletin of the New York Academy of Medicine, 49,* 501-509.

Kilcoyne, N., Richter, R., & Alsup, P. (1974). Adolescent hypertension. I: Detection and prevalence. *Circulation, 50,* 758.

Kotchen, J. M., Kotchen, T. A., Schwertman, N. C. & Kuller, L. H. (1974). Blood pressure distributions of urban adolescents. *American Journal of Epidemiology, 99,* 315-324.

Krantz, D. S. & Manuck, S. B. (1984). Acute psychophysiologic reactivity and risk of cardiovascular disease: A review and methodologic critique. *Psychological Bulletin, 96,* 435-464.

Langford, H. G. (1981). Is blood pressure different in Black people? *Postgraduate Medical Journal, 57,* 749-754.

Langford, H. G., Watson, R. L., & Douglass, B. A. (1980). Factors affecting blood pressure in population groups. *Transactions of the Association of American Physicians, 63,* 135-146.

Langford, H. G., Langford, F. P. J., & Tyler, M. (1985). Dietary profile of sodium, potassium, and calcium in U.S. Blacks. In W. D. Hall, E. Saunders, & N. B. Shulman (Eds.), *Hypertension in Blacks: Epidemiology, pathophysiology & treatment,* 49-57. Chicago, IL: Year Book Medical Publishers.

Lazarus, R. S. (1978). A strategy for research on psychological and social factors in hypertension. *Journal of Human Stress, 4(3),* 34-40.

Lazarus, R. S., & Launier, R. (1978). Stress-related transactions between person and environment. In L. A. Pervin & M. Lewis (Eds.), *Perspectives in interactional psychology.* NY: Plenum Press.

Light, K. C. (1987). Psychosocial precursors of hypertension: Experimental evidence. *Circulation, 76* (Suppl. I), 67-76.

Light, K. C., Sherwood, A., Obrist, P., James, S., Strogatz, D. & Willis, P. (August, 1986). Comparisons of cardiovascular and renal responses to stress in Black and White normotensive and borderline hypertensive men. Paper presented at the American Psychological Association Convention, Washington, D. C.

Lovenberg, W., Bruckwick, E. A., Alexander, R. W., Horwitz, D. & Kaizer, H. R. (1974). Evaluation of serum dopamine-beta-hydroxylase activity as an index of sympathetic nervous activity in man. In E. Usdin (Ed.) *Neuropsychopharmacology of monoamines and their regulating enzymes.* NY: Raven Press.

Luft, F. C., Grim, C. E., Fineberg, N., and Weinberger, M. C. (1979). Effects of volume expansion and contraction in normotensive Whites, Blacks, and subjects of different ages. *Circulation, 59,* 643-650.

Luft, F. C., Grim, C. E., Higgins, J. T., and Weinberger, M. H. (1977). Differences in response to sodium administration in normotensive White and Black subjects. *Journal of Laboratory and Clinical Medicine, 90*, 555-562.

Luft, F., Grim, C., & Weinberger, M. (1985). Electrolyte and volume homeostasis in Blacks. In W. D. Hall, E. Saunders, & N. Shulman (Eds.), *Hypertension in Blacks: Epidemiology, pathophysiology & treatment*, 115-131. Chicago, IL: Year Book Medical Publishers.

Mann, S., Millar-Craig, M. W., & Raftery, E. B. (1985). Superiority of 24-hour measurement of blood pressure over clinic values in determining prognosis in hypertension. *Clinical Experimental Hypertension. 7(2 & 3)*, 279.

Manuck, S. B. & Proietti, J. M. (1982). Parental hypertension and cardiovascular response to cognitive and isometric challenge. *Psychophysiology, 19*, 481-489.

Matthews, K., Weiss, S., Detre, T., Dembroski, T., Falkner, B., Manuck, S., & Williams, R. (Eds.) (1986). *Handbook of stress reactivity and cardiovascular disease.* NY: J. Wiley & Sons.

McCarron, D. A., Morris, C. D., & Cole, C. (1982). Dietary calcium in human hypertension. *Science, 217*, 267-269.

McGee, D. P. (1976). An introduction to African psychology: Melanin, the physiological basis for psychological oneness. In L. M. King, V. J. Dixon, & W. W. Nobles (Eds.), *African philosophy: Assumptions & paradigms for research on Black persons*, 215-222. Los Angeles, CA: Fanon Research & Development Center.

Miller, J. Z. & Grim, C. E. (1983). Heritability of blood pressure. In T. A. Kotchen, J. M. Kotchen & J. Wright (Eds.), *High blood pressure in the young*, 79-90. Boston, MA:

Miller, J. Z., Grim, C. E., Connelly, P. M., and Weinberger, M. H. (1979). Association of blood groups with essential and secondary hypertension: A possible association of the MNS system. *Hypertension, 1*, 493-497.

Moll, P. P., Harburg, E., Burns, T. L., Schork, M. A., & Ozgoren, F. (1983). Heredity, stress and blood pressure, a family set approach: The Detroit project revisited, *Journal of Chronic Diseases, 36(4)*, 317-328.

Mongeau, J. G., & Biron, P. (1981). The influences of genetics and of household environment in the transmission of normal blood pressure. *Clinical and Experimental Hypertension, 3(4)*, 593-596.

Morell, M. A., Shapiro, D., Myers, H. F., Goldstein, I., & Armstrong, M. (In press). Prevailing states versus recurrent activation models of psychophysiologic responses to behavioral states in Black and White normotensive males. *Psychophysiology*, (Abstract).

Murphy, J. K., Alpert, B. S., Moes, D. M., & Somes, G. (1986). Race and cardiovascular reactivity: A neglected relationship *Hypertension, 8*, 1075-1083.

Myers, H. F. (1982). Stress, ethnicity and social class: A model for research on Black populations. In E. E. Jones & S. Korchin (Eds.), *Minority mental health*, 118-148. NY: Holt, Rhinehart & Winston.

Myers, H. F. (Chair) et al. (1984). Summary of workshop III: Working group on socioeconomic and sociocultural influences in coronary heart disease in Blacks. *American Heart Journal, 108(3, Part 2)*, 706-710.

Myers, H. F. (1985). Coronary heart disease in Black populations: Current research, treatment and prevention needs. *Health & Human Services Secretary's Task Force Report on Black and minority health, Vol. IV: Cardiovascular and Cerebrovascular Diseases.*

Myers, H. F. (August, 1986). Family contributions in essential hypertension in Blacks. Paper presented at the American Psychological Association Convention, Washington, D.C.

Myers, H. F., Morell, M., Shapiro, D., Goldstein, I., & Armstrong, M. (1985). Biobehavioral stress reactivity in Black and White normotensives. *Psychophysiology, 22(5),* 605-606, (Abstract).

Myers, H. F., Shapiro, D., McClure, F., & Daims, R. (May, 1986). Caffeine and stress reactivity in Black & White males. Paper presented at the Western Psychological Association Convention, Seattle, Washington.

Nash, J., Jorgensen, R., Lasser, N., & Hymowitz, N. (March, 1985). The effects of race, gender and task on cardiovascular reactivity in unmedicated, mild hypertensives. Paper presented at the Society of Behavioral Medicine meeting, New Orleans.

National Black Health Care Providers Task Force on High Blood Pressure Education and Control Report (1980). U.S. Department of Health & Human Services, NIH Publ. No. 80-1474.

National Center for Health Statistics Report (1977). *Blood pressure levels of persons 6-74 years: United States, 1971-1974.* Vital and Health Statistics, Series 11, No. 203, DHEW Pub. HRAPHS 78-1648. Washington, D.C.: Government Printing Office.

National Center for Health Statistics Report (1981). *Hypertension in adults 25-74 years of age: United States, 1971-1975.* Vital and Health Statistics, Series 11, No. 221. DHHS Publ. PHS 81-1671. Washington, D.C.: Government Printing Office.

Neaton, J. D., Kuller, L. H., Wentworth, D., & Borhani, N. O. (1984). Total mortality and cardiovascular mortality in relation to cigarette smoking among Black and White males followed up for five years. *American Heart Journal, 108(3, Part 2),* 759-769.

Nesser, W. B., Tyroler, H. A., & Cassel, J. C. (1971). Social disorganization and stroke mortality in the Black population of North Carolina. *American Journal of Epidemiology, 93,* 166-175.

Obrist, P. A. (1981). *Cardiovascular physiology: A perspective.* NY: Plenum Press.

Obrist, P. A., Gaebelein, C. J., Teller, E. S., Langer, A. W., Grignolo, A., Light, K. C., & McCubbin, J. A. (1978). The relationship among heart rate, carotic dp/dt and blood pressure in humans as a function of type of stress. *Psychophysiology, 15,* 102.

Ostfeld, A. M., & Shekelle, R. B. (1967). Psychological variables and blood pressure. In J. Stamler, R. Stamler, & T. N. Pullman (Eds.), *The epidemiology of hypertension.* NY: Grune & Stratton.

Page, I. H. (1960). The mosaic theory of hypertension. In F. Bock & P. Cottier (Eds.), *Essential hypertension.* Berlin.

Patterson, O. (1983). The nature, causes and implications of ethnic identification. In C. Fried (Ed.), *Minorities: Community and identity,* 25-50. NY: Springer-Verlag.

Pickering, T. G., Harshfield, G. A., Kleinert, H. B., Banks, S., & Laragh, J. H. (1982). Comparisons of blood pressure during normal daily activities, sleep, and exercise in normal and hypertensive subjects. *JAMA, 247,* 992-996.

Pickering, T. G., Harshfield, G. A., Devereaux, R. B., & Laragh, J. H. (1985). What is the role of ambulatory blood pressure monitoring in the management of hypertensive patients. *Hypertension, 7,* 171-187.

Prineas, R. J., Gillum, R. F., Horibe, H. & Hannan, P. J. (1980). The Minneapolis Children Blood Pressure Study, Part 2: Multiple determinants of children's blood pressure. *Hypertension, 2(Suppl I),* I-25-28.

Prineas, R. J., & Gillum, R. (1985). U.S. epidemiology of hypertension in Blacks. In W. D. Hall, E. Saunders, & N. B. Shulman, (Eds.), *Hypertension in Blacks: Epidemiology, pathophysiology and treatment,* 17-36. Chicago, IL: Yearbook Medical Publishers.

Robertson, D., Frolich, J. C., Carr, R. K., Watson, J. T., Hollifield, J. W., Shanel, D. G., & Oates, J. A. (1978). Effects of caffeine on plasma renin activity, catecholamines and blood pressure. *New England Journal of Medicine, 298,* 181-186.

Rose, R. J., Miller, J. Z., Grim, C. E., & Christian, J. C. (1979). Aggregation of blood pressure in the families of identical twins. *American Journal of Epidemiology, 109(5),* 503-511.

Rose, R. J. et al. (1980). Heritability of blood pressure: Analysis of variance in MZ twin parents and their children. *Acta Geneticae Medicae-Et-Gemellological, 29,* 143-149.

Rowland, D., DeGiovanni, J., McLeary, R., Watson, R., Stallard, T., & Littler, W. (1982). Cardiovascular response in Black and White hypertensives. *Hypertension, 4,* 817-820.

Russel, R. P., & Massi, A. T. (1973). Significant associations of adrenal cortical abnormalities with essential hypertension. *American Journal of Medicine, 54,* 44.

Schachter, J., Kuller, L. H. & Perfetti, C. (1984a). Blood pressure during the first five years of life: Relation to ethnic group (Black or White) and to parental hypertension. *American Journal of Epidemiology, 119,* 541-553.

Schachter, J., Kuller, L. H. & Perfetti, C. (1984b). Heart rate during the first five years of life: Relation to ethnic group (Black or White) and to parental hypertension. *American Journal of Epidemiology, 119,* 554-563.

Schneiderman, N. (1983). Behavior, autonomic function, and animal models of cardiovascular pathology. In T. Dembroski, T. Schmidt, & G. Blumchen (Eds.), *Biobehavioral bases of coronary heart disease.* Basel: Karger.

Schneiderman, N. (August, 1986). Race, gender and reactivity in the Miami Minority Hypertension Project. Paper presented at the American Psychological Association Convention, Washington, D.C.

Schneiderman, N., Kaufman, P., & Carver, C. (Eds.) (In press). *Research in cardiovascular behavioral medicine: A handbook of research methods, measurement and experimental design.* NY: Plenum.

Schwartz, G. E., Shapiro, A. P., Redmond, D. P., Ferguson, D. C. E., Ragland, D., & Weiss, S. M. (1979). Behavioral medicine approaches to hypertension: An integrative analysis of theory and research. *Journal of Behavioral Medicine, 2(4),* 311-364.

Shapiro, D., & Goldstein, I. (1982). Biobehavioral perspectives on hypertension. *Journal of Consulting & Clinical Psychology, 50(6),* 841-858.

Shapiro, D., & Goldstein, I. (In press). The effects of stress and caffeine on hypertensives. *Psychophysiology.*

Shapiro, D., Lane, J. D., & Henry, J. P. (1986). Caffeine, cardiovascular reactivity and cardiovascular disease. In K. A. Matthews, S. M. Weiss, T. Detre, T. M. Dembroski, B. Falkner, S. B. Manuck, & R. B. Williams (Eds.), *Handbook of stress, reactivity and cardiovascular disease*, 311-328. NY: J. Wiley & Sons.

Shulman, N. B. (1985). Renal disease in hypertensive Blacks. In W. D. Hall, E. Saunders, & N. B. Shulman (Eds.), *Hypertension in Blacks: Epidemiology, pathophysiology and treatment*, 106-112. Chicago, IL: Yearbook Medical Publishers.

Speers, M. A., Kasl, S. W., Freeman, D. H., & Ostfeld, A. M. (1986). Blood pressure concordance between spouses. *American Journal of Epidemiology, 123* 818-829.

Stamler, J. (1980). Hypertension: Aspects of risk. In *Hypertension update: Mechanism, epidemiology, evaluation and management*, 22-37. Bloomfield, NJ: Health Learning Systems.

Steptoe, A., Melville, D., & Ross, A. (1984). Behavioral response demands, cardiovascular reactivity and essential hypertension. *Psychosomatic Medicine, 46*, 33-48.

Strickland, T. (1986). Caffeine and stress reactivity as a function of race and parental history in normotensive females. Unpublished Doctoral Dissertation, University of Georgia.

Syme, S. L. (1979). Psychosocial determinants of hypertension. In Onesti, E., & Klint, C. (Eds.), *Hypertension: Determinants, complications and intervention.* NY: Grune & Stratton.

Syme, S. L., Oakes, T. W., Friedman, G. D., Feldman, R. Siegelaub, A. B., & Collen, M. (1974). Social class and racial differences in blood pressure. *Public Health Briefs: American Journal of Public Health, 64(6)*, 619-620.

Thompson, G. E. (May, 1980). Hypertension: Implications of comparisons among Blacks and Whites. *Urban Health*, 31-33.

Tyroler, H. A., Heyden, S., & Hames, C. G. (1975). Weight and hypertension: Evans County studies of Blacks and Whites. In O. Paul (Ed.), *Epidemiology and Control of Hypertension*, 177-204. N.Y.: Stratton Intercontinental Medical Book Corp.

Tyroler, H. A., & James, S. A. (1978). Blood pressure and skin color. *American Journal of Public Health, 68*, 1170-1172.

Tyroler, H. A., Knowles, M. G., Wing, S. B., Logue, E. E., Davis, C. E., Heiss, G., Heyden, S., & Hames, C. G. (1984). Ischemic heart disease risk factors and twenty-year mortality in middle-aged Evans County Black males. *American Heart Journal, 108(3, Part 2)*, 738-747.

U.S. Department of Health, Education & Welfare: National Center for Health Statistics and National Center for Health Research,(1978). DHEW Publication No. (PHS) 78-123.

U.S. Department of Health & Human Services, (August, 1986). Cardiovascular and bronocular diseases. *Report of the Task Force on Black & Minority Health,IV*, 1. U.S. Government Printing Office.

Venter, C., Joubert, P., & Styrdom, W. (1985). The relevance of ethnic differences in hemaodynamic responses to the head-up tilt maneuver to clinical pharmacological investigations. *Journal of Cardiovascular Pharmacology, 7*, 1009-1010.

Voors, A. W., Foster, T. A., Frerichs, R. R., Webber, L. S., and Berenson, G. S. (1976). Studies of blood pressures in children, ages 5-14 years in a total biracial community: The Bogalusa Heart Study. *Circulation, 54*, 319-327.

Voors, A. W., Webber, L. S. & Berenson, G. S. (1980). Racial contrasts in cardiovascular response tests for children from a total community. *Hypertension, 2*, 686-694.

Voors, A. W., Webber, L. S., Frerichs, R. R. and Berenson, G. S. (1977). Body height and body mass as determinants of basal blood pressure in children: The Bogalusa Heart Study. *American Journal of Epidemiology, 106*, 101-108.

Washington, E., & McCloud, V. (1982). The external validity of research involving American minorities. *Human Development, 25*, 334-339.

Watkins, L. O. (1984). Worldwide experience: Coronary artery disease and hypertension in Black populations. *Urban Health, 13*, 30-35.

Watkins, L. O., & Eaker, E. (1986). Population and demographic influences on reactivity. In K. Matthews, S. Weiss, T. Detre, T. Dembroski, B. Falkner, S. Manuck, & R. Williams (Eds.), *Handbook of stress, reactivity and cardiovascular disease*, 85-107. NY: J. Wiley & Sons.

Watson, R. Y., Langford, H. G., Abernethy, J., Barnes, T. Y., & Watson, M. J. (1980). Urinary electrolytes, body weight, and blood pressure: Pooled cross-sectional results among four groups of adolescent females. *Hypertension, 2(Suppl. I):I*, 93-98.

Watt, G. (1986). Design and interpretation of studies comparing individuals with and without a family history of high blood pressure. *Journal of Hypertension, 4(1)*, 1-7.

Weiner, H. (1979). *The psychobiology of essential hypertension*. NY: Elsevier.

Zinner, S. H., Levy, P. S., & Kass, E. H. (1971). Familial aggregation of blood pressure in childhood. *New England Journal of Medicine, 284*, 401-404.

Zinner, S. H., Rosner, B., Oh. W., & Kass, E. H. (1985). Significance of blood pressure in infancy: Familial aggregation and predictive effect on later blood pressure. *Hypertension, 7(3, Part I)*, 411-416.

Glossary

Adrenal Cortex—A structure located within the adrenal glands that produces steroid hormones (e.g., cortisol, aldosterone) which are crucial to blood pressure regulation.

Aldosteronism—Abnormality of electrolyte metabolism (e.g., calcium, potassium, sodium, etc.) caused by excessive secretion of aldosterone.

Alpha-adrenergic—Neurotransmitter receptor sites throughout the vasculature that when stimulated result in the constriction of the blood vessels. Vascular constriction results in increased blood pressure.

Autonomic nervous system (ANS)—the portion of the nervous system concerned with regulation of the activity of cardiac muscle, smooth muscle, and glands.

Beta-adrenergic—Neurotransmitter receptor sites located throughout the vasculature system that when stimulated result in the expansion or dilation. Vasodilation results in blood pressure reduction.

Beta-blockade—Introduction of chemical agents that prevent excitation of the beta-adrenergic receptors.

Biobehavioral—Research approach that investigates the concurrent effect of behavioral and psychosocial factors which influence biological mechanisms.

Catecholamines—Compounds that mimic the physiological effects of adrenergic stimulation such as nonrepinephrine and epinephrine. They facilitate "flight or fight" responses.

Coarctation—Refers to the stricture or contraction of a blood vessel (e.g., coarctation of the aorta).

Cold pressor test—Task involving the introduction of a hand or other body part into ice-water, and the measurement of subsequent physiological changes (e.g., blood pressure, heart rate).

Coronary Heart Disease (CHD)—Diseases of the heart and blood vessels.

Diuretics—Pharmacologic agents that promote the production of urine as a means of reducing blood pressure by decreasing body fluid volume.

Dopamine-beta-hydroxylase (DBH)—Enzyme involved in the biosynthesis of the catecholamine norepinephrine.

End-stage renal disease—Kidney disease marked by a loss of at least 80% of the kidneys' ability to filter waste products. This condition results in a buildup of toxic substances in the blood which can be fatal.

Endocrine—Pertaining to glands and other structures that produce and secrete hormones into the circulatory system.

Forearm vascular resistance—An index of vasoconstriction of blood vessels in the forearm skeletal muscle. This measure is obtained after the introduction of a stressor.

Glomerular filtration rate—The volume of waste formed by the kidney per unit of time (e.g., milliliters/minute).

Hemodynamic—Pertaining to factors (e.g., dimensions of vessels and the viscosity of blood) which influence the flow of blood through the cardiovascular system.

Hyperreactivity—Excessive or exaggerated physiological response to stress. This pattern of response is believed to be associated with enhanced risk for hypertension and other cardiovascular diseases.

Left Ventricular Hypertrophy—Enlargement of the left ventricle of the heart.

Mineralocorticoid—Group of corticosteroids, primarily aldosterone, which are principally involved in the regulation of electrolyte and water balance via their influence on ion transport in the kidneys.

Morbidity—Condition of being diseased or sick. Morbidity rate refers to the number of persons in a population who are afflicted by a specific disease in a given period of time (e.g., one year).

Mortality—Death rate in a population for a specific disease or for all diseases in a given period of time (e.g., CHD death rate in Blacks, ages 60-75 in 1985-1987).

Neurohormonal—Condition where both neural and hormonal factors influence a physiological outcome.

Pathophysiology—The physiological basis or processes underlying disordered functioning (e.g., the pathophysiology of hypertension).

Pheocromocytoma—Vascular tumor of the medulla of the adrenal gland. This tumor causes increased secretion of epinephrine and nonrepinephrine.

Plasma renin—Enzyme that is stored and secreted by the kidney. It plays a significant role in the regulation of blood pressure.

Pressor—Response to a stimulus or stressor indicated by increases in blood pressure.

Psychotropic Medication—Drugs that modify or affect mental states.

Radiographic—Pertaining to x-rays of internal structures of the body.

Renal Functioning—Functioning of the kidneys.

Stress-reactivity—Hemodynamic (i.e., blood pressure) biochemical (e.g., catecholamines), and/or psychological (e.g., anxiety) responses to stressors which are generally introduced and measured in a controlled laboratory setting.

Type A behavior pattern—Behavior pattern characterized by hard-driving, aggressiveness, ambitiousness, restlessness, and functioning under self-imposed time pressure. This behavior pattern is associated with increased risk for coronary heart disease.

Vasoconstriction—The reduction of the diameter of a blood vessel, especially constriction of arterioles which results in decreased blood flow and increased blood pressure.

ALCOHOLISM AND DRUG ADDICTION AMONG BLACK ADULTS

Marva Lloyd Redd

Introduction

Individuals who digest alcohol or use other drugs may become unwilling victims of drug abuse. Alcoholism and other drug addictions do not respect race, age, religion, or national origin; drug abuse premeates all personality types, economic strata, and age groups. Thus, it is impossible to give a composite picture of the typical alcoholic or addict—there is none. What we do have, however, are groups of people who have a tendency to be at a greater risk for becoming alcoholic or drug addicted and who have higher rates of drug abuse. Typically, Black Americans have been identified as such a group, particularly Black adult males. Sociologically, this is partly attributed to different cultural attitudes toward drunkenness and "getting high". There are also those for whom the consequences of alcoholism and drug addiction are compounded by their precarious positioning in society. Historically, this applies to Black Americans whose positioning has meant social and economic deprivations based on race.

Alcoholism and other drug addictions reap havoc on the lives of their victims. The focus of this paper is primarily on alcoholism and the Black male, with a brief description of other drug addictions. Both alcoholism and other drug addictions are discussed separately with a comparative analysis of differences between Whites, Blacks, and other ethnic groups. The primary issues under consideration are: How prevalent are alcoholism and other drug addictions among Blacks and are there age-related factors which help to explain their drug use patterns?

Alcohol Abuse, Alcoholism, and Related Problems

Scope of the Problem

During the 1980s, there has been increased unemployment with its

351

accompanying stresses. Economically, Blacks have been among those hardest hit; they have one of the highest unemployment rates in this country and those who are employed often fear losing their jobs. When pressures such as these mount, it is not uncommon for those affected to attempt to relieve their anxiety by drinking alcohol. According to the tension-reduction theory, this is a reactive way of handling stress which oftentimes results in alcoholism. In such situations, alcoholism often begins with occasional relief drinking, progressing to regular, heavy drinking, and finally escalating to pathological drinking.

Alcoholism breeds both physical and psychological dependence. The physical addiction begins with increased tolerance to alcohol, followed by decreased tissue tolerance. Psychologically, the alcoholic begins to think, then believe, that he needs alcohol to function. This progression often occurs unknowingly, usually over a period of years. While there is public information about alcohol consumption, there are individuals who remain unaware of its addicting properties and deleterious effects on the body. They believe alcoholism is something that happens to someone else, as they consume greater quantities of alcohol in an attempt to reduce emotional pain. As these patterns continue, alcohol may be used to such excess that the ability to function is substantially impaired. Hence, alcoholism is most often defined as impaired functioning in such vital areas as work, family life, health, and social life which is related to one's alcohol consumption (Maddux and Voorhees, 1987).

Alcoholism is one of our nation's major physical and mental health debilitators. Kinney and Leaton (1978) report that: (1) an alcoholic's mortality rate is two and one-half times greater than a nonalcoholic, (2) an alcoholic's life expectancy is shortened ten to twelve years, (3) rates of violent deaths are higher for alcoholics, (4) thirty-six million persons are affected by relationships with an active alcoholic, (5) alcohol is involved in approximately thirty thousand highway deaths annually, (6) one-third of suicides are alcohol-related, (7) one-half of homicides are alcohol-related, and (8) twenty percent of all hospitalizations are alcohol-related. Kinney and Leaton (1978) also found that the annual cost of alcoholism to society exceeds twenty-four billion dollars. These costs include lost production, health and medical, motor vehicle accident damages, and alcoholism services, including legal and social welfare expenditures. Needless to say, the human sufferings caused by injury and death associated with alcohol abuse are incalculable.

Royce (1981) estimated that there were approximately nine million alcoholics in the United States. A decade ago the estimate was five million alcoholics (Brecher, 1972). By conservative estimates, alcoholics are primarily male although some observers argue that there are equal numbers of male and female alcoholics (Kinney and Leaton, 1978). The alcoholic population is thought to be employable or employed, with skid row persons comprising a mere 5 percent (Kinney and Leaton, 1978). Among this

5 percent, many were employed and resided in intact families during some period in their lives. For some, the loss of materialistic possessions and family ties were visible consequences of pathological alcohol consumption.

Few studies exist regarding the prevalence of alcoholism among Black males. Among them, Clark and Midanik (1982) in a national probability survey of persons 18 years of age and older, found that heavy drinkers and problem drinkers were as common among Blacks who drank as among Whites. However, an earlier study of treatment statistics from a systematic survey of consecutive admissions to a general medical ward of a metropolitan teaching hospital concluded that alcoholism was twice as prevalent among Blacks (Barchha et al. 1968). These conclusions were based on an analysis of data on 392 subjects, of whom 194 were Black. Also, Rimmer et al. (1971) investigated 259 subjects (24 percent Black) admitted to treatment in two Midwestern hospitals, one private and one public, and found a higher rate of alcohol consumption among Blacks. But dissimilar results were obtained from a 1984 national survey of drinking patterns. This analysis indicated that the drinking patterns of Black and White males were quite similar (Herd, no date). Few differences were found between the two groups.

Young Black males have been found to have higher treatment admission rates than Whites in the same age group. Rosenblath et al. (1971) analyzed data on 567 subjects (60 percent Black) admitted for treatment of alcohol withdrawal symptoms. These investigators concluded that, given the population, the ratio of admissions among Black subjects was higher than their representation in the general population. Similar findings were documented by Hornstra and Udell (1973) who analyzed data for 1,360 subjects (24 percent Black) admitted to a private or public psychiatric hospital. They also found that Blacks represented a greater percentage of admissions than their representation in the general population. The majority of subjects in these investigations were males.

Etiological Factors in Alcoholism Development

Black men, like other cultural groups, report drinking for a variety of reasons. From a cultural perspective, Harvey (1985) states that frustration, alcohol availability, and permissiveness toward alcohol consumption contribute to alcohol abuse among Blacks. German (1973) linked high rates of alcoholism among Blacks living in the ghetto directly to debilitating economic and social conditions which create a self-perpetuating cycle. According to Frazier (1962), Blacks drink to escape the harsh realities of their existence. For some Blacks, overindulgence and heavy drinking are means of overcoming feelings of frustration, hopelessness, and worthlessness. It is Frazier who coined the term "narcotize" to describe the anesthetic effects which alcohol has on Blacks who are attempting to forget their social and economic frustrations.

Larkins (1965), in a historical analysis, contends that Blacks drink heavily to facilitate their adjustment to racial stress and discrimination, which are constant reminders of color conscious America. A similar view advanced by Maddox et al. (1964, 1968) contends that many Black males drink to compensate for feelings of social inadequacy. Supporting this view, McClelland (1972) maintains that alcohol helps the Black male adjust in a society where resources and opportunities are limited.

In contrast, Robins's et al. (1968) longitudinal investigation of drinking problems among urban Black males attributed drinking problems to familial and personal factors rather than to power needs. Heavy drinking among subjects was found to be a means of compensating for, and coping with, the effects of being reared in an unstable familial situation. A later investigation by King et al. (1969) supported some of these findings. They found that unstable home situations and deviances were predictors of heavy drinking in adult life. These investigators acknowledged, however, that the consequences of discrimination contribute to the weakening of support systems among Blacks and create environmental conditions which encourage alcohol consumption to relieve stress and frustration.

Sterne and Pittman (1972) also explained motivational factors in alcohol use among Blacks. In an inner city public housing complex, data were analyzed on 404 subjects from 320 households, the majority of whom were Black. For these subjects, alcohol was found to serve two functions: as an utilitarian function, it helped them to forget the hardships of daily living which were often associated with racism and discrimination; as convivial drinking it served a purely social function; alcohol was a catalyst which fueled conversation and provided incentives to socialize.

Actually, utilitarian and convivial drinking are both common among Black adult males of all ages. However, convivial drinking has been identified as especially characteristic of some older Black men. Meyers et al. (1985/1986) surveyed 928 older adults, 60 years and older living in urban areas. Blacks in the sample who were 75 years old and older who drank reported drinking mostly for convivial purposes to enhance sociability. Also among this group, an association was found between optimism and drinking—those with the lowest expectations regarding leisure and work activities tended to abstain from alcohol.

Patterns of Alcohol Consumption

In addition to etiological considerations related to whether or not Black males drink to relieve stress or whether they drink for utilitarian or convivial purposes, the literature also identifies specific drinker and abuser patterns. In *Alcohol and the Negro: Explosive Issues*, Larkins (1965) examined structural factors which impacted upon alcohol consumption patterns among Blacks. These factors included: (1) the legislative measures enacted to control the circumstances under which free Blacks consumed alcoholic beverages, (2) the triangular slave trade which involved an international exchange of slaves for liquor and products to make liquor, and (3) the system of slavery which encouraged slave owners to limit alcohol consumption among Blacks to specific times. As a result of these controls, both Coggins (1979) and Harper (1976) suggested that when allowed to drink alcohol, slaves frequently abused it. Indeed, abuse and drunkenness were expected.

Many of the drinking patterns of Black men today are described as models of past drinking behaviors exhibited by slaves and free Blacks. Harper (1976) suggested that Blacks' drinking characteristics, just like their unique rhythm of speech and dance and distinct use of words and style of dress, reflect an accumulation of ethnic and cultural experiences. He also suggested that contemporary Blacks frequently drink on holidays or weekends, much like the "after harvest" and "special occasion" drinking of Blacks during slavery.

A similar pattern is described by Coggins (1979) who identified two extreme categories of drinking among Blacks: heavy drinking and abstinence. Consistent drinking patterns among Black men, however, have not been empirically verified. Blacks report varying patterns of alcohol consumption—bender, daily, and weekend drinking. Rimmer et al. (1971) reported that the metropolitan Blacks in their sample were mostly bender drinkers who drank daily during binges, usually in the mornings. Vitols (1968) examined cultural factors in the make-up of alcoholics admitted to a southern state-funded hospital for treatment and found that Blacks were primarily weekend drinkers.

Supporting both of these findings, Feldman et al. (1974) examined data for 2,286 alcoholics from units at two metropolitan-based mental health centers. In one center, the population was basically low-income inner city residents (59 percent Black). These subjects described themselves as regular drinkers throughout the week and on weekends. Upper income rural Blacks in Mississippi, however, reported a somewhat different pattern of drinking. These Blacks drank mostly on week nights, usually after work, and on weekends (Benjamin, 1976). In contrast, Meyers et al. (1985/1986) found that regular drinking was uncommon among elderly respondents surveyed. Their study found that only a small percentage (6 percent) of subjects reported drinking daily, one or more drinks. An analysis of the data suggest that there may be regional, socioeconomic, and age related differences in drinking patterns among Black men.

In addition to comparisons of drinking patterns among Blacks, some researchers have investigated differences in drinking patterns among Blacks and other ethnic groups. One investigation published by

355

Caetano (1984) surveyed 4,167 subjects—1,206 Blacks (38 percent males), 2,327 Whites (44 percent males), and 634 Hispanics (42 percent males)—who resided in Northern California. Caetano found that male drinking patterns across ethnic groups were similar, notwithstanding the fact that attitudes about alcohol use were different with Black subjects having a more liberal attitude than White.

Information regarding differences in alcohol consumption rates between Black and White men also vary. Lower rates were identified in earlier investigations with some subsequent investigations revealing higher rates and others finding no differences when comparing consumption rates among Black and White males. Jellinek and Keller (1952) reported that Blacks had a lower rate of heavy drinkers than Whites. Malzberg (1955) found that among Black and White native born metropolitan subjects there were less intemperate drinkers than among persons born elsewhere. Rimmer's et al. (1971) study yielded different findings: Black subjects were found to have higher consumption rates than White. Harper (1983) reviewed two different studies and concluded that there were no differences between Black and White males in alcohol consumption rates. To wit:

> In a random sample of 2,746 subjects, Cahalan and Cisin (1968) included a limited proportion of Black Americans (approximately 8 percent). The data were collected throughout the United States in late 1964 and early 1965. Data in drinking practices were analyzed according to religion, ethnicity, income, social class, age, sex, education, and geographic region. In reference to race, a very brief presentation of the findings indicated no significant difference between rates of White and rates of Black non-drinkers and heavy drinkers (Harper, 1983, p. 25).

A 1984 national survey conducted by Herd (no date) of drinking patterns among Blacks supported Harper's findings. Herd reporting subgroup data collected on 725 Black and 743 White men (total sample 5,221) living in households of the United States (excluding Alaska and Hawaii) concluded that overall there were more similarities than differences between the two groups. However, Herd also identified differences between Black and White men when examining drinking patterns and age distribution. Fewer young Black men between 18-29 years of age (17 percent) than White men (33 percent) were found to be frequent heavy drinkers. Among Black men 30-39 years old, there was a substantial increase in alcohol consumption, however, drinking patterns in that age group approximated those of Whites in the same age group. Interestingly, however, the pattern changes after age 39. Black men over 40 years old were mostly abstainers and/or infrequent drinkers whereas drinking increased among White men:

> Nearly three-quarters of Black men over 60 years of age report that

they are abstainers or drink less than once a month. The rise of abstention among Blacks is matched by comparatively higher rates of frequent drinking in the population of White men. Hence among men aged 50-59 years, almost three times as many Whites as Blacks are occasional higher maximum drinkers and among those over 60, more than three times as many Whites report drinking frequently but in small quantities (Herd, no date, p. 10).

When consuming alcoholic beverages, regardless of frequency or amount, it has been noted by Harper (1976) that Black men, particularly lower income Blacks, prefer higher priced liquors. A disproportionate amount of money is often spent on alcohol, considering the percentage of Blacks in the general population and the amount of their expendable income. As with many other materialistic possessions, these alcohol purchases are often made instead of more saliently needed items. Paradoxically, higher priced liquor is generally not purchased because of a desire for a particular flavor of beverage. In fact, Vitols (1968) reported that Black subjects, more than White, do not have a preference for a particular beverage. The ability to purchase these beverages and to make them available to friends is considered a status symbol.

It is obvious that alcohol serves many functions—a tension reducer, ego booster, and a social enhancer. During earlier years when segregation limited access to public facilities, private clubs, and taverns, alcohol also served as a symbol of deprivation. Compensating for these restrictions, Black men frequently created their own places to drink and to socialize: dives, homes, street corners, vacant lots, sidewalks, and abandoned buildings became places to congregate, drink, get high, and socialize. Group drinking and drinking in social settings thus became common among Blacks, particularly Black males, who tended to drink with friends or in familial situations (Harper, 1983).

Public drinking by young Black males, as displayed in predominantly Black communities, was often encouraged by the presence of liquor establishments which were usually White owned and located in close proximity to residential areas (Harper, 1976). This practice is reportedly a residual from the prohibition era, when moonshine stills were frequently located in Black neighborhoods. Today liquor businesses are often still visible in predominantly Black ghetto areas and thrive basically on the meager incomes of local residents.

Onset of Problematic Drinking

In contrast to drinking patterns, some consistency was found in empirical findings related to onset of problematic drinking among Black males. Some researchers found that this kind of drinking started earlier among Black than White subjects. Over a nine year period, Strayer (1961) collected data on 1,308 subjects admitted to treatment at an urban-based alcoholism clinic. Although the small number of Blacks in the sample—44 of 1,308 subjects—severely restricted drawing inferences, Strayer (1961) was able to conclude that the onset of excessive drinking was shorter for Black than White subjects. Along a similar line, Vitols (1968) found that the onset of acute and persistent alcoholism started at an earlier age among Black than White subjects. More specifically, symptomatic drinking among Blacks was found by Rimmer et al.(1971) to start five years earlier than for other ethnic groups.

Adding another dimension to the discussion, Viamontes and Powell (1974) found that both the onset of drinking and loss of control over drinking were earlier for Black than for White subjects. This conclusion was reached after analyzing data for 200 subjects (100 Black and 100 White) admitted to a long term alcoholism treatment program at a mental health center. Supporting these findings, Strauss et al. (1974) reported that alcoholism was generally highest among older subjects, between 45 and 54 years old, except for Black subjects who tended to be younger. They concluded this after analyzing clinical and epidemiological data for 312 subjects admitted to a psychologically oriented treatment facility. Subjects were selected from a population of about 180,000 persons living in a catchment area with a ratio for Blacks of 7:1.

A later investigation, however, indicates a different trend. Edwards (1985) surveyed 100 urban older adults which included Black males. Case records, interviews, and questionnaires were used to abstract data. Final results indicated that most respondents started drinking heavily between 55 and 64 years of age which is during a time period when alcohol consumption is expected to decline as part of the normal maturation process. Also, after surveying more than 2,000 (8 percent Black) subjects, Caetano (1984) found alcohol-related problems increased in older age groups. Those 30-39 years old reported more alcohol-related problems than those 18-29 years old. Noteworthy is that the opposite trend existed among White male subjects.

Consequences of Pathological Alcohol Consumption

Regardless of the time period involved from social to pathological drinking, the onset of problematic drinking, including loss of control, can result in severe consequences. Negative consequences related to alcohol consumption, such as illnesses, legal problems, and early deaths are especially characteristic of young Black males. Chances of committing alcohol-related crimes and having social problems are high among Blacks between 18 and 30 years of age (Lowman, et al., no date). Livingston (1985) determined that Black subjects are at a greater risk for developing primary and secondary health and behavioral problems associated with their alcohol abuse. These health problems include: (1) a greater propensity for delirium tremens (Rimmer et al., 1971), (2) earlier onset of delirium tremens (Vitols, 1968), (3) more hallucinations and convulsions (Viamontes and Powell, 1974), (4) major medical complications (German, 1973), (5) high cirrhotic death rates (Alcohol Epidemiologic Data Systems, 1980), (6) more psychosomatic complaints (Vitols, 1968), (7) severe neuroses and psychoses (Malzberg, 1955; Vitols, 1968), and (8) high rates of esophageal cancer (Herd, 1986).

German (1973) assessed the extent and nature of medical problems among 122 subjects (83 percent Black) admitted for detoxification. Among 92 percent of the subjects, he found one or more of the following major medical complications: heart, hepatic, neurological, and gastrointestinal abnormalities. In addition, a significant number suffered from malnutrition, anemia, and trauma. Also between 1969-71 for Black males 35-44 years old the incidence of esophageal cancer was 10 times that of Whites and among older age groups the rate for Black males was four times that of White males (Herd, 1986). Furthermore, since 1978, deaths from cirrhosis of the liver increased among Blacks (Lowman et al., no date). Quoting statistics from the U.S. Alcohol Epidemiologic Data Reference Manual (1980), Lowman et al., (no date, p. 57) reported that:

> In 1978, cirrhosis death rates rose steeply among Blacks in their twenties. Where a parallel ascent did not occur among Whites until after the age of 35. Among Black males 25 to 34 years of age, cirrhotic death rates were several times higher than for White males the same age. For all ages, the cirrhotic death rate for Black Americans was nearly twice that for White Americans.

After surveying 46,471 subjects (8 percent Black), Malzberg (1955) found that among Blacks alcoholic psychoses ranked high for first admissions. Likewise, Vitols's (1968) investigation revealed that Black subjects had more neurotic defenses than White subjects. Depressive and suicidal behaviors, however, were less prevalent among Black than White subjects (Vitols, 1968), although drinkers demonstrated more depressive behaviors than nondrinkers among both Black and White subjects (Neff, 1986). Also, blackouts occurred less frequently among Black than White subjects (Vitols, 1968).

As these investigations illustrate, there are enormous physical and psychological consequences of alcohol abuse which may shorten life expectancy. Also, there are legal consequences of alcohol abuse which may be life threatening. For example, according to Hyman (1968) who studied data in Columbus, Ohio and Santa Clara County, Blacks between 20-64 years of age were twice as likely to be arrested for driving while intoxicated as other men in the same age group. However, although many people assume that there is a strong association between alcohol and other criminal offenses such as homicides, Watts and Wright (1983) described research in this area as relatively new. Also, much of the research involves local rather than national data. Gary (1983) reported being unable to locate any national data which exclusively delineated homicidal statistics for Blacks.

Nevertheless, some of the existing crime data suggest an association between alcohol consumption and crime among Black men in metropolitan areas. Gary (1983) postulated that income and age are crucial variables in understanding this phenomenon. After reviewing crime related data, Gary (1983, p. 143) surmised that:

> ...murders among the middle and upper income groups are committed by White men over thirty years of age and alcohol consumption is rarely involved. In homicides among lower income persons, the murderer is often a Black man under thirty years of age and alcohol is implicated in more than 50 percent of the cases.

Harper (1976) surveyed four metropolitan cities—Atlanta, Cleveland, Miami, and Washington, D.C. He analyzed data on the blood alcohol content of autopsied homicidal victims many of whom were Black males. This investigation suggested a relationship between these homicides and alcohol consumption. About 50 percent of all victims were under the influence of alcohol at the time of their death. In Atlanta, of the 214 victims, 63 percent were under the influence of alcohol; of the 272 victims in Cleveland, 55 percent were under the influence of alcohol; of the 145 victims in Miami, 49 percent were under the influence of alcohol; and among the 255 victims in Washington, D.C., 49 percent were under the influence of alcohol. Furthermore, Harper (1977) concluded that alcohol-related homicides were greater for Black males under 30 years of age than for Whites in the same age group.

After analyzing data on social factors related to the development of alcoholism among Black males, Robins et al. (1968) and Lewis et al. (1985) concluded that alcoholism and antisocial behavior were associated. According to King et al. (1969), Blacks' legal problems as well as crimes resulting in imprisonment appear to be alcohol-related. Grisby (1963) analyzed data on Black prisoners in Florida's Raiford State Prison and found that 33 percent of offenses happened while subjects were under the influence of alcohol. Data from the above studies suggest that Blacks may become aggressive when drinking, with the outcome sometimes being violent and antisocial behaviors.

Herd (1986) reports somewhat different findings. This investigator postulates that there are few differences between Blacks and Whites who commit serious alcohol-related crimes:

> Black property offenders over 40 are only slightly less likely than Whites to have been drinking. Among those having committed crimes against the person, older Black offenders are about as likely as Whites to have been drinking. However, among young offenders—who are

overrepresented in prison populations—Blacks were less likely than Whites to have been drinking at the time of the crime...Blacks were less likely than Whites to have been drinking heavily. (Herd, 1986, p. 102).

There are also empirical investigations on behavior while intoxicated which suggest that Blacks may not become aggressive when drinking. Intoxicated Black subjects, more than their White counterparts, were found to be gregarious, talkative, and happy (Strayer, 1961). Black alcoholic subjects were also found to be less defensive and distressed than their nonalcoholic counterparts (Walters et al., 1984) which perhaps can best be explained by degree of intoxication. For example, in the earlier stages of intoxication when the senses are beginning to be affected and inhibitions lowered, there may be a feeling of well- being. As the level of intoxication increases, there may be less emotional control resulting in the release of pent-up feelings which may include anger and frustration.

An issue closely linked to crime and alcohol abuse is the connection between overall mortality rates and alcohol consumption among Blacks. Generally, there are higher mortality rates among alcoholics than nonalcoholics. Alcoholics also have a shorter life expectancy than nonalcoholics, with Blacks having an even shorter life expectancy. Combs-Orme et al. (1985) studied mortality rates among 1,289 Black and White alcoholics. Among these subjects, the overall mortality rate for a 5 to 9 year period was 22 percent, with Blacks in the sample dying at a younger age. This suggests that Black alcoholics never get to be older Americans because they die at a young age. Data were also examined on 644 Black and White alcoholics (42 percent Black) comparing death rates and occupational prestige variables. Deaths among Blacks in the high prestige group were significantly higher while mortality rates among Whites were significantly higher within the middle-prestige groups. For upper-class Blacks, it appears that alcohol consumption as a stress reliever may be a deadly tension reducer.

Utilization of Alcoholism Treatment Networks

Alcoholics actually have few choices: reduced productivity, incapacitating illnesses, early deaths, or recovery which often means abstinence from all mood altering chemicals. Those choosing recovery may seek help from a variety of resources, which include other alcoholics or professionally trained staff working in alcoholism treatment programs. These treatment programs vary in type but generally are classified as inpatient, outpatient, or day treatment facilities. Harper (1983) suggests that limited knowledge of alcoholism, a tendency not to seek help voluntarily, and less knowledge of available social services sometimes interferes with the entry of Blacks into treatment networks.

Benjamin et al. (1977) surveyed 113 Black heads of households in a southern community to ascertain their attitudes toward alcohol abuse, alcoholism, and treatment. A majority of these respondents considered alcohol abuse and alcoholism to be treatable; some, however, believed that alcoholics were hopeless and, therefore, could not be helped. Rural respondents reported relying heavily on family networks to handle drinking problems. On the other hand, small town and city residents infrequently reported that interfamilial assistance was a viable alternative for handling alcohol-related problems. Yet, although ambivalent, when introduced to alcoholism treatment, Black subjects generally accepted hospitalization much more gracefully than White subjects (Vitols, 1968). Blacks also participated more in treatment activities as demonstrated by the frequency of clinic contacts, group therapy attendance, and diagnostic services received; but often remained in treatment a shorter period of time than Whites (Lowe and Alston, 1973; Strayer, 1961).

Although treatment stay for Blacks is sometimes shorter than for Whites, as discussed in the scope of the problem, research investigations indicate that Blacks tend to have higher admission rates to treatment with alcohol-related diagnoses than Whites (Herd, 1986: Malzberg, 1944,; NIAAA, 1982, 1983: Rosenblath et al., 1971; and Towle, 1974).

> Black Americans are currently overrepresented in the alcohol treatment system, particularly in the urban areas of the Northeast. The excess involvement of Blacks in the alcohol treatment system is consistent with the high rates of psychiatric hospitalization for alcohol problems described for urban, migrant Blacks in earlier decades. Within the current alcohol treatment system, Blacks appear to be modestly overrepresented in programs. In contrast, they appear greatly overrepresented in programs designed for persons in the lower socioeconomic strata, such as public inebriates (Herd, 1986, p. 118).

Recent investigations for 1977-1980 and 1982 have shown that Blacks comprise 15 to 18 percent of alcoholism and/or combined alcoholism treatment programs although they are only 11 percent of the general population (NIAAA, 1980, 1982, 1983). Blacks have also been found to be overrepresented in employee assistance programs as well as driving while intoxicated programs (Towle, 1974). Various reasons have been given for these occurrences, including poor social and economic conditions, chronic institutionalization of Blacks in psychiatric hospitals and the criminal justice system, poor nutrition and health conditions, and the use of alcohol treatment facilities as welfare and rehabilitation programs (Malzberg, 1944; Rosenblath et al., 1971; Herd, 1986).

In addition to being overrepresented in alcoholism treatment programs, Black males are admitted for alcoholism treatment at a younger age than White males (Combs-Orme, 1985; Gorwitz, et al. 1970; Gross et al., 1972; Hornstra and Udell, 1973; Locke and Duvall, 1964; Viamontes and Powell, 1974; Zax et al., 1967). Combs-Orme et al. (1985) in a study of mortality rates among 1,289 Black and White alcoholics admitted to psychiatric and general hospital facilities in the St. Louis area found that the mean age of Blacks was 39.4 years old and 48.4 years old for Whites. Earlier investigations reveal similar results. Viamontes and Powell (1974) studied 100 Black and White male alcoholics in a treatment facility in the St. Louis area and found that the mean age of Blacks in the sample was 37 years old while the mean age for White subjects was 46 years old. As with the overrepresentation of Blacks in treatment, a variety of factors have been identified as contributing to Black males entering treatment at a younger age than Whites. Among them high unemployment, negative reactions to problems of early adulthood, inadequate family support networks, different bodily processing of alcohol and subsequent development of alcoholism, and poor nutrition among lower socioeconomic Blacks which speeds up the development of alcohol-related diseases (Gross et al., 1972; Locke & Duvall, 1964; Rimmer et al., 1971; Viamontes and Powell, 1974).

A different pattern, however, emerges in older Black and White males. Both Gorwitz et al. (1970) and Gross et al. (1972) found that fewer Blacks than Whites in the older age groups were admitted to treatment for alcoholism. Black males were found to enter treatment at a younger age than Whites but their admission rates declined with advancement in age while the admission rates for Whites substantially increased:

> Gross et al. (1963) reported that in a sample of 147 male patients, Blacks had a mean age that was 8 years younger than Whites. In a later study of 567 men (Gross et al., 1972) Blacks were also found to be approximately 8 years younger than Whites. There were twice as many Black patients in the 20-34 age group; yet, in the oldest age groups, there were nearly three times as many White, as Black patients (Herd, 1986, p. 96).

This occurrence may be related to the high incidences of alcohol-related medical problems and high mortality rates among Black male alcoholics. Actually, Black male alcoholics may die before becoming classified as older adults. For those persons surviving chronic heavy drinking, there may be the development of life threatening physical problems which require medical treatment in a general hospital. In such situations, the alcoholism may become a secondary diagnosis which is not reported as part of regular alcohol-related data.

Drug Addiction

Prevalence

Thus far we have examined the impact of one primary drug, alcohol, on the lives of Black males. There are, however, other drugs that have negative consequences. Although their use is not as widespread, these drugs are just as devastating. It is also more difficult to assess the prevalence of these drugs because related statistics often are derived from illegal activities which result in arrests or are obtained from investigations of publicly funded treatment programs. Meanwhile, there are those who abuse a variety of licit and illicit drugs who never come to the attention of legal authorities or are treated in private treatment facilities. Furthermore, some persons contend that drug prevalence data are biased because they reflect current political, social, and legal trends (Johnson, et al. 1976). Because Blacks are frequently overrepresented in criminal arrests and subsequent imprisonment, their representation in national data may be exaggerated.

Historically, drug abuse is identified with lower income ghetto Black males, particularly illegal drug use such as opiates. During the 1960s and 1970s, however, this perception started to erode as drug problems became more visible among middle and upper income Blacks and Whites. Surveying 19,948 military enrollees, of which 7 percent were Black, Callan and Patterson (1973) found few differences between Blacks and Whites in overall drug use. An examination of multi-drug use patterns among subjects revealed a 31 percent usage rate for Blacks compared to a 32 percent usage rate for Whites. Reporting results from a national survey, O'Donnell et at. (1976) also concluded that differences between drug use among Blacks and Whites were diminishing. Today, fewer differences can be found between Black and White drug users in such areas as illegal activity, mortality rates, and extent of drug use. But despite these recent trends, much of the research indicates that some drug abuse continues to be predominantly a minority experience (Staples, 1976). In some urban Black communities, as much as 10 percent of the total population is addicted to drugs (Gary, 1983).

Drug Usage Patterns

Although Blacks are most often associated with opiate use (Mandel and Bordatto, 1980), a variety of other drugs are abused. For example, the metropolitan police department of St. Louis (Lackla, 1985) which serves an area highly populated by Blacks (45 percent Black) identified the most commonly abused drugs as: (1) marijuana, (2) pharmaceuticals—preludin, dilaudid, and talwin, (Ts and Blues), (3) cocaine, (4) phencyclidine (PCP/whack), (5) heroin, (6) methadrine, and (7) lysergic acid diethylamide (LSD). Among St. Louis's "Whack" users, aggressive and violent behaviors have been found to be especially prevalent among young Black males. Examining other parts of the country, particularly in the California area, increasingly Blacks are identified with use of a cocaine derivative called crack which can be cheaply produced. There are some reports that crack has been a longstanding problem in the Black community, but did not receive media attention until it filtered into White communities.

Because both adults and juveniles are employed to sell "rock", a name used to describe crack, its use is thought to be an especially dangerous phenomenon. In many cities, dealers are primarily juveniles who man crack houses, also known as "rock houses", where a rock can be purchased for as little as $10.00 (*Newsweek*, March 17, 1986, pp. 59,60). Thus the once highly priced cocaine is now readily available for a mere fraction of its prior cost. Because of its easy accessibility to both youth and adults alike and because of the crime and violence associated with its use, some law enforcement officers believe that the cocaine battle has already been lost, particularly in some Black communities (*Newsweek*, March 17, 1986, p. 60):

> Rock is a word with special significance to the 500,000 Black residents of Central Los Angeles. To them, "rock" is an affordable, plentiful, and uniquely marketed form of cocaine free base...But to law enforcement officials, politicians, drug experts, and treatment providers, "rock" has come to symbolize the outcropping of a new epidemic, one that has been reflected by a doubling of admissions into state and county funded treatment programs, and has resulted in waves of violent crimes...Rock cocaine has made the once expensive "basing" of cocaine an easy and affordable option in poorer communities once dominated by heroin, PCP, and alcohol (*U.S. Journal on Alcohol and Drug Abuse, 1985*).

A survey of drug arrest records in a large metropolitan area in Ohio indicated that of 2,393 drug-related arrests, Black males were most often arrested for narcotics and barbiturate abuse while Whites were mostly arrested for marijuana, hallucinogen, and amphetamine abuse (Petersen, et al., 1975). Similar results were reported by Nail et al. (1974) who in an exploratory investigation of 833 military males, found that over 80 percent of Blacks sampled had a history of heroin use and few used hallucinogens. Another study conducted by Kleinman and Lukoff (1975) indicated that sampled Blacks and Whites had about the same use rate for marijuana. Blacks, however, were less likely to be polydrug users.

When considering the issue of age and drug use Kleinman and Lukoff (1975) found more parallels. For both Blacks and Whites drug use decreased with increasing age. The young were heavier drug users than middle-aged persons (age 18-29 years, age 30-49 years) who were more frequent users than older persons (age 59 years and older). Factors contributing to this pattern may be similar to those found among alcoholics—shorter mortality rates among drug abusers. There is also the element of imprisonment which limits the accessibility of drugs for both Blacks and Whites. Finally, there are the elements of increased family and job responsibilities as well as declining health which may affect the extent of drug use.

Consequences of Drug Abuse

It remains that drug abuse and its related social, economic, and legal consequences are more apparent in Black than White communities. In addition to the devastating socioeconomic and sociofamilial consequences, drug abusers risk being arrested for their illegal drug use. This is particularly true of Blacks, who are eight times more likely than Whites to be arrested for illicit drug use (Gary, 1983).

The United States Department of Justice (1980) reported that among 516,142 persons arrested for drug violations in 1979, 21.8 percent were Black (Gary, 1983, p. 141). Arrest and imprisonment, which are among the gravest consequences of illicit drug use, still continue to disproportionately befall Black males (Mandel, 1974).

As with alcoholics, drug addicts have higher mortality rates. Joe et. al. (1982) analyzed national data on 3,324 Black and White daily opiod addicts treated in community-based programs and found that death rates were 3 to 14 times higher than in the general population. Furthermore, these investigators concluded that age was the only reliable predictor of mortality rates among those surveyed. Younger addicts, those 30 years old and under, were more likely to die from drug-related deaths than older addicts whose deaths were mostly attributed to natural causes.

Drug Abuse Treatment

Just as with alcoholics, treatment for drug addiction is important to the recovering process. Unlike alcoholism treatment, however, addiction treatment is often, though not always, associated with the type of drug abused. For example, opiod addiction which is prevalent among Blacks, often is associated with detoxification, methadone maintenance, and supportive outpatient services. Opiod addicts are also, however, sometimes treated in residential treatment programs. Treatment of other drug addictions are often associated with drug free outpatient clinics and residential programs sometimes referred to as therapeutic communities. Methadone treatment and therapeutic communities are more common to publicly funded, community-based programs than to the hospital-based chemical dependency units which now proliferate and treat a range of drug abuse problems and addictions.

In an investigation of drug abuse treatment modalities, Joe et al. (1982-1983) concluded that outpatient detoxification was the least effective. After surveying 1,812 Black and White male opiod addicts, Simpson and Savage (1981/1982) also found that outcomes for methadone maintenance, therapeutic community, and drug-free outpatient treatment were not significantly different; however, clients in outpatient detoxification had notably poorer treatment outcomes.

From admissions to some publicly funded drug treatment programs, investigators have found similar demographic characteristics and presenting problems. Craig (1980) analyzed data on 322 applicants to a veteran drug treatment program and identified a typical narcotic addict seeking treatment as 30 years old, married, a Black male with an 11th grade education and a GED that was acquired while in prison. Drug habits tended to span 8 to 9 years and many were multiple drug users, abusing both alcohol and marijuana.

Furthermore as with alcoholics, medical problems were common among drug addicts in treatment. Ladner et al. (1975) examined drug-related complaint data for persons admitted to a large urban hospital and found that both Blacks and Anglos were at risk for addiction problems but that Blacks were also at risk for medical problems associated with their drug use. This is a crucial factor because medical problems tend to complicate the recovering process because they often have to be addressed before therapeutic issues related to treatment can be seriously explored.

Once treatment commences, retention problems are common among drug addicts. However, among Blacks, investigators found variable attrition rates. Wexler and de Leon (1977) surveyed 809 residents (81 percent male; 64.9 percent Black) in a community-based program and found that Blacks were less likely than Whites to drop out of treatment. Steer (1983) also concluded after reviewing data on 110 patients, mean age 24 years to 34 years, that Whites dropped out of treatment more frequently than Blacks. But Linn et al. (1979) found equal drop out rates (63 percent) among Blacks and Whites. Also, factors affecting retention in treatment were quite different among Blacks and Whites. Blacks were more intrinsically motivated, being mostly influenced by their perceptions of the treatment milieu as accepting and caring, while whether or not Whites remained in treatment related more to their personal motivation and adjustment to life in general (Linn et al., 1979).

Regardless of the type of treatment, McLellan (1983) concluded that age was the only reliable predictor of treatment retention. This was concluded after analyzing 113 studies linking patient characteristics to methadone maintenance treatment. McLellan (1983) found that those tending to remain in treatment were 25 years old, Black males, and married. Being a part of an intact family and being young seemed to enhance treatment retention.

Implications and Conclusions

In many ways, the drug epidemic of the 1980s as it is sometimes called, has some validity—not necessarily because the use of drugs other than alcohol has increased substantially, but because some highly addictive drugs are more accessible to, and affordable by, both adults and youth. Yet, it is alcohol that continues to be the primary drug of abuse. Because alcohol is a legal drug, there is not the same kind of stigma associated with its use as with the use of controlled substances. Also, the alcoholic can often easily conceal dependence behind respectable social and ceremonial uses of alcohol while other drug uses and/or abuses, whether over-the-counter medications or controlled substances, frequently are labeled as deviant behaviors.

For Black males, the stigma associated with alcohol and other drug abuse is critical regardless of the nature or extent of the abuse. It is inconsequential that recent research data indicate that Black drinking patterns, in terms of consumption and frequency, approximate the population at large. When we consider that many Black families are below the federally defined poverty line; that unemployment rates are rising and there are limited opportunities for Blacks in professional and highly skilled jobs; that there is an increase in divorce and separation among Black families resulting in more female headed households; and that there is a continued escalation of Black on Black crime usually involving young Black males; Blacks can ill-afford any physical and psychological impairment because of drug abuse.

When examining alcohol or other drug abuse, a major concern for Black men is that using drugs often breeds violence and tragedy not just for the abuser but for family members and the community as well. Furthermore, many human resources are lost by acts of violence which are inflicted by drug impaired perpetrators whose victims often are also drug impaired. The sad part, however, remains that in many Black families seldom is the act associated with drug abuse. Drug impaired family members are often protected and cared for by family members who may scorn or excuse their drug use. When that person is a male, there is frequently little said as family members pretend that all is well, tolerate a lessening in the male's role in the family, and/or experience continuous emotional and sometimes physical abuse as a result of the abusers erratic behavior.

There are few empirically identified age-related factors which explain alcohol or other drug use patterns among Blacks. However, it has been determined that both alcoholics and other drug abusers, especially young Black males, have high mortality rates, entering treatment with major medical problems. Major medical problems include high rates of esophageal cancer which is common among middle-age Blacks. Correspondingly, cirrhosis deaths are high and increasing among young Black males. Also, although Blacks tend to start drinking and using other drugs at an older age than Whites, problematic drinking requiring treatment commences at a younger age for Blacks than Whites with the actual onset of alcoholism being shorter for Black than for White males. Furthermore, alcohol-related problems appear to increase with age among Blacks and younger Blacks tend to commit more alcohol-related crimes than older Blacks. Also, homicides among lower income persons are frequently committed by young Black males and alcohol is usually involved in these crimes.

Mounting a meaningful awareness strategy to overt these kinds of alcohol and other drug related problems among Blacks of all ages is hampered by the scarcity of national and longitudinal data. Much of the existing data are one-dimensional, focusing on specific aspects of drug use and abuse, comparing males in different age groups but ignoring specific maturational issues. Robins and Murphy (1967) are among the few investigators to examine childhood factors and familial characteristics in light of subsequent drug abuse patterns among Black male adults. Pre-selected male respondents were identified while in elementary school, and subsequently interviewed at 30-35 years of age to determine prevalence of drug use. Of the original sample, 95 percent were located. Among those, 50 percent had used some drug illegally and 10 percent of the sample were addicted to heroin. For most respondents using drugs, marijuana was the gateway drug to heavier, more extensive drug use. These researchers concluded that a combination of delinquency, dropping out of high school, and an absent father characterized those most vulnerable to heroin addiction. Neither economic status nor elementary school performance were found to be predictive of future drug use.

Unlike the Robins and Murphy (1967) investigation, most existing research does not examine the same subjects during different periods over time to assess age-related issues. It is this kind of data which can give valuable information regarding alcohol and other drug abuse among maturing Black males and help to better understand and impact this phenomenon. If the drug epidemic of the 1980s is to be lessened, more empirical data are needed to support the need for research, prevention, and treatment programs which address the motivational issues which are relevant for Black males of all ages. If drug abuse is to be successfully abated among Black males, regardless of age, alcohol and other drug prevention and treatment programs are desperately needed which address the specific needs of the Black male as he progresses through the maturational process. Because Black males frequently enter treatment at a young age, it is important that there be a focused diagnostic assessment process and comprehensive treatment planning (Redd, 1984). This is especially crucial when considering that Black males are overrepresented in treatment programs.

During the 1980s there has been a substantial reduction in publicly funded alcoholism and other drug treatment programs. Meanwhile, pay-for-services, hospital-based programs which require insurance, have increased. Such a trend is disastrous in today's society because there are many people who do not have insurance and who are unable to pay for expensive hospital care. In prior years such persons were estimated to be minimal. During the 1980s there are many more than the 5 percent skid row alcoholics or drug addicts who are unable to pay for treatment. Consider for example the new poor who find themselves without health insurance coverage because of loss of employment and a regular income. This is particularly true of Black males because when layoffs occur they are often among the first to be terminated because they have the least seniority. Thus more affordable inpatient and outpatient treatment options which address the needs of Blacks are needed. There is ample room for both publicly and privately funded drug abuse treatment programs.

References

Alcohol Epidemiologic Data Systems (AEDS) (1980). *Cirrhosis of the liver mortality in the United States. Each State and County and selected SMSA's*. U. S. Alcohol Epidemiologic Data Reference Manual. Section 2. Rockville, MD. National Institute on Alcohol Abuse and Alcoholism.

Barchha, R., Stewart, M. A., & Guze, S. B. (1968). The prevalence of alcoholism among general hospital ward patients. *American Journal of Psychiatry, 125,* 681-684.

Benjamin, R. (1976). Rural Black folk and alcohol. In F. Harper (Ed.), *Alcohol abuse in Black America*, pp. 50-60. Alexandria, Virginia: Douglass.

Benjamin, R., & Rao, V. P. (1977). Alcohol-related problems and intra-familial management among Blacks. Jackson State University, Conference (SWSA) Southwestern Sociological Association.

Brecher, E. M. (1972). *Licit and illicit drugs. Canada Limited: Boston, Little, Brown.*

Caetano, R. (1984). Ethnicity and drinking in Northern California: A comparison among Whites, Blacks, and Hispanics. *Alcohol and alcoholism, 19* (1), 31-44.

Cahalan, D., & Cisin, I. H. (1968). American drinking practices: Summary of findings from a national probability sample. *Quarterly Journal of Studies on Alcohol, 29,* 130-151.

Callan, J. P., & Patterson, C. D. (1973). Patterns of drug abuse among military inducters. *American Journal of Psychiatry, 130* (3), 260-264.

Clark, W. B., & Midanik, L. (1982). Alcohol use and alcohol problems among U.S. adults: Results of the 1979 national survey. In National Institute on Alcohol Abuse and Alcoholism. *Alcohol consumption and related problems*, pp. 3-52. Alcohol and Health Monograph No. 1. DHHS Pub. No. (ADM) 82-1190. Washington, D.C.: Supt. of Docs. U.S. Government. Print. Off.

Coggins, P. C. (1979). Culture specific recommendations for meeting the needs of minority alcoholics. Washington, D.C.: Original paper presented at a forum of the National Council on Alcoholism, Inc.

Combs-Orme, T., Taylor, J. R., & Robins, L. N. (1985). Occupational prestige and mortality in Black and White alcoholics. *Journal of Studies on Alcohol, 46* (5), 443-446.

Craig, R. J. (1980). Characteristics of inner city heroin addicts applying for treatment in a Veterans Administration Hospital drug program. *International Journal of the Addictions, 15* (3), 409-418.

Edwards, D. W. (1985). An investigation of the use and abuse of alcohol and other drugs among 50 aged male alcoholics and 50 aged female alcoholics. *Journal of Alcohol and Drug Education, 30* (2), 24-30.

Feldman, J., SU, W. H., Kaley, M. M., & Kissin, B. (1974). Skid row and inner-city alcoholics—a comparison of drinking patterns and medical problems. *Quarterly Journal of Studies on Alcohol, 35,* 565-576.

Frazier, E. F. (1962). *Black bourgeoise*. New York: Collier.

Gary, L. E. (1983). The impact of alcohol and drug abuse on homicidal violence. In T. D. Watts & R. Wright (Eds.), *Black alcoholism: Towards a comprehensive understanding*, pp. 136-151. Springfield, Illinois: Charles C. Thomas.

German, E. (1973). Medical problems in chronic alcoholics. *Journal of Chronic Diseases, 26,* 661-668.

Gorwitz, K., Bahn, A., Warthen, F., & Cooper, M. (1970). Some epidemiological data on alcoholism in Maryland: Based on admissions to psychiatric facilities. *Quarterly Journal of Studies on Alcohol, 31,* 423-443.

Grigsby, S. (1963). Raiford study: Alcohol and crime. *Journal of Criminal Law and Criminology, 54,* 296-306.

Gross, M., Halport, E., Sabot, L., & Polizos, P. (1963). Hearing disturbances and auditory hallucinations in the acute alcoholic pyschoses. Tintinitus: Incidence and significance. *Journal of Nervous and Mental Disease, 137* (5), 455-465.

Gross, M., Rosenblath, S., Lewis, E., Chartoff, S., & Malenowski, B. (1972). Acute alcoholic psychoses and related syndromes: Psychosocial and clinical characteristics and their implications. *British Journal of Addiction, 67,* 15-31.

Harper, F. D. (1976). Alcohol and crime in Black America. In F. Harper (Ed.), *Alcohol abuse and Black America*. Alexandria, Virginia: Douglas.

Harper, F. D. (1977). Alcohol use among North American Blacks. In Y. Israel, F. Glaser, H. Kulant, R. Popham, W. Schmidt, & R. Smart (Eds.), *Research advances in alcohol and drug problems, 4*, pp. 349-366. New York: Plenum Press.

Harper, F. D. (1983). Alcohol use and alcoholism among Black Americans: In T. D. Watts & R. Wright (Eds.), *Black alcoholism: Towards a comprehensive understanding*, pp. 19-36. Springfield, Illinois: Thomas.

Harper, F. D. (1976). *Alcohol abuse and Black America*. Alexandria, Virginia: Douglas.

Harvey, W. B. (1985). Alcohol abuse and the Black community: A contemporary analysis, special issues: Social thought on alcoholism. *Journal of Drug Issues, 15* (1), 81-91.

Herd, D. (No date). Sub-group differences in drinking patterns among Black and White men: Results from a national survey.(pp. 1-36). Alcohol Research Group, School of Public Health, University of California, Berkeley, California.

Herd, D. (1986). A review of drinking patterns and alcohol problems among U.S. Blacks. Report of the Secretary's Task Force—Black and minority health, U.S. Department of Health and Human Services. (pp. 77-140).

Hornstra, R. K., & Udell, B. (1973). Psychiatric services and alcoholics. *Missouri Medicine, 70,* 103-107.

Jellinek, E., & Keller, M. (1952). Rates of alcoholism in the United States of America. *Quarterly Journal of Studies on Alcohol, 13,* 49-59.

Hyman, M. (1968). The social characteristics of persons arrested for driving while intoxicated. *Quarterly Journal of Studies on Alcohol, 4,* 138-177.

Joe, G. W., Lloyd, R. M., Simpson, D. D., & Singh, B. K. (1982/1983). Recidivism among opiod addicts after drug treatment. An analysis by race and tenure in treatment. *American Journal of Drug and Alcohol Abuse, 9* (4), 371-382.

Joe, G. W., Lehman, W., & Simpson, D. D. (1982). Addict death rates during a four-year post treatment follow-up. *American Journal of Public Health, 72* (7), 703.

Johnson, B., & Nishi, S. M. (1976). Myths and realities of drug use by U.S. minorities. In P. Iiyama, S. M. Nishi, & B. Johnson (Eds.), *Drug use and abuse among U. S. minorities,* pp. 3-68. New York: Praeger.

King, L. J., Murphy, G. E., Robins, L. N., & Darvish, H. (1969). Alcohol abuse: A critical factor in the social problems of Negro men. *American Journal of Psychiatry, 125,* 1682-1690.

Kinney, J., & Leaton, G. (1978). *Loosening the grip.* St. Louis, Missouri: C. V. Mosby.

Kleinman, P., & Lukoff, I. F. (1975). *Generational status, ethnic group and friendship networks: Antecedents of drug use in a ghetto community.* New York: Columbia University School of Social Work, Center for Socio-Cultural Studies in Drug Use.

Lackla, S. (1985). *Drug abuse: Challenge of 1985 and beyond.* St. Louis Metropolitan Police Department.

Ladner, R., Page, W., & Lee, M. L. (1975). Ethnic and sex effects on emergency ward utilization for drug-related problems: A linear model analysis. *Journal of Health and Social Behavior, 16* (3), 315-325.

Larkins, J. (1965). *Alcohol and the Negro: Explosive issues.* Zebulon, North Carolina: Record.

Lewis, C. E., Robins, L., & Rice, J. (1985). Association of alcoholism with antisocial personality in urban men. *Journal of Nervous Mental Disorders, 173* (3), 166-167.

Linn, M. W., Shane, R., Webb, N. L., & Pratt, T. C. (1979). Cultural factors and/in drug abuse treatment. *International Journal of the Addictions, 14* (2), 259-280.

Livingston, I. L. (1985). Alcohol consumption and hypertension: A review with suggested implications. *Journal of the National Medical Association, 77* (2), 129-135.

Locke, B., & Duvall, H. (1964). Alcoholism among first admissions to Ohio public hospitals. *Quarterly Journal of Studies on Alcohol, 25* (3), 521-534.

Lowe, G. D., & Alston, J. P. (1973). An analysis of racial differences in services to alcoholics in a southern clinic. *Hospital and Community Psychiatry, 24,* 547-551.

Lowman, C., Harford, T. C., & Kaelber, C. T. (No date). Alcohol use among Black senior high school students. In *Alcohol and Youth: Facts for planning,* National Clearinghouse for Alcohol Information/National Institute on Alcohol Abuse and Alcoholism. Rockville, Maryland, pp. 56-65.

Maddox, G. L., & Borinski, E. (1964). Drinking behavior of Negro collegians: A study of selected men. *Quarterly Journal of Studies on Alcohol, 25,* 651-668.

Maddox, G. L., & Williams, J. R. (1968). Drinking behavior of Negro collegians. *Quarterly Journal of Studies on Alcohol, 29,* 117-129.

Maddux, R. B., & Voorhees, L. (1987). *Job performance and chemical dependency: A practical guide for managers and supervisors.* Los Altos, California: Crisp.

Malzberg, B. (1944). Statistics of alcoholic mental diseases. *Religious Education, 39,* 23-30.

Malzberg, B. (1955). Use of alcohol among White and Negro mental patients: Comparative statistics of first admissions to New York State Hospitals. *Quarterly Journal of Studies on Alcohol, 16,* 668-680.

Mandel, J. (1974). The cost of drug policy to minorities. *Agenda, 4* (1), 36-46.

Mandel, J., & Bordatto, O. (1980). Dawn: A second look—its impact on minorities and public policy. *American Journal of Drug and Alcohol Abuse, 7* (3&4), 361-377.

McCelland, D. (1972). *The drinking man.* New York: Free Press.

McLellan, T. A. (1983). Patient characteristics associated with outcome. *National Institute on Drug Abuse: Treatment research monographs, 83-1281,* 500-529.

Meyers, A. R., Hingson, R., Mucatel, M., Heeren, T., & Goldman, E. (1985-1986). The social epidemiology of alcohol use by urban older adults. *International Journal of Aging and Human Development, 21* (1), 49-59.

Nail, R. L., Gunderson, E. K., & Arthur, R. J. (1974). Black-White differences in social background and military drug abuse patterns. *American Journal of Psychiatry, 131* (10), 1097-1102.

National Institute on Alcohol Abuse and Alcoholism (1982). *National alcoholism program information system statistical report on NIAAA funded treatment programs for calendar year 1980,* National Institute on Alcohol Abuse and Alcoholism: Author.

National Institute on Alcohol Abuse and Alcoholism (1980). *National drug and alcoholism treatment utilization survey, comprehensive report.* National Institute on Alcohol Abuse and Alcoholism: Author.

National Institute on Alcohol Abuse and Alcoholism (1983). *National drug and alcoholism treatment utilization survey, comprehensive report.* National Institute on Alcohol Abuse and Alcoholism: Author.

Neff, J. A. (1986). Alcohol consumption and psychological distress among U.S. Anglos, Hispanics and Blacks. *Alcohol and alcoholism, 21* (1), 111-119.

Newsweek (1986). Kids and cocaine, *107,* 58-63.

O'Donnell, J. A., Voss, H., Clayton, R., Slatin, G., & Room, R. (1976). *Young men and drugs—a nationwide survey.* National Institute on Drug Abuse Research Monograph Series 5. Rockville, Maryland: National Institute on Drug Abuse.

Petersen, D. M., Schwirian, K. P., & Bleda, S. E. (1975). *The drug arrest, 13* (1), 106-110.

Redd, M. L. (1984). *Alcoholism treatment outcomes.* (Dissertation). St. Louis, Missouri: Washington University.

Rimmer, J., Pitts, F. N., Reich, T., & Winokur, G. (1971). Alcoholism II. sex, socioeconomic status and race in two hospitalized samples. *Quarterly Journal of Studies on Alcohol, 32,* 942-952.

Robins, L. N., & Murphy, G. E. (1967). Drug use in a normal population of young Negro men. *American Journal of Public Health, 57* (9), 1580-1596.

Robins, L. N., Murphy, G. E., & Breckenridge, M. B. (1968). Drinking behavior of young urban Negro men. *Quarterly Journal of Studies on Alcohol, 29,* 657-684.

Rosenblath, S. M., Gross, M. M., Broman, M., Lewis, E., & Malenowski, B. (1971). Patients admitted for treatment of alcohol withdrawal syndromes. *Quarterly Journal of Studies on Alcohol, 32,* 104-115.

Royce, J. E. (1981). *Alcohol problems and alcoholism: A comprehensive survey.* New York: Free Press.

Simpson, D. D., & Savage, L. J. (1981/1982). Client types in different drug abuse treatments: Comparisons of follow-up outcomes. *Ameican Journal of Drug and Alcohol Abuse, 8* (4), 401-418.

St. Louis Post Dispatch (1986). Eaps: Help for troubled employees. Section C., pp. 1 & 8.

Staples, R. (1976). *Introduction to Black sociology.* New York: McGraw-Hill.

Steer, R. A. (1983). Retention in drug-free counseling. *International Journal of the Addictions, 18* (8), 1109-1114.

Sterne, M., & Pittman, D. (1972). *Drinking patterns in the ghetto* (Unpublished report), (1 &2). St. Louis, Missouri: Washington University, Social Science Institute.

Strauss, J. S., Wolfe, D., Ord, A. V., & Geoghegan, R. (1974). Inpatient alcoholics: Characteristics and needs. *Comprehensive Psychiatry, 15,* 205-212.

Strayer, R. A. (1961). Study of the Negro alcoholic. *Quarterly Journal of Studies on Alcohol, 22,* 111-123.

Towle, L. H. (1974). Alcoholism treatment outcomes in different populations. In M. Chafetz (Ed.), Proceedings of the fourth annual alcoholism conference of the National Institute on Alcohol Abuse and Alcoholism. Washington, D.C., NIAAA.

U.S. Department of Justice (1980). Crime in the United States. Washington, D.C.: U.S. Government Printing Office.

U. S. Journal on Alcohol and Drug Abuse (1985). "Rock" cocaine hits L.A. (excerpt).

Viamontes, J. A., & Powell, B. J. (1974). Demographic characteristics of Black and White male alcoholics. *International Journal of the Addictions, 9,* 489-494.

Vitols, M. M. (1968). Culture patterns of drinking in Negro and White alcoholics. *Diseases of the nervous system, 29,* 391-394.

Walters, G. D., Greene, R. L., & Jeffrey, T. B. (1984). Discriminating between alcoholic and nonalcoholic Blacks and Whites on the MMPI. *Journal of Personality Assessment, 48* (5), 486-488.

Watts, T. D., & R. Wright (Eds.) (1983). *Black alcoholism: toward a comprehensive understanding.* Springfield, Illinois: Charles Thomas.

Wexler, H. K., & de Leon, G. (1977). The therapeutic community: Multivariate prediction of retention. *American Journal of Drug Abuse, 4* (2), 145-151.

Zax, M., Gardner, E., & Hart, W. (1967). A survey of the prevalence of alcoholism in Monroe County, New York. *Quarterly Journal of Studies on Alcohol, 28* (2), 316-327.

LIFE CONTROL THEORY: A PERSPECTIVE ON BLACK ATTITUDES TOWARD DEATH AND DYING

Maurice Jackson

Introduction

Death and dying are the beginning and the end, the major parameters of the life cycle. Given the importance of death in any group it is surprising that there have been few efforts to explain the character of Black death and dying. The relative lack of information virtually precludes the possibility of this paper reporting tests of well-founded hypotheses. Instead, it will begin to bring together some facts and traditional explanations and present the beginning of a new theory, life control theory. Specifically this paper will discuss: 1) current knowledge of Black death and dying; 2) past explanations of Black death and dying; and 3) life control theory.

Current Knowledge

As far as we can tell, the facts of death for Blacks are extraordinary (Jackson, 1972). Beginning with the capturing and buying of Africans for slavery, through slavery and Reconstruction to modern times, a time period which involved capital punishment, lynchings and some wars, death rates for Blacks have been relatively high.

Recent information indicates this is still the case. There is a general consensus among researchers that the Black death rate has been higher than the White rate. Blacks have a higher death rate at all ages than do White Americans (Blackwell, 1975). Blacks have a higher death rate than Whites in virtually every disease category (Pinkney, 1975). Demographers attribute great importance to mortality, and they have discovered that the Black death rate has remained different from that of the larger society over time (Farley, 1970). This has been true of death relative to birth rates in different stages of population change. The theory of demographic transition has been utilized to describe changes in contemporary populations in terms of four stages. Generally, in the first stage high birth and death

375

rates prevail. At this level the high death rates neutralize the high birth rates. The second stage is one in which birth rates remain high but death rates fall due to improvement of technology, increase in agricultural output and changes in medicine. During the third stage the fall of death rates is even more rapid than in the second stage while birth rates may begin to decline. In the fourth stage the death rate is stabilized at a low level and the birth rates decline to a low level.

The Black population of the United States has had a different demographic history. In the first stage (early 19th century) death rates were very high but birth rates were even higher. In the second stage (late 19th century) poor health conditions are said to have resulted in the decline in the birth rates. But there were only modest improvements in mortality.

The control of certain contagious diseases such as yellow fever, cholera, malaria, and typhoid fever was seen as responsible for the decrease in death rates. The death rate declined more slowly than the fertility rate. In the third stage (from 1935 to 1955) death rates were substantially reduced, and birth rates continued to climb until the late 1950s. In the fourth stage, since the late 1950's, birth rates have been increasing because of the development of better health, control of disease, education, and contraception; but there has been no general improvement in the level of mortality. Thus, it seems reasonable to assume that these historical and current differentials in pattern of mortality rates imply something about differences in which Blacks and Whites relate to life and death.

Past Explanations

Typical explanations of Black death and dying have tended to be of two types: common sense, and multi-factorial. The common sense view asserts that until recently Blacks have wished for death rather than accepting, defying, or denying it as members of the larger society have. The reasoning goes something like this: A life of oppression for Blacks produced so much misery that only through death could the effects of their hardship be overcome. Consequently, it is claimed that Blacks developed faith in the hereafter as a place where things would be much better. In effect, this view assumed that oppressed people tend to wish for death because their lives are unbearable, while their oppressors fear death because life is so precious for them. But ideas like "we shall overcome" have meant that Blacks have wanted to live a good life here on earth. Death, then, did and does not hold power as a way for Blacks to escape from life (Kastenbaum and Aisenberg, 1972). Logically, if Blacks had centered their lives on the hereafter, if death was used to overcome life's disapppointments, and if death were an escape hatch, then Blacks would have embraced death by taking their lives in great number to reach the hereafter. Facts do not support this view.

Much of the information from songs, poetry, and other literature growing out of the Black experience reveals a Black emphasis on death and dying that is this-worldly rather than other-worldly (Jackson, 1972).

Sacred and Secular Norms

The purpose of this account is not to add another horror story to the academic literature. It is rather, to delineate a few of the more dramatic reasons for the meaning that death may have for Blacks. With this as background, the foreground of the ways in which death is handled by Black people will be explored.

There are at least two alternatives. First is that set of expectations which can be described as the sacred norm. This norm specifies that Black people should attend to the supernatural and metaphysical concerns surrounding and following death, while de-emphasizing things of this world. Death in this context would provide an escape from this world. The sacred norm assumes that Black people cannot deal effectively with death as a phenomenon in this world and, therefore, should look to and glorify another world, an afterworld.

A different set of expectations form the secular norm, which specifies that Black people should view death as part of the normal life process, as an inevitable event in a naturalistic context, occurring in the world of experience. Death should be accepted as a frequent companion, and Black people would not need to de-emphasize it by focussing upon a supernatural world. The secular norm assumes that death should be interpreted as natural, in spite of its obvious highly disturbing social and emotional impact.

The sacred-secular norm distinction somewhat parallels Vernon's temporal (this-world) and spiritual (other-world) interpretations of death (Vernon, 1970). However, these orientations can better be seen as obligatory, hence normative. The terms "sacred" and "secular" also carry Durkheim's meaning of "things put aside" and "things not put aside" respectively (Durkheim, 1926). The question, then, is do Black people feel obliged to treat death as a thing put aside from this world (the sacred norm) or as something very much a part of this world (the secular norm)?

The usual interpretation of the behavior and rituals with which Blacks approach death is that they represent virtually the epitome of the sacred approach. It will be shown why this is not the case, that indeed the very opposite is true, and that lack of historical and sociological understanding has severely limited the ability to interpret the significance of this behavior and these rituals. Even in Africa, belief in the power of the ancestral dead to affect the lives of their descendents was widespread

377

(Herskovits, 1958). Although many contemporary behavioral scientists might consider this to be a superstition, the intent is not to debate the truth of the beliefs, but to use the example to indicate the kind of naturalistic continuity that existed between those on earth and those who had died.

Spirituals and Poetry

Since academic reports are lacking, the literature of Black people will be considered, beginning with spirituals and developing through more contemporary writings. The spirituals themselves are probably the form of Black literature most open to varied interpretation. Rather than symbolizing the other-worldly phenomena that emerges from a literal translation, they should be considered as a covert form of desire for freedom, with death simultaneously representing actual death and freedom—with the obvious realization that the only freedom most of the slaves would find was to occur with death. In that light, consider the words of "Swing low, sweet chariot," with the dual symbolism of death and freedom, although sung in the context of traditional Christianity. It is not difficult to realize the consequences, had the slaves expressed their desire for freedom from slavery in more overt fashion.

Thus Brown (1958, p. 279-289) concludes that references to troubles on earth are far more numerous in Negro spirituals than are references to freedom in a Christian form of heaven. He goes further: "It is only a half-truth to see the spirituals as other-worldly. 'You take dis worl', and give me Jesus' is certainly one of the least of the refrains. In the spirituals the slave took a clear-eyed look at this world, and he revealed in tragic poetry what he saw."

Fisher (1969) is in agreement. He states that "Negroes did not sing other-worldly songs like White people" (p. 182). While plantation missionaries stressed other-worldliness, not one spiritual "reflected interest in anything other than a full life here and now" (Fisher, 1969, p. 137). Even the frequent references to heaven could readily be interpreted as symbolizing a place on earth away from slavery: "Negro slaves ordinarily believed that Africa was heaven," (Fisher, 1969, p. 146), and that heaven within the United States was in the North.

Familiarity with death emphasized in the spirituals, expresses the secular norm of death with which the Blacks were so familiar. First as Fisher (1969) states, Blacks were prepared to accept death. Second, familiarity with death is shown in the interpretation of death as another life on earth (Fisher, 1969). Here death provides a continuity with life. As a matter of fact, until the first half of the nineteenth century, Black people preferred to believe in African reincarnation rather than in Christian immortality. The popularity of the famous spiritual based upon the death and rising of Lazarus gives support to this view.

In many spirituals, neither a secular nor a sacred view of death was evident. Nonetheless, the themes of death as freedom, rest, departure, and finding peace were all very common.

"Resting in the arms of Jesus" produces the image of a warm human relationship, not a mystical fantasy.

Poetry written by Black authors complements this discussion of the meaning of death found in the spirituals. Paul Lawrence Dunbar (1899) continues the theme of intimate familiarity with death, an expression of the secular norm, in his poem *A Death Song*. In the poem he draws a picture of familiar physical surroundings in describing a death scene. The poem also specifies certain favorite conditions under which death is acceptable: "If I's layin' 'mong de t'ings I's allus knowed." Finally, the poem contains a definition of death as rest and release, a secular theme.

Claude McKay, in his famous poem *If We Must Die*, written in 1919, offers another definition of death which highlights the secular norm. He relates death to social relationships in this world. Death can be noble—or it can be ignoble, a death for hogs. The preferred type of death for Black people is a noble death, even though it means that Blacks, outnumbered and outpowered, die in fighting back.

Around the same time, James Weldon Johnson illustrated the secular norm of death by defining death, as did Dunbar, as a time of rest. In his *Go Down Death*, he says that "She is not dead," but that she has found rest through closeness with Jesus. Later in the same poem, Johnson writes of death as a reward for laboring "long in my vineyard."

A more recent poem *When I Am Dead* by Owen Dodson (1970, p. 285) explores the familiarity theme of the secular norm through underscoring familiar physical surroundings.

Black Literature

The emphasis upon the secular norm of death is also found in contemporary literature written by Black people. For example, Claude Brown (1965, p. 48-49) in *Manchild in the Promised Land* pointed to another definition of death as a reward, specifically for masculinity. Funerals in Harlem vary, depending upon the "toughness" of the individual involved. Among other things, funerals are ways to reward Blacks who stand up to other people, especially White people. Brown stated:

> The best (church) songs were sung at the funerals for the 'bad niggers'. I learned that a bad nigger didn't take shit from 'nobody' and that even the 'crackers' didn't mess with him....

> One day I went to a funeral for a bad nigger. A lot of people were

there, and most of them had heard about him but were seeing him for the first time. I guess they were scared to see him while he was still alive and still bad.... At his funeral, lot of ladies cried, and the preacher talked about him real loud for a long time. Before the preacher started talking, somebody sing 'Before this Time Another Year' and 'Got On My Traveling Shoes.' When the preacher finished talking about him, they took the casket outside and put it down in the ground. I have seen people do that before, but I didn't think they would do it this time. It just didn't seem like the right way to treat a bad nigger, unless being dead made him not so bad any more....

Somebody would sing real good at Grandpa's funeral, and a lot of people would be there. It would have to be a big funeral, because Grandpa was a real bad and evil nigger when he was a young man.

A final example of the Black norm of death as a commentary on social relationships is found in Redding's (1951, pp. 13-15) description of the death of a White person. In it Redding shows how his own life as a Black person affected his view of death. Here, the death of a White person seen as symbolic of antagonistic White, was defined as partially satisfying.

On looking out of the window of the college building at something which moved in the yard below, Redding reports:

There would have been no shock in seeing a woman of the neighborhood dressed only in a ragged slip, but a powdery snow had fallen the night before and the day was bitter cold. When I saw the woman, who seemed quite young, she was lurching and staggering in the rear of the yard. A dog must have followed her out of the house, for one stood by the open door watching and flicking it's tail dubiously. The woman's face was stiff and vacant, but in her efforts to walk her body and limbs jerked convulsively in progressive tremors. I could not tell whether she was drunk or sick as she floundered in the snow in the yard. Pity rose in me, but at the same time something else also—a gloating satisfaction that she was White. Sharply and concurrently felt, the two emotions were of equal strength, in perfect balance, and the corporeal I fixed in a trance at the window, oscillated between them.

When she was within a few steps of the outhouse, the poor woman lurched violently and pitched face downward in the snow. Somehow utterly unable to move, I watched her convulsive struggles for several minutes. The dog came down the yard meanwhile, whinning piteously, and walked stiff-legged around the White and almost naked body. The woman made a mess in the snow and then lay still.

Finally I turned irresolutely and went into the corridor. There was the entrance door and near it the telephone. I could have gone out and a few steps would have brought me to the yard where the woman lay and I could have tried to rouse someone or myself taken her into the house. I went to the telephone and called the police.

He read in the newspaper the next morning that a twenty-six year old woman had died of exposure followed by an epileptic seizure, suffered while alone.

Redding concluded that his experience as a Negro in America had fostered his reaction to a dying White person. In his word, "The experience of my Negroness, in a section where such experiences have their utmost meaning in fear and degradation, cancelled out humaneness."

It is the opinions of other scholars that not only is the Black American conception of death this-worldly but it reflects the African conception that the spiritual world is not separate from ongoing activities (Staples, 1976). Some observations which support this view are the enormous number of funeral parlors, the high regard for undertakers, and the ways in which death is related to "style and status" found in the Black communities like Harlem (Harrington, 1962).

The Multi-factor Approach

Students of Black death and dying have tended to study either what they regarded as the excessively high death rates of Blacks or the trends in death rates. The death rates are explained by a range of factors: disease; (Holmes, 1937), ignorance, limited time, small income, poor health, poor ventilation, poor food and water, disease, little health education, and lack of hospital facilities (Woodson, 1930); poor heredity, neglect of infants, bad dwellings, poor food, bad ventilation, lack of outdoor life, lack of measures to prevent spread of diseases, climate, ignorance of laws of health, poor exercise, and insufficient clothes, poverty, poor housing overcrowdedness, and lack of widespread health education (DuBois, 1967); informal social control, isolation, low literacy, and cultural backwardness (Johnson, 1966); poverty, housing problems caused by overcrowding, and lack of widespread health education (Cayton and Drake, 1966).

There are difficulties with the factor approach. One problem that can develop in the specification of responsible factors is that they may result in contradictions. For instance, isolation is said to be one of those factors in the rural areas and overcrowdedness, its opposite, in the urban areas. Another problem is the great specificity and limited generalizability of the various factors.

Scholars who study trends in Black death rates tend to describe the change or persistence in rates (Farley, 1970; Frazier, 1949; Holmes, 1937; Myrdal, 1944). Factors such as control of contagious diseases are seen as responsible for the death rate of Blacks over time (Farley, 1970).

Generally studies of Black death and dying tend to highlight problems in the Black community as the source of Black mortality. But death is not merely a result of problems. Everyone dies. Not only that but concentration on the Black community tends to ignore the social sources of facts in the community that exist outside it. Hence, any theory will be an improvement if it circumvents the multifactor approach and the concentrations on problems within the Black community as the cause of Black death and dying. An approach which avoids the multi-factor approach by being more systematic and general will be discussed. The theory will emphasize the effects of the larger society rather than the effects of the problems of the Black community on death and dying within it.

Life Control Theory

Life control theory is designed to provide a more adequate explanation by, in part, overcoming some of the problems with previous explanations of Black death and dying. It is based on a few assumptions. First it is assumed that most members of all groups are typically oriented toward survival or that survival is a fundamental objective. This does not mean that all groups survive as the objective may not be achievable for certain reasons.

Death is an indicator of the survival of a group in much the same way that law is an indicator of types of social solidarity, according to Durkheim (1960). Solidarity, however, is of secondary importance to survival of a group in that it is one of the means to survival.

Survival has not been given the attention it deserves in sociology although it tends to be a matter of interest to many observers of the Black community. Indeed, Thompson (1974) sees survival as the most fundamental aspect of the experience of Blacks in the United States.

Of the early European founders of sociology, Herbert Spencer (1969, 1895) stands out in his emphasis on survival. Spencer focused on the concept "survival of the fittest" to explain what he considered to be differences in the ability of European and African races, among other races, to survive. He claimed that Africans were physically, emotionally, and intellectually less fit than Europeans and, therefore, were not as likely to survive. As societies evolved, the less fit, such as Africans, would become extinct. The racism in this view is painfully obvious. One can imagine how surprised Spencer would be by the fact that ancestors of the least fit race survived the eras of slavery, Reconstruction, Black Codes, and Jim Crow. He would be equally surprised if he could see the vigor of American Blacks today under very trying circumstances. This is a time of great crisis for American Blacks: they are losing land, employment positions, higher educational positions, and government programs in which they once participated.

Life control theory differs from Spencer's theory of survival in not assuming as he did that the fittest survive. It tends to follow Darwin

(1967) by assuming that valid comparisons and determinations with respect to survival can only be made between living and extinct beings not between living ones. At this point it is obvious that Black Americans not only have survived very difficult life circumstances but continue to do so. They have done so in ways that bring credit to them physically, intellectually, and emotionally. In short, who survives is an open question. Survival, however, relates directly to the extent to which members of groups can control their life circumstances.

Many sociologists as proponents of functional theory have regarded maintenance or survival as the prime fact of societies. However, they tend to take survival for granted and to concentrate on explaining the contributions, positive and negative, that units make to it. Survival, itself, is basically unanalyzed.

Life control theory assumes survival to be much more problematic. It is not a fixed point of reference but a changeable phenomenon. This character of survival does not mean that members of a society or group have to adjust or adapt. It is a fact to be taken into account as they strive to control their situation.

Secondly, it is assumed that in order to survive, members of groups must have sufficient control of their life circumstances. Life control theory, then, rests upon a central fact of life of Blacks specifically and people in general. Most people try to exert control over their lives. To generate a more general explanation than the multifactor ones, it makes sense to look for a common feature of Black lives over time and space and to look for that feature in the larger society. An important common fact is that Blacks have tended to be controlled externally and coercively by application of various rules (laws, mores, and folkways). Slavery, Black Codes, and Jim Crow laws are historical examples of rigorous control imposed externally on Blacks. Throughout history in the United States, Blacks were denied the rights, theoretically and practically, that citizens of the society enjoyed. The liberties they experienced were determined by the will of other persons.

Today the situation is one in which Blacks continue to experience less control over their lives than Whites as a result of their relatively powerless minority status (Henry and Short, 1964). To say this in another way, the differential death rates of Blacks and Whites are based on poorer living conditions of Blacks which are a reflection of a power imbalance in which Whites have not only preempted resources but have controlled Blacks. In effect, those with less control will have fewer resources and higher rates of dying.

A third assumption is that life control theory is more general than contemporary sociological theories. At the risk of oversimplifying these theories and ignoring the many differences between them, they can be characterized as varieties of life control theory: A) functional theory focuses upon the consequences a group has for gaining or losing control by a society; B) conflict theory points to the way conflict facilitates or fails to facilitate the acquisition of control; C) power theory analyzes the way in which a group gains control over other groups, and the ways in which they control; D) exchange theory emphasizes the reciprocity of relationships which may or may not result in the gaining of control; E) symbolic interaction theory depicts the way in which symbols may or may not bring about control; and F) labeling theory deals with the way in which labels assist in the acquisition or loss of control. The conditions under which control is gained or lost still needs specifying.

A fourth assumption of life control theory is that Black Americans have generated and continue to generate their own norms at the same time norms controlling much of their behavior have been developed by the larger society. Consequently, the behavior of Blacks has been and is over-regulated not under-regulated. Much of the work on slavery has misunderstood this point. Blacks were said to be disorganized in slavery. The characterization of Blacks as disorganized extends to the present time. It is, however, this very conception that has led, in part, to excessive regulation by the larger society. Differences of Blacks from Whites have either been characterized as deviant or as pathological. These views, too, result in efforts to correct Black individuals and groups.

A more adequate description is that Blacks lead over-controlled lives rather than under-controlled ones. What makes for over-control are the formal and informal, public and private norms generated in the larger society. Typically, these norms are seen as the reigning ones.

An aspect of this external control is enforcement. Strict enforcement of norms may be seen as another indicator of excessive regulation. In fact, operating norms are thought to be effective with regard to behavior to the extent to which they are enforced. Facts such as the concern that Blacks have had with police brutality and excessive use of deadly force and the greater proportion of Black children who are formally physically punished in public schools point to overregulation. But this formal over-regulation is only part of the picture. Blacks, relative to White members of society, are overregulated with respect to informal rules (mores and folkways) to the extent that they are generated outside the Black community and added to those produced within the Black community.

Summary

In this paper I have attempted to promote interest in research which can expand our knowledge of Black attitudes toward death and dying. Life control theory has been proposed as a theoretical model for looking at Black death and dying. It offers a way of viewing Black life and that appreciates it as one *not* dominated by general attitudes of death fears and wishes or death defiance, death acceptance, and death denial but by attitudes that promote sense of control in lives where control is frequently imposed by outsiders.

References

Blackwell, J. E. (1975). *The Black community: Diversity and unity*. New York: Dodd Mead.

Brown, C. (1965). *Manchild in the promised land*. New York: The New American Library.

Brown, S. A. (1958). In L. Hughes & A. Bontemps (Eds.), *Book of Negro folklore*. New York: Dodd, Mead and Co.

Cayton, H. R., & Drake, S. C. (1966). *Black metropolis*. London: Jonathan Cape.

Clark, K. B. (1965). *Dark ghetto*. New York: Harper and Row.

Darwin, C. (1967). *Origin of species*. Cambridge: Harvard University Press.

Demeny, P., & Gingerich, P. (1967). A reconsideration of Negro-White mortality differentials in the United States. *Demography, 4(2)*.

DuBois, W. E. B. (1967). *The Philadelphia Negro*. New York: Schocken.

Dunbar, P. L. (1899). A death song. *Lyrics of the hearthside*. New York: Dodd, Mead and Co..

Durkheim, E. (1960a). *The division of labor in society* (translated by George Simpson). Illinois: The Free Press.

Durkheim, E. (1926). *The elementary forms of religious life*. New York: The MacMillan Co.

Farley, R. (1970). *Growth of the Black population*. Chicago: Markham.

Fisher, M. M. (1969). *Negro slave songs in the United States*. New York: The Citadel Press.

Frazier, E. F. (1949). *The Negro in the United States*. New York: The Macmillan Co.

Harrington, M. (1962). *The other America*. Baltimore: Penguin.

Henry, A. F., & Short, J. F. (1964). *Suicide and homicide*. New York: Free Press.

Herskovits, M. J. (1958). *The myth of the Negro past*. Boston: Beacon Press, Pp. 197-207.

Holmes, S. J. (1937). *The Negro's struggle for survival*. Berkeley: University of California Press.

Jackson, M. (1972). The Black experience with death. *Omega, 3(2)* 203-209.

Johnson C. S. (1966). *The shadow of the plantation*. Chicago: University of Chicago Press.

Johnson, J. W. (1927). *Go down death*. In J. W. Johnson, *God's trombones*. New York: The Viking Press.

Kastenbaum, R., & Aisenberg, R. (1972). *The psychology of death*. New York: Springer Publishing Co.

McKay, C. (1970). If we must die. In C. T. Davis & D. Walden (Eds.), *On being Black*. Greenwich: Fawcett, 1970.

Myrdal, G. (1944). *An American dilemma*. New York: Harper Brothers.

Pinkney, A. (1975). *Black Americans*. New York: Prentice-Hall.

Redding, J. S. (1951). *On being Negro in America*. Indianapolis: Bobbs-Merrill.

Spencer, H. (1969a). *The study of sociology*. Ann Arbor: The University of Michigan Press.

Spencer, H. (1895b). *The principles of sociology*, v. 1-2. New York: D. Appleton and Company.

Staples, R. (1976). *Introduction to Black studies*. New York: McGraw-Hill.

Thompson, D.C. (1974). *Sociology of the Black experience*. Wesport: Greenwood Press.

Vernon, G. M. (1970). *Sociology of death*. New York. The Ronald Press Company, 1970.

Part V
The Future

BLACKS IN AN AGING SOCIETY*

Rose C. Gibson

The welfare of the Black family is a major influence on Black adult development and aging. At the same time dominant social trends, such as the aging of our society, affect the well-being of the Black family. What, then, lies ahead for the Black family of the future? Blacks in every age group today are confronted with their own set of critical social problems, problems that, if not attended to effectively, will have serious consequences for the Black family both in the near future and well beyond.

This chapter will concern itself with these specific social problems and their impact on Black children, teenagers, the middle-aged, and elderly, as well as with the implications they pose for our society as a whole. Identifying the more critical social problems by summarizing census data and the findings of my own research—based on *The National Survey of Black Americans* (NSBA)[1] (see notes at end of chapter)and on other major national studies—will give us a useful starting point.

There are several reasons why the problems confronting various age groups of Black Americans may be diffcult to resolve. First, the absolute number of Blacks is smaller—and will always be smaller—than that of Whites, and smaller groups can have more difficulty making their voices heard.[2] (This must be balanced against the fact that small groups without power or wealth can wield influence through the use of special voting patterns, lobbies, and coalitions with other groups; or by posing an imminent public threat, as Blacks did during the civil disturbances of the 1960s and 1970s, and as victims of Acquired Immune Deficiency Syndrome (AIDS) do today.) Second, advocacy movements on behalf of particular age, income, occupation, or gender groups have usually focused on the needs of the majority within the group, even when the needs of its minority are vastly different.[3] Third, we have customarily focused legislative and societal attention on only a single group or issue at a time.[4] Finally, the relation between the absolute size and social position of a group seems to determine its importance as a "special group."[5]

These characteristic ways of focusing societal attention—coupled with the disproportionate growth of the elderly White population, which is better positioned socially—could have profound and deleterious effects on the Black family of tomorrow.[6]

*Reprinted with permission of *Daedalus*, Journal of American Academy of Arts and Sciences. *The Aging Society*, Vol. 115, No. 1, Winter 1986, Cambridge, Massachusetts.

Let us explore some possible solutions to these problems, as well as reasons why these solutions might not be forthcoming. Let us then speculate about how our failures today might affect the future economic, social, physical, and psychological welfare of the Black family.

The Changing Demography of Black Americans

The first obstacle confronting the Black family in the aging society lies in the absolute numbers of Blacks compared with that of Whites. The number of Blacks age sixty-five and over has been increasing faster than the number of Whites of those ages, but elderly Blacks comprise—and always will comprise—a smaller group in absolute numbers than comparable Whites. This Black-White comparison of absolute numbers holds true in all age groups. Based on sheer numbers, this means that, age for age, Whites may fare better when pitted against Blacks for benefits, services, and programs as our society ages.

If we look at the two groups in our population most in need of help, children and the elderly, we find that the young outnumber the old in the Black population, while the reverse is true for Whites, the number of White elderly (age sixty-five and over) is larger than that of White children under five years of age, and of White teenagers from fifteen to nineteen years of age (U.S. Dept. of Commerce, 1986).

According to Jacob Siegel and Maria Davidson's 1984 monograph for the Census Bureau, this difference in proportions at younger and older ages stems from the higher fertility of Black women, as well as from Blacks' higher mortality at mid-life. That the number of White children is decreasing while the number of White elderly is increasing means that there will continue to be a greater ratio of elderly to children among Whites. This will not be the case among Blacks. Although the number of Black elderly is increasing, the number of Black children is slowly decreasing, and there will continue to be a greater ratio of children to elderly among Blacks for some time to come. Theoretically, then, the burden of support for the elderly of both races could fall disproportionately on the shoulders of today's Black youth as they age. But as the Black underclass has a higher rate of reproduction than the Black middle class (as John Reid points out in his 1982 report), a majority of Black youth will be born poor and without the personal resources as adults to be the mainstays of growing numbers of dependent elderly in an aging society.

The ratio of dependent Blacks (under fifteen years of age and over sixty-four) to working-age Blacks (ages sixteen to sixty-four) will be greater than will be the case for Whites, and this will serve to heighten the Black burden of dependency. The situation will be exacerbated if the labor-force participation of middle-aged Blacks continues to decline.

Individuals aged seventy-five and older constitute a section of the Black population that is growing disproportionately. (There is, in fact, a racial mortality crossover effect at about that age, a subject to which we shall return.) The most rapidly growing group of the Black elderly are women who are eighty and over, and it is they who have the longest average remaining lifetime. In 1978, Black women at age eighty could expect 11.5 years more of life, in contrast to 8.8 for Black males, 8.8 for White females, and 6.7 for White males. These race-by-gender differences are not new; they were observable as early as 1900 (U.S. Department of Health & Human Services, 1987).

Certainly, the demographies of Blacks and Whites are changing, but, as we have noted, the small absolute numbers of Blacks in every age group may hinder them from gaining societal focus on their particular social problems—that is, unless we begin to recognize those problems in a larger context: as an urgent task our society can ignore only at its peril. The problems of Black children become especially important when we realize that, by virtue of their group size relative to White children, it is they who have the greater potential for bearing responsibility for the dependent in an aging society.

It is the problems of these Black children that we shall first consider.

Black Children at Risk in an Aging Society

Infants and Children

The major social problems confronting Black children today are poverty, inadequate health care, and poor quality of education—three conditions that are closely related. Nearly 50 percent of Black children live in poverty, which means that the Black child has a fifty-fifty chance of growing up underprivileged, undereducated, and unemployed. It is these very Black children who, as adults, will be expected to assume proportionately more responsibility for supporting the dependent Black and White elderly than their White counterparts. For this reason alone, today's Black children should be of particular concern to majority group members. Otherwise, society's indifference, or its simple lack of attentiveness, could produce Black family heads who are poor in money, in education, and in health—conditions that could seriously undermine not only the economic stability of the Black family of the future, but also their ability to support those of us who will look to them for assistance.

The percentage of poor Black children is even higher in households headed by a woman. What is more, large segments of the low-income Black population are not even being reached by most of the major govern-

391

ment income-transfer programs for the poor and jobless. According to a report by Robert Hill in 1981, among Black households with incomes under $6,000, only 51 percent received food stamps; 39 percent were covered by Medicaid, 33 percent lived in public housing; 25 percent received rent subsidies; 25 percent received free school lunches; and only 22 percent received Supplemental Security Income (SSI). Another reason for the continuing poverty of Black children is the roll-back since 1979 of such major anti-poverty programs as Aid to Families with Dependent Children (AFDC) and food stamps.

Marian Wright Edelman of the Children's Defense Fund notes that, when compared with White children, Black children are more likely to be in poor health, twice as likely to have no regular source of health care, more likely to be seriously ill when they finally see a doctor, five times as likely to have to rely on hospital emergency rooms or outpatient clinics and twice as likely to be born to mothers who have had no prenatal care. Thirteen percent of all Black children are born with low birth weights, a factor that is associated with poor prenatal care and makes them more vulnerable as a group to mortality, prematurity, and mental retardation.

In spite of these disturbing conditions, shrinking federal funding and restrictive eligibility requirements have limited the effectiveness of federal health-care programs. For example, 16 percent of Black children are not covered by either Medicaid or private insurance. The Early Periodic Screening, Diagnosis, and Treatment program (EPSDT), which makes preventive care available to low-income children, renders ineligible those children who fail to qualify for Medicaid. This means that about five million poor children living in two-parent families do not meet the requirements for EPSDT. The Child Health Assurance Plan repeatedly failed to pass Congress until 1984, when a mini-version that reflected budget cuts and further reductions was passed. And the Special Supplemental Food Program for Women, Infants, and Children (WIC), a program that provides baby formula, diet supplements, and checkups for poor pregnant and nursing women and small children, is underfunded and has a steadily growing waiting list.

The curtailment of programs that are of special benefit to the health of Black infants and children is at once a moral matter and a cost-benefit issue. A case in point is the WIC program, which has demonstrably reduced some of the negative effects of low birth weight. The moral issue is whether we have the right to eliminate health-care strategies that are known to have positive effects, and thus to determine which groups of children will have access to "the good life" and which will not. Alan Pifer (1986) has many times raised the question whether life-sustaining equipment and methods used to keep the very old infirm alive (sustenance that is perhaps desired by neither the patient nor the family) are justified in view of the great need for food supplements to pregnant underprivileged women.

Black children also receive poorer-quality educations than do White children. Evelyn Moore of the National Black Child Development Institute reports that Black children are more than twice as likely to have their educations delayed by two or more years; three times as likely to be assigned to classes for the "educable mentally retarded"; twice as likely to be suspended, expelled, or given corporal punishment; twice as likely to drop out of school; twice as likely to be behind grade level; and more likely to score below the mean on national standardized tests, but only half as likely to be labeled gifted. In 1981, John Ogbu of the University of California at Berkelely suggested that inferior education for Black children is a function of several subtle mechanisms: negative teacher attitudes and low expectations (teachers believe that Blacks are less intelligent than Whites); biased testing and classification; biased tracking or ability grouping; biased textbooks and inferior curricula; inadequate academic and career guidance; biased channeling into special education classes; the employment of less qualified teachers in Black schools; and cutbacks in federal aid to education and programs—such as Headstart— that were successful in preparing Black children for better academic performance.

The danger is that the curtailment of major anti-poverty, healthcare, and education programs that especially benefited Black children might be accelerated by the increasing needs and demands of the rapidly growing group of Whites age sixty-five and over for similar types of programs. Samuel Preston of the University of Pennsylvania points out that child-welfare programs (such as AFDC) have already been rolled back, while programs benefiting the elderly (such as Social Security) have been maintained or expanded. He suggests that this is happening because entitlements are negotiated from demographic strength, and the elderly are simply more numerous than children—and their numbers are increasing. Furthermore, he states that the White elderly do not vote on behalf of children's welfare, and that they most assuredly do not vote for "other children's" (i.e., minority children's) welfare.

The effect of this erosion of child-welfare programs and increasing competition from other groups is that Black children may not develop the resources of affluence, health, and education to live as independent adults. Moreover, as we have noted, the diminishing numbers of White children and the increasing numbers of White elderly make today's Black children the burden-bearers of tommorrow—those who, as adults, will theoretically have more of a burden than their White counterparts in supporting the dependent. It is somewhat ironic, then, that the anti-poverty insulation, the health care, and the quality of education that Black children receive is far inferior to that of their White counterparts, and that Black children of today, a group with great potential for contributing to an aging society, are themselves in jeopardy partly *because* of an aging society.

Teenagers

Teenage pregnancies and out-of-wedlock births are especially disturbing problems among Black teenage women. The rate of Black teenage (age fifteen through seventeen) childbearing in 1979 was more than three times the White rate: 77 per 1000, versus 25 per 1000. As John Reid reports, the proportion of births out-of-wedlock has increased from 90 percent to 93 percent for Black women age fifteen through seventeen and from 36 to 42 percent for a comparable group of White women. In spite of this situation, few inroads have been made into the problem of Black teenage pregnancy. If these trends continue, however, increasing numbers of young Black women will be raising children without fathers in the home. Niara Sudarkasa presents evidence that Black families headed by women can be highly functional, and the statement here must not be miscontrued to mean that Black families headed by women are, by definition, dysfunctional.[7] The issue is economic. Black families headed by women with no male present are making up larger and larger segments of the Black poor than are Black husband-wife families. According to Reynolds Farley of the University of Michigan, over one-half of Black female-headed families lived below the poverty level in 1982, in contrast to only 19 percent of Black husband-wife families.

Programs and services that provide continuing education, job training, and child care for these teenage unwed mothers could help lift them out of poverty. But as they are now constituted, child-care programs tend to benefit higher-income women more than those with lower incomes. Evelyn Moore suggests that child care for poor Black mothers is in fact a kind of "Catch-22" situation, in which rigid income cut-off levels for eligibility act as disincentives to full-time work, so that many Black families must remain poor if they are to obtain quality child care. (It is interesting to note that child care became a national concern only when White mothers began to join the labor force in numbers.) In an aging society, where larger and larger number of elderly Whites will demand continuing education, training for labor-force reentry, and their own day-care facilities, the needs of poor Black unwed mothers may well go unmet.

Teenage Black men have their own set of problems, including vulnerability to homicide, incarceration, and constantly high rates of unemployment. A Black male youth is five times as likely as a White male youth to be a victim of homicide (frequently as a result of police intervention) and twice as likely to be detained in a juvenile or adult correctional facility. A Black youth is three times as likely as a White youth to be unemployed. A Black student who graduates from high school has a greater chance of being unemployed than a White student who dropped out of elementary school. A Black college graduate is as likely to be unemployed as a White high-school dropout. James McGhee of the National Urban League has stated that the current estimate of 50 percent unemployment for Black youths is probably an underestimation: 70 percent is more likely. This might mean that an overwhelming majority of today's Black teenage men *will never work in any sustained or beneficial way in their lifetimes.* If that is an accurate assessment, they will arrive at adulthood and old age with even fewer skills and poorer lifetime work experiences than their parents and grandparents, for whom unemployment rates in youth were not nearly so high.

The increasing loss of Black men through death and incarceration in youth and as a result of the failure to find employment may portend the virtual disappearance of the Black male from the Black family and, as Charles Willie of Harvard University suggests, further dissolution of the Black family in the future.[8]

Homicide, incarceration, and unemployment, inextricably bound, dictate a hand-in-glove approach to preventive counseling and vocational training programs. Yet Black youth are underrepresented in counseling programs and overrepresented in training courses that are geared toward low-wage, low-upward-mobility, and low-demand jobs (less than 15 percent of electronics students are Black, for example, as against 65 percent of textile-production students). David Swinton of the Clark College Policy Center suggests that the solution to the unemployment problem of young Black males lies less with job training than with the creation of suitable jobs. Yet the needs of burgeoning numbers of older White workers—for counseling services, for the creation of new types of jobs and for new training programs to facilitate them—may deter the possibility of creating those new jobs and job-training programs that focus specifically on the needs of disadvantaged Black youth.

When viewed as a single phenomenon, the plights of the masses of Black infants, children, and teenagers today might mean that the Black family of the twenty-first century will be more economically disadvantaged than was its counterpart in the preceding century—a disturbing possibility indeed.[9]

Blacks at Midlife: Another Group at Risk

Middle-aged Blacks (aged forty-five to sixty-four) represent a segment of the Black family that is at risk in an aging society. The critical social problems of the masses of middle-aged Blacks today are divorce, separation, difficulties in psychological adjustment, low morale as workers, and declining physical abilities accompanied by decreases in labor-force participation. These fairly new social trends are creating the "unretired-retired," a new type of Black retiree (Gibson, 1987; Jackson and Gibson, 1986). If these work and retirement problems are characteristic of a life stage of Blacks, the Black middle-aged worker will be at an increasingly greater risk as the pool of older White workers grows in an aging society. Work and retirement may need reconceptualizing both for the benefit of these early retirees and for the economic welfare of their families.

Divorce and Separation

Divorce and separation are on the rise in Black America. By mid life, only 55 percent of Blacks are married and living with a spouse, in contrast to 79 percent of Whites—figures that are due in part, of course, to the greater mortality of Blacks than Whites at earlier ages. The rise in the divorce ratio has been more dramatic for Black than for White women (from 104 versus 56 in 1970, to 265 versus 128 in 1982). Findings from a study I completed in 1983 using the NSBA to compare the mental health of middle-aged and elderly Blacks, suggest that divorced and separated Black women are also among the least well-off of Blacks at mid life on several measures of stress, distress, and morale. One of the reasons for these psychological states may be economic. Paul Glick, former senior demographer with the Census Bureau, pointed out that in 1979 only 29 percent of Black women who had sole custody of young children were awarded child support payments (as compared with 59 percent for their counterparts in all other races); fewer Black women than women of other races who were awarded child support payments actually received them (5/8 versus 3/4); and very few divorced Black women were awarded alimony. Disrupted marriage thus takes a disproportionate economic and psychological toll on Black American women at mid-life.

Mental Health Status

Middle age may be the most tumultuous time of life for Blacks, partly because the tasks of middle age are particularly difficult for Blacks today.[10] Current thought assumes that good feelings accrue about oneself as one accomplishes the major tasks of mid life, some of which are assessing one's accomplishments, pinpointing one's position in society relative to others, and feeling mastery for the first time over one's own life and social environment. Blacks may fare less well than Whites in these self-appraisals. Measuring one's accomplishments might be particularly difficult when racial discrimination in the marketplace has put a lid on the achievements of those Blacks who are now at middle age. These may be the single group of Blacks today for whom accomplishments fall shortest of aspirations. Younger middle-class Blacks may be better able to bridge the gap between aspirations and accomplishments because of their greater opportunities, and elderly Blacks may have a smaller gap because their aspirations have already been lowered by the time they reach old age. To aspire and not to reach, a quality that is thus more characteristic of middle-aged Blacks than others, may be particularly stressful.

With respect to assessing one's position in society, while Whites at mid life are at the pinnacle of their careers and incomes, today's mid life Blacks are in straitened circumstances. They are keenly aware of their lower socioeconomic positions relative to younger (age thirty to forty-four) middle-class Blacks—those beneficiaries of the social changes of the 1970s—and relative to middle-aged Whites as well. For middle-aged Whites, the reverse is true; they are higher in socioeconomic position than either younger Whites or their Black age-mates. Middle-aged Blacks, then, find themselves in the least advantaged position, whether they compare themselves to middle-aged Whites or young Black adults.

Feelings of mastery over one's social environment are theoretically at their peak in mid life, but this model may also be inappropriate for middle-aged Blacks. Career development was not possible in the jobs today's middle-aged Blacks held when they were young, and there were few opportunities available to develop skills that would be marketable in a high-tech society. Occupying low-level jobs, they are also unable to manipulate their work environments to accommodate their declining physical abilities; they have few economic cushions of savings or investments on which to fall back. Hence, the work environment becomes more hostile and difficult, rather than easier to negotiate, and feelings of competence and mastery are unlikely to be at their high point.

Findings from several of my studies support the idea that feelings of personal efficacy are highest for older Whites while in the labor force but highest for older Blacks when they leave it. In our 1986 study of the work and retirement experiences of Blacks age fifty-five and over, Professor James Jackson of the University of Michigan's Institute for Social Research and I found that feelings of control over one's own life were higher among those Blacks who had left the labor force than among those who were still workers. Similarly, in my 1982 study of older Black and White women from *The Panel Study of Income Dynamics*,[11] I found that feelings of control decreased as the White women retired but increased as the Black women retired. These opposite feelings of personal efficacy were related to the contrasting realities of the jobs the women left—fulfilling White-collar jobs on the one hand, and restrictive household jobs on the other.

The mental-health status of Blacks at mid life is poorer than that of Blacks at late life. My 1983 mental-health study, noted earlier, revealed this to be true by several measures of stress, distress, and morale. Blacks at mid life, for example, were more likely than Blacks at late life to have serious personal problems (stress); to have interpersonal problems (with spouses, children, marriage, and divorce); and to experience extreme feelings of nervous breakdown (distress). Stress proved to be more intricately tied to physical health among the middle-aged than among the elderly.

Attaching physical complaints to emotional problems peaks among Blacks at mid life. And, perhaps not coincidentally, the death rate from stress-related diseases is also greatest during this time of life among Blacks. The middle-aged were not only more stressed and distressed than the elderly, but also less well-off with respect to morale—they were not as satisfied with their lives, and they were less likely to be happy.

The Black middle-aged who were the most likely to be stressed and distressed were women, members of the underclass, the divorced, and the separated. With respect to stress, distress, and morale, mid-life Black women appear to be at higher psychological risk than mid-life Black men.

The Black underclass is also at serious risk in mid life. As income and education decrease, stress and distress increase.

The most disadvantaged in that regard were those with incomes of less than $5,000 a year and those with less than an eleventh-grade education. The divorced and separated were the most likely of the marital groups to be seriously stressed and distressed.

Although the Black underclass is more likely to be stressed and distressed, the Black middle-class is more likely to have low morale. At particular risk in regard to morale—life dissatisfaction and unhappiness—were women who could be considered well-off: those with incomes over $20,000, those who are college graduates, those in professional occupations, and those living in the suburbs. We might speculate that their low morale is due to the fact that they have set high goals for themselves and are experiencing wide gaps between these goals and their accomplishments. They may also be measuring themselves against the younger Black women, aged thirty to forty-four, who made the quantum leaps in education, occupation, and income in the decade between 1970 and 1980.

Clearly, Blacks at mid life have special problems of stress and distress and those middle-aged with limited economic and social resources are the most likely to be confronted with them. Since it is the more affluent, on the other hand, who are more likely to have problems of morale, family counseling services and programs carefully designed to address the different mental health needs of under- and middle-class Blacks at mid life will be needed in the coming decades. But increasing numbers of the White elderly will also need family counseling services, as will the growing numbers of White families that consist of several generations living together.

Competition for mental-health resources and mental-health dollars during the next decades may not only involve the White elderly versus teenage Blacks versus middle-aged Blacks, but might also pit groups within the Black middle-aged community against each other. This sort of competition could be minimized if counseling services were designed to address the problems of Blacks comprehensively—across the life cycle and as family units.

Reconceptualizing Work and Retirement

Nearly 40 percent of nonworking Blacks age fifty-five and over can be categorized as the "unretired-retired," individuals who appear and behave as if they were retired, but do not call themselves such. My 1987 study of the retirement definitions of older Blacks identified this group as the most needy of the Black middle-aged. Because they do not meet the traditional retirement criteria—of chronological age, a clear line between work and nonwork, income from retirement sources, and their own realization that they are retired—this very needy group finds itself screened out of major retirement research and deprived of the retirement-benefit planning and policy that stem from that research.

Who are these "unretired-retired"? They are older Black workers, many in early mid life, who are making a gradual exodus out of the labor force mainly for reasons of physical disability. Among the middle-aged, disability in most categories increased more for Blacks than for Whites over the past twelve years, while over the past twenty-six years, decreases in labor-force participation were more dramatic for Black men and increases in the labor force more dramatic for White women (Gibson, 1986b; U.S. Department of Labor, 1982). The disturbing possibility is that, beginning at about age fifty-five—barring radical social intervention such as equalizing employment opportunities and creating jobs that would accommodate their declining physical abilities—a large group of older Blacks will never work again in any systematic way; their work lives will effectively be over. In order to assure that they receive some type of benefits, "retirement" age may need to be moved back for older Blacks in the aging society—and eventually for other groups as well.[12]

One of the most interesting findings of the study James Jackson and I conducted was that, for many Blacks, the retirement years are often the happiest and most secure of their lives. This finding is in direct contrast to the results of several empirical studies of work and retirement that indicate that the elderly would benefit from remaining in the work force, and would in fact prefer to do so rather than to retire at the traditional cut-off point of age sixty-five. In his study of the retirement of Black and White men, for example, Herbert Parnes found that the morale of White retirees was lower than that of older White workers even after controlling for income, age, and health. The NSBA data, in contrast, reveal that the reverse is true for older Blacks: retirees have higher morale than workers. There are at least two possible reasons for this. First, the combination of declining physical abilities of older Blacks, coupled with their restriction to strenuous and distasteful jobs at the bottom of the job hierarchy that do not accommodate their infirmities, makes work as it is now structured more punishing. Second, many Blacks in retirement can look forward for the first time in their lives to the reliability of a monthly check coming in from Social Security plus SSI benefits. The truth is that for a majority of older Blacks it is not work, but retirement, that promotes adjustment.

If current trends in disability and early labor-force withdrawal continue, there is a distinct possibility that, by the middle of the twenty-first century Blacks will "cease" working and begin "retirement" *before* mid life. This will pose problems on the policy level: should we call this group "retired," in spite of the fact that they do not meet the traditional criteria, so that we can provide them with some type of special benefits when their work lives are over? The problem intensifies when we realize that growing numbers of White retirees who will be living longer will also need income supplements. We need to investigate new ways of supporting burgeoning numbers of Black and White nonworkers.

It is also possible that the lines between work and nonwork will become even more blurred as older Blacks work more sporadically as a result of competition with growing numbers of older Whites for the scarce jobs that accommodate the declining physical capacities of older workers. Because disability pay is a mainstay of these middle-aged Blacks who are leaving the labor force, the disability role may replace the retirement role. The result would be an increase in importance of disability-pay legislation over Social Security legislation for the economic welfare of Blacks—especially when the proposed age of eligibility changes, as is now planned under Social Security. At this time, there will be an even longer wait between the end of work lives and the beginning of benefits, and growing numbers of Black males simply will not live long enough to collect their benefits. Given the shorter life spans of Blacks, this raises an even more fundamental issue—are age-based policies in general inappropriate for the masses of Blacks in an aging society?

All of these work and retirement factors mean that, because the Black family may be top-heavy with nonworking dependents, its welfare may be seriously threatened as we approach the twenty-first century. Certainly, middle-aged Blacks face a number of serious challenges and adjustments at this time of their lives. Middle age, then, may be likened to a proving ground, a battle from which only the victorious emerge—those who are physically and psychologically fit and get to play out old age. For Blacks who survive these crises, old age may actually be a less stressful time than mid life. It should not be surprising, therefore, that Blacks age seventy-five and over are regarded as psychological as well as physical survivors.

The Black Elderly in an Aging Society

Attempts to solve the major problems of today's elderly may encounter roadblocks in the form of the needs of increasing numbers of their

White counterparts, who are living longer but in poorer health. If inadequate health care and insufficient economic support for the Black elderly continue, the burden of caring for them may fall squarely on the shoulders of younger Blacks, the masses of whom may be ill-equipped, as we have already pointed out, to bear the responsibility. A balancing factor, however, might be the notable psychological assets of these very old Blacks.

The racial mortality crossover might be a case in point. The crossover refers to the fact that, up to about age eighty, Whites can expect to live longer than Blacks, but after that age, Blacks can expect to live longer than Whites. There are several speculations as to why this is so. First, Blacks at advanced ages may be a more biologically select group—those who survived inadequate medical care earlier in life. It is also possible that aging is retarded in some ways among Blacks at advanced ages—a possibility that might be attributed to race differences in aging at the cellular level. A third possibility is that Blacks are especially insulated in some way at more advanced ages against the leading killer diseases—heart disease, cancer, stroke, and generalized arteriosclerosis. It is also possible that social factors might account for differences in the mortality of older Blacks and Whites. This idea is buttressed by certain parallels we see between the lives of older Blacks in our society and the lives of the very old in other countries—Equador, Russia, and Turkey. Some of these similarities lie in environment, diet, the kind of sustained physical labor that continues over a lifetime and lasts well into old age, and role constancy—a certain maintenance of positions of esteem within the family and social circle as age progresses.

Certain psychological factors may also serve to decrease the vulnerability of older Blacks to disease and thus to mortality. These might include more positive attitudes toward life, effective ways of handling stress, and the use of special help-seeking patterns in times of great need (Gibson, 1982; Gibson and Jackson, 1988; Chatters, Taylor and Jackson, 1985). A good deal of recent research, including that of Stanislav Kasl and Lisa Berkman in 1981, suggests that each of these sets of social and psychological factors does indeed buffer the onset of certain diseases. In short, some particular insights might be gained into the racial mortality crossover by examining the biomedical, social, and psychological data of elderly Blacks.

Even though these Black survivors lack the attributes of financial security, adequate education, and marital company (more Black then White elderly live without spouses), they seem to sustain themselves psychologically as they age. Certainly, in terms of one gross measure of adjustment—suicide—older Blacks fare well. In my analysis of data from the National Center for Health Statistics, I found that suicide rates among the elderly, ranking from lowest to highest, are ordered as follows: Black females, Black males, White females, and White males. Older Black women are the most likely to be poor and the least likely to end their own lives; older White men are the least likely to suffer poverty and the most apt to die by their own hands. There is also an apparent correlation between suicide and prayer as a coping response to worry: elderly Black women are least likely to commit suicide and most likely to use prayer as a coping resource, while elderly White men are most inclined toward suicide and least inclined toward prayer. Black men and White women fall between these extremes. I suspect that it is the communal as well as the intrinsic aspects of prayer that are helpful to older Blacks; "getting together to get things done." And as Emile Durkheim has suggested, greater bonding to social groups increases social integration and thus psychological well-being.

A recurring theme in several of my research studies is that not all aspects of old age have negative connotations for Blacks. Elderly Whites have somewhat higher morale than elderly Blacks in most of the major national studies, but if we consider the great disparities between the races in functional health, income, education, and marital harmony, the gap in morale is not commensurate with the gap in resources. Is something putting a floor under the morale of elderly Blacks? Is it merely a matter of long practice, of long experience in meeting adversity? Or have they found particular resources and strategies that sustain them? My 1982 analysis of national data collect in 1957 and again in 1976 suggests that some of the effective mechanisms of Blacks may lie, not only in the role religion plays in their lives, but in their use of special patterns of help-seeking as they adapt to old age. In terms of using informal support networks in times of distress, older Black Americans drew from a more varied pool of informal helpers than did their White counterparts, both in middle and late life, and were more versatile in interchanging these helpers one for another as they approached old age. Whites, in contrast, were more likely to limit help-seeking to their spouses in middle life, and when their spouses were no longer available for this support, to confine their attempts to replace it by calling only on single family members as they approached old age.

In spite of their economic and physical handicaps, the Black elderly—the psychological survivors—may turn out to be part of the salvation of the Black family of the future. The unusual strengths of very old Black women (who are perhaps, not so coincidentally, experiencing the most rapid growth of all 80+ groups, considered by sex and race) are well-known. Elderly Black women have been a wellspring of support and nurturance over time, as Maya Angelou so eloquently asserted in her forward to Emily Wilson and Susan Mullally's 1983 book, *Hope and Dignity*:

> They have overcome the cruel roles into which they had been cast by racism and ignorance. They have wept over their hopeless fate and defined destiny by creating hope anew. They have nursed by force a

nation of hostile strangers, and wrung from lifetimes of mean servitude and third class citizenship a dignity of indescribable elegance.

It is interesting that recent findings of empirical studies are beginning to substantiate these very words and thoughts. The rapid growth of this group, coupled with the growing tendency of Black families to be without men, may mean that a modal Black family of the future (there could be other modes as well) will be composed of several generations of women. Publicly funded programs and services could encourage these roles of older Black women as surrogate parents in families without fathers present. This would not be an unfamiliar role, for historically many have taken responsibility for raising the children of others—their own grandchildren, the children of other family members and friends, and the children of their White employers.

In summary, the renowned strengths of the Black family will be put to a severe test as our society ages, and as larger and more powerful groups compete for limited resources. No age group of Black Americans will be insulated against this effect: Black infants, children, teenagers, the middle-aged, and the elderly each has particular economic, social, physical and/or psychological vulnerabilities—problems that if not attended to may have profound and deleterious effects on the welfare and structure of the Black family, and, in turn, on Black adult development and aging. Yet, there are enormous strengths within the Black family's own ranks, and while the concerns are grave, the hopes are also great as we approach the twenty-first century.

It goes without saying, of course, that policies and programs that ameliorate the poverty of, improve the health care of, and create equal opportunities for Black Americans of all ages will help the most to solve the problems of the Black family in an aging society. The absence of sound knowledge about the effects of an aging society on the welfare of Blacks in the future makes it premature to recommend specific policy or program changes that might buffer these effects. Systematic diagnosis and examination is needed; without them, policies and programs are bound to fall short and go awry. What is required is a programmatic approach that will allow researchers and policy-makers from diverse disciplines and areas of interest to work together to identify and offer solutions to the problems. A monitoring of changes in the demographies of Black and White Americans is basic, and the following specific areas are in need of particular scrutiny: (1) the Black infant, (2) the Black child, (3) the Black teenager, (4) the Black middle-aged, and (5) the Black elderly.

As I conceive it, this project would emerge in three stages over several years. The major objective of the first stage would be to verify scientifically some of the suppositions scholars are making about the critical problems that face each of these Black age groups, and their eventual effects on the Black family. The goal of the second stage would be to integrate the disparate findings of each part of the project, using the best scientific methods available. Stage three would pose a set of policy recommendations based on the findings of stage two.

Those of us who are vitally interested in the future of the Black family, Black adult development, and Black aging can only urge that such studies will be undertaken, and that helpful policies will be formulated as a result. Without this kind of intensive study and informed intervention, the problems of the Black family can only worsen in the aging society.

Notes

1. The *National Survey of Black Americans* is the first national probability sample of the adult Black population that is truly representative of Blacks in the continental United States. See James S. Jackson and Gerald Gurin, *National Survey of Black Americans* (Ann Arbor, MI: Institute for Social Research, University of Michigan, 1979).

2. Samuel Preston suggests that the power of special-interest groups to influence public decisions is a function of the size of the group, the wealth of the group, and the degree to which that size and wealth can be mobilized for concerted action. See Samuel Preston, "Children and the Elderly: Divergent Paths for America's Dependents," presidential address to the Population Association of America, Minneapolis, MN, May 1984.

3. The Displaced Homemaker's Program is a case in point. The program was designed to address the work and training needs of mid-life women, but it failed to address the particular problems of Black women at mid life because it was targeted at housewives who had never worked. Black women have historically been workers.

4. John Naisbitt, monitoring social change by using content analysis of newspapers over the years, documents the fact that our closed social system handles only a limited number of concerns at a time. He cites examples of issues of racism being replaced by issues of sexism, and sexism by ageism. Congress acted at the crest of each movement. See John Naisbitt, *Megatrends* (New York: Warner Books, 1982), pp. xxiv-xxvii.

5. Preston, op. cit., commenting on the problems of the elderly, suggests that higher-positioned, larger groups tend to elicit focus on their problems. This means that Blacks of all ages, being less numerous and lower-positioned socially, might have difficulty gaining attention as a "problem group" (barring the group's potential as a public threat).

6. This is not to say that the Black family is dysfunctional, for its strengths are well known. See, for example, Robert B. Hill, *The Strengths of Black Families* (New York: Emerson Hall, 1972).
7. See Niara Sudarkasa, in Rose C. Gibson, Ed., *Blacks in an Aging Society: Proceedings of the Carnegie Corporation Conference*, held at Ann Arbor, MI, Oct. 16, 1984.
8. There is serious debate among scholars of the Black family as to whether "dissolution" should be used in describing conditions in Black families. While there is agreement that the Black family is not a pathological form of the American family, but rather takes on a variety of functional forms that might be different from the "norm," there is disagreement as to whether "dissolution" can take on strictly economic meaning. Willie attaches an economic meaning based on the fact that certain types of Black families—families headed by women—are overrepresented among the Black poor. See C. Willie in Rose C. Gibson, Ed., op. cit.
9. The civil rights movement, although it worked to secure voting and other civil rights, did not fully address the economic conditions of Blacks in America. It is the opinion of some that middle-class Blacks benefitted more than other Blacks, and that poverty among the masses remains unattenuated, creating a small Black elite and a massive Black underclass. See, for example, William J. Wilson, *The Declining Significance of Race* (Chicago: University of Chicago Press, 1978).
10. For a discussion of several tasks at mid life, see Bernice Neugarten, "The Awareness of Middle Age," in Bernice Neugarten, Ed., *Middle Age and Aging* (Chicago: University of Chicago Press, 1968).
11. The *Panel Study of Income Dynamics* is a major national ongoing economic study in its fifteenth year of data collection. See James N. Morgan, *Panel Study of Income Dynamics* (Ann Arbor, MI: Institute for Social Research, University of Michigan, 1968).
12. This phenomenon of an increasing group of subjectively unretired Blacks could be an omen for other groups of older Americans. Certainly this seems possible if we take as precedent the occurences of negative social phenomena that appeared first in the Black community and were then manifested in White America: two good examples of this are drug abuse and the high incidence of out-of-wedlock births. If we perceive these as a pattern, then we might speculate that the observed changes in work and retirement patterns among Blacks are a kind of forewarning to the society at large.
13. Data collected originally by Gerald Gurin, Joseph Veroff, and Sheila Feld in *Americans View Their Mental Health* (Ann Arbor, MI: Institute for Social Research, University of Michigan, 1957, 1976).

References

Chatters, L. M., Taylor, R. J., & Jackson, J. S., (1985). Size and composition of the informal helper networks of elderly Blacks. *Journal of Gerontology, 40*(2), 605-614.

Gibson, R. C. (1982). Blacks at middle and late life: Resources and coping in F. Berardo (Ed.), *The Annals of The American Academy of Political and Social Science. 464,* 79-90. Sage Publications: California.

Gibson, R. C. (1986). Blacks in an aging society. *Daedalus 115.*

Gibson, R. C. (1986). Perspectives on the Black family. In A. Pifer and D.L. Bronte (Eds.), *Our aging society: Paradox and promise.* W.W. Norton Publishers.

Gibson, R. C. (1986). *Blacks in an aging society.* The Carnegie Corporation: New York.

Gibson, R. C. (1987). Reconceptualizing retirement for Black Americans. *The Gerontologist.*

Gibson, R. C. (1987). Defining retirement for Black Americans. In D. E. Gelfand, & C. Barresi (Eds.). *Ethnicity and aging.* Springer Publications.

Gibson, R. C. & Jackson, J. S. (1988). Health, physical functioning, and informal support among the Black elderly. *The Milbank Memorial Fund Quarterly 65,* Supplement 2.

Jackson, J. & Gibson, R. C. (1986). Work and retirement among the Black elderly. In Zena Blau (Ed.), *Current perspectives on aging and the life cycle.* V. 1, pp. 193-222. JAI Press Inc.

Pifer, A. & Bronte, L. (Eds.) (1986). *Our aging society: Paradox and promise.* New York: W.W. Norton.

U.S. Department of Commerce, Bureau of the Census. (N.D). *Projections of the Population of the United States, by Age, Sex, and Race: 1983 to 2080,* Series P-25, No. 952, pp. 38, 105-6. Washington, D. C.: Author.

U.S. Department of Labor, Bureau of Labor Statistics, Labor Force Statistics. (1982). *Current Population Survey: A Databook.* Vol. 1. Bulletin 2096—Tables A-3 and A-4. Washington, D.C.: Author.

U.S. Department of Health and Human Services, Public Health Service. (1987). *Health United States.* Washington, D.C.: Author.

Biographical Sketches and Indexes

Biographical Sketches

NORMAN B. ANDERSON is an Assistant Professor, Department of Psychiatry, Duke University Medical Center, a Research Psychologist at the Durham Veterans Administration Medical Center GRECC, and a Senior Fellow of the Duke Center for the Study of Aging and Human Development. He received his doctorate in clinical psychology at the University of North Carolina, Greenboro in 1983. He has received a number of prestigious honors and awards for his research, including a Rockefeller Foundation Research Fellowship, and New Investigator Awards from both the Society of Behavioral Medicine and the National Institutes of Health. Dr. Anderson is an active scholar with numerous publications on cardiovascular reactivity and hypertension in Blacks. This research is currently being funded by the John D. and Catherine T. MacArthur Foundation.

PHILLIP J. BOWMAN is currently on leave from the University of Illinois, Urbana-Champaign where he is an Assistant Professor in both Psychology and Afro-American Studies. While on leave, he is a Senior Research Fellow at the University of Michigan with funding from the Ford Foundation Post-doctoral Fellowship Program. He received the Ph.D. in Social Psychology from the University of Michigan, where he worked for several years as a Research Scientist with the Institute for Social Research. At the Institute, he was a Study Director on three National Studies of Black Americans which focused on mental health issues, general family dynamics, and the school to work transition.

Dr. Bowman has numerous articles, book chapters, reviews and technical reports on topics such as race-related socialization, motivation and academic performance, joblessness and discouragement among Black Americans, post-industrial displacement and family role strains, and the nature of Black psychology. He is a frequent reviewer for scholarly journals, a research consultant, and is especially interested in linking theory and research to public policy issues.

BENJAMIN BOWSER is from New York's Harlem and received his Ph.D. in Sociology from Cornell University (1976). Since 1975 he has served in a variety of administrative and research roles at Cornell University, The Western Interstate Commission for Higher Education, Santa Clara University and Stanford University. He is currently on the faculty at California State University at Hayward in Sociology, is Associate Editor of

409

Sage Race Relations Abstracts (U.K.) and co-editor of *Impacts of Racism on White Americans* (1981) and *Census Data for Small Areas of New York City* (1981). He is presently doing ethnographic research in San Francisco and completing a longitudinal study of the decline of Harlem.

LINDA M. CHATTERS, Ph.D. is an Assistant Professor in the School of Public Health and a Faculty Associate at the Institute for Social Research, The University of Michigan. Her research interests include subjective well-being and quality of life evaluations, family support networks, the use of religion as a coping resource, and survey research methodology. Her research appears in *Psychology and Aging, Journal of Gerontology, The Gerontologist, Social Work,* and *The Journal of Black Studies.* Dr. Chatters' research is supported by a First Independent Research Support and Transition (First) Award (R29 AGO7179) from the National Institute on Aging.

RUPPERT A. DOWNING, is an Associate Professor and Director of Field Instruction, University of Illinois School of Social Work at Urbana-Champaign. He completed undergraduate (B.A.) and graduate studies (MSW) at Purdue University and the University of Illinois, respectively.

He has rendered services to public and professional organizations at the local, state, and national levels including the Family Service Association of America, the Council on Social Work Education, the National Committee on Part-time Social Work Education, and the Childrens Home and Aid Society of Illinois.

As a social work practitioner, Mr. Downing has worked in the areas of Community Mental Health, Health, Child Welfare, Correctional Services, and Family Life Education. His scholarly work includes publications in professional journals, chapters in social work textbooks; and research on Black self-help groups, oral history, and Black elderly utilization of social services. Mr. Downing was recently appointed to membership on the Council on Social Work Education's International Social Welfare Education Committee.

ROSE GIBSON received her Ph.D. from the University of Michigan and is a former National Institute of Aging Postdoctoral Fellow in Statistics, Survey Research Design and Methodology on Minority Populations. She is a Faculty Associate at the Institute for Social Research and an Associate Professor in the School of Social Work at the University of Michigan. Dr. Gibson has participated in several pioneering national surveys, is the author of *Blacks in An Aging Society,* and has published widely in such journals as *The Milbank Quarterly, Daedalus, The Annals of The*

American Academy of Political and Social Science, and *The Gerontologist.* She is a member of the National Institute of Mental Health Initial Scientific Review Group on Life Course, Prevention, and Aging. She is on the editorial boards of the *Journal of Aging and Health, Journal of Aging and Social Policy, The Gerontologist, The Journal of Minority Aging;* Consulting Editor for *Social Work;* and reviewer for such journals as *The Milbank Quarterly* and *The Journal of Gerontology.* Her major research interest is in sociocultural factors in aging.

WINSTON E. GOODEN is Associate Professor of Psychology at Fuller Theological Seminary, Graduate School of Psychology where he teaches, provides clinical supervision and does psychotherapy. He received his doctorate in Clinical Psychology from Yale University. He is doing research on psychological development in adulthood with a particular focus on mid-life. An ordained minister, Dr. Gooden provides consultation, workshops and conferences to Black Churches in the greater Los Angeles area.

ALGEA OTHELLA HARRISON is Professor of Psychology at Oakland University in Rochester, Michigan. She received her B.S. from Bluefield State College in Bluefield, West Virginia, and the M.A. and Ph.D. (1970) from the University of Michigan. Professor Harrison has been a Visiting Professor of Psychology at the University of the Virgin Islands and the University of California, Los Angeles. Her scholarly activities in developmental psychology have focused on cognitive and psychosocial development among Black children, while her scholarly activities in Women's Studies have investigated interrole conflicts among Black women. She has made numerous presentations at national conventions, written several book chapters, and published articles in various professional journals, including *Child Development* and *Psychology of Women Quarterly.* She is well known for her efforts as a member of planning committees for the national meetings on Empirical Research in Black Psychology and the Society for Research in Child Development. Professor Harrison has been a reviewer for research proposals and professional journals, including a membership on the Editorial Board of Child Development from 1983-86.

JAMES S. JACKSON was named Associate Dean of the University of Michigan's Rackham School of Graduate Studies in 1987. He has been at the University of Michigan since 1971 and is currently a Professor of Psychology, Research Scientist at the Institute for Social Research, and Faculty Associate at the Center for Afro-American and African Studies, and the Gerontology Institute. In 1986-87 he was a National Research Council/Ford Foundation Senior Postdoctoral Fellow at the Groupe D'Etudes en Sciences Sociale, Paris, France. Dr. Jackson received his undergraduate degree in psychology from Michigan State University, his M.A. degree in psychology from the University of Toledo in 1970 and his Ph.D. in Social Psychology from Wayne State University in 1972. Since 1977 he has been the Director of the Program for Research on Black Americans in the Research Center for Group Dynamics, Institute for Social Research. He is currently a member of several scientific review panels including the National Academy of Sciences Committee on the Status of Black Americans: 1940-1980, a National Cancer Institute Scientific Panel on Black/White cancer survival differences, an European Economic Community Study on Immigration and Racism; and he chairs the Gerontological Society Task Force on Racial Minority Group Aging. He is a past chair of the NIH Human Development II Review Panel and former member of the National Academy of Sciences Committee on Aging. He is married and has two daughters.

MAURICE JACKSON, Ph.D., deceased, was a Professor of Sociology at the University of California, Riverside.

ARTHUR JONES is a clinical psychologist currently engaged in full-time independent practice in Denver, Colorado. Before entering private practice, Dr. Jones taught clinical psychology at Sangamon State University (Springfield, Illinois), Bowling Green (Ohio) State University and the University of Colorado School of Medicine. Dr. Jones has had a long-standing interest in African American psychology, reflected in his teaching, publications, and ongoing clinical work. For the past few years he has been immersed in the study and practice of Jungian psychology, and has begun to play a role in forging a synthesis between the concepts of Jungian psychology and the emerging body of literature and clinical practice in African and African-American psychology. He views the spiritual emphasis of both these theoretical traditions as particularly pertinent to clinical work with African Americans and to African-American life generally.

REGINALD L. JONES is Professor, Department of Afro-American Studies, and Adjunct Professor, Graduate School of Education, University of California at Berkeley. He received the A.B. cum laude in Psychology from Morehouse College, the M.A. in Clinical Psychology from Wayne State University, and the Ph.D. in Psychology from The Ohio State University. He has been a clinical psychologist in military and state hospitals;

Professor and Vice-Chair, Department of Psychology, the Ohio State University; Professor and Chair, Department of Education, University of California, Riverside; and Professor and Director, University Testing Center, Haile Sellassie I University, Addis Ababa, Ethiopia. He has also taught at UCLA and at Miami, Fisk, and Indiana Universities. In 1971-72 he was National Chair of the Association of Black Psychologists.

Dr. Jones has produced 28 instructional videotapes in Black Psychology, written more than 200 articles, chapters, reviews and technical reports, and edited more than a dozen books, including *Black Psychology* (third edition, in press), *Sourcebooks on the Teaching of Black Psychology*, and *Black Adolescents*. From 1979-1983 he was editor of *Mental Retardation*, an official journal of the American Association on Mental Retardation.

Professor Jones' special honors include the Citation for Distinguished Achievement from The Ohio State University; the J. E. Wallace Wallin Award from the Council for Exceptional Children; the Distinguished Faculty Award, Black Alumni Council, University of California Alumni Association; the Education Award of the American Association on Mental Retardation; the Loetta Hunt Award from Ohio State; and on two occasions, the Scholarship Award of the Association of Black Psychologists.

SYED MALIK AL-KHATIB (aka Cedric X Clark) is currently Associate Professor of Communications at Marist College in Poughkeepsie, New York. A former Chairman of the Black Studies Department at San Francisco State University and The State University of New York at New Paltz, Dr. Khatib has taught at Stanford University, University of San Francisco and Princeton University. Among Dr. Khatib's scholarly achievements is membership on the editorial board of *The Journal of Black Psychology*, past editor of *The Journal of Social Issues* and listings in *Who's Who in the West* and *Who's Who Among Black Americans*.

Prior to his teaching career Dr. Khatib has served as a Peace Corps Volunteer to Nigeria. He has traveled widely in Europe, Africa, India, and the Middle East.

Dr. Khatib's publications include: *Black Studies or the Study of Black People, The Shockley-Jensen Thesis: A Contextual Appraisal, Critical Elements of Black Mental Health, Voodoo or IQ: An Introduction to African Psychology, Television and Social Controls* and *The Concept of Legitimacy in Black Psychology*. His publications have appeared in: *Playboy, Ebony, Scientia, Black World, Television Quarterly*, and *The Journal of Black Psychology*, among others.

Dr. Khatib received his Ph.D. in Communication from Michigan State University and held a post-Doctoral Fellowship at the Annenberg School of Communications at the University of Pennsylvania. His most recent publication is entitled *The Reduction of Cognitive Conflict Through the*

413

Spatial Displacement of Discrepant Attitudinal Objects, published in *The Journal of Intergroup Relations* (Vol. *XV*, No. 4, 1988).

CAROLYN BENNETT MURRAY is an Associate Professor in the Psychology Department and Ethnic Studies Program at the University of California, Riverside. She received her doctorate in Social Psychology from the University of Michigan, where she has returned on two separate occasions as a post-doctoral fellow. She has also been a post-doctoral fellow in Aging, Mental Health and Culture at the Institute on Aging, Portland State University, and during the 1985-86 academic year was a post-doctoral Ford Fellow in the Psychology Department at the University of California, Los Angeles. Her research and published work spans two areas: (1) attribution and affective consequences of negative stereotypic expectations for academic achievement, and (2) social support among the minority elderly

HECTOR F. MYERS, Ph.D. is an Associate Professor of Psychology and Co-Director of the Minority Mental Health Training Program in the Department of Psychology at UCLA; and Director of the Biobehavioral Laboratory at the Charles R. Drew University of Medicine and Science. Dr. Myers is an active researcher with numerous research articles and book chapters on stress and the mental and physical health of Black adults and families to his credit. His most recent research has been on the role of psychosocial stress in the development of essential hypertension in Blacks, and he is a frequent consultant to federal agencies in the development and evaluation of research initiatives on the health status and well-being of Black Americans. Dr. Myers is currently involved in a collaborative effort to develop and test a culturally-adapted, behavioral skill based parent training program as a primary prevention tool for Black families.

THOMAS A. PARHAM, Ph.D., is Director of the Career Planning and Placement Center, and adjunct faculty member at the University of California in Irvine.

Dr. Parham grew up in Southern California, and received his Bachelor's degree in Social Ecology from the University of California, Irvine. He completed his Master's degree in Counseling Psychology at Washington University in St. Louis, and received his Ph.D. in Counseling Psychology at Southern Illinois University at Carbondale.

Dr. Parham is an active member of the Association of Black Psychologists, and also has affiliations with the American Psychological Association, and the American Association for Counseling and Development. He also serves on the editorial board of the *Journal of Multi-Cultural Counseling and Development*.

For the past nine years, Dr. Parham has focused his research efforts in the area of Psychological Nigrescence, and has authored several articles in the area. While research in the area of racial identity development remains his primary focus, his current efforts are devoted to co-authoring a book entitled, *The Psychology of Blacks*.

HOWARD P. RAMSEUR is a psychologist with the Psychiatry Service of the Medical Department at the Massachusetts Institute of Technology and is in private practice in Cambridge, Massachusetts. He received his doctorate in Personality and Developmental Psychology from Harvard University; was a pre-doctoral Fellow in Psychology (Psychiatry) at Massachusetts General Hospital, and a post-doctoral Fellow at the Psychiatry Service of M.I.T.'s Medical Department. Dr. Ramseur was Acting Director of Outpatient Department/Emergency Services at the Dr. Solomon Carter Fuller, C.M.H.C. in Boston, Massachusetts, and an Assistant Professor of Psychology at the University of Massachusetts at Boston. He is a member of the Association of Black Psychologists, American Psychological Association, and the Consortium for Research on Black Adolescents (C.R.O.B.A.). Dr. Ramseur has done research and writing that examines psychological health as well as racial identity among Black adolescents and adults. He is currently investigating factors that affect Black academic and work-place achievement.

MARVA LLOYD REDD, Ph.D. has seventeen years of work experience in social services which includes family counseling as well as individual and group therapy. Areas of specialization include alcohol and other drug abuse counseling with adults and youth. Dr. Redd is a graduate of Washington University where she received a Ph.D. in Sociology. She also has a Master's degree in Rehabilitation Counseling from Boston University and a Bachelor of Arts degree from Hampton Institute. Currently, she is employed as Program Director of a county-wide youth agency in St. Louis County, Missouri that provides prevention and intervention services.

JANICE E. RUFFIN is Director of Counseling and Psychological Services, and Assistant Professor, at Baruch College, City University of New York. She is also a psychologist in private practice. Dr. Ruffin received her doctorate in Clinical Psychology from the Graduate School, City University of New York. She had an extensive career in psychiatric nursing before becoming a psychologist. She combined clinical work in community mental health centers with teaching graduate students in psychiatric nursing. Dr. Ruffin has held faculty positions at New York University, Yale University, and Rutgers University, and has published numerous articles on minority health care, Blacks in nursing, and racial issues in psychotherapy.

TONY L. STRICKLAND is Assistant Professor of Psychology and Psychiatry and Research Scientist in the Biobehavioral Laboratory in the Department of Psychiatry at the Charles R. Drew University of Medicine and Science, and Assistant Professor of Psychology and Psychiatry in the Department of Psychiatry at UCLA. He received his Ph.D. in Clinical Psychology from the University of Georgia in 1986, and is presently engaged in an active research program on stress-reactivity in cardiovascular disease and affective disorders in Blacks. He is the author of several research articles on this topic.

ROBERT JOSEPH TAYLOR, Ph.D. is an Assistant Professor in the School of Social Work and a Faculty Associate at the Institute for Social Research, The University of Michigan. His research interests include family and non-kin assistance networks, formal and informal help-seeking for personal problems, racial group identification and socialization, and the determinants of religious participation. His work has been published in the *Journal of Gerontology*, *Journal of Marriage and the Family*, *The Gerontologist*, *Social Work*, *Review of Religious Research*, and *Journal of Black Studies*. Dr. Taylor is the recipient of a First Independent Research Support and Transition (First) Award (R29 AGO8656) from the National Institute on Aging.

NAMES INDEX

Abboud, F.M., 325, 338
Abrahams, R., 119, 144
Adams, D.L., 192, 209
Akbar, N., 122, 139, 144, 306, 307
Aldridge, D.P., 278, 279, 293
Allen, D., 3, 28
Allen, V., 117, 144
Allen, W.R., 78, 81, 95, 117, 121, 123, 125, 142, 143, 144, 251, 263
Alston, J.P., 201, 203, 209
Anderson, N.B., 311, 313, 315, 322, 325, 330, 331, 333, 335, 338
Andrews, F.M., 193, 197, 199, 203, 210
Angel, R., 251, 252, 253, 267
Annest, J.L., 318, 338
Antonucci, T.C., 144, 246, 247, 248, 258, 261, 267
Aschenbrenner, J., 253, 254, 262, 263, 268
Ashante, M.K., 118, 122, 144
Atchley, R.C., 285, 286, 293
Auletta, K., 119, 139, 144

Baer, D.E., 336, 339
Bailey, E.J., 280, 281, 282, 283, 293
Baldwin, J., 122, 140, 144, 152, 165
Ball, R.E., 204, 205, 210
Bancroft, G., 96, 113
Banfield, E., 7, 28
Bang, K.M., 283, 284, 294
Baratz, J.C., 122, 144
Barbarin, O., 217, 218, 221, 232, 233, 235, 238
Barchha, R., 353, 370
Barnes, E.J., 225, 228, 238
Barnett, R., 123, 142, 145
Barnett, R.C., 93, 113
Baruch, G.K., 123, 145
Battle, S.F., 276, 277, 294
Battles, P.B., 126, 145
Beaver, M.L., 287, 294
Becker, G., 6, 28
Beckett, J.O., 93, 95, 96, 104, 106, 107, 113
Bell, B., 202, 210
Bell, D., 6, 28
Benedek, T., 32, 60
Benenson, H., 105, 106, 113
Bengston, V., 3, 28
Bengston, V.L., 203, 210, 245, 258, 268
Benjamin, R., 355, 362, 370
Berenson, G.S., 332, 339
Berry, M.F., 122, 139, 145

Bibring, G.L., 32, 60
Billingsley, A., 251, 268
Blackwell, J.E., 280, 294, 375, 385
Blassingame, J., 95, 113
Bloom, M., 156, 165, 273, 294
Bluestone, B., 6, 14, 28
Blumberg, L., 253, 254, 268
Bonacich, E., 6, 14, 28
Bonham, G.S., 320, 339
Boserup, E., 94, 113
Bowman, P.J., 117-150, 121, 123, 124, 125, 128, 129, 130, 135, 136, 139, 140, 142, 145, 234, 238
Bowser, B.P., 3-30
Boyle, E., 317, 320, 333, 339
Branch, L.G., 261, 268
Brazelton, T.B., 104, 113
Brecher, E.M., 352, 370
Brookins, G.K., 109, 113
Brown, C., 379, 385
Brown, J.O., 280, 284, 294
Brown, S.A., 378, 385
Buhrmann, M.V., 306, 307
Burlew, A.K., 93, 103, 106, 107, 109, 113
Butler, R.N., 160, 161, 162, 165

Caetano, R., 356, 358, 370
Callan, J.P., 364, 370
Campbell, A., 191, 194, 197, 199, 201, 202, 203, 204, 206, 210
Cannon, M., 120, 145
Cantor, M.H., 249, 259, 261, 262, 268
Carp, F.M., 201, 210
Cayton, H.R., 381, 385
Cazenave, N.A., 117, 118, 121, 124, 125, 131, 145
Cervantes, R.C., 221, 238
Chatters, L.M., 132, 141, 145, 191-213, 204, 205, 206, 210, 249, 260, 264, 268, 401, 406
Chestang, L.W., 274, 294
Chiriboga, D.A., 202, 210
Chorofas, D., 6, 28
Chrysant, S., 315, 339
Clark, K., 16, 28
Clark, K.B., 120, 135, 145, 385
Clark, M.L., 230, 238
Clark, V., 331, 339
Clemente, F., 201, 203, 210, 265, 268
Coggins, D.C., 355, 371
Colarusso, C., 59, 60

Combs-Orme, T., 361, 362, 371
Comptroller General of the U.S., 172, 185
Cooper, R., 316, 317, 339
Copeland, E.T., 107, 113
Costa, Jr., D.T., 59, 60
Craig, R.J., 367, 371
Cross, Jr., W.E., 41, 60, 151, 152, 154, 155,
    164, 165, 217, 225, 227, 228, 229, 230,
    235, 238
Curry, C.L., 313, 339
Czaja, S.J., 201, 210

Dancy, J., 287, 294
Davis, A., 8, 28, 94, 96, 113
Davis, G., 158, 159, 165
Devore, W., 274, 294
Diamond, E.L., 321, 339
Diener, E., 192, 197, 198, 199, 200, 201, 203,
    208, 210
Dimsdale, J.E., 328, 339
Ditto, B., 323, 339
Dohrenwend, B.S., 321, 339
Dollard, J., 5, 28
Donnenwerth, G.V., 203, 210
Dono, J.E., 245, 261, 262, 268
Dowd, J.A., 167, 185
Dowd, J.J., 196, 199, 200, 210
Downing, R.A., 273-295, 288, 292, 294
Drake, S.C., 17, 24, 28, 122
Dressler, W.W., 234, 238
Du Bois, W.E.B., 16, 28, 122, 145, 381, 385
Dun, S.V., 282, 294
Durbin, R., 143, 145
Durkheim, E., 377, 382, 385
Duvall, E., 131, 145

Edmonds, R., 129, 146
Edwards, D.E., 358, 371
Edwards, O.L., 232, 238
Ehrlich, I.F., 204, 210
Elder, G., 3, 28
Elliot, R.S., 323, 339
Ellison, R., 157, 165
Epstein, C., 102, 107, 108, 113
Epstein, C.F., 36, 37, 60
Epstein, F.H., 317, 339
Erikson, E.H., 32, 33, 60, 73, 89, 126, 128,
    130, 131, 133, 134, 136, 137, 146, 152,
    160, 161, 165, 220, 238, 298, 307
Eron, L.D., 123, 135, 146
Evans, G., 284, 294
Ewart, C.K., 336, 340

Falkner, B., 323, 329, 340

Farley, R., 375, 381, 385
Farrell, W., 117, 146
Fasteau, M., 117, 146
Feagin, J., 253, 254, 263, 268
Feldman, J., 355, 371
Finnerty, F.A., 312, 313, 340
Fisher, B.M., 287, 294
Fisher, M.M., 378, 385
Fleming, J., 108, 113
Folkow, B., 323, 340
Foner, A., 290, 291, 294
Franklin, J.H., 117, 146
Frazier, E.F., 8, 9, 12, 26, 28, 122, 146, 251,
    254, 265, 268, 302, 307, 353, 371, 381,
    385
Frederickson, M., 323, 328, 335, 340
Freeman, R., 28, 29
Frieze, I., 37, 60
Frey, W.H., 171, 176, 185
Fulbright, K., 107, 113

Gaines-Carter, P., 159, 165
Gallatin, J., 135, 137, 146
Gallup Report, 265, 268
Galvin, Y.R., 57, 60
Garfinkel, R., 92, 114
Gary, L.E., 117, 118, 119, 120, 121, 125, 136,
    137, 140, 146, 238, 360, 364, 366, 371
Gauain, J.M., 256, 268
Gentry, W.D., 321, 340
George, A., 233, 238
George, J.C., 219, 234, 239
George, L.K., 55, 60, 126, 146, 192, 196, 197,
    198, 199, 210
George-Abeyie, D., 120, 135, 136, 137, 146
German, E., 353, 359, 371
Gibbs, J.T., 227, 229, 230, 239
Gibson, G.S., 311, 340
Gibson, J.T., 128, 142, 146
Gibson, R., 233, 235, 239
Gibson, R.C., 256, 264, 268, 389-406, 395,
    399, 401, 406
Giddings, P., 92, 95, 96, 97, 103, 114
Giele, J., 2, 32, 37, 60
Gillum, R.F., 312, 313, 315, 316, 320, 331,
    340
Glaab, C., 7, 29
Glasgow, D., 23, 29
Glasgow, D.G., 120, 130, 146
Glazer, N., 122, 146
Glenn, N.D., 201, 210
Glick, P., 27, 29
Goldberg, H., 117, 146
Goode, W.J., 124, 128, 142, 146

Gooden, W., 35, 60, 63-89, 69, 89
Gorwitz, K., 362, 363, 371
Gould, K.H., 278, 294
Gould, R., 156, 165
Gould, R.L., 32, 61
Governor's Task Force on Black and
    Minority Health, 283, 295
Greeley, A.M., 265, 268
Green, L., 125, 129, 130, 146
Greenberg, W., 327, 340
Greenstadt, L., 327, 340
Grier, W., 223, 225, 239
Griffin, Q.D., 231, 232, 239
Grigsby, S., 360, 371
Grim, C.E., 311, 315, 316, 318, 320, 325, 326,
    340
Grolnick, L., 336, 340
Gross, M., 362, 363, 371
Gump, J., 93, 109, 114
Gurin, P., 129, 140, 146, 157, 165, 229, 239
Guterman, S., 225, 239
Gutman, H., 8, 10, 29, 251, 268
Gwaltney, J., 9, 29

Hafner, R.J., 336, 340
Hagestad, G., 195, 211
Hagestad, G.O., 249, 268
Hall, W.D., 314, 331, 335, 340
Hamilton, R.N., 132, 146
Hanft, R., 284, 294
Hannerz, U., 122, 139, 147
Hapgod, F., 117, 147
Harburg, E., 311, 317, 321, 334, 341
Harding, V., 139, 147
Hare, B., 276, 294
Hare, N., 139, 147
Harel, Z., 173, 180, 181, 185
Harley, S., 95, 96, 114
Harpen, F.D., 137, 147, 355, 356, 357, 360,
    361, 371
Harrell, J.P., 41, 61, 321, 341
Harrington, M., 381, 385
Harris, L., 177, 178, 185
Harrison, A.O., 91-115, 91, 93, 106, 107,
    110, 114, 235, 239
Harrison, B., 7, 11, 29
Harrison, J., 117, 147
Harvey, W.B., 353, 371
Hatchett, D., 129, 135, 147
Havighurst, R., 161, 166
Hayes, C.G., 316, 317, 341
Hays, W., 254, 269
Heckler, M.H., 117, 120, 137, 147
Heiss, J., 227, 239

Henry, A.F., 383, 385
Hendricks, L., 147
Herd, D., 359, 360, 362, 372
Herskovits, M.J., 122, 128, 139, 147, 378, 385
Hetherington, E., 119, 147
Herzog, A.R., 192, 194, 195, 197, 198, 199,
    201, 204, 207, 211
Heyman, D.K., 265, 269
Hill, E., 26, 29
Hill, R., 122, 125, 138, 139, 147, 172, 173,
    173, 175, 177, 185
Hill, R.B., 37, 61
Himes, J., 204, 211
Hirsch, C., 251, 265, 269
Hofferth, S.L., 251, 253, 256, 269
Hoffman, S., 117, 147
Hogan, D.P., 319, 341
Holahan, C.J., 234, 239
Hollenberg, N.K., 323, 341
Holmes, D., 289, 294
Holmes, S.J., 381, 385
Hood, E., 101, 114
Horan, P.M., 198, 211
Homstra, R.K. 362, 372
Horowitz, A., 261, 269
Hotline, 279, 294
House, J., 202, 211
Houston, L., 230, 239
Howard-Caldwell, C.S., 137, 147
Howenstein, L.S., 110, 114
Hughes, F.P., 126, 147
Huych, M.H., 126, 147
Hyman, M., 359, 372
Hypertension Detection & Followup
    Program Cooperative Group, 312,
    318, 320, 334, 341

Iglehart, J.K., 284, 294

Jackson, B., 151, 166
Jackson, J., 36, 61, 395, 406
Jackson, J.J., 132, 147, 172, 178, 185, 200,
    203, 211, 261, 269, 292, 293, 294, 319,
    341
Jackson, J.S., 132, 140, 147, 176, 179, 185,
    191, 193, 195, 197, 199, 201, 203, 204,
    205, 207, 211
Jackson, M., 167, 177, 181, 186, 200, 211,
    375, 377, 385
Jaffee, D., 97, 98, 114
Jahoda, M., 218, 220, 239
James, S.A., 311, 318, 319, 321, 341
Janson, P., 194, 205, 211
Jellinek, E., 356, 371

Jenkins, A., 41, 61
Jennings, R.M., 141, 147
Jensen, G.F., 225, 239
Joe, B.E., 286, 294
Joe, G., 366, 367, 372
Johnson, B., 364, 372
Johnson, C., 8, 9, 29, 381, 385
Johnson, R., 289, 294
Jones, A.C., 297-307, 297, 299, 303, 307
Jones, E.E., 217, 239
Jones, L., 21, 29
Jones, R., 138, 139, 148
Jorgenson, R.S., 323, 341
Jung, C.G., 306, 307

Kahn, R.L., 124, 142, 148, 248, 269
Kain, J.T., 29
Kaplan, N.M., 323, 341
Kaplan, M.B., 135, 136, 148
Kardiner, A., 215, 223, 224, 239
Karon, B.P., 223, 239
Kart, C.S., 172, 186
Kase, S.V., 319, 341
Kastenbaum, R., 376, 385
Katz, S.H., 332, 341
Kaufman, R., 26, 29
Keil, C., 122, 148
Keil, J.E., 317, 318, 342
Keith, P.M., 110, 114
Kennedy, C.E., 273, 294
Kennedy, T.R., 254, 255, 262, 269
Kenyatta, J., 139, 148
Kessler, R.C., 120, 123, 140, 148, 319, 342
Kilcoyne, M.M., 314, 332, 342
Kilmer, D.C., 273, 295
Kimmel, D., 126, 148
King, L.J., 354, 360, 372
Kinney, J., 352, 372
Kivett, V.R., 203, 211
Kleinman, P., 365, 372
Komaroff, A.C., 232, 239
Kotchen, J.M., 332, 342
Kovel, J., 56, 61, 298, 307
Kozma, A., 192, 196, 198, 211
Krantz, D.S., 322, 323, 342
Krigel, L., 117, 148
Kunar, K., 6, 29
Kunjufu, J., 120, 121, 148

Lackla, S., 364, 372
Ladner, J., 253, 262, 263, 269, 367, 372
Lambing, M.L.B., 265, 269
Lampherc, L., 104, 114
Land, K.C., 197, 211

Landry, B., 105, 110, 114
Langford, H.G., 312, 314, 315, 316, 342
Larkins, J., 354, 372
Larson, R., 192, 212
Lawton, M.P., 196, 212
Layng, A., 122, 148
Lazarus, R., 219, 222, 239
Lazarus, R.S., 202, 212, 321, 322, 342
Lee, C.C., 231, 232, 239, 240
Lee, G.R., 247, 269
Lemann, N., 17, 29
Levine, L.W., 122, 139, 148
Levinson, D., 33, 45, 46, 58, 61, 152, 156, 161, 166
Levinson, D.F., 63, 89
Levinson, D.J., 279, 295
Lewis, C.E., 360, 372
Liebow, E., 64, 89, 120, 131, 140, 148, 262, 263, 269
Light, K.C., 325, 329, 331, 335, 342
Lindsay, I., 199, 212
Linn, M.W., 203, 212, 367, 372
Lipman, A., 203, 212
Litwak, E., 261, 262, 269
Livingston, I.L., 358, 372
Locke, B., 362, 363, 372
Lohmann, N., 192, 212
Looney, J.G., 231, 232, 240
Lopata, H.Z., 251, 269
Lovenberg, W., 316, 342
Lowe, G.D., 262, 372
Lowman, C., 358, 359, 373
Luft, F.C., 311, 315, 325, 326, 335, 342, 343
Luther, A., 6, 29
Luther, X., 302, 303, 307
Lykes, M.B., 235, 240

Maddox, G.L., 352, 354, 373
Malcolm X, 152, 166
Malone, B.L., 56, 61
Malson, M.R., 94, 114
Malzberg, B., 356, 359, 362, 373
Mandel, J., 364, 366, 373
Mangum, G.L., 130, 148
Mann, S., 324, 343
Mannheim, K., 3, 29
Manuck, S.B., 323, 343
Manton, K., 182, 183, 186
Manuel, R.C., 177, 186
Marshall, P., 303, 307
Marsiglio, W., 131, 148
Martin, E., 254, 255, 262, 263, 269
Martineau, W., 253, 254, 263, 264, 269
Maslow, A., 219, 240

Masuda, M., 202, 212
Matney, W.C., 170, 173, 176, 178, 179, 186
Matthews, K., 322, 323, 343
Mbiti, J., 141, 148
McAdoo, H.P., 107, 109, 114, 117, 148, 257, 261, 264, 269
McAdoo, J.L., 121, 131
McCarron, D.A., 315, 343
McCarthy, J., 224, 225, 227, 228, 240
McCelland, D., 354, 373
McGee, D.P., 317, 343
McGoldrick, M., 303, 307
McLellan, T.A., 367, 373
Mead, M., 4, 8, 29, 141, 148
Meadows, K.I., 253, 254, 263, 269
Merton, R.K., 124, 125, 128, 135, 142, 148
Messer, M., 203, 212
Meyer, C.H., 273, 295
Meyers, A.R., 354, 355, 373
Michalos, A.C., 199, 200, 212
Miller, I.W., 137, 148
Miller, J.Z., 316, 317, 318, 343
Miller, K.S., 73, 119, 120, 148
Miller, W., 58, 122, 135, 139, 148
Milliones, J., 151, 166
Minall, C.H., 259, 270
Mitchell, J.S., 251, 253, 270
Moll, P.P., 317, 343
Mongeau, J.G., 318, 343
Monik, E., 299, 307
Moon, M., 252, 270
Moore, H.B., 223, 240
Morell, M.A., 326, 343
Morgan, J.N., 251, 252, 253, 256, 270
Morris, A., 121, 122, 139, 148, 264, 270
Morris, J.N., 196, 212
Mortiner, J.T., 103, 107, 108, 115
Moynihan, D., 251, 254, 270
Mullins, E.T., 108, 109, 115
Munnicks, M., 168, 186
Murphy, J.K., 332, 343
Murray, C., 9, 29
Murray, C.B., 167-187
Murray, S.R., 107, 109, 115
Mutran, E., 259, 270
Myers, H.F., 311-349, 318, 319, 321, 322, 326, 327, 336, 343, 344
Myers, L.J., 122, 148
Myrdal, G., 122, 148
Myrdal, G., 15, 29

Nagi, S., 180, 186
Nail, R.L., 365, 373
Nash, J.J., 328, 344

National Association of Social Workers, 292, 295
National Black Health Care Providers Task Force on High Blood Pressure Education & Control Report, 311, 312, 314, 318, 344
National Caucus & Center on Black Aged, Inc., 167, 172, 177, 179, 180, 181, 184, 186
National Center for Health Statistics, 180, 182, 185, 186
National Center for Health Statistics Report, 312, 331, 344
National Council on Aging, 167, 169, 186, 199, 203, 212
National Institute on Alcohol Abuse & Alcoholism, 362, 373
National Urban League, 167, 186
Neaton, J.D., 314, 344
Neff, J., 233, 240
Neff, J.A., 359, 373
Neighbors, H.W., 120, 121, 149, 233, 235, 258, 264
Nelson, H.M., 265, 270
Nesser, W.B., 321, 344
Neugarten, B.L., 142, 144, 156, 166, 196, 212, 279, 295
Newsweek, 365, 373
Nichols, L., 117, 149
Nickens, H., 284, 295
Nicols, M.D., 279, 295
Nobles, W., 122, 138, 140, 142, 240, 303, 307
Northcott, H.C., 106, 115

Obleton, N.B., 92, 109, 115
O'Brien, E.M., 280, 295
Obrist, P.A., 321, 323, 344
O'Donnell, J.A., 364, 373
Ortega, S.T., 196, 200, 203, 204, 212
Ostfeld, A.M., 321, 344

Parham, T.A., 151-166, 152, 166, 230, 240
Patterson, O., 316, 317, 344
Pearce, D., 97, 102, 115
Pearlin, L., 124, 128, 135, 142, 149
Perun, P.J., 32, 61
Peterson, J.A., 286, 295
Pettigrew, T.F., 171, 186, 217, 223, 240
Phillips, M., 170, 173, 176, 177, 186
Pickering, T.G., 324, 337, 345
Pierce, C., 217, 240
Pifer, A., 392, 406
Pinkey, A., 375, 385
Pleck, E., 80, 117, 149

Pleck, J., 76, 117, 149
Porche, L.M., 152, 166
Powell, D.H., 126, 130, 135, 149
Price, B., 6, 29
Prineas, R.J., 312, 332, 345
Pugh, R.W., 38, 61

Ragan, P., 4, 29
Rainwater, L., 251, 270
Ramseur, H.P., 215-241, 229, 231, 240
Rapoport, R.N., 105, 115
Redd, M.L., 351-374, 370, 373
Redding, J.S., 380, 385
Register, J.C., 200, 203, 212
Reich, M., 6, 29
Riley, M.W., 169, 186
Riley, N., 129, 149
Rimmer, J., 353, 355, 356, 358, 359, 363, 374
Robertson, D., 345
Robins, L.N., 354, 360, 369, 374
Rockville, M.D., 238
Rodgers-Rose, L.F., 36, 61
Roscow, I., 195, 212
Rose, A., 5, 29
Rose, R.J., 318, 345
Rosenblath, S.M., 353, 362, 374
Rossi, A., 31, 32, 37, 61
Rossi, R.J., 197, 212
Rowland, D., 337, 345
Royce, J.E., 352, 374
Rubenstein, D.I., 203, 212, 251, 270
Rubin, R., 119, 149
Ruffin, J.E., 31-61, 35, 61
Russel, R.P., 316, 345
Rutledge, E.O., 93, 94, 115
Rutter, M., 237, 240
Ryan, W., 120, 149

Sarbin, T.R., 124, 142, 149
Sasaki, M.S., 265, 270
Sauer, W., 203, 204, 205, 212
Schachter, J., 332, 345
Schaie, K.W., 200, 212
Schneiderman, N., 323, 325, 329, 345
Schnessler, K.F., 191, 192, 208, 213
Schwartz, G.E., 322, 323, 345
Scott, P.B., 96, 97, 100, 104, 107
Seligman, M.E.D., 137, 149
Shaiken, H., 6, 29
Shanas, E., 249, 251, 259, 270
Shapiro, D., 322, 327, 345, 346
Shimkin, D., 254, 262, 270
Shinn, M., 119, 149
Shulman, N.B., 313, 333, 346

Siegel, S.J., 169, 186
Simmons, S.J., 287, 295
Simms, M.C., 92, 97, 102, 115
Smelser, N.J., 31, 61, 130, 149
Smith, M.B., 218, 240, 241
Smith, W.D., 18, 241
Soldo, B., 170, 186
Somerville, R.M., 276, 295
Spaights, E., 23, 29
Speers, M.A., 336, 346
Spencer, H., 382, 386
Spreitzer, E., 203, 213
Stack, C.B., 21, 30, 254, 255, 262, 263, 270
Stamler, J., 314, 318, 320, 346
Stanford, E.P., 259, 270
Staples, R., 26, 30, 36, 61, 105, 115, 117, 118,
   120, 125, 149, 364, 374, 381, 386
Statistical Abstract of the U.S. 1986, 98, 99,
   100, 101, 115
Steer, R.A., 367, 374
Stein, M., 13, 60
Steptoe, A., 323, 346
Sterne, M., 354, 374
Stevenson-Long, J., 126, 149, 279, 295
Stewart, J., 120, 149
Stewart, W., 35, 61
Strauss, J.S., 358, 374
Strayer, R.A., 357, 358, 361, 362, 374
Strickland, T., 327, 331, 335, 346
Sudarkasa, N., 122, 138, 141, 149, 150
Sutherland, R., 8, 30
Sweet, J.A., 251, 270
Syne, S.L., 311, 312, 318, 321, 334, 346

Taenber, K.E., 171, 186
Talley, T., 167, 186
Taylor, R.J., 118, 121, 132, 133, 141, 150,
   245-271, 250, 257, 258, 259, 261, 264,
   265, 266, 270
Taylor, R.L., 224, 225, 227, 241
Taylor, S., 35, 61
Terborg-Penn, R., 95, 96, 115
Thernstrom, S., 10, 30
Thomas, A., 223, 241
Thomas, C., 151, 166
Thomas, R.J., 289, 295
Thompson, D.C., 382, 386
Thompson, G., 291, 295
Thompson, G.E., 312, 313, 346
Thurow, L., 6, 30
Tienda, M., 251, 252, 253, 271
Tines, N.Y., 6, 29
Tinney, J.S., 122, 150
Torres-Gil, F., 285, 286, 295

Touraine, A., 6, 30
Towle, L.H., 362, 374
Triandis, H.C., 122, 150
Troll, L.E., 126, 131, 150, 246, 258, 271
Turner, B.B., 37, 61
Turner, C., 157, 166, 278, 295
Tyler, F., 231, 241
Tyroler, H.A., 314, 317, 333, 346

U.S. Bureau of the Census, 171, 173, 175, 176, 181, 186, 187
U.S. Commission on Civil Rights, 177, 187
U.S. Department of Commerce, 102, 115
U.S. Department of Commerce, Bureau of the Census, 10, 11, 14, 16, 18, 19, 22, 30, 390, 406
U.S. Department of Health & Human Services, Public Health Service, 391, 406
U.S. Department of Justice, 366, 374
U.S. Department of Labor, Bureau of the Census, 399, 406
U.S. Senate Special Committee on Aging, 171, 180, 182, 187

Valentine, B., 120, 136, 150
Valliant, G., 33, 52, 61, 79, 85, 89
Van Hoose, W.H., 126, 150
Vaughan, D.A., 205, 213
Venter, C., 325, 346
Vernon, G.M., 377, 386
Veroff, J., 194, 195, 201, 204, 213, 225, 244
Viamontes, J.A., 359, 362, 363, 374
Vitols, M.M., 357, 358, 359, 362, 374
Voors, A.W., 332, 347

Walker, A., 91, 115
Walters, G.D., 361, 374
Walton, H.W., 117, 121, 150

Washington, D.C., 38, 61
Washington, E., 319, 347
Watkins, L.O., 316, 317, 318, 331, 347
Watson, R.Y., 347
Watson, W.H., 177, 187
Watt, G., 317, 347
Watts, T.D., 359, 374
Weaver, J.L., 277, 295
Weiner, H., 311, 347
Welsing, F., 274, 295
Wertheimer, B.M., 95, 96, 115
West, J.M., 139, 150
Wexler, H.K., 367, 374
White, R., 230, 241
Wilcox, C., 241
Wilkins, R., 152, 166
Wilkinson, D., 117, 120, 137, 150
Williams, B.S., 176, 187
Williams, I., 151, 166
Williams, J.A., 251, 271
Williams, M., 284, 295
Willie, C.V., 278, 295
Wilson, W.J., 30, 129, 130, 150
Witt, D.D., 196, 204, 213
Wolfgang, M.E., 135, 150
Wood, V., 196, 213
Wool, H., 130, 150
Wright, B., 230, 241
Wright, G., 6, 30

Yancey, W., 227, 241
Yearwood, L., 121, 122, 150
Yonmans, E.G., 203, 213

Zacks, H., 279, 295
Zahan, D., 298, 307
Zax, M., 362, 374
Zinner, S.H., 317, 347

SUBJECT INDEX

Activity perspective on subjective
well-being, 198
Adaptive cultural resources 137-139
early adulthood, 140
middle adulthood, 140
old age, 141
preadult years, 139-140
Adaptation, stress
appraisal, 232-233
coping styles, 235-236
external coping resources, 233
internal coping resources, 234
Adult development, research
approaches to study of, 31-33
Advocacy services, Black aged, 291-293
Afro-American folk culture, 25
Age cohorts
fifty-two to seventy-one, 12-14
forty-two to fifty-one, 14-20
seventy two and older, 8-12
thirty-five to forty-four, 20-23
Age cohorts, subjective well being
and, 205-208
Age status and subjective well-being, 204
Aging society, Blacks in, 389-406
elderly, 400-404
infants and children, 391-393
middle-adulthood, 395-400
teenagers, 394-395
Age thirty mothers, 42
A.T.T. See Age Thirty Transition,
35, 39, 52
Age Thirty Transition (A.T.T.), 35, 39, 52
Black women and, 52
Alcoholism
consequences, 358-361
etiological factors in, 353-354
onset, 357-358
patterns of consumption, 354-357
scope of problem, 351-353
treatment networks, 361-363

Baby boomers, 20-23
Biobehavioral perspective, essential
hypertension, 322-324
Biological differences, essential
hypertension, 315-316
Black Aged, lifespan perspective,
essential hypertension, 333-334
Black consciousness, transformation of,
151-166

Black elderly
geographic distribution and mobility,
170-171
health, 180-181
housing, 172-173
income status, 176-178
labor force participation, 178-180
life cycle approach to, 167-169
living arrangements, 173-175
marital status, 175-176
mental health, 182-183
population characteristics, 170
social indices and, 167-187
surveys of, 169-183
Black identity, traditional
theories, 223-226
Black males
alcohol abuse, 353-363
drug addiction, 364-368
Black man as hero, 87
Black men
coping and, 118, 121
ethnicity and, 118, 121-122
oppression and, 118, 120-121
pathology and, 118, 119-120
research perspectives on, 117-123
role strain, 117-150
Black Norm, 225
Black personality, traditional theories,
223-226
Black Rage, 224
Black-White differences, essential
hypertension, 311-315
Black women
during decades of sixties and
seventies, 96
during decade of World War I, 96
during reconstruction, 95-96
images of, 91
life span issues, 92-94
participation and labor market, 91
historical review of, 94-98
role models, 92-93
Black women's adult development
male-female relations and, 36
occupational patterns and, 37-38
sociocultural context of, 35-36
socio-historical perspectives on, 37-38
Black working women, 91-115
demographic trends, 98-102
effect of family on, 108-111

effect on family, 104-108
employment rates, 98-100
family life, 103-104
income distribution, 101-102
life span issues, 92-94
occupational and educational
attainment, 100-101

Caffeine and stress, 326-328
Cardiovascular stress reactivity, 324-325
Careerists, 42
Children and youth, lifespan
perspective, essential hypertension,
331-333
Church support networks, Blacks, 264-266
Civil rights movement, 14
Cofigurative cultural change, 5-6
Community, 17, 20
Community change, 16
Community change, effects of, 7
Comparative trends, subjective
well-being, 202-204
Competent personality, 230-232
Concept of balance, 306
Convoys of social support, 248-250
Coping, Black men and, 118, 121, 141
Coping styles
Black women and, 50-51
Cross model, 151, 152
Cultural changes, phases of, 4-6
Cultural transformation, 5

Death and dying, Blacks
Black literature, 379-381
current knowledge, 375-376
Life Control Theory, 382-384
past explanations, 376-377
multi-factor approach, 381-382
sacred and secular norms, 377-378
spirituals and poetry, 378-379
Deindustrialization, impact
on Afro-Americans, 26
Demography of Black Americans,
changing, 390-391
Desegregation, 24
Developmental tasks, Adult life cycle, 41,
273-274
Disengagement and subjective
well-being, 198
Double jeopardy, Black elderly
and, 167-187, 199-200
Dream phase
male school teachers and, 68-69
street men and, 65-67

Drug Addiction
consequences of, 366
patterns of, 364-366
scope of problem, 351-353
treatment, 366-368

Early Adulthood, 274-279
adaptive cultural resources, 140
maladaptive response pattern,
135-136
work role strain and, 129-131
Early Adult development, Black men,
63-89
E.A.T. See Early Adult Transition,
35, 39
Early Adult Transition, (E.A.T.) 35, 39
Black women and, 59
E.A.W. See Entering the Adult World, 35,
39
Economy, impact of, 6-7
Economy, participation in, 26
Economic racism, 24
Economic sufficiency, Black elderly,
289-291
Elderly, 400-404
Elders, 25
Encounter racial identity attitude, 154-155
Entering the Adult World (E.A.W.), 35, 39
Essential hypertension, 311-349
biobehavioral perspective on, 322-324
biological differences, 315-316
genetic familial factors, 316-318
Black-White differences in, 311-315
research, pitfall of, 321-322
sociocultural differences, 320-321
socioeconomic status differences,
318-319
sociopsychological differences,
320-321
Ethnicity, Black men and, 118, 121-122, 141
Eurocentric value structure,
racial identity and, 161
Evolution of life structures, Black women,
43-44

Familial support networks
ethnographic research on, 254
kinship networks, 253-254
living arrangements, 251-253
Family, formation of
male school teachers, 76-78
street men and, 73-76
Feminization of poverty, 97
Folk culture, 21

Forming an occupation
  Black women and, 45
Forming a dream
  Black women and, 44-45, 49-50
Forming a marriage and family
  Black women and, 45-46
Forming mentor relationships,
  Black women and, 45
Full transitions, 48

Gender differences in subjective
  well-being, 204
Generational effects, 3-30
Genetic familial factors, essential
  hypertension, 316-318
Glossary, essential hypertension, 347-349
Great Society programs, 9, 27

Health and subjective well-being, 204
Health care manpower, 284-285
Health education, 283-284
Health, elderly, 180-181
Health services, middle adulthood, 280-285
Housing, elderly, 172-173
Housing,
  fifty-two to seventy one cohort, 14
  seventy two and over cohort, 11-12
Human services, 273-295
Human services, early adulthood
  adoption services, 278
  family life education, 276
  family planning, 277-278
  federal programs, 287
  genetic counseling, 276-27
  health services, 280-285
  later adulthood, 286
  middle adulthood, 279
  retirement planning, 285-286
Hypertensive, Blacks
  biobehavioral research on, 324-334
  reactivity, within group variability,
    330-331

Ideal model, psychological
  health, 218
Immersion-emersion racial identity
  attitudes, 155
Income, Black-White differences in, 18, 19
Income status, elderly,
  176-178
Infants and children, 391-393
Influence of the majority culture,
  ˚clinical case example, 301-303
Informal social support, 245-271

Informal support, non-kin, 261
Influence of traditional African-American
  culture, clinical care,
  example of, 303-304
Integenerational differences
  seventy-two and older cohort, 8-12
Integrators, 42
Internalization racial identity
  attitudes, 155
Intimacy, development in adulthood, 85

Judgment theories of subjective
  well-being, 200

Kin support, theories of, 261-262

Labor force participation,
  Black women and, 36-47
  declining, 27
  elderly, 178-180
Late Adulthood, levels of
  racial identity, 160-164
Later Adulthood, 286-293
Learned helplessness, role strain
  related, 137
Legislative initiative, 292-293
Levinson's theory
  Black women and, 52-55
    limitations for Black men, 87-88
    limitation for understanding
      Black women, 53-55
Life choices, racial identity and, 50
Life Control Theory, 382-384
Life cycle approach, Black
  elderly, 167-169
Life cycle, conceptions of
  Erickson's stages, 32
Life span development, problems
  affecting field, 31
Life span perspectives, essential
  hypertension
  Black adults, 333
  Black aged, 333-334
  children and youth, 331-333
Life style behavior, 280-282
Life span theories
  Levinson's life structure paradigm,
    33-35
  Normative crisis model, 32
  Stage, 32
  Timing of events models, 32
Limited transitions, 48
Living arrangements,
  elderly, 173-175

Mainstream social science theories,
challenges to, 215-216
Maladaptive response patterns,
Black males, 133-135
early adulthood, 135-136
middle adulthood, 136-137
old age, 137
preadult years, 135
Marital status,
elderly, 175-176
"Mark of Oppression", 224
Marriage, formation of
male school teachers, 76-78
"street men", 73-76
Media images, 5
Mental health
Black elderly, 182-183
Mentors
male school teachers and, 69
street men and, 67-68
Methodology for life cycle study,
168
Middle Adulthood, 279-286
adaptive cultural resource, 140
divorce and separation, 396
levels of racial identity, 156-160
maladaptive response patterns,
136-137
mental health status ,396-398
provider role strain and, 131-132
work and retirement, 399
Middle Class, 12, 16, 25-26
Midlife Transition (M.L.T.), 35
Black women and, 48, 59
full transition, 48
limited transitions, 48
modified transitions, 48
M.L.T. See Midlife transition,
35
Modeling in program utilization,
Black aged, 288-289

Negotiation initiative, 291-292
"Negro" folk traditions, 13
Negro youth, portrayals of, 15
New Deal, the, 27
Nigrescence, 151-166
Non-kin support providers, ethnographic
research on, 262-263
Non-kin support, theories of, 261-262
Normative crisis model, 32
Normotensive Adults, study of, 325-328
caffeine and stress, 326-328
physical stressors, 328

psychosocial stressors, 328-330
Novice phase,
Black men and, 65-78
Black women and, 44, 54

Occupational life
male school teachers, 81-84
"street men", 79-81
Occupations, formation of
male school teachers and, 71-73
"street men", and 70-71
Old Age
adaptive cultural resource, 141
elderly role strain and, 132-133
maladaptive response patterns, 137
Openness to experience, Black women
and, 59
Opportunity generation, 15-16
Oppression, Black men and, 118, 120-121,
141

Pathology
Black men and, 118, 119-120, 141
Personal experience and endowments,
clinical case example of, 304-306
Physical stressors, essential hypertension,
328
Post-figurative cultural change, 5
Post-figurative social control, 24
Post-industrial era, 6
Post-industrialists, 6
Preadulthood
male student role strain and, 128-129
Preadult years
adaptive cultural resources, 139-140
maladaptive response patterns,
135-136
Pre-encounter racial identity
attitudes, 154
Prefigurative cultural change, 4-5
Pre-retirement planning, middle
adulthood, 285-286
Professional Black women, stages of
development, 31-61
Professional work, racial identity
and, 50
Psychological functioning, Black
adults
clinical applications, 298-307
model of, 298
Psychological health
ideal model, 218
social/cultural context, 217-218
universal models, 219-223

Psychologically healthy Black
    adults, 215-241
Psychosocial stressors
    essential hypertension, 330
    normotensive adults, 326
Psychotherapy, Black Adults, 297-307

Quality of life, 191-213

Race consciousness, 8, 24
Race unity, 24
Racial differences
    subjective well-being, 202-204
    support exchange, 256-257
Racial discrimination, 5
Racial identity, 151-166, 228-230
    Black women and, 56-58
    Cross model of, 151-152
    levels of
    late adulthood, 160-164
    middle adulthood, 156-160
    stages for Black women, 56-58
Racial identity attitudes
    encounter, 154-155, 158-159, 162
    immersion-emersion, 155, 159-160,
        162-163
    internalization, 155, 160, 163
    pre-encounter, 154, 157-158, 161-162
Racial oppression, 9
Racial self-esteem, 41
Racism, Black women and, 51
Reactions to racial oppression,
    clinical case examples, 298-301
Research, directions for
    Black adult development, 88
Research needs
    Black children, 403-404
    Black elderly, 403-404
    Black infants, 403-404
    Black middle-aged, 403-404
    Black teenagers, 403-404
    subjective well-being, 208-209
    support networks, 266-267
Research, pitfalls of, essential
    hypertension, 321-322
Resource Analysis and subjective
    well-being, 205-208
Responsible research, 292
Retirement planning, middle
    adulthood, 285
Role Adaptation
    Black men and, 117-150
    theoretical model of, 123-126
Role strain

Black men and, 117-150
    developmental issues, male, 126-128
    elderly, 132-133
    preadulthood, 128-129
    provider, 131-132
    student, preadulthood, 128-129
    theoretical model of male, 123-126
    work, early male adulthood, 129-131

Sacred and Secular norms, 377-378
S.D. See Settling Down, 35, 39, 52
Self-concept, 227
Self, concept of, Jungian, 306
Self-discovery, Black women and, 53, 59
Self-esteem, 227-228
Self-protection, Black women and, 53, 59
Settling Down (S.D.) 35, 39, 52,
    Black women and, 47-48, 53, 54
Social/cultural context, 217-218
Social generation, 3, 4, 24-25
Social indicators and, 204
Social indicators of subjective
    well-being, 205-206
Social indices, elderly, 167-187
Social security, 291
Social support
    age difference in, 247-248
    convoys, 248-250
    life course perspectives, 246-247
Sociocultural differences, essential
    hypertension, 320-321
Socioeconomic status and subjective
    well-being, 204
Socioeconomic status differences,
    essential hypertension, 318-319
Sociopsychological differences,
    essential hypertension, 320-321
Spirituality, Black adults, 306-307
Split Labor Market, 26
Stage theories, 32
Stages of development, Black professional
    women, 31-61
"Street men", 64
Stress, 311-349
    appraisal, 232-233
    coping styles, 235-236
    external coping resources, 233
    internal coping resources, 234
Stress and subjective well-being,
    202
Student role strain, 128-129
Subjective well-being, 191-213
    activity perspective, 198
    age cohort and, 205-208

age status and, 204
aging and, 202
comparative trends, 202-204
correlates of, 204-205
disengagement perspective, 198
gender differences and, 204
health and, 204
history of research, 196-197
interpretations of, 197-198
judgment theories of, 200
predictors of, 204-205
racial differences, 202-204
research analyses of, 205-208
research needs, 208-209
resource models of, 198-199
social indicators and, 205-206
socioeconomic status and, 204
stress and, 202
Subjective well-being models
life span issues in, 195-196
Suburban movement of Blacks, 171
Support exchanges, racial differences in,
256-257
Support networks, 245-271
Support networks
aging Blacks, 259-261

Blacks, 257-259, 263-264
Surveys, elderly, 169-183
Symbolism in program and service
utilization, Black aged, 288

Teenagers, 394-395
Timing of events models, 32
Black women and, 55
Treatment, drug addiction, 366-368
Treatment networks, alcoholism, 361-363

Underclass, Black participation in, 24, 25
Urban Black families, kinship networks,
253-254
Urbanization, 5
Urbanization, impact on Afro-American
life, 10

Work role strain, male, early adulthood,
129-131
World of work,
fifty-two to seventy-one cohort, 13-14
forty-two to fifty-one cohort, 14
seventy-two and older adults, 9-11
thirty-five to forty-four cohort, 20-23